FOR USE
IN
LIBRARY
ONLY

Women's Diaries, Journals, and Letters

GARLAND REFERENCE LIBRARY
OF THE HUMANITIES
(Vol. 780)

To my mother, JoAnn Cline

WOMEN'S DIARIES, JOURNALS, AND LETTERS
An Annotated Bibliography

Cheryl Cline

Garland Publishing, Inc. • New York & London
1989

Library of Congress Cataloging-in-Publication Data

Cline, Cheryl, 1954–
Women's diaries, journals, and letters : an annotated bibliography / Cheryl Cline.
p. cm. — (Garland reference library of the humanities ; vol. 780)
Includes indexes.
ISBN 0–8240–6637–5 (alk. paper)
1. Women—Biography—Bibliography. 2. Autobiography—Bibliography. 3. Women—Diaries—Bibliography. 4. Women—Correspondence—Bibliography. I. Title.
Z7963.B6C55 1989
[CT3230]
016.92072—dc19 89–1197
CIP

Printed on acid-free, 250-year-life paper
Manufactured in the United States of America

CONTENTS

PREFACE

This bibliography lists published private writings of appreciable length, including those published as articles or as extracts in larger works. Most of the works listed are in English; however, writings in French, Spanish, German, Portuguese, and other languages are also included. I decided to include foreign-language material because I wanted to list the original editions of private writings which had been translated. These led me to others which had not been translated, and I could not bear to leave them out. Some of the important works in the field of private writing, such as Peter Boerner's TAGEBUCH and LE JOURNAL INTIME by Beatrice Didier, have not been translated into English.

The private writings of some authors, Colette and George Sand among them, have not been translated in their entirety. Others, such as the letters of Madame de Sevigne, have enjoyed a lively publishing history in both English and the original language. However, if a definitive edition has not been published, the text will vary a great deal from one edition to the next. This will be reflected in translations of the works. Translations may, in fact, be based upon not one but two or even three editions in the original language. Thus, while some titles will have English counterparts that bear at least nominal resemblance to the orginal (Liane de Pougy's MES CAHIERS BLEUS/MY BLUE NOTEBOOKS), many will not.

I have not tried to define "diary" or "letter" in any strict sense, though I have tried to stay as close as possible to personal, private writing. The largest grey area is the travel narrative. It has long been a practice for authors to write a "diary" or "letters home" after they had returned home, and no doubt many of the travel books listed here were composed in this way. However, most were at least re-written from notes taken while actually traveling, and of course, many of them are quite genuine.

Neither have I tried to compile a list of "good" diaries and letters. Private writings cannot be judged good on literary merit alone. The diary of Nannie Stillwell Jackson, for example, has no literary appeal whatsoever. The importance of her diary lies in its very dullness: in the endless, repetative, wearying detail of her life on a subsistence farm. An unreadable diary may be useful to social historians, psychologists, or linguists.

Authors are listed under the names by which they are best known. Thus, Margaret Fuller is listed under Fuller, not Ossoli, her married name. Women well-known by more than one name are listed under what appears to be the best known, and cross-referenced with the others. "Piozzi, Hester Lynch Salusbury Thrale" will direct the reader to "Thrale, Hester Lynch Salusbury, later Piozzi." Many times, a woman's best-known name is the one under which her diary or correspondence is published, even though she may have subsequently married (or remarried). She will be listed by the name which appears on the title page.

In ordering foreign names, the article is ignored except where the name is best known in an Anglicized form (DuPont, Lafayette). Last names begining with "Mc" are treated as if they were spelled "Mac." The works of anonymous authors are listed together under "Anonymous," and ordered alphabetically by title.

Single-author studies of a diarist or letter-writer are listed under her name; for example, studies of A DIARY FROM DIXIE are listed under Mary Chesnut. Such works are listed together under the heading "critical works" in the Index of Narratives by Subject. All four indices direct the reader to specific entry numbers.

In addition to the bibliographies listed in Part I, the following sources were helpful in compiling this bibliography: AMERICA HISTORY AND LIFE (Santa Barbara: ABC-CLIO, Inc.,1980); THE BRITISH LIBRARY GENERAL CATALOG OF PRINTED BOOKS TO 1975 (London: K.G. Saur, 1983-); WOMEN IN AMERICAN HISTORY: A BIBLIOGRAPHY,

Cynthia E. Harrison (Santa Barbara: ABC-CLIO, 1972); WOMEN IN SPANISH AMERICA: AN ANNOTATED BIBLIOGRAPHY FROM PRE-CONQUEST TO CONTEMPORARY TIMES, Meri Knaster (Boston: G.K. Hall, 1977); THE NATIONAL UNION CATALOG OF THE LIBRARY OF CONGRESS (New York: Mansell, 1978-); THE NEW YORK PUBLIC LIBRARY REFERENCE DEPARTMENT SUBJECT CATALOG OF THE WORLD WAR I COLLECTION (Boston: G.K. Hall); PEOPLE IN BOOKS, Margaret E. Nicholson (New York: H.W. Wilson, 1969); BIBLIOGRAPHY OF BRITISH HISTORY: THE EIGHTEENTH CENTURY, 1714-1789, Stanley Pargellis, and D.J. Medley (Oxford: The Clarendon Press, 1951); THE ARTHUR AND ELIZABETH SCHLESINGER LIBRARY ON THE HISTORY OF WOMEN IN AMERICA: THE MANUSCRIPT INVENTORIES AND THE CATALOGS OF MANUSCRIPS, BOOKS AND PICTURES (Cambridge, Mass.: Radcliffe College/G.K. Hall, 1973); and THE CATALOG OF THE SOPHIA SMITH COLLECTION (Boston: G.K. Hall, 1975).

I would like to thank Jane Begos, with whom a collaboration in the early stages of this project unfortunately fell through. I would also like to thank the staff at the Main Library of the University of California at Berkeley, especially the library pages, and Mrs. Joyce M. Ford, who granted me stack privileges when I belatedly asked for them. Most of all I would like to thank my husband, Lynn Kuehl, for support beyond all reason, and for his help editing the final draft of the manuscript.

INTRODUCTION

I: WOMEN'S LETTERS AND DIARIES

Anais Nin wrote of her diary that it:

> ...helped me to make the separation between my real self and the role-playing a woman is called upon to do. The roles which were imposed on me as a woman by my culture--from two different cultures, the Latin and then later the American--I fulfilled. I did what I called my duty. But at the same time the diary kept my other self alive, it showed what I really wanted, what I really felt, what I really thought. [1]

In the privacy of their diaries, or in letters to trusted confidants, women have revealed what they "really felt," what they thought, believed, desired, or held important as they lived through the large events of history or the small rituals of everyday life. Not every woman is able, as Nin was, to make the separation between her "real self" and the role-playing expected of her as a woman. Yet the conflict is there. A Lucy Stone or a Sybilla Aleramo may publicly resist the constraints of traditional womanhood; a Eugenie de Guerin may try to bring her inner self in line with the orthodox femininity decreed by her God; and a Julia Ward Howe may attempt a balance, as countless other women have done; but whether women rebel, submit, or compromise, they are always conscious of the limitations and expectations placed upon them because of their sex. It is here, at the point of conflict between women's selves and Woman's role, as well as in the strategies brought to the battle by women in different times and different cultures, that the contradictions of women's lives are best illuminated. The conflict appears, muted or raging, in women's letters and diaries from the eleventh century to the present.

Women's private writings yield an abundance of what has often been called "trivia" but what we may also call "history." Helena Morely's diary is steeped in the Catholicism of rural Brazil; her life is markedly different from that of Ellen Strang, an Iowa farm girl. The richness of detail found in such diaries--not just the details but the diarists' response to them--tell us as much about a society as population charts or military histories. This seems obvious. Yet until recently women's private writings have been ignored, except to serve as background color for the standard histories. When women's lives are brought into the foreground, our view of history is not only more complete: it changes. What we know as history is deepened, broadened, and ultimately, redefined.

The first-person accounts of women who made the overland journey are perhaps the most fully examined of women's private writings. Studies of women on the frontier, such as those by Lillian Schlissell, Glenda Riley, Annette Kolodny, and Jeannie McKnight, as well as newly edited or newly discovered diaries and letters such as those published in the COVERED WAGON WOMEN series edited by Kenneth Holmes, have extended the body and scope of the literature of the Westward Movement. Women's private writings have gained new importance in other fields as well. Paul C. Rosenblatt examines women's writing for the light it sheds upon nineteenth century mourning and twentieth century grief theories; Ketaki Kushari Dyson includes women's accounts in her study of British citizens in nineteenth century India, and William Henry Irving acknowledges women's contribution to English letter-writing as a literary form.

If women's private writings are being mined for what they can tell us about history, they are also being taken increasingly seriously as life-writing. Less than fifteen years ago, when Estelle Jelinek began writing her dissertation on the tradition of women's autobiography, very little had been written on the subject. Today women's autobiography is a thriving field, and like much of women's studies, it is interdisciplinary, drawing upon history, literature, linguistics, sociology, psychology, librarianship and archival research.

At the heart of all of this new activity are new theories of what constitutes a good or even a real autobiography. In the past, letters and diaries, with a few exceptions (George Sand's JOURNAL, the letters of Madame de Sevigne) have been placed outside the boundaries of autobiography; boundaries which have been drawn by men. Jelinek argues that as women's lives have been different from men's, so have their autobiographies differed. She and other feminist critics have challenged theories of formal autobiography and located traditions of female autobiography in correspondence and in the diary.

The diary and the letter share similarities, but they differ in one important respect: that of intended audience. Diaries, to simplify a great deal, are primarily written for an audience of one. Since no one else will read it, the diarist can write freely and honestly what is on her mind or in her heart. She is the central figure, and everyone else--mothers, husbands, children--are secondary characters, perceived through her eyes, interpreted through the pages of her book. This is what Robert Fothergill calls the book of the self.

Letters can be said, as Sir Arthur Ponsonby does, "to have two parents, the writer and the recipient." [2] When reading letters, the personalities of two people, often more, must be taken into account, as well as the relationship between them, which directs and colors their correspondence. One writer's letters to different people can reveal many facets of her personality and character.

These two forms expand to encompass a great deal. If at one end of the spectrum stands the secret diary and the private letter, at the other stands the community journal and the "dispatch," both of which stand just this side of the newspaper column and the letter to the editor. Along this continuum lie Japanese poetic diaries, travel accounts, family correspondence, prison letters, account books, pregnancy journals, children's copy-books, and others, each with its own distinctive qualities and different possibilities for research.

Of all the kinds of private writing, domestic account books are the least personal, the least concerned with the self. They tell us little about the personality of the writer, almost nothing of her feelings, her dreams, her hopes and disappointments, even of her activities, except second-hand, through notations of their costs. However, as Cynthia Huff observes, "The extensive keeping of accounts in diaries shows the scope of women's managerial functions and business acumen." [3] In addition, each careful entry of income earned, expenditures for household items, repairs and upkeep, wages for servants, or travel expenses, adds detail to a picture of women's daily lives.

The diary of Mercy Goodwin Bodfish is a fairly typical example of another kind of account book, the family chronicle. To Bodfish, as to many eighteenth and nineteenth century women, fell the duty of family historian. Hers is not a private journal but a family history recorded in diary form; the first entry records the birth of her father, an event which she obviously could not have witnessed. In terse entries she records births, marriages, deaths, religious and community events, and the details of the family business, all serving to mark the movement of the Bodfish family through history.

Letter-writing duties for the family generally fell to women as well. Lady Stanley of Alderly was so good at letter-writing she was assigned the duty at the age of twelve, and though perhaps precocious, she was only one of countless women who have acted as family scribe from the seventeenth century until well into the twentieth. Their efforts were particularly crucial during the nineteenth century; women kept up the correspondence that linked family members as they migrated all over the globe. These letters not only kept strong the feelings of love and kinship, they were family "dispatches," carrying news and chronicling the family's life in new lands.

Travel journals and letters have always been popular, since, as Thomas Mallon writes, "even those people not given to the desire to record the details of the everyday will find in themselves the impulse to hoard the sights and sounds of places to which they may never return."[4] Armchair travelers, too, delight in the sights and sounds of places they may never see. The peoples of nineteenth century Africa, the landscape of Heian Japan, the top of Everest, the source of the Nile; all of these are captured vividly by the best travel writers.

The Victorians were intrepid travelers, prolific travel writers, and enthusiastic readers of travel books. They recognized that a travel book is not just about places but about people, and from the Victorians onward the personality of the author becomes a key ingredient in a good travelogue. Cribbing from Baedeker or Fodor's is not enough. A good travel book must also, according to Catherine Barnes Stevenson, "appeal to readers by offering autobiographical and psychological insights: inward views of the traveller's responses to physical hardships, danger, emotional stress in an alien environment."[5]

Stevenson, who has studied women travelers from 383 AD to the present, and Mary Russell, who focuses on Victorian women in Africa, observe that women's travel writings differ from those of men on several crucial points. "The male African traveller," Stevenson writes, "emerges from his own narrative...as a heroic figure; the female traveller, however is calculatedly unheroic."[6] Women are less inclined than men to view travel as an opportunity to confront and dominate a new land. Instead, women "develop strategies of accomodation," to deal with the unfamiliar or the dangerous. In traveling--often alone--to distant and unknown countries, women endured the same hardships and faced them with the same courage as men. Yet in their published travel books they tended to downplay both, often with a dash of humor.[7]

The male traveler almost always had a clear destination in mind or goal to accomplish. Women, on the other hand, have been more inclined to follow a more random, leisurely route, to "dawdle along the road, pausing to stop and stare and ruminate upon the idiosyncracies of life."[8] More so than men, women travelers observed the customs and commented in detail upon the daily lives of the peoples among whom they traveled.

For many of these women, the lure of adventure proved greater than the pull of tradition, but they took this conflict much to heart. The way of life chosen by "lady travelers" such as Isabella Bird and Lady Florence Baker required skills and capabilities at odds with prevailing ideals of femininity. "Forced by circumstances to be hardy, courageous, and decisive, these women developed personae which, while still consciously ladylike, had a masculine authority and competence."[9] Many women travelers were ambivalent about their new personae; proud of their achievements, they nevertheless clung to many of the traditional notions of feminine propriety. While their lives and adventures were held up as models for "The New Woman," many of them found the label repugnant. Even today, some women who travel for adventure will insist they are not feminists.

Women who undertook householding abroad as wives and daughters of diplomats, "China Merchants," or British civil servants may not have considered themselves heroic. Yet taking on what Stevenson calls "the housewife's burden" required a special brand of heroism:

> The exhausting attempt to manage a household under insupportable domestic conditions and to adjust psychologically to an inimical land--this is the heroism of which...many women travellers write."[10]

The housewife's burden also loomed large in the lives of women who emigrated to frontier settlements in North America, Africa, New Zealand, Australia, and South America. For women on the frontier, as for women travelers, everything was in upheaval: work roles, social expectations, the very "emotional fabric of women's lives."[11] Many women in frontier settlements experienced a sense of dislocation, even of alienation. The sense of dislocation was greater for women than for men, as Lillian Schlissel argues, because, "first of all, the determination to make the two-thousand mile journey was not one made by the women,"[12] many of whom made the Westward journey under protest. Men viewed emigration as an opportunity to better their lives, but the quality of women's lives often seemed to suffer on the frontier. They were expected to perform roughly the same duties they had at home--cooking, cleaning, caring for infants, making clothing--but with fewer amenities. In addition, they had to take on some of the "men's work": loading and unloading wagons, driving teams of oxen, standing guard at night. Women worked harder on the frontier.[13]

Frontier women had to deal with the same ambivalence about women's roles and propriety that confronted the lady traveler. They too had to reconcile Victorian notions of ladylike behavior with the rough-and-tumble life on the frontier. This was often complicated by family conflicts. In many frontier families, ambivalence over women's roles was a source of tension between mothers and daughters, since the younger women tended to look upon frontier life as an opportunity to behave in a more independent manner. They were more likely to try on new roles and to view the journey as an adventure, while their elders clung to traditional values and behavior. Yet despite generational tensions, despite hardships and dislocation, many women, young and old, did find frontier life to be an adventure; a journey not only to a new land but perhaps to a new self.

If the freedom of travel can inspire women to take up the pen, so can confinement. One of the most famous diaries in history was written in the confinement of an attic--the "secret annex" where for two years Anne Frank and her family hid from the Nazis during the German occupation of Holland.

Prison comes automatically to mind when one thinks of confinement and women have written their share of prison letters and journals. Prisoners are often forbidden to write, and much prison writing is done secretly and smuggled out, or kept hidden until the prisoner is liberated. Natalie Stark Crouter kept a secret diary during the two years she was interned by the Japanese during World War II; an act which, had it been discovered, was punishable by death (death was also the penalty for writing in the Nazi concentration camps). That Crouter and others risked their lives by writing secretly suggests how important diaries can be to prisoners. Lynn Z. Bloom, who edited Crouter's diary, writes that prison diaries can be a "valuable means of maintaining a necessary sense of self, of being in touch with external reality."[14] Prisoners write to maintain their sanity.

Prison letters, when not forbidden, are always monitored. Political prisoners, knowing their letters will be read by censors, will sometimes include political messages in them, in hopes of educating their captors and perhaps even winning them over to the prisoner's cause.

Prison letters and diaries have often been written (or published) to bear witness for the author's cause against injustice of a brutal authority. The letters and diaries of Etty Hilesum, a Dutch Jew who died at Auchwitz, the letters of Constance Markievicz, an Irish Nationalist arrested for leading the Easter Rebellion of 1916, and the diary of Barbara Deming, jailed for taking part in a civil rights march through the business district of Albany, Georgia, all bear testimony to their authors' resistance to tyranny, to her belief in her cause, and, in Hilesum's case, to her courage in the face of death.

One does not have to be literally in jail to be imprisoned. Disability and chronic illness may confine a woman as surely as any lock and key. Alice James wrote her famous journal while confined to bed by real and imagined illnesses. Katharine Butler Hathaway, who wrote under the *nom de plume* "the Little Locksmith," had a short stature and painfully curved spine which caused her both mobility and respiratory problems. Bedridden and confined to one room, she turned to art (she was aware of the symbolism in her interest in miniature objects) and to writing.

"Confinement" was also once a euphemism for pregnancy. In the nineteenth century, when matters of pregnancy and childbirth were taboo in polite society, it was considered unseemly for a woman who too obviously "showed" to appear in public. Housebound and in an unmentionable condition, many women confided in their diaries. Cynthia Huff has found these to be meticulously detailed accounts and suggests they may be the best source of information about nineteenth century childbirth practices.[15]

In our society today, pregnancy is not the taboo subject it once was. Pregnancy diaries are more commonly published, such as those by Charlotte Hirsh,

Susan Lapinski, and Phyllis Chesler, whose book WITH CHILD was a bestseller in the United States. Women are no longer shut away from public life during pregnancy, and confinement as a metaphor has largely disappeared from pregnancy accounts, to be replaced by the image of the journey. The trials of a difficult pregnancy, especially if the mother-to-be is strongly religious, are often laid out for the reader as a sort of Pilgrim's Progress. Pregnancy is a time for soul-searching, and even those who choose to adopt a child, as Nan Bauer Maglin did, sometimes feel the need to explore their feelings about motherhood in a diary. They too may describe the process as a journey into the unknown.

Diary-writing has long been considered a useful tool for self-development, each era and each social mileu defining "self-development" in its own way. From the Puritan journal of the seventeenth century to the modern "intensive journal," diaries have been seen as instructional to the soul, both to write and to read.

The earliest self-improvement journals were religious. As Sir Arthur Ponsonby rather testily notes, it is to the religious motive that we owe the "immense number of diaries given up to self-disparagement, repentance, prayer and supplication. The Puritans, the Covenanters and the Quakers were taught by means of diaries to watch themselves, correct themselves, to mark out their course of life, and note any deflections from the straight path."[16]

Published Quaker journals were carefully edited to form instructional and inspirational narratives, after the example of the official version of George Fox's journal, published at the end of the seventeenth century. Metta L. Winter outlines the typical Quaker journal:

> A demonstration of the miracle of the Inner Light created in the writer's life, including the successive steps by which he or she obtained spiritual harmony; recounting of religious crises and how these were resolved; and the carrying out of the commands of the Spirit in outward action and an account of the resulting inner peace."[17]

Winter brings the Quaker journal into the twentieth century by suggesting that contemporary Friends make use of the rich tradition of the Quaker Journal. Modern writers have advantages over their ancestors, benefitting from the insights of psychology, which help illuminate the processes of journal-writing. Because Friends' journals are no longer required to be submitted to the meeting for editing and publication, the modern Quaker is free to write "both copiously and without censorship, making the most effective use of the journal's experimental dimension."[18]

Winter is not the only writer to bring together the idea of the Quaker confessional journal and modern psychological diary. In PRIVATE CHRONICLES, Robert Fothergill writes:

> It may be argued that the practice of self-examination in moral terms, which is seldom absent from even the most "secular" diaries, may derive in fact from the Puritan equation of serious self-communing with strict examination of conscience. What other business has a man with his inner secret self, if not the business of improving it?[19]

That the modern journal of conscience has much in common with the early religious journals is apparent from some of the titles of recent "how-to" books on diary writing: THE NEW DIARY: HOW TO USE A JOURNAL FOR SELF-GUIDANCE AND EXPANDED CREATIVITY; ONE TO ONE: SELF-UNDERSTANDING THROUGH JOURNAL WRITING; LIFE STUDY: EXPERIENCING CREATIVE LIVES THROUGH THE INTENSIVE JOURNAL; and of course, KEEPING A SPIRITUAL JOURNAL.

Ira Progoff's statement of purpose at the begining of AT A JOURNAL WORKSHOP is not, despite its secular, psychoanayltical phraseology, far removed from that of the early Quakers:

> The INTENSIVE JOURNAL workbook is specifically designed to provide an instrument and techniques by which persons can discover within themselves the resources they did not know they possessed. It is to enable them to draw the power of deep contact out of the

> actual experience of their lives so that they can recognize their own identity of the universe as they experience it...The specific means of achieving this contact with the inner resources of one's life is by the regular and disciplined use of the INTENSIVE JOURNAL with its progressive exercises. The effective principle operating in this is that, when a person is shown how to reconnect himself with the contents and continuity of his life, the inner thread of movement by which his life has been unfolding reveals itself to him by itself. Given the opportunity, a life crystallizes out of its own nature, revealing its meaning and its goal."[20]

To find oneself or to find God; to expand one's creativity or to examine one's conscience; whatever the purpose of keeping such a diary, one thing is clear: The journal of conscience is concerned with the inner secret self and the business of improving it.

Diary writing has also been employed by religious and secular teachers as a means to educate the young; to help lead them into the religious fold or to instruct them in the social responsibilities of their elders. Cynthia Huff calls such journals "behavior books."[21] Written as part of the child's daily lessons, they contained regular entries upon the child's lessons, religious instruction, domestic affairs of the household (in which she, as a girl, would be instructed to take part), and her relationships with family and friends. Since the chief purpose of the behavior books was to mold the character of the young, self-expression was encouraged but closely monitored.

As Huff observes, the primary relationship treated in the child's diary was that with her teacher, whether a governess, as in the case of Marjorie Fleming (her governess, Isabella Keith, was also her cousin), or her mother, as in the case of Louisa May Alcott. The nineteenth-century child diary, Huff stresses, really comprises _two_ autobiographies, that of the child, and that of her teacher. The teacher dictated and shaped the form and the content of the child's diary, as well as corrected errors in spelling, punctuation, composition, and penmanship. We are reminded of Isabella's presence when Marjorie Fleming states, "love is a papithatic thing as well as troublesome & tiresome but O Isabella forbid me to speak about it" or acknowledges, "this page is far from being well written." Sometimes Isabella writes directly in the diary: "Marjorie must write no more journal till she writes better." This stern injunction is followed by handwriting exercises.[22]

Louisa May Alcott's mother is also present in Alcott's diary. The young Louisa asked her mother to write something in her journal, and received a lecture on the proper use of a diary:

> Dear Louy--your handwriting improves very fast. Take pains and do not be in a hurry. I like to have you make observations about our conversations and your own thoughts. It helps to express them and to understand your little self. Remember, dear girl, that a diary should be an epitome of your life. May it be a record of pure thought and good actions, then you will indeed be the precious child of your loving mother.[23]

Louisa strove mightily to keep to this standard, but she had her lapses, as did Marjorie:

> To day I affronted myself before Miss Margaret and Miss Isa Crawford and Mrs. Craford & Miss Kermical which was very naughty but I hope that there will be no more evil in all my journal.[24]

Though kept in check, the diarist's personality often breaks out from behind rote descriptions of lessons and self-disparaging resolutions. Too often however, the diaries of children (as well as their letters) have been all but buried in sentimentality by their adult editors. Certainly the naivete and innocence of childhood writing can be charming, but its charm can be overemphasized to the detriment of the diary's other qualities. Once rescued from such sentimentality, childhood diaries have much to offer. The dual autobiography suggested by Cynthia Huff is but one example of the direction new research into the private writings of children might take.

Women's letters and diaries can also be considered as autobiographical art in the fullest sense of the word. Correspondence has been called a woman's art, and certainly, some of the best letter-writers have been women: Madame de Sevigne, Madame de Stael, George Sand. From its begining, letter-writing was considered to be an informal art, one that was supposed to be natural, spontaneous, unplanned, unstudied; in other words, artless. In reality, a great deal of effort and artistry went into producing these effects, especially during the eighteenth century, when letter writing reached its maturity as an art form. As Howard Anderson and Irvin Ehrenpreis comment, "the letters that the eighteenth century judged its best are not thoughtless outpourings; their charm and their power, as well as their very appearance of spontaneity, are the result of considerable, if varied, art."[25]

Diary-writing has also been considered as an art, and the same qualities of spontaneity, effortlessness and "artlessness" are prized in a good diary. Just as with good letter writing, these effects are learned, practiced, and perfected. Some writers--Anais Nin, Alice James, Madame de Sevigne--are able to take it a step further, and to raise their diary or their letters from the art of self-expression to an expressive art.

The line dividing private writings and fiction is thin and often crossed. In eighteenth century Europe, the popularity of the familiar letter rose in tandem with the epistolary novel, and for a long time the relationship between the two was casual. It was not uncommon for an author to include fictitious letters in a volume of her correspondence or for an editor to slip spurious letters into a work. The first two editions of Lady Mary Wortley Montagu's Turkish Embassy letters contained many that are spurious (and the "real" letters were composed by Lady Montagu, based on her correspondence). Whole volumes of bogus letters have been published under an author's name, such as those attributed to Madame de Pompadour.

Also popular were letter writing manuals,

sometimes called letter-writers or miscellanies. As entertaining as they were instructional, the letter-writing manuals pretended to be collections of real letters "found" by the editor, hidden away in a chest (THE LADIES CASKET BROKE OPEN) or waylaid enroute to its destination (THE POST-BOY ROBB'D OF HIS MAIL). These books stood midway between the epistolary novel and the true anthology. The pretexts for the collections were obviously fictitious, as were most of their contents; yet often, among the letters ascribed to Marie Antoinette or Mary Stuart, lurked one or two genuine missives.

Earlier still, the Japanese poetic diary flourished in Heian Japan. Women excelled in this form to such a degree that Earl Miner locates the beginings of modern Japanese literature in their writings. These diaries were not private (in the sense of "secret"), since they were passed around to be read, but they did deal with private matters--especially love affairs--which we today might hesitate to broadcast to the world, at least while they were still in progress. The books grew in the way diaries do, in installments, over a period of time, so that the lovers' stories were allowed to unfold as they happened. The poems set down in them--THE GOSSAMER DIARY contains over three hundred--added an artistic dimension. The resulting blend of autobiography, poetry, and correspondence, crosses boundaries between private and public, between life and art, and between solitary writing and shared correspondence.

Modern authors also see connections between the diary, the letter, and art. Suzanne Juhasz examines the work of Kathleen Fraser, who writes fiction based on her journal, and argues that Fraser and other feminist writers who attempt to use the diary as a source and a model for poetry and stories are faced with a dilemma: how can writing meant for a public audience maintain its private quality? Or the other way around, how can "writing for oneself become writing for others without losing its essence?"[26] According to Juhasz, the public and the private can only be fused if:

> the traditional concept of wall--of private
> and public as separate and mutually

> exclusive places--is replaced by a recognition of connection, of fluid boundaries, of a space somewhere between private and public that partakes of both.[27]

To Anais Nin the diary and fiction appear as a duality; the two forms "run in parallel lines," each enhancing the other:

> I was writing better in the notebooks because I was writing outside, in the formal work, and I was writing more authentically in the novels because I sustained the informal, improvised living contact with my relationships, cities, the present.[28]

It is also clear that she meant her Diary, in its edited form at least, to be a literary work. There is nothing artless about her diary, still less in her editing of the diary for publication:

> It was the experience of the novelist which helped me to edit the diary. It was the fiction writer who knew when the tempo lagged, when details were trivial, when a description was a repetition. I changed nothing essential, I only cut the extraneous material, the overload.[29]

The Russian poet Zinaida Hippius believed writing letters and diaries to be a creative act no different from that of writing poetry. For her, the power of language was sacrosanct.

> No one knows what a part of me my letters are! What a rare gift! Rare, indeed. Even if they are poor I impart to them what I have, with pain in my heart, with faith in my words.[30]

Writers of less artistic power have felt that their words carried their feelings. But it is the poet who says, "my words, when they contain my feelings, are of the same substance as my flesh."[31] Hippius' conviction is echoed in the words of another Russian poet, Marina Tsvetayeva: "For me, the word _is almost the same_ as feeling; the innermost thing."[32] If the word is the innermost thing, of the same substance as one's flesh, categories such as "private" and "public" are irrelevant. For Hippius and Tsvetayeva, and for other writers, such categories did not exist; they made none of the usual distinctions between their letters, their diaries, and their art.

II: PROBLEMS IN EDITING

"Divide them up how you will," Sir Arthur Ponsonby wrote, "into ancient and modern, social, political, travel, or personal, instrospective, or objective, within each category there is infinite variety with just the slender but very distinct link that all these men and women have felt impelled to keep a book, in which periodically to write down something about themselves."[33] Between a woman's impulse to write down something of herself and ours to read it stands a host of intermediaries: editors, publishers, executors. All of these, but particularly the editor, may take a hand in shaping the published text. In light of this, it seems neither wise nor sensible to approach a published text as if it represented an author's original words. The publishing history of a text, the editorial methods used to prepare it for publication, and the relationship between an editor and an author must all be taken into account.

Private writings edited for a public audience present a number of problems. The first, naturally, regards completeness. Elizabeth Hampsten, writing about unpublished writings held in libraries and historical societies, finds one question "vital to any critical examination of writing that was not intended for publication: how complete is what we have?"[34]

War, flood, fire, the vicissitudes of life, and perhaps worst of all, indifferent descendants, all play their part in making what we have less than complete. Most diaries are consigned to oblivion, by chance and by design. Letters, once read and answered, are often thrown away, or else kept carelessly. Often, letters never reach their intended destination. Letters go astray even in the best of times, but during wartime or periods of social upheaval, letters may be seized, censored, or simply lost in the confusion. Unless letters are drafted in a diary, as Eliza Pinckney's were, correspondence does not exist all of a piece, but as many separate pages, sheets, notes, cards, and scraps of paper. If collected at all, its unity is fragile and often temporary. It is rare that a correspondence survives completely intact.

The destruction of an author's papers after her death is commonplace. Ted Hughes, to cite a recent example, burned portions of Sylvia Plath's journals which included passages written up to two days before her suicide because he "did not want her children to have to read them."[35] Just as commonly, writers destroy their papers themselves. Louisa May Alcott revised her journal at different times during her life, destroying parts of it along the way, and Clara Schumann consigned a good many of her letters to the fire before her daughter persuaded her to save them. If an author cannot bring herself to destroy her papers, she may ask an executor to do so after her death. Jane Austen left instructions that her private papers be burned, and Rose Macaulay directed her executors to destroy any personal papers found in her apartment after her death--with the result that while her side of the correspondence survived to be published in LETTERS TO A SISTER, those of her sister Jean did not. (Jean also destroyed a number of Macaulay's letters to her before turning the remainder over for publication.)

When "what we have" is then published, another vital question arises: how complete is _this edition_ of an author's private writings? What, we may ask, has been left out? "No editor can be trusted not to ruin a diary,"[36] Sir Arthur Ponsonby wrote, and the same can be said of the editors of letters. The most sensitive and careful editors, in cutting what they may feel unimportant, irrelevant, repetitious or even "too personal," walk a very fine line. They may end up, for all their good intentions, ruining the work.

Many editors have been neither sensitive nor careful. Editors have cut manuscripts they felt were too long; padded those they thought too short; re-arranged material to suit themselves; bowdlerized writings which revealed the less-than-perfect character of their authors. Too often, they have destroyed the originals once the edited version was published.

The rather brutal editorial treatment the letters of Eliza Fay received after her death is not uncommon. Fay, an Englishwoman, followed her husband to India in the 1880's; after separating from him, she spent the next thirty years living and traveling in India, Europe, and North America. She compiled an autobiography from her letters, which remained unpublished at her death. The administrator of her estate, feeling the manuscript too long, cut what he thought uninteresting and published a much shortened version.[37] This version, among other things, entirely deletes the last twenty years of Fay's life, now irrevocably lost, since the editor destroyed both her manuscript and her original letters.

The urge to make a "good story" out of a diary that seems rambling and disjointed, or from a correspondence too far-ranging or voluminous, is the motive which guides many an editor's blue-pencil (we are fortunate that not all editors are as thorough as Eliza Fay's). While many diaries and letters are written around a theme (such as pregancy journals) or an event (letters on an elk hunt), most private writings _are_ disjointed and far-ranging. In this case, material _may_ be extracted from them and shaped into a more cohesive narrative.

Virginia Woolf's A WRITER'S DIARY, compiled from her diary by Leonard Woolf, is one well-known example of editing for story. The book could more properly be called "Extracts from a writer's diary on the subject of writing." It contains "practically everything which referred to her own writing," as well as sections of practice writing, selected descriptive passages which "give the reader an idea of the direct impact upon her mind of scenes and persons, i.e., of the raw material of her art," and comments on what she was reading. The book thus created "throws light upon Virginia Woolf's intentions, objects, and methods as a writer"; it makes no attempt to present a whole and entire picture of Woolf's character.[38] Similar editorial methods, using extracts to focus on one aspect of an author's life or character, were used in Julia Ward Howe's WALK WITH GOD, extracts from her journal which deal with her religion; and GEORGE ELIOT'S FAMILY LIFE AND LETTERS, excerpts from her correspondence focusing on her relationships with her family.

Famous and prolific writers often have more than one story to tell, and their private writings may fall more naturally into several narratives. Fanny Burney's diary can be divided into at least two without doing violence to the text: the story of her life as Lady-In-Waiting at the court of George III and the story of her friendships with Mrs. Thrale and Dr. Johnson. Likewise, Fanny Kemble's diary of her career in the Theatre and her journal-expose of life on a Georgia plantation are two separate and distinct stories. Prolific letter writers such as Elizabeth Barrett Browning or Madame de Stael present different sides of their character to different people, and it is fitting that each correspondent should have his or her own volume.

Editing for story is perhaps most obvious in the case of love letters. Love letters are often set off from the rest of a writer's correspondence, to stand as a self-contained story. They are likely to be pruned of mundane matters as well, because if love affairs are embarassing to editors who would keep an author's reputation untarnished, so are business affairs unwanted in a volume of love letters. Thus, references to household and business matters were deleted from the courtship letters of Margaret Tyndall and John Winthrop so as not to intrude upon the unfolding story of a Puritan courtship and marriage.

The desire to control the story told by a woman's private writings is nowhere more apparent than in those which have been out-and-out bowdlerized. Today, doctoring a text to portray an author in a more favorable light is considered unconscionable in any serious edition of an author's papers. But earlier editors had no qualms about cleaning up an author's private writings to match an idealized public persona. Family and friends have the most at stake in insuring that an author's reputation is well-polished for posterity. They are most often the executors of an author's papers, and sometimes an author's first (or only) editors as well. Countless "memorial" editions to "loving mothers," "deceased sisters," and "pious servants of Jesus Christ" were--and still are--compiled by family and friends upon an author's death. Most of these can be counted upon to portray the author in the best light possible.

To protect the reputation of a woman author means, in most cases, to protect her from charges of unchastity, or worse, sexual deviance. Bowdlerized versions of the private writings of Margaret Fuller and Emily Dickinson demonstrate the lengths to which editors will go to forestall such charges. THE MEMOIRS OF MARGARET FULLER, edited by Ralph Waldo Emerson, William H. Channing, and James Freeman Clarke, stands almost as a textbook case of editorial pathology. According to Robert Hudspeth, editor of the reconstructed edition of her letters, Fuller's three friends employed a rather heavy-handed method of cut-and-paste, often working with the original letters. They blotted out some passages "with gobs of purple ink," scissored out others, rearranged, wrote over passages, and inserted their own phrasing and comments. All of this was done in "an attempt to make Fuller intellectually safer and sexually acceptable, her marriage normal, her son legitimate." [39]

Not surprisingly, the private writings of lesbians have been subjected to bowdlerization of the protective sort. Fuller's writings about her love for women were among those excised by her editors in order to make her "sexually acceptable." Similar passages were delet- ed from the letters of Emily Dickinson, and for the same reasons. Lillian Faderman [40] describes in great detail the removal of such problematic passages from Emily Dickinson's letters to Sue Gilbert. It is clear from the deleted passages that Dickinson felt more passion towards Gilbert than early editors of her letters felt was "normal." And it was a relative who first edited Dickinson's letters for publication: Martha Dickinson Bianchi was Dickinson's niece--and Sue Gilbert's daughter.

Controversy does sometimes attend the publication of a bowdlerized text, and may even rage through two or three editions. The first edition of the letters of Jane Welsh Carlyle, which appeared shortly after her death, was not altogether well received. Critics felt

Thomas Carlyle's eagerness to put his wife's letters into print was a little unseemly, and the rosy picture of the Carlyle's marriage presented by the published letters was met with some skepticism. In fact, the letters *were* edited to portray their marriage as less rocky than it was. Thomas Carlyle's nephew, Alexander Carlyle, disliked the deception and published a newly edited volume to set the record straight. Unfortunately, *this* editor manipulated his material to portray their relationship in a more *negative* light. It was not until much later that an edition was published which printed Carlyle's words as she had written them, and which let readers draw their own conclusions.

When a woman's papers are edited to tell someone *else'* story, her own is often given short shrift. Their diaries and correspondence may be cut or shaped to fit into the *Life* of a husband, brother, father, or colleague. The letters between Samuel Butler and his sister May, for example, are presented to reveal *his* character, not hers; in an early edition of the letters of Charles and Mary Lamb, Mary is nowhere mentioned in the introduction; and Lady Judith Montefiore's journals were severely pruned, paraphrased, re-written in the third person, and combined with those of her husband.

There are of course many cases where this does not happen, where correspondence is edited to reveal a relationship between equals. This is true of the published letters of Emma Goldman and Alexander Berkman and of the correspondence of Gertrude Stein and Carl Van Vechten. In Carl Van Doren's edition of the correspondence of Benjamin Franklin and his sister Jane Mecom, and in later editions of the letters of Abigail and John Adams the private papers of public figures are weighed in relation *to each other*, and found to be of equal value. If history perceives John Adams and Benjamin Franklin to be the more important figures, Abigail Adams and Jane Mecom are hardly negligible. A wife or a sister need not be hidden in the shadow of a great man.

It is more common, however, for a wife's papers or a daughter's to be pressed into service of a male-oriented concept of history. The editor of the papers of Mary Moffat and her husband Robert, nineteenth-century missionaries to South Africa, cut most of the "purely personal" matter from Mary's letters, such as "gossip" and "trivial" news of family and friends, since he felt these things irrelevant to a history of the mission at Kuruman. The resulting book, comprised of the official journal required by all missionaries in the field (written by Robert) and those parts of Mary's letters which deal strictly with mission affairs, reflects the formal, official, male idea of history. Papers edited in this way not only do violence to the writings of the individual woman, but to history as well.

Women can also be buried in published collections of family papers. Early collections sometimes omitted the full names of women diarists and letter writers, even in genealogies. Biographical information is even more stingily given out, so that at times, it can be difficult to trace a woman through subsequent marriages. Apparently, a "Lady Elizabeth" had no existence of her own, save as the wife of the man under consideration at the moment, whether he be Sir Henry or Sir George.

To be considered a mere adjunct to a more important male is better, however, than to not be considered at all. This was almost the fate of Harriet Thompson, the wife of a Union officer during the Civil War. The couple wrote to each other throughout the war, but while her husband's letters describing his experiences in the war were published, her letters relating "the trials and vicissitudes of a childless young wife," were almost forgotten. The journal and letters of Lady Florence Baker were also tardily published. This energetic nineteenth century traveler was for a long time known only through her husband's books because her own journal and letters were not published until 1972. Surprisingly, Martha Washington's letters have not yet been collected, and only sporadically published, save by the Mt. Vernon Ladies Association, which has worked to remedy this omission by publishing Washington's letters in their quarterly Journal.

If on the one hand, we must ask what is left out of the published version of an author's private writings, we might ask of some works, "what has been added?" Sketchy narratives are often expanded into fuller, more readable, more enjoyable accounts. A woman caught up in a tense and unpredictable situation may have time to only write brief entries in a diary; later she may wish to flesh them out by memory. May Sinclair, whose JOURNAL OF IMPRESSIONS IN BELGIUM was written from notes and memory, observes in her introduction to the book that circumstances seldom allowed regular journal-keeping:

> "in the last week in the siege of Antwerp, when the wounded were being brought to Ghent by the hundreds, when the fighting came closer and closer to the city, and at the end, when the Germans were driving you from Ghent to Bruges to Ostend and from Ostend to Dunkirk, you could not sit down to write your impressions, even if you were cold-blooded enough to want to. It was as much as you could do to scribble the merest note of what happened in your day book." [41]

It was customary for travelers to expand sketchy accounts into full-blown narratives in the form of letters, diaries, or journal-letters. Some were entirely contrived, but most were at least written from notes taken at the time, no matter how sketchy or brief. Diaries and letters were often combined for publication, or rewritten in the form of either one or the other. "Letters to Friends at Home" was often a polite fiction, since the letter and diary forms were popular throughout the eighteenth and nineteenth centuries. They were pleasing to readers because they provided a feeling of immediacy; and they were convenient to writers because they were easily mastered forms, ones with which most people were familiar, even if they were not professional writers. They had probably received lessons in both as part of their education, and could more or less confidently cast their narratives in either form.

More ambitious writers may see in their private writings the seeds of a literary work. That Mary Boykin Chesnut considered the editing and publication of A DIARY FROM DIXIE a serious literary undertaking is clear from the many manuscipt versions she left behind. Her original diary, only recently published, consisted of brief notes written during the Civil War, from her plantation in South Carolina and as a traveller in different parts of the South. She expanded and revised the diary, obviously with purely literary intentions, several times during her life, all of them presented as a "spontaneous" diary. Four different versions of the work, aside from the original notes, surivive.

Narratives are also combined with others to form entirely new texts. In the most self-effacing editing of this kind, the author allows her text to be subsumed into that of another--usually, but not always, her husband. Fanny Stevenson kept a diary of a sea cruise made with her husband Robert Louis Stevenson, chiefly to keep an up-to-date account when he neglected his own diary. When her own diary of the cruise was published, she cut from it most of the passages which had been adapted and added to his. Other collaborations are more even-handed. The descriptive notes taken by Elizabeth Agassiz while on an expedition with Louis Agassiz were edited together with his more scientific ones and published jointly under the title A JOURNEY IN BRAZIL. It is almost impossible to separate out who wrote what--even the authors confessed they had forgotten which of them wrote many of the passages--but credit is given to both. Women sometimes join with other women to publish "diaries in duo" as Flora and Benoite Groult titled their book. Sarah Ponsonby and Eleanor Butler, the Irish "romantic friends" known as the Ladies of Llangollen, kept a joint diary, though little of it remains. We do, however, have the full diary kept by another female couple, Edith Cooper and Katherine Bradley. Their JOURNAL OF MICHAEL FIELD, as well as their letters to Robert Browning and all of their poetry, whether written jointly or separately, was published under their pseudonym.

To create a journal where none existed is possibly the ultimate editorial act. I do not mean forgery, but the gathering together of scattered material into something that can be called a "journal." Perhaps the most famous posthumously created journal is that of Katherine Mansfield. Mansfield did not keep a journal in the usual sense of the word; even the brief journals she began from time to time are fragmentary jottings, and she rarely kept them up for more than a few weeks at a time. THE JOURNALS OF KATHERINE MANSFIELD came into being entirely through the work of her husband, the publisher John Middleton Murray. C.K. Stead explains that the material in the SCRAPBOOK and the two versions of the JOURNAL published by Murray came from one collection of papers:

> This collection consisted of four ordinary and rather empty diaries for the years 1914, 1915, 1920 and 1922; about thirty notebooks containing fragments of stories, scenes, snatches of conversation, ideas, notes from reading, quotations, calculations of household finances, unposted letters; and finally, about one hundred loose sheets of equally heterogeneous material.[42]

Mansfield's journals present, in Stead's words, "a sort of metaphysical puzzle...how can Katherine Mansfield be 'author' of a book of which, as such, she was unaware?" Stead does not hold that the JOURNAL is entirely the work of Murray but comes to the conclusion that the "essential unity" of Mansfield's private writings would enable it to fall together into a good book no matter how it was arranged. "The material has, it must be admitted, the fascination of a kitset which can be assembled in different ways to produce instant--and genuine--art."[43]

The "kitset" method was also used by Ruth Limmer to create the autobiography of Louise Bogan. What Limmer calls "a mosaic" is compiled from

> "...journals, notebook entries, poems (some never before published), sentences and paragraphs from her criticism, portions of letters, a lecture, answers to questions (in one case, questions she herself posed), short stories, recorded conversations, scraps of paper..."[44]

In a similar manner, Lenore Marshall began shaping her autobiography in the form of a journal from a lifetime of collected fragments (the task was finished by Janice Thaddeus after Marshall's death); and Stan Steiner brought together the fragmented lifetime writings of Bonita Wa Wa Calachaw, which she had written on cheap drawing pads, "envelopes from welfare checks, leaflets, advertising folders, a broadside announcing a 'Minstrel Show' of the Harlem Elks' Club in 1924."[45] These editorial creations are as much a "book of the self" as any "real" diary, yet they have come into being in a manner more akin to the editing of a volume of letters. Scattered, fragmented, it is only under the hands of an editor that they come to reveal the unfolding story of a woman's life.

An editor can be careful or insensitive; rigorously faithful to the text or unscrupulously intent upon shaping it to fit a cardboard pattern of its author. It has been said that every biography is also an autobiography--of its author. Those who edit the private writings of others have also revealed their own personalities and prejudices. While new, meticulously accurate editions of women's private writings are invaluable, the older editions should not be discarded out of hand because they are "bad." Behind their faults and inconsistencies lie societal values and expectations which might well serve as background for the author's own life. What editors have chosen to highlight or suppress can be used as a measure of women's changing roles and place in society through history.

"In journals and diaries, letters and scraps, we hear the voices of our predecessors speaking for themselves," Elizabeth Hampsten writes. "We read because we want to know what was on their minds."[46] In their private writings, in diaries or in letters to trusted confidants, women have felt most free to speak for themselves. Whether we read them in order to mine them for the minutiae of daily life or to set them in their rightful place in the canon of great life writings, it is certain that women's voices add to our knowledge and understanding of our culture and those of centuries past.

NOTES

1. Nin, Anais, "The Personal Life Deeply Lived," in Hinz, Evelyn J., A WOMAN SPEAKS: THE LECTURES, SEMINARS, AND INTERVIEWS OF ANAIS NIN (Chicago: Swallow Press, 1975), 154.

2. Ponsonby, Arthur, ENGLISH DIARIES (London: Methuen, 1923), xxi.
3. Huff, Cynthia, BRITISH WOMEN'S DIARIES (New York: AMS Press, 1985), xxi.
4. Mallon, Thomas, A BOOK OF ONE'S OWN (New York: Ticknor & Fields, 1984), 42.
5. Stevenson, Catherine Barnes, WOMEN TRAVEL WRITERS IN AFRICA (Boston: Twayne Publishers, 1982), 6.
6. Stevenson, WOMEN TRAVEL WRITERS IN AFRICA, 160.
7. Stevenson, WOMEN TRAVEL WRITERS IN AFRICA, 160.
8. Russell, Mary, THE BLESSINGS OF A GOOD THICK SKIRT: WOMEN TRAVELLERS AND THEIR WORLD (London: Collins, 1986), 211.
9. Stevenson, WOMEN TRAVEL WRITERS IN AFRICA, 4.
10. Stevenson, WOMEN TRAVEL WRITERS IN AFRICA, 17.
11. Schlissel, Lillian, "Mothers and Daughters on the Western Frontier," FRONTIERS 3:2 (1978), 29.
12. Schlissel, "Mothers and Daughters on the Western Frontier," 30.
13. Schlissel, "Mothers and Daughters on the Western Frontier," 30.
14. Bloom, Lynn Z., "The Diary as Popular History, JOURNAL OF POPULAR CULTURE 9:4 (Spring, 1976), 797.
15. Huff, Cynthia, "Chronicles of Confinement: Reactions to Childbirth in British Women's Diaries," WOMEN'S STUDIES INTERNATIONAL FORUM 10:1 (November, 1987), 63.
16. Ponsonby, ENGLISH DIARIES, 8.
17. Winter, Metta L., "Heart Watching Through Journal Keeping," FRIENDS JOURNAL (November 1, 1980), 11.
18. Winter, "Heart Watching Through Journal Keeping," 12.
19. Fothergill, Robert, PRIVATE CHRONICLES (New York: Oxford University Press, 1974), 17.
20. Progoff, Ira, AT A JOURNAL WORKSHOP (New York: Dialogue House Library, 1976), 10.
21. Huff, BRITISH WOMEN'S DIARIES, xxv.
22. Smyth, Clifford, MARJORIE FLEMING'S BOOK (New York: Boni & Liveright, n.d.), 33, 72, 80.
23. Quoted in Moffat, Mary Jane and Charlotte Painter, REVELATIONS: DIARIES OF WOMEN (New York: Random House, 1974), 31.
24. Smyth, MARJORIE FLEMING'S BOOK, 76.
25. Anderson, Howard and Irvin Ehrenpreis, THE FAMILIAR LETTER IN THE EIGHTEENTH CENTURY (Lawrence: University of Kansas Press, 1966), 273.

26. Juhasz, Susanne, "The Journal as Source and Model for Feminist Art: The Example of Kathleen Fraser," FRONTIERS 8:1 (1984), 16.
27. Juhasz, "The Journal as Source and Model for Feminist Art," 16.
28. Nin, Anais, "The Diary Versus Fiction," in Webber, Jeannette and Joan Grumman, WOMAN AS WRITER (Boston: Houghton Miflin, 1978), 41.
29. Nin, "The Diary Versus Fiction," 45.
30. Pachmuss, Temira, BETWEEN PARIS AND ST. PETERSBURG: SELECTED DIARIES OF ZINAIDA HIPPIUS (Urbana: University of Chicago Press, 1975), 66.
31. Pachmuss, BETWEEN PARIS AND ST. PETERSBURG, viii.
32. Feinstein, Elaine, A CAPTIVE LION: THE LIFE OF MARINA TSVETAYEVA (New York: E.P. Dutton, 1987), 133.
33. Ponsonby, MORE ENGLISH DIARIES (London: Methuen, 1927), 4.
34. Hampsten, Elizabeth, READ THIS ONLY TO YOURSELF (Bloomington: University of Indiana Press, 1982), 8.
35. McCullough, Frances, THE JOURNALS OF SYLVIA PLATH (New York: The Dial Press, 1982), xiii.
36. Ponsonby, MORE ENGLISH DIARIES, 5.
37. Fay, Eliza, ORIGINAL LETTERS FROM INDIA (London: Hogarth Press, 1925).
38. Woolf, Virginia, A WRITER'S DIARY (New York: Harcourt Brace Jovanovich, c.1953), viii-ix.
39. Hudspeth, Robert, THE LETTERS OF MARGARET FULLER (Ithaca: Cornell University Press, 1983), 61.
40. Faderman, Lillian, "Emily Dickinson's Letters to Sue Gilbert," MASSACHUSETTS REVIEW 18:2 (Summer, 1977), 197-225.
41. Sinclair, May, JOURNAL OF IMPRESSIONS IN BELGIUM (London: Hutchinson, 1915).
42. Stead, C.K., THE LETTERS AND JOURNALS OF KATHERINE MANSFIELD: A SELECTION (London: Penguin, 1977) 13.
43. Stead, THE LETTERS AND JOURNALS OF KATHERINE MANSFIELD, 14.
44. Limmer, Ruth, JOURNEY AROUND MY ROOM: THE AUTOBIOGRAPHY OF LOUISE BOGAN (New York: Viking Press, 1980), xx.
45. Steiner, Stan, SPIRIT WOMAN: THE DIARIES AND PAINTINGS OF BONITA WA WA CALACHAW (New York: Harper & Row, 1980), 80.
46. Hampsten, READ THIS ONLY TO YOURSELF, 14-15.

WOMEN'S DIARIES, JOURNALS, AND LETTERS

I. BIBLIOGRAPHIES

1. Addis, Patricia K. THROUGH A WOMAN'S I: AN ANNOTATED BIBLIOGRAPHY OF AMERICAN WOMEN'S AUTO-BIOGRAPHICAL WRITINGS, 1946-1976. Metuchen, N.J.: Scarecrow Press, 1983. 607p.

Lists autobiographies, diaries and journals, memoirs, reminiscences, travel accounts, and collections of letters.

2. Arksey, Laura, Nancy Pries, and Marcia Reed, ed. AMERICAN DIARIES: AN ANNOTATED BIBLIOGRAPHY OF PUBLISHED AMERICAN DIARIES AND JOURNALS. Detroit: Gale Research Co., 1983. 2 vols.

3. Batts, John Stuart. BRITISH MANUSCRIPT DIARIES OF THE NINETEENTH CENTURY: AN ANNOTATED LISTING. Totowa, N.J: Rowman and Littlefield, 1976. 345p.

4. Begos, Jane Dupree. ANNOTATED BIBLIOGRAPHY OF PUBLISHED WOMEN'S DIARIES. Pound Ridge, N.Y.: The Author, 1977. 66p.

5. Bitton, Davis. GUIDE TO MORMON DIARIES AND AUTO-BIOGRAPHIES. Provo, Utah: Brigham Young University Press, 1977. 416p.

Lists published and unpublished diaries.

6. Breton, Arthur J. A GUIDE TO THE MANUSCRIPT COLLECTIONS OF THE NEW YORK HISTORICAL SOCIETY. Westport, Conn.: Greenwood Press, 1972. 2 vols.

Diaries are indexed.

7. Brinton, Howard Haines. QUAKER JOURNALS: VARIETIES OF RELIGIOUS EXPERIENCE AMONG FRIENDS. Wallingford, Penn.: Pendle Hill Publications, 1972. 130p.

8. Donovan, Lynn Bonfield. "Day By Day Records: Diaries from the California Historical Society Library." CALIFORNIA HISTORICAL SOCIETY QUARTERLY 54:4 (Winter, 1975), 359-372 and 56:1 (Spring, 1977), 72-81.

Describes manuscript diaries in the Society's holdings, with an emphasis on women and Native Americans.

9. Forbes, Harriet. NEW ENGLAND DIARIES, 1602-1800. A DESCRIPTIVE CATALOGUE OF DIARIES, ORDERLY BOOKS, AND SEA JOURNALS. Topsfield, Mass.: Privately Printed, 1923. 439p.

Lists published and unpublished works.

10. Goodbody, Olive C. "Irish Quaker Diaries." JOURNAL OF THE FRIENDS HISTORICAL SOCIETY 50:2 (1962) 51-64.

Lists and describes diaries, journals and reminiscences dated 1697-1864, held by the Religious Society of Friends, Dublin, Ireland.

11. Havelice, Patricia Pate. AND SO TO BED: A BIBLIOGRAPHY OF DIARIES PUBLISHED IN ENGLISH. Metuchen, N.J.: Scarecrow Press, 1987. 698p.

12. Hinding, Andrea. WOMEN'S HISTORY SOURCES: A GUIDE TO ARCHIVES AND MANUSCRIPT COLLECTIONS IN THE UNITED STATES. Associate editor: Ames Sheldon Bower. Consulting editor: Clarke A. Chambers. New York and London: R.R. Bowker Co., in association with the University of Minnesota. 2 vols.

Diaries are indexed.

13. Huff, Cynthia. BRITISH WOMEN'S DIARIES: A DESCRIPTIVE BIBLIOGRAPHY OF SELECTED NINETEENTH CENTURY WOMEN'S MANUSCRIPT DIARIES. New York: AMS Press, 1985. 139p.

Interpretive bibliography. Lists major elements in diarist's life, content, format, and stylistic features, and divides works under the headings Aristocracy, Gentry, Professional-Commercial, Intelligentsia, and Religious.

14. Lesbian Herstory Archives. "Journal Writing from a Lesbian Perspective." LESBIAN HERSTORY ARCHIVES NEWSLETTER 6 (July, 1980), 22.

15. MacPike, E.F. "American and Canadian Diaries, Journals, and Note-Books." BULLETIN OF BIOGRAPHY 18 (1944), 91-92, 107-115, 156-158.

16. Matthews, William. AMERICAN DIARIES: AN ANNOTATED BIBLIOGRAPHY OF AMERICAN DIARIES WRITTEN PRIOR TO THE YEAR 1861. Berkeley, Calif.: University of California Press, 1945. 383p.

17. ------. BRITISH DIARIES: AN ANNOTATED BIBLIOGRAPHY OF BRITISH DIARIES WRITTEN BETWEEN 1442 AND 1942. Berkeley, Calif.: University of California Press, 1950. 339p. Reprinted by Peter Smith, Glouster, Mass., 1967.

18. ------. CANADIAN DIARIES AND AUTOBIOGRAPHIES. Berkeley, Calif.: University of California Press, 1950. 130p.

19. ------. AMERICAN DIARIES IN MANUSCRIPT, 1580-1954: A DESCRIPTIVE BIBLIOGRAPHY. Athens, Ga.: University of Georgia Press, 1974. 176p.

Capsule descriptions and locations of over 5,000 manuscript diaries.

20. Nolen, Anita L. "The Feminine Presence: Women's Papers in the Manuscript Division." QUARTERLY JOURNAL OF CONGRESS 32 (October, 1975), 348-365

Describes manuscript holdings in the Library of Congress, including correspondence and diaries.

21. Rhodes, Carolyn H., ed. FIRST PERSON FEMALE AMERICAN: A SELECTED AND ANNOTATED BIBLIOGRAPHY OF THE AUTOBIOGRAPHIES OF WOMEN LIVING AFTER 1950. Associate editors: Mary Louise Briscoe and Ernest L. Rhodes.

Troy, New York: The Whitston Publishing Co., 1980. 404p. (American Notes & Queries Supplement, Vol. II.)

Includes diaries and compilations of personal writings.

22. Sakala, Carol. WOMEN OF SOUTH ASIA: A GUIDE TO RESOURCES. Foreword by Maureen L.P. Patterson. Millwood, N.Y.: Kraus International Publications, 1980.

Descriptive bibliography. Includes "Libraries, Archives and Other Resources in India for the Study of Women," by Geraldine Forbes; "Libraries, Archives and Other Resources in Pakistan for the Study of Women," by Emily Hodges; "Libraries, Archives and Other Resources in Bangladesh for the Study of Women," by Sirajul Islam, and "Library Resources in the United Kingdom for the Study of Women in South-east Asia," by Carol Sakala.

23. Thomas, Evangeline, ed. WOMAN RELIGIOUS: A GUIDE TO REPOSITORIES IN THE UNITED STATES. Edited with the assistance of Joyce L. White and Lois Wachtel. New York and London: R.R. Bowker Co., 1983. 329p.

Descriptive list of religious communities and their archives. Manuscript diaries and journals are indexed.

24. Thomas, William Sturgis. AMERICAN REVOLUTIONARY DIARIES, ALSO JOURNALS, NARRATIVES, AUTOBIOGRAPHIES, REMINISCENCES AND PERSONAL MEMOIRS. Catalogued and described with an index of places and events. New York, 1923. 46p.

25. Wilson, Joan Hoff and Lynn Bonfield Donovan. "Women's History: A Listing of West Coast Archival and Manuscript Sources." CALIFORNIA HISTORICAL QUARTERLY 55:1 (Spring, 1976), 74-83 and 55:2 (Summer, 1976), 170-185.

Survey of major primary sources located in West Coast libraries. Gives locations and lists of holdings.

II. CRITICAL WORKS

26. Allport, Gordon W. "Diaries and Letters." In THE USE OF PERSONAL DOCUMENTS IN PSYCHOLOGICAL SCIENCE. New York: Social Science Research Council, 1942. p.95-110.

Discusses the use of diaries and letters in psychological studies and in therapy.

27. Anderson, Howard, Philip B. Daghlian, and Irvin Ehrenpreis. THE FAMILIAR LETTER IN THE EIGHTEENTH CENTURY. Lawrence, Kans.: University of Kansas Press, 1966. 306p.

Contains: Howard Anderson, "The Familiar Letter in the Eighteenth Century: Some Generalizations," and Robert Halsband, "Lady Mary Wortley Montagu as a Letter Writer."

28. L'Association International des Etudes Françaises. "Les Journaux Intimes." CAHIERS DE L'ASSOCIATION INTERNATIONALE DES ÉTUDES FRANÇAISES 17 (March, 1965), 97-168, plus disscussion, 269-286.

29. Baldwin, Christina. ONE TO ONE: SELF UNDERSTANDING THROUGH JOURNAL WRITING. New York: M. Evans, 1977. 186p.

How-to book on journal writing, concentrating on its therapeutic uses, and slanted towards women.

30. Belloc, Hilaire. "On Diaries." In CONVERSATION WITH AN ANGEL AND OTHER ESSAYS. New York and London: Harper & Bros., 1929. p.220-227.

Humorous essay on the diary form. Discusses author intent, "lying," unintentional truths, and the historical uses of diaries.

31. ------. "On Diarists." In THE SILENCE OF THE SEA AND OTHER ESSAYS. New York: Sheed & Ward, 1940.

Short humorous essay on the reasons why people write diaries and why other people read them.

32. Beresford, John. "Diarists of the Eighteenth Century." In STORM AND PEACE. London: Cobden-Sanderson, 1936. p.107-134.

Includes discussion of Dorothy Wordsworth's early journal and the diary of Fanny Burney.

33. Bernfeld, S. TREIB UND TRADITION IM JUGENDALTER: KULTURPSYCHOLOGISCHE STUDIEN AN TAGBÜCHERN. Leipzig: J.A. Barth, 1931. 181p.

34. Bloom, Lynn Z. "The Diary as Popular History." JOURNAL OF POPULAR CULTURE 9:4 (Spring, 1976), 794-807.

Discusses the contribution of the common person to history through diary writing, based on the diary of Natalie Stark Crouter, an American interned in the Philippines by the Japanese during World War II. Contains excerpts from Crouter's diary.

35. Boerner, Peter. TAGEBÜCH. Stuttgart: J.B. Metzlersche Verlagsbüchhandlüng, 1969. 90p.

Discusses the diary from psychoanalytic, literary, and historical points of view and provides extensive bibliographic information.

36. Bolitho, Hector. A BIOGRAPHER'S NOTEBOOK. New York: Macmillan, 1950. 213p.

Includes a chapter on the letters of Marie of Roumania; a chapter on the letters and diaries of Louise, Duchess of Saxe-Coburg-Gotha; and a chapter on the diaries of seven Quaker women.

37. Bonnat, Jean-Louis, Mireille Bossis and Helen Girard. ÉCRIRE-PUBLIÉR-LIRE: LES CORRESPONDANCES. PROBLEMATIQUE ET ÉCONOMIE D'UN "GENRE LITTERAIRE." Actes du Coloque International. Publication de l'Universite de Nantes. Novembre, 1983. 474p.

Eighteen essays and six round table discussions on the letter form, as a literary genre and as it relates to history, literature, psychology, biography and autobiography. Includes: J. Brengues, "La Correspondance Amoureuse et le Sacre"; M. de Saint-Laurent, "Cent Lieues et Dix-Huit Jour: des Lettres d'Amour, en 1884"; A. Roger, "La Lettre d'Amour et l'Effémnation Épistolaire"; M. Schneider, "De L'Épistolaire au Theorique: l'Accidentellement Vivant"; R. Karst Matausch, "De la Lettre aux Lettres: Réflexions sur la Genese de l'Écriture Épistolaire chez George Sand"; K. Wingard, "Correspondance et Litterature Épistolaire: George Sand en 1884"; N. Rogers, "George Sand et la Lettre Fictive/Réelle: Étude Stylistique"; S. Lecointre, "Pour une Théorie du Texte des Correspondances (G. Sand)"; M. Bossis, "La Correspondance comme Figure de Compromis"; M.C. Grassi, "Un Example d'Analyse Sérielle: Les Correspondances Intimes de la Noblesse Française"; P. Dumonceaux, "Le XVIIe Siècle: Aux Origines de la Lettre Intime et du Genre Épistolaire"; A. Pages, "La Communication Circulaire"; and J. Delabroy, "Le Courant de la Plume: Mythe et Vérité de La Correspondance (l'Example G. Flaubert--G. Sand). Round Table discussions: "Porquoi Éditer?"; "Correspondances d'Artistes: Lectures"; "Rapports de la Correspondance a l'Oeuvre"; "La Lettre Document: Approche Interdisciplinaire"; "Les Correspondances d'Artistes et leurs Productions"; and "Des Images et des Sons pour Correspondre."

38. Broc, Vicomte de. LE STYLE ÉPISTOLAIRE. Paris: Librairie Plon, Plon-Nourrit et Cie., Imprimeurs-Éditeurs, 1901. 291p.

Includes discussion of Madame de Sévigné, Madame de Maintenon, and Madame de Deffand and her correspondents.

39. Bryant, David. "Revolution and Introspection: The

Appearance of the Private Diary in France." EUROPEAN STUDIES 8 (April, 1978), 259-272.

The appearance of the introspective journal in France is tied to the Age of Revolution; between the years 1774 and 1824, and especially after 1789, the genuinely private, inward-looking diary made its appearance, a departure from the more outward-looking chronicles of the external world which came before it.

40. ------ "Réflexions sur le Journal Intime." BULLETIN DE LA SOCIÉTÉ NEOPHILOLOGIQUE/BULLETIN OF THE MODERN LANGUAGE SOCIETY 82:1 (1981), 66-74.

41. Buhler, Charlotte. "Judentagebüch und Lebenslauf. Zwei Madchentagebücher Mit Einer Einlietung." QUELLEN UND STUDIEN ZUR JUGENDKÜNDE, Vol. 9. Jena: Fischer, 1934.

Comparative study of two adolescent diaries by girls.

42. ------. "Drie Generationen im Judentagebüch." QUELLEN UND STUDIEN ZUR JUGENDKÜNDE, Vol. 11. Jena: Fischer, 1934. 184p.

Comparative analysis of the diaries of three girls of succeeding generations, born between 1873 and 1910.

43. Cargas, Harry J. and Roger J. Radley. KEEPING A SPIRITUAL JOURNAL. Garden City, N.Y.: Doubleday/ Nazareth Books, 1981.

44. Casewit, Curtis W. THE DIARY: A COMPLETE GUIDE TO JOURNAL WRITING. Allen, Tex.: Argus Communications, 1982. 146p.

How-to book on journal writing, using examples from famous diaries and from the author's own journal.

45. Centre Aixois de Recherches Italiennes. LA CORRESPONDANCE: ÉDITION, FONCTIONS, SIGNIFICATION. Actes du Colloque Franco-Italien, Aix-En-Provence, 5-6, Octobre, 1983. Aix-En-Provence: Université de

Provence, 1984. 233p.

Contains twelve critical essays on French and Italian letters, including J.L. Bonnat, "Un Écran et ses Négatifs: La Correspondance"; J.L. Vissière, "Prête-moi ta plume...": Les Manuels de Correspondance"; J. Basso, "Quelques Reflexions sur les Lettres en Italien Publiees entre 1538 et 1662"; J. Lacrox, "Correspondance au XIXe Siecle"; and A. Arlslan, "L'Archivio Inedito della Corrispondenza de Neera (Anna Radius Zuccari)."

46. Culley, Margo. "Women's Diary Literature: Resources and Directions in the Field." LEGACY: A NEWSLETTER OF NINETEENTH CENTURY WOMAN WRITERS 1:1 (Spring, 1984), 4-5.

47. Dainard, J.A. EDITING CORRESPONDENCE: PAPERS GIVEN AT THE FOURTEENTH ANNUAL CONFERENCE ON EDITORIAL PROBLEMS, UNIVERSITY OF TORONTO, 3-4 NOVEMBER 1978. New York and London: Garland Publishing, 1979. 124p.

Five papers on the methods and problems of editing correspondence, by editors of the papers of Sir Walter Scott, Benjamin Disraeli, Jean-Jacques Rousseau and Emile Zola. Includes Wilmarth S. Lewis, "Editing Familiar Letters."

48. Davey, Samuel. "The Study of Familiar Letters as an Aid to History and Biography." TRANSACTIONS OF THE ROYAL SOCIETY OF LITERATURE, Series 2, Vol. 22 (1906), 21-31.

49. Didier, Beatrice. LE JOURNAL INTIME. Paris: Presses Universitaires de France, 1976. 198p.

Study of the diary from historical, sociological, psychoanalytical, and literary points of view.

50. Didion, Joan. "On Keeping a Notebook." In WOMAN AS WRITER. Edited by Jeanette L. Webber and Joan Grumman. Boston: Houghton Mifflin Co., 1978. p.147-153.

Didion keeps a notebook rather than a proper diary. Her entries are evocative rather than an accurate factual record of experience.

51. Dobbs, Brian. DEAR DIARY: SOME STUDIES IN SELF-INTEREST. London: Elm Tree Books, 1974. 229p.

52. Drew, Elizabeth. THE LITERATURE OF GOSSIP: NINE ENGLISH LETTERWRITERS. New York: W.W. Norton & Co., 1964. 254p.

Contains chapters on Dorothy Osborne, Lady Mary Wortley Montagu, and Jane Welsh Carlyle.

53. Duckett, Eleanor Shipley. WOMEN AND THEIR LETTERS IN THE EARLY MIDDLE AGES. Northampton, Mass.: Smith College, 1965. 28p. (Katherine Asher Engel Lectures, 1964).

54. Dyson, Ketaki Kushari. A VARIOUS UNIVERSE: A STUDY OF THE JOURNALS AND MEMOIRS OF BRITISH MEN AND WOMEN IN THE INDIAN SUBCONTINENT, 1765-1856. Delhi: Oxford University Press, 1978. 406p.

Overview, similiar to Sir Arthur Ponsonby's works on British diaries (items 94, 95, and 96). Reviews journals, prints extracts, and gives historical and biographical background of each work. Includes Jemima Wicksted Kimberly, Eliza Fay, Mary Martha Sherwood, Maria Dundas Graham, Maria, Lady Nugent, and an anonymous woman.

55. Ehrenpreis, Irvin, and Robert Halsband. THE LADY OF LETTERS IN THE EIGHTEENTH CENTURY. PAPERS READ AT A CLARK LIBRARY SEMINAR JANUARY 18, 1969. Los Angeles: William Andrews Clark Memorial Library, University of California, Los Angeles, 1969. 55p.

Contains two papers. "Letters of Advice to Young

Spinsters," by Ehrenpreis discusses Jonathan Swift's views on women, based on a study of letters written by Swift, Esther Johnson, and Esther Vanhomrigh. "Ladies of Letters of the Eighteenth Century" by Halsband is concerned with the careers of Elizabeth Montagu, Lady Mary Wortley Montagu, Mary Astell, Dorothy Osborne, Elizabeth Carter, Hannah More, and others. Discusses their views on writing and the publication of their work, and their correspondence, and concludes that as letter writers they became women of letters.

56. Fothergill, Robert A. PRIVATE CHRONICLES: A STUDY OF ENGLISH DIARIES. New York: Oxford University Press, 1974. 214p.

Critical introduction to the genre and to the great diaries. Includes discussion of the diaries of Elizabeth Barrett Browning, Fanny Burney, Lady Charlotte Bury, Lady Eleanor Butler, Jane Welsh Carlyle, Lady Frederick Cavendish, Lady Anne Clifford, Mary Countess Cowper, George Eliot, Celia Fiennes, Marjorie Fleming, Caroline Fox, Lady Margaret Hoby, Elizabeth Lady Holland, Ivy Jacquier, Alice James, Fanny Kemble, Katherine Mansfield, Anais Nin, Beatrix Potter, Frances Lady Shelley, Hester Lynch Thrale Piozzi, Queen Victoria, Beatrice Webb, Virginia Woolf, and Dorothy Wordsworth.

57. Girard, Alain. LE JOURNAL INTIME ET LA NOTION DE PERSONNE. Paris: Presses Universitaires de France, 1963. 638p.

Psychological and sociological study of the personal journal and the concept of the self.

58. Godwin, Gail. "A Diarist on Diarists." ANTAEUS 21/22 (Spring/Summer, 1976), 50-56.

Godwin has kept a diary since age thirteen. Discusses privacy, truth in diary-writing, the diary as an unfolding of a private, personal history, and the differences between the processes of writing a diary and writing fiction.

59. Görner, Rudiger. DAS TAGEBÜCH: EINE EINFÜHRUNG. Munich: Artemis, 1986. 128p.

60. Grasser, Albert. DAS LITERARISCHE TAGEBÜCH: STUDIEN UBER ELEMENTS DES TAGEBÜCHS ALS KUNSTFORM. Saarbrucken: West-Ost Verlag, 1955. 142p.

61. Halsband, Robert. "Editing the Letters of Letter Writers." VIRGINIA UNIVERSITY BIBLIOGRAPHIC SOCIETY STUDIES IN BIBLIOGRAPHY 11 (1958), 23-37.

Outlines problems encountered in editing correspondence, based on the author's experience in editing the letters of Lady Mary Wortley Montagu.

62. Hampsten, Elizabeth. READ THIS ONLY TO YOURSELF: THE PRIVATE WRITINGS OF MIDWESTERN WOMEN, 1880-1910. Bloomington, Ind.: Indiana University Press, 1982. 242p.

Study of letters and diaries of North Dakota women; differs from other studies of women's personal writings in that Hampsten made a study of one collection instead of choosing the writings according to a particular topic. Discusses differences between the private writings of men and women, and between writers of different classes. Contains lengthy excerpts, chiefly from unpublished sources.

63. Hedges, Elaine. "The Nineteenth Century Diarist and Her Quilts." FEMINIST STUDIES 8:2 (Summer, 1982), 293-299.

Notes that making scrapbooks is a salvage art not unlike that of quilting, and discusses similarities between the diary and the quilt. Includes brief quotes from published and unpublished diaries on the subject of quilting; among those quoted are Anna Green Cook and Sarah Connell Ayer.

64. Hocke, Gutav R. DAS EUROPAISCHE TAGEBÜCH. Wiesbaden: Limes Verlag, 1963. 1135p.

Contents: Buch 1: Gründmotive Europlaischer

Tagebücher; Beivrage zur Vergleichenden Literatur-geschichte. Buch 2: Anthologie Europlaische Tagebücher.

65. Hoffmann, Leonore and Margo Culley. WOMEN'S PERSONAL NARRATIVES: ESSAYS IN CRITICISM AND PEDAGOGY. New York: The Modern Language Society of America, 1985. 244p.

Includes Margo Culley, "Women's Vernacular Literature: Teaching the Mother Tongue"; Virginia Walcott Beauchamp, "Letters as Literature: The Prestons of Baltimore" and "Letters and Diaries: The Persona and the Real Woman--A Case Study"; Susan S. Kissel, "Writer Anxiety versus the Need for Community in the Botts Family Letters"; and "Preparing a Collection of Regional Autobiographical Materials for Use in the Composition Classroom"; Annette Kolodny, "Captives in Paradise: Women on the Early American Frontier"; John Schilb, "The Usefulness of Women's Nontraditional Literature in the Traditional Literature-and-Composition Course"; Dure Jo Gillikin, "A Lost Diary Found: The Art of the Everyday"; Susan Waugh, "Women's Shorter Autobiographical Writings: Expression, Identity, and Form"; Elizabeth Hampsten, "Editing a Woman's Diary: A Case Study. Also includes "The Diary of Amelia Buss" and "The Letters of Delina Hooper."

66. Holcombe, James P. LITERATURE IN LETTERS; OR, MANNERS, ART, CRITICISM, BIOGRAPHY, HISTORY, MORALS, ILLUSTRATED IN THE CORRESPONDENCE OF EMINENT PERSONS. New York: D. Appleton & Co., 1866. 520p.

67. Hornbeak, Katherine. THE COMPLETE LETTER WRITER IN ENGLAND, 1568-1800. Northampton, Mass.: Smith College, 1934. 150p.

Study and bibliography of letter-writing manuals and epistolary miscellanies. Manuals and miscellanies purported to be anthologies of authentic letters, but were more often fictitious compilations.

68. Hudson, Arthur K. ENGLISH LETTER WRITERS.

Exeter: A. Wheaton, 1951. 266p.

General history of letter-writing in England.

69. Irvine, Lyn L., ed. TEN LETTER WRITERS. London: Leonard and Virginia Woolf, 1932. 230p.

Study of the great letter writers, with chapters on Madame du Deffand, Dorothy Osborne, Madame de Sévigné, Jane Welsh Carlyle, and Henrietta Frances Spencer, Countess of Bessborough.

70. Irving, William Henry. THE PROVIDENCE OF WIT IN THE ENGLISH LETTER WRITERS. Durham, N.C.: Duke University Press, 1955. 382p.

Includes chapters on Lady Mary Wortley Montagu, Lady Suffolk, and the Bluestockings; with brief discussions of Lady Hervey, Margaret, Duchess of Newcastle, Dorothy Osborne, Hester Lynch Thrale Piozzi, Madame de Sévigné, Elizabeth Singer Rowe, and others.

71. Jelinek, Estelle C., ed. WOMEN'S AUTOBIOGRAPHY: ESSAYS IN CRITICISM. Bloomington, Ind.: Indiana University Press, 1980. 274p.

Includes: Lynn Z. Bloom and Orlee Holder, "Anais Nin's DIARY in Context." Jelinek's introduction, "Women's Autobiography and the Male Tradition," contains remarks on the diary as a particularly appropriate form for women.

72. Johnson, Edgar. ONE MIGHTY TORRENT: THE DRAMA OF BIOGRAPHY. New York: Stackpole Sons, 1937. 595p. New York: Macmillan Co., 1955. 591p.

Includes several essays on personal writing. In "Memoirs and Diaries," he discusses the differences between the two, and notes that a diary can in some cases stand on its own as biography. In "The Heyday of the Letter Writers," he traces the history of the post in England, and the development of letter writing as a literary form, using Madame de Sevigne and Lady Mary

Wortley Montagu as examples. Includes a chapter on the correspondence of Lady Wortley Montagu.

73. Johnston, James C. BIOGRAPHY, THE LITERATURE OF PERSONALITY. With an introduction by Gamaliel Bradford. New York and London: The Century Co., 1927. 312p.

Includes a discussion of memoirs and diaries, noting that diaries are more useful from the standpoint of biography (rather than history) than are memoirs, since the point of the diary is self-revelation. Maintains that Fanny Burney was a better self-observer than Samuel Pepys and that Eugenie de Guerin was more relevatory than Defoe.

74. Juhasz, Susanne. "The Journal as a Source and Model for Feminist Art: The Example of Kathleen Fraser." FRONTIERS: A JOURNAL OF WOMEN STUDIES 8:1 (1984), 16-20.

Examines the ways in which Fraser, a poet, uses the journal as a source and model for art, an example of feminist writers' attempts to integrate the public and private realms.

75. Kagle, Steven E. AMERICAN DIARY LITERATURE, 1620-1799. Boston: Twayne Publishers, 1979. 203p.

Includes discussion of the diaries of Sarah Kemble Knight, Sally Wister, Nancy Shippen, and Margaret Morris.

76. Kaschnitz, Marie Luise. DAS TAGEBÜCH DES SCHRIFTSTELLERS. Mainz: Verlag der Akademie der Wissenschaften und der Literatur, in Kommission bei F. Steiner, Wiesbaden, 1965. 14p.

77. Koyano, Jun'ichi. HEIAN KOKI JORYU NIKKI NO KENKYU. Tokyo: Kyoiku Shuppan Senta, Showa 58 [1983]. 360p.

Includes discussion of THE DIARY OF MURASAKI

SHIKIBU, THE SARASHINA DIARY (by Sugawara no Takasue no Musume), and THE EMPEROR HORIKAWA DIARY (by Sanuki no Suke).

78. Kuhn-Osius, K. Eckhard. "Making Loose Ends Meet: Private Journals in the Public Realm." GERMAN QUARTERLY 54:2 (March, 1981), 166-176.

79. Lee, L.L., and Merrill Lewis, eds. WOMEN, WOMEN WRITERS AND THE WEST. Troy, New York: The Whitston Publishing Co., 1979. 252p.

Contains: McKnight, Jeannie. "American Dream, Nightmare Underside: Diaries, Letters and Fiction of Women on the American Frontier," and Elinore Lentz, "Homestead Home: The Letters of Elinore Pruitt Stewart."

80. Levin, Susan M. "What Did You Do In The War, Mommy?" HELICON NINE: A JOURNAL OF WOMEN'S ARTS AND LETTERS 2:1 (Summer, 1980), 16-21.

Compares the journals of two women writing during the American Revolution: Sally Wister, a young patriot, and Baroness Fredericke Riedesel, the wife of a German Officer fighting with the British Army.

81. Litto, Victor del, comp. LE JOURNAL INTIME ET SES FORMES LITTERAIRES. Actes du Colloque de Septembre, 1975. Paris and Geneva: Librarie Droz, 1978. 330p.

Includes: Michel Gilot, "Quelques pas Vers le Journal Intime"; Perre Reboul, "Niveaux d'Intimite dans les Ecritures de George Sand"; Michel David, "Le Problème du Journal Intime en Italie"; Gilbert Bosetti, "L'Intimite du Journal Pavesien: Écrire Pour Vivre"; Michel Baude, "Une Structure Isolité: Les Anniversaires dans le Journal Intime (Réstif de la Bretonne et Azais)"; Jean-Pierre Collintet, "L'Auteur du Journal Lecteur et Juge du Journal des Autres"; Peter Boerner, "Place du Journal das La Litteraire Moderne"; Jacques Chocheyras, "La Place de Journal Intime dans un

Typologie Linguistique des Formes Litteraires"; Beatrice Didier, "Pour une Sociologie du Journal Intime"; Gerald Ranaud, "Le Journal Intime: de la Redaction à la Publication. Essai d'Approche Sociologique d'un Genre Litteraire"; and Marie-Françoise Luna, "L'Auture Lieu du Moi Étude sur Trois Journaux de Jeunes Filles (Bashkirtseff, Nin, "Grête" Lainer)."

82. Mallon, Thomas. A BOOK OF ONE'S OWN: PEOPLE AND THEIR DIARIES. New York: Ticknor & Fields, 1984. 318p.

Makes brief mention of Enid Bagnold, Marie Bashkirtseff, Simone de Beauvoir, Helen Bevington, Dora Carrington, Anne Frank, Lady Augusta Gregory, Karen Horney, Alice James, Fanny Kemble, Amelia Stewart Knight, Selma Lagerlöf, Gretchen Lainer, Anne Morrow Lindbergh, Katherine Mansfield, George Sand, Queen Victoria, Ellen Weeton, Virginia Woolf, Dorothy Wordsworth, and others.

83. Meriwether, James B., ed. SOUTH CAROLINA WOMEN WRITERS. Spartanburg, S.C.: The Reprint Co., 1979.

Contains: Edwin Arnold III, "Women Diarists and Letter Writers of 18th Century South Carolina"; Delle Mullen Craven, "The Unpublished Diaries of Mary Moragne Davis"; C. Vann Woodward, "What is the Chesnut Diary?" George F. Hayhoe, "Mary Boykin Chesnut's Journal: Visions and Revisions"; Eileen Gregory, "The Formality of Memory: A Study of the Literary Manuscripts of Mary Boykin Chesnut"; and Elizabeth Nuhlenfeld, "Literary Elements in Mary Chesnut's Journal."

84. Metzger, Deena, and Barbara Myerhoff. "Dear Diary (Or, Listening to the Silent Laughter of Mozart While the Beds are Unmade and the Remains of Breakfast Congeal on the Table)." CHRYSALIS 7 (1979), 39-49.

Discusses the journal as a literary genre, as an activity, and as a ritual for the creation of the self. Points out its use in therapy and its importance to the women's movement as a source of shared knowledge.

85. Miller, Marilyn Jeanne. THE POETICS OF NIKKI BUNGAKU: A COMPARISON OF THE TRADITIONS, CONVENTIONS, AND STRUCTURE OF HEIAN JAPAN'S LITERARY DIARIES WITH WESTERN AUTOBIOGRAPHICAL WRITINGS. New York: Garland Publishing, 1985. 412p.

86. Miner, Earl. JAPANESE POETIC DIARIES. Berkeley, Calif.: University of California Press, 1969. 211p.

History and criticism of the Japanese poetic diary, containing discussion of and excerpts from the diaries of Izumi Shikibu and an anonymous woman.

87. ------. "Literary Diaries and the Boundaries of Literature." YEARBOOK OF COMPARATIVE AND GENERAL LITERATURE 21 (1972), 46-51.

In tenth-century Japan the diary emerged as prose fiction and provided the formal basis of a number of classical works; in eleventh-century Japan, women dominated literature, and the poetic diary was a popular form.

88. Moriya, Shogo. HEIAN KOKI NIKKI BUNGAKURON: SARASHINA NIKKI, SANUKI NO SUKE NIKKI. Tokyo: Shintensha, Showa 58 [1983] 326p.

Discusses THE SARASHINA DIARY (by Sugawara no Takasue no Musume) and THE EMPEROR HORIKAWA DIARY (by Sanuke no Suke).

89. Neimark, Edith D., and Caroline Stead. "Everyday Thinking by College Women: Analysis of Journal Entries." MERRILL-PALMER QUARTERLY 27 (October, 1981), 471-488.

90. Nin, Anais. "At a Journal Workshop." In IN FAVOR OF THE SENSITIVE MAN AND OTHER ESSAYS. London: Harvest Books, Harcourt Brace Jovanovich, 1976. p.98-104.

91. O'Brien, Kate. ENGLISH DIARIES AND JOURNALS. London: W. Collins, 1943. 48p.

Brief survey of the great English diarists, including Fanny Burney, Dorothy Wordsworth, Queen Victoria, Caroline Fox, and Katherine Mansfield.

92. ------. "Writers of Letters." ESSAYS AND STUDIES 9 (1956). Being Volume 9 of the New Series of Essays and Studies Collected for the English Association by Sir George Hamilton. p.7-20.

On the pleasures of reading the great letter writers, with discussion of Madame de Sévigné, Charlotte Bronte, and the love letters of Robert and Elizabeth Barrett Browning.

93. Perry, Ruth. WOMEN, LETTERS AND THE NOVEL. New York: AMS Press, 1980. 218p.

Deals with the role of women in the development of the familiar letter and the epistolary novel.

94. Ponsonby, Arthur. ENGLISH DIARIES: A REVIEW OF ENGLISH DIARIES FROM THE SIXTEENTH TO THE TWENTIETH CENTURY. With an introduction on diary writing. London: Methuen & Co., 1923. 447p.

Includes reviews of and extracts from the diaries of Mary Browne, Fanny Burney, Lady Charlotte Bury, Elizabeth Byrom, Lady Mary Coke, Mary Countess Cowper, George Eliot, Celia Fiennes, Caroline Fox, Elizabeth Fry, Elizabeth Lady Holland, Fanny Kemble, Lady Eleanor Butler and Sarah Ponsonby, Frances Lady Shelley, Mary Shelley, and Queen Victoria.

95. ------. MORE ENGLISH DIARIES: FURTHER REVIEWS OF DIARIES FROM THE SIXTEENTH TO THE NINETEENTH CENTURY. With an introduction on diary reading. London: Methuen & Co., 1927. 250p.

Includes reviews of and extracts from the diaries of Lady Anne Clifford, Margaret Lady Hoby, and Dorothy Wordsworth.

96. ------. SCOTTISH AND IRISH DIARIES FROM THE

SIXTEENTH TO THE NINETEENTH CENTURY. With an introduction. London: Methuen & Co., 1927. 192p.

Scottish and Irish diaries are separated from the English diaries because of space considerations only. Includes reviews of and extracts from the diaries of Marjorie Fleming, Jane Cameron, Anne Chalmers, Jane Welsh Carlyle, Mary Rich Countess of Warwick, Elizabeth Frecke, and Lady Arabella Denny.

97. Prado, Holly. "Journal Writing: Where it Can Go From Where it Is." Presented at the Conference, "The Diary, the Journal, The Autobiography, February 11-13, 1977." NEW: A BEYOND BAROQUE FOUNDATION PUBLICATION: ARTS & LETTERS 8:3 (May, 1977), 44-47.

98. Progoff, Ira. AT A JOURNAL WORKSHOP: THE BASIC TEXT AND GUIDE FOR USING THE INTENSIVE JOURNAL. New York: Dialogue House Library, 1976. 320p.

Text for the author's journal writing workshops, which focus on the therapeutic use the journal as a vehicle for self-improvement.

99. ------. LIFE-STUDY: EXPERIENCING CREATIVE LIVES BY THE INTENSIVE JOURNAL METHOD. New York: Dialogue House Library, 1983. 302p.

100. Rainer, Tristine. THE NEW DIARY: HOW TO USE A JOURNAL FOR SELF GUIDANCE AND EXPANDED CREATIVITY. Preface by Anais Nin. Los Angeles: J.P. Tarcher, distributed by St. Martin's Press, 1978. 323p.

How-to book on diary writing, chiefly concerned with the diary as an aid to self-awareness, inner liberation, and creativity.

101. Redford, Bruce. THE CONVERSE OF THE PEN: ACTS OF INTIMACY IN THE EIGHTEENTH-CENTURY FAMILIAR LETTER. Chicago: University of Chicago Press, 1986. 252p.

Includes "Lady Mary Wortley Montagu: The Compass of the Senecan Style," and "Samuel Johnson and Mrs. Thrale: The 'Little Language' of the Public Moralist."

102. Robertson, Jean K. THE ART OF LETTER WRITING: AN ESSAY ON THE HANDBOOKS PUBLISHED IN ENGLAND DURING THE SIXTEENTH AND SEVENTEENTH CENTURIES. Liverpool: University Press; and London: Hodder & Stoughton, 1943. 80p.

Survey and bibliography of letter-writers, or manuals, published between 1568 and 1700.

103. Rosenblatt, Paul C. BITTER, BITTER TEARS: NINETEENTH CENTURY DIARISTS AND TWENTIETH CENTURY GRIEF THEORIES. Minneapolis, Minn.: University of Minnesota Press, 1983. 201p.

Examines patterns of grief in nineteenth-century United States and Canada, based on descriptions of grief found in published and unpublished private diaries, including those of Dolly Lunt, Elisabeth Koren, Molly Dorsey Sanford, Mary Richardson Walker, Harriet Sherrill, and others. An appendix deals with the ethics of using private diaries for study, and with the particular problems women diarists have had in keeping their diaries private, free from the prying eyes of male family members, especially husbands.

104. Rule, Jane. "Letters." In OUTLANDER. Tallahassee, Fla.: The Naiad Press, 1981. p.191-198.

Stresses the importance of preserving personal letters to Lesbian life and history, and tells of her decision to include letters written to her in her archives when the time comes to dispose of her papers.

105. Salvan, Albert J. "Private Journals in French Literature." AMERICAN LEGION OF HONOR MAGAZINE 25 (1954), 201-214.

106. Schlissel, Lillian. "Women's Diaries on the Western Frontier." AMERICAN STUDIES 18:1 (Spring, 1977), 87-100.

Explores women's experience of the westward movement, using their diaries as a source.

107. ------. "Mothers and Daughters on the Western Frontier." FRONTIERS: A JOURNAL OF WOMEN'S STUDIES 3:2 (Summer, 1978), 20-33.

Examining the diaries of women who made the overland trip to Oregon, Schlissel concludes that more hardships and psychic dislocation occurred for older women who made the trip during childbearing years than for young women and new brides; and that the mother-daughter bonds served to provide a sense of stability and continuity with the past at the same time it established a web of obedience and obligation. Based on the diaries of Elizabeth Dixon Geer, Lydia Milner Waters, Mollie Dorsey Sanford, and others.

108. ------. "Diaries of Frontier Women: On Learning to Read the Obscured Patterns." In WOMEN'S PLACES: FEMALE IDENTITY AND VOCATION IN AMERICAN HISTORY. Edited by Mary Kelley. Boston: G.K. Hall, 1979. p.53-66.

109. ------. WOMEN'S DIARIES OF THE WESTWARD JOURNEY. Preface by Carl N. Degler. Gerda Lerner, supervising editor. New York: Schocken Books, 1982. 262p.

Discusses the hazards of pregnancy, traveling with small children, cholera epidemics, Indian hostility, and the dangers to men which left many women to file widow's claims at the end of the journey. Concludes that women felt a great deal more ambivalence about immigration than did men. Contains extracts from the diaries of Catherine Haun, Lydia Allen Rudd, Amelia Stewart Knight, and Jane Gould Tourtillot.

110. Vuolo, Brett Harvey. "Pioneer Diaries: The Untold Story of the West." MS. MAGAZINE 3:2 (May, 1975), 32-36.

Essay on the author's grandmother's diary, which describes the life of her great-grandmother. Includes brief excerpts from the diaries of frontier women.

111. Vuliamy, C.E. ENGLISH LETTER WRITERS. London:

Collins, 1945. 48p.

Brief but lively survey includes discussion of Sarah Jennings Duchess of Marlborough, Lady Henrietta Frances Spencer Countess of Bessborough, the Paston Letters, Lady Mary Wortley Montagu, Mrs. Elizabeth Montagu, Dorothy Osborne, Hester Lynch Thrale Piozzi, Mrs. Delany, Charlotte Bronte, Jane Welsh Carlyle, Queen Victoria, Queen Elizabeth I, and Gertrude Bell.

112. Wilson, Edmund. "Three Confederate Ladies: Kate Stone, Sarah Morgan, Mary Chesnut." In PATRIOTIC GORE: STUDIES IN THE LITERATURE OF THE AMERICAN CIVIL WAR. New York: Oxford University Press, 1962. p.258-298.

Studies three Civil War diaries, comparing their different experience of Southern "feudal" life, and their responses to its destruction during the War.

113. Winter, Metta L. "'Heart Watching' Through Journal Keeping." FRIENDS JOURNAL (November 1, 1980) 10-12.

Examines the Quaker journal as a vehicle for confession, self-examination, and charting spiritual progress, as well as for proselytizing and for strengthening bonds between widespread Quaker communities.

114. WOMEN'S STUDIES INTERNATIONAL FORUM 10:1 (1987), 1-97.

Special issue on women's autobiography. Includes: Dale Spender, "Journal on a Journal;" Suzanne L. Bunkers, "Faithful Friend: Nineteenth-Century Midwestern American Women's Unpublished Diaries;" Liz Stanley, "Biography as Microscope or Kaleidoscope? The Case of 'Power' in Hannah Cullwick's Relationship with Arthur Munby;" Treva Broughton, "Margaret Oliphant: The Unbroken Self;" Alice A. Deck, "Whose Book is this Anyway: Authorial Versus Editorial Control in Harriet Jacobs' INCIDENTS IN THE LIFE OF A SLAVE GIRL, WRITTEN BY HERSELF" (which makes use of Jacobs' correspondence); Cynthia A. Huff, "Chronicles of Confinement: Reactions to Childbirth in British Women's Diaries;" Lynn Z. Bloom, "Till Death Do Us Part: Men's and Women's Interpretations of Wartime Internment;" Jane DuPree Begos, "The Diaries of Adolescent Girls;" and Joanne E. Cooper, "Shaping Meaning: Women's Diaries, Journals, and Letters--the Old and the New."

III. ANTHOLOGIES

115. Aitken, James, ed. ENGLISH DIARIES OF THE XVI, XVII AND XVIII CENTURIES. Harmondsworth, Middlesex, England: Penguin Books, 1941. 155p.

Includes letters by Fanny Burney, Elizabeth Byrom, Mary Countess Cowper, and Celia Fiennes.

116. ------. ENGLISH DIARIES OF THE XIX CENTURY, 1800-1850. Harmondsworth, Middlesex, England: Penguin Books, 1944. 160p.

117. ------. ENGLISH LETTERS OF THE XVIII CENTURY. Harmondsworth, Middlesex, England, and New York: Pelican Books, 1946. 185p.

Includes letters of Lady Mary Wortley Montagu, Mrs. Delany, and Fanny Burney.

118. ------. ENGLISH LETTERS OF THE XIX CENTURY. Harmondsworth, Middlesex, England: Pelican Books, 1946. 188p.

Includes letters of Hannah More, Jane Welsh Carlyle, Charlotte Bronte, and Harriet Martineau.

119. [American Antiquarian Society]. AMERICAN WOMEN'S DIARIES. New York: Readex Film Products, 1984. Reels 1-21: New England Diaries.

Ruth Henshaw Bascom (1824-1910), Susan E.P.B. Forbes, Caroline Barrett White (1820-1915), Abigail Gardner Drew (1777-1868), Hanna Davis Gale, Louisa Adams Park (1773-1813), Sally Ripley, and Martha "Patty" Rogers (1761-1840).

120. Argyll, John George Edward Henry Douglas Sutherland Campbell, Duke of, ed. INTIMATE SOCIETY LETTERS OF THE EIGHTEENTH CENTURY. London: S. Paul, 1910. 2 vols.

121. Bahr, Hans Walter, comp. and ed. DIE STIMME: DIE MENSCHEN BRIEFE UND AUFZEICHNÜNGEN AUS DER GANZEN WELT, 1939-1945. Munich: R. Piper & Co. Verlag 1962. 600p.

Includes Edith Stein (1891-1942), Ruth Metz (1922-1944), Simone Weil, and Virginia Woolf.

122. Bamford, Francis, ed. DEAR MISS HEBER: AN EIGHTEENTH-CENTURY CORRESPONDENCE. With introductions by Georgia and Sacheverell Sitwell. London: Constable & Co., 1936. 293p.

Letters written to Mary Heber of Weston (1758-1809) by Mary Curzon, Elizabeth Iremonger, Dorothea Lady Banks, Elizabeth Drake, Rebecca Penyston, Elizabeth Bland, and Mariana Drake.

123. Barton, Arnold, ed. LETTERS FROM THE PROMISED LAND: SWEDES IN AMERICA, 1840-1914. Minneapolis: Published by the University of Minnesota Press for the Swedish Pioneer Historical Society, 1975. 344p.

Documentary history. Includes extracts from the letters and diaries of Christina Kallstrom, Rosalie Roos, Mary Stephenson, Ida Lindgren, Emma Huhtasaari, Emma Anderson, Mrs. Mandus Swenson, and several anonymous women.

124. Bedfordshire Historical Record Society. SOME BEDFORDSHIRE DIARIES. Streatley, England: Bedfordshire Historical Record Society, 1960. Volume 40. 256p.

Includes diaries of Christian Williamson (d. 1720), Elizabeth Brown (1754-1793), and Catherine Young Maclear, and a letter from Australian pioneer Priscilla Dodson.

125. Behrens, Katja. FRAUENBRIEFE DER ROMANTICK.

Herausgegeben und mit einem nachwort. Frankfurt am Main: Insel Verlag, 1981, 1982. 448p.

Extracts from the correspondence of German Romantic women authors. Includes Karoline von Gunderode, Bettina von Arnim, Rahel Varnhagen, Caroline Schlegel-Schelling, Dorothea Veit-Schlegel, and Susette Gontard.

126. Berger, Josef and Dorothy Berger, eds. DIARY OF AMERICA: THE INTIMATE STORY OF OUR NATION, TOLD BY 100 DIARISTS--PUBLIC FIGURES AND PLAIN CITIZENS, NATIVES AND VISITORS--OVER THE FIVE CENTURIES FROM COLUMBUS, THE PILGRIMS AND GEORGE WASHINGTON TO THOMAS EDISON, WILL ROGERS AND OUR OWN TIME. New York: Simon & Schuster, 1957. 621p.

Includes Sarah Kemble Knight, Anna Green Winslow, Elizabeth Fuller, Fanny Kemble, Catherine Elizabeth Havens, Louisa May Alcott, Susan Shelby Magoffin, Amelia Stewart Knight, Charlotte Forten, Rose O'Neal Greenhow, Mary Boykin Chesnut, Laura Jernegan, Julia Newberry, Claire Consuelo Sheridan, Dorothy Black, and Simone de Beauvoir.

127. ------. SMALL VOICES: A GROWNUP'S TREASURY OF SELECTIONS FROM THE DIARIES, JOURNALS AND NOTEBOOKS OF YOUNG CHILDREN. New York: P.S. Ericksson, 1966. 305p.

Includes Anaïs Nin, Mary Scarborogh Paxson, Esther Edwards, Emily Wortis, Opal Whitely, Euphemia Mason Olcott, Maggie Owen, Sallie Hester, Margaret O'Brien, Marian Cuca, Marjorie Fleming, Louisa May Alcott, Sylvia McNeely, Harriet Spencer Countess of Bessborough, Mary Garfield, "Tishy," Marie Bashkirtseff, Laura Jernegan, Susan Robben, Catherine Elizabeth Havens, Anna Green Winslow, Marilyn Bell, Caroline Cowles Richards, Tatyana Tolstoy, Susy Clemens, Gretchen Lainer, and Margaret Emily Shore.

128. Bickley, Francis Lawrence. AN ENGLISH LETTER BOOK. London: G. Chapman, 1925. 226p.

Includes Lady Anne Vernon, Princess Mary, Anne

Countess of Warwick, Elizabeth Queen of Bohemia, Brilliana Lady Harley, Princess Elizabeth, Sarah Churchill Duchess of Marlborough, Bridget Noel, Mary Princess of Orange, Elizabeth Montagu, Hannah More, Queen Charlotte, Anna Seward, The Hon. Miss Grimston, Elizabeth Craven Margravine of Anspach, and others.

129. Blassingame, John W., ed. SLAVE TESTIMONY: TWO CENTURIES OF LETTERS, SPEECHES, INTERVIEWS AND AUTOBIOGRAPHIES. Baton Rouge: Louisiana State University Press, 1977. 777p.

Contains letters for the most part not printed in the collections by Carter G. Woodson (item 263) or Robert S. Starobin (item 240). One hundred eleven letters, 1736-1864, from fifty-five correspondents; thirty of them by women, including some by Lucy Skipwith (see item 326).

130. Bottger, Fritz. FRAUEN IN AUFBRUCH: FRAUENBRIEFE AS DEM VORMARZ UND DER REVOLUTION VON 1848. Darmstädt: Luchterhand, 1979. 571p.

Includes Jeanette Straus-Wöhl, Annette von Droste-Hulshoff, Bettina von Arnim, Henriette Feuerbach, Emma Herwegh, Clara Schumann, Elise Lensing, Fanny Lewald-Stähr, Johanna Kinkel, and Jenny Marx.

131. ------. ZU NEUEN UFERN: FRAUENBRIEFE VON DER MITTE DES 19. JAHRHUNDERTS BIS ZUR NOVEMBERREVOLUTION 1918. Berlin: Verlag der Nagion, 1981. 575p.

Includes letters of Malwida von Meysenbug, Marie von Ebner-Eschenback, Marie Hesse, Bertha von Suttner, Lou Andreas-Salomé, Paula Modersöhn-Becker, Ricarda Huch, Kathe Köllwitz, Rosa Luxemburg, and Clara Zetkin.

132. Brockway, Wallace, and Keith Winer, eds. A SECOND TREASURY OF THE WORLD'S GREAT LETTERS. A MIXED MAILBAG INCLUDING INTIMATE EXCHANGES AND CYCLES OF CORRESPONDENCE BY FAMED MEN AND WOMEN OF HISTORY AND THE ARTS. Selected, edited, with historical settings

and biographical settings. Together with a preferatory note by M. Lincoln Schuster. New York: Simon & Schuster, 1941. 636p.

Includes Catherine of Siena, Joan of Arc, Queen Elizabeth I, Dorothy Osborne, Christina of Sweden, Madame de Sevigne, Queen Anne, Lady Mary Wortley Montagu, Madame de Pompadour, Catherine the Great, Madame de Stael, Dolly Madison, Jane Austen, Jane Welsh Carlyle, George Sand, Charlotte Bronte, Jenny Lind, Harriet Beecher Stowe, Florence Nightengale, Louisa May Alcott, Julia Ward Howe, and Katherine Mansfield.

133. Bryant, Arthur. POSTMAN'S HORN: OR AN ANTHOLOGY OF THE LETTERS OF THE LATTER 17TH CENTURY ENGLAND. London: Home and Van Thal, 1946. 319p.

Includes Lady Anne North of Tostock, Lady Elizabeth Bradshaigh, Mary Thelwall, Lady Jane Shakerley, Lady Elizabeth Dryden, Lady Anne Hambleton, Barbara Villiers, Elizabeth Bodville, Ursula Hull, Ann Pigot, Nancy Denton, The Hon. Mrs. Margaret Sherard, Mall Eure, Mary Eure, Mrs. Elizabeth Legh, Lady Mary Coke, Elizabeth Duchess of Albemarle, Elizabeth Dobson, Mrs. Penelope Denton, Arundel Penruddock, Mrs. Edmund Mary Verney, Frances Stuart Duchess of Richmond, Elizabeth Beaumont, Mrs. Elizabeth Preston, Katherine Shakerley, Nell Gwyn, Mrs. Margaret Elmes, Princess Mary of England, Lady Rachel Russell, and Lady Peg Elmes.

134. Cahen, Albert. LETTRES DU XVIIIe SIÈCLE: LETTRES CHOISIES DE VOLTAIRE, MADAME DU DEFFAND, DIDEROT, MADAME ROLAND ET DE DIVERS AUTEURS. Publiées avec une introduction, des notices, et des notes. Paris: Collin, 1923. 536p.

135. Chapelan, Maurice, ed. ANTHOLOGIE DU JOURNAL INTIME. Temoins d'Eux-Mêmes. Avec introduction et notices. Paris: R. Laffont, 1947. 639p.

136. Charnwood, Dorothea Mary Roby (Thorpe) Barness,

ed. CALL BACK YESTERDAY: A BOOK OF OLD LETTERS CHOSEN FROM HER COLLECTION WITH SOME MEMOIRS OF HER OWN AND A PREFACE BY SIR JOHN SQUIRE. London: Eyre and Spottiswoode, 1937. 320p.

137. Clarke, Patricia. THE GOVERNESSES: LETTERS FROM THE COLONIES, 1862-1882. London: Hutchinson, 1985. 236p.

Letters from British emigrants to Australia.

138. Connor, Eva G., ed. LETTERS TO CHILDREN. New York: Macmillan Co., 1938. 247p.

Includes Catherine of Aragon, Mary Queen of Scots, Henrietta Maria, wife of Charles I of England, Mrs. Delany, Abigail Adams, Hannah More, Mary Lamb, Dolly Madison, Dorothy Wordsworth, Jane Austen, Mary Russell Mitford, Baroness Bunsen, Abba May Alcott, Mrs. Nathaniel Hawthorne, George Sand, Harriet Beecher Stowe, George Eliot, Clara Wieck Schumann, Emily Dickinson, Louisa May Alcott, and Kate Greenaway.

139. Conrad, Heinrich, ed. FRAUENBRIEFE VON UND AN HERMANN FURSTEN PUCKLER-MUSKAW. Aus dem Nachlas neu herausgegeben von Heinrich Conrad. München: G. Müller, 1912. 370p.

Includes letters of Bettina von Arnim, Ida Grafin Hahn-Hahn (1805-1880), and Eugènie Marlet (1825-1887).

140. Culley, Margo. A DAY AT A TIME: THE DIARY LITERATURE OF AMERICAN WOMEN FROM 1764 TO THE PRESENT. New York: The Feminist Press, 1985. 341p.

Extracts from the diaries of Mary Vial Holyoke, Abigail Abbot Bailey, Elizabeth Sandwith Drinker, Nancy Shippen, Elizabeth Fuller, Margaret Van Horn Dwight, Sarah Peirce Nichols, Rebecca Cox Jackson, Carolina Keyser Preus, Amelia Stewart Knight, Helen Marnie Stewart, Eliza Frances Andrews, Annie Holmes Ricketson,

Helen Ward Brandeth, Mary Dodge Woodward, Fannie Hardy, Mary Maclane, Elizabeth Ashe, Edith O. Clark, Juanita Harrison, Eslanda Goode Robeson, Nell Giles Ahern, Abigail Lewis, Barbara Deming, Joan Frances Bennett, Bonita Wa Wa Calachaw Nunez, Joyce Mary Horner, Barbara Smith, and one anonymous woman.

141. Curie, Eve, Philippe Barres, and Raoul de Roussy de Sales, eds. THEY SPEAK FOR A NATION: LETTERS FROM FRANCE. Translated by Drake and Denise DeKay. Garden City, N.Y.: Doubleday Doran Co., 1941. 238p.

Letters soldiers, nurses, refugees, children, and prisoners of war during World War II. The letters are printed anonymously.

142. Dannett, Sylvia G.L., ed. NOBLE WOMEN OF THE NORTH. New York and London: Thomas Yoseloff, 1959. 419p.

Collection of letters and extracts from the diaries of Northern women who went South as nurses during the Civil War.

143. Davies, Margaret Llewelyn. MATERNITY: LETTERS FROM WORKING-WOMEN. Collected by the Women's Co-Operative Guild. Preface by the Rt. Hon. Herbert Samuel, MP. London: G. Bell & Sons, 1915. Reprinted with a new introduction by Gloden Dallas. London: Virago Press, 1978. 212p.

Letters from members of the Women's Co-Operative Guild written in 1914 to Margaret Llewelyn Davies, General Secretary of the Guild, in response to an appeal for direct experiences of childbirth and motherhood. The letters are heartfelt, personal documents on a subject not then thought fit for public discussion.

144. Dawson, William J., and Conigsby W. Dawson, eds. THE GREAT ENGLISH LETTER WRITERS. With introductory

essays and notes. New York: F.H. Revell Co., and New York and London: Harper & Bros., 1908. 2 vols.

Volume 1 includes Charlotte Bronte, Jane Welsh Carlyle, and Mary Wortley Montagu.

145. D'Oyley, Elizabeth. ENGLISH LETTERS. With a preface by George Gordon. London: E. Arnold, 1928. 255p.

146. ------. ENGLISH DIARIES. With a preface by George Gordon. London: Arnold, 1935. 253p.

147. Drury, Clifford Merrill, ed. FIRST WHITE WOMEN OVER THE ROCKIES: DIARIES, LETTERS AND BIOGRAPHICAL SKETCHES OF THE SIX WOMEN OF THE OREGON MISSION WHO MADE THE OVERLAND JOURNEY IN 1836 AND 1838. With introductions and editorial notes. Glendale, Calif.: A.H. Clarke, 1963-1966. 2 vols.

Volume 1: Narcissa Prentiss Whitman, diaries and letters 1836-1837; Eliza Hart Spalding, diary 1837-1840 and letter, 1842; Mary Augusta Dix Gray, letters and diary, 1838-1842, and Sarah Gilbert Smith, the only one not known to have kept a diary. Volume 2: Mary Richardson Walker, diary 1838-1848; Myra Fairbanks Eells, diary 1838; and the overland diaries of Myra Eells and Mary Walker, April-September, 1838. Volume 3: Sarah White Smith, diary and letters, 1838-1839.

148. Dublin, Thomas, ed. FARM TO FACTORY: WOMEN'S LETTERS, 1830-1860. New York: Columbia University Press, 1981. 191p.

Collection of letters written by women who left rural New England to work in the factory towns.

149. Dunaway, Philip and Mel Evans, eds. A TREASURY OF THE WORLD'S GREAT DIARIES. Introduction by Louis Untermeyer. Garden City, New York: Doubleday & Co., 1957. 586p.

Includes Louisa May Alcott, Marie Bashkirtseff, Fanny Burney, Mary Boykin Chesnut, Sarah Morgon Dawson, Celia Fiennes, Marjorie Fleming, Anne Frank, Wanda Gag, Lady Charlotte Elizabeth Guest, Sarah Kemble Knight, Selma Lagerlof, Dolly Sumner Lunt, Katherine Mansfield, Julia Newberry, George Sand, Kathleen Lady Scott, Countess Sophie Tolstoy, Queen Victoria, Virginia Woolf, and Dorothy Wordsworth.

150. Evans, Elizabeth, ed. WEATHERING THE STORM: WOMEN OF THE AMERICAN REVOLUTION. New York: Charles Scribner's Sons, 1975. 372p.

Includes Jemima Condict Harrison, Martha I'ans Walker, Margaret Hill Morris, Sarah Wister, Elizabeth Sandwith Drinker, Grace Growden Galloway, Mary Gould Almy, Jane Young Ferguson, Anna Rawle Clifford, Deborah Sampson Gannett, and Elizabeth Foote Washington.

151. Fischer, Christiane, ed. LET THEM SPEAK FOR THEMSELVES: WOMEN IN THE AMERICAN WEST, 1849-1900. Archon: Shoe String Press, 1977. 345p.

Includes Mary Ballou, Abby Mansur, and Rachel Haskell.

152. Forbes-Robertson, Diana, and Roger W. Straus, Jr. WAR LETTERS FROM BRITAIN. With a foreword by Vincent Sheean. New York: G.P. Putnam's Sons, 1941. 240p.

Letters written during World War II. Includes Lady Diana Cooper, Helen Kirkpatrick, Edith J. Lyttleton, Constance Spry, Bessie Porter, Elspeth Huxley, Rebecca West, Myra Hess, Dorothy Black, Mrs. Leslie Banks, Lady Colefax, Mrs. Kate Gielgud, and many anonymous women.

153. Francia, Ennio. DELFINA DE CUSTINE, LOUISA STOLBERG, GIULETTA RECAMIER À CANOVA: LETTERE INÉDITE. Roma: Edizioni de Storia e Letteratura, 1972. 174p.

Letters of Delphine de Sabran, Marquise de Custine

(1770-1826), Louise Maximilienne Caroline, Countess of Albany 1752-1824), and Jeanne Francoise Julie Adelaide Bernard Rècamier (1777-1849) to Antonio Canova.

154. Franklin, Penelope. PRIVATE PAGES: DIARIES OF AMERICAN WOMEN, 1830'S--1970'S. New York: Ballantine Books, 1986. 491p.

Extracts from published and unpublished diaries. Includes Marion Taylor, Yvonne Blue, Kate Tomibe, Annie Burnham Cooper, Martha Lavell, Azalia Emma Peet, Winifred Willis, Eleanor Cohen Seixas, Martha Shaw, Carole Bovoso, Marie Barrows, Ethel Robertson Whiting, and Deborah Norris Logan.

155. Fraser, Antonia. LOVE LETTERS: AN ANTHOLOGY CHOSEN BY ANTONIA FRASER. New York: Alfred A. Knopf, 1977. 245p.

Includes Margery Brews, Marie Bashkirtseff, Jane Welsh Carlyle, Rosa Luxemberg, Esther Vanhomrigh, Dora Carrington, Queen Mary II, Emily Bardach, Dorothy Osborne, Sophia Peabody, Julie de Lespinasse, Juliette Drouèt, Ellen Terry, Zelda Fitzgerald, Lady Pelham, Catherine of Aragon, Czarina Alexandrina, Elizabeth Hervey, Lucrezia Borgia, Lady Shigenari, Heloise, Mary Wollstonecraft, Dorothy Thompson, Sarah Bernhardt, and Marie d'Agoult.

156. Fyfe, J.G., ed. SCOTTISH DIARIES AND MEMOIRS. With an introduction by Professor J.D. Mackie. Stirling, Scotland: Eneas MacKay, 1942. 2 vols.

Includes Margaret Calderwood of Polton, Lady Anne Barnard, and Eliza Dawson Fletcher.

157. Gallup, Donald. THE FLOWERS OF FRIENDSHIP: LETTERS WRITTEN TO GERTRUDE STEIN. New York: Alfred A. Knopf, 1953. 403p.

Letters 1895-1946 by Mabel Dodge Luhan, Sylvia Beach, Edith Sitwell, Natalie Clifford Barney, Gertrude Atherton, Ellen Glasgow, Clare Booth Luce, Mildred Aldrich, Janet Flanner, and others.

158. Gentry, Curtis, ed. FIFTY FAMOUS LETTERS OF HISTORY. New York: Thomas Y. Crowell Co., 1930. 188p.

Includes Empress Agrippina, Anne Boleyn, Mary Queen of Scots, Queen Elizabeth I, Madame de Sevigne, Jane Welsh Carlyle, and Princess Alice of England.

159. Godfrey, Kenneth W., Audrey M. Godfrey and Jill M. Derr. WOMEN'S VOICES: AN UNTOLD HISTORY OF THE LATTER-DAY SAINTS. Salt Lake City: Deseret Book Co., 1982.

Includes extracts from the diaries of Eliza Marie Partridge Smith Lyman (1820-1886), Mary Haskin Parker Richards (1823-1860), and Patty Bartlett Sessions (1795-1892).

160. Grant, Amy Gordon, ed. LETTERS FROM ARMAGEDDON: A COLLECTION MADE DURING THE WORLD WAR. Boston and New York: Houghton Mifflin Co., 1930. 295p.

Collection of anonymous letters by Canadians serving in World War I, including nurses and relief volunteers. Includes lengthy extracts from the letters of the editor's sister, Muriel Grace Galt, 1914-1919, which record her experiences as a nurse in France, Egypt, and India.

161. Graves, Anna Melissa. BENVENUTO CELLINI HAD NO PREJUDICE AGAINST BRONZE: LETTERS FROM WEST AFRICA. Baltimore, Md.: Privately printed by the Waverly Press, 1943. 175p.

Documents the author's travels in West Africa through letters to her from West Africans, including Chrissie Kesseadoo, 1931-1932; Elizabeth Olivierre, 1937; Adelaide Casely-Hayford and Gladys Casely-Hayford, 1931-1936.

162. ------. BOTH DEEPER THAN AND ABOVE THE MELEE: LETTERS FROM EUROPEANS. Baltimore, Md.: Privately printed by the Waverly Press, 1945. 422p.

163. Greenhill, Basil and Ann Giffard, eds. WOMEN

UNDER SAIL: LETTERS AND JOURNALS CONCERNING EIGHT WOMEN TRAVELLING OR WORKING ON SAILING VESSELS BETWEEN 1829 AND 1949. Newton Abbot, Devon, England: David & Charles, n.d. 213p.

Includes Mary Molesworth, Mary Jane Saunders, Jessie Campbell, Martha Matilda Birnie Johnstone, Thomazene Williams, Annie Slade, Rachel Henning, and Anne Stanley Gwynneth Moss.

164. Hahner, June E., ed. WOMEN IN LATIN AMERICA: THEIR LIVES AND VIEWS. Los Angeles, Calif.: UCLA Latin American Center Publications: University of California at Los Angeles, 1976. 181p.

Includes Micaela Bastidas Puyucahua, Fanny Calderon de la Barca, Helena Morely, and Maria Carolina de Jesus.

165. Hale, John, ed. SETTLERS: BEING EXTRACTS FROM THE JOURNALS AND LETTERS OF EARLY COLONISTS IN CANADA, AUSTRALIA, SOUTH AFRICA AND NEW ZEALAND. London: Faber & Faber, 1950. 408p.

Includes Frances Stewart and Bridget Lacy of Canada, Elizabeth Macarthur and Mary Thomas of Australia, Lady Anne Barnard of South Africa, and Charlotte Godley of New Zealand.

166. Hamalian, Leo, ed. LADIES ON THE LOOSE: WOMEN TRAVELERS OF THE 18TH AND 19TH CENTURIES. New York: Dodd, Mead & Co., 1981. 256p.

Includes Mary Wollstonecraft, Margaret Fuller, Lady Mary Wortley Montagu, Lady Hester Stanhope, Lady Ann Blunt, and Isabella Lucy Bird.

167. Hampsten, Elizabeth. TO ALL INQUIRING FRIENDS: LETTERS, DIARIES, AND ESSAYS IN NORTH DAKOTA, 1880-1910. Grand Forks, N.Dak.: Department of English, University of North Dakota, 1979. 243p.

Includes extracts from the letters and diaries of North Dakota women.

168. Harding, Rachel and Mary Dyson, eds. A BOOK OF CONDOLENCES FROM THE PRIVATE LETTERS OF ILLUSTRIOUS PEOPLE. With a foreword by Madeleine L'Engle and a preface by Ann Farrer. New York: Continuum, 1981. 185p.

Includes Charlotte Bronte, Jane Welsh Carlyle, Mary Baker Eddy, George Eliot, Queen Elizabeth I, Joyce Grenfell, Mrs. M. Hartley, Jessica Mitford, Lady May Wortley Montagu, Elizabeth Myres, Ruth Plant, Elizabeth Purefoy, Madame de Sévigné, Edith Sitwell, Queen Victoria, Ellen Willmott, and Virginia Woolf.

169. Harrison, Ada M., ed. GREY AND SCARLET: LETTERS FROM THE WAR AREAS BY ARMY SISTERS ON ACTIVE SERVICE. With a foreword by Her Majesty Queen Mary, and an introduction by Dame Katherine Jones. London: Hodder & Stoughton, 1944. 200p.

Letters written during World War I by members of Queen Alexandra's Imperial Military Nursing Service and Territorial Army Nursing Service.

170. Hashomer Hatzair Collective. YOUTH AMIDST THE RUINS: A CHRONICLE OF JEWISH YOUTH IN THE WAR. New York: Published for the Hashomer Hatzair Collective by Scopus Publishing Co., 1941. 117p.

Includes extracts from the diaries and letters of soldiers, refugees, and young Jews living in occupied cities during World War II. The writers are generally identified by their first names only.

171. Hawkins, Richmond Laurin, comp. NEWLY DISCOVERED FRENCH LETTERS OF THE SEVENTEENTH, EIGHTEENTH AND NINETEENTH CENTURIES. Cambridge, Mass.: Harvard University Press, 1933. 288p.

Includes Anne Lefevre, Madame de Maintenon, Rachel (Elisa Felix), George Sand, and others.

172. Hellerstein, Erna Olafson, Leslie Parker Hume and Karen M. Offen, eds. VICTORIAN WOMEN: A DOCUMENTARY ACCOUNT OF WOMEN'S LIVES IN NINETEENTH CENTURY ENGLAND,

FRANCE AND THE UNITED STATES. Prepared under the auspices of the Center for Research on Women at Stanford University. Stanford, Calif: Stanford University Press, 1981. 534p.

Includes previously unpublished documents, and extracts from the published writings of Nellie Weeton, Kate Stanley, Caroline Clive, Mary Abigail Chaffe Abell, and others.

173. Henry, Sondria and Emily Taitz. WRITTEN OUT OF HISTORY: A HIDDEN LEGACY OF JEWISH WOMEN REVEALED THROUGH THEIR WRITINGS AND LETTERS. New York: Bloch Publishing Co., 1978. 293p.

Includes Donna Sarah, Lady Maliha, Esperanza Malchi, Lady Judith Montefiore, Rebecca Gratz; letters found in the Cairo Geniza; and extracts from the Prague Ghetto Letters, 1619.

174. Hoffman, Nancy, ed. WOMAN'S "TRUE" PROFESSION: VOICES FROM THE HISTORY OF TEACHING. Old Westbury, N.Y.: The Feminist Press, and New York: McGraw-Hill Book Co., 1981. 327p.

Writings of American teachers. Includes Mary Swift, Sarah Chase, Lucy Chase, Julia Rutledge, Mary Ames, Charlotte L. Forten, Laura M. Towne, Sallie Holley, Mary E. Adams, Ellen P. Lee, and Mary S. Adams.

175. Holliday, Laurel. HEART SONGS: THE INTIMATE DIARIES OF YOUNG GIRLS. Guerneville, Calif.: Bluestocking Books, 1978. 191p. New York: Methuen, 1980. 181p.

Includes extracts from the adolescent diaries of Anaïs Nin, Maggie Owen Wadelton, Kathie Gray, Gretchen Lainer, Selma Lagerlöf, Marie Bashkirtseff, Nellie Ptaschkina, Matilda von Buddenbroch, and Flora and Benôite Groult.

176. Holmes, Kenneth, ed. and comp. COVERED WAGON WOMEN: DIARIES AND LETTERS FROM THE WESTERN TRAILS,

1840-1890. Glendale, Calif.: Arthur H. Clark Co., 1983. Volume 1: 1840-1849. 272p.

First of a projected series of ten volumes of rare and previously unpublished documents. Includes Betsey Bayley, Anna Maria King, Tabitha Brown, the Donner Party Letters, Phoebe Stanton, Rachel Fisher, Elizabeth Dixon Smith, Patty Sessions, Keturah Belknap, Sallie Hester, and Louisiana Strentzel.

177. Hunt, R.N. Carew, ed. UNPUBLISHED LETTERS FROM THE COLLECTION OF JOHN WILD. New York: The Dial Press; and London: Lincoln MacVeagh, 1930.

Includes Frances Sheridan, Elizabeth Pennington, Hannah Cowley, Eva Maria Viletti Garrick, Lady Emma Hamilton, Queen Caroline of Brunswick, and Maria Edgeworth.

178. Hurd, Charles and Eleanor Hurd, eds. A TREASURY OF GREAT AMERICAN LETTERS: OUR COUNTRY'S LIFE AND HISTORY IN LETTERS OF ITS MEN AND WOMEN. New York: Hawthorn Books, 1961. 320p.

Includes Abigail Adams, Mrs. Samuel Harrison, Dolly Madison, Ellen Bigelow, Dame Shirley (Louise Clappe), Susan B. Anthony, Jane Addams, Mary Baker Eddy, and Edna St. Vincent Millay.

179. Ihringer, Bernhard. FRAUENBRIEFE ALLER ZEITEN. Stuttgart: C. Krabbe, 1910. 413p.

180. Ingpen, Ada, ed. WOMEN AS LETTER-WRITERS: A COLLECTION OF LETTERS. London: Hutchinson, 1909. 444p.

Includes Margaret Paston, Anne Boleyn, Mary Queen of Scots, Lady Rachel Russell, Lady Mary Wortley Montagu, Queen Elizabeth I, Dorothy Osborne, Esther Vanhomrigh, Elizabeth Montagu, Mary Delany, Elizabeth Carter, Hester Chapone, Hester Lynch Thrale Piozzi, Anna Letitia Barbauld, Catherine Clive, Hannah More, Anna Seward, Fanny Burney, Lady Emma Hamilton, Mary

Wollstonecraft, Sarah Siddons, Maria Edgeworth, Lady Harriet Hesketh, Sydney Owenson Lady Morgan, Amelia Opie, Lucy Aikin, Ann Godwin, Jane Taylor, Mary Lamb, Angelica Kaufman, Dorothy Wordsworth, Susan Ferrier, Elizabeth Inchbald, Marjory Fleming, Jane Austen, Mary Russell Mitford, Mary Shelley, Lady Anne Barnard, Mary Howitt, Lady Caroline Lamb, Felicia Dorothea Hemans, Joanna Baillie, Harriet Martineau, Sara Coleridge, Jane Welsh Carlyle, The Countess of Blessington, Elizabeth Gaskell, Lady Lucy Duff-Gordon, Charlotte Bronte, Sarah Austin, Margaret Fuller, Lady Hester Stanhope, Harriet Beecher Stowe, Agnes Strickland, Anna Jameson, Fanny Kemble, Elizabeth Barrett Browning, George Eliot, and Christina Rossetti.

181. Johnson, R. Brimley, ed. BLUESTOCKING LETTERS. London: John Lane, the Bodley Head, 1926. 282p.

Includes Elizabeth Montagu, Mrs. Vesey, The Hon. Mrs. Boscawen, Hester Chapone, and Elizabeth Carter.

182. Jones, Katharine M., ed. HEROINES OF DIXIE. Indianapolis, Ind.: Bobbs-Merrill Co., 1955. 430p.

Includes Judith Brockenbrough McGuire, Mary Boykin Chesnut, Cornelia Peake McDonald, Kate Cumming, Sarah Morgan, Julia LeGrand, Mary Ann Loughborough, Susan Bradford, Phoebe Yates Pember, Mary Ann Harris Gray, and Eliza Frances Andrews.

183. ------. THE PLANTATION SOUTH. Indianapolis, Ind.: Bobbs-Merrill Co., 1957. 412p.

Includes Dolly Madison, Frederika Bremer, Almira Coffin, Frances Anne Kemble, Ella Gertrude Clanton Thomas, Mahala Eggleston Roach, and Mrs. Issac H. Hillard.

184. ------. LADIES OF RICHMOND, CONFEDERATE CAPITOL. With an introduction by Clifford Dowdey. Indianapolis, Ind.: Bobbs-Merrill Co., 1962. 364p.

Includes Margaret Sumner McLean, Mary Boykin

Chesnut, Judith Brockenbrough McGuire, Elizabeth L. Van Lew, Cornelia Peake McDonald, Virginia Clay, Julia Gardener Tyler, Varina Howell Davis, Kate Mason Rowland, Mary Curtis Lee, Emma Mordecai, Phoebe Yates Pember, and others.

185. Kobler, Franz, ed. A TREASURY OF JEWISH LETTERS: LETTERS FROM THE FAMOUS AND HUMBLE. Second ed. New York: Publication of the East and West Library issued by Farrar, Straus & Young, 1953. 2 vols.

186. ------. LETTERS OF THE JEWS THROUGH THE AGES FROM BIBLICAL TIMES TO THE MIDDLE OF THE 18TH CENTURY. Edited with an introduction, biographical notes and historical comments. Second edition. New York: East and West Library, 1978. 2 vols.

Includes Lady Maliha, Donna Sarah, Esperanza Malchi, the women of the Prague Ghetto, 1619, and others; considers Gluckel of Hamlin as a letter-writer.

187. Korn, Alfons L. THE VICTORIAN VISITERS: AN ACCOUNT OF THE HAWAIIAN KINGDOM, 1861-1866. INCLUDING THE JOURNAL LETTERS OF SOPHIA CRACROFT, EXTRACTS FROM THE JOURNALS OF LADY FRANKLIN, AND DIARIES AND LETTERS OF QUEEN EMMA OF HAWAII. Honolulu: University of Hawaii Press, 1958. 351p.

Includes writings of Sophia Cracroft (b.1816), Jane Griffin, Lady Franklin (1792-1875), and Emma, Consort of Kamehameha IV, King of the Hawaiian Islands (1836-1885).

188. Leinster, Emilia Mary Lennox, Duchess of Fitzgerald, ed. CORRESPONDENCE. Dublin: Stationery Office, 1949-1957. 3 vols.

Volume 1: Letters of Emily, Duchess of Leinster. Volume 2: Letters of Lady Sarah Lennox Napier. Volume 3: Letters of Lady Louise Conolly.

189. Lerner, Gerda. THE FEMALE EXPERIENCE: AN AMERICAN DOCUMENTARY. Indianapolis, Ind.:

Bobbs-Merrill Educational Publishing, 1977. 509p.

Documentary history. Includes Louisa May Alcott, Mary Putnam Jacobi, Martha Coffin Wright (1806-1878), Ellen Wright Garrison (1840-1931), Harriet Beecher Stowe, Emily Rakestraw Robinson, Lucy Stone, Sarah Stone, Catherine M. Sedgwick, Mary R. Lewis, Marian Louise Moore, Lucy Chase, Sarah Christie Stevens (1844-1920), Lena Morrow Lewis, Belva Lockwood, Mary Dyer, and Marian Louise Moore.

190. LESBIAN HOME JOURNAL: DIARIES, LETTERS AND DREAMS. Seattle: Working On It Lesbian Press, Summer, 1976. 64p.

Collection of extracts from the private writings of Lesbians; writers are identified by first name only.

191. "Letters of Presidents of the United States and 'Ladies of the White House'." PENNSYLVANIA MAGAZINE OF HISTORY AND BIOGRAPHY 25:3 (1901), 355-365; 25:4 (1901), 527; 26:1 (1902), 115-125.

Includes letters of Martha Washington, Abigail Adams, Dolly Madison, Louisa C. Adams, Rachel Jackson, Anna Harrison, Julia Gardiner Tyler, Mrs. James Polk, Betty T. Bliss, Abigail Fillmore, and Mary Todd Lincoln.

192. LETTRES DE MADEMOISELLE DE MONTPENSIER, DE MESDAMES DE MOTTEVILLE ET DES MONTMORENCY DE MADEMOISELLE DUPRÉ ET DE LA MARQUISE DE LAMBERT. Accompagnés de notices biographiques et de notes éxplicatives. Paris: Leopold-Collin, 1806.

Includes Isabelle de Harville de Montmorency, (1629-1712). Anne Marie Louise d'Orléans, Duchesse de Montpensier (1627-1693), Françoise Langlois Bertaut, Dame de Motteville, (1651-1689), and Anne Thérèse de Marguenat de Courcelles, Marquise de Lambert (1647-1733).

193. Lewis, W.S., Robert A. Smith and Charles H.

Bennett, eds. HORACE WALPOLE'S CORRESPONDENCE WITH HANNAH MORE, LADY BROWNE, LADY MARY COKE, LADY HERVEY, LADY GEORGE LENNOX, ANNE PITT, LADY SUFFOLK, MARY HAMILTON (MRS. JOHN DICKINSON). New Haven: Yale University Press, 1961. 528p. (Yale Edition of Walpole's Correspondence, vol. 31).

194. Lifshin, Lyn, ed. ADRIADNE'S THREAD: A COLLECTION OF CONTEMPORARY WOMEN'S JOURNALS. New York: Harper & Row, 1982. 333p.

Includes Lin Lifshin, Maxine Kumin, Carol Mont Parker, Rachel De Vries, Kay Morgan, Sharon Wysocki, Barbara Moraff, Alix Kates Schulman, Marge Piercy, Bibi Wein, Leslie Ullman, Gail Godwin, Sylvia Plath, Eleanor Coppola, Michele Murray, Susan Kinnicutt, Carol Dine, Judith Minty, Mary Elsie Robertson, Kate Green, Margaret Ryan, Nan Hunt, Anne Sexton, Kathleen Spivack, Judith McDaniel, Geneen Roth, Diane Kendig, L.L. Zieger, Florinda Colavin-Bridges, Judith Hemschemeyer, Darlene Myers, Nancy Esther James, Elaine Starkman, Michelle Herman, Sarah Arvio, Janet Gluckman, Carol Bly, Janice Eidus, Mary Ann Lynch, Ida Nudel, Toi Derricotte, Miriam Sagan, Linda Hogan, Sandra Alcosser, Rita Mae Brown, Denise Levertov, Linda Pastan, Deborah Robson, and Patricia Hampl.

195. Lucas, E.V., ed. THE GENTLEST ART: A CHOICE OF LETTERS BY ENTERTAINING HANDS. New York: The Macmillan Co., 1913. 422p.

Includes Marjorie Fleming, Hannah More, Mary Guilhermin, Jane Austen, Dame Dorothy Brown, Anna Seward, Maria Edgeworth, Lady Mary Wortley Montagu, and Lady Pelham.

196. ------. THE SECOND POST: A COMPANION TO THE GENTLEST ART. Sixth Ed. London: Methuen & Co., 1919. 266p.

197. ------. POST BAG DIVERSIONS. New York and London: Harper & Bros., 1934. 259p.

Letters written to Lucas, 1903-1933. Includes

Elizabeth Asquith, Princess Antoine Bibesco, Barbara Chase, Helen Keller, Mrs. W.K. Clifford, Mary Edwards, Lady (Ian) Hamilton, Gertrude Jekyll, Lady Jekyll, Mrs. Andrew Lang, Margaret Mackail, Lady Noble, and Mrs. H. Watkins.

198. Luce, Iris, ed. LETTERS FROM THE PEACE CORPS. Washington, D.C.: Robert B. Luce, Inc., 1964. 135p.

Letters by Peace Corps volunteers to their families, fellow volunteers, and to the Peace Corps Headquarters, during the 1950's and 1960's. Nine women are included.

199. Luchetti, Cathy Lee, and Carol Olwell. WOMEN OF THE WEST. St. George, Utah: Antelope Island Press, 1982. 240p.

Includes extracts from the diaries of Mary Richardson Walker, Miriam Davis Colt, Sister Mary Catherine Cabareaux, Kitturah Penton Belknap, and Bethina Owens-Adair; and from the letters of Elinore Pruitt Stewart.

200. Lutz, Alma, ed. WITH LOVE, JANE: LETTERS FROM AMERICAN WOMEN ON THE WAR FRONTS. New York: The John Day Co., 1945. 199p.

Letters written by women during World War II.

201. Lyell, Laetitia, ed. A MEDIAEVAL POST-BAG. London: Jonathan Cape, 1934. 320p.

Contains a good introductory survey of the familiar letter in the fifteenth century ("Private Letters and Their Writers in the Fifteenth Century," pp. 13-25) and extracts from the correspondence of the Stonor Family (Dame Elizabeth Stonor), from the Plumpton Correspondence (Katherine Chadderton, Maude Rose and Dorothy Plumpton), from the Paston Correspondence (Elizabeth Clere, Margaret Paston, Dame Elizabeth Brews, Margery Brews), from the Shillingford Correspondence (Joan Pelham, Jane Roos), from the Cely Papers and from the Marchall Correspondence.

202. McCord, Shirley S. TRAVEL ACCOUNTS OF INDIANA, 1679-1961. A COLLECTION OF OBSERVATIONS BY WAYFARING FOREIGNERS, ITINERANTS, AND PERIPATETIC HOOSIERS. Indiana Historical Collections, Volume 47. 331p.

Includes Mrs. Lydia Bacon, Harriet Williams Sawyer, Amelia M. Murray, and Caroline C. Barnum.

203. Maison, Andre, comp. ANTHOLOGIE DE LA CORRESPONDANCE FRANÇAISE. Etablié, prefacé et annoteé par André Maison. Lausanne: Éditions Récontre, 1969. 7 vols.

Comprehensive collection of the great French letter writers. Volume 1 includes Marguerite de Navarre, Catherine de Médicis, Jeanne d'Albret, Marie Stuart, Marguerite de Valois, Louise de Coligny, Sainte Jeanne de Chantal, Marie de Médicis, Catherine de Vivonne Marquise de Rambouillet, Mère Angelique, Mère Agnes, Anne Doni d'Attichy, Comtesse de Maure, Jeanne Hurault de Hospital, Dame de Choisy, Marie de Rohan, Duchesse de Chevreuse, Julie Lucine d'Angennes de Montausier, Anne Bigot Corneuel, and Madèleine de Scudèry. Volume 2 includes: Marie de Hautefort, Marèchale de Shomberg, Ninon de Lenclos, Anne de Gonzague de Cleves, Anne Geneviève de Bourbon, Duchesse de Longueville, Charlotte Saumaise de Chazan, Comtesse de Brègy, Madame Gilbert Pascal Périer, Mere Anelique de Saint-Jean-Arnauld, Marie Gigualt de Bellefonds de Villars, Jacqueline Pascal, Madame de Sévigné, Anne Marie Louise d'Orléans, Duchesse de Montpensier, Isabelle de Harville de Montmorency, Madame de Scudèry, Marie Madeleine Pioche de la Vergne, Comtesse de Lafayette, Madame de Maintenon, Marie-Angélique de Gue-Bagnols de Coulanges, Françoise Athenais de Rouchechouart de Mortemart de Montespan, La Princesse des Ursins, Madèleine Reneé de Gaureau de Mont, and Françoise Louise de la Baume le Blanc, Duchesse de la Vallière. Volume 3 includes: La Comtesse de Grignan, Anne Marguerite le Valois de Villette de Murçay, Comtesse de Caylus, Pauline Adhemar de Monteil de Grignan de Simiane, Anne Louise Bénédicté de Bourbon, Duchesse du Main, Claudine Alexandrine Guèrin, Marquise de Tencin, Margueritte Jeanne Cordier de Launay de Staal, Marie Adèlaide de Savoie, Duchesse de Bourgogne, Marie-Thérèse Quenaudon Piron (Mlle. de Bar), Adrienne Couvreur (or Lecouvreur), Charlotte Élisabeth Gèoffrin, and Gabrièlle Émilie le Tonnelièr de Bréteuil, Marquise de Châtelet. Volume 4 includes: Thérèse Deshayes de la Popelinière, Marie Thérèse Walpurgis Amèlie Christine d'Autriche, Marie Anne Françoise de Noailles Comtesse de la Mark, Jeanne Antoinette Poisson, Marquisse de Pompadour, Marie Antonie Walpurgis, Princesse de Bavière, Madame d'Épinay, Catherine II, Empress of Russia, Julie de Lespinasse, Louise Honorine Crozat du Chatel, Duchesse de Choiseul, Sophie Jeanne Armande Élisabeth Septimanie de Vignerot du Plessis-Richélieu, Comtesse d'Egmont, Isabelle Agnes Élisabeth van Tuyll van Serooskerken, Dame de Saint-Hyacinthe, Madame de Charrière, Amèlie Panckouke Suard, Marie Jeanne Philipon, Madame Roland de la Platière, Marie Antoinette Josephe de Lorraine, Archiduchesse d'Autriche, and Louise Julie Carreau Talma. Volume 5 includes: Germaine de Staël, Charlotte Corday, Pauline de Beaumont, Madame de Rémusat, Princess Lieven, Celeste Buisson de la Vigne, Vicomtesse de Chateaubriand, Claire Rose Louise Bonne de Kersaint, Duchesse de Durfort-Duras, Anna Petrovna Soymonof Swetchine, Hortense Therese Sigismonde Sophie Alexandrine Allart de Méritens, Marceline Felicité Désbordes-Valmore, and Pauline Marie Michelle Fredérique Ulirique de Montmorin-Saint Harem, Comtesse de Beaumont. Volume 6 includes: George Sand, Éugenie Henriette Augustine Agoult, Juliette Drouét, and Mère Bénedicté de Gobineau. Volume 7 includes: Marie Bashkirtseff, Colette, and Marie Éugenia Ignacia Augustina de Guzman y Palafox, Comtesse de Teba (l'Impèratrice Éugenie).

204. Marcus, Jacob R., comp. THE AMERICAN JEWISH WOMAN: A DOCUMENTARY HISTORY. New York: KTAV Publishing House, and Cincinnati, Ohio: American Jewish Archives, 1981. 1047p.

Includes Abigail Bilhah Levy Franks (1696-1756),

Miriam Gratz, Esther Hart, Rebecca Franks, Abigail Minis, Frances Hart Shetfall (1740-1820), Rachel Myers, Rebecca Samuel, Anna Barnett, Joyce Myers (1737-1824), Rachel Mordecai Lazarus, Rebecca Gratz, Sally Etting, Esther Shetfall, Rebecca Cohen, Anna Marks, Eleanor H. Cohen, Getty Bechmann, Maimie Pinzer, and many anonymous women.

205. Mason, Edward T, ed. BRITISH LETTERS, ILLUSTRATIVE OF CHARACTER AND SOCIAL LIFE. New York and London: G.P. Putnam's Sons, the Knickerbocker Press, 1888. 3 vols.

Includes Jane Welsh Carlyle, Sarah Siddons, Hester Lynch Thrale Piozzi, Eleanor Butler and Sarah Ponsonby, Madame de Genlis, Maria Edgeworth, Mary Lamb, Elizabeth Lady Holland, Mary Delany, Mrs. Pendarves, Elizabeth Carter, Hannah More, Mrs. Trench, Sara Coleridge, Lucy Aiken, Anna Letitia Barbauld, Lady Sidney Owenson, Lady Morgan, Caroline Norton, Anne Grant, Mary Russell Mitford, Lady Mary Wortley Montagu, Caroline Frances Cornwallis, Lady Sommerville, Mary Berry, and Caroline Clive.

206. Mason, Mary Grimley, and Carol Hurd Green. JOURNEYS: AUTOBIOGRAPHICAL WRITINGS BY WOMEN. Boston: G.K. Hall, 1979. 228p.

Includes discussion and extracts from the personal writings of Lady Mary Wortley Montagu, Mrs. Jarena Lee, Sara Coleridge, Lady Ann Blunt, Beatrice Webb, H.D. (Hilda Doolittle), and Susan Sontag.

207. Maxton-Graham, Joyce Anstruther, comp. WOMEN OF BRITAIN: LETTERS FROM BRITAIN. Introduction by Jan Struther. New York: Harcourt Brace & Co., 1941. 334p.

Collection of letters from British women written during World War II. The letters are anonymous, and personal details have in many cases been deleted.

208. Megroz, R.L., ed. LETTERS OF WOMEN IN LOVE: DISCLOSING THE FEMALE HEART FROM GIRLHOOD TO OLD AGE.

Boston and New York: Houghton Mifflin Co., and Cambridge, England: The Riverside Press, 1929. 318p.

Includes Abigail Adams, Dorothy Osborne, Esther Vanhomrigh, Jane Welsh Carlyle, Elizabeth Barrett Browning, Margaret Paston, Mary Shelley, Margaret, Duchess of Newcastle, Heloise, George Sand, Mary Wollstonecraft, Hester Lynch Thrale Piozzi, Madame de Stael, Marjorie Fleming, Lady Mary Wortley Montagu, Margaret Fuller, Maria Edgeworth, Christina Rossetti, Jane Austen, and Dorothy Wordsworth.

209. Merriam, Eve, comp. GROWING UP FEMALE IN AMERICA: TEN LIVES. Garden City, N.Y.: Doubleday & Co., 1971. 308p.

Contains brief excerpts from the letters of Eliza Southgate Bowne and Dolly Madison, from the diaries of Sarah Kemble Knight and Maria Mitchell, and from the journal of Mary Ann Webster Loughborough.

210. Millet, Kate, introduction. CATERPILLARS: JOURNAL ENTRIES BY ELEVEN WOMEN. With a introduction by Kate Millet. No Place (Berkeley, Calif.?): Epona Press, 1977. 137p.

In 1975, Millet taught an extension course in Women in Literature at the University of California at Berkeley. She assigned a journal to be written and to be read in class. This book contains excerpts from the journals kept by students, and was edited by women in the class.

211. Moffat, Mary Jane and Charlotte Painter, eds. REVELATIONS: DIARIES OF WOMEN. New York: Random House, 1974. 411p.

Excellent general introduction to women's diaries. Moffat's essay on the reasons women write diaries, and Painter's afterword on the function of the diary in bridging the gap between life and art provides a good framework for the presentation of extracts from the diaries of Louisa May Alcott, Sylvia Ashton-Warner, Marie

Bashkirtseff, Ruth Benedict, Emily Carr, Mary Boykin Chesnut, Madame Dostoëvsky, George Eliot, Joanna Field, Marjorie Fleming, Anne Frank, Loran Hurnscott, Alice James, Carolina Maria de Jésus, Fanny Kemble, Kathe Kollwitz, Selma Lagerlöf, Katherine Mansfield, Martha Martin, Anaïs Nin, Charlotte Painter, Nellie Ptaschkina, George Sand, Frances Karlen Santamaria, Evelyn Scott, Florida Scott- Maxwell, Hannah Senesh, Sei Shonagon, Gertrude Stein, Sophia Tolstoy, an unknown Japanese woman, Virginia Woolf, and Dorothy Wordsworth.

212. Moffat, Mary Jane, ed. IN THE MIDST OF WINTER: SELECTIONS FROM THE LITERATURE OF MOURNING. New York: Random House/Vintage Books, 1982. 274p.

Includes excerpts from the diaries of Toby Talbot, Anne Phillipe, and Virginia Woolf.

213. Morgan, Dale. OVERLAND IN 1846: DIARIES AND LETTERS OF THE CALIFORNIA-OREGON TRAIL. Georgetown, Calif.: Talisman Press, 1963. 2 vols.

214. Mulder, William and A. Russell Mortensen, eds. AMONG THE MORMONS: HISTORICAL ACCOUNTS BY CONTEMPORARY OBSERVERS. New York: Alfred A. Knopf, 1967. 482p.

Includes Charlotte Haven, Sarah Hall Haven, Martha Hall Scott, and Elizabeth Wells Randall.

215. Myres, Sandra L., ed. HO FOR CALIFORNIA: WOMEN'S OVERLAND DIARIES FROM THE HUNTINGTON LIBRARY. San Marino, Calif.: Huntington Library, 1980. 314p.

Includes extracts from the diaries of Mrs. Jane McDougal, Mary Stuart Bailey, Helen Carpenter, Harriet Bunyard, and Mrs. Maria Shrode.

216. Nicolson, Marjorie Hope. CONWAY LETTERS: THE CORRESPONDENCE OF ANNE, VISCOUNTESS CONWAY, HENRY MORE, AND THEIR FRIENDS, 1642-1684. Collected from manuscript sources and edited with a biographical account. New Haven, Conn.: Yale University Press; and

London: Humphrey Milford, Oxford University Press, 1930. 517p.

Correspondence of Anne Finch Conway, Viscountess Conway (1631-1679).

217. O'Farrell, Patrick. LETTERS FROM IRISH AUSTRALIA, 1825-1929. Text of Letters edited by Brian Trainor. Sydney, Australia: New South Wales University Press, and Belfast: Ulster Historical Foundation, 1984. 244p.

History of Irish immigrants in Australia based on and including extracts from private correspondence. Includes letters of Elizabeth Jane Matthews Crawford.

218. Omori, Annie Shepley, trans., and Kochi Doi. DIARIES OF COURT LADIES OF OLD JAPAN. With an introduction by Amy Lowell. Boston: Houghton Mifflin, and Cambridge: The Riverside Press, 1920. 195p. Tokyo: Kenkyusha, 1935, 1963. 209p. New York: AMS Press, 1970 (reprint of the 1920 edition), 200p.

Presents the poetic diaries of three contemporaries of the Heian period: THE SARASHINA DIARY, the DIARY of Lady Murasaki and the DIARY of Izumi Shikibu.

219. Payne, Karen, ed. BETWEEN OURSELVES: LETTERS BETWEEN MOTHERS AND DAUGHTERS, 1750-1982. Boston: Houghton Mifflin Co., 1983. 416p.

Includes Helen Claes, Sylvia Plath, Edith Summerskill, Anne Sexton, Jessie Bernard, Jackie Page, Charlene Baldridge, Nan Hunt, Terry Wolverton, Sarah Grace, Lady Mary Wortley Montagu, Frederika Bremer, George Sand, Harriet Martineau, Elizabeth Blackwell, Lucy Stone, Florence Nightengale, Louisa May Alcott, Susan B. Anthony, Mary Putnam Jacobi, Queen Victoria, Calamity Jane, Olive Schreiner, Crystal Eastman, Helen Keller, Lella Secor, Vera Brittain, Winifred Holtby, Amelia Earhart, Constance Lytton, Hannah Senesh, Hilde Coppi, Rose Schlosinger, Maired Nugent, Isa Kogon,

Robin Morgan, Nan Baur Maglin, Elaine Starkman, Judy Green Herbsreit, Mrs. Colbert, Brooke Jacobson, Susan Abbott, Jackie Lapidus, Isak Dinesen, Chungmi Kim, Susan Meulander Faulkner, Marion Cohen, Joannie Fritz, Anne Scott, and others given by first name only.

220. Pearce, T.M., ed. LITERARY AMERICA: THE MARY AUSTIN LETTERS. Westport, Conn., and London: Greenwood Press, 1979. 296p.

Correspondence preserved in the Mary Austin Collection at the Henry E. Huntington Library, San Marino, California. Includes letters of Ina Donna Coolbrith, Anna Howard Shaw, Fannie Hurst, Alice Corbin Henderson, Ruth St. Denis, Amy Lowell, Kate Douglas Wiggin, Mabel Dodge Luhan, Frances Perkins, Marianne Moore, Willa Cather, Elizabeth Connor Lindsay, and Una Jeffers.

221. Ponsonby, Arthur, comp. THE LITTLE TORCH: QUOTATIONS FROM THE DIARIES OF THE PAST FOR EVERY DAY OF THE YEAR. Selected and with an introduction by Arthur Ponsonby (Lord Ponsonby of Shulbrede). With 12 portraits and decorations from the signs of the Zodiac by Thomas Poulton. London: George Routledge & Sons, 1938. 410p.

222. Radel, Jutta. LIEBE MUTTER, LIEBE TOCHTER: FRAUENBRIEFE AUS 3 JAHRHUNDERTS. Mit einem vorwort von Joseph Auslander. München: Rogner und Bernhard, 1980. 190p. Frankfurt: Ullstein, 1982. 189p.

223. Rees, Bryon Johnson, ed. NINETEENTH CENTURY LETTERS. New York: Charles Scribner's Sons, 1919. 543p.

Includes Maria Edgeworth, Mary Lamb, Jane Welsh Carlyle, Elizabeth Barrett Browning, and George Eliot.

224. Rhys, Earnest. LETTERS FROM LIMBO. London: J.M. Dent & Sons, 1936. 289p.

Letters written chiefly to Rhys, including letters

by Olive Schreiner, Grace Rhys, Winifred Holtby, Hilda Schuster, Sylvia Lind, Virginia Woolf, Hilda Vaughn, Mary Gardener, and Stella Rhys.

225. Richardson, Mrs. Abby (Sage), ed. OLD LOVE LETTERS: OR, LETTERS OF SENTIMENT WRITTEN BY PERSONS EMINENT IN ENGLISH LITERATURE AND HISTORY. Boston: J.R. Osgood, 1883. 322p.

226. Riding, Laura. EVERYBODY'S LETTERS. With an editorial postscript. London: A. Barker, 1933. 253p.

Anthology of letters written to Riding. Correspondents are identified by first name only.

227. Riordan, Jim, trans. LETTERS FROM THE DEAD: LAST LETTERS FROM SOVIET MEN AND WOMEN WHO DIED FIGHTING THE NAZIS, 1941-1945. Translated from the Russian. Moscow: Progress Publishers, 1965. 232p.

228. Saint René Taillandier, René Gaspard Ernest, ed. LETTRES INÉDITES DE J.C.L. SISMONDI, DE M. DE BONSTETTEN, DE MADAME DE STAEL ET DE MADAME DE SOUZA À MADAME LA COMTESSE D'ALBANY. Publiée avec une introduction. Paris: Michel Lévy Frères, 1863. 406p.

Includes letters of Madame de Staël and Adelaide Marie Emilie Filleul, Comtesse Flahaut, Marqueza do Sousa Botelho Mourao e Vasconcellos (1761?-1836).

229. Sainte Beuve, C.-A. THE REIGN AND AMOURS OF THE BOURBON REGIME. A BRILLIANT DESCRIPTION OF THE COURTS OF LOUIS XIV, AMOURS, DEBAUCHERY, INTRIGUES, AND STATE SECRETS, INCLUDING SUPPRESSED AND CONFISCATED MANUSCRIPTS; THE CORRESPONDENCE OF MADAME, PRINCESS PALATINE. Preceeded by introductions from C.-A. Sainte Beuve. Unexpurgated rendition into English. New York: Privately Printed for members of the Versailles Historical Society, 1889. 326p.

Contains correspondence of Marie Adelaide de Savoie, Duchess de Bourgogne, Elizabeth Charlotte, Duchesse d'Orleans, and Francoise d'Augigne, Marquise de Maintenon.

230. Saintsbury, George, ed. A LETTER BOOK: SELECTED WITH AN INTRODUCTION ON THE ART OF LETTER-WRITING. London: G. Bell & Sons, and New York: Harcourt Brace & Co., 1922. 306p.

Includes Eleanor, Duchess of Burgandy, the Paston family, Lady Mary Sidney, Dorothy Osborne, Lady Mary Wortley Montagu, Jane Welsh Carlyle, Elizabeth Barrett Browning, and Fanny Kemble.

231. Sanders, Margaret, comp. INTIMATE LETTERS OF ENGLAND'S QUEENS. New York: Pitman Publishing Corp, 1956, and London: Museum Press, 1957. 234p.

Includes Catherine of Aragon, Anne Boleyn, Jane Seymour, Anne of Cleves, Catherine Howard, Catherine Parr, Lady Jane Grey, Mary I, Elizabeth I, Anne of Denmark, Henrietta Maria, Catherine of Braganza, Mary Beatrice of Modena, Mary II, Queen Anne, Caroline of Brandenburg- Anspach, Charlotte Sophia of Mecklenburg-Strelitz, Caroline of Brunswick, Adelaide of Saxe-Meiningen, and Queen Victoria.

232. Sanger, Margaret, ed. MOTHERHOOD IN BONDAGE. New York: Brentano's: Publishers, 1928. 446p.

Collection of letters written to Sanger from mothers, fathers, and physicians in response to her birth control campaigns. Letters deal with issues of girl mothers, poverty, illness and maternity, forced motherhood, miscarriage and infant death, and the loneliness of "confinement." An appendix presents an analysis by Mary Sumner Boyd of the some five thousand letters, classified according to geographic distribution, economic status, mother's age, number of children, frequency of childbirth, and number of miscarriages and stillbirths.

233. Schuster, Lincoln M., ed. A TREASURY OF THE WORLD'S GREAT LETTERS. FROM ANCIENT DAYS TO OUR OWN TIME, CONTAINING THE CHARACTERISTIC AND CRUCIAL COMMUNICATIONS AND INTIMATE EXCHANGES AND CYCLES OF CORRESPONDENCE OF MANY OF THE OUTSTANDING FIGURES OF

WORLD HISTORY, AND SOME NOTABLE CONTEMPORARIES. New York: Simon & Schuster, 1940. 1968. 562p.

Includes Empress Agrippina, Heloise, Madame de Sévigné, Madame du Barry, Elizabeth Barrett Browning, Emily Dickinson, and Sarah Bernhardt.

234. Scoones, W. Baptiste, ed. FOUR CENTURIES OF ENGLISH LETTERS. SELECTIONS FROM THE CORRESPONDENCE OF ONE HUNDRED AND FIFTY WRITERS FROM THE PERIOD OF THE PASTON LETTERS TO THE PRESENT DAY. London: C. Kegan Paul & C., 1880. 573p.

Letters 1450-1859. Includes Margaret Paston, Margaret of Anjou, Queen Elizabeth I, Queen Henrietta Maria, Lady Rachel Russell, Lady Mary Wortley Montagu, Hester Lynch Thrale Piozzi, Mrs. Elizabeth Montagu, Mary Moser, Hannah More, Fanny Burney, Mary Wollstonecraft, Maria Edgeworth, Lucy Aiken, Lady Blessington, and Harriet Martineau.

235. Sears, Clara Edicott. GLEANINGS FROM OLD SHAKER JOURNALS. Boston and New York: Houghton Mifflin, 1916.

236. Slavik, Bedrich. SRDCE A DOBA: LISTY CESKYCH ZEN. Usporadal Slavik. Praha: Nakl. Atlas, 1942. 397p.

Letters of Ěliska Krasnohorská, Hana Kvapilová, Zdenka Braunerová, Blahoslavená Anežka, Královna Kunhuta, Zuzana Cerninova Z Harasova a Jejídcera Eliška Myslikova z Chudenic, Magdalena Dobromila Rettigová, Božena Němcová, Marie Ventová a Bohuslava Rajska, Marie Riegrova, Karolina Světlá and Sofie Podlipská.

237. Snow, Edward, ed. WOMEN OF THE SEA. New York: Dodd, Mead & Co., 1962. 272p.

Collection of biographies of sea-faring women, based on interviews and journals. Includes extracts from the journals of Azuba Bearse Handy, a whaler's wife at sea, 1852-1853; Hannah Rebecca Crowell Burgess, navigator and wife of a mariner, 1852-1856; and Alice Snow, 1883.

238. SO'S YOUR OLD LADY 20 (April,1978). 3-26.

Special issue of a feminist-lesbian journal devoted to extracts from diaries by Lesbian writers. Includes Quimetta Perle, Sue Hoffman, Ellen Anthony, Astrid Bergie, Karen Stenback, Kathy McConnell, Judith McDaniel, Toni McNaron, Constance Wolfe, Barb Jensen, Nancy Erickson, Audrey Ewart, Pamella Farley, Elle Anthony, Pat Blain, and several anonymous women.

239. Sprigg, June. DOMESTICK BEINGS. Illustrated and annotated. New York: Alfred A. Knopf, 1984. 143p.

Stories of and extracts from diaries of seven American women: Anna Green Winslow, Abigail May, Jemima Condict, Martha Ballard, Rebecca Dickinson, Mary Wright Cooper, and Abigail Adams.

240. Starobin, Robert S., ed. BLACKS IN BONDAGE: LETTERS OF AMERICAN SLAVES. New York: New Viewpoints, 1974. 196p.

Documents gathered from unpublished sources, and divided into four sections: The Black Elite; Report on Slave Life; Protest, Escape and Rebellion; and After Slavery. Includes letters by Hannah Valentine, Bella de Rosset, Sarah Boon, Rose Hill, Hannah Grover, Levina Johnson, Mrs. Anne Eliza James, and Henrietta Fullor.

241. Sterling, Dorothy. WE ARE YOUR SISTERS: BLACK WOMEN IN THE NINETEENTH CENTURY. New York: W.W. Norton, 1984.

Includes many letters of Black women, including a chapter of letters from slave women; letters of Harriet Jacobs, Sarah L. Forten, Sarah M. Douglas, Anna Douglas, Rosetta Brown, Josephine Brown, Mary A. Shadd, Mary A. Cary, Sarah Parker Remond, Emma Brown, Susan Bruce, Nancy Ruffin, Sojourner Truth, Harriet Tubman, Sarah G. Stanley, Edmonia Highgate, and others; and extracts from the diaries of Francis Rollin, Mary Virginia Montgomery, Laura Hamilton Murray, and Ida B. Wells.

242. Sternberg, Janet, ed. THE WRITER ON HER WORK. New York and London: W.W. Norton & Co., 1980. 265p.

Includes extracts from the journals of Michele Murray, Susan Griffin and Janet Burroway.

243. Stopes, Marie Charlotte Carmichael, ed. MOTHER ENGLAND: A CONTEMPORARY HISTORY; SELF-WRITTEN BY THOSE WHO HAVE NO HISTORIAN. London: J. Bale, Sons & Danielsson, 1929. 296p.

Letters received by Dr. Stopes in response to her birth control book, MARRIED LOVE (1926), from working mothers of Great Britain.

244. ------. DEAR DR. STOPES: SEX IN THE 1920'S. Edited by Ruth Hall. London: Deutsch, 1978. 218p. Harmond, Middlesex, England, and New York: Penguin Books, 1981. 222p.

245. Sutherland, Elizabeth, ed. LETTERS FROM MISSISSIPPI. Preface by James W. Silver. New York: McGraw-Hill, 1965. New York: New American Library (Signet), 1966. 214p.

Letters written by volunteers in the Summer Freedom Project, who went to Mississippi in 1964 to work for the Civil Rights Movement. Includes letters of fifty-six women.

246. Szladits, Lola L., comp. OTHER PEOPLE'S MAIL: LETTERS OF MEN AND WOMEN OF LETTERS SELECTED FROM THE HENRY W. AND ALBERT A. BERG COLLECTION OF ENGLISH AND AMERICAN LITERATURE. New York: New York Public Library, 1973. 96p.

Reproduces one letter each by sixteen authors, with facsimile reproductions of the originals. Includes a letter from Jane Austen to her sister Cassandra (written backwards), one from Charlotte Bronte to Ellen Nussey, one from Emily Dickinson to Benjamin Kimbal, one from Virginia Woolf to Barbara Hiles Bagenal, and one from Elinor Wylie to Horace Wylie.

247. Tiersot, Julien, ed. LETTRES DE MUSICIENS. ÉCRITES EN FRANÇAIS DU XVe AU XXe SIÈCLE. Turin: Bocca Frères Éditeurs, 1924. Première Série (de 1480 a 1830).

Includes Caroline Branchu, Josephine Grassini, Madame Saint Aubin, Madame Gavaudan, Madame Dabadie, Madame Grassari, Madame Bigottini, Madame Dugazon, and Madame Gothier.

248. ------. LETTRES DE MUSICIENS. ÉCRITES EN FRANÇAIS DU XVe AU XXe SIÈCLE. (DE 1831 À 1885). Paris: Librarie Felix Alcan, Fratelli Bocca, n.d.

Includes Olympe Rossini, Pauline Duchambage, and George Sand.

249. Vanderpoel, Emily Noyes, comp. CHRONICLES OF A PIONEER SCHOOL FROM 1792 TO 1833: BEING THE HISTORY OF MISS SARAH PIERCE AND HER LITCHFIELD SCHOOL. Edited by Elizabeth C. Barney Buel. Cambridge, Mass.: Massachusetts University Press, 1903. 465p.

Collection of school diaries. Includes Charlotte Sheldon (1780-ca. 1840), Lucy Sheldon (1788-1889), Mary Ann Bacon (1797-1815), Caroline Chester (1801-1870), Eliza Ogden, Jane R. Lewis, and Mary L. Wilbor (b. 1806)

250. ------. MORE CHRONICLES OF A PIONEER SCHOOL, FROM 1792 TO 1833. Cambridge, Mass.: Massachusetts University Press, 1920.

251. Van Doren, Charles, ed. LETTERS TO MOTHER. Great Neck, N.Y.: Channel Press, 1959. 350p.

Letters by daughters include Margaret Fuller, Saint Catherine of Sienna, Gertrude Bell, Amelia Earhart, Harriet Martineau, Joyce Kilmer, Susan Lamb, Marjorie Fleming, an anonymous Union Nurse, Susan B. Anthony, Florence Nightengale, Queen Elizabeth I, Marie Antoinette, Empress Frederick, Louisa May Alcott, and George Sand.

252. Van Doren, Dorothy, ed. THE LOST ART: LETTERS OF SEVEN FAMOUS WOMEN. New York: Coward McCann, 1929. 356p.

Mary Wortley Montagu, Abigail Adams, Mary Wollstonecraft, Jane Austen, Jane Welsh Carlyle, Margaret Fuller, and Charlotte Bronte.

253. Van Thal, Herbert, comp. THE ROYAL LETTER BOOK: BEING A COLLECTION OF ROYAL LETTERS FROM THE REIGN OF WILLIAM I TO GEORGE IV. Edited with a prefatory note. With a foreword by Arthur Bryant. London: The Cresset Press, 1937. 313p.

Includes Empress Matilda, Eleanor of Aquitaine, Isabella, Queen Dowager of Spain, Philippa, Queen of Portugal, Joanna, Countess of Westmoreland, Margaret of Anjou, Elizabeth Woodville, Elizabeth, sister of Edward IV, Elizabeth of York, Katherine of Aragon, Anne Boleyn, Katherine Parr, Margaret of Scotland, Lady Jane Grey, Mary I, Elizabeth I, Anne of Denmark, Queen Henrietta Maria, Elizabeth, Electress of the Palatinate, Mary of Modena, Mary II, Queen Anne, Charlotte of Mecklenburg-Strelitz, Caroline Matilda of Denmark, Caroline Princess of Wales, Caroline of Brunswick, Princess Charlotte, Princess Elizabeth, Mary, Duchess of Gloucester, Adelaide of Saxe-Meiningen, and Queen Victoria.

254. Walter, Edward Lorraine, ed. CLASSIC FRENCH LETTERS. New York: Henry Holt & Co., and Boston: C. Schoenhof, 1894. 214p.

Includes Madame de Sévigné, Madame de Maintenon, and Madame du Deffand.

255. Wayne, Philip, ed. THE PERSONAL ART: AN ANTHOLOGY OF ENGLISH LETTERS. London and New York: Longmans, Green, 1949. 242p.

Includes letters of Jane Austen, Lady Elizabeth Bradshaigh, Charlotte Bronte, Fanny Burney, Jane Welsh Carlyle, Harriet Cavendish, Kitty Clive, Ann Constable,

Maria Edgeworth, Mrs. M. Elmes, Marjorie Fleming, Lady Gardiner, the Hon. Maria Holroyd, Mary Lamb, Lady Mary Wortley Montagu, Dorothy Osborne, the Duchess of Queensborough, Lady Rachel Russell, Sarah Siddons, Mrs. Thrale, and Lady Trevelyan.

256. West, Jessamyn, comp. THE QUAKER READER. New York: The Viking Press, 1962. 523p.

Includes extracts from the diaries of Elizabeth Buffam Chase, Elizabeth Fry, and Caroline Fox; and from the correspondence of Hannah Whitall Smith.

257. Wheeler, G.C., comp. TO MOTHER. New York: E.P. Dutton, 1934. 324p.

Includes Lady Harriot Eliot, Lady Caroline Lamb, Harriet Martineau, Lady Harriet Howard Duchess of Sutherland, Sophia Hawthorne, and Florence Nightengale.

258. Wiley, Bell I., ed. SLAVES NO MORE: LETTERS FROM LIBERIA, 1833-1869. Lexington, Ky.: The University Press of Kentucky, 1980. 349p.

Letters of ex-slaves who emigrated to Liberia. Contains the letters of the Minor-Blackford family (Mary Ann Minor), the Skipwith family, the Page-Andrews family (Peggy Potter), the McDonnough family (Mary Jackson, Bridget McDonnough, Nancy Smith McDonnough, Julia Smith McDonnough, and Harriet Fuller McDonnough) the Ross family (Sarah J. Woodson), the Rice family, and the ex-slaves of Robert E. Lee (Rosabella Burke).

259. Willard, Barbara, comp. "I--": AN ANTHOLOGY OF DIARISTS. Illustrated by John Sergeant. London: Chatto & Windus, 1972. 189p.

260. Wolfe, Allis Rosenberg. "Letters of a Lowell Mill Girl and Friends: 1845-1846." LABOR HISTORY 17:1 (Winter, 1976), 96-102.

Five letters to Harriet Robinson; four from her friends Marie and Laura Currier of Wentworth, New

Hampshire, and one from Miss H.E. Beck, a mill worker. Gives a picture of the lives of New England women who went to work in the mill towns.

261. Wolfe, Susan J. and Julia Penelope Stanley. THE COMING OUT STORIES. Foreword by Adrienne Rich. Watertown, Mass.: Persephone Press, 1980. 251p.

Extracts from the private writings of Lesbians, including Judith Niemi, Ellen Roe Anthony, Caryl B. Bently, Judith McDaniel, Julia Penelope Stanley, Minnie Bruce Pratt, Janet Sipe, and Wendy Judith Cutler.

262. Wood, Mary Ann, ed. LETTERS OF ROYAL AND ILLUSTRIOUS LADIES, FROM THE COMMENCEMENT OF THE TWELFTH CENTURY TO THE CLOSE OF THE REIGN OF QUEEN MARY. London: H. Colburn, 1846. 3 vols.

263. Woodson, Carter, G., ed. THE MIND OF THE NEGRO AS REFLECTED IN LETTERS WRITTEN DURING THE CRISIS, 1800-1860. First published in 1926 by the Association for the Study of Negro Life and History. Reissued, 1969, by Russell & Russell, a division of Antheneum Publishing Co., N.Y., by arrangement with the Association for the Study of Negro Life and History. 672p.

Private and public letters from Black Americans to the American Colonization Society, to antislavery workers and agencies, and to private citizens. The Introduction presents eight letters of Phillis Wheatley to Miss Arbour Tanner.

264. Wormely, Katherine Prescott, ed. and trans. THE CORRESPONDENCE OF MADAME, PRINCESS PALATINE, MOTHER OF THE REGENT, OF MARIE-ADELAIDE DE SAVOIE, DUCHESSE DE BOUGOGNE, AND OF MADAME DE MAINTENON, IN RELATION TO ST.-CYR. Preceeded by introductions from C.A. Sainte-Beuve. Versailles edition. Boston: Hardy, Pratt & Co., 1899.

IV. FAMILY COLLECTIONS

265. Andrews, Marietta Minnigerode, comp. SCRAPS OF PAPER. New York: E.P. Dutton & Co., 1929. 381p.

Papers of an American family. Includes extracts from the journal of Mrs. Henry Grafton Dulany, 1862-1863; from the correspondence of Kate Powell, 1863; from the diary of Miss Frances Westwood Ellzey, during the Civil War, and from the correspondence of Lucy Minnigerode from Kiev, Russia, 1914-1915.

266. Anglesey, George Charles Henry Victor Paget, Marquess. THE CAPEL LETTERS. BEING THE CORRESPONDENCE OF LADY CAROLINE CAPEL AND HER DAUGHTERS WITH THE DOWAGER COUNTESS OF UXBRIDGE FROM BRUSSELS AND SWITZERLAND, 1814-1817. With an introduction by Sir Arthur Bryant. London: Jonathan Cape, 1955. 248p.

Correspondence of Caroline Paget, Lady Capel (1773-1847) and her daughters, Maria Capel, later Marquis d'Epinassy (1797-1856), Mary Capel (1808-18-?), Louisa Heneage Paget (d.1914), and Jane (Mary) MacLoughlin (1805-1849) with Jane Champagne Paget, Countess of Uxbridge (1742-1817).

267. Armstrong, Margaret. FIVE GENERATIONS: LIFE AND LETTERS OF AN AMERICAN FAMILY, 1750-1900. New York and London: Harper & Bros., 1930. 425p.

Biography of a New York family, based on and including letters by Margaret Marshall Armstrong, Abigail de Hart Mayo, Catherine Armstrong, Jane Currie, Margaret Livingston Stuyvesant, Anna Cooper, Rose

Armstrong, Mrs. Thomas Hewson, Clara Foster, Elizabeth Ramsay, Julia Keen Fish, Dolly Madison, Margaret Salter, Emily Salter, Charlotte Williams, Ellen Wilkins, Sarah Ward Armstrong, and Helen Neilson Armstrong.

268. Bacon, Georgeana Woolsey and Eliza Woolsey Howland, eds. LETTERS OF A FAMILY DURING THE WAR FOR THE UNION 1861-1865. New Haven, Conn.: Tuttle, Morehouse & Taylor, 1899. 2 vols.

Papers of an American family. Includes letters by Jane Eliza Newton Woolsey, Abby Howland Woolsey, Jane Stewart Woolsey, Mary Woolsey Howland, Georgeana Murison Woolsey, Eliza Woolsey Howland, Harriet Roosevelt Woolsey and Caroline Carson Woolsey.

269. Bagshaw, William H.A. THE BAGSHAWES OF FORD: A BIOGRAPHICAL PEDIGREE. London: Mitchell & Hughes, 1886. 610p.

Papers of an English family. Includes the religious diary of Catherine Bagshawe (1760-1818).

270. Baker, Donald E., ed. "The Conine Family Letters, 1849-1851: Employed in Honest Business and Doing the Best We Can." INDIANA MAGAZINE OF HISTORY 69:4 (1973), 320-365.

Letters written to Mrs. Mary Anne Conine Seymour, from her father, her brother, and her sisters Jane, Emily, and Catherine.

271. ------. "The Conine Family Letters, 1852-1863: Just Think How We Scattered." INDIANA MAGAZINE OF HISTORY 70:2 (1974), 122-178.

272. Balfour, Sir James. LETTERS TO KING JAMES THE SIXTH FROM THE QUEEN, PRINCE HENRY, PRINCE CHARLES, THE PRINCESS ELIZABETH AND HER HUSBAND, FREDERICK, KING OF BOHEMIA, AND THEIR SON, PRINCE FREDERICK HENRY. From the originals in the Library of the Faculty of Advocates. Edinburgh: Printed by T. Constable, 1835.

273. Benedict, Claire. FIVE GENERATIONS (1785- 1923). BEING SCATTERED CHAPTERS FROM THE HISTORY OF THE COOPER, POMEROY, WOOLSON AND BENEDICT FAMILIES, WITH EXTRACTS FROM THEIR LETTERS AND JOURNALS. London: Ellis, 1930.

Papers of an American family. Includes extracts from the letters of Hannah Peabody Chandler Woolson, Emma Cornelia Pomeroy Woolson, Jane Stoors Cooper, and Susan Fenimore Cooper; from the diary of Hannah Cooper Pomeroy Woolson; and from the diaries and letters of Georgiana Pomeroy Wilson, Constance Fenimore Cooper, and Clara Woolson Benedict.

274. Bernard, Jessie Shirley. SELF PORTRAIT OF A FAMILY: LETTERS BY JESSIE, DOROTHY LEE, CLAUDE AND DAVID BERNARD. With commentary by Jessie Bernard. Boston: Beacon Press, 1978. 344p.

Sociologist Bernard uses the letters of her family to explore the parent-child bond and family psychology and dynamics, with special emphasis on the problems facing a single (widowed) working mother.

275. Bessborough, Earl of, and A. Aspinall, eds. LADY BESSBOROUGH AND HER FAMILY CIRCLE. London: John Murray, 1940. 307p.

Diary of Henrietta Frances Spencer Ponsonby, Countess of Bessborough (1761-1821) edited together with family letters.

276. Betham, Ernest, ed. A HOUSE OF LETTERS: BEING EXCERPTS FROM THE CORRESPONDENCE OF MISS CHARLOTTE JERNINGHAM (THE HONORABLE LADY BEDINGFELD), LADY JERNINGHAM, COLERIDGE, LAMB, SOUTHEY, BERNARD, AND LUCY BARTON, AND OTHERS, WITH MATILDA BETHAM; AND FROM DIARIES AND VARIOUS SOURCES, AND A CHAPTER UPON LANDOR'S QUARRELL WITH CHARLES BETHAM AT LLANTHONY. ALSO NOTES OF SOME PHASES IN THE EVOLUTION OF AN ENGLISH FAMILY. A new edition. London: Jarrolds, 1905?. 291p.

277. Betts, Edwin Morris and James Adam Bear, Jr. THE

FAMILY LETTERS OF THOMAS JEFFERSON. Columbia, Mo.: University of Missouri Press, 1966. 506p.

Includes letters of Jefferson's daughters: Martha Jefferson Randolph (1772-1836), Mary Jefferson Eppes (1778-1804), Anne Cary Randolph Bankhead (1791-1826), Ellen Wayles Randolph Coolidge (1796-1876), and Cornelia Jefferson Randolph (1799-1871).

278. Birkbeck Family. A PIONEER FAMILY: THE BIRKBECKS IN ILLINOIS, 1818-1827. London: Jonathan Cape, 1953.

Papers of an English Quaker family who established an utopian community in Illinois. Includes correspondence of Elizabeth Birkbeck and Prudence Birkbeck.

279. Blake, Alice Elizabeth, ed. MEMOIRS OF A VANISHED GENERATION, 1813-1855. With an introduction by Lady St. Helier. London and New York: John Lane, 1909. 308p.

Letters written by members of the family of Admiral Edmond Sexton Perry Knox and that of his son, General Thomas Edmond Knox.

280. Boggs, Marion Alexander, ed. THE ALEXANDER LETTERS, 1787-1900. Savannah, Ga.: Privately Printed for G.J. Baldwin, 1910. 387p. Reprinted with a foreword by Richard Barksdale Harwell. Athens, Ga.: University of Georgia Press, 1980. 387p.

Letters of an American family. Includes Sarah Hillhouse Gilbert (d.1855), and her children: Louisa Frederika Alexander Gilmer (1824-1895), Sarah Gilbert Alexander Lawton (1826-1897), Harriet Virginia Alexander Cumming (1828-1910), Marion Brackett Alexander Boggs (1842-1901), and Alice Van Yeveren Alexander Haskell (1848-1902).

281. Bond, R. Warwick, ed. THE MARLAY LETTERS, 1778-1820. London: Constable & Co., 1937. 476p.

Papers of an English family. Includes letters of Catherine Dawson, later Lady Bury (1762-1851), Hannah

Maria Townley Dawson, Comtesse de Seissan, Lady Louisa Conolly, Miss Mary Dawson, Lady Sarah Napier, Lady Dunally, Miss Louisa Tisdall, and Miss Ellis Cornelia Knight (1757-1837). Also includes letters by Maria Edgeworth, Jane Austen, Lady Charlotte Napier, Sidney, Lady Morgan, Lady Charlotte Bury, Amelia Opie, Madame de Stael, and Caroline Lamb.

282. Bonstelle, Jessie and Marian DeForest. LITTLE WOMEN LETTERS FROM THE HOUSE OF ALCOTT. Boston: Little, Brown & Co., 1914. 197p.

A sentimental view of life at the Alcott home as seen through early family letters, the diaries of the Alcott children, and poems. Contains some extracts from the diary of Louisa May Alcott.

283. Bovoso, Carole. "Discovering My Foremothers." MS. MAGAZINE 6:3 (September, 1977), 56-59.

A Black American writes on her foremothers, drawing upon extracts from the diaries of her great grandmother, Frances Ann Rollin (1847-1901), and her great aunt, Iona Rollin Whipper (1872-1953).

284. Boykins, Edward, ed. TO THE GIRLS AND BOYS: BEING THE DELIGHTFUL, LITTLE-KNOWN LETTERS OF THOMAS JEFFERSON TO AND FROM HIS CHILDREN AND GRANDCHILDREN. Selected, with historical notes. New York: Funk & Wagnalls, 1964. 210p.

Includes letters by Martha Jefferson (1772-1836), Mary Jefferson (1778-1876), Ellen Wayles Randolph (1796-1876), Cornelia Jefferson Randolph (1799-1871), and Ann Cary Randolph (1791-1826).

285. Butterfield, L.H., ed. THE ADAMS FAMILY PAPERS: ADAMS FAMILY CORRESPONDENCE. Wendell D. Garrett, Associate Editor. Marjorie E. Sprague, Assistant Editor. Cambridge, Mass.: The Belknap Press of Harvard University Press, 1963-1965. 6 vols.

Includes Abigail Smith Adams, Abigail Adams Smith, Abigail Brown Brooks Adams (1808-1889), Marian Hooper

Adams, Elizabeth Smith Shaw (1750-1815), Hannah Quincy Storer (1736-1826), Mary Smith Cranch (1741-1811), Hannah Storer Green, Elizabeth Palmer Cranch (1748-1814), Mary Palmer (1746-1791), and Mercy Otis Warren.

286. Byrne, Muriel St. Clair, ed. THE LISLE LETTERS. Chicago: University of Chicago Press, 1981. 6 vols.

Letters of an English family living during the reign of Henry VIII.

287. ------. THE LISLE LETTERS: AN ABRIDGMENT. Selected and arranged by Bridget Boland. Foreword by Hugh Trevor-Roper. Chicago: University of Chicago Press, 1983.

Includes letters by Honor Grenville Plantagenet, Viscountess Lisle (1493/5-1566), Anne Basset (c.1521-1557), Jane Basset, Katherine Bassett (b.1517 or 1519/20), Mary (Marie) Basset (1522/5-1598), Anne Rouaud, Madame de Bours, Jane Boyes Ryngeley, Soeur Anthoinette De Saveuses, Mary Uvedale, and Dame Elizabeth Shelley, Abbess of St. Mary's, Winchester.

288. Cameron, Kenneth Neill. SHELLEY AND HIS CIRCLE, 1773-1822. Cambridge, Mass.: Harvard University Press, 1961. 2 vols.

Chiefly the letters of the Wollstonecraft, Godwin, and Shelley families. Includes letters by Mary Wollstonecraft, Margaret Nicholson, Mary Robinson, Elizabeth Inchbald, Mary Jane Godwin, and Mary E. Robinson; and extracts from the diary of Harriet Grove.

289. Campbell, Gerald, comp. EDWARD AND PAMELA FITZGERALD: BEING SOME ACCOUNT OF THEIR LIVES, COMPILED FROM THE LETTERS OF THOSE WHO KNEW THEM. London: E. Arnold, 1904. 256p.

Includes extracts from the diaries of Lady Sophia Fitzgerald (d.1826) and Lady Lucy Fitzgerald Foley (1771-1851).

290. Carson, William G.B., ed. "Secesh." MISSOURI HISTORICAL SOCIETY BULLETIN 23:2 (1967), 119-145.

Extracts from the correspondence, 1861-1863, of the Lane family of St. Louis, Missouri, Confederate sympathizers. "Secesh" is short for "Successionist." Includes letters of Mary, Anne, and Sarah Lane.

291. Chart, D.A., ed. THE DRENNAN LETTERS. BEING A SELECTION FROM THE CORRESPONDENCE WHICH PASSED BETWEEN WILLIAM DRENNAN, M.D. AND HIS BROTHER-IN-LAW AND SISTER, SAMUEL AND MARTHA MCTIER, DURING THE YEARS 1776-1819. Belfast: H.M. Stationery Office, 1931. 432p.

Letters of an Irish family. Includes letters of Martha Drennan McTier.

292. Chatterton, Georgiana, Lady. MEMOIRS, PERSONAL AND HISTORICAL OF ADMIRAL LORD GAMBIER, WITH ORIGINAL LETTERS FROM WILLIAM PITT THE FIRST LORD CHATHAM, LORD NELSON, LORD CASTLEREAGH, LORD MULGRAVE, HENRY FOX THE FIRST LORD HOLLAND, THE RIGHT HON. GEORGE CANNING, ETC. Edited from family papers. London: Hurst & Blackett, 1861. 2 vols.

Includes letters of Hannah More and extracts from the journal of Lady Featherstonhaugh of Uppark, Sussex.

293. Cholmondeley, R.H., ed. THE HEBER LETTERS, 1783-1832. London: The Batchworth Press, 1950. 355p.

Letters of Reginald Heber, Bishop of Calcutta and his family. Includes Elizabeth Heber, Emily Heber (1821-1901), Harriet Heber (1824-1899), Mary Baylie Heber (d.1774), and Mary Allanson Heber.

294. Clark, Mrs. Godfrey, ed. GLEANINGS FROM AN OLD PORTFOLIO. CONTAINING SOME CORRESPONDENCE BETWEEN LADY LOUISA STUART AND HER SISTER CAROLINE, COUNTESS OF PORTARLINGTON, AND OTHER FRIENDS AND RELATIONS. Edinburgh: Privately Printed for D. Douglas, 1895-1898.

Correspondence between Louisa, Lady Stewart

(1757-1851), Caroline Stuart Dawson, Countess of Portarlington (d.1813), and others.

295. Cline, C.L. THE OWL AND THE ROSSETTIS: LETTERS OF CHARLES A. HOWELL AND DANTE GABRIEL, CHRISTINA AND WILLIAM MICHAEL ROSSETTI. University Park and London: Pennsylvania State University Press, 1977. 61p.

Includes six letters from Christina Rossetti to Howell. Some of Howell's correspondence was written by his wife, Frances Catherine Howell.

296. Cohen, Lucy. LADY DE ROTHSCHILD AND HER DAUGHTERS, 1821-1931. London: John Murray, 1937. 354p.

Extracts from the diaries of Lady Louisa Montefiore de Rothschild (1821-1910), Lady Constance de Rothschild Battersea (1843-1931), and the Hon. Mrs. Annie de Rothschild York (1844-1926).

297. Crafts, James M. and William F. Crafts. THE CRAFTS FAMILY. Northampton, Mass.: Gazette Printing Co., 1893.

Includes extracts from the diary of Betsey Heath (1769-1813).

298. Curtis, Caroline Gardiner, ed. CARY LETTERS. Cambridge, Mass.: Printed at the Riverside Press, 1891.

Includes the diary of Margaret Cary (1719-1762) and the diary of Anne M. Cary.

299. Davis, Norman. THE PASTON LETTERS: A SELECTION IN MODERN SPELLING. With an introduction, notes, and glossary. Oxford: Oxford University Press, 1963. 288p.

300. ------. PASTON LETTERS AND PAPERS OF THE FIFTEENTH CENTURY. Oxford: Oxford at the Clarendon Press, 1971. 2 vols.

Authoritative edition. Personal and business

correspondence of a medieval English family, begining about 1420 and ending in 1503. Includes the letters of Agnes Paston (d.1479), Margaret Paston (d.1484), Elizabeth Paston, later Poynings and Brown, Margery Paston, later Calle (d. not later than 1479), Anne Paston, later Yelverton (d.1494 or 1495), and Margery Brews Paston (d.ca.1495).

301. Dow, George F. HOLYOKE DIARIES. Salem, Mass.: Essex Institute, 1911.

Includes the diaries of Margaret Holyoke (1763-1825), Elizabeth Holyoke (1771-1789), Mary Vial Holyoke (1737-1802), Priscilla Holyoke (1739-1782), and Susanna Holyoke Ward (1779-1860).

302. Eland, G. PUREFOY LETTERS, 1735-1753. London: Sidgwick & Jackson, 1931. 2 vols.

Includes letters of Elizabeth Fish Purefoy (1672-1765).

303. Faugère, M.P. LETTRES, OPUSCULES ET MEMOIRES DE MADAME PÉRIER ET DE JACQUELINE, SOEURS DE PASCALE, ET DE MARGUERITE PERIER, SA NIECE. Publiées sur les manuscrits origineaux. Paris: Chez A. Vaton, 1845. 490p.

Includes writings of Gilberte Pascal Périer, (1620-1685), Jacqueline Pascal (1625-1661) and Marguerite Périer (1646-1733).

304. Freemantle, Anne, ed. THE WYNNE DIARIES. London: Oxford University Press, 1935-1940. 3 vols.

Diaries of a Scottish family; Eugenia Wynne, later Campbell (b.1780), Elizabeth Wynne, later Freemantle (1779-1857), and Harriet Wynne. Edited from over 62 volumes.

305. ------. THE WYNNE DIARIES, 1789-1820. Passages selected by Anne Freemantle. New York, London and Toronto: Geoffry Cumberlege, Oxford

University Press, 1952. 551p.

Abridged version of the 1935-1940 edition.

306. Gardiner, Dorothy, ed. THE OXINDEN LETTERS, 1607-1642. BEING THE CORRESPONDENCE OF HENRY OXINDEN OF BARHAM AND HIS CIRCLE. London: Constable & Co., 1933. 328p.

Includes letters by Margaret Lady Oxinden, Lady Katherine Eastday Sprakeling (d.1627), Katherine Oxinden (1587-1642), Margery Tilghman (b.1587), Frances Saunders (b.1590), Hanna Pettit (1599-1641), Elizabeth Sprakeling (d.1581), Elizabeth Oxinden Dalison (b.1610), Mary Lady Peyton, Anne Peyton Oxinden (b.1612), Margaret Peyton Kent, Anne Peyton Hales, Ann Oxinden Master (b.1607), Mary Culling Denwood (b.1610), Leah C. Huffam (b.1618), Ellen C. Wood (b.1621), and Katherine C. Oxinden (b.1624).

307. Grant, James, ed. SEAFIELD CORRESPONDENCE FROM 1685-1708. Edinburgh: Printed at the University Press by T. and A. Constable for the Scottish History Society, 1912. 497p. (Scottish History Society, Second Series, Vol. 3.)

Includes letters by Anne Countess of Findlater, Mary Hamilton Countess of Findlater, Lady Mary Graham, Anne Duchess of Hamilton, Marie Marchioness-Dowager of Huntly, Anne Lindsay, wife of the Duke of Rothes, Anna Countess of Seafield, Martha Stevenson, and others.

308. Gray, Almira. PAPERS AND DIARIES OF A YORK FAMILY, 1764-1839. London: Sheldon Press; New York and Toronto: Macmillan Co., 1927. 292p.

Includes extracts from the diaries of Faith Hopwood Gray (1751-1826).

309. Grosvenor, Hon. Mrs. Caroline Susan Theodora Stuart-Wortley, ed. THE FIRST LADY WHARNCLIFFE AND HER FAMILY, (1779-1856). By her grandchildren Caroline Grosvenor and the late Charles Beilby, Lord Stuart of

Wortley. London: William Heinemann, 1927. 2 vols.

Family letters woven into a narrative, centering on Elizabeth Caroline Mary Creighton Stuart-Wortley-Makenzie, Baroness Wharncliffe (1799-1856). Includes letters by the Countess of Bessborough, Elizabeth Foster Hervey Duchess of Devonshire, Princess Marie Clothilde, Catherine Wortley Talbot, Louisa Stuart Wortley, Lady Louisa Hervey Hawkesbury, and others.

310. Harcourt, Edward William. THE HARCOURT PAPERS. Oxford: Printed for Private Circulation, 1880-1905.

Includes extracts from the diary of Lady Anne Harcourt (1608?-1642) for the years 1649-1661.

311. Hemlow, Joyce. THE HISTORY OF FANNY BURNEY. London: Oxford at the Clarendon Press, 1958. 528p.

Family biography based on and including extracts from the papers of Fanny Burney, Charlotte Anne Burney Frances Broom (1761-1838), Marianne Frances, and Charlotte Francis Barrett.

312. Herbert, Lord,[Baron Sidney Charles Herbert], ed. HENRY, ELIZABETH AND GEORGE (1734-1780). LETTERS AND DIARIES OF HENRY, TENTH EARL OF PEMBROKE, AND HIS CIRCLE. London: Jonathan Cape, 1939. 576p.

Includes extracts from the correspondence of Elizabeth Spencer Herbert, Countess of Pembroke (1737-1831) and Lady Charlotte Herbert (1773-1784).

313. ------. PEMBROKE PAPERS (1780-1794). LETTERS AND DIARIES OF HENRY, TENTH EARL OF PEMBROKE AND HIS CIRCLE. London: Jonathan Cape, 1950. 509p.

Includes extracts from the correspondence of Charlotte, Queen of England, and Elizabeth Spencer Herbert, Countess of Pembroke.

314. Herskowitz, Leo and Isidore S. Meyer, eds. LEE MAX FRIEDMAN COLLECTION OF AMERICAN JEWISH COLONIAL

CORRESPONDENCE: LETTERS OF THE FRANKS FAMILY, 1733-1748. Waltham, Mass.: American Jewish Historical Society, 1968.

Includes letters of Abigail Franks (1696-1756).

315. Howard, Eliot, comp. ELIOT PAPERS. London: E. Hicks, Jr., 1895.

Papers of an English Quaker family. Includes extracts from a diary by Mariabella Eliot for 1759 and extracts from the diary of Mary Weston (1712-1766).

316. Howe, Mark Anthony DeWolfe, ed. THE ARTICULATE SISTERS: PASSAGES FROM JOURNALS AND LETTERS OF THE DAUGHTERS OF PRESIDENT JOSIAH QUINCY OF HARVARD UNIVERSITY. Cambridge, Mass.: Harvard University Press, 1946. 249p.

Includes extracts from the journals of Eliza Susan Quincy, 1814-1821; Mary Sophia Quincy, 1829; Anna Cabot Lowell Quincy, 1833 and 1834; and from the journal and letters of Margaret Morton Quincy, later Greene, 1824-1828.

317. Johnson, R. Brimley. FANNY BURNEY AND THE BURNEYS. London: S. Paul & Co., 1926. 407p.

Selection from the papers of the Burney family, including extracts from the diary of Fanny Burney and Susan Burney Phillips, 1755-1800.

318. Judd, Jacob. CORRESPONDENCE OF THE VAN CORTLANDT FAMILY OF CORTLANDT MANOR, 1815-1848. Tarrytown, New York: Sleepy Hollow Press/Sleepy Hollow Restorations, 1981. 652p.

Includes extracts from the correspondence of Cornelia Beekman, Magdalen Stevenson, Eliza Treat, Anne Stevenson Van Cortlandt, Sarah Van Wyck, Ann Varick, Joanna Van Wyck, Catherine Van Wyck, Eliza T. Sharp, Mary Van Cortlandt, Gertrude Van Cortlandt Beekman, and Margaret Stuyvesant.

319. Kennon Family. "Kennon Letters." VIRGINIA MAGAZINE OF HISTORY AND BIOGRAPHY 31:1 (January, 1924), to 40:2 (April, 1932).

Letters of Elizabeth B. Kennon, Sally S. Kennon Sinclair, Rachel Mordecai, and Samuel Mordecai, 1809-1816.

320. Kingsford, Charles Lethbridge. STONOR LETTERS AND PAPERS. London: Offices of the Camden Society, 1919. 2 vols. (Royal Hist. Soc., Camden, 3rd. Ser.)

Printed from the original documents in the Public Record Office, Ancient Correspondence, XLVI. Includes the letters of Elizabeth Stonor, first wife of Sir William Stonor; Annys Wydeslade, second wife of Sir William Stonor; Dame Ann Stonor, his third wife; Margery Hampden; Mary Barantyne; Queen Elizabeth Woodville; Jane Stonor, and Dame Katherine Arundell.

321. Knight, William Angus, ed. LETTERS OF THE WORDSWORTH FAMILY, FROM 1787 TO 1855. Boston and London: Ginn and Co., 1907. 3 vols. Reprinted, New York: Haskell House Publishers, 1969. 3 vols.

322. Litchfield, Henrietta. EMMA DARWIN: A CENTURY OF FAMILY LETTERS, 1792-1896. New York: D. Appleton & Co., 1915. 2 vols.

Papers of an American family. Volume One contains letters and journals written by members of the Allen, Wedgewood and Darwin families. Volume 2 contains the life and letters of Emma Darwin (b.1808).

323. Loines, Elma, ed. THE CHINA POST-BAG OF THE SETH LOW FAMILY OF SALEM AND NEW YORK, 1829-1873. Manchester, Maine: Falmouth Publishing House, 1953. 324p.

Papers of an American merchant family. Includes letters by Harriet Low (1809-1878), Ellen Porter Low (1827-1898), Mary Porter Low (1786-1872), Mary Anne Low Archer (1808-1851), Anne Bedell Low, and Sarah Lyman. Also includes Harriet Low's journal for 1829-1834.

324. McLachlan, H. RECORDS OF A FAMILY, 1800-1933. PIONEERS IN EDUCATION, SOCIAL SERVICE AND LIBERAL RELIGION. Manchester University Press, 1935. 240p.

Papers of the Beard family of Great Britain. Includes extracts from the journal of Mary Dendy (b.1855), and from the correspondence of Mary Shipman Beard and of Helen Dendy Bosanquet.

325. Meier, Olga. THE DAUGHTERS OF KARL MARX: FAMILY CORRESPONDENCE, 1866-1898. Translated and adapted by Sheila Rowbotham. New York and London: Harcourt Brace Jovanovich, 1977. 342p.

Includes letters by Jenny Marx Longuet (1844-1883), Laura Marx LaFarge, and Eleanor Marx Aveling.

326. Miller, Randall M., ed. DEAR MASTER: LETTERS OF A SLAVE FAMILY. Ithaca, N.Y., and London: Cornell University Press, 1978. 281p.

Letters of a Black American family, the Skipwiths. Some members were freed to emigrate to Liberia; others settled on an absentee-owned plantation in Alabama. Includes letters by Diana, Matlilda S., and Lucy Skipwith.

327. Myers, Robert. THE CHILDREN OF PRIDE: A TRUE STORY OF GEORGIA AND THE CIVIL WAR. New Haven, Conn.: Yale University Press, 1972. 1845p.

328. ------. THE CHILDREN OF PRIDE: SELECTED LETTERS OF THE FAMILY OF DR. CHARLES COLCOCK JONES FROM THE YEARS 1860-1868, WITH THE ADDITION OF SEVERAL PREVIOUSLY UNPUBLISHED LETTERS. A new, abridged edition. New Haven, Conn., and London: Yale University Press, 1984. 671p.

Papers of an American family. Includes letters by Mary Jones Jones, Mary Sharp Jones Mallard, Laura Elizabeth Maxwell Buttolph, Susan Mary Jones Maxwell Cumming, and extracts from the journal of Mary Jones and Mary S. Mallard, December, 1864--January, 1865.

329. Newton, Evelyn Caroline Bromley-Davenport Legh, Baroness, ed. LYME LETTERS, 1660-1760. London: William Heinemann, 1925. 341p.

Family letters of Richard Legh of Lyme and his wife Elizabeth Legh (d.1728), of England. Contains many letters by their eldest daughter, Lettice Legh (1663-1719).

330. Onslow, Sibella Macarthur. SOME EARLY RECORDS OF THE MACARTHURS OF CAMDEN. Sydney: Angus & Robertson, 1914. 496p.

Papers of an Australian immigrant family who settled in New South Wales. Includes letters of Elizabeth Macarthur-Onslow (1840-1911).

331. Phillips, Marion G. and Valerie Phillips Parsegian, eds. RICHARD AND RHODA: LETTERS FROM THE CIVIL WAR. Washington, D.C.: Legation Press, 1981. 112p.

Chiefly letters between Rhoda McConnell Phillips (1844-1921), and her husband, Richard Covel Phillips, with letters by Deborah Phillips (b.1846), Olive Phillips, Sarah Triphene Phillips (b.1849), Bettie Moore Phillips, Amanda Anabel Phillips, and Lydia Ann McConnell Phillips (b.1846).

332. Raitt, Helen and Mary Collier Wayne, eds. WE THREE CAME WEST: A TRUE CHRONICLE. San Diego, Calif.: Tofua Press, 1974. 250p.

Letters of Margaret Collier Graham, her husband Donald Graham, and her sister Eliza Jane Collier, emigrants to California from Iowa and Illinois.

333. Richardson, Ethel M. LONG FORGOTTEN DAYS LEADING TO WATERLOO. London: Heath Cranton, 1928. 403p.

Papers of an Irish family of Stratford, County Kildare. Includes letters of Mary Walsh Stratford, Elizabeth Baisley Stratford, Martha Neale Stratford,

Lady Amelia Stratford, Viscountess Powerscourt, Harriot Westenra Wingfield Vernor, and Mary Cairnes Murray; and extracts from the diary of Harriot Westenra Wingfield.

334. Riley, Glenda. "The Morse Family Letters: A New Home in Iowa, 1856-1862." ANNALS OF IOWA 45:3 (Winter, 1980), 212-221.

Includes letters of Sara Morse (1831-1916).

335. Riley, Paul D., ed. "Cather Family Letters, 1895." NEBRASKA HISTORY 54:4 (Winter, 1973), 585-618.

Papers of the family of American author Willa Cather. Contains letters by Franc Amanda Smith Cather (1846-1922), Carrie Cather (1876-1960), Wilella Payne (1822-1960), and Jennie Boak Cather (1850-1931).

336. Roehm, Marjorie Catlin. THE LETTERS OF GEORGE CATLIN AND HIS FAMILY: A CHRONICLE OF THE AMERICAN WEST. Berkeley, Calif.: University of California Press, 1966. 463p.

Includes letters by Polly Catlin, Eliza Catlin Dart (1798-1866), Abigail Catlin Sayre, Mary Dart, Clara Catlin Gregory, Mary Catlin Hartshorn (1802-1848), Theodosia Catlin, and Fannie Dubois Chase.

337. Ross, Janet, ed. THREE GENERATIONS OF ENGLISH WOMEN. MEMOIRS AND CORRESPONDENCE OF SUSANNAH TAYLOR, SARAH AUSTIN AND LADY DUFF GORDON. London: T. Fisher Unwin, 1892. New, revised and enlarged edition, 1893. 571p.

Correspondence of Susannah Cook Taylor (1755-1823), her daughter Sarah Taylor Austin (1793-1867), and her granddaughter Lucie Austin, Lady Duff Gordon (1821-1869), with the diary of Sarah Austin for 1841-1843.

338. Rossetti, William, ed. FAMILY LETTERS OF CHRISTINA AND GEORGINIA ROSSETTI. With some supplementary letters and appendices. London: Brown,

Langham; New York: Charles Scribner's Sons, 1908. 242p.

Selection of Rossetti family letters, 1843-1894. Includes correspondence of Sophie Cayley, 1852-1883, and a diary kept on behalf of Christina Rossetti's mother, Francesca Rossetti, 1881-1886. The latter is in Christina Rossetti's handwriting; the composition and diction appears to be hers as well.

339. Searle, Arthur, ed. BARRINGTON FAMILY LETTERS, 1628-1632. London: Offices of the Royal Historical Society, University College, 1983. (Camden fourth series, Vol. 28) 269p.

Chiefly letters written to Lady Joan Barrington (d.1641) by Lady Judith Barrington, Lady Anne Barrington, Lady Mary Eden, Lady Mary Eliot, Lady Joan Barrington Everard, Lady Mary Barrington Gerrard, Jane Whaley Hook, Lady Elizabeth Barrington Masham, and Lady Joan Attham St. John.

340. Shorter, Clement. THE BRONTES, LIFE AND LETTERS. BEING AN ATTEMPT TO PRESENT A FULL AND FINAL RECORD OF THE LIVES OF THE THREE SISTERS, CHARLOTTE, EMILY JANE AND ANNE BRONTE, FROM THE BIOGRAPHIES OF MRS. GASKELL AND OTHERS, AND FROM NUMEROUS UNPUBLISHED MANUSCRIPTS AND LETTERS. New York: Charles Scribner's Sons, 1908. 2 vols.

Enlarged and revised edition of Shorter's previous work, CHARLOTTE BRONTE AND HER CIRCLE. Contains over thirteen hundred letters by the Bronte sisters.

341. Skemp, John Rowland, ed. LETTERS TO ANNE: THE STORY OF A TASMANIAN FAMILY TOLD IN LETTERS TO ANNE ELIZABETH LOVELL (MRS. THOMAS KEARNEY) BY HER BROTHERS AND SISTER AND OTHER RELATIVES DURING THE YEARS 1846-1872. Edited by her grandson. Melbourne, Australia: Melbourne University Press, 1956. 1622p.

Letters of a pioneer Australian family. Includes letters by Sophia Cato Lovell, Emma Lovell, Margaret Lovell Kearney, Fanny Kearney, and Louisa Lovell.

342. Spark, Muriel. THE LETTERS OF THE BRONTES: A SELECTION. Norman, Okla.: University of Oklahoma Press, 1954. 208p.

Chiefly letters of Charlotte Bronte, with some letters by Maria Branwell, and Emily, Anne, Branwell, and Patrick Bronte.

343. Stapleton, Thomas, ed. PLUMPTON CORRESPONDENCE. A SERIES OF LETTERS CHIEFLY DOMESTIC, WRITTEN IN THE REIGN OF EDWARD IV, RICHARD III, HENRY VII AND HENRY VIII. Edited...from Sir Edward Plumpton's book of Letters. With notices historical and biographical of the family of Plumpton. London: Printed for the Camden Society by J.B. Nichols and Son, 1839. 312p.

Correspondence 1460-1548 of Sir William Plumpton, his son Sir Robert Plumpton and "other members of the family," including Agnes Plumpton, wife of Sir Robert, Isabell Plumpton, his second wife, Elizabeth Pole, Dorothye Plumpton, Ann Abbott, Katherine Chadderton, and Maud Rose.

344. Stifler, James Madison. "MY DEAR GIRL": THE CORRESPONDENCE OF BENJAMIN FRANKLIN WITH POLLY STEVENSON, GEORGIANA AND CATHERINE SHIPLEY. New York: George H. Doran co., 1927. 279p.

Correspondence between Franklin and Mary "Polly" Stevenson Hewson, Georgiana Shipley Hare-Naylor, and Catherine Louisa Shipley, from about 1757 to 1786.

345. Stirling, Anna Maria Diana Wilhelmina Pickering, comp. THE LETTER-BAG OF LADY ELIZABETH SPENCER-STANHOPE. COMPILED FROM THE CANNON HALL PAPERS, 1806-1873. London: John Lane, the Bodley Head; New York: John Lane Co.; Toronto: Bell & Cockburn, 1913. 2 vols.

Includes letters by Marianne Stanhope, Isabella Spencer-Stanhope, and Lady Elizabeth Wilhelmina Spencer Stanhope.

346. Thompson, Edward Maunde, ed. CORRESPONDENCE OF

THE FAMILY OF HATTON. BEING CHIEFLY LETTERS ADDRESSED TO CHRISTOPHER, FIRST VISCOUNT HATTON, A.D. 1601-1704. Westminster, England: Printed for the Camden Society, 1878. 2 vols. (Camden Series Two, Vols. 22-23.)

Includes letters by Lady Elizabeth Hatton (d.1672), Elizabeth Bodville, Lady Catherine Lyttelton, Lady Elizabeth Berkeley, Lady Frances Hatton, Anne Montague, and Ann, Countess of Manchester.

347. Tiffany, Nina M., ed. Assisted by Susan I. Lesley. LETTERS OF JAMES MURRAY, LOYALIST. Boston, 1901.

Papers of a Colonial American family. Includes letters of Elizabeth Murray Smith (1726-1785), to James Murray and extracts from her diary of travel in England and Scotland, 1769-1770; and letters of Mrs. Henry Barnes and Elizabeth Murray Robbins.

348. Todd, Sheryl, ed. ALL EIGHT WENT. COMPILED FROM THE DIARIES OF ELOISE JAMESON, BERNICE JAMESON TODD, HETTY JOY JAMESON AND HETTY JAMESON ELMORE. Edited by Sheryl Todd under the direction of Bernice Jameson Todd, with help and advice from Adelaide Jameson David. Illustrated by Joy Gilbert Jameson. Santa Monica, Calif.: Sheryl Todd Graphic Design, 1977. 225p.

Extracts from the diaries written on a world tour undertaken by the Jameson family in 1910-1911.

349. Troxell, Janet Camp. THREE ROSSETTIS: UNPUBLISHED LETTERS TO AND FROM DANTE GABRIEL, CHRISTINA, WILLIAM. Cambridge, Mass.: Harvard University Press, 1937. 216p.

Family correspondence 1873-1891.

350. Tuckerman, Bayard. NOTES ON THE TUCKERMAN FAMILY OF MASSACHUSETTS, AND SOME ALLIED FAMILIES. Boston: Privately Printed, 1914. 263p.

Papers of an American family. Includes extracts

from the diaries of Margaret Graves Cary (1719-1762).

351. Verney, Frances Parthenope Nightengale, Lady, comp. MEMOIRS OF THE VERNEY FAMILY. Compiled from the letters and illustrated with portraits at Claydon House. London and New York: Longmans, Green & Co., 1892-1899. 4 vols.

Extensive history of the family, drawing upon extracts from the correspondence of Mary Blacknall Verney (fl. 1639), her guardian, Mrs. Wiseman, Margaret Pulteny, and Lady Denton.

352. Verney, Margaret Maria Williams-Hay, Lady, ed. VERNEY LETTERS OF THE EIGHTEENTH CENTURY. From the manuscripts at Claydon House. London: E. Benn, 1930. 2 vols.

Contains letters of Elizabeth Palmer Verney, first wife of Sir John Verney, and her children Mary Verney, Elizabeth Verney Adams, and Margaret Verney; of Elizabeth, Lady Verney, later Viscountess Fermanagh, third wife of Sir John Verney; of Lady Cary Gardiner Strewkley and her children Penelope, Carolina, Isabella and Katherine Strewkley; and of Margaret Gardiner, Margaret Adams, Isabella Adams, Mary Lloyd, Ruth Lloyd, and others

353. Warden of Wadham College, Oxford, ed. LETTERS, HITHERTO UNPUBLISHED, WRITTEN BY MEMBERS OF SIR WALTER SCOTT'S FAMILY TO THEIR OLD GOVERNESS. London: E.G. Richards, 1905. 164p.

Includes twenty-eight letters by Charlotte Sophia Scott Lockhart (1799-1837), and twelve by Anne Scott (1803-1833).

354. Webb, Maria Lamb, ed. THE FELLS OF SWARTHMOOR HALL AND THEIR FRIENDS. WITH AN ACCOUNT OF THEIR ANCESTOR, ANNE ASKEW, THE MARTYR. A PORTRAITURE OF RELIGIOUS AND FAMILY LIFE IN THE 17TH CENTURY, COMPILED CHIEFLY FROM ORIGINAL LETTERS AND OTHER DOCUMENTS,

NEVER BEFORE PUBLISHED. London: W. Bennet, 1865.

Letters of an English Quaker family, 1546-1702. Includes letters of Anne Askew (burned as a heretic in 1546), Margaret Fell, Mary Pease, Margaret Rous, Elizabeth Stubbs, Margaret Fox, Margaret Fawcett, Princess Elizabeth, Sarah Fell (later Mead), Susanna Fell, Gulielma Maria Penn, Mary Loner, and Anna Maria Countess of Horne.

355. Wise, Thomas James, M.A. Oxon, and John Alexander Symington. THE BRONTES: THEIR LIVES, FRIENDSHIPS AND CORRESPONDENCE. Oxford: Printed at the Shakespeare Head Press and Published for the Press by B. Blackwell, 1932. 4 vols.

Amalgamation of previous biographies, including that by Mrs. Gaskell, with previously unpublished letters, into one complete biography of all three Bronte sisters. Contains one hundred new letters by Charlotte Bronte, and letters by her mother, Maria Branwell, and her friend Elizabeth Nussey.

356. Wister, Fanny Kemble, ed. THAT I MAY TELL YOU: JOURNALS AND LETTERS OF THE OWEN WISTER FAMILY. Wayne, Penn.: Haverford House, 1979. 276p.

Includes extracts from the letters of Sarah Butler Wister and from her Civil War diary (including her 1889 annotations); and extracts from the correspondence of Mary Channing Wister, wife of American author Owen Wister.

357. Woodforde, Dorothy Heighes, ed. WOODFORDE PAPERS AND DIARIES. With an introduction. London: Peter Davies, 1932. 259p.

Extracts from the diaries of a diary-writing family related to James Woodforde, author of DIARY OF A COUNTRY PARSON. Includes extracts from the diaries of Mary Woodforde, 1684-1680, Nancy Woodforde (1757-1830) 1792, Anne Woodforde, 1818; and from the letters and diary of Julia Woodforde (1789-1873), 1818.

358. Wyndham, Hon. Maud Mary Lyttleton. CHRONICLES OF THE EIGHTEENTH CENTURY. FOUNDED ON THE CORRESPONDENCE OF SIR THOMAS LYTTLETON AND HIS FAMILY. London: Hodder, 1924. 2 vols.

Extracts from the correspondence of Christian Lyttleton, Hester Lyttleton, and Molly Lyttleton. The family's correspondence with Mrs. Elizabeth Montagu is included in Volume Two.

V. DIARIES, JOURNALS, LETTERS

359. Anonymous. A WAR NURSE'S DIARY: SKETCHES FROM A BELGIAN FIELD HOSPITAL. New York: The Macmillan Co., 1918. 115p.

Diary of nursing work during World War I.

360. Anonymous [Wife of Namiki-Shi]. "A Woman's Diary." In KOTTO: BEING JAPANESE CURIOS, WITH SUNDRY COBWEBS. Lafcadio Hearn. London and New York: Macmillan Co., 1902, 1910. 251p. Boston: Houghton Mifflin, 1922. 251p.

Diary 1895-1900 by a Japanese woman whose identity is unknown. Describes an arranged marriage to a poor widower, Namiki-Shi. The marriage is successful, but the couple live in extreme poverty. Three children born to them die in infancy, the diarist outliving the last born by only two weeks.

361. Anonymous. "An Independent Voice: A Mill Girl From Vermont Speaks Her Mind." Edited by Loriman S. Brigham. VERMONT HISTORY 41:3 (1973), 142-146.

Letters written by a young woman who went in 1851 to work in a Massachusetts textile mill, to earn money to attend Oberlin College. Only her first name--Lucy Ann--is known.

362. Anonymous. DIARY OF A NURSING SISTER ON THE WESTERN FRONT, 1914-1915. Edinburgh and London: William Blackwood & Sons, 1915. 300p.

Diary August 18, 1914--May 26, 1915 of an English

member of the Voluntary Aid Detachment, written while on Station Duty at Le Mans, on an Ambulance train at Ypres, Boulogne, Rouen and Nueve Chappelle, and with a field Ambulance at the Front. Includes a description of winter and Christmas in the trenches.

363. Anonymous. FOUR TO FOURTEEN. BY A VICTORIAN CHILD. London: Robert Hale, 1939. 157p.

Diary of an English girl, begun at about ten years old. The chief interest in the diary, according to the editor, is the diarist's patient acceptance of injustice and cruelty, and the unconsciousness which which the atmosphere of the household in which she lived is disclosed.

364. Anonymous. THE GOSSAMER YEARS: A DIARY BY A NOBLEWOMAN OF HEIAN JAPAN. Translated and edited by Edward Seidensticker. Vermont: Charles E. Tuttle Co., 1974. 201p.

Japanese poetic diary. Describes twenty-one years in the life of a mid-Heian Fujiwara noble-woman, known today as the Mother of Michitsuna. Her name and her date of birth are not known. The work is roughly contemporary to Lady Murasaki's TALE OF GENJI and the PILLOW BOOK OF SEI SHONAGON.

365. Anonymous. LETTERS FROM A FRENCH HOSPITAL. Boston and New York: Houghton Mifflin Co., 1917. 96p.

Letters of an English nurse working near the front in France, written to her uncle, July 31, 1915--September 17, 1916.

366. Anonymous. LETTERS FROM A NEW ENGLAND VILLAGE. Edited by Ellen Chase. Baltimore: The Southworth Press, 1929. Reprinted from the New England Quarterly 2:1 (1929), 140-149.

Extracts from letters written by an unnamed young woman, 1850-1852 (from age 22 to 24). Describes life in a country parsonage in Worcester County.

367. Anonymous. MADEMOISELLE MISS: LETTERS FROM AN AMERICAN GIRL SERVING WITH THE RANK OF LIEUTENENT IN A FRENCH HOSPITAL AT THE FRONT. With a preface by Dr. Richard C. Cabot. Boston: W.A. Butterfield, 1916. 102p.

368. Anonymous. NOTEBOOKS OF A SPINSTER LADY, 1878-1903. London and New York: Cassell & Co., 1919. 319p.

Extracts from a social diary, consisting of "anecdotes, incidents and conversations that amused or were of interest to her," with running commentary by the editor, also anonymous.

369. Anonymous. RESPECTFULLY YOURS, ANNIE: LETTERS OF A LONDON COOK. Introduced by Sylvia Brockway. New York: E.P. Dutton & Co., 1942. 230p.

Domestic war-time letters, September 3, 1939--October 11, 1941, from a cook employed by the Brockway family. Describes air-raids, food shortages and rationing, and social life in London that continued under the shadow of the war. The Brockways left England for the U.S. in July, 1939 and remained there for the duration of the war.

370. Anonymous. "South Korea: Letters from Solitary." Edited by Matthew Seiden. MS. MAGAZINE 4:2 (August, 1975), 91-92.

Prison letters from a student to her mother. She was arrested in March, 1974, during a demonstration protesting the constitution of South Korea and urging a return to the previous democratic constitution.

371. Anonymous. THOSE WAR WOMEN. BY ONE OF THEM. New York: Coward-McCann, 1929. 283p.

Diary February--August, 1919 of an American entertainer with the Women's Division of the American Expeditionary Forces in France.

372. Anonymous. "War Diary of a Union Woman in the

South." In FAMOUS ADVENTURES AND PRISON ESCAPES OF THE CIVIL WAR. Edited by George Washington Cable. New York: The Century Company, 1893, 1911. 338p.

Civil war diary, December 1, 1860--August 20, 1863, by a Union woman who remained in the Confederacy, residing in New Orleans and Mississippi. She was present at the Siege of Vicksburg.

373. Anonymous. WOMAN UNDER FIRE: SIX MONTHS IN THE RED ARMY: A WOMAN'S DIARY AND EXPERIENCES OF REVOLUTIONARY RUSSIA. Foreword by Reginald J. Dingle. London: Hutchinson and Co., 1930. 286p.

374. Aberdeen and Temair, Ishbel Maria Marjoribanks Gordon, Marchioness d', 1857-1939. British feminist, political hostess and philanthrophist. THE CANADIAN JOURNAL OF LADY ABERDEEN, 1893-1898. Edited with an introduction by John T. Saywell. Toronto: Champlain Society, 1960. 517p. (Publications of the Champlain Society, 38.)

Social diary. Her husband, John Gordon, Marquess of Aberdeen and Temair, served as Governor-General of Canada from 1893 to 1898.

375. Abernon, Helen Venetia Duncombe Vincent, Viscountess d', b. 1866. RED CROSS AND BERLIN EMBASSY, 1915-1926. EXTRACTS FROM THE DIARIES OF VISCOUNTESS D'ABERNON. London: John Murray, 1946. 152p.

Diary of war work during World War I.

376. Abutsu, Nun d. 1283. Japanese poetic diarist and wife of poet Fujiwara Tamie. "The Izayoi Nikki (1277-1280)." Edwin O. Reischauer. In TRANSLATIONS FROM EARLY JAPANESE LITERATURE. Edwin O. Reischauer and Joseph K. Yamagiwa. Cambridge, Mass.: Published for the Harvard-Yenching Institute by Harvard University Press, 1951. p.3-135.

Poetic diary of travel from Kyoto to Kamakura,

with poems to her children, comments on correspondence with friends in Kyoto, and quotes from many of the poems exchanged in these letters. The diary is also known as THE DIARY OF THE WANING MOON and THE TRAVELS OF ABUTSU.

377. Abzug, Bella S., b. 1920. American politician. BELLA! MS. ABZUG GOES TO WASHINGTON. Edited by Mel Ziegler. New York: Saturday Review Press, 1972. 314p.

Public diary of Abzug's first year in Congress, 1971.

378. Adair, Cornelia Wadsworth. Irish-American wife of John Adair, a partner with Charles Goodnight in the JA Ranch in Texas. MY DIARY: AUGUST 30TH TO NOVEMBER 5TH, 1874. Introduction by Montagu K. Brown. Illustrated by Malcolm Thurgood. Austin, Tex., and London: University of Texas Press, 1965. 125p.

Travel diary of trip from her estate in Ireland to America, then cross-country on a buffalo-hunting trip with her husband.

379. Adams, Abigail Smith, 1744-1818. American feminist and wife of John Adams, second President of the United States. LETTERS OF MRS. ADAMS, THE WIFE OF JOHN ADAMS. With an introductory memoir by her grandson, Charles Frances Adams. Boston: C.C. Little and J. Brown, 1840. 447p. Second ed., 1840. 2 vols.

Letters 1761-1816.

380. ------. FAMILIAR LETTERS OF JOHN ADAMS AND HIS WIFE ABIGAIL, DURING THE REVOLUTION. WITH A MEMOIR OF MRS. ADAMS. Charles Frances Adams. New York: Hurd & Houghton, 1876. 424p.

381. ------. NEW LETTERS OF ABIGAIL ADAMS, 1788-1801. Edited with an introduction by Stewart Mitchell. Boston: Houghton Mifflin, and Cambridge, England: The Riverside Press, 1947. 281p. Reprinted, Westport, Conn.: Greenwood Press, 1973. 281p.

One hundred forty-one previously unpublished letters written to her sister, Mary Smith Cranch, during John Adams's Vice Presidency and Presidency.

382. ------. THE ADAMS-JEFFERSON LETTERS: THE COMPLETE CORRESPONDENCE BETWEEN THOMAS JEFFERSON AND ABIGAIL AND JOHN ADAMS. Edited by Lester J. Cappon. Chapel Hill: Published for the Institute of Early American History and Culture at Williamsburg, Virginia, by the University of North Carolina Press, 1959. 2 vols.

Letters 1777-1826.

383. ------. THE BOOK OF ABIGAIL AND JOHN: SELECTED LETTERS OF THE ADAMS FAMILY, 1762-1784. Edited by L.H. Butterfield, Marc Friedlaender and Mary-Jo Kline. Cambridge, Mass.: Harvard University Press, 1975. 411p.

Intended to illuminate the private lives and characters of Abigail and John Adams; the selection leans more toward their daily lives than towards their involvement in historical events. Includes extracts from her diary, letters to her sisters Mary Smith Cranch and Elizabeth Shaw, and letters and extracts from the diary of her daughter, Abigail Adams Smith.

384. ------. "Conflicting Demands in Correspondence: Abigail Adams on Women's Rights." Judy C. Pearson. TODAY'S SPEECH 23:4 (Fall, 1975), 29-33.

Discusses differences between Adams's letters to John Adams and Mercy Otis Warren on women's rights, citing apparent inconsistencies and differences in rhetoric between the two sets of letters. Those to Warren are more direct, logical, and to the point, and in them Adams outlines arguments which she later uses in letters to John Adams. Pearson compares these sequences in light of the conflicting demands encountered by feminists who address themselves to intimate males on the subject of women's rights.

385. Adams, Marian Hooper, 1843-1885. American

political hostess, pioneer woman photographer, and wife of historian Henry Adams. THE LETTERS OF MRS. HENRY ADAMS, 1865-1883. Boston: Little, Brown & Co., 1936. 587p.

Social diaries describe her nine trips away from home in Boston and Beverly Farms--two voyages abroad and seven winters in Washington, D.C.

386. Agassiz, Elizabeth Cabot Cary, 1822-1907. American educator, founder and first president of Radcliffe College, and wife of naturalist Louis Agassiz. A JOURNEY IN BRAZIL. Louis and Elizabeth Agassiz. Boston: Ticknor & Fields, 1868. 540p. Reprinted, New York: Frederick A. Praeger, 1969.

Account of the Thayer Expedition to Brazil, April, 1865--August, 1866. Elizabeth's descriptive journal of the journey is combined with Louis's scientific notes; it is difficult to tell where her writing leaves off and his begins.

387. ------. ELIZABETH CARY AGASSIZ: A BIOGRAPHY. Lucy Allen Paton. With illustrations. Boston: Houghton Mifflin, and Cambridge, England: The Riverside Press, 1919. 423p.

Letters 1838-1907, and extracts from her diary. The first half of the book is concerned with her married life and the work of her husband; the second half with the founding of Radcliffe College.

388. Agoult, Marie Catherine Sophie de Flavigny, Comtesse d'., 1805-1876. French historian and feminist who wrote under the pseudonym Daniel Stern, and lover of Franz Liszt. CORRESPONDANCE DE LISZT ET DE LA COMTESSE D'AGOULT, 1833-1840. Publiee par M. Daniel Ollivier. Paris: B. Grasset, 1933.

389. ------. AUTOUR DE MADAME D'AGOULT ET DE LISZT (ALFRED DE VIGNY, EMILE OLLIVIER, PRINCESS DES BELGIOJOSO). Lettres publiée avec un introduction et notes par David Ollivier. Paris: B. Grasset, 1941.

390. ------. UNE CORRESPONDANCE ROMANTIQUE: MADAME D'AGOULT, FRANZ LISZT, HENRI LEHMANN. Presentée par Solange Joubert. Paris: Flammarion, 1947. 236p.

391. ------. MARIE D'AGOULT: SON MARI, SES AMIS. CORRESPONDANCE ET DOCUMENTS INÉDITES. Jacques Vier. Paris: Editions du Cedre, 1950. 142p.

392. Aikin, Lucy, 1781-1864. English historian, biographer and children's author. MEMOIRS, MISCELLANIES AND LETTERS OF LUCY AIKIN: INCLUDING THOSE ADDRESSED TO THE REVEREND DR. CHANNING FROM 1826 TO 1842. Edited by Philip Hemery Le Breton. London: Longman, Green, Longman, Roberts & Green, 1864. 440p.

393. ------. CORRESPONDENCE OF WILLIAM ELLERY CHANNING, D.D., AND LUCY AIKIN, FROM 1826 TO 1842. Edited by Anna Letitia Le Breton. Boston: Roberts Bros., 1874. 426p.

394. Aikman, Louisa Susannah Wells, 1755-1831. American colonist. JOURNAL OF A VOYAGE FROM CHARLESTON, SOUTH CAROLINA TO LONDON, UNDERTAKEN DURING THE AMERICAN REVOLUTION. BY A DAUGHTER OF AN EMINENT AMERICAN LOYALIST IN THE YEAR 1778 AND WRITTEN FROM MEMORY ONLY IN 1779. New York: New York Historical Society, 1906. 121p. Reprinted, New York: Arno Press, 1968. 121p.

Loyalist diary, May-August, 1778. Written a year after the events, but according to AMERICAN DIARIES (1983) it follows a daily diary pattern.

395. Aissé, Charlotte Elizabeth, 1694-1733. French beauty and letter-writer. LETTRES DE MLLE. AISSÉ A MME. C.... QUI CONTIENNENT PLUSIEURS ANECDOTES DE L'HISTOIRE DU TEMPS DÉPUIS L'ANNÉE 1726 JUSQU'EN 1733. Précédés d'un Narré Très-court de l'Histoire de Mlle. Aisse, pour Servir a l'Intellligence de ses Lettres. Avec des notes, dont quelques-unes sont de M. de Voltaire. Paris: Chez La Grange, 1787. 242p.

Letters to Julie Pelissary Calandrini, (fl.1695-1729).

396. ------. LETTRES DE MADEMOISELLE AISSÉ À MADAME CALANDRINI. Précédeés d'une notice par A. Piedagnel. Paris: Librarie Des Bibliophiles, 1878. 183p.

397. ------. LETTRES DE MADEMOISELLE AISSÉ À MADAME CALANDRINI. Nouvelle édition critique; publiée avec une introduction, des notes et des documents inédits par Henri Courteault. Avant-propos par Robert de Flers. Paris: Édition de la Bonne Ideé, 1926.

398. ------. LETTRES DE MADEMOISELLE AISSÉ À MADAME CALANDRINI. 5th ed., revisée et annotée par M.J. Ravenel. Avec une notice par M. Saint-Beuve. Paris: Gerdes, 1846. 325p. Reissued, 1853, with "Lettres diverses" by Mme. du Deffand, Mme. de Crequy and others. Reprinted, Paris: Stock, Delamain et Boutelleau, 1943. 205p.

399. Albany, Charlotte Stuart, Duchess of, d. 1789. English-German Daughter of Charles III and Louise, Countess of Albany. THE LIFE AND LETTERS OF H.R.H. CHARLOTTE STUART, DUCHESS OF ALBANY, ONLY CHILD OF CHARLES III. Francis John Angus Skeet. London: Eyre and Spottiswoode, Publishers, 1832. 175p.

Biography comprised of letters and extracts from letters. Describes life at the Courts of Europe.

400. Albany, Louise Maximiliane Caroline Emanuele Stuart, Princess of Stolberg, calling herself Countess of, 1752-1824. German-born Italian salonist, wife of Charles James Edward Stuart and mistress of Italian poet Count Victor Alfieri. LETTERE INÉDITE DI LUIGIA STOLBERG, CONTESSA D'ALBANY À UGO ROSCOLO, E DELL' ABATE LUIGI DI BREME ALLA CONTESSA D'ALBANY. Publicate da Comillo Antona. Traversi e da Domenico Bianchini. Rome: E. Molino, 1887. 275p.

401. ------. LE PORTEFEUILLE DE LA COMTESSE D'ALBANY (1806-1824). Lettres mises en ordre, et publiées avec un portrait par Leon G. Pèlissier. Paris: Albert Fontemoing, 1902. 726p.

402. ------. LETTRES INEDITES DE LA COMTESSE D'ALBANY A SES AMIS DE SIENNE. Lettres mises en ordre et publiées par Léon G. Pèlissier. Toulouse: Édition Private, 1904-1915. 3 vols

Volume 1: Lettres à Teresa Regoli Mocenni et au Chanoine Luti, 1797-1802. Volume 2: Lettres à l'Archiprêtre Luti et à Vittorio Mocenni, 1802-1809. Volume 3: Lettres à Alessandro Cerretani, 1803-1820.

403. ------. THE LAST STUART QUEEN: LOUISE, COUNTESS OF ALBANY; HER LIFE AND LETTERS. Herbert M. Vaughn. London: Duckworth & Co., 1910. 359p.

Correspondence with connecting biographical text. Contains an appendix of seven letters in French to Signora Teresa Mocenni and the Arch-Priest Luti not included in LES LETTRES INEDITES...A SES AMIS DE SIENNE.

404. ------. LETTRES DE LA COMTESSE D'ALBANY AU CHEVALIÉR DE SOBIRATS. Suivies de quelques pièces inedites ayant rapport à elle, editées par le Marquis de Ripert-Montclar. Monaco: Imprimérie de Monaco, 1916. 138p.

405. Albret, Jeanne d', Queen of Navarre, 1528-1572. French Daughter of Marguerite de Navarre, and mother of King Henry IV of France. LETTRES DE LA ROYNE DE NAVARRE, AU ROI, A LA ROYNE SA MÈRE, A MONSIEUR FRÈRE DU ROI, A MONSIEUR LE CARDINAL DU BOURBON SON BEAU-FRÈRE, ET LA ROYNE D'ANGLETERRE. Rochelle: Barthèlemy Berton, 1569. London: Microfilm copy made by the British Museum Photographic Service, nd. Collation of orginal, 128p.

406. ------. LETTRES DE ANTOINE DE BOURBON ET DE JEANNE D'ALBRET. Publiées pour la Société de l'Histoire de France, par M. de Rochambeau. Paris: Renouard, 1877.

407. Alcott, Louisa May, 1832-1888. American author. LOUISA MAY ALCOTT: HER LIFE, LETTERS AND JOURNALS. Edited by Ednah D. Cheney. Boston: Roberts Bros., 1891. 404p. Reprinted, Boston: Little, Brown & Co., 1919.

Letters and journals edited together chronologically, 1843-1886. Alcott revised and destroyed parts of her journals in later life; and most of her correspondence was destroyed, according to her wishes.

408. ------. BRONSON ALCOTT'S FRUITLANDS: WITH TRANSCENDENTAL WILD OATS, BY LOUISA MAY ALCOTT. Compiled by Clara Endicott Sears. Boston: Houghton Mifflin, 1915. 185p.

"Transcendental Wild Oats" is a fictionalized, humorous account of her father's unsuccessful utopian farming experiment, Fruitlands. Also contains a brief childhood diary kept by Anna Bronson Alcott (b.1831), June-September, 1843.

409. ------. TRANSCENDENTAL WILD OATS AND EXCERPTS FROM THE FRUITLANDS DIARY. Introduction by William Henry Harrison. Illustrations by J. Streeter Fowke. Harvard, Mass.: Harvard Common Press, 1975, 1981. 92p.

"Transcendental Wild Oats" followed by a childhood diary written for the period, August--September, 1843.

410. Aldrich, Mildred, d. 1928. American journalist. A HILLTOP ON THE MARNE: BEING LETTERS WRITTEN JUNE 3--September 8, 1914. Boston and New York: Houghton Mifflin Co., and Cambridge, England: The Riverside Press, 1915. 187p.

War letters to an unamed friend in the U.S., begining with Aldrich's move into a house on the Marne, seeking a "quiet refuge," which was almost immediately disturbed by war.

411. ------. ON THE EDGE OF THE WAR ZONE: FROM THE BATTLE OF THE MARNE TO THE ENTRANCE OF THE STARS AND STRIPES. Boston: Small, Maymard & Co., 1917. 311p.

Continuation of above. Letters to a friend in the U.S., September 6, 1914--April 8, 1917.

412. ------. THE PEAK OF THE LOAD: THE WAITING MONTHS

ON THE HILLTOP FROM THE ENTRANCE OF THE STARS & STRIPES TO THE SECOND VICTORY ON THE MARNE. Boston: Small, Maynard & Co., 1918. 277p.

Continuation of above. Letters to a friend in the U.S., April 20, 1917--Remembrance Day, 1918.

413. Aleramo, Sibilla, pseud. for Rina Pierangeli Faccio, 1876-1960. Italian poet, author, journalist and feminist. UN AMORE INSOLITO: DIARIO, 1940-1944. Con una lettura de Lea Melandri e Una Cronologia della Vita dell' Auturice. Scelta e cura di Alba Morino. Milano: Feltrinelli, 1979. 476p.

414. ------. DIARIO DE UNA DONNA. INEDITI 1945-1960. Milan: Feltrinelli, 1978. 485p.

415. ------. LETTERE D'AMORE A LINA. SIBILLA ALERAMO. A cura di Alessandro Cenni. Milan: Savelli, 1982. 92p.

Letters to Lina Poletti.

416. Alexander, Evelina Throop Martin, b. 1843. American Army wife. "Evy Alexander: The Colonel's Lady at Ft. McDowell." Edited by Sandra L. Myres. MONTANA: MAGAZINE OF WESTERN HISTORY 24:3 (1974), 26-38.

Background and excerpts from letters, 1868-1869. An Army wife describes life at Ft. McDowell in Arizona Territory.

417. ------. CALVARY WIFE: THE DIARY OF EVELINE M. ALEXANDER, 1866-1867. BEING A RECORD OF HER JOURNEY FROM NEW YORK TO FORT SMITH TO JOIN HER CALVARY-OFFICER HUSBAND, ANDREW J. ALEXANDER, AND HER EXPERIENCE WITH HIM ON ACTIVE DUTY AMONG THE INDIAN NATIONS AND IN TEXAS, NEW MEXICO AND COLORADO. College Station, Tex.: A.&M. University Press, 1977. 175p.

418. Alexander, Frances Gordon Paddock. American; and Lady Evelyn Murray Cobbold, b. 1867. English. WAYFARERS IN THE LIBYAN DESERT. New York and London: G.P. Putnam's Sons; and London: A.L. Humphreys, 1912. 127p.

Travel diary. The American edition appeared under Alexander's name; the English edition under Cobbold's.

419. Alexandra, Empress Consort of Nicholas II, Emperor of Russia, 1872-1918. PIS'MA IMPERATRITSY ALEKSANDRY FEDOROVNY K IMPERATORU NIKOLAIU II. [Perevod s angliiskago V.D. Nabokova.] Berlin: Slovo, 1922. 2 vols.

420. ------. LETTERS OF THE TSARITSA TO THE TSAR, 1914-1916. With an introduction by Sir Bernard Pares, K.B.E. London: Duckworth & Co., 1923. 478p. New York: McBride, 1924. 478p. Reprinted, Stanford, Calif.: Hoover Institution Press, 1973. 462p.

421. ------. THE NICKY-SUNNY LETTERS: CORRESPONDENCE OF THE TSAR AND TSARITSA, 1914-1917. Hattiesburg, Miss.: Academic International, 1970. 2 vols. in one.

Selection reprinted from THE LETTERS OF THE TSAR TO THE TSARITSA, 1914-1917 (London, 1929), and THE LETTERS OF THE TSARITSA TO THE TSAR, 1914-1916 (London, 1923), chosen to illuminate the intimate details of the daily lives of the Tsar and Tsaritsa during World War I and the Russian Revolution. The letters have been re-translated from the official Russian edition. The Tsar and Tsaritsa generally wrote in English.

422. Alice, Consort of Louis IV, Grand Duke of Hesse-Darmstadt, 1843-1878. English daughter of Queen Victoria. ALICE, GROSSHERZOGIN VON HESSEN UND BEI RHEIN, PRINZESSIN VON GROSSBRITTANIEN UND IRLAND. MITTHEILUNGEN AUS IRHEN LEBEN UN AS IRHEN BRIEFEN. Darmstadt: A. Bergstrasser, 1884. 431p.

423. ------. ALICE, GRAND DUCHESS OF HESSE, PRINCESS OF GREAT BRITAIN AND IRELAND. BIOGRAPHICAL SKETCH AND LETTERS. London: John Murray, 1884. 415p. New York: G. Munro, 1884. 212p. New York and London: G.P. Putnam's Sons, 1884. 407p.

Letters to her mother, Queen Victoria.

424. ------. ALICE, GRAND DUCHESS OF HESSE, PRINCESS

OF GREAT BRITAIN AND IRELAND, LETTERS TO HER MAJESTY THE QUEEN. With a memoir by H.R.H. Princess Christian. Leipzig: B. Tauchnitz, 1885. 2 vols. London: John Murray, 1885. 342p.

425. Allart de Méritens, Hortense, 1801-1879. French author. "Les Correspondants d'Hortense Allart de Meritens: Sainte-Beuve, Madame d'Agoult, Documents Inédits." REVUE DE PARIS (September 15, 1907), 289-330.

426. ------. HORTENSE ALLART DE MÉRITENS DANS SES RAPPORTS AVEC CHATEAUBRIAND, BÉRANGER, LAMÉNNAIS, SAINTE-BEUVE, GEORGE SAND, MADAME D'AGOULT (DOCUMENTS INÉDITES). Portraits et autobiographes. Léon Seché. Paris: Société du Mercure de France, 1908. 329p.

Contains letters to George Sand, Charles-Augustin St. Beuve, and others, and extracts from letters, with commentary.

427. ------. LETTRES INEDITES À SAINTE-BEUVE (1841-1848). Avec une introduction et des notes par Léon Seché. Paris: Société du Mercure de France, 1908. 340p.

Letters to Charles Augustin Sainte-Beuve.

428. ------. LETTRE INEDITE À GINO CAPPONI. Petre Ciureanu. Genoa: Tolozzi, 1961.

429. ------. HORTENSE ALLART ET ANNA WOODCOCK (CON LETTERE INEDITE). A cura di Petre Ciureanu. Genoa: Tolozzi, 1961.

430. ------. NOUVELLES LETTRES À SAINTE-BEUVE (1832-1864) PAR HORTENSE ALLART. Les Lettres de la collection Lovenjoul. Textes réunis, classés et annotés par Lorin A. Uffenbecke. Geneva: Librairie Droz, 1965. 175p.

Letters which came to light after the publication of LETTRES INEDITES À SAINTE-BEUVE (1908) and meant as a companion to that volume.

431. Allen, Harriet Trowbridge, d. 1877. American author. TRAVELS IN EUROPE AND THE EAST DURING THE YEARS 1858-1859 AND 1863-186. Printed for private circulation. New Haven, Conn.: Tuttle, Morehouse & Taylor, 1879. 506p.

Travel account written from a journal, and letters written to family and friends at home.

432. Allen, Mary Montcrieff. TRAVEL DIARY, 1835-1837. EUROPE AND THE MIDDLE EAST. Charleston, S.C.: South Carolina Historical Society, n.d. Microfiche (9x12 cm.).

433. Allibone, Susan, 1813-1854. American. A LIFE HID WITH CHRIST IN GOD: BEING A MEMOIR OF SUSAN ALLIBONE, CHIEFLY COMPILED FROM HER DIARY AND LETTERS. Alfred Lee. Philadelphia: J.B. Lippincott, 1856. 295p.

Includes a religious diary, 1833-1854.

434. Alliluyeva, Svetlana Stalina, b. 1926. Russian author and daughter of Josef Stalin. TWENTY LETTERS TO A FRIEND. Translated from the Russian by Prescilla Johnson McMillan. New York: Harper & Row, 1967. 246p.

Autobiography in the form of letters, written over one month's time in 1963 to friends in Moscow, and not originally intended for publication.

435. Almy, Mary Gould, 1735-1808. American Quaker and Loyalist. "Mrs. Almy's Journal." NEWPORT HISTORICAL MAGAZINE 1 (1880-1881), 17-36.

Diary July-August, 1778 describes the occupation of Newport, Rhode Island, by the British Army. Although she was a Loyalist, her husband fought with the Revolutionary Forces.

436. Alsop, Susan Mary Jay Patten, b. 1918. American wife of diplomat William Patten. TO MARIETTA FROM PARIS, 1945-1960. Garden City, N.Y.: Doubleday & Co., 1975. 370p.

Journal-letters written to her friend Marietta Tree describe social life in European literary, social, and diplomatic circles in the years after World War II.

437. Ambler, Mary Cary. American. "Diary of Mary Ambler, 1770." G.B. Ambler. VIRGINIA MAGAZINE OF HISTORY AND BIOGRAPHY 45 (1937), 152-170.

Social and travel diary, September--October, 1770.

438. Ames, Blanche Butler, 1847-1939. American wife of Mississippi Governor Adelbert Ames. CHRONICLES OF THE NINETEENTH CENTURY: FAMILY LETTERS OF BLANCHE BUTLER AND ADELBERT AMES, MARRIED JULY 21ST, 1870. Compiled by Blanche Butler Ames, 1935. Clinton (?), Mass.: 1957. 2 vols.

Consists chiefly of Blanche Butler's family letters and love letters to Adelbert Ames.

439. Ames, Mary, 1831-1903. American teacher. FROM A NEW ENGLAND WOMAN'S DIARY IN DIXIE IN 1865. Springfield, Mass.: Plimpton Press, 1906. 125p. Reprinted, New York: Negro Universities Press, 1969.

Account of work with the Freedmen's Bureau, teaching newly freed slaves on Edisto Island, South Carolina, May, 1865--September, 1866.

440. Amory, Katherine, 1731-1777. American colonist and Loyalist. THE JOURNAL OF MRS. JOHN AMORY, 1775-1777. Edited by Martha C. Codman. Boston: Privately Printed 1923. 101p.

Loyalist diary, May 1775--March 1777, written during the American Revolution by a Boston woman staying in London.

441. Anderson, Isabel Weld Perkins, b. 1876. American. ZIGZAGGING. Boston and New York: Houghton Mifflin, 1918. 269p.

Reminiscences written from a diary, includng extracts from the original, of work in a district hospital six miles from the trenches during World War I; with the American Red Cross in the Army Zone; and of work assisting the Queen of Belgium in an operating room.

442. Andreas-Salomé, Louise Lelia, 1861-1937. Russian-German philospher, author, and psychoanalyst. RAINER MARIA RILKE / LOU ANDREAS-SALOMÉ: BRIEFWECHSEL. Mit erlauterungen und einem Nachwört, herausgegeben von Ernst Pfeiffer. Zurich: M. Niehans, 1952. 651p. New edition, Frankfurt am Main: Insel Verlag, 1975. 643p.

443. ------. IN DER SCHULE BEI FREUD: TAGEBÜCH EINES JAHRES 1912-1913. Aus dem nachlass herausgegeben von Ernst Pfeiffer. Zurich: M. Niehans, 1958. 300p.

444. ------. THE FREUD JOURNAL OF LOU ANDREAS-SALOMÉ. Translated and with an introduction by Stanley A. Leavy. New York: Basic Books, 1964. 211p.

Translation of item 443.

445. ------. SIGMUND FREUD / LOU ANDREAS SALOMÉ: BRIEFWECHSEL. Herausgegeben von Ernst Pfeiffer. Frankfurt am Main: S. Fissher, 1966. 291p.

446. ------. SIGMUND FREUD AND LOU ANDREAS-SALOME: LETTERS. Edited by Ernst Pfeiffer. Translated from the German by William and Elaine Robson-Scott. New York: Harcourt Brace Jovanovich; and London: Hogarth Press/Institute of Psycho-Analysis, 1972. 244p.

Translation of item 445. Correspondence 1912-1936 between Freud and "an authoress of note, who became his pupil and collaborator."

447. ------. EINTRAGUNGEN: LETZTE JAHRE. LOU ANDREAS-SALOMÉ. Herausgegeben und mit einem Nachwört Versehen von Ernst Pfeiffer. Frankfurt am Main: Insel Verlag, 1982. 141p.

Account of Andreas-Salomé's last years and death.

448. Andrews, Eliza Frances, 1840-1931. American author, botanist and teacher. ELIZA FRANCES ANDREWS: THE WAR-TIME JOURNAL OF A GEORGIA GIRL, 1864-1865. Edited by Spencer Bidwell King. New York: D. Appleton & Co., 1908. 387p. Macon, Ga.: The Ardivan Press, 1960. 396p. Atlanta, Ga.: Cherokee Publishing Co., 1976.

Diary of a trip from her home in Washington, D.C., (her father, Judge Garnett Andrews, was a Unionist) to a family plantation in Georgia. Describes destruction by Union Troops, and the breakup of the Confederacy in the last months of the war. Her diary is highly literate and has been compared to that of Mary Boykin Chesnut.

449. Andrews, Ellen Miriam Gibson, 1849-1921. American. HUDSON DIARY, 1896-1900. Transcribed and edited by Willis Harry Miller. Hudson, Wis: Wisconsin Star-Observer, Printer, 1968. 51p.

Religious and social diary, 1896-1900, of a resident of Hudson, Wisconsin.

450. Angle, Helen M. Blondel, b. 1871. American. THE LOG OR DIARY OF OUR AUTOMOBILE VOYAGE THROUGH MAINE AND THE WHITE MOUNTAINS, WRITTEN BY ONE OF THE SURVIVORS. Stamford, Conn.: R.H. Cunningham, 1910. 91p.

451. Angoulême, Marie Thérèse Charlotte, Duchesse d', 1778-1851. French princess; eldest daughter of Marie Antoinette and Louis XVI. JOURNAL DE LA DAUPHINE, 5 OCTOBRE 1789--SEPTEMBRE 1792. Corrigé et annotée par Louis XVIII. Journal entierement inédit, publiée par les soins de la famille Hué. Introduction par le Baron Imbert de Saint Amand. Paris: Firmin-Didot, n.d.

During the French Revolution, Duchesse d'Angouleme was imprisoned in the Temple and later exchanged for prominent Republican prisoners in Austria.

Angoulême, Louise de Savoie, Duchesse d'. See: Louise de Savoie, Duchesse d'Anglouléme.

452. Anne, Queen of Great Britain, 1665-1714. LETTERS OF TWO QUEENS. By Lt.-Col. the Hon. Benjamin Bathurst. London: R. Holden & Co., 1924.

Personal letters of Queen Anne and Queen Mary II (1662-1694), daughters of King James II, chiefly to Frances, daughter of Sir Allen Apsley, later the wife of Sir Benjamin Bathurst. Queen Anne's Letters date from 1679, when she was fifteen; Queen Mary's probably begin about the year 1671 or 1672, when she was nine.

453. ------. THE LETTERS AND DIPLOMATIC INSTRUCTIONS OF QUEEN ANNE. Edited by Beatrice Curtis Brown. London: Cassell and Co., 1935. 451p.

Almost all of her personal correspondence and a small selection of her official letters, 1679-1714.

454. Anspach, Elizabeth Berkeley, Baroness Craven, afterwards Margravine of, 1750-1828. English author. A JOURNEY THROUGH THE CRIMEA TO CONSTANTINOPLE: IN A SERIES OF LETTERS FROM THE RIGHT HONOURABLE ELIZABETH LADY CRAVEN, TO HIS SERENE HIGHNESS THE MARGRAVE OF BRANDEBOURGE, ANSPACH AND BAREITH. WRITTEN IN THE YEAR MDCCLXXXVI. Dublin: H. Chamberlaine, 1789. 415p.

Travel letters, 1785-1786.

455. ------. REMARKS IN A JOURNEY THROUGH THE CRIMEA, BY LADY CRAVEN. SELECTED FROM HER ELEGANT LETTERS, INTERSPERSED WITH DESCRIPTIVE ACCOUNTS BY VARIOUS AUTHORS. London: Printed by J.S. Barr, 1791. 226p.

456. Anthony, Susan Brownell, 1820-1906. American feminist and suffragist. THE LIFE AND WORK OF SUSAN B. ANTHONY: INCLUDING PUBLIC ADDRESSES, HER OWN LETTERS AND MANY FROM HER CONTEMPORARIES. Indianapolis: Bobbs-Merrill Co., 1898-1908. 3 vols.

457. Anthony, Susanna, 1726-1791. American devout. THE LIFE AND CHARACTER OF MISS SUSANNA ANTHONY, WHO

DIED IN NEWPORT (RHODE ISLAND) JUNE 23 MDCCXCI, IN THE SIXTY-FIFTH YEAR OF HER AGE. CONSISTING CHIEFLY IN EXTRACTS FROM HER WRITINGS WITH SOME BRIEF OBSERVATIONS ON THEM. Edited by Samuel Hopkins. Printed at Worcester, Mass.: Hartford, 1769. Reprinted by Hudson and Goodwin, 1799. 187p.

Contains extracts from a religious diary.

458. Antrim, Louisa Jane McDonnell, Countess of, 1855-1949. English Lady in Waiting. LOUISA, LADY IN WAITING: THE PERSONAL DIARIES AND ALBUMS OF LOUISA, LADY IN WAITING TO QUEEN VICTORIA AND QUEEN ALEXANDRA. Compiled and Edited by Elizabeth Longford. London: Jonathan Cape, 1979. 213p.

Court diary. Longford summarizes and quotes from the diaries.

459. Apple, Jacki, and Martha Wilson. American artists. "Correspondence Between Jacki Apple and Martha Wilson, 1973-1974." HERESIES 2 (May, 1977), Patterns of Communication and Space Among Women Issue. 43-47.

Correspondence between two performance artists connected with the Franklin Furnace Archive for Artists's books in New York City. Includes brief extracts from their journals which deal with their impressions of each other and of their correspondence.

Arblay, Frances Burney, Madame d'. See: Burney, Fanny.

460. Arbuthnot, Harriet Fane, 1793-1834. English wife of diplomat Charles Arbuthnot. THE JOURNAL OF MRS. ARBUTHNOT, 1820-1832. Edited by Frances Bamford and the Duke of Wellington. London: Macmillan, 1950. 2 vols.

Social diary 1820-1832, records important political events of the day, especially respecting the careers of her husband, George Canning, Robert Stewart, Viscount Castlereagh, and of Arthur, 1st Duke of

Wellington. The first paragraph of her diary ends: "I begin with the reign of George the 4th, the 1st of February, 1820"--George III had died January 29.

461. Arlet, Suzanne. French. L'INDIVINCIBLE AU THÉÂTRE: PAGES DE JOURNAL INTIME. Les Sables-d'Olone: Pinson, 1979. 117p.

462. Armstrong, Henrietta Esther Caroline, 1862-1944. South African nurse and hospital administrator. CAMP DIARY OF HENRIETTA ESTHER CAROLINE ARMSTRONG: EXPERIENCES OF A BOER NURSE IN THE IRENE CONCENTRATION CAMP, 6 APRIL--11 OCTOBER, 1901. With an introduction, editing of the text and historical notes by Thariza van Rensburg. Pretoria: Human Sciences Research Council, 1980. 211p.

Compassionate and realistic account of hospital work among Boer refugees during the second Anglo-Boer War by the founder and head of the Irene Voluntary Nurses Corps of Pretoria. Heavily documented, annotated, and illustrated with photographs.

463. Arnauld, Jacqueline Marie Angélique [Religious name: Angélique Marie de Sainte-Magdeleine, known as Mère Angélique], 1591-1661. French nun and Abbess. EXTRAITS DES LETTRES DE LA MÈRE MARIE- ANGÉLIQUE ARNAULD. Divisés en deux parties. Leyde: Chez William de Groot, 1734. 292p.

464. ------. LES LETTRES DE LA REVERENDE MÈRE MARIE-ANGÉLIQUE ARNAULD, ABBESSE ET RÉFORMATRICE DE PORT-ROYAL. Utrecht: Aux Depens de la Compagnie, 1742-1744. 3 vols.

465. Arnauld, Jeanne Catherine Agnes [Religious name: Agnes de Saint-Paul, known as Mère Agnes], 1593-1671. French Jansenist nun and Abbess. LES LETTRES DE LA MÈRE AGNES ARNAULD, ABBESSE DE PORT-ROYAL. Publiée par P. Faugère. Chez Benjamin Duprat, 1858. 10 vols.

466. Arnim, Bettina von [Katharina Elisabeth Ludovica Magdalena Brentano von Arnim], 1785-1859. German

reformer, intellectual and letter writer. GOETHE'S CORRESPONDENCE WITH A CHILD. FOR HIS MONUMENT. Berlin: printed by Trowitzsh & Son, 1837-1839. 3 vols. London: Orme, Brown, Green & Longmans, 1837-1839. Reprinted, London: Ticknor & Fields, 1859. 504p.

Correspondence of von Arnim with Goethe's mother, Elizabeth Goethe, 1807-1808; correspondence with Goethe from 1807; and extracts from her diary.

467. ------. THE DIARY OF A CHILD. Berlin: Printed by Trowitzsh & Son, 1838; and London: Longmans, Green, 1838? 325p.

Also published as part three of Goethe's CORRESPONDENCE WITH A CHILD.

468. ------. GUNDERODE: CORRESPONDENCE OF FRAULEIN GUNDERODE AND BETTINE VON ARNIM. Translated by Margaret Fuller. Boston: E.P. Peabody, 1842. 106p.

469. ------. GOETHES BRIEFWECHSEL MIT EINEM KINDE. Seinem denkamal von Bettina von Arnim. Mit einer einleitung von Franz Brummer. Leipzig: Pr. Reclam, 1890. 583p.

470. ------. BETINNAS BRIEFWECHSEL MIT GOETHE. Auf Grund ihres handschriftlichen nachlass nebst zeitgenussischen dockumenten uber ihr personalisches verhaltnis zue Goethe, zum ersten mal herausgegeben von Reinhold Stieg. Leipzig: Insel-Verlag, 1922. 455p.

471. ------. BETTINA IN IHREN BRIEFEN. Ausgewählt von Hartmann Goertz. Leipzig: Insel-Verlag, 1935. 86p. (Insel-Bucherei No. 466.)

472. ------. BETTINA VON ARNIM UND RUDOLPH BAIER, UNVER- OFFLENTLICHTE BRIEFE UND TAGEBÜCHAUFZEICHNUNGEN. Herausgegeben von Kurt Gassen. Greifswald: L. Bamberg, 1937.

473. ------. DIE ANDACHT ZUM MENSCHENBILD: UNBEKANNTE BRIEFE VON BETTINE BRENTANO. Herausgegeben von

Willhelm Schellberg un Friedrich Fuchs. Jena: E. Diederichs, 1942. 378p.

Letters to Friedrich Karl von Savigny and Gunda Brentano von Savigny (1780-1863).

474. ------. WERKE UND BRIEFE. Herausgegeben von Gustav Konrad. Frechen: Bartmann-Verlag, 1959-1963. 5 vols. (in four).

475. ------. ACHIM UND BETTINA VON ARNIM IN IHREN BRIEFEN. BRIEFWECHSEL ACHIM VON ARNIM UND BETTINA BRENTANO. Herausgegeben von Werner Vortriede, mit einder einleitung von Rudolf Alexander Schröder. Frankfurt am Main: Suhrkamp, 1961. 2 vols.

476. ------. DER BRIEFWECHSEL ZWISCHEN BETTINE BRENTANO UND MAX PROKOP VON FREBERG. Herausgegeben und kommentiert von Sibylle von Steinsdorff. Berlin and New York: De Gruyten, 1972. 356p.

477. ------. DIE GUNDERODE. Mit einem essay von Christa Wolf. [Amerkungen und Register von Heinz Amelung, neu durchgesehen]. Frankfurt am Main: Insel-Verlag, 1982. 519p.

478. ------. DER BRIEFWECHSEL BETTINE VON ARNIMS MIT DEN BRUDERN GRIMM, 1838-1841. Herausgegeben von Hartwig Schultz. Frankfurt am Main: Insel-Verlag, 1985. 418p.

Correspondence with Jacob and Wilhelm Grimm.

479. ------. BETTINE VON ARNIM WERKE UND BRIEFE IN DREI BANDEN. Herausgegeben von Walter Schmitz und Sibylle von Steindorff. Frankfurt Am Main: Deutscher Klassiker Verlag, 1986.

480. ------. BETTINE UND ARNIM: BRIEF DER FREUNDSCHAFT UND LIEBE. Herausgegeben, eingeführt und kommentiert von Otto Betz und Veronika Straub. Frankfurt Am Main: Knecht, 1986.

Volume 1: 1806-1808.

481. Arnold, Annemarie, b. 1909. German religious teacher. YOUTH MOVEMENT TO BRUDERHOF: LETTERS AND DIARIES OF ANNEMARIE NE WACHTER, 1926-1932. Edited by the Hutterian Brethren, Woodcrest Bruderhof. Foreword by Anna Mow. Rifton, N.Y. and Robertsbridge, U.K.: Plough Publishing House/Hutterian Brethren, 1986. 234p.

Early writings record her childhood and school days, her involvement in the German Youth Movement, her religious conversion, and her life as a teacher in the religious community of the Hutterian Brethren, against the backdrop of the rise of Nazism.

482. Arthur, Malvina, 1832-1916. American sister of U.S. President Chester Alan Arthur. "The Diaries of Malvina Arthur: Windows into the Past of Our 21st President." Thomas C. Reeves. VERMONT HISTORY 38:3 (1970), 177-188.

483. Ashe, Elizabeth H., 1869-1954. American physician, health-worker and Red Cross Volunteer. INTIMATE LETTERS FROM FRANCE DURING AMERICA'S FIRST YEAR OF WAR. San Francisco: Philopolis Press, 1918. 122p.

484. ------. INTIMATE LETTERS FROM FRANCE AND EXTRACTS FROM THE DIARY OF ELIZABETH ASHE, 1917-1919. Revised and enlarged. San Francisco: Bruce Brough Press, 1931.

Ashe was called by the Red Cross to form the first pediatric unit to be sent to France during World War I. Her hospital, set up for women and children, was eventually turned over to military use.

485. Ashton-Warner, Sylvia, b. 1905. New Zealand novelist and educator. TEACHER. New York: Simon & Schuster, 1963. 191p.

Notebook-diary of teaching in a Maori school. Fuses personal writing with a documentation of her theory of the Key Vocabulary, an innovative method of teaching children to read using a system of personal and individualized "key words."

486. ------. MYSELF. New York: Simon & Schuster, 1967. 239p.

Further account of her teaching in Maori schools, somewhat fictionalized. Includes an account of a love affair, and of her determination to have a "room of one's own,"--in her case, a reconditioned cottage--in which to work.

487. Asquith, Cynthia Mary Evelyn Charteris, Lady, 1877-1960. English daughter-in-law of Prime Minister Herbert Henry Asquith. DIARIES: 1915-1918. Edited by E.M. Horsley. Foreword by L.P. Hartley. London: Hutchinson, 1968. New York: Alfred A. Knopf, 1969. 529p.

Social diary.

488. Asquith, Margot [Margaret Emma Alice Tennant Asquith], Countess of, 1864-1945. Scottish political and social personality, hostess and author. Wife of English Prime Minister Herbert Henry Asquith. MY IMPRESSIONS OF AMERICA. New York: George H. Doran Co., 1922. 217p.

489. ------. PLACES & PERSONS. London: Thornton Butterworth, 1925. 288p.

Includes "A Little Diary of a Journey to Egypt in 1891," published separately in 1921; "Impressions of America," a diary of travel in the U.S. in 1922 and published separately in 1922; and accounts of travel in Spain in 1923 and Italy in 1924 which appear to have been rewritten from a diary.

490. Assheton, Susan, b.1767. American daughter of a distinguished Philadelphia family. "Susan Assheton's Book." Edited with a preface by Joseph M. Beatty. PENNSYLVANIA MAGAZINE OF HISTORY AND BIOGRAPHY 55:1 (1931), 174-186.

Private social diary, 1801-1832. Gives details of national events, activities of visiting Royalty, and family affairs, and throws some sidelights upon educational and religious practices in Philadelphia during the first part of the nineteenth century.

491. Atherton, Gertrude Franklin Horn, 1857-1948. American author. LIFE IN THE WAR ZONE. New York: Systems Printing Co., 1916. 24p.

World War I diary.

492. ------. "Your Picture Hangs In My Salon: The Letters of Gertrude Atherton and Ambrose Bierce." Emily Leider. CALIFORNIA HISTORICAL QUARTERLY 25:4 (Winter, 1981/1982), 332-349.

Discussion of the rocky correspondence between the two authors, with some brief extracts from Atherton's letters.

493. Atkins, Mary, 1819-1882. American educator. Principal and proprietor of the Benecia Seminary for Young Ladies, the founding institution of Mills College. THE DIARY OF MARY ATKINS: A SABBATICAL IN THE 1860'S. Introduction by Aurelia Henry Reinhardt. Mills College: Eucalyptus Press, 1937. 46p.

Short diary of a cruise in the Pacific, from San Francisco to Shanghai, November 19, 1863--March 4, 1864.

494. Atkins, Thomasina, pseud. American. THE LETTERS OF THOMASINA ATKINS, BY A PRIVATE (W.A.C.) ON ACTIVE SERVICE. With a foreword by Mildred Aldrich. New York: George H. Doran Co., 1918. 162p.

War letters. "Thomasina Atkins" was a general nickname given to women in the active service.

495. Atkinson, Florence. American teacher who emigrated to Argentina. "The Diary of Florence Atkinson." Eugene G. Sharkey. JOURNAL OF THE RUTGERS UNIVERSITY LIBRARY 34:1 (1970), 23-27.

Discussion of the diary Atkinson kept in the 1880's as a teacher in Argentina.

496. Auger du Breuil, Anne. French author. AU GRE DES JOURS. Paris: Cercle Litteraire de l'Avenue Foch, 1981. 202p.

497. Augusta, Duchess of Saxe-Coburg-Saalfield, 1757-1831. IN NAPOLEONIC DAYS: EXTRACTS FROM THE PRIVATE DIARY OF AUGUSTA, DUCHESS OF SAXE-COBURG-SAALFIELD, QUEEN VICTORIA'S MATERNAL GRANDMOTHER, 1806-1821. Selected and translated by H.R.H. The Princess Beatrice. London: John Murray, 1941. 237p.

498. Austen, Jane, 1775-1817. English author. LETTERS OF JANE AUSTEN. Edited with an introduction and critical remarks by Edward, Lord Brabourne. London: R. Bentley & Sons, 1884. 2 vols.

First published edition of her letters.

499. ------. LETTERS OF JANE AUSTEN. Selected from the compilation of her nephew, Lord Brabourne, by Sarah Chauncey Woolsey. Boston: Little, Brown & Co., 1892, 1903. 333p.

500. ------. FIVE LETTERS FROM JANE AUSTEN TO HER NIECE, FANNY KNIGHT, PRINTED IN FACSIMILE. New York and Oxford: The Clarendon Press, 1924. 22p.

Edition of 250 copies. Letters to Lady Fanny Catherine Knight (1793-1882).

501. ------. THE LETTERS OF JANE AUSTEN. Selected with an introduction by R. Brimley Johnson. London: John Lane, and New York: Lincoln MacVeagh, the Dial Press, 1925. 190p.

Selections from the Lord Brabourne edition.

502. ------. JANE AUSTEN'S LETTERS TO HER SISTER CASSANDRA AND OTHERS. Edited and collected by R.W. Chapman. London and New York: Oxford University Press, 1932. Reprinted with corrections, 1964, 1979. 519p.

First complete edition.

503. ------. JANE AUSTEN: SELECTED LETTERS 1796-1817. Selected and edited by R.W. Chapman. London, New York and Toronto: Oxford University Press, 1955. 266p.

Selection of about one-third of Austen's letters, taken from item 502 above, designed as an introduction to her life and letters. Includes a section of letters from her sister, Cassandra Austen (1773-1845) to Fanny Knight on Austen's death.

504. ------. LETTERS AND MANUSCRIPTS IN THE PIERPONT MORGAN LIBRARY. The Pierpont Morgan Library, 1975. 30p. plus facsimiles (4p.).

Catalog of an exhibition held in 1975. Describes letters and prints an evocative sentence or two from each. Lists two letters by Cassandra Elizabeth Austen, and presents facsimiles of three letters.

505. Avakian, Elizabeth, b. 1943. American author and feminist. TO DELIVER ME OF MY DREAMS. Millbrae, Calif.: Les Femmes/Celestial Arts, 1975. 91p.

Journal begun as Avakian's Master's thesis in psychology. Explores the female point of view in psychology and literature, and her own growing consciousness as a feminist.

506. Ayer, Sarah Newman Connell, 1791-1835. American. DIARY OF SARAH CONNELL AYER. ANDOVER AND NEWBURYPORT, MASSACHUSETTS; CONCORD AND BOW, NEW HAMPSHIRE; PORTLAND AND EASTPORT, MAINE. Portland, Maine: Lefavor-Towwer Co., 1910. 404p.

Domestic and religious diary November, 1805--March, 1835.

507. Ayscough, Florence Wheelock, 1878-1942. American author and companion to American poet Amy Lowell. FLORENCE AYSCOUGH AND AMY LOWELL: CORRESPONDENCE OF A FRIENDSHIP. Edited with a preface by Harley Farnsworth MacNair. Chicago: University of Chicago Press, 1945. 288p.

Literary correspondence of Ayscough and Lowell, 1917-1925; of Ayscough and Ada Russell, 1925-1926; and selections from Lowell's correspondence with Harriet Monroe, 1918-1920.

508. Bacheracht, Thérèse von. German author. THÉRÈSE VON BACHERACHT UND KARL GUTZKNOW: UNVEROFFENTLICHTE BRIEFE (1842-1849). Herausgegeben von Werner Vordtriede. Munich: Kossell, 1971. 255p.

509. Backhouse, Hannah Chapman Gurney, 1787-1850. English Quaker. EXTRACTS FROM THE JOURNAL AND LETTERS OF HANNAH CHAPMAN BACKHOUSE. London: Privately Printed by R. Barrett, 1858. 291p.

Includes letters and diary of travels in the United States, 1830-1835.

510. Bacon, Alice Mabel, 1858-1918. American author and teacher in a school for girls in Japan. A JAPANESE INTERIOR. Boston: Houghton Mifflin Co., 1893. 272p.

Letters 1888-1889 describe life in Japan.

Bacon, Jane Meautys Cornwallis, Lady. See: Cornwallis, Jane Meautys, later Bacon.

511. Bacon, Lydia B. Stetson, 1786-1853. American wife of Lt. Josiah Bacon of the American Revolutionary Forces. THE BIOGRAPHY OF MRS. LYDIA B. BACON. Boston: Massachusetts Sabbath School Society, 1856. 348p.

Edited from her letters and journal, 1811-1853.

512. ------. "Mrs. Lydia B. Bacon's Journal, 1811-1812." Edited by Mary M. Crawford. INDIANA MAGAZINE OF HISTORY 59:4 (December, 1944), 376-386; and 60:1 (March, 1945), 59-79.

Bacon accompanied her husband on his tour of duty in the War of 1812. Her journal as it appears in THE BIOGRAPHY OF LYDIA B. BACON (1856) is heavily edited; this version is taken from the original manuscript.

513. Baerg, Anna. Russian-born Mennonite and immigrant to Canada after the Russian Revolution. "The Diary of Anna Baerg." Peter J. Dyck. MENNONITE LIFE 28:4 (1973), 121-125.

Extracts from her diary, 1917-1923.

514. Bagehot, Eliza Wilson, 1832-1921. English wife of historian Walter Bagehot. THE LOVE LETTERS OF WALTER BAGEHOT AND ELIZA WILSON, WRITTEN FROM 10 NOVEMBER, 1857 TO 23 APRIL, 1858. Edited by their sister, Mrs. Russell Barrington. London: Faber & Faber, 1933. 203p.

515. ------. "Surrender to Subservience: An Introduction to the Diaries and Journals of Eliza Wilson Bagehot." Sister A. Martha Westwater. INTERNATIONAL JOURNAL OF WOMEN'S STUDIES 1:5 (September-October, 1978), 517-529.

Discussion of her journal and diary, with extracts 1851-1921. Bagehot, the wife and daughter of famous men, is presented as an example of those women who should have been great but were not, because they were not able to overthrow the traditional assumptions of women's roles.

516. Bagnold, Enid Algerine, b. 1889. English novelist. A DIARY WITHOUT DATES. London: William Heinemann, 1918. New York: William Morrow, 1935. 145p. Reprinted with a new introduction by Monica Dickens, London: Virago Press, 1978. 127p.

Diary of hospital work during World War I.

517. ------. LETTERS TO FRANK HARRIS AND OTHER FRIENDS. Edited with an introduction by R.P. Lister. Andoversford, England: Whittington Press, and London: Heinemann, 1980. 77p.

518. Bailey, Abigail Abbot, 1746-1815. American. MEMOIRS OF MRS. ABIGAIL BAILEY, WHO HAD BEEN THE WIFE OF MAJOR ASA BAILEY...WRITTEN BY HERSELF...TO WHICH ARE

ADDED, SUNDRY ORIGINAL BIOGRAPHICAL SKETCHES. Edited by Ethan Smith. Boston: Samuel T. Armstrong, 1815. 275p.

Not properly a diary, but a reminiscence written as a journal account of her struggles with a husband who became increasingly violent and destructive. Bailey was eventually granted a divorce.

519. Baker, Florence, Lady. Hungarian explorer and wife of explorer Sir Samuel Baker. MORNING STAR: FLORENCE BAKER'S DIARY OF THE EXPEDITION TO PUT DOWN THE SLAVE TRADE ON THE NILE, 1870-1873. Anne Baker. Foreword by Sir Ronald Wingate. London: William Kimber, 1972. 240p.

Diary kept while traveling with her husband and his nephew, Julian Baker, in the region of the Upper Nile. Includes a biography, extensive notes, and explanatory text.

Baker, Ida Constance. See: L.M.

520. Baker, Janet. English opera singer. FULL CIRCLE: AN AUTOBIOGRAPHICAL JOURNAL. With photographs by Zoe Dominic. London: Julia Macrae / Franklin Watts, and New York: Franklin Watts, 1982. 270p.

Diary 1981-1982 of her final season of stage work, beginning with a production of ALCESTE in September, 1981, through a production of MARY STUART, and ending with her last perfomance in ORFEO in July, 1982. Baker kept the diary in response to requests to write her autobiography; she preferred instead to put one year of her life "under the microscope." Though a record of her last year, it's also representative: "a mixture of opera, concerts, recitals and travel."

521. Baker, Silvia. ALONE AND LOITERING: PAGES FROM AN ARTIST'S TRAVEL-DIARY, 1938-1944. With illustrations by the author and a comment by Clough Williams-Ellis. London: P. Davies, 1946. 163p.

522. Balascheff, Marie [Mariia Grigor'evna Dantakuzen

Balasheva]. Russian daughter of a member of the American Diplomatic Corps during the 1920's. THE TRANSPLANTING: A NARRATIVE FROM THE LETTERS OF MARIE BALASCHEFF, A RUSSIAN REFUGEE IN FRANCE. Edited by Martha Genung Stearns. New York: Macmillan Co., 1928. 251p.

Journal-letters written to a friend in the U.S. July-15, 1923--August, 1925, describe refugee life in Constantinople, Serbia, and finally France. Partly reminiscences, partly a daily record of life in Le Crotoy, France, where she settled.

Balch, Emily Tapscott Clark. See: Clark, Emily.

523. Baldwin, Abigail Pollard, 1798-1876. American wife of a Presbyterian minister. "Selections from the Plymouth Diary of Abigail Baldwin, 1853-1854." VERMONT HISTORY 40:3 (Summer, 1972), 218-223.

Extracts from a diary written after her return home from a twenty-month residence in Texas, a place she loathed and called "a land of little gratitude." Details of daily life, religious thoughts, and her great relief to be home despite a harsh Vermont winter and family tragedy.

524. Baldwin, Marian. American. CANTEENING OVERSEAS, 1917-1919. New York: The Macmillan Co., 1920. 200p.

War letters June 30, 1917--June 9, 1919, of a Y.M.C.A. volunteer working in France.

525. Ball, Hannah, 1733-1792. English devout. MEMOIRS OF MISS HANNAH BALL...EXTRACTED FROM HER DIARY OF THIRTY YEARS EXPERIENCE; IN WHICH THE DEVICES OF SATAN ARE LAID OPEN, THE GRACIOUS DEALINGS OF GOD WITH HER SOUL, AND ALL HIS SUFFICIENT GRACE, ARE EXEMPLIFIED IN HER USEFUL LIFE AND HAPPY DEATH. Joseph Cole. York: Wilson, Spence, & Mawman, 1796. 71p. Revised and enlarged by John Parker, with a preface by the Reverend Thomas Jackson, London: John Mason, 1839. 180p.

Religious diary, 1767-1792.

526. Ballard, Martha Moore, 1735-1812. American midwife. THE HISTORY OF AUGUSTA, MAINE. VOLUME ONE: FIRST SETTLEMENT AND EARLY DAYS AS A TOWN, 1607-1847. INCLUDING THE DIARY OF MRS. MARTHA MOORE BALLARD, 1785 TO 1812. Edited by Charles Elventon Nash. Augusta, Maine: Charles E. Nash & Son, 1904. 612p.

Contains extracts from the diary of Martha Ballard, 1785-1812. Domestic diary, including town news and gossip, and accounts of her work as a midwife.

527. Balléroy, Charlotte Madeléine Émilie Le Fébvre de Caumartin, Marquise de la Cour de Balléroy, d. 1749. French letter-writer and wife of the first Marquis of Balleroy. LES CORRESPONDANTS DE LA MARQUISE DE BALLÉROY. D'Après les originaux inedits de la Bibliotheque Nazarine, avec des notes et une introduction historique sur le maisons de Caumartin et de Balléroy. Par le Comte Edouard de Barthèlemy. Paris: Hachette et Cie., 1883. 2 vols.

Letters of an important French eighteenth-century letter writer, to the Baron de Breteuil, the Abbot of Guitaut, the Chevalier de Girardin, and others.

528. Ballou, Mary. American frontier settler in California. I HEAR THE HOGS IN MY KITCHEN: A WOMAN'S VIEW OF THE GOLD RUSH. Edited by Archibald Hanna. New Haven, Conn.: Yale University Press, printed for Frederick W. Beinecke, 1962. 13p.

Extract from a journal, December 1851, and a letter to her son, October 30, 1852. Describes the voyage to California via Panama, and life on the California frontier.

529. Bancroft, Elizabeth Davis, b. 1803. American wife of historian and statesman George Bancroft. LETTERS FROM ENGLAND, 1846-1849. New York: Charles Scribner's Sons, 1904. 224p.

Social letters of a diplomat's wife, written in the form of a diary and sent to relatives in the U.S.

530. Banning, Margaret Culkin, b. 1891. American novelist. SALUD! A SOUTH AMERICAN JOURNAL. With drawings by Rafaelo Busoni. New York and London: Harper & Bros., 1941. 372p.

Travel diary, January 18--February 27, 1941, written while traveling through Columbia, Ecuador, Peru, Chile, Argentina and Brazil.

531. ------. LETTERS FROM ENGLAND, SUMMER, 1942. New York and London: Harper & Bros., 1943. 315p.

Letters written while travelling in England just before the U.S entered World War II, June 5--July 1, 1942, as part of a goodwill effort to further relations between the English and American people. She tours factories, attends Red Cross meetings, meets literary and political luminaries, and comments a great deal om women and war work.

532. Barbour, Martha Isabella Hopkins, 1824-1888. American. JOURNALS OF THE LATE BREVET MAJOR PHILIP NORBOURNE BARBOUR, CAPTAIN IN THE 3RD REGIMENT, UNITED STATES INFANTRY, AND HIS WIFE, MARTHA ISABELLA HOPKINS BARBOUR, WRITTEN DURING THE WAR WITH MEXICO, 1846. Edited by Rhoda Van Bibber Tanner Doubleday. New York and London: G.P. Putnam's Sons, 1936. 187p.

Diary July 1--October 4, 1846 kept while staying with relatives in Texas while her husband fought in the War with Mexico. Much of the diary deals with her husband, her pride in his advancement in the military, and how much she misses him; her own life is one of genteel domesticity--"As usual I have been sewing, reading, and sleeping"--she ends one entry. Her husband was killed in battle in 1846.

533. Barclay, Grace [pseud. for Lydia Minturn Post]. American wife of an Officer in the American Revolutionary Forces. GRACE BARCLAY'S DIARY; OR, PERSONAL RECOLLECTIONS OF THE AMERICAN REVOLUTION. A PRIVATE JOURNAL PREPARED FROM AUTHENTIC DOMESTIC SOURCES. Edited by Sidney Barclay (pseud.). New York: Anson

D.F. Randolph, 1859, 1866. 251p. New York: Rudd & Carleton, 1859. Reprinted, Port Washington, N.Y.: The Kennikat Press, 1970.

Diary 1776-1783, including description of the occupation of Long Island by the British.

534. Barkley, Frances Hornby Barkley, d. 1845. Wife of Captain William Barkley, a trader who discovered the Strait of Juan de Fuca. "The Mystery of Mrs. Barkley's Diary: Notes on the Voyage of the 'Imperial Eagle,' 1786-1787." BRITISH COLUMBIA HISTORICAL QUARTERLY 6:1 (1942), 31-47.

Barkley was the first European woman to visit the Pacific Northwest. Documents the mystery of her diary, which was written on a the Voyage of 1786-1787 and which is thought to have been destroyed in a fire in 1909. Seeks to prove the diary did exist, citing collateral quotes and textual evidence that her reminiscences were written from a diary.

535. ------. "Documents Relating to the Mystery of Mrs. Barkley's Diary. I: Extracts from the Diaries of Frances Hornby Barkley. II: Extracts from the Reminiscences of Frances Hornby Barkley." BRITISH COLUMBIA HISTORICAL QUARTERLY 6:1 (1942), 49-59.

Presents extracts from portions of her diary which were published, comparing them to parallel sections of her reminiscences.

536. Barnard, Anne Lindsay, Lady, 1750-1825. Scottish author and poet. SOUTH AFRICA A CENTURY AGO: LETTERS WRITTEN FROM THE CAPE OF GOOD HOPE (1797-1801) BY THE LADY ANNE BARNARD. Edited with a memoir and brief notes by W.H. Wilkins. London: Smith, Elder & Co., 1901. 316p.

Memoir followed by letters, chiefly to Henry Dundas. Describes life in colonial South Africa; she married Sir Andrew Barnard, first Colonial Secretary to the Colony of the Cape of Good Hope. Lady Barnard acted as First Lady of Cape Colony, performing many of the social duties which usually fell to the wife of the Governor.

537. ------. BARNARD LETTERS, 1778-1824. Edited by Anthony Powell. London: Duckworth, 1928. 319p.

Letters by Sir Andrew Francis Barnard, Thomas Barnard, and Lady Anne Barnard. Lady Anne's letters date from 1806 (Sir Andrew died in 1807).

538. ------. LETTERS OF LADY ANNE BARNARD TO HENRY DUNDAS FROM THE CAPE AND ELSEWHERE, 1793-1803; TOGETHER WITH HER JOURNAL OF A TOUR INTO THE INTERIOR AND CERTAIN OTHER LETTERS. Newly edited with an introduction and notes by A.M. Levin Robinson. Cape Town: A.A. Balkema, 1973. 303p.

Henry Dundas was Secretary of State for War, Treasurer of the British Navy, and President of the Board of Control, during the earliest period of British occupation of South Africa.

539. Barnitz, Jennie Platt, 1841-1927. American army wife. LIFE IN CUSTER'S CALVARY: DIARIES AND LETTERS OF ALBERT AND JENNIE BARNITZ, 1867-1868. Edited by Robert M. Utley. London and New Haven, Conn.: Yale University Press, 1977. 302p.

Extracts from their letters and diaries, edited together chronologically to give an account of Army life on the American frontier.

540. Barr, Amelia Edith Huddleston, 1831-1919. American novelist. ALL THE DAYS OF MY LIFE: AN AUTOBIOGRAPHY. THE RED LEAVES OF A HUMAN HEART. New York and London: D. Appleton, 1913. 527p.

Autobiography; describes life as the daughter of an English Methodist minister, emigrating to the United States, work as a teacher and a writer. Includes extracts from a Civil War diary, and diary extracts dealing with her writing.

541. Barrington, Emilie Isabel Wilson. English. THROUGH GREECE AND DALMATIA: A DIARY OF IMPRESSIONS RECORDED BY PEN & PICTURE. London: Adam and Charles Black, 1912. 263p.

Travel diary, written in September of an unspecified year.

542. Bascom, Ruth Henshaw, 1722-1848. American artist. "Diaries." In SOME AMERICAN PRIMITIVES: A STUDY OF NEW ENGLAND FACES AND FOLK PORTRAITS. Clara E. Sears. Boston, 1941. Reprinted, Port Washington, New York, the Kennikat Press, 1968. p.118-125.

Brief extracts from her diary, 1830-1837, concerning portraits she painted during that time.

543. ------. A NEW ENGLAND WOMAN'S PERSPECTIVE ON NORFOLK, VIRGINIA, 1801-1802: EXCERPTS FROM THE DIARY OF RUTH HENSHAW BASCOM. Edited, with an introduction, by A.C. Roeber. Worcester, Mass.: American Antiquarian Society, 1979. Reprinted from the PROCEEDINGS OF THE AMERICAN ANTIQUARIAN SOCIETY 88:2 (October, 1979), 277-325.

544. Bashkirtseff, Marie [Mariia Konstantinova Bashkirtseva], 1860-1884. Russian-French artist. Her diary, which she wrote for posterity, is a classic in the genre of the French Journal Intime. THE JOURNAL OF A YOUNG ARTIST. Translated by Mary J. Serrano. New York: Cassell & Co., 1889. 434p.

545. ------. JOURNAL OF MARIE BASHKIRTSEFF. Translated from the French by A.D. Hall and G.B. Heckel. Chicago and New York: Rand, McNally & Co., 1890. 825p.

Diary 1873-1884, begining when Bashkirtseff was twelve, and continuing to her death in 1884 of tuberculosis. Her adolescent diary describes the life of a Russian Emigre family in Paris; school, social affairs and friendships. Her later diary describes Parisian social, literary and artistic circles. Her diary is intensely introspective and self-conscious; Bashkirtseff was very concerned with diary writing as a creative activity and as a record for posterity.

546. ------. LETTERS OF MARIE BASHKIRTSEFF. Translated by Mary J. Serrano. New York: Cassell Publishing Co., 1891. 340p.

Letters 1868-1891, to her family and to Emile Zola, Baron Saint-Amand, M. Edmond de Goncort, and others.

547. ------. LAST CONFESSIONS OF MARIE BASHKIRTSEFF, AND HER CORRESPONDENCE WITH GUY DE MAUPASSANT. With a foreword by Jeanette L. Gilder. New York: Frederick A. Stokes Co., 1901. 157p. Also published as THE FURTHER MEMOIRS OF MARIE BASHKIRTSEFF, TOGETHER WITH A CORRESPONDENCE BETWEEN GUY DE MAUPASSANT AND MARIE BASHKIRTSEFF. London: G. Richards, 1901. 172p.

Extracts from her journal, 1883-1884, with selections from her correspondence with de Maupassant for the same period.

548. ------. THE NEW JOURNAL OF MARIE BASHKIRTSEFF: FROM CHILDHOOD TO GIRLHOOD. Translated by Mary J. Safford. New York: Dodd, Mead & Co., 1912. 141p.

549. ------. LETTRES DE MARIE BASHKIRTSEFF. Avec quatre portraits, des autographes et une préface par Francois Coppée. Paris: Bibliothèque Charpentier, 1922. 282p.

550. ------. I KISS YOUR HANDS: THE LETTERS OF GUY DE MAUPASSANT AND MARIE BASHKIRTSEFF. Illustrated by Danuta Laskowska. London: Rodale Press, 1954. 47p.

Part of a series of illustrated miniature books.

551. ------. THE JOURNAL OF MARIE BASHKIRTSEFF. Translated by Mathilde Blind. With a new introduction by Rozsika Parker and Griselda Pollock. London: Virago Press, 1985. 716p.

552. Bassett, Hannah, 1815-1855. American Quaker. MEMOIRS OF HANNAH BASSETT, WITH EXTRACTS FROM THE DIARY. Lynn, Mass.: W.W. Kellogg, Printer, 1860. 72p.

Quaker diary.

553. Bayard, Martha Pintard. American wife of an Ambassador to England during the American Revolution. JOURNAL OF MARTHA PINTARD BAYARD, LONDON, 1794-1797. Edited by Samuel Bayard Dodd. New York: Dodd, Mead & Co., 1894. 141p. Reprinted by Scholarly Press, 1976.

Social diary by a diplomat's wife.

554. Bayly, Katherine, 1721-1774. Irish. "Diary." PROCEEDINGS OF THE ROYAL SOCIETY OF ANTIQUARIES OF IRELAND, 5th Series, Volume 8 (1898), 141-154.

Biography and extracts from her diary, October, 1721--April, 1756 describe domestic and society life in Dublin. According to Matthews (BRITISH DIARIES) her diary is particularly interesting for its description of plays and the theatre.

555. Beard, Mary Payne. American mother of historian Charles Beard. "Old School Days on the Middle Border, 1849-1859: The Mary Payne Beard Letters." Edited by Peter A. Soderbergh. HISTORY OF EDUCATION QUARTERLY 8:4 (1968), 497-504.

Presents two letters from Beard to her son.

556. Beaumarchais, Marie-Thérèse Amelie Willermaula (or Willermawla) Caron, Dame de, 1751-1816. French wife of Pierre Augustin Caron de Beaumarchais. MADAME DE BEAUMARCHAIS, D'APRÈS SA CORRESPONDENCE INÉDITE. Louis Bonneville de Marsangy. Paris: Calmann Lévy, 1890.

557. ------. LETTRES INÉDITES DE BEAUMARCHAIS, DE MADAME DE BEAUMARCHAIS, ET LEUR FILLE EUGENIÉ. Publiées d'apres les origineaux de la "Clements Library" par Gilbert Chinard. Paris: A. Margraff; and Baltimore: The Johns Hopkins Press, 1929. 139p.

558. Beauvoir, Simone de, b.1908. French author, philosopher, and long-time companion of Jean-Paul Sartre. L'AMERIQUE AU JOUR LE JOUR. Paris: P. Morihien, 1948. 390p.

559. ------. AMERICA DAY BY DAY: JANUARY--May, 1947. Translated by Patrick Dudley. New York: Grove Press, 1953. 337p.

Diary of travel in America. Retrospectively written, reconstructed from notes, letters, and memory, "but scrupulously exact. I have respected the chronological order of my astonishments, admirations, indignations, hesitations, and mistakes."

560. Beck, Frances. American. THE DIARY OF A WIDOW. Boston: Beacon Press, 1965. 142p.

561. Bedford, Mary du Caurroy Tribe, Duchess of, 1865-1937. THE FLYING DUCHESS: THE DIARIES AND LETTERS OF MARY, DUCHESS OF BEDFORD. Edited with an introduction by John, Duke of Bedford. London: MacDonald, 1968. 216p.

562. Beemer, Eleanor. American. MY LUISENO NEIGHBORS: EXCERPTS FROM A JOURNAL KEPT IN PAUMA VALLEY, NORTHERN SAN DIEGO COUNTY, 1934 TO 1974. Ramona, Calif.: Acoma Books, 1980. 91p.

563. Belknap, Kitturah Penton, 1820-1913. American frontier settler. "Family Life on the Frontier: The Diary of Kitturah Penton Belknap." Edited by Glenda Riley. ANNALS OF IOWA 44:1 (Summer, 1977), 31-51.

Chronicles her family's 1839 journey by covered wagon from Ohio to an Iowa homestead near the Des Moines River, and life there to 1847. In 1848, the family moved westward to Oregon.

564. Bell, Deborah, 1668/9-1738. English Quaker and wife of John Bell. A SHORT JOURNAL OF THE LABOURS AND TRAVELS OF THAT FAITHFUL SERVANT OF CHRIST, DEBORAH BELL. London: Printed and sold by Luke Hinde, at the Bible in George-Yard, Lombard Street, 1762. 71p.

Quaker diary, 1707-1737; account of travels and ministry in England.

565. ------. A SHORT JOURNAL OF THE LABOURS AND TRAVELS IN THE WORK OF THE MINISTRY OF CHRIST, DEBORAH BELL. London: J. Phillips, 1776. 100p.

566. ------. "Journal." FRIENDS LIBRARY 5 (1841), 1-23.

567. Bell, Gertrude Margaret Lowthian, 1868-1926. English scholar, poet, archeologist, art critic, linguist, explorer, and British Civil Servant in the Middle East. LETTERS OF GERTRUDE BELL. Selected and edited by Lady Bell (Florence Eveleen Eleanore Oliffe Bell). New York: Boni and Liveright, 1927. 2 vols.

Letters 1874-1926 give an account of Bell's youth and school days, her travels to what was then Persia, mountaineering excavations with Sir William Ramsay in Asia Minor, her years as Oriental Secretary, and her experiences during World War I.

568. ------. THE EARLIER LETTERS OF GERTRUDE BELL. Edited and collected by Elsa Richmond. London: E. Benn; New York: Liveright Publishing Corp, 1937. 347p.

Letters from her early years which had not come to light when the previous volume was in preparation. Letters 1868-1892 describe her school days, early friendships, college, and life in Roumania, England, and Iran (Persia).

569. Belloc, Elizabeth Rayner Parkes, 1828-1924. English feminist, suffragist, and journalist. I, TOO, HAVE LIVED IN ARCADIA: A RECORD OF LOVE AND CHILDHOOD. Marie Belloc Lowndes. New York: Dodd, Mead & Co., 1942. 318p.

First volume of Marie Belloc-Lowndes' autobiography, in which she tells the story of her mother's marriage and widowhood. Based on and includes extracts from the diaries of Elizabeth Parkes Belloc with her mother and mother-in-law, 1867-1881.

570. Bender, Flora Isabelle, b. 1848. American frontier settler. "Notes by the Way: Memoranda of a Journey Across the Plains from Bell Creek, Washington County, to Virginia City, Nevada Territory, May 7 to August 4, 1863." NEVADA HISTORICAL SOCIETY QUARTERLY 1:4 (July, 1958), 144-174p.

Diary by the fifteen-year-old daughter of a tailor-turned-farmer who moved the family to Nevada for health reasons, and to get a better education for his children.

571. Benedict, Ruth Fulton, 1887-1948. American anthropologist. AN ANTHROPOLOGIST AT WORK: THE WRITINGS OF RUTH BENEDICT. Edited by Margaret Mead. New York: Houghton Mifflin, 1951. 583p.

Short anthropological writings; selected correspondence with Mead, Edward Sapir and Franz Boaz; letters from the field; extracts from her diaries and journals, and other autobiographical writings.

572. ------. "The Unconfined Role of the Human Imagination: A Selection of Letters. Richard Chase and Ruth Benedict, 1945-1946." Judith Modell. AMERICAN STUDIES 23:2 (Fall, 1982), 49-65.

In 1945, Chase asked Benedict to serve on his dissertation committee. They discussed his dissertation by mail, with "special frankness and heat" once Benedict had tactfully resigned from the committee. The letters are reproduced in facsimile.

573. Benedictsson, Victoria, 1850-1888. Swedish Author. STORA BOKEN. Utg. under redaktion av Christina Sjoblad. [S.L.]: Cavefors, 1978.

Diary 1882-1884.

574. Benson, Margaret, 1865-1916. LIFE AND LETTERS OF MAGGIE BENSON. By her brother, Arthur Christopher Benson. London and New York: Longmans; and London: John Murray, 1917. 445p.

575. Benson, Stella, d. 1933. British novelist. "Stella Benson: Letters to Laura Hulton, 1915-1919." Edited with an introduction by William Brandon. THE MASSACHUSETTS REVIEW 25:2 (Summer, 1984), 225-246.

Letters to long-time friend Laura Hulton, a physician and psychiatrist, whom Benson had met through her work in the Suffrage Movement. The letters printed here were chiefly written from the United States.

576. Bentley, Anna Briggs. American Quaker frontier settler. "Correspondence of Anna Briggs Bentley from Columbia County, 1826." Edited by Bayly Ellen Marks. OHIO HISTORY 78 (Winter, 1969), 38-45.

Diary-letter, August 17-27, 1826, extracted from a voluminous unpublished correspondence. Gives a woman's view of frontier life in Ohio. Bentley had travelled there with her husband, by wagon and on foot.

577. Bentley, Toni. American dancer with the New York City Ballet. WINTER SEASON: A DANCER'S JOURNAL. New York: Random House, 1982. 150p.

578. Berenson, Mary Smith Costelloe, 1864-1945. American art critic and wife of art critic Bernard Berenson. MARY BERENSON: A SELF-PORTRAIT FROM HER LETTERS AND DIARIES. Edited by Barbara Strachey and Jayne Samuels. London: Victor Gollancz, 1983. 319p. New York: W.W. Norton, 1984. 336p.

579. Berg, Mary, b. 1924. Polish Jew. WARSAW GHETTO: A DIARY. New York: L.B. Fisher, 1945. 253p.

Berkeley, Elizabeth, later Margravine of Anspach. See: Anspach, Elizabeth Berkeley, Margravine of.

580. Berkeley, Maud, 1859-1949. English. MAUD: THE DIARY OF A VICTORIAN WOMAN. Adapted by Flora Fraser. Introduction by Elizabeth Longford. San Francisco: Chronicle Books, 1985. 192p.

581. Bernstein, Aline Frankau, 1881-1955. American

stage and costume designer. MY OTHER LONELINESS: LETTERS OF THOMAS WOLFE AND ALINE BERNSTEIN. Edited by Suzanne Stutman. Chapel Hill, N.C.: University of North Carolina Press, 1983. 390p.

Letters 1925-1932 record a love affair between two talented and complex artists, and give a picture of the literary and dramatic circles of the period.

582. Berry, Katherine Fiske, b. 1877; and Maria Berry. Americans. Daughter and mother of a Maine family of missionaries to Japan. KATIE-SAN: FROM MAINE PASTURES TO JAPAN SHORES. Cambridge, Mass.: Dresser, Chapman & Grimes, 1962. 285p.

Account of missionary work in Japan through Maria Berry's diaries and letters, 1877-1890; Katie's diaries and letters, 1890-1893; and Katie's letters home from a return visit to Japan, 1919-1920. Since Katie was an only child, much of her mother's writings concern her.

583. Berry, Mary, 1763-1852. British author. EXTRACTS OF THE JOURNALS AND CORRESPONDENCE OF MISS BERRY FROM THE YEAR 1783 TO 1852. Edited by Lady Theresa Lewis. London: Longmans, Green, 1865. 3 vols. Reprinted, New York: AMS Press, 1971. 3 vols.

Extracts from a journal Berry kept as a "sort of shorthand account" of her life, and correspondence with the Duchess of Devonshire, the Princess of Wales, Madame de Stael, Lady Elizabeth Stuart, and others. Journal extracts and letters are edited together chronologically.

584. ------. VOYAGES DE MISS BERRY À PARIS, 1782-1836. Traduit par Mme. la Duchesse de Broglie. Paris: A Boblot, 1905. 314p.

Excerpts from EXTRACTS FROM THE JOURNALS AND CORRESPONDENCE OF MISS BERRY..., relating to her travels in France.

585. ------. THE BERRY PAPERS. BEING THE

CORRESPONDENCE HITHERTO UNPUBLISHED OF MARY AND AGNES BERRY, 1763-1852. Lewis Melville. London: John Lane, the Bodley Head; and New York: John Lane Co., 1914. 448p.

Includes material not in the Lewis edition. Chiefly letters between Mary and Agnes Berry (1764-1852), with letters from Maria Edgeworth and Thomas and Jane Welsh Carlyle, and a long series of letters exchanged between Mary Berry and the Hon. Mrs. Damer.

586. ------. HORACE WALPOLE'S CORRESPONDENCE WITH AGNES AND MARY BERRY AND BARBARA CECILIA SETON. Edited by W.S. Lewis and A. Dayle Wallace, with the assistance of Charles H. Bennett and Edwine M. Martz. New Haven, Conn.: Yale University Press and London: Humphrey Milford, Oxford University Press, 1944. 2 vols. (The Yale Edition of Horace Walpole's Correspondence, Vols. 11, 12.)

Volume 1 includes letters to and from Mary and Agnes Berry (1764-1852), October 14, 1788--December, 1791.

587. Bettle, Jane, 1773-1840. American Pennsylvania Quaker. EXTRACTS FROM THE MEMORANDUMS OF JANE BETTLE, WITH A SHORT MEMOIR RESPECTING HER. Second edition. Philadelphia: J. and Kite, 1843. 116p.

Contains extracts from a Quaker Journal.

588. Bevington, Helen Smith, b. 1906. American poet, essayist and professor of English at Duke University. ALONG CAME THE WITCH: A JOURNAL IN THE 1960'S. New York: Harcourt Brace Jovanovich, 1976. 223p.

Literary notebook 1960-1969, containing essays, poems, and journal entries.

589. ------. THE JOURNEY IS EVERYTHING: A JOURNAL OF THE SEVENTIES. Durham, N.C.: Duke University Press, 1983. 208p.

Literary notebook of essays, poems, and journal entries, arranged in monthly segments.

590. Bibesco, Marthe Lucie Lahovary, Princesse, b. 1887. Roumanian novelist and essayist. LA VIE D'UNE AMITIÉ: MA CORRESPONDANCE AVEC L'ABBE MUGNIER, 1911-1944. Paris: Librarie Plon, 1951-1955. 2 vols.

591. Bigelow, Glenna Lindsley. American. LIÉGE, ON THE LINE OF MARCH: AN AMERICAN GIRL'S EXPERIENCE WHEN THE GERMANS CAME TO BELGIUM. New York: John Lane, 1918. 156p.

Diary of life in Belgium during World War I.

592. Birchall, Emily Jowitt, 1852-1884. English gentlewoman. THE DIARY OF A COUNTRY SQUIRE: EXTRACTS FROM THE DIARIES AND LETTERS OF DEARMAN AND EMILY BIRCHALL. Chosen and introduced by David Very. Gloucester: Alan Sutton Publishing Co., 1983. 242p.

Extracts from the letters and diary of Emily, the wife of Dearman Birchall, 1872-1884. Describes the life of an English country gentlewoman and her family.

593. Bird, Isabella [Isabella Lucy Bird Bishop], 1831-1904. English traveller and philanthropist. THE ENGLISHWOMAN IN AMERICA. London: John Murray, 1856. 464p. New edition, with a foreword and notes by Andrew Hill Clark. Madison: University of Wisconsin Press, 1966. 497p.

Lively chronicle of travel in North America, based on her journal and letters.

594. ------. A LADY'S LIFE IN THE ROCKY MOUNTAINS. London: John Murray, 1879. New edition, with an introduction by Daniel Boorstin. Norman, Okla.: University of Okalahoma Press, 1960. 249p.

Letters written in the autumn and early winter of

1873 as Bird travelled by train and horseback from California across the Rocky Moutains to Denver. She participates in a cattle roundup and is trapped by bad weather for a month, living in a mountain cabin with a young miner.

595. ------. UNBEATEN TRACKS IN JAPAN: AN ACCOUNT OF TRAVELS ON HORSEBACK IN THE INTERIOR, INCLUDING VISITS TO THE ABORIGINES OF YEZO AND THE SHRINES OF NIKKO AND ISE. London: John Murray, 1880. 2 vols.

Travel letters written on a trip she undertook in 1878 for health reasons. She travelled for some months in the interior of the main island of Japan. From Nikko northwards, her route was "altogether off the beaten track, and had never been traversed in its entirety by any European."

596. ------. THE HAWAIIAN ARCHEPELAGO: SIX MONTHS AMONG THE PALM GROVES, CORAL REEFS AND VOLCANOES OF THE SANDWICH ISLANDS. Second edtion. John Murray, 1876 and New York G.P. Putnam's Sons, 1881. 318p. Reprinted with the title SIX MONTHS IN THE SANDWICH ISLANDS BY ISABELLA LUCY BIRD. Honolulu, Hawaii: University of Hawaii Press for Friends of the Library Hawaii, 1964. 278p.

Letters written to a "near relation" in England, probably her sister, and printed as they were written, with a few omissions and abridgments. Again travelling for her health, she journeyed from Hawaii to the mainland United States, across the Rocky Mountains to Denver, Colorado. The latter part of this trip is described in A LADY'S LIFE IN THE ROCKY MOUNTAINS.

597. ------. JOURNEYS IN PERSIA AND KURDISTAN. INCLUDING A SUMMER IN THE UPPER KARUN REGION AND A VISIT TO THE NESTORIAN RAYAHS. New York: G.P. Putnam's Sons, and London: John Murray, 1891. 2 vols.

Diary-letters January 1--December 13, 1890.

598. ------. AMONG THE TIBETANS. With illustrations by Edward Whymper. London: Religious Tract Society, and New York and Chicago: Fleming H. Revell Co., 1894. 159p.

599. ------. THE YANGTZEE VALLEY AND BEYOND: AN ACCOUNT OF TRAVELS IN CHINA, CHIEFLY IN THE PROVINCE OF SZE CHUAN AND AMONG THE MANT-TZE OF THE SOMO TERRITORY. London: John Murray, 1899. 557p. New York: G.P. Putnam's Sons, 1900. 2 vols.

Diary-letters, photographs, and notes from a brief diary, edited to form a travelogue of journeys in China, undertaken for recreation and interest, after some months of "severe travelling" in Korea. Entries are not dated.

600. ------. JOURNEY TO TRUCKEE. REPRINTED FROM A LADY'S LIFE IN THE ROCKY MOUNTAINS; A SERIES OF LETTERS WRITTEN BY ISABELLA LUCY BIRD TO HER SISTER IN ENGLAND, AND PUBLISHED IN 1879 BY JOHN MURRAY, LONDON. Berkeley, Calif.: The Elkus Press, 1945. 13p.

Birney, Josephine Young Churchill. See: Young, Josephine.

601. Bishop, Elizabeth, 1911-1979. American poet; and Marianne Moore, 1887-1972, American poet. "Words Worth a Thousands Postcards: The Bishop/Moore Correspondence." Lynn Keller. AMERICAN LITERATURE 55:3 (October, 1983), 405-429.

Extracts from the Bishop-Moore correspondence reveals the extent of Moore's influence on Bishop's poetry, and a strong friendship between the two poets which lasted until Moore's death.

Bishop, Isabella Lucy Bird. See: Bird, Isabella.

602. Bishop, Nan; Sarah Hamilton, and Clare Bowman. Americans. NAN, SARAH AND CLARE: LETTERS BETWEEN

FRIENDS. New York: Avon Books, 1980. 300p.

Letters between women who became friends in 1966 while all three were drama students. They went their separate ways in 1967, but their lives took parallel courses. The six months of correspondence, begun in 1977, covers a crucial period of readjustment and reassessment in all three women's lives.

603. Blackford, Susan Leigh, 1833-1903. American southern Confederate landowner. MEMOIRS IN AND OUT OF THE ARMY IN VIRGINIA DURING THE WAR BETWEEN THE STATES. Compiled by Mrs. Susan Leigh Blackford from original and contemporaneous correspondence and diaries and edited exclusively for the private use of their family by her husband, Charles Minor Blackford. Lynchburg, Va.: J.P. Bell Co., Printers, 1894-1896. 2 vols.

Letters between Charles and Susan Blackford, 1816-1865.

604. ------. LETTERS FROM LEE'S ARMY: MEMOIRS OF LIFE IN AND OUT OF THE ARMY IN VIRGINIA DURING THE WAR BETWEEN THE STATES. Annotated by Charles Minor Blackford. Edited and abridged for publication by Charles Minor Blackford III. New York: Charles Scribner's Sons, 1947. 312p.

Abridged version of the 1894 edition.

605. Blackmore, Rebeccah Crosthwaite Ridley, d. 1864. American Civil War diarist. "Behind the Lines in Middle Tennessee, 1863-1865: The Journal of Bettie Ridley Blackmore." Edited by Sarah Ridley Trimble. TENNESSEE HISTORICAL QUARTERLY 12:1 (March, 1953), 48-80.

Vivid description of life behind Union Lines. Her husband, George Blackmore, and four of her brothers were serving in the Confederate Army. Her mother continued the diary to February 12, 1865, after Blackmore's death in 1864.

606. Blaine, Catherine, 1829-1908. American teacher

and wife of the first Methodist minister in Seattle, Washington. MEMOIRS OF PUGET SOUND: EARLY SEATTLE, 1853-1856. THE LETTERS OF DAVID AND CATHERINE BLAINE. Edited by Richard A. Seiber. Fairfield, Wash.: Ye Galleon Press, 1978. 220p.

Courtship letters, and letters to relatives during the early years of her marriage describe life in frontier Seattle, church work, and teaching at Seattle's first public school. Includes Blaine's journal of the voyage from the East Coast to Seattle via the Isthmus of Panama.

607. Blaine, Harriet Bailey Stanwood, 1828-1903. American wife of James G. Blaine, Secretary of State under Presidents James A. Garfield and Chester A. Arthur. LETTERS OF MRS. JAMES G. BLAINE. Edited by Harriet S. Blaine Beale. New York: Duffield & Co., 1908. 2 vols.

Letters 1869-1899. Memorial edition intended for family members. A comment from the introduction is perhaps significant: "With gratitude I realize that she, who never gave a thought to herself, living only the lives of others, who was content to be used, absorbed, obliterated if need be, in her service of love, lives once more in these rescued leaves...."

608. Blake, Catherine. Canadian wife of William Hume Blake, Solicitor-General under the Baldwin-La Fontaine Administration. "Notes and Documents: The Riots of 1849 in Montreal." CANADIAN HISTORICAL REVIEW 15 (1934), 283-288.

Short diary account of the April, 1849 riots in Montreal caused by Lord Elgin's assent to the Rebellion Losses Bill.

609. Blessington, Marguerite Power Farmer Gardiner, Countess of, 1789-1849. British diarist, novelist and social figure. JOURNAL OF A TOUR THROUGH THE NETHERLANDS TO PARIS, IN 1821. London: Printed for Longman, Hurst, Rees, Orme and Brown, 1822. 171p.

610. ------. THE IDLER IN ITALY. London: H. Colburn, 1839. 3 vols.

Travel diary.

611. ------. THE IDLER IN FRANCE. London: Henry Colburn, Publisher, 1841. 2 vols.

Travel diary.

612. ------. THE LITERARY LIFE AND CORRESPONDENCE OF THE COUNTESS OF BLESSINGTON. London: T.C. Newby, 1855. 3 vols. New York: Harper & Bros., 1855. 2 vols.

Volume 1 is a biography based on and including extracts from her personal writings. Volume 2 contains her correspondence with Teresa Gamba Gucciola (later La Marquise de Boissy), Letitia Elizabeth Landor, Walter Savage Landor, the Duke of Wellington, Sir Edward Bulwer-Lytton, Captain Maryatt and Madame du Deffand.

613. ------. A JOURNAL OF CONVERSATIONS WITH LORD BYRON. Boston: W. Veazie, 1859. 381p.

Not precisely a journal, but a record of conversations with Byron, based on her diary kept at Genoa, April-July, 1823.

614. ------. LADY BLESSINGTON AT NAPLES. Edited by Edith Clay. Introduction by Sir Harold Acton. London: Hamish Hamilton, 1979. 170p.

Abridged selection from THE IDLER IN ITALY, 1823-1826. Social and travel diary.

Blixen, Karen Dinesen, Baroness. See: Dinesen, Isak.

615. Blood, Jane Wilkie Hooper, 1845-1898. American Mormon frontier settler. JANE WILKIE HOOPER BLOOD: AUTOBIOGRAPHY AND ABRIDGED DIARY. Edited by Ivy Hooper Blood. Logan: J.P. Smith Printing, 1966.

Mormon diary, 1880-1898.

616. Blücher von Wahlstatt, Evelyn Mary Stapleton-Bretherton, Furstin von, b. 1876. English wife of Prince Blucher of Germany. AN ENGLISH WIFE IN BERLIN: A PRIVATE MEMOIR OF EVENTS, POLITICS, AND DAILY LIFE IN GERMANY THROUGHOUT THE WAR AND THE SOCIAL REVOLUTION OF 1918. New York: E.P. Dutton & Co., 1920. 336p.

Diary August, 1914--February, 1919. Princess Blücher's memoir is as non-partisan as circumstances permitted. She had relatives fighting on both sides, and she worked, with Princes Pless and Princess Munster, to care for British prisoners and wounded.

617. Bluh, Bonnie Charles. American feminist. WOMAN TO WOMAN: EUROPEAN FEMINISTS. Brooklyn, N.Y.: Starogubski Press, 1974. 317p.

Travelogue/diary of Bluh's journey through Europe, which she undertook in order to interview feminists of many countries. Includes many letters written to Bluh upon her return to the U.S.

618. Bodfish, Mercy Goodwin, 1752-1803. American daughter of Samuel Goodwin, an early settler and landowner in Maine. "Some Records of Samuel Goodwin of Pownalborough, Maine, and His Descendents." NEW ENGLAND HISTORICAL AND GENEALOGICAL REGISTER 67:1 (1913), 27-32.

Includes the diary of Mercy Bodfish. Not a personal diary, but one-line entries detailing family affairs and vital statistics of the community, 1785-1816. According to Harriet Forbes (item 9) the manuscript is written in two different hands, and the earliest date in the diary is that of the birth of her father in 1716.

619. Bodichon, Barbara Leigh Smith, 1827-1891. English feminist, reformer, and intimate of George Eliot. AN AMERICAN DIARY, 1857-1858. Edited from the manuscript by Joseph W. Reed, Jr. London: Routledge & Kegan Paul, 1972. 198p.

Travel diary. During her trip she lectured on

women's rights, and also argued the subject in her journal. She was concerned with the rehabilitation of Blacks after emancipation, and discusses in her journal Black churches, schools, and the social barriers Black people faced after slavery ended.

620. Bogan, Louise, 1897-1970. American poet and literary critic. WHAT THE WOMAN LIVED: SELECTED LETTERS OF LOUISE BOGAN, 1920-1970. Edited by Ruth Limmer. New York: Harcourt Brace Jovanovich, 1973. 401p.

Literary correspondence to friends, publishers and editors, selected from over 1,000 extant letters.

621. ------. JOURNEY AROUND MY ROOM: THE AUTOBIOGRAPHY OF LOUISE BOGAN. A mosaic by Ruth Limmer. New York: The Viking Press, 1980. 197p.

Assemblage of journal and notebook entries, memoirs, short stories, poetry, extracts from correspondence, and other material, framed by a "meditation" Bogan wrote in 1932 called "Journey Around My Room."

622. Boggs, Mary Jane. American. "Rambles Among the Virginia Mountains: The Journal of Mary Jane Boggs, June, 1851." Edited by Andrew Buni. VIRGINIA MAGAZINE OF HISTORY AND BIOGRAPHY 77:1 (1969), 78-111.

Travel diary; a "literary novice" describes the Shenandoah Valley and its inhabitants.

623. Bompas, Charlotte Selina Cox, 1830-1917. Canadian missionary and wife of the first Bishop of Selkirk. A HEROINE OF THE NORTH. MEMOIRS OF CHARLOTTE SELINA COX BOMPAS, WIFE OF BISHOP SELKIRK (YUKON). WITH EXTRACTS FROM HER JOURNALS AND LETTERS. London: Society for Promoting Christian Knowledge; and New York and Toronto: The Macmillan Co., 1929. 187p.

Missionary diary and letters.

624. Bonaparte, Elisabeth Patterson, 1785-1879.

American first wife of Jerome Bonaparte, King of Westphalia. THE LIFE AND LETTERS OF MADAME BONAPARTE. Eugene L. Didier. New York: Charles Scribner's Sons, 1879. 276p.

The marriage between Elisabeth Patterson and Jerome Bonaparte, youngest brother of Napoleon Bonaparte, caused an international scandal, and was annulled in France at the insistence of Napoleon.

625. Bonaparte, Marie, Princess, 1882-1962. Psychoanalyst. FIVE COPY-BOOKS WRITTEN BY A LITTLE GIRL BETWEEN THE AGES OF SEVEN AND A HALF AND TEN. WITH COMMENTARIES. Translated by Nancy Proctor-Gregg (Volumes 2-4 translated by Eric Mosbacher). London: Imago, 1953. 4 vols.

626. Bonheur, Rosa (Marie Rosalie), 1822-1899. French painter and sculptor. REMINISCENCES OF ROSA BONHEUR. Edited by Theodore Stanton. New York: D. Appleton and Co., 1910. 413p. Reprinted, New York: Hacker Art Books, 1976.

Biography based on extracts from letters by Bonheur and others. Includes two chapters of letters printed in their entirety; one of family letters, and one of letters to friends.

627. Borden, Courtney Louise Letts. American wife of explorer John Borden. THE CRUISE OF THE "NORTHERN LIGHT": EXPLORATION AND HUNTING IN THE ALASKAN AND SIBERIAN ARCTIC, BY MRS. JOHN BORDEN; IN WHICH THE SEA-SCOUTS HAVE A BIG ADVENTURE. New York: Macmillan Co., 1928. 317p.

Account of the Borden-Field Museum Arctic expedition of 1927.

628. Bost, Sophie Bonjour, 1835-1920. Swiss pioneer immigrant to America. LES DERNIERS PURITANS, PIONNIERS AMERIQUE, 1851-1920. LETTRES DE THÉODORE BOST ET SOPHIE BONJOUR. Presentées par Charles Marc-Bost. Préface d'Yves Berger. Paris: Hachette et Cie., 1977. 439p.

629. ------. A FRONTIER FAMILY IN MINNESOTA: LETTERS OF THEODORE AND SOPHIE BOST, 1851-1920. Edited and translated by Ralph H. Bowen. Minneapolis, Minn.: University of Minneapolis Press, 1981. 391p.

Based on the Marc-Bost edition. "Familiar, if unusually vivid and detailed, picture of the Minnesota farming frontier in the 1850's and the ensuing decades."

630. Boswell, Anabella Innes, 1826-1916. Australian pioneer settler. ANABELLA BOSWELL'S JOURNAL. Edited with an introduction by Morton Herman. Sydney, London, and Melbourne: Angus & Roberston, 1965. 179p.

Autobiography, with extracts from a diary of her early years in London, and full entries for her later life in Australia, 1839-1848. Vivid description of growing up on the Australian frontier.

631. Bosworth, Joanna Shipman. American. A TRIP TO WASHINGTON, 1834. PAPERS OF JOANNA SHIPMAN BOSWORTH, BEING THE DIARY OF A CARRIAGE TRIP MADE IN 1834 BY CHARLES SHIPMAN AND HIS DAUGHTERS, JOANNA AND BETSY, FROM ATHENS, OHIO, TO PHILADELPHIA, BALTIMORE, AND WASHINGTON; AND A FAMILY HISTORY. Privately published by Henry M. Dawes, December 25, 1914. 44p.

632. Botta, Anne Charlotte Lynch, 1815-1891. American author and literary hostess. MEMOIRS OF ANNE C.L. BOTTA, WRITTEN BY HER FRIENDS. WITH SELECTIONS FROM HER CORRESPONDENCE AND FROM HER WRITINGS IN PROSE AND POETRY. Compiled by V. Botta. New York: J. Selwin Tait & Sons, 1894. 459p.

Includes extracts from her letters and diary.

633. Boulnois, Helen Mary. English. INTO LITTLE THIBET. London: Simpkin, Marshall, Hamilton, 1923. 256p.

Travel diary. Describes a journey through India and Tibet, probably in 1921 or 1922.

634. Bowen, Clarissa Walton Adger, 1837-1915. American. DIARY OF CLARISSA ADGER BOWEN. ASTABULA PLANTATION, 1865, WITH EXCERPTS FROM OTHER FAMILY DIARIES AND COMMENTS BY HER GRANDDAUGHTER CLARISSA WALTON TAYLOR AND MANY OTHER ACCOUNTS OF THE PENDLETON-CLEMSON AREA, SOUTH CAROLINA, 1776-1889. Edited by Mary Stevenson. Foundation for Historic Restoration in Pendleton Area, 1973. 126p.

635. Bowen, Helen Gilman. American. MOUNT SHASTA OR BUST: A FAMILY TRAVELOGUE IN THE 1890'S. Los Angeles, Calif.: Bowen, 1978. 189p.

636. Bower, Anna Catherine, b. 1768. English. DIARIES AND CORRESPONDENCE OF ANNA CATHERINE BOWER. London: Printed for Private Distribution by Bickers & Son, 1903. 175p.

Contains extracts from a travel diary, June, 1787--February, 1789, written while travelling in France and Belgium.

637. Bowles, Jane Auer, 1917-1973. American author and wife of author Paul Bowles. OUT IN THE WORLD: THE SELECTED LETTERS OF JANE BOWLES, 1935-1970. Edited by Millicent Dillon. Santa Barbara, Calif.: Black Sparrow Press, 1985. 319p.

Literary correspondence. Early letters cover Bowles' teenage years in Greenwich Village, her marriage to Paul Bowles, and the publication of TWO SERIOUS LADIES; later letters deal with her decision to go to Morocco, life in Paris, New York, and Tangier, her struggle with writer's block, her stroke, and her last writings from a convent hospital in Malaga.

638. Bowne, Eliza Southgate, 1783-1809? American. A GIRL'S LIFE EIGHTY YEARS AGO: A SELECTION FROM THE LETTERS OF ELIZA SOUTHGATE BOWNE, 1783-1809. Edited with an introduction by Clarence Cook. New York: Charles Scribner's Sons, 1887. 239p.

Thoughtful and intelligent letters by a young

woman from a wealthy Maine family, who admitted admiration for "many of the sentiments" of Mary Wollstonecraft while remaining leery of her "principles."

639. Boyle, Laura. English wife of a Colonial Officer stationed in Africa. DIARY OF A COLONIAL OFFICER'S WIFE. Oxford: Alden Press, 1968. 175p.

Diary 1916-1917, written while living with her husband David Boyle in Ashanti and the Gold Coast.

640. Boylston, Helen Dore. SISTER: THE WAR DIARY OF A NURSE. New York: I. Washburn, 1927. 202p.
World War I diary.

641. Braddon, Mary Elizabeth, 1837-1915. English novelist. "Devoted Disciple: The Letters of Mary Elizabeth Braddon to Sir Edward Bulwer-Lytton, 1862-1873." Robert Lee Wolf. HARVARD LITERARY BULLETIN 22 (April, 1974), 129-161.

Bradford, Martha Wilmot. See: Wilmot, Catherine.

642. Bradford, Phoebe George, 1794-1840. American wife of Whig editor Moses Bradford. "Phoebe George Bradford Diaries." Edited by Emerson W. Wilson. DELAWARE HISTORY 16:1 (1974), 1-21; 16:2 (1974), 132-151; 16:3 (1974), 244-267; and 16:4 (1974), 337-357.

Selections from a private diary, 1832-1839 deal with life on the Bradfords' Mt. Harmon plantation in Maryland, social and church affairs.

643. Bradford, Ruth. American daughter of a Sea Captain and shipping merchant. "MASKEE!" THE JOURNAL AND LETTERS OF RUTH BRADFORD, 1861-1872. Hartford, Conn.: The Prospect Press, 1938. 162p.

Bradford journeyed with her father to China when he took the position of Consul at Amoy. Her journal describes the sea voyage to China and life there,

1861-1863; and the voyage home, 1863-1864. Letters cover the period 1861-1864 and a later journey to China, 1870-1872. "Maskee" is a mid-nineteenth century Anglo-Chinese term meaning roughly "what the Hell!"

644. Bradley, Amy Owen. American nurse. BACK OF THE FRONT IN FRANCE: LETTERS FROM AMY OWEN BRADLEY, MOTOR DRIVER OF THE AMERICAN FUND FOR FRENCH WOUNDED. Boston: W.A. Butterfield, 1918. 155p.

War letters, October 31, 1916--May 5, 1918, to family in America. Bradley was still in France at the time the book was published. Describes nursing work near the trenches.

645. Brame, Caroline, 1847-1892. French. LE JOURNAL INTIME DE CAROLINE BRAME. Enquete de Michelle Perrot et Georges Ribeil. Paris: Montalba, 1985. 252p.

Social and religious diary of a young woman of an upper-middle class Parisien family, 1864-1868. Includes letters written to her husband from Belgium during the Franco-Prussian War, 1871.

646. Brandt van Warmelo, Johanna, b. 1876. South African nurse. HET CONCENTRATIEKAMP VAN IRENE. Amsterdam: Kaapstad, 1905.

One of two surviving personal documents of the Irene Concentration Camp in South Africa, written during the second Anglo-Boer War. The other is by Henrietta Armstrong (Item 462). Brandt van Warmelo was a nurse under Armstrong's supervision in the Irene Voluntary Nurses Corps.

647. Branson, Ann, 1808-1891. American Quaker. JOURNAL OF ANN BRANSON, A MINISTER IN THE GOSPEL IN THE SOCIETY OF FRIENDS. Philadelphia: W.H. Pile's Sons, Printers, 1892. 408p.

648. Brasil de Assis, Cecilia, b. 1899. American wife of Brazilian political theorist J.F. Brasil de Assis. DIARIO DE CECILIA BRASIL ASSIS: PERIODO 1916-1928.

Introducao, selecao e notas de Carlos Reverbel. Porto Alegre: L.& P.M. Editores, 1983. 208p.

649. Brassey, Anne (or Annie) Allnutt, Baroness, 1839-1887. English travel author. AROUND THE WORLD IN THE YACHT "SUNBEAM," OUR HOME ON THE OCEAN FOR ELEVEN MONTHS. With illustrations chiefly after drawings by the Hon. A.Y. Bingham. New York: H. Holt & Co., 1879. 479p. Published in England under the title A VOYAGE IN THE "SUNBEAM"; OUR HOME ON THE OCEAN FOR ELEVEN MONTHS. London: Longmans, Green & Co., 1881. 492p. Reprinted, Chicago and New York: Belford, Clarke & Co., 1886. 488p.

Diary 1876-1877, of a world cruise from England to Rio de Janeiro, around the Straits of Magellan to Tahiti, Hawaii, Japan, China, Ceylon, returning through the Red Sea and the Mediterranean to England. Lady Brassey accompanied her husband, Thomas Brassey, on yearly voyages on their yacht, "Sunbeam;" extracts from her journals of the voyages were published in lavishly illustrated editions.

650. ------. SUNSHINE AND STORM IN THE EAST: OR, CRUISES TO CYPRUS AND CONSTANTINOPLE. With upwards of 100 illustrations chiefly from drawings by the Hon. A.Y. Bingham. London: Longmans, Green & Co., 1880. 448p.

Travel diary, 1874 and 1878, describing two cruises in the East, and the changes which occured between the two visits, for Lady Brassey, a change "from all that was bright and glittering to all that was dull and miserable and wretched."

651. ------. IN THE TRADES, THE TROPICS AND THE ROARING FORTIES: 14,000 MILES IN THE "SUNBEAM" IN 1883. With 292 illustrations engraved on wood by G. Pearson and J. Cooper after drawings by R.T. Pritchett. New York: H. Holt & Co., 1885. 523p.

Travel diary, 1883, describing a cruise to Madeira, Trinidad, Venezuela, Jamaica, the Bahamas, Bermuda, and the Azores.

652. ------. THE LAST VOYAGE: THE LAST VOYAGE TO INDIA AND AUSTRALIA, IN THE "SUNBEAM" BY THE LATE LADY BRASSEY. Illustrations by R.T. Pritchett and from photographs. London and New York: Longmans, Green & Co., 1889. 490p.

Journal of an eleven-month cruise around India.

653. Braudy, Susan. American. BETWEEN MARRIAGE AND DIVORCE: A WOMAN'S DIARY. New York: William Morrow, 1975. 239p.

654. Brawne, Fanny [Frances Brawne, afterwards Lindon]. English lover of poet John Keats; and Frances Keats, afterwards Llanos. English sister of John Keats. LETTERS OF FANNY BRAWNE TO FANNY KEATS, 1820-1824. Edited with a biographical introduction by Fred Edgcumbe. With a preface by Maurice Buxton Forman. New York: Oxford University Press, 1937. 103p.

Correspondence between the two women was begun after Keat's death, at his request.

655. Brayton, Patience, 1733-1794. American Quaker. A SHORT ACCOUNT OF THE LIFE AND RELIGIOUS LABORS OF PATIENCE BRAYTON, LATE OF SWANSEY, IN THE STATE OF MASSACHUSETTS. MOSTLY SELECTED FROM HER OWN MINUTES. New York and London: W. Phillips, 1802. 144p.

Quaker diary, July 9, 1771--September 14, 1787 describes travels in Pennyslvania, Maryland, Georgia, and in Great Britain.

656. Breckenridge, Juanita, 1860-1946. American minister and minister's wife. "The Problem of Professional Careers for Women: Letters of Juanita Breckenridge, 1872-1893." Edited by Carol Kammen. NEW YORK HISTORY 55:3 (1974), 281-300.

Breckenridge was a minister of the Congregational Church of Brookton, New York but gave up her ministry upon her marriage to Fred E. Bates, also a minister. Her letters, which return repeatedly to the problem of woman's place in organized Protestant religion, are presented to exemplify the lives of women whose aspirations were lofty but whose public achievement was limited, who lived traditional domestic lives but whose attempts at professions outside the home suggests tensions within them worthy of study.

657. Breckinridge, Lucy Gilmer, later Bassett. American daughter of Virginia Congressman James Breckinridge. "Dusky Wings of War: The Journal of Lucy G. Breckinridge, 1862-1864." Mary D. Robertson. CIVIL WAR HISTORY 23:1 (March, 1977), 26-51.

Journal of life at Grove Hill, in the Shenandoah Valley of Virginia, by "a cultured, witty, high-spirited, loving and often wistful" diarist.

658. ------. LUCY BRECKINRIDGE OF GROVE HILL: THE JOURNAL OF A VIRGINIA GIRL, 1862-1864. Edited by Mary D. Robertson. Kent, Ohio: Kent State University Press, 1979. 235p.

Confederate Civil War diary. Chronicles events of the war, records her thoughts on religion, love and marriage, and her frustration with the position of women. Breckinridge's diary compares well with Mary Chesnut's A DIARY FROM DIXIE and Robert Cole's collection THE CHILDREN OF PRIDE.

659. Bremer, Frederika, 1801-1865. Swedish author and reformer. NEW SKETCHES OF EVERY-DAY LIFE: A DIARY. Translated from the Swedish by Mary Howitt. New York: Harper, 1844. 134p.

Translation of EN DAGBOK and of STID OCH FRED (STRIFE AND PEACE).

660. ------. FREDERIKA BREMER'S WORKS. Translated by Mary Howitt. London: H.G. Bonn, 1852-1853. 3 vols.

Volume 2 contains her diary.

661. ------. HEMMIN I DEN NYA VERLDEN. EN DAGBOK I BREF, SKAIFUA UNDER TVENNE ARS RESOR I NORRA AMERIKA

OCH PA CUBA. Stockholm: P.A. Norstedt & Soner, 1853-1854. 3 vols.

662. ------. THE HOMES OF THE NEW WORLD: IMPRESSIONS OF AMERICA. Translated by Mary Howitt. New York: Harper & Bros., 1854. 2 vols.

Journal-letters written to her sister describe America and American social customs during her travels there in 1849-1853.

663. ------. LIFE, LETTERS AND POSTHUMOUS WORKS OF FREDERIKA BREMER. Edited by her sister, Charlotte Bremer. Translated from the Swedish by Fredr. Milow. The poetry marked with an asterisk translated by Emily Nonnen. New York: R. Worthington, 1868, 1880. 439p.

664. ------. AMERICA OF THE FIFTIES: LETTERS OF FREDERIKA BREMER. Selected and edited by Adolph B. Benson. New York: The American-Scandinavian Foundation, 1924. 344p.

Selections from THE HOMES OF THE NEW WORLD (1854).

665. Breshkovsky, Catherine [Ekaterina Kinstantinovna Verigo Breshko-Breshkovskaia], 1844-1934. Russian revolutionary and member of the Preliminary Parliament of Russia, 1917. THE LITTLE GRANDMOTHER OF THE RUSSIAN REVOLUTION: REMINISCENCES AND LETTERS OF CATHERINE BRESHKOVSKY. Edited by Alice Stone Blackwell. Boston: Little, Brown, 1918. 348p.

Political letters, 1909-1917. to Julia Ward Howe, Emma Goldman, Alice Stone Blackwell, and others, whom she met on a visit to the U.S. in 1904.

666. Brett, Dorothy, b. 1883. American literary figure. LAWRENCE AND BRETT: A FRIENDSHIP. Philadelphia: J.B. Lippincott, 1933. 300p. London: M. Secker, 1933. 287p. New edition, with a new introduction, prologue and epilogue by John Manchester, Santa Fe, N.Mex.: Sunstone Press, 1974. 300p.

Loving apostrophy to D.H. Lawrence, based on and

written in the form of a diary. Reminiscences of literary life in England, New Mexico, Mexico, and Capri.

667. Bridgman, Eliza Jane Gillett. American missionary to China. DAUGHTERS OF CHINA: OR, SKETCHES OF DOMESTIC LIFE IN THE CELESTIAL EMPIRE. New York: Carter, 1853. 234p.

Diary of missionary work in the 1840's. Bridgman established a school for girls in China.

668. Bright, Abbie, b. 1848. American farmer. "Roughing it on Her Kansas Claim: The Diary of Abbie Bright, 1870-1871." Edited by Joseph W. Snell. KANSAS HISTORICAL QUARTERLY 37:3 (1971), 233-268 and 37:4 (1971), 394-428.

Diary September, 1870--June, 1871, written while visiting her brother in Indiana in 1870, and while visiting her brother Philip in Kansas, where she took out a claim for herself of 160 acres. Describes frontier life in Indiana and Kansas, and her work as a schoolteacher.

669. Brittain, Vera Mary, 1893-1970. English author, journalist and peaceworker; wife of political philospher George Catlin. See item 1507. CHRONICLE OF YOUTH: THE WAR DIARY, 1913-1917. Edited by Alan Bishop with Terry Smart. Preface by Clare Leighton. New York: Morrow, 1982. 382p.

Brittain used this diary as the base for TESTAMENT OF YOUTH (1933) and quoted freely from it in the first seven chapters, but she intended to publish it separately. Provides a contrast to TESTAMENT OF YOUTH as it presents a day-by-day account of the suspense and anguish of the war close up, where TESTAMENT OF YOUTH gives a perspective of the war from the point of view of a historian looking backwards.

670. ------. CHRONICLE OF FRIENDSHIP: DIARY OF THE THIRTIES, 1932-1939. Edited by Alan Bishop. London: Victor Gollancz, 1986. 448p.

671. Broglie, Albertine Ida Gustavine de Stael-Holstein, Duchesse de, 1797-1838. LETTRES DE LA DUCHESSE DE BROGLIE, 1814-1838. Publiées par son fils le Duc de Broglie. Paris: Calmann Levy, 1896. 838p. Reproduced in microfiche, New York: Bibliotheque Nationale, distributed by Clearwater Publishing Company. 4 fiches (105x148 mm).

672. Bronte, Charlotte, 1816-1855. English novelist. THE LIFE OF CHARLOTTE BRONTE. Elizabeth C. Gaskell. With an introduction by Clement Shorter. London: Humphrey Milford, Oxford University Press, 1875. 476p. New edition, with an introduction by May Sinclair. London: J.M. Dent & Sons, and New York: E.P. Dutton & Co., 1908, 1933. 411p.

Biography chiefly comprised of extracts from Bronte's correspondence.

673. ------. CHARLOTTE BRONTE AND HER CIRCLE. Clement K. Shorter. New York: Dodd, Mead & Co., 1896. 512p.

Based on the Gaskell edition. Includes previously unpublished material; juvenalia, family papers, and many new letters.

674. ------. THE LOVE-LETTERS OF CHARLOTTE BRONTE TO CONSTANTIN HEGER. T.J. Wise, 1914. 43p.

675. Brooke, Mildred, later Hoover, 1872-1940. American historian. MILDRED CREW BROOKE: AN UNFINISHED MANUSCRIPT OF REMINISCENCES AND SOME EXTRACTS FROM HER DIARY. With interpolations and an epilogue. [Edited by Theodore J. Hoover.] Casa del Oso, Calif.: Privately Printed [at Davenport, Calif., by T.J. Hoover], 1940. 110p.

Brooke wrote on California local history; her reminiscences were meant as a personal document for her friends.

676. Brooks, Anne M. American. THE GRIEVING TIME: A

MONTH BY MONTH ACCOUNT OF RECOVERY FROM LOSS. Wilmington, Del.: Delapeake Publishing, 1982. 40p.

677. ------. THE GRIEVING TIME: A YEAR'S ACCOUNT OF RECOVERY FROM LOSS. Garden City, N.Y.: Dial Press, 1985. 40p.

Diary of a widow, probably written in 1980; deals with grief over the death of her husband.

678. Brown, Emma Jane Frazey. American mother of Josephine Edith Brown. "Soldier of the 92nd Illinois: Letters of William H. Brown and His Fiancee, Emma Jane Frazey." Edited by Vivian C. Hopkins. BULLETIN OF THE NEW YORK PUBLIC LIBRARY 73:2 (February, 1969), 114-136.

Courtship Letters written during the Civil War, September, 1862--May,1867. They were married in 1867 and moved west from Illinois to Iowa by covered wagon in 1871.

679. Brown, Josephine Edith. American farmer. "Diary of an Iowa Farm Girl: Josephine Edith Brown, 1892-1901." Edited by Vivian C. Hopkins. ANNALS OF IOWA 42:2 (Fall, 1973), 126-146.

Diary of a fourteen-year old farm girl growing up in the pioneer community of Shelby, Iowa.

680. Brown, Laura. American. "A Young Girl in the Missouri Border War." Dorothy Brown Thompson. MISSOURI HISTORICAL REVIEW 58:1 (1963), 55-69.

Letters 1859-1864. Brown attended Monticello, a young ladies seminary at Godfrey, Illinois; during vacations she lived with a married sister near Mexico, Missouri. These letters to her brother were written as an outlet for her "troubled thinking." At first personal, they gradually become filled with news about the border warfare.

681. Brown, Polly Guion, 1783-1871. American. "Diary

of a 19th Century Lass." Ann Barry. SEVENTEEN 36 (1977), 118-122.

682. Brown, Sally, b. 1807; and Pamela Brown, b. 1816. THE DIARIES OF SALLY AND PAMELA BROWN, 1832-1838, AND HYDE LESLIE, 1887, PLYMOUTH NOTCH, VERMONT. Edited by Blanche Brown Bryant and Gertrude Elaine Baker. Springfield, Vt.: William L. Bryant Foundations, 1970. 176p.

683. Browne, Charlotte, fl. 1754. English nurse in the American Revolution. "With Braddock's Army: Mrs. Browne's Diary in Virginia and Maryland." Fairfax Harrison. VIRGINIA MAGAZINE OF HISTORY AND BIOGRAPHY 32:4 (1924), 305-320.

Travel and wartime diary 1754-1757. Browne accompanied her brother, an officer in Braddock's Expeditionary Force, from London to Fort Cumberland, Virginia. Harrison places her diary alongside Mrs. Grant of Laggan (items 1335, 1336), Janet Schaw (item 2418), and Madame de Riedesel (items 2306, 2307). Only those portions of her diary relating to Virginia and Maryland are excerpted here.

684. ------. "The Journal of Charlotte Browne, Matron of the General Hospital with the English Forces in America, 1754-1756." In COLONIAL CAPTIVES, MARCHES AND JOURNEYS. Edited by Isabel Caulder. Published under the auspices of the National Society of Colonial Dames of America. New York: Macmillan Co., 1935. Reprinted, Port Washington: Kennikat Press, 1967. p.169-198.

685. Browne, Mary, 1807-1833. English. DIARY OF A GIRL IN FRANCE IN 1821. With illustrations by herself. Introduction by Euphemia Stewart Browne. Edited by Cdr. the Hon. H.N. Shore, R.N. New York: E.P. Dutton, and London: John Murray, 1905. 188p.

Travel diary written on a visit to France with her family in 1821. Browne disliked France intensely.

686. Browning, Elizabeth Barrett Barrett, 1806-1861. English poet and wife of poet Robert Browning. LETTERS OF ELIZABETH BARRETT BROWNING, ADDRESSED TO RICHARD HENGIST HORNE. With commentaries on contemporaries. Edited by Townshend S.R. Mayer. London: R. Bentley and Son, 1877. 2 vols.

Hengist was a poet who collaborated with Browning on the preparation of A NEW SPIRIT OF THE AGE (London, 1844) and POEMS OF GEOFFRY CHAUCER MODERNIZED (London: 1841). Their correspondence began in 1838 and continued until her marriage.

687. ------. THE LETTERS OF ROBERT BROWNING AND ELIZABETH BARRETT BARRETT, 1845-1846. Edited by Frederic G. Kenyon. New York and London: Harper & Bros., 1899. 2 vols.

First edition of the Barrett-Browning letters. Prints the correspondence between them in its entirety, but contains many textual errors and little annotation.

688. ------. ELIZABETH BARRETT BROWNING: LETTERS TO HER SISTER, 1846-1859. Edited by Leonard Huxley, LL.D. London: John Murray, 1929; and New York: E.P. Dutton & Co., 1930. 344p.

One hundred and seven letters to her sisters not included in the Kenyon edition, chiefly to Henrietta Barrett Cook (d.1860), with a few addressed to Arabella Barrett.

689. ------. TWENTY-TWO UNPUBLISHED LETTERS OF ELIZABETH BARRETT BROWNING AND ROBERT BROWNING ADDRESSED TO HENRIETTA AND ARABELLA MOULTON-BARRETT. New York: United Features Syndicate, 1935. 89p. Reprinted, New York: Haskell House Publishers, 1971. 89p.

690. ------. FROM ROBERT AND ELIZABETH BROWNING: A FURTHER SELECTION OF THE BARRETT-BROWNING FAMILY CORRESPONDENCE. Edited with introduction and notes by William Rose Benet. London: John Murray, 1936. 144p.

Twenty-two hitherto unpublished letters addressed to Elizabeth Barrett Browning's sisters.

691. ------. ANDROMEDA IN WIMPOLE STREET: CONTAINING EXTRACTS FROM THE LOVE LETTERS OF ELIZABETH AND ROBERT BROWNING. Dormer Creston [D.J. Baynes]. London: Eyre & Spottiswoode, 1950. 284p.

692. ------. ELIZABETH BARRETT TO MISS MITFORD: THE UNPUBLISHED LETTERS OF ELIZABETH BARRETT BARRETT TO MARY RUSSELL MITFORD. Edited and with an introduction by Betty Miller. London: John Murray; and New Haven, Conn.: Yale University Press, 1954. 284p.

Selection of 142 of 430 extant letters, 1836-1846 (52 previously published in the Kenyon edition). This edition ends with Elizabeth Barrett's marriage, though the correspondence continues after this date.

693. ------. UNPUBLISHED LETTERS OF THOMAS DE QUINCEY AND ELIZABETH BARRETT BROWNING. Edited from the originals in the Gray Collection, Auckland Public Library, by S. Musgrove. Auckland: Auckland University College, 1954. 37p. Reprinted, Folcroft, Penn.: Folcroft Press, 1969. 37p.

694. ------. ELIZABETH BARRETT TO MR. BOYD: UNPUBLISHED LETTERS OF ELIZABETH BARRETT BROWNING TO HUGH STUART BOYD. Introduced and edited by Barbara P. McCarthy. London: John Murray; and New Haven, Conn.: Published for Wellesley College by Yale University Press, 1955. 299p.

695. ------. LETTERS OF THE BROWNINGS TO GEORGE BARRETT. Edited by Paul Landis with the assistance of Ronald E. Freeman. Urbana, Ill.: University of Illinois Press, 1958. 392p.

Letters to Elizabeth Barrett Browning's brother. Her letters to George Barrett are more political and worldly than those written to her sisters.

696. ------. DIARY BY ELIZABETH BARRETT BROWNING.

Edited with an introduction and notes by Philip Kelley and Ronald Hudson. Includes psychoanalytical observations by Robert Coles. Athens, Ohio: Ohio University Press, 1969. 405p.

Diary 1821-1832 and letters to Hugh Stuart Boyd, 1831-1832. The editors note the diary illuminates the letters Browning wrote to Boyd, and the letters in some measure amplify references made in the diary; therefore, all extant letters to Boyd for the period are printed in an Appendix.

697. ------. THE LETTERS OF ROBERT BROWNING AND ELIZABETH BARRETT BARRETT, 1845-1846. Edited by Elvan Kintner. Cambridge, Mass.: The Belknap Press of Harvard University Press, 1969. 2 vols.

Complete and definitive edition. Based on the Kenyon edition, but edited from original manuscript letters, with annotations and corrections.

698. ------. HOW DO I LOVE THEE? THE LOVE LETTERS OF ROBERT BROWNING AND ELIZABETH BARRETT. Selected and with an introduction by V.E. Stack. New York: G.P. Putnam's Sons, 1969. 230p.

Courtship letters, 1845-1846, dating from their first acquaintance to the eve of their wedding.

699. ------. THE BROWNINGS: LETTERS AND POETRY. Selected and with an introduction by Christopher Ricks. Illustrated by Barnett I. Plotkin. Garden City, N.Y.: Doubleday, 1970. 726p.

700. ------. THE BROWNINGS TO THE TENNYSONS: LETTERS FROM ROBERT BROWNING AND ELIZABETH BARRETT BROWNING TO ALFRED, EMILY, AND HALLAM TENNYSON, 1852-1889. Edited by Thomas J. Collins. Waco, Tex.: Armstrong Browning Library, 1971. 59p. (Baylor Browning Interests, No. 22.)

701. ------. "Ruskin and the Brownings: Twenty Five Unpublished Letters." BULLETIN OF THE JOHN RYLANDS

LIBRARY 54 (1972), 314-356.

Includes two letters from Elizabeth Barrett Browning to John Ruskin.

702. ------. INVISIBLE FRIENDS: THE CORRESPONDENCE OF ELIZABETH BARRETT BARRETT AND BENJAMIN ROBERT HAYDON, 1842-1845. Edited by Willard Bissell Pope. London: Oxford University Press, 1939. 78p. New edition, Cambridge, Mass.: Harvard University Press, 1972. 200p.

Browning never met the artist Haydon, but they carried on a brief correspondence.

703. ------. "A Report on the Published and Unpublished Letters of Elizabeth Barrett Browning to Mary Russell Mitford." Meredith R. Raymond. BROWNING INSTITUTE 1 (1973), 37-62.

Description of the correspondence and what it reveals of the relationship between the two women. Discusses developments in the editing and publication of the letters, and lists manuscript holdings.

704. ------. ELIZABETH BARRETT BROWNING'S LETTERS TO MRS. DAVID OGILVY, 1849-1861. WITH RECOLLECTIONS BY MRS. OGILVY. Edited by Peter N. Heydon and Philip Kelley. New York: Quadrangle/The New York Times Book Co., and the Browning Institute, 1973. 220p. London: John Murray, 1974. 220p.

Letters document a substantial and intimate personal relationship between the two women, and the life of the Anglo-Florentine community of the late 1800's. Eliza Ann Harris Dick Ogilvy (1822-1912) was a Scottish poet.

705. ------. "Elizabeth Barrett Browning and Her Brother Alfred: Some Unpublished Letters." Ronald Hudson. BROWNING INSTITUTE STUDIES 2 (1974), 135-160.

Discussion of the relationship between Browning

and her younger brother Alfred Price Barrett Moulton-Barrett, printing eight letters, 1855-1859.

706. ------. THE BARRETTS AT HOPE END: THE EARLY DIARY OF ELIZABETH BARRETT BROWNING. Edited with an introduction by Elizabeth Berridge. London: John Murray, 1974. 276p.

707. ------. THE BROWNING'S CORRESPONDENCE: A CHECKLIST. Compiled by Philip Kelley and Ronald Hudson. New York: The Browning Institute; and Arkansas City, Kans.: The Wedgestone Press, 1978. 498p.

Descriptive, chronological list of all known published and unpublished letters of the Brownings.

708. ------. "The Browning's Correspondence: Supplement No. 1 to the Checklist." Philip Kelley and Ronald Hudson. BROWNING INSTITUTE STUDIES 6 (1978), 163-168. Supplement No. 2: BROWNING INSTITUTE STUDIES 7 (1979), 173-187. Supplement No. 3: BROWNING INSTITUTE STUDIES 8 (1980), 161-176. Supplement No. 4: BROWNING INSTITUTE STUDIES 9 (1981), 161-172. Supplement No. 5: BROWNING INSTITUTE STUDIES 10 (1982), 163-168.

709. ------. "The Inconvenience of Celebrity: An Unpublished Letter from Elizabeth Barrett Browning to Mary Russell Mitford." Lucien L. Agosta. BROWNING SOCIETY NOTES 8 (April, 1978), 11-13.

710. ------. THE BROWNING'S CORRESPONDENCE. Edited by Philip Kelley and Ronald Hudson. Winfield, Kans.: Wedgestone Press, 1984-1987. 4 vols.

Letters 1809-1840. Definitive edition. Further volumes in preparation.

Burnet, Margaret Kennedy, Lady. See: Kennedy, Margaret, Lady

711. Bryan, Mary Edwards, 1842-1913. American author. "A Georgia Authoress Writes Her Editor: Mrs. Mary E.

Bryan to W.W. Mann, 1860." Edited by James S. Patty. GEORGIA HISTORICAL SOCIETY QUARTERLY 41:4 (December, 1957), 416-431.

Four letters from a popular novelist to the editor of THE GEORGIA COURIER. The letters throw light on Georgia life on the eve of the Civil War, upon persons and events prominent in Georgia literature and journalism in 1860, and upon Bryan's own background, attitudes, activities, and ideas on literature.

712. Buchanan, Sophia Bingham. American wife of a Union Officer during the Civil War. "Letters to the Front: A Distaff View of the Civil War." George M. Blackburn. MICHIGAN HISTORY 49:1 (1965), 53-67.

War-time letters written by a highly literate and expressive woman to her husband, Captain John Claude Bingham, serving in the Union Army. Letters reveal the anxieties and trials suffered by women left behind as men fought the war.

713. Buddenbroch, Mathilde. Swiss cousin of Religious reformer John Calvin. LE JOURNAL DE MARGUERITE. Translated from the German by L. Louis-Filliol. Geneva: A. Cherbuliez, 1875.

Diary of a woman who lived in German-speaking Switzerland at the time of the Protestant Reformation.

Bull, Maria Lucia. See: Guerard, Maria Lucia Bull.

714. Bullitt, Ernesta Drinker. American. AN UNCENSORED DIARY FROM THE CENTRAL EMPIRES. Garden City, N.Y.: Doubleday Page & Co., 1917. 205p.

War diary, describing travel in Germany, Belgium and Austria-Hungary, May 14--September 18, 1916. Bullitt was inspired by the Revolutionary War diary of her ancestor, Elizabeth Sandwith Drinker, to write an account of her own wartime experiences.

715. Bulwer-Lytton, Rosina Doyle Wheeler, Baroness

Lytton, 1802-1882. English novelist and wife of author Sir Edward Bulwer-Lytton. UNPUBLISHED LETTERS OF LADY BULWER-LYTTON TO A.E. CHALON, R.A. With an introduction and notes by S.M. Ellis. London: E. Nash, 1914. 315p.

Letters to Alfred Edward Chalon.

716. Bunke, Tamara, "Tania," 1940?-1968. Argentinian revolutionary, journalist, and undercover agent. TANIA: LA GUERILLERA INVOLVIDABLE. Havana, Cuba: Instituto del Libro, 1970. 335p.

717. ------. TANIA: THE UNFORGETTABLE GUERILLA. THE SCRAPBOOK OF A YOUNG GIRL WHO WORKED FOR THE REVOLUTION IN CUBA AND DIED WITH CHE IN THE BOLIVIAN JUNGLE. Edited by Marta Rojas and Mirta Rodriguez Calderon. New York: Vintage Books/ Random House, 1971. 212p.

Journal entries, letters, and photographs.

718. Bunsen, Frances, Baroness, 1791-1876. LIFE AND LETTERS OF FRANCES, BARONESS BUNSEN. Edited by Augustus J.C. Hare. London: Daldy Ibister, 1879. 2 vols.

Biography comprised chiefly of letters. Hare notes, however, that thousands of letters have been necessarily omitted.

719. Bunting, Hannah Syng, 1801-1832. American Methodist. MEMOIR, DIARY AND LETTERS OF MISS HANNAH SYNG BUNTING OF PHILADELPHIA. Compiled by T. Merritt. New York: T. Mason and G. Lane, 1837. 2 vols.

Religious diary, 1818-1832.

720. Bunyard, Harriet, d. 1900. American frontier settler. "Diary of Miss Harriet Bunyard: From Texas to California in 1868." Edited by Percival J. Cooney. HISTORICAL SOCIETY OF SOUTHERN CALIFORNIA QUARTERLY 13 (1924), 92-124.

Overland diary, April 29--October 24, 1868, written at the age of nineteen.

Burge, Dolly Sumner Lunt. See: Lunt, Dolly Sumner.

721. Burlingame, Lettie Lavilla, 1859-1890. American lawyer. LETTIE LAVILLA BURLINGAME: HER LIFE PAGES, STORIES, POEMS AND ESSAYS. INCLUDING A GLIMPSE OF HER SUCCESS AS THE FIRST LADY LAWYER OF WILL COUNTY, ILLINOIS, THE HOME OF HER GIRLHOOD. ALSO AS PRESIDENT, UP TO THE TIME OF HER DEATH, OF THE FIRST "EQUAL SUFFRAGE ASSOCIATION" OF JOLIET, ILLINOIS, TO WHICH SHE DEDICATED HER LAST WORK, A SUFFRAGE SONG, WORDS AND MUSIC, "PUT ON THE ORANGE RIBBON," ETC. ETC. Arranged for publication by her mother, O.C. Burlingame. Joliet, Ill.: J.E. Williams & Co., 1895. 374p.

Burnet, Margaret Kennedy, Lady. See: Kennedy, Margaret, Lady

722. Burnett, Frances Hodgson [Frances Eliza Hodgson Burnett], 1849-1924. English-American novelist and juvenile author. THE ROMANTICK LADY, FRANCES HODGSON BURNETT: THE LIFE STORY OF AN IMAGINATION. Vivian Burnett. New York and London: Charles Scribner's Sons, 1927. 423p.

Biography based on and including excerpts from her correspondence with family, friends, colleagues and editors.

723. Burney, Fanny [Madame Frances Burney d'Arblay], 1752-1840. English novelist and Lady-In-Waiting at the court of George III. THE DIARY AND LETTERS OF MADAME D'ARBLAY, 1778-1840. By her niece [Charlotte Barrett]. London: H. Colburn, 1842-1846. 7 vols. New edition, London: Hurst & Blackett, 1854. 7 vols. New edition with a preface and notes by Austin Dobson, London and New York: Macmillan & Co., 1904-1905. 6 vols.

Begins with the publication of EVELINA (1778).

724. ------. MEMOIRS OF MADAME D'ARBLAY...COMPILED FROM HER VOLUMINOUS DIARIES AND LETTERS, AND FROM OTHER SOURCES. Mrs. Helen Berkeley [pseud. for Anna Cora Ogden Mowatt Ritchie]. New York: J. Mowatt & Co., 1844. 2 vols. in one.

725. ------. FANNY BURNEY AND HER FRIENDS: SELECT PASSAGES FROM HER DIARY AND OTHER WRITINGS. Edited by Leonard Benton Seeley. With nine illustrations after Reynolds, Gainsborough, Copley, and West. London: Seeley and Co.; and New York: Scribner and Welford, 1890. 331p. Reprinted, Detroit: Gale Research Co., 1969. 331p.

726. ------. JOHNSONIA: ANECDOTES OF THE LATE SAMUEL JOHNSON, LL.D., BY MRS. PIOZZI, RICHARD CUMBERLAND, BISHOP PERCY AND OTHERS, TOGETHER WITH THE DIARY OF DR. CAMPBELL AND EXTRACTS FROM THAT OF MADAME D'ARBLAY. Newly collected and edited by Robina Napier. London and New York: George Bell & Sons, 1892.

727. ------. THE EARLY DIARY OF FRANCES BURNEY, 1768-1778. WITH A SELECTION FROM HER CORRESPONDENCE, AND FROM THE JOURNALS OF HER SISTERS SUSAN AND CHARLOTTE BURNEY. Edited by Annie Raine Ellis. London: George Bell & Sons, 1889.

Early diary not included in the Barrett edition; correspondence for 1768-1778; letters from Susan Elizabeth Burney to Fanny Burney, 1778-1779; and letters and fragments of the journal of Charlotte Ann Burney, 1777-1787.

728. ------. DIARY AND LETTERS OF FRANCES BURNEY, MADAME D'ARBLAY. Revised and edited by Sarah Chauncey Woolsey. Boston: Little, Brown and Co., 1902. 2 vols.

729. ------. DR. JOHNSON AND FANNY BURNEY: BEING THE JOHNSONIAN PASSAGES FROM THE WORKS OF MADAME D'ARBLAY. With an introduction and notes by Chauncey Brewster Tinker. New York: Moffat, Yard & Co., 1911. 252p. Reprinted, Westport, Conn.: Greenwood Press, 1970. 252p.

Taken from the Barrett edition, the Ellis edition, and the MEMOIRS of Doctor Burney.

730. ------. THE DIARY AND LETTERS OF MADAME D'ARBLAY (FRANCES BURNEY). Edited and selected, with a preface and notes by Muriel Masefield. London: George Routledge & Sons, 1931. 336p.

Excerpts emphasize the period begining with the publication of EVELINA (1778), and Burney's life as Lady-In-Waiting to Queen Charlotte.

731. ------. THE QUEENY LETTERS: BEING LETTERS ADDRESSED TO HESTER MARIA THRALE BY DOCTOR JOHNSON, FANNY BURNEY AND MRS. THRALE-PIOZZI. Edited by the Marquis of Landsdowne. New York: Farrar & Rinehart, 1934. 275p.

"Queeny" was the nickname given to Hester Maria Thrale, daughter of Hester Lynch Thrale Piozzi.

732. ------. THE DIARY OF FANNY BURNEY. Edited by Lewis Gibbs. New York: E.P. Dutton Co., 1940. 416p.

Abridged version of the DIARY, based on the Barrett edition.

733. ------. JOURNALS OF FANNY BURNEY (MADAME D'ARBLAY). Edited by Joyce Hemlow and Althea Douglas. London: Oxford University Press, 1972-1975. 6 vols.

Definitive edition. Burney heavily edited her papers; this edition restores them to their original form. Social and Court diary and Letters, 1791-1812.

734. ------. THE STORY OF FANNY BURNEY: AN INTRODUCTION TO THE DIARY AND LETTERS OF MADAME D'ARBLAY. Muriel Agnes Masefield. Cambridge, England: University Press, 1927. Reprinted, New York: Haskell House Publishers, 1974. 160p.

735. ------. THE FAMOUS MISS BURNEY: THE DIARIES AND LETTERS OF FANNY BURNEY. Edited by Barbara G. Schrank and David J. Supino. New York: Minerva Press, 1976. 335p.

Selections from the Diary and letters covering the entire span of Burney's writing. An excellent introduction to the larger work.

736. ------. FANNY BURNEY: SELECTED LETTERS AND

JOURNALS. Edited by Joyce Hemlow. Oxford: Clarendon Press; New York: Oxford University Press, 1986. 366p.

737. Burney, Fanny Anne (later Wood). English great-niece of author Fanny Burney. A GREAT NIECE'S JOURNALS. BEING EXTRACTS FROM THE JOURNALS OF FANNY ANNE BURNEY (MRS. WOOD) FROM 1830 TO 1842. Edited with a preface and notes by her grand-daughter, Margaret S. Rolt. London: Constable & Co., 1926. 359p.

738. Burns, Amanda McDowell, b. 1839. American teacher. FIDDLES IN THE CUMBERLANDS. By Amanda McDowell and Lela McDowell Blankenship. New York: R.R. Smith, 1943. 310p.

Diary 1861-1866, written at Cumberland Institute, White County, Tennessee, where Burns taught; augmented by narrative chapters and additions by Blankenship.

739. Burns, Susan. American. "Journal of a Trip from Philadelphia to Salisbury, North Carolina in 1848." Edited by Merl E. Reed. MISSISSIPPI QUARTERLY 21:1 (Winter, 1967-1968), 71-77.

Journal of a trip by steamship, rail, and coach. Reed notes that Burns' description of the class structure of North Carolina, based on the architecture and construction of the houses, is particularly noteworthy.

740. Burr, Esther Edwards, 1732-1758. American diarist and wife of Reverend Aaron Burr. ESTHER BURR'S JOURNAL. Edited by Jeremiah Eames Rankin. Washington, D.C.: Woodward & Lathrop, 1903. 100p.

Diary 1741-1757.

741. ------. "Journal of Esther Burr, 1754-1757." Josephine Fisher. NEW ENGLAND HISTORICAL QUARTERLY 3:2 (April, 1930), 297-315

Attempts to correct the impression given by Rankin

(item 740.) that Burr was a stiff, correct, humorless woman, and cites what Fisher calls Rankin's clumsy paraphrasing of Burr's journal. The journal is written as journal-letters to Miss Sally Prince of Boston, and describes Parrish life of a minister's wife, the War with France, 1754-1757, politics, and the early days of Princeton.

742. Burr, Theodosia, later Alston, 1783-1813. American society belle and daughter of U.S. Vice President Aaron Burr. CORRESPONDENCE OF AARON BURR AND HIS DAUGHTER THEODOSIA. Edited with a preface by Mark Van Doren. New York: Covici-Friede, 1929. 349p.

Edition of 500 copies.

743. ------. "An Intercourse of the Heart: Some Little Known Letters of Theodosia Burr." Dorothy Valentine Smith. NEW YORK HISTORICAL SOCIETY 36 (January, 1953).

Selection of letters written to Burr's half-brother, John Barstow Prevost.

744. Bury, Charlotte Campbell, Lady, 1775-1861. English Lady-in-Waiting. DIARY ILLUSTRATIVE OF THE TIMES OF GEORGE THE FOURTH. INTERSPERSED WITH ORIGINAL LETTERS FROM THE LATE QUEEN CAROLINE, AND FROM VARIOUS OTHER DISTINGUISHED PERSONS. London: H. Colburn, 1838-1839. 4 vols.

745. ------. THE DIARY OF A LADY-IN-WAITING, BY LADY CHARLOTTE BURY. BEING THE DIARY ILLUSTRATIVE OF THE TIMES OF GEORGE THE FOURTH, INTERSPERSED WITH ORIGINAL LETTERS FROM THE LATE QUEEN CAROLINE AND FROM OTHER DISTINGUISHED PERSONS. Edited by A. Francis Steuart. London and New York: John Lane Co., 1908. 2 vols.

746. Bury, Elizabeth, 1644-1720. English diarist and wife of Nonconformist Minister Samuel Bury. AN ACCOUNT OF THE LIFE AND DEATH OF ELIZABETH BURY. CHIEFLY COLLECTED OUT OF HER OWN DIARY. TOGETHER WITH HER FUNERAL SERMON BY THE REVEREND MR. WILLIAM TONG AND HER

ELEGY BY THE REVEREND MR. J. WATTS. Bristol: J. Penn, 1720. 244p.

Religious diary, 1693-1720.

747. Bury, Priscilla Susan Faulkner. English painter. "Mrs. Edward Bury (Née Priscilla Susan Faulkner), Botanical Artist." Nora F. McMillan. JOURNAL OF THE SOCIETY FOR THE BIBLIOGRAPHY OF NATURAL HISTORY 5:1 (1968), 71-75.

Letters between Bury and William Roscoe.

748. Bussy, Dorothy Strachey. English translator of André Gide. CORRESPONDANCE ANDRÉ GIDE--DOROTHY BUSSY. Édition etablié et presenteé par Jean Lambert. Notes de Richard Tedeschi. Paris: Gallimard, 1979. 3 vols.

Letters 1918-1951.

749. ------. SELECTED LETTERS OF ANDRÉ GIDE AND DOROTHY BUSSY. Edited by Richard Tedeschi. Introduction by Jean Lambert. New York: Oxford University Press, 1983. 316p.

750. Butler, America Rollins, 1826-1910. American frontier settler. "Mrs. Butler's 1853 Diary of the Rogue River Valley." Edited by Oscar Osburn Winther and Rose Dodge Gayley. OREGON HISTORICAL QUARTERLY 41:4 (December, 1940), 346-349.

Overland diary written on the journey to Yreka, California, and then to the Rogue River Valley in southern Oregon. Describes life on the family's farm in Oregon.

751. Butler, Eleanor, Lady, 1739-1829 and Sarah Ponsonby, 1754-1831. Irish romantic friends. THE HAMWOOD PAPERS OF THE LADIES OF LLANGOLLEN AND CAROLINE HAMILTON. Edited by Mrs. G.H. Bell. London: Macmillan & Co., 1930. 417p.

Joint domestic diary, 1785 and 1788-1790, of which

only fragments remain. Butler and Ponsonby eloped together in 1778, and lived as a couple 53 years, until Eleanor's death. Theirs is considered "the great success story" of eighteenth-century female romantic friendships.

752. ------. LIFE WITH THE LADIES OF LLANGOLLEN. Compiled and edited by Elizabeth Mavor. Hammondsworth: Viking Press, 1984. 238p.

753. Butler, Elizabeth Southerden Thompson, Lady, 1850-1933. English military painter. FROM SKETCH-BOOK AND DIARY. Illustrated by the author. London: Adams and Charles Black, 1909.

Account of travels in Africa, Italy, and Ireland.

754. ------. LETTERS FROM THE HOLY LAND: A DESCRIPTION OF TRAVEL IN PALESTINE. London: Adams and Charles Black, 1912. 84p.

Travel letters, February-March of an unspecified year.

755. Butler, Mary, "May," 1841-1916. Sister of Samuel Butler. THE CORRESPONDENCE OF SAMUEL BUTLER WITH HIS SISTER MAY. Edited with an introduction by Daniel F. Howard. Berkeley, Calif., and Los Angeles: University of California Press, 1962. 265p.

Contains excerpts from letters by May Butler, though Howard is more concerned with those of Samuel Butler.

756. Buxton, Victoria Alexandrina, Lady, Later Lady de Bunsen, b. 1874. LADY VICTORIA BUXTON: A MEMOIR, WITH SOME ACCOUNT OF HER HUSBAND. By the Rt. Hon. George W.E. Russell. London: Longmans, Green, & Co., 1919. 238p.

Biography based on and including letters and "memorandums." Describes life at Court.

757. Byrom, Elizabeth, 1722-1801. English daughter of

theologian John Byrom. THE PRIVATE JOURNAL AND LITERARY REMAINS OF JOHN BYROM. Edited by Richard Parkinson. Manchester, England: The Cheetham Society, 1854-1857. (Vols. 32, 34, 40, and 44; Byrom's diary in Vol. 44).

Public diary, August, 1745--January, 1746, much of it dealing with the Jacobite Rebellion, with which she and her father sympathized.

758. Byron, Anne Isabella Millbanke Byron, Baroness, 1792-1860. English philanthropist and wife of poet George Gordon, Lord Byron. THE LIFE AND LETTERS OF ANNE ISABELLA, LADY NOEL BYRON. From Unpublished Papers in the Possession of the Late Ralph, Earl of Lovelace. Ethel Colburn Mayne. With an introduction and epilogue by Mary, Countess of Lovelace. New York: Charles Scribner's Sons, 1929. 501p.

Biography based on and including correspondence, 1811-1860, concentrating on the years of her marriage to Byron and its dissolution. Appendix 1 contains letters written during the early months of their engagement, September-October, 1814.

759. Calderón de la Barca, Frances Erskine Inglis, 1804-1882. Scottish traveler and wife of Spanish diplomat Angel Calderón de la Barca. LIFE IN MEXICO DURING A TWO YEARS RESIDENCE IN THAT COUNTRY. With a preface by W.H. Prescott. London: Chapman & Hall, 1843. 437p. Boston: Little, Brown & Co., 1843. 375p.

Account based on letters, describing travel in Mexico and life there as the wife of a diplomat.

760. ------. LA VIDA EN MEXICO. Nota preliminar por Artemio del Vale Arízpe. Traducción de Enrique Martinez Sobral. Mexico: Libro Mexico, 1958. 2 vols.

761. ------. LA VIDA EN MEXICO DURANTE UNA RESIDENCIA DE DOS ANOS EN ÉSE PAIS. Traducción y prologo de Felipé Teixidor. Mexico: Editorial Porrua, 1959. 601p.

762. ------. LIFE IN MEXICO: THE LETTERS OF FANNY

CALDERÓN DE LA BARCA. WITH NEW MATERIAL FROM THE AUTHOR'S PRIVATE JOURNAL. Edited and annotated by Howard T. Fisher and Marion Hall Fisher. Garden City, N.Y.: Doubleday/Anchor Press Books, 1970. 834p.

LIFE IN MEXICO developed from letters to relatives, which were in turn based on a journal kept while travelling in Mexico. Only two of three volumes of this journal survive. Definitive edition, incorporating portions of her journal not used in the original edition. Includes extensive notes, background material, photographs, and bibliography.

763. Calderwood, Margaret Steuart, 1715-1774. Scottish resident of Polton, Midlothian. LETTERS AND JOURNALS OF MRS. CALDERWOOD OF POLTON, FROM ENGLAND, HOLLAND, AND THE LOW COUNTRIES IN 1756. Edited by Alexander Fergusson. Edinburgh: D. Douglas, 1884. 386p.

Travel account, describing life at Court, written from a diary and letters, June--December 1756. Except for the first few pages, the letters are not dated; however, the dailiness is retained.

764. Calisher, Hortense, b. 1911. American Jewish novelist and short story writer. HERSELF: AN AUTO-BIOGRAPHICAL WORK. New York: Arbor House, 1972. 398p.

Contains an abridged version of a journal written in 1958 while on a lecture tour of Japan.

765. Callcott, Maria Dundas Graham, Lady, 1785-1842. English traveller, diarist and political figure at the Portuguese Court. JOURNAL OF A RESIDENCE IN INDIA. Edinburgh: A. Constable, 1812. 211p. Second edition, 1813. 215p.

766. ------. JOURNAL OF A RESIDENCE IN CHILE, DURING THE YEAR 1822; AND A VOYAGE FROM CHILE TO BRAZIL IN 1823. London: Printed for Longman, Hurst, Rees, Orme, Brown, and Green, 1824. 512p. Reprinted with a new introduction by A.C. Wilgus, New York: Frederick A. Praeger, 1969. 512p.

767. ------. MARIA, LADY CALLCOTT, THE CREATOR OF "LITTLE ARTHUR." Rosamund Brunel Gotch. London: John Murray, 1937. 319p.

Contains extracts from diaries and letters.

768. ------. "Correspondencia Entre Maria Graham e a Imperatriz Dona Leopoldina e Cartas Anexas." BRAZIL BIBLIOTHECA NACIONAL 60 (1940), 29-65.

769. ------. JOURNAL OF A VOYAGE TO BRAZIL, AND RESIDENCE THERE, DURING PART OF THE YEARS 1821, 1822, AND 1823. London: Longman, Hurst, Rees, Orme, Brown, and Green, 1824. 335p. Reprinted with a new introduction by A.C. Wilgus, London: Frederick A. Praeger, 1969. 335p.

Account of a voyage with her first husband, Captain Thomas Graham of the British Royal Navy. Political diary dealing with many of the major events surrounding Brazil's fight for independence from Portugal.

770. ------. JOURNAL, 1827. From the Ashmolean Museum, Oxford, England. Oxford Microform Publications, n.d. 9 microfiches (105x148 cm).

771 Callender, Hannah, 1737-1801. American Quaker Colonist.. "Extracts from the Diary of Hannah Callender." George Vaux. PENNSYLVANIA MAGAZINE OF HISTORY AND BIOGRAPHY 12:4 (1888), 432-456.

Diary 1758-1762.

772. Cameron, Evelyn. English-born Montana frontier settler. "The Intimate Vision of Evelyn Cameron." Donna M. Lucey. GEO 5:1 (January, 1983), 66-79.

Discussion of and extracts from a diary, 1893-1928, of frontier life on a pony ranch owned by Cameron and her husband. Illustrated by photographs taken by Cameron.

773. Cameron, Lucy Lyttelton Butt, 1781-1858. British

novelist. THE LIFE OF LUCY LYTTELTON CAMERON. PARTLY AN AUTOBIOGRAPHY, AND FROM HER PRIVATE JOURNALS. Edited by her eldest son [Charles Cameron]. London: Darton & Co., 1862. 572p.

774. Campan, Jeanne Louise Henriette Genet, 1752-1822. French educator and Lady-In-Waiting to Marie Antoinette. JOURNAL ANECDOTIQUE DE MADAME CAMPAN, OU SOUVENIRS RECUEILLIS DANS SES ENTRETIENS. Par M. Maigne. Suivi d'une Correspondance inedite de Madame Campan avec son fils. Paris: Baudouin Freres, 1824. 250p.

775. ------. THE PRIVATE JOURNAL OF MADAME CAMPAN. COMPRISING ORIGINAL ANECDOTES OF THE FRENCH COURT; SELECTIONS FROM HER CORRESPONDENCE, THOUGHTS ON EDUCATION, &TC. Edited by M. Maigne. London: H. Colburn, 1825. 440p.

776. ------. CORRESPONDANCE INEDITE DE MADAME CAMPAN AVEC LA REINE HORTENSE. Publiée avec notes et introduction par J.A.C. Buchon. Paris, 1835; and Brussels: Meline, 1835. 2 vols.

777. ------. MADAME CAMPAN À ÉCOUEN. ÉTUDE HISTORIQUE ET BIOGRAPHIQUE. D'APRES DES LETTRES INÉDITES CONSERVÉS AUS ARCHIVES NATIONALES ET A LA GRANDE-CHANCELLERIE DE LA LÉGION D'HONNEUR. Précédeé d'un notice sur le Chateau d'Écouen. Par Louis Bonneville de Marsangy. Paris: H. Champion Librairie de la Société de l'Histoire de Paris. Pontoise: Alex. Seyes, Librairie, 1879. 343p.

Documents relating to the founding of Ecouen, a school founded by Napoleon I for the daughters and sisters of the Officers of the Legion of Honor. He appointed Madame Campan Superintendent. Letters are for the most part taken from CORRESPONDANCE INEDITE DE MADAME CAMPAN AVEC LA REINE HORTENSE (1835).

778. Campbell, Mrs. Patrick, pseud. for Beatrice Stella Tanner Patrick, 1865-1940. English stage actress. MY LIFE AND SOME LETTERS, BY MRS. PATRICK CAMPBELL. New York: Dodd, Mead and Co., 1922. 451p.

Autobiography. Most of the letters are from her correspondents, including Sarah Bernhardt, George Bernard Shaw, Ellen Terry, and Campbell's daughter, Stella Campbell.

779. ------. BERNARD SHAW AND MRS. PATRICK CAMPBELL: THEIR CORRESPONDENCE. Edited by Alan Dent. New York: Alfred A. Knopf, 1952. 385p.

Letters 1899-1939 by "an intellectual giant and a great and beautiful actress, a pair whose brilliance of mind and of personality dominated the English-speaking stage for fifty years."

780. Canfield, Sarah E. American army wife. "An Army Wife on the Upper Missouri: The Diary of Sarah E. Canfield, 1866-1868." Edited by Ray H. Mattison. NORTH DAKOTA HISTORY 20 (1953), 191-220.

781. Cannon, Luella Wareing, b. 1888. American Mormon missionary. MY CUP RUNNETH OVER. Salt Lake City: Privately printed by the author, 1969. 494p.

Mormon autobiography and missionary diary, 1888-1968.

782. Cannon, Martha Hughes, 1857-1932. American Mormon, physician, and first woman Senator in the United States. "The Goose Hangs High: Extracts from the Letters of Martha Hughes Cannon." Constance L. Lieber. UTAH HISTORICAL QUARTERLY 48:1 (1980), 37-48.

Extracts from letters written from England, 1885-1887. Cannon had exiled herself to prevent her husband's arrest for polygamy; she was his plural fourth wife.

783. Capper, Florence Crawford, b. 1868. American publisher and wife of Kansas Governor

Arthur Capper. "A Kansas Romance of the Gay Nineties." Homer Edward Socolofsky MIDWEST QUARTERLY 3 (October, 1961), 81-93

Describes the courtship of Florence Crawford and Arthur Capper, drawing upon excerpts from their diaries, June, 1891--November, 1892.

784. Caraway, Hattie Ophelia Wyatt, 1878-1950. American politician. SILENT HATTIE SPEAKS: THE PERSONAL JOURNAL OF SENATOR HATTIE CARAWAY. Edited by Diane D. Kincaid. Westport, Conn., and London: Greenwood Press, 1979. 151p.

Public Diary, written on Senate stationery, describes daily Senate activities. Sketchy entries from December 14, 1931, shortly after she took office, to May, 1932, and even briefer entries for January, 1934.

785. Carlyle, Jane Welsh, 1801-1866. English literary figure and wife of English historian Thomas Carlyle. LETTERS AND MEMORIALS OF JANE WELSH CARLYLE. Prepared for publication by Thomas Carlyle. Edited by James Anthony Froude. London: Longmans, Green, 1883. 3 vols. New York: Charles Scribner's Sons, 1903. 3 vols.

First published edition, annotated by Thomas Carlyle and heavily edited by Froude. Diary extracts, 1855-1856, are included in Volume 2.

786. ------. EARLY LETTERS OF JANE WELSH CARLYLE, TOGETHER WITH A FEW OF LATER YEARS AND SOME OF THOMAS CARLYLE. All hitherto unpublished. Edited by David G. Ritchie. London: Swan Sonnenshein & Co., 1889.

Fifty-five letters, 1819-1866, chiefly addressed to the editor's great-aunt, Eliza Stoddard.

787. ------. NEW LETTERS AND MEMOIRALS OF JANE WELSH CARLYLE. Annotated by Thomas Carlyle and edited by Alexander Carlyle, with a introduction by Sir James Crichton-Browne. London and New York: John Lane, the Bodley Head, 1903. 2 vols.

Letters which, according to the editor, James Anthony Froude "mutilated or put aside." A lengthy introduction is devoted to a criticism of Froude's handling of Carlyle's papers, and to clearing up what the editor believes to be mistakes and misinformation about the Carlyles' marriage.

788. ------. THE LOVE LETTERS OF THOMAS CARLYLE AND JANE WELSH. Edited by Alexander Carlyle. London: John Lane, 1908, 1909. 2 vols.

Love letters, 1821-1826.

789. ------. JANE WELSH CARLYLE: LETTERS TO HER FAMILY, 1839-1863. Edited by Leonard Huxley. London: John Murray, 1924. 390p.

Selection of 165 letters from the volumes edited by James Anthony Froude and Alexander Carlyle, and from previously unpublished correspondence with her family.

790. ------. LETTERS OF JANE WELSH CARLYLE TO JOSEPH NEUBERG, 1848-1862. Edited with an introduction and notes by Townsend Scudder. London and New York: Oxford University Press, 1931. 42p.

Correspondence with a business man who felt things of the mind and spirit should be "neglected by no man, not even under the pressing demands of a business career." He became friends of the Carlyles in 1848.

791. ------. JANE WELSH CARLYLE: A NEW SELECTION OF HER LETTERS. Arranged by Trudy Bliss. London: Victor Gollancz, 1950. 355p.

Selection taken from previous editions, including those by James Anthony Froude, Alexander Carlyle, and Leonard Huxley.

792. ------. I TOO AM HERE: SELECTIONS FROM THE LETTERS OF JANE WELSH CARLYLE. With an introduction and notes by Alan and Mary McQueen Simpson. Cambridge, Mass.: Cambridge University Press, 1977. 306p.

793. ------. THOMAS AND JANE: SELECTED LETTERS FROM THE EDINBURGH UNIVERSITY LIBRARY COLLECTION. Edited by Ian Campbell. Edinburgh: Published by Friends of Edinburgh University Library for its members, 1980. 102p.

794. ------. THE COLLECTED LETTERS OF THOMAS AND JANE WELSH CARLYLE. Duke-Edinburgh edition. General editor, Charles Richard Sanders. Co-editor, Kenneth J. Fielding. Duke University Press, 1970-1987. Volume 8 (January 1835--June 1836), 1980. 364p.; and Volume 9 (July 1836--December 1837) 1981. 434p.

Definitive edition of the Carlyle correspondence; supersedes all previous publications so far as the text of the letters is concerned.

795. Carnegie, Mrs. V.M. A KENYAN FARM DIARY. Edinburgh and London: W. Blackwood & Son, 1930. 271p.

Diary 1919-1928.

796. Carolina Maria, Consort of Ferdinand I, King of the Two Sicilies, 1752-1818. CORRESPONDANCE INÉDITE DE MARIE-CAROLINE, REINE DE NAPLES ET DE SICILE, AVEC LE MARQUIS DE GALLO (1792-1806). Publiée par M. le Commandant Weil. Paris: Plon-Nourrit, 1911. 71p.

797. Caroline Matilda, Queen Consort of Christian VII, King of Denmark and Norway, 1751-1775. MEMOIRS OF AN UNFORTUNATE QUEEN. INTERSPERSED WITH LETTERS, WRITTEN BY HERSELF, TO SEVERAL OF HER ILLUSTRIOUS RELATIONS AND FRIENDS. London: J. Bew, 1776. 260p.

798. Carr, Emily, 1871-1945. Canadian artist and author. HUNDREDS AND THOUSANDS: THE JOURNALS OF EMILY CARR. Toronto and Vancouver: Clarke, Irwin & Co., 1966. 332p.

Chronicles her work as an artist and presents her philosophy of aging; she began her journal at age fifty-eight.

799. ------. M.E.: A PORTRAYAL OF EMILY CARR. Edythe

Hembroff-Schlelcher. Toronto: Clarke, Irwin Co., 1969. 123p.

Short biographical sketch and letters to Hembroff-Schlelcher, 1933-1940.

800. ------. "Letters from Emily Carr." W.F. Blissett. UNIVERSITY OF TORONTO QUARTERLY 41:2 (1972), 93-150.

Letters 1937-1944 to Ruth Humphrey, then a professor of literature at Victoria College.

801. Carr, Mary Francis. American Shaker. SHAKERS: A CORRESPONDENCE BETWEEN MARY FRANCES CARR OF MOUNT HOLLY CITY AND A SHAKER SISTER, SARAH LUCAS OF UNION VILLAGE. Edited by R.W. Pelham. Union Village, Ohio, 1868. 24p. Cincinatti, P.T. Shultz, 1869. 23p. Springfield, Mass., 1870. 23p.

802. Carraud, Zulma (Tourangin), 1796-1889. UNPUBLISHED CORRESPONDENCE OF HONORE DE BALZAC AND MADAME ZULMA CARRAUD, 1829-1850. London: John Lane, 1937. 400p.

803. ------. HONORE DE BALZAC: CORRESPONDANCE AVEC ZULMA CARRAUD, (1829-1850). Preface par Marcel Bouteron. Paris: A. Colin, 1935. 352p. Nouvelle édition revisée et augmenteé, avec notes et commentaires par Marcel Bourteron, Paris: Gallimard, 1951. 305p.

804. Carriera, Rosalba, 1675-1757. Italian portrait artist. JOURNAL DE ROSALBA CARRIERA PENDANT SON SOJOURN À PARIS EN 1720 ET 1721. Publiée en Italien par Vianelli. Traduit, annotée et augmenteé d'une biographie et des documents inédits sur les artistes et les amateurs du temps par Alfred Sensier. Paris: J. Techener, 1863. 569p.

805. ------. ROSALBA CARRIERA. Vittorio Malamani. Bergamo: Instiuto d'Arti Grafiche, 1910.

Monograph which includes Carriera's Paris diary, 1720-1721.

806. ------. ROSALBA'S JOURNAL AND OTHER PAPERS. Austin Dobson. London: Oxford University Press, 1926. Reprinted, Freeport, N.Y.: Books for Libraries Press, 1976.

807. ------. ROSALBA CARRIERA: LETTERE, DIARI, FRAMMENTI. Bernadina Sani. Firenze: L.S. Olschki, 1985. 2 vols.

808. Carrington, Dora Houghton, 1893-1932. English artist and member of the Bloomsbury Group. CARRINGTON: LETTERS AND EXTRACTS FROM HER DIARIES. Chosen and with an introduction by David Garnett. With a biographical note by Noel Carrington. New York: Holt, Rinehart and Winston, 1970, 1971. 514p.

Literary letters, 1915-1932 to Lytton Strachey, Noel Carrington, Rosamond Lehmann, David Garnett and others.

809. Carrington, Margaret Irvin Sullivant. American wife of a frontier Army officer. AB-SA-RA-KA, HOME OF THE CROWS: BEING THE EXPERIENCES OF AN OFFICER'S WIFE ON THE PLAINS, AND MARKING THE VICISSITUDES OF PERIL AND PLEASURE DURING THE OCCUPATION OF THE NEW ROUTE TO VIRGINIA CITY, MONTANA, 1866-1867, AND THE INDIAN HOSTILITIES THERETO; WITH OUTLINES OF THE NATURAL FEATURES AND RESOURCES OF THE LAND, TABLE OF DISTANCES, MAPS, AND OTHER AIDS TO THE TRAVELER, GATHERED FROM OBSERVATION AND OTHER RELIABLE SOURCES. Philadelphia: J.B. Lippincott, 1860. Revised and enlarged edition published under the title AB-SA-RA-KA, LAND OF MASSACRE, London and Philadelphia: J.B. Lippincott, 1879. 378p.

Extracts from a diary, 1866-1867. Entries are for the most part rewritten from the original but keep the daily, dated form. The enlarged edition contains additional "aids to the traveler," and historical information; the new title reflects the escalation of the Indian Wars in the region between 1866 and 1879.

810. Carroll, Gladys Hasty, b. 1904. American

novelist. TO REMEMBER FOREVER: THE JOURNAL OF A COLLEGE GIRL, 1922-1923. Boston: Little, Brown & Co., 1963. 306p.

Account of Carroll's Sophomore year at Bates College, Maine, compiled from her journal, letters, and college newspaper articles.

811. Carter, Elizabeth, 1717-1806. English author and Bluestocking. A SERIES OF LETTERS BETWEEN MRS. ELIZABETH CARTER AND MISS CATHERINE TALBOT, FROM THE YEAR 1741 TO 1770. TO WHICH ARE ADDED, LETTERS OF MRS. ELIZABETH CARTER TO MRS. VESEY, BETWEEN THE YEARS 1763 AND 1787. Published from the originals in the possession of the Reverend Montagu Pennington. Edited by Montagu Pennington. London: F.C.& J. Rivington, 1809. 4 vols.

Correspondence with Bluestockings Catherine Talbot (c.1720-1770) and Elizabeth Vesey (1715?-1791). Mrs. Carter and Miss Talbot met in 1741, and collaborated on a translation of Epictetus.

812. ------. LETTERS FROM MRS. CARTER TO MRS. MONTAGU, BETWEEN THE YEARS 1755 AND 1800, CHIEFLY UPON LITERARY AND MORAL SUBJECTS. Edited by Montagu Pennington. Published from the originals in the possession of the Reverend Montagu Pennington. London: Printed for F.C. and J. Rivington by R.&R. Gilbert, 1817. 3 vols. Reprinted, New York: AMS Press, 1973.

Letters to English author and literary figure Elizabeth Montagu.

813. Carter, Lillian, b. 1898. American mother of U.S. President James Carter. AWAY FROM HOME: LETTERS TO MY FAMILY. Lillian Carter and Gloria Carter Spann. New York: Simon & Schuster, 1977. 155p.

Letters from India, where Carter worked as a Peace Corps Volunteer. She joined at the age of sixty-seven.

814. Caruso, Dorothy. Wife of opera singer Enrico Caruso. A PERSONAL HISTORY, BY DOROTHY CARUSO. New

York: Hermitage House, 1952. 191p.

Part reminiscence, part diary. Sections of the reminiscences are written in diary form, but in the past tense.

815. Cary, Agnes. EMPRESS EUGENIE IN EXILE. New York: The Century Co., 1920. 368p.

Diary of ten months Cary spent with the Empress Eugenie in 1886.

816. Cary, Harriet. American Civil War Diarist. "Diary of Miss Harriet Cary, Kept by Her from May 6, 1862 to July 24, 1862." TYLER'S QUARTERLY 9:2 (1927), 104-115 and 12:3 (1931), 160-173.

Confederate diary by a resident of Williamsburg, Virginia. The diary begins, "The repudiated stars and stripes are now waving over our town, and humiliated I feel, we bow our heads to Yankee despotism."

817. Case, Adelaide Teague, b. 1887. English religious author and wife of a British Colonial Officer stationed in India. DAY BY DAY AT LUCKNOW: A JOURNAL OF THE SEIGE OF LUCKNOW. London: R. Bentley, 1858. 348p.

Diary of the Seige of Lucknow during the Indian Mutiny of 1857-1858.

818. Cassatt, Mary Stevenson, 1844-1926. American Impressionist painter. CASSATT AND HER CIRCLE: SELECTED LETTERS. Edited by Nancy Mowll Matthews. New York: Abbeville Press, 1984. 360p.

Selection of letters, (208 of 1,100) 1860-1926, which concentrates on those which offer the greatest insight into the development of Cassatt's art.

819. Castle, Barbara, b. 1911. English politician and journalist. THE CASTLE DIARIES, 1974-1976. London: Weidenfeld and Nicolson, 1980. 788p.

Public diary, chronicling her years as a Cabinet Minister under Prime Minister Harold Nicolson. Castle was a member of the House of Commons for twenty-four years.

820. ------. THE CASTLE DIARIES, 1964-1970. London: Weidenfeld and Nicolson, 1984. 858p.

Public diary of English Cabinet Activities. The diary has been "pruned" for publication, but the original has been bequeathed to Bradford University, England.

821. Cates, Tressa R. American. THE DRAINPIPE DIARY. New York: Vantage Press, 1957. 273p.

Secret diary, 1941-1945 of a civilian nurse interned by the Japanese in the Philippines during World War II.

Catez, Elizabeth. See: Elizabeth de la Trinite.

822. Cather, Willa Sibert, 1873-1947. American novelist and short story writer. WILLA CATHER IN EUROPE: HER OWN STORY OF THE FIRST JOURNEY. Introduction and incidental notes by George N. Kates. New York: Alfred A. Knopf, 1956. 178p.

Travel diary, 1902.

823. ------. WILLA CATHER IN PERSON: INTERVIEWS, SPEECHES, AND LETTERS. Selected and edited by L. Brent Bohlke. Lincoln, Nebr.: University of Nebraska Press, 1986. 202p.

824. Catherine II, Empress of Russia, 1729-1796. JOSEPH II UND KATHARINA VON RUSSLAND. IHR BRIEFWECHSEL. Herausgegeben von Alfred, Ritter von Arneth. Wien: W. Braumuller, 1869. 393p.

825. ------. LEOPOLD II, FRANZ II, UND CATHARINA. IHRE CORRESPONDENZ, NEBST EINER EINLEITUNG: ZUR GESCHICHTE DER POLITIK LEOPOL'S II. Herausgegeben von Adolf Beer. Leipzig: Duncker & Humbolt, 1874. 259p.

826. ------. BRIEFWECHSEL ZWISCHEN HEINRICH, PRINZ VON PREUSSEN UND KATHARINA II VON RUSSLAND. Dr. Richard Kravel. Berlin: A Duncker, 1903. 178p.

827. ------. DER BRIEFWECHSEL ZWISCHEN DER KAISERIN KATHARINA II VON RUSSLAND UND JOHANN GEORGE ZIMMERMANN. Herausgegeben von Eduard Bodeman. Hannover: Hahn, 1906.

Correspondence with Johan George, Ritter von Zimmermann (1728-1795). The letters are in French.

828. ------. LES LETTRES DE CATHERINE II AU PRINCE DE LIGNE (1780-1796). Publiées avec quelques notes par le Princesse Charles de Ligne. Bruxelles et Paris: G. Van Oest et Cie., 1924. 236p.

Letters to Charles Joseph, Prince de Ligne (1735-1814).

829. ------. CORRESPONDENCE OF CATHERINE THE GREAT WHEN GRAND DUCHESS, WITH SIR CHARLES HANBURY-WILLIAMS AND LETTERS FROM COUNT PONIATOWSKI. Edited and translated by the Earl of Ilchester and Mrs. Langford-Brooke. London: Thornton Butterworth, 1928. 288p.

Correspondence July 31, 1756--June, 1757 with Sir Charles, British Ambassador at the Court of Empress Elizabeth from 1755-1757, and letters from Stanislaus-Augustus, King of Poland, then Count Poniatowski.

830. ------. DOCUMENTS OF CATHERINE THE GREAT: THE CORRESPONDENCE WITH VOLTAIRE AND THE INSURRECTION OF 1767, IN THE ENGLISH TEXT OF 1768. Edited by W.F. Reddaway. Cambridge, England: The University Press, 1931. 349p.

Correspondence with Voltaire, 1763-1777. Catherine's authorship of the letters has been questioned.

831. ------. VOLTAIRE AND CATHERINE THE GREAT: SELECTED CORRESPONDENCE. Translated with Commentary,

notes and introduction by A. Lentin. With a foreword by Elizabeth Hill. Cambridge, England: Oriental Research Partners, 1974. 186p.

832. Catherine de Medicis, Consort of Henry II, King of France, 1519-1589. CATHERINE DE MEDICIS: LETTRES. Publiées par M. le Comte Hector de la Ferrière. Paris: Imprimerie Nationale, 1880-1943. 11 vols.

Volumes 1-5 edited by Hector de la Ferriere-Percy. Volumes 6-10 edited by Gustave Bageunault de Puchesse. Volume 11 compiled by Eugene Lelong and Lucien Auvray, and edited by Andre Lesort. Letters 1533-1588.

833. Catherine, Queen Consort of Jerome Bonaparte, King of Westphalia, 1783-1835. CORRESPONDANCE INEDITE DE LA REINE CATHERINE DE WESTPHALIE, NÉE PRINCESSE DU WURTEMBERG AVEC SA FAMILLE ET CELLE DU ROI JEROME, LES SOUVERAINES ETRANGERS ET DIVERS PERSONAGES. Publiée par le Baron Albert du Casse. Paris: E. Bouillon, 1893. 398p.

834. Catherine, Consort of William I, King of Wurtemberg, 1788-1818. SCENES OF RUSSIAN COURT LIFE: BEING THE CORRESPONDENCE OF ALEXANDER I WITH HIS SISTER CATHARINE. Translated by Henry Havelock. Edited with an introduction by the Grand Duke Nicholaus. London: Jarrolds, 1915. 331p.

Appendices include extracts from the MEMOIRS of the Princess Lieven and letters of the Empress Maria.

835. Cavell, Edith, 1865-1915. English nurse and resistance worker during World War I. EDITH CAVELL. Rowland Ryder. London: Hamish Hamilton, 1975. 278p.

Includes a chapter on a short diary, written in April and May of 1915 and found thirty years after the War. Presents extracts for two days in 1915. Also presents extensive extracts from Cavell's correspondence. Cavell was arrested by the Germans in 1915 and executed for treason.

836. Cavendish, Lucy Caroline Lyttelton, Lady

Frederick, 1841-1925. English Maid of Honor to Queen Victoria. DIARY OF LADY FREDERICK CAVENDISH. Edited by John Bailey. London: John Murray, 1927. 2 vols.

Court diary, 1856-1882. Gives a picture of contemporary politics and social life in London and in the country.

837. Caylus, Marie Marguerite le Valois de Villette de Murcay, Comtesse de, 1673-1729. French author, aristocrat, and niece of Madame de Maintenon. SOUVENIRS ET CORRESPONDANCE DE MADAME DE CAYLUS. Edition complete publiee avec une annotation historique, biographique et litteraire et un index analytique par Emile Raunie. Paris: Bibliotheque Charpentier, 1889. 344p.

838. Chace, Elizabeth Buffum, 1806-1899; and Lucy Buffum Lovell, 1809-1895. American abolitionists. TWO QUAKER SISTERS. FROM THE ORIGINAL DIARIES OF ELIZABETH BUFFUM CHACE AND LUCY BUFFUM LOVELL. With an introduction by Malcolm R. Lovell. Foreword by Rufus M. Jones. New York: Liveright Publishing Corp, 1937. 183p.

Antislavery reminiscences by Elizabeth, and a diary of motherhood and infant mortality by Lucy.

839. Chacel, Rosa. Spanish author and critic. ALCANCIA: ROSA CHACEL. Barcelona: Seix Barral, 1982. 2 vols.

Volume 1 (Ida), 1940-1966. Volume 2 (Vuelta), 1967-1981.

840. Chaix, Marie, b. 1942. French author. UN 21 AVRIL À NEW YORK: JOURNAL 1980-1982. Paris: Éditions Seuil, 1986. 202p.

841. Chalmers, Anne, later Hanna, 1813-1891. Scottish daughter of religious leader Reverend Thomas Chalmers. LETTERS AND JOURNALS OF ANN CHALMERS. Edited by her daughter [Mrs. Matilda Grace Hanna Blackie]. London: The Chelsea Publishing Co., 1923. 209p.

Letters written to her life-long friend Anne

Parker (later Lady Cardwell) and a journal written on a trip to England in 1830. Only the girlhood letters, 1826-1828, between Chalmers and Lady Cardwell have been published.

842. Chambers, Charlotte Ludlow, d. 1821. American. MEMOIR OF CHARLOTTE CHAMBERS. By her grandson, Lewis H. Garrard. Philadelphia: Privately Printed for the Author, 1856. 135p.

Contains extracts from her letters and a diary, 1796-1821, giving a picture of the early settlement of Cincinnati, Ohio.

843. Chapone, Hester, 1727-1801. English author and Bluestocking. THE WORKS OF MRS. CHAPONE. Now first collected. London: John Murray, 1807. 4 vols.

Volumes I and II comprise a biography of Chapone, including extracts from her correspondence. Volume III contains correspondence with Samuel Richardson and others. Volume IV contains her correspondence with Elizabeth Carter.

844. Charlotte Augusta of Wales, Consort of Prince Leopold of Saxe-Coburg-Saalfeld, 1796-1817. ROYAL CORRESPONDENCE: OR, LETTERS, BETWEEN HER LATE ROYAL HIGHNESS THE PRINCESS CHARLOTTE, AND HER ROYAL MOTHER, QUEEN CAROLINE OF ENGLAND, DURING THE EXILE OF THE LATTER. DEVELOPING MANY OF THE MOST MYSTERIOUS AND IMPORTANT TRANSACTIONS CONNECTED WITH THE EVENTFUL LIFE, AND FATAL CATASTROPHE OF HER MAJESTY'S DEATH, AS WELL AS RELATING TO OTHER DISTINGUISHED CHARACTERS IN THE KINGDOM. London: Jones and Co., 1822. 188p.

Includes correspondence with Caroline Amelia of England, and Elizabeth, Queen Consort of George IV.

845. ------. LETTERS OF THE PRINCESS CHARLOTTE, 1811-1817. Edited by A. Aspinall. London: Home and Van Thal, 1949. 254p.

Letters chiefly to her closest friend, Miss Mercer

Elphinstone. An introduction covers her life until her marriage, and presents extracts from early letters.

846. Chase, Josephine Streeper, 1835-1894. American Mormon and Sunday School teacher. "The Josephine Diaries: Glimpses of the Life of Josephine Streeper Chase, 1881-1894." Edited by Fae Decker Dix. UTAH HISTORICAL QUARTERLY 46:2 (1978), 167-183.

Diary of daily domestic life in Utah by a plural wife (second wife of George Ogden Chase) and mother of sixteen.

847. Chase, Lucy, 1822-1909; and Sarah Chase. American Quaker teachers. DEAR ONES AT HOME: LETTERS FROM CONTRABAND CAMPS. Edited by Henry L. Swint. Nashville, Tenn.: Vanderbilt University Press, 1966. 274p.

Letters to family and friends in New England describe teaching newly freed slaves in Craney Island Negro schools, in mainland Virginia, and elsewhere, 1861-1870.

848. Châteauroux, Marie-Anne de Mailly-Neslé, Duchesse de, 1717-1744. French mistress of Louis XV. CORRESPONDANCE INÉDITE DE MADAME DE CHATEAUROUX AVEC LE DUC DE RICHELIEU, LE MARÉCHAL DE BELLE-ISLE, M.M. DUVERNEY, DE CHAVIGNI, MADAME DE FLAVACOURT ET AUTRES. Précédeé d'une notice historique sur la Vie de Madame de Chateauroux, par Madame Gacon-Dufor. Paris, 1806. 2 vols.

Châtelet, Gabrielle Emilie de Tonnelier de Breteuil. See: Du Châtelet, Gabrielle Emilie de Tonnelier de Breteuil, Marquise.

849. Chatterton, Henrietta Georgiana Marcia Lascelles, Lady, 1806-1876. English author. MEMOIRS OF GEORGIANA, LADY CHATTERTON. WITH SOME PASSAGES FROM HER DIARY. Edward Heneage Dering. London: Hurst and Blackett, 1878. 309p. London: Art and Book Co., 1901. 279p. London: R.&T. Washbourne, 1911. 279p.

Extracts from a literary diary, 1837-1859.

850. Chesler, Phyllis, b. 1940. American psychologist, feminist and scholar. WITH CHILD: A DIARY OF MOTHERHOOD. New York: T.Y. Crowell, 1979. 304p.

Diary of a first pregnancy and first year of motherhood.

851. Chesnut, Mary Boykin Miller, 1823-1886. American diarist. A DIARY FROM DIXIE, 1859-1861. Edited by Isabella D. Martin and Myra Lockett Avary. New York: Peter Smith, 1929. 423p.

Chesnut's diary is regarded by many as one of the fullest, most perceptive, and liveliest Confederate accounts of the Civil War.

852. ------. A DIARY FROM DIXIE. Edited by Ben Ames Williams. New York: Houghton Mifflin, 1949. 572p.

853. ------. "Mary Boykin Chesnut: Southern Intellectual." In CONFEDERATE WOMEN. Bell Irvin Wiley. Westport, Conn., and London: Greenwood Press, 1975. 204p.

Comparison of the text of the diary as edited by Chesnut and by Ben Ames Williams, and of William's fictionalized version, A HOUSE DIVIDED (1947).

854. ------. MARY CHESNUT'S CIVIL WAR. Edited by C. Vann Woodward. New Haven, Conn., and London: Yale University Press, 1981. 886p.

First definitive edition of Chesnut's diary, drawing upon four surviving manuscript versions.

855. ------. "Mary Boykin Chesnut: The Making of a Reputation." George F. Hayhoe. THE MISSISSIPPI QUARTERLY 35:1 (Winter, 1981/1982), 60-72.

Discusses the literary career of Chesnut's DIARY.

856. ------. THE PRIVATE MARY CHESNUT: THE UNPUBLISHED CIVIL WAR DIARIES. C. Vann Woodward and

Elisabeth Muhlenfeld. Oxford and New York: Oxford University Press, 1984. 292p.

Complete text of the authentic, original and previously unpublished Civil War diary, February 18, 1861--June 26, 1865. Her published diary was really a memoir based on this diary, expanded and written in a diary style.

857. Child, Lydia Maria Francis, 1802-1880. American author and social reformer. CORRESPONDENCE BETWEEN LYDIA MARIA CHILD AND GOVERNOR WISE AND MRS. MASON OF VIRGINIA. Boston: American Anti-Slavery Society, 1860. 28p.

858. ------. LETTERS OF LYDIA MARIA CHILD. With a biographical introduction by John G. Whittier, and an appendix by Wendell Phillips. Boston: Houghton Mifflin Co., 1882, 1883. 280p. Reprinted, New York: Arno Press, 1969. 280p.; New York: AMS Press, 1971. 280p.

Memorial selection of her letters, 1817-1880, comprising only a fraction of her correspondence.

859. ------. "Letters of a Massachusetts Reformer to an Indiana Radical." James A. Barnes. INDIANA MAGAZINE OF HISTORY 26:1 (March, 1930), 46-60.

Correspondence 1862-1878 between Child and George V. Julian, one of her closest friends in the "Free Soil" Party. Barnes notes the publication of the letters will add little information about the Civil War, but that letters from extremists on both sides will give readers insight into the emotional element which played an important role in the War.

860. ------. LYDIA MARIA CHILD: SELECTED LETTERS, 1817- 1880. Edited by Milton Meltzer and Patricia G. Holland. Francine Krasno, Associate Editor. Cambridge, Mass.: University of Massachusetts Press, 1982. 610p.

Personal and formal letters to John Brown,

Margaret Fuller, William Lloyd Garrison, Angelina Grimke, and others, reflecting Child's primary private and public concerns: abolition, marriage reform, labor and capitalism, and women's rights. Heavily annotated.

861. ------. THE COLLECTED CORRESPONDENCE OF LYDIA MARIA CHILD, 1817-1900. Edited by Patricia G. Holland and Milton Meltzer. Millwood, N.Y.: Kraus Microforms, 1980. 97 microfiches (105 x 148mm) and clothbound guide.

Over two thousand letters on microfiche and a printed guide which provides a biography of Child and a bibliography of works by and about her.

862. Chimay, Emilie Louise Marie Françoise Josephine de Pellapra de Riquet, Princesse de, 1808-1859. Illegitimate daughter of Napoleon Bonaparte and wife of Prince Joseph de Chimay, Envoy of Leopold I. LETTRES D'UNE FILLE DE NAPOLEON (FOUNTAINBLEU ET WINDSOR), 1853-1859. Publiée par la Princesse Bibesco. Paris: Editions Flammarion, 1933. 248p.

Letters and the "Journal Intime de Princesse de Chimay," p.199-248.

863. ------. LETTERS FROM THE FRENCH AND ENGLISH COURTS, 1853-1859, BY THE PRINCESSE DE CHIMAY. Presented by Princesse Marthe Bibesco. Translated from the French by Hamish Miles. London: Jonathan Cape, 1934. 159p.

Court letters, written to her children during the years her husband was Envoy. Includes an extract from the JOURNAL of Empress Marie-Louise.

864. Choiseul-Praslin, Fanny [Francoise Altarice Rosalba Sebastiani], Duchesse de, 1807-1847. EXTRAITS DE LETTRES DE MADAME LA DUCHESSE DE PRASLIN ET AUTRES PIÉCES MANUSCRITS TROUVÉES DANS SES PAPIERS. Paris: Imprimèrie Royale, 1847. 86p.

865. Christie, Agatha, pseud. for Dame Agatha Mary

Clarissa Miller Christie Mallowan, 1891-1976. English writer of mystery fiction. COME TELL ME HOW YOU LIVE. London: Collins, 1946. 192p. Reprinted, New York: Dodd, Mead & Co., 1974. 192p.

Undated journals describe several trips to the Middle East with her husband, English archeologist Sir Max Mallowan, on archeological digs undertaken in the years before World War II.

866. Churchill, Jeanette Jerome, Lady, 1854-1921. American-born wife of Lord Randolph Spencer Churchill and mother of Sir Winston Churchill. JENNIE: LADY RANDOLPH CHURCHILL: A PORTRAIT WITH LETTERS. Peregrine Churchill and Julian Mitchell. New York: St. Martin's Press, 1974. 239p.

Letters 1873-1921, begining with the courtship letters of Jeanette Jerome and Lord Randolph Churchill.

867. Churchill, Marianne. English immigrant to Natal. A MERCHANT FAMILY IN EARLY NATAL: DIARIES AND LETTERS OF JOSEPH AND MARIANNE CHURCHILL. WITH A NARRATIVE OF PIONEERING TRAVELS TO POTCHEFSTROOM AND THE SOUTPENSBERG. With contemporary illustrations by Marianne Churchill. Selected, edited and introduced by Daphne Child. Cape Town: A.A. Balkema, 1979. 198p.

Extracts from a pioneer diary, 1857-1858. Churchill emigrated to Natal with her brother in 1850.

868. Churchill, Matilda Faulkner, b. 1840. English missionary to India. LETTERS FROM MY HOME IN INDIA. BEING THE CORRESPONDENCE OF MRS. GEORGE CHURCHILL (1871-1916). Edited and arranged by Grace McLeod Rogers. New York: George H. Doran Co., 1916. 305p.

869. Clairmont, Clara, "Claire," Mary Jane, 1798-1879. English literary figure. Daughter of William Godwin, step-sister of Mary Wolstonecraft Shelley, and mistress of Lord Byron. THE JOURNALS OF CLAIRE CLAIRMONT. Edited by Marion Kingston Stocking with the assistance of David Makenzie Stocking. Cambridge, Mass.: Harvard University Press, 1968. 571p.

Four journals, 1814-1827. The primary interest of her journals lies in the light they shed on the Shelley family, from the time of Percy Shelley's elopement with Mary Godwin in 1814, to his death in 1822. This edition is as complete as possible, annotated, documented, and lightly edited.

870. ------. "The Mark of X in Claire Clairmont's Journal." Marcel Kessel. PUBLICATIONS OF THE MODERN LANGUAGE ASSOCIATION OF AMERICA 66 (December, 1951), 1180-1183.

Hitherto mysterious illnesses are explained by Kessel's decoding of Claimont's mark of "X" next to dates in her journal to keep track of her menstrual periods. Kessel uses these markings to disprove the theory that a child bearing the name Elena Adelaide Shelley was Clairmont's child by Percy Bysshe Shelley.

871. ------. "The Journal and Notebooks of Claire Clairmont, Unpublished Passages." Lorraine Robertson. KEATS-SHELLEY MEMORIAL BULLETIN 4 (1952), 35-48.

Extracts, with commentary, of previously unpublished portions of Clairmont's journal.

872. ------. "Claire Clairmont's Lost Russian Journal and Some Further Glimpses of Her Later Life." Herbert Huscher. KEATS-SHELLEY MEMORIAL BULLETIN 6 (1955), 35-47.

Transcription of a diary presumed lost. Presents extracts December 21, 1826--January 30, 1827, and includes a brief discussion of her later life.

873. Clancy, Ellen. English. A LADY'S VISIT TO THE GOLD DIGGINGS OF AUSTRALIA IN 1852-1853. WRITTEN ON THE SPOT. Edited by Patricia Thompson. London: Angus & Robertson, 1963. 160p.

Diary of gold-seeking adventures in Australia by a girl who, according the the editor, noticed everything, enjoyed everything, wrote busily in her diary, collected facts and figures, involved herself in various adventures with abandonned wives and orphaned children, fell in love, got married--and found some gold.

874. Clappe, Louise Amelia Knapp Smith, "Dame Shirley," 1819-1906. American author and teacher who traveled among the mining camps of frontier California. THE SHIRLEY LETTERS FROM THE CALIFORNIA MINES IN 1851-1852; BEING A SERIES OF TWENTY-THREE LETTERS FROM DAME SHIRLEY (MRS. LOUISE AMELIA KNAPP SMITH CLAPPE) TO HER SISTER IN MASSACHUSETTS AND NOW REPRINTED FROM THE PIONEER MAGAZINE OF 1854-1855. With synopses of the letters, a foreword, and many typographical and other corrections and emendations. Thomas C. Russell, together with an "Appreciation" by Mrs. M.V.T. Lawrence...San Francisco: Printed by T.C. Russell, 1922. 350p.

Letters written from Rich Bar, a failing and almost deserted mine on the Feather River, and later from Indian Bar. Rich and perceptive descriptions of the life of early California gold miners.

875. ------. LETTERS OF DAME SHIRLEY. Edited by Carl I. Wheat. San Francisco: Grabhorn Press, 1933. 2 vols. (limited letterpress edition).

876. ------. THE SHIRLEY LETTERS FROM THE CALIFORNIA MINES. With an introduction and notes by Carl I. Wheat. New York: Alfred A. Knopf, 1949. 216p.

877. ------. THE SHIRLEY LETTERS, BEING LETTERS WRITTEN IN 1851-1852 FROM THE CALIFORNIA MINES. By "Dame Shirley." With an introduction by Richard E. Oglesby. Santa Barbara, Calif., and Salt Lake City, Utah: Peregrine Smith, 1970. 198p.

878. Clark, Anne. American ambassador's wife. AUSTRALIAN ADVENTURE: LETTERS FROM AN AMBASSADOR'S WIFE. Foreword by Dame Zara Holt. South Melbourne, Australia: Macmillan of Australia, 1969. 232p.

Letters 1965-1967 to family and friends in America.

879. Clark, Edith O. American teacher and Wyoming State Superintendent of Public Instruction. "The Diary of Edith O. Clark." ANNALS OF WYOMING 39:2 (1967), 217-244.

Diary of building a log cabin near Buffalo, Wyoming.

880. Clark, Eleanor, b. 1913. American author and wife of Robert Penn Warren. EYES, ETC.: A MEMOIR BY ELEANOR CLARK. New York: Pantheon Books, 1977. 175p.

Struck by sudden blindness, Clark began a diary as a place to deal with her feelings about her disability.

881. Clark, Emily, later Balch, 1893-1953. American journalist and editor. INGENUE AMONG THE LIONS: THE LETTERS OF EMILY CLARK TO JOSEPH HERGESHEIMER. Edited with an introduction by Gerald Langford. Austin, Tex.: University of Texas Press, 1965. 221p.

Literary letters, 1921-1924, written almost daily, to keep Hergesheimer informed on her "precarious and often hilarious stint in the editor's chair" of the Southern literary magazine THE REVIEWER.

882. Clark, Helen E. American frontier settler. TWO DIARIES: THE DIARY AND JOURNAL OF CALVIN PERRY CLARK WHO JOURNEYED BY WAGON TRAIN FROM PLANO, ILLINOIS TO DENVER AND VICINITY OVER THE SANTA FE TRAIL IN THE YEAR 1859, TOGETHER WITH THE DIARY OF HIS SISTER HELEN E. CLARK WHO MADE A SIMILAR JOURNEY BY THE NORTHERN ROUTE IN THE YEAR 1860. Denver: Denver Public Library, 1962. 91, 44p.

Clark's diary is inverted, with the title: THE DIARY OF HELEN E. CLARK WHO JOURNEYED BY WAGON TRAIN FROM PLANO, ILLINOIS TO DENVER AND VICINITY OVER THE NORTHERN ROUTE IN THE YEAR 1860. Overland diary, April-June, 1860.

883. Clark, Laura Downs, 1798-1863. American doctor's wife. "The Original Diary of Mrs. Laura Downs Clark.

Wakeman, Ohio." THE FIRELANDS PIONEER 21 (1920), 2309-2326.

Diary June-October, 1818, chronicling pioneer life in Firelands, Ohio. William Matthews calls this an excellent and detailed diary.

Clarke, Caroline Cowles Richards. See Richards, Caroline Cowles.

884. Clarke, Mary McGowan. American frontier settler and wife of author Charles Francis Clarke. TO FORM A MORE PERFECT UNION: THE LIVES OF CHARLES FRANCIS AND MARY CLARKE FROM THEIR LETTERS, 1847-1871. Herbert Oliver Brayer. Glendale, Calif.: The Arthur H. Clark Co., and Albuquerque, N.Mex.: University of New Mexico Press, 1941. 233p.

885. Clawson, Mary. American. LETTERS FROM JERUSALEM. London and New York: Abelard-Schumann, 1957. 224p.

Clawson traveled to Jerusalem in 1953 with her husband, an agricultural economist. Describes a two-year's residence, including letters from the first year, June, 1953--June, 1954.

886. Clemm, Mrs. American aunt and mother-in-law of Edgar Allan Poe. "Mrs. Clemm and Henry Wadsworth Longfellow." Steven Allaback. HARVARD UNIVERSITY BULLETIN 18:1 (1970), 32-42.

Letters written to Longfellow, with commentary.

887. Clemson, Floride, later Lee, 1842-1871. American granddaughter of John C. Calhoun. A REBEL CAME HOME: THE DIARY OF FLORIDE CLEMSON. TELLS OF HER WARTIME ADVENTURES IN YANKEELAND, 1863-1864, HER TRIP HOME TO SOUTH CAROLINA, AND LIFE IN THE SOUTH DURING THE LAST FEW MONTHS OF THE CIVIL WAR AND THE YEAR FOLLOWING. Edited by Charles M. McGee, Jr. and Ernest M. Lander, Jr. Columbia, S.C.: University of South Carolina Press, 1961. 153p.

Diary written in Bladensburg, Beltsville, and Baltimore, Maryland, January 1, 1863--December 11, 1864, and at home in Pendleton, South Carolina, January 1--October 24, 1865, with occasional entries to 1869.

888. ------. "A Confederate Girl Visits Pennsylvania, July-September 1863." Ernest M. Lander, Jr. WESTERN PENNSYLVANIA HISTORICAL MAGAZINE 49:2 (1966), 111-126 and 49:3 (1966), 197-211.

Clemson was a transplanted southerner who lived in Maryland. In December, 1864, she secured a pass to visit her home town of Pendleton, South Carolina. Letters to her mother describe the countryside, her relatives, family feuds, and her deep faith in the Confederate cause.

889. Clifford, Anne Herbert, later Countess of Pembroke, 1590-1676. English wife of Richard Sackville, 3rd Earl of Dorset, and later Philip Herbert, 4th Earl of Pembroke and Montgomery; and ancestress of Victoria Sackville-West. THE DIARY OF LADY ANNE CLIFFORD. With an introductory note by Victoria Sackville-West. London: William Heinemann, 1923. 112p.

Partly reminiscences, partly a diary of her life with her first husband, 1603-1619. The text was taken from an eighteenth-century transcript; the original was probably destroyed.

890. ------. "The Diary of Lady Anne Clifford: A Study of Class and Gender in the Seventeenth Century." Katherine Hodgkin. HISTORY WORKSHOP: A JOURNAL OF SOCIALIST AND FEMINIST HISTORIANS 19 (Spring, 1985), 148-161.

For the first thirty years of her life, Lady Clifford fought for the right to inherit her father's estate; having obtained them, devoted the last thirty years to the control of her tenants. These two aspects of her life raise questions about class and gender relations and the different types of oppression entailed by each.

891. Clive, Catherine, 1711-1785. English actress. THE LIFE OF MRS. CATHERINE CLIVE. WITH AN ACCOUNT OF HER ADVENTURES ON AND OFF THE STAGE. A ROUND OF HER CHARACTERS. TOGETHER WITH HER CORRESPONDENCE. Percy Fitzgerald. London: A. Reader, 1888. 112p.

Chiefly business correspondence with David Garrick, 1768-1777, and some brief notes to others.

892. Clive, Caroline Meysey-Wigley, 1801-1873. British author. CAROLINE CLIVE: FROM THE DIARY AND FAMILY PAPERS OF MRS. ARCHER CLIVE. Edited by Lady Mary Clive. London: David Higham Associates, the Bodley Head, 1949. 286p.

893. Clough, Margaret Morley, 1803-1827. English missionary to Ceylon. EXTRACTS FROM THE JOURNAL AND CORRESPONDENCE OF THE LATE MRS. MARGARET MORLEY CLOUGH. With an introduction by Adam Clarke. London: J. Mason, 1829. 174p.

Missionary diary, 1823-1826.

894. Coatsworth, Elizabeth Jane, b. 1893. American poet and children's author. PERSONAL GEOGRAPHY. ALMOST AN AUTOBIOGRAPHY. A Janet Greene Book. Brattleboro, Vt.: Stephen Greene Press, 1976. 192p.

895. Cobb, Mary Blackburn, 1773-1802. English Baptist. EXTRACTS FROM THE DIARY AND LETTERS OF MRS. MARY COBB. London: C.&R. Baldwin, 1805. 324p.

Religious diary, 1792-1802.

Coburg, Louise, Princess von. See: Louise, Princess of Belgium.

896. Cohen, Fanny Yates. American Civil War Diarist. "Fanny Cohen's Journal of Sherman's Occupation of Savannah." Spencer B. King, Jr. THE GEORGIA HISTORICAL QUARTERLY 41:4 (December, 1957), 407-416.

Civil War diary begining December 21, 1864, the

day General Sherman's troops entered Savannah, and ending January 3, 1865.

897. Cohen, Marion Deutsche, b. 1943. American poet. THE SHADOW OF AN ANGEL: A DIARY OF A SUBSEQUENT PREGNANCY FOLLOWING NEO-NATAL LOSS. Las Colinas, Tex.: Liberal Press, 1986. 136p.

898. Coke, Jane Wharton Holt, Lady, 1706-1761. English daughter of the first Marquis of Wharton. LETTERS FROM LADY JANE COKE TO HER FRIEND MRS. EYRE AT DERBY, 1747-1758. Edited by Mrs. Ambrose [Florence Ada Monica Buckston] Rathbone. London: S. Sonnenschein, 1899. 169p.

899. Coke, Mary Campbell, Lady, 1726-1811. Scottish daughter of John, Duke of Argyll. THE LETTERS AND JOURNALS OF LADY MARY COKE. Edited by J.A. Home. Edinburgh: D. Douglas, 1889-1896. 4 vols.

Diary 1756-1774, written as letters to her sister, Lady Strafford, but not usually sent. The BIBLIOGRAPHY OF BRITISH HISTORY (1951) notes that seventeen volumes of her journals remain unpublished.

900. Colenso, Frances (Bunyon), 1816-1898. English wife of John Colenso, Bishop of Natal. COLENSO LETTERS FROM NATAL. Arranged with comments by Wyn Rees. Pietermaritzburg: Shuter and Shooter, 1958. 400p.

Letters 1865-1893 to Lady Mary Lyell and to Katherine Lyell. The letters focus upon three themes: the perservation of a united imperial Church, race problems, and the daily lives of a English Colonial family in Natal.

901. Coleridge, Mary Elizabeth, 1861-1907. English novelist and poet; grand-niece of Samuel Coleridge. GATHERED LEAVES FROM THE PROSE OF MARY E. COLERIDGE. With a memoir by Edith Sichel. New York: E.P. Dutton & Co., 1910. 338p.

Collection of short stories, essays, poems, and extracts from letters and diaries, 1882-1907.

902. Coleridge, Sara Coleridge, 1802-1852. English author and wife of Samuel Coleridge. MINNOW AMONG THE TRITONS: MRS. SARA T. COLERIDGE'S LETTERS TO THOMAS POOLE, 1799-1834. Edited by Stephen Potter. Bloomsbury, England: Nonesuch Press, 1934. 186p. Reprinted, New York: AMS Press, 1973. 185p.

Forty-two letters to her friend and confidant Thomas Poole, written at about the time of her separation from Samuel Coleridge.

903. ------. MEMOIR AND LETTERS OF SARA COLERIDGE. Edited by her daughter [Edith Coleridge]. New York: Harper & Bros., 1874. 528p. Second edition, London: Henry S. King & Co., 1873. 2 vols. Reprinted, New York: AMS Press, 1973. 528p.

904. ------. SARA COLERIDGE AND HENRY REED. REED'S MEMOIR OF SARA COLERIDGE; HER LETTERS TO REED, INCLUDING HER COMMENT ON HIS MEMOIR OF GRAY. Edited by Leslie Nathan Broughton. London: Humphrey Milford, Oxford University Press, and Ithaca, N.Y.: Cornell University Press, 1937. 117p.

905. Colette, Sidonie Gabrielle, 1873-1954. French novelist and short story writer. UNE AMITIÉ INATTENDUE. CORRESPONDANCE DE COLETTE ET DE FRANCIS JAMMES. Introduction et notes de Robert Mallet. Paris: Éditions Emile-Paul Frères, 1945. 75p.

Correspondence 1904-1906 with the French Catholic writer, centering on their mutual love of nature.

906. ------. LETTRES À HELENE PICARD. Texte établi et annotée par Claude Pichois. Paris: Éditions Flammarion, 1958. 232p.

Letters between Picard and Colette, 1920-1942, and between Colette and Marguerite d'Escola on the death of Picard, 1945-1946.

907. ------. LETTRES À MARGUERITE MORENO. Texte établi et annotée par Claude Pichois. Paris: Éditions Flammarion, 1959. 356p.

Letters 1923-1947 to Colette's friend of over fifty years. Includes a few of Moreno's letters to Colette.

908. ------. LETTRES DE LA VAGABONDE. Texte établi et annotée par Claude Pichois et Roberte Forbin. Paris: Éditions Flammarion, 1961. 293p.

909. ------. LETTRES AU PETITE CORSAIRE. Texte établi et annotée par Claude Pichois et Roberte Forbin. Préface de Maurice Goudeker. Paris: Editions Flammarion, 1963. 153p.

Letters to French writer, traveller and film maker Renee Hamon. Includes extracts from Hamon's journal, which is chiefly about Colette.

910. ------. EARTHLY PARADISE: AN AUTOBIOGRAPHY, DRAWN FROM HER LIFE-TIME WRITINGS. Robert Phelps. Translated by Herman Briffault, Derek Coltman, and others. New York: Farrar, Straus & Giroux, 1966. 505p.

911. ------. LETTRES À SES PAIRS. Texte établi et annotée par Claude Pichois et Roberte Forbin. Paris: Éditions Flammarion, 1973. 454p.

Letters to friends and colleagues, including Jean Cocteau, Gyp, Alfred Jarry, Paul Valèry, Charlotte Lyses, Anna de Noailles, Marie Noël, and others, 1894-1953.

912. ------. LOOKING BACKWARDS: RECOLLECTIONS. Translated from the French by David Le Vay. With an introduction by Maurice Goudeket. Bloomington and London: Indiana University Press, 1975. 214p.

Translation of JOURNAL À REBOURS and DE MA FENÊTRE. Includes extracts from a journal of life in Paris during the Occupation in World War II, from DE MA FENÊTRE; and two excerpts from JOURNAL À REBOURS, "Pre War," and "The Flight from Paris."

913. ------. LETTERS FROM COLETTE. Selected and translated by Robert Phelps. New York: Farrar Straus Giroux, 1980. 214p.

Letters taken from the five French volumes edited by Claude Pichois and Roberte Forbin.

914. ------. EN TOURNÉE: CARTES POSTALES A SIDO. SUIVI DE, NOTES DE TOURNÉES. Préface de Michel del Castillo. Notes de Michel Remy-Bieth. Paris: Persona, 1984. 111p.

915. ------. LETTRES À SA FILLE / SIDO. PRÉCÉDÉ DE LETTRES INÉDITES DE COLETTE. Prefaces de Bertrand de Jouvenel, Jeannie Malige et Michelle Sarde. Paris: Des Femmes, 1984. 520p.

916. ------. LETTRES À MOUNE ET AU TOUTOUNET (HELENE JOURDAN-MORHANGE ET LUC-ALBERT MOREAU), 1929-1954. Texte établi et prefacee par Bernard Villaret. Paris: Des Femmes, 1985. 405.

Letters to Helene Jourdan-Morhange (b.1888) and Luc-Albert Moreau (1882-1948).

917. Collette, Elizabeth van Horne, 1776-1846. American frontier settler. JOURNEY TO THE PROMISED LAND: JOURNAL OF ELIZABETH VAN HORNE COLLETTE. Pittsburgh: Historical Society of Western Pennsylvania, 1939. 23p.

Overland diary, written in 1807 by the daughter of a Baptist Minister.

918. Collins, Catharine Wever. American Wife of a U.S. Calvary Officer. AN ARMY WIFE COMES WEST: LETTERS OF CATHARINE WEVER COLLINS, 1863-1864. Edited by Agnes Wright Spring. Denver, 1954. 33p. Reprinted from COLORADO MAGAZINE 31:4 (1954), 241-273.

Collins left home in Ohio in 1863 to visit her husband, Colonel William O. Collins, then Commanding the Eleventh Ohio Voluntary Calvary at Fort Laramie, Colorado Territory. Letters to family describe hardships of travel, meeting other pioneers, life at Fort Laramie, and the danger of Indian attack.

919. Colt, Miriam Davis, b. 1817. American frontier

settler. WENT TO KANSAS: BEING A THRILLING ACCOUNT OF AN ILL-FATED EXPEDITION TO THAT FAIRY LAND, AND ITS SAD RESULTS. TOGETHER WITH A SKETCH OF THE LIFE OF THE AUTHOR, AND HOW THE WORLD GOES WITH HER. By Mrs. Miriam Davis Colt. Watertown: Printed by L. Ingalls and Co., 1862. 294p. Reprinted, Ann Arbor, Mich.: University Microfilms, Inc, 1966. 294p.

Account of settling in Kansas, told in a diary and letters, 1856-1862.

920. ------. A HEROINE OF THE FRONTIER: MIRIAM DAVIS COLT IN KANSAS, 1856. EXTRACTS FROM MRS. COLT'S DIARIES. Edited with an introduction by J. Christian Bay. Cedar Rapids, Iowa: Privately Printed for the Friends of the Torch Press, 1941. 58p.

921. Comly, Rebecca, b. 1773. American Quaker colonist and wife of educator John Comly. JOURNALS OF THE LIFE AND RELIGIOUS LABORS OF JOHN COMLY, LATE OF BYBERRY, PENNSYLVANIA. Published by his children. Philadelphia: T.E. Chapman, 1853. 645p.

Contains extracts from Rebecca Comly's journal, 1797-1829.

922. Conant, Charlotte Howard, 1862-1925. American teacher. A GIRL OF THE EIGHTIES: AT COLLEGE AND AT HOME. FROM THE FAMILY LETTERS OF CHARLOTTE HOWARD CONANT, AND FROM OTHER RECORDS. By Martha Pike Conant and others. Boston and New York: Houghton Mifflin; and Cambridge, England: The Riverside Press, 1931. 262p.

Letters from Wellesley College, 1880-1884; from Northfield Seminary in Massachusetts and from Rutland, Vermont, where she taught, 1884-1887; and from her home in Greenfield, Massachusetts, 1887-1892.

923. Condict, Jemima, later Harrison, 1754-1779. American colonial. JEMIMA CONDICT: HER BOOK. BEING A TRANSCRIPT OF THE DIARY OF AN ESSEX COUNTY MAID DURING THE REVOLUTIONARY WAR. Newark, N.J.: The Carteret Book Club, 1930. 73p.

924. Constant de Rebeque, Rosalie de, 1758-1835. French wife of statesman Benjamin Constant, and intimate of Madame de Stael. LETTRES DE ROSALIE DE CONSTANT ÉCRITES DE LAUSANNE À SON FRÈRE CHARLES LE CHINIOIS EN 1798. Publiées et annotées par Suzanne Roulin. Lausanne: F. Rouge, 1948. 137p.

925. ------. BENJAMIN ET ROSALIE CONSTANT: CORRESPONDANCE, 1786-1830. Publiée avec une introduction et des notes par Alfred et Suzanne Roulin. Paris: Gallimard, 1955. 369p.

926. Cook, Anna Maria Green, 1844-1936. American Confederate diarist. THE JOURNAL OF A MILLEDGEVILLE GIRL, 1861-1867. Edited by James C. Bonner. Athens, Ga.: University of Georgia Press, 1964. 131p.

927. Cooke, Lucy Rutledge. American frontier settler. CROSSING THE PLAINS IN 1852: NARRATIVE OF A TRIP TO "THE LAND OF GOLD" AS TOLD IN LETTERS WRITTEN DURING THE JOURNEY. Modesto, Calif.: Privately Printed, 1923. 94p.

928. Cooley, Elizabeth Ann, 1825-1848. American frontier settler. "From Virginia to Missouri in 1846: The Journal of Elizabeth Ann Cooley." Edward D. Jervey and James E. Moss. MISSOURI HISTORICAL REVIEW 60:2 (January, 1966), 162-206.

The first part of her journal, 1842-1846, which deals with her life in Virginia to the time of her marriage, is not printed, but is discussed. Excerpts deal with her journey to Texas and ultimately to Missouri.

929. Cooper, Caroline Ethel. Australian. BEHIND THE LINES: ONE WOMAN'S WAR, 1914-1918. THE LETTERS OF CAROLINE ETHEL COOPER. Edited and with an introduction by Decie Denholm. London: Jill Norman & Hobhouse, 1982. 311p.

930. Cooper, Diana, b. 1892. English actress and wife of diplomat and statesman Duff Cooper. THE RAINBOW

COMES AND GOES. Boston: Houghton Mifflin; and Cambridge, England: The Riverside Press, 1958. 271p.

Autobiography and extracts from letters. Describes work in hospitals during World War I, and courtship with Duff Cooper.

931. ------. THE LIGHT OF COMMON DAY. London: Hart-Davis, 1959. 264p. Boston: Houghton Mifflin; and Cambridge, England, The Riverside Press, 1959. 264p. Harmondsworth, Middlesex: Penguin Books, 1963. 233p.

Continuation of her autobiography. Includes extracts from letters, 1923-1939, describing diplomatic travel with her husband in America, cruises in the Mediterranean and the Balkans, and the beginings of World War II.

932. ------. TRUMPETS FROM THE STEEP. Boston: Houghton Mifflin; and Cambridge, England: The Riverside Press, 1960. 268p.

Continuation of her autobiography. Describes travel in America, life in the English countryside and at the British Embassy in Lisbon, in extracts from letters, 1944-1954.

933. ------. A DURABLE FIRE: THE LETTERS OF DUFF AND DIANA COOPER, 1913-1950. Edited by Artemis Cooper. London: Collins, 1983. 332p. London: Hamish Hamilton, 1985. 332p.

934. Cooper, Mary, 1714-1778. American Farmer. THE DIARY OF MARY COOPER: LIFE ON A LONG ISLAND FARM, 1768-1773. Edited by Field Horne. New York: Oyster Bay Historical Society, 1981. 84p.

935. Cooper, Mary Hanson, 1786-1812. English Methodist. MEMOIR OF THE LATE MRS. MARY COOPER OF LONDON, WHO DEPARTED THIS LIFE, JUNE 22, 1812, IN THE TWENTY-SIXTH YEAR OF HER AGE. EXTRACTED FROM HER DIARY AND EPISTOLARY CORRESPONDENCE. Adam Clarke. New York: J. Soule and T. Mason for the Methodist Episcopal

Church in the United States, Abraham Paul, Printer, 1816. 161p. Boston: Wells and Lilly, 1819. 276p. London: J. Butterworth & Son, 1822. 260p. New York: N. Bangs and J. Emory, 1825. 165p. New York: B. Waugh and T. Mason, 1832. 240p.

Extracts from a Methodist diary, 1809-1812.

936. Cooper, Mary Sarson Winfield, 1813-1851. English Methodist. MEMORIALS OF MRS. MARY SARSON COOPER, LATE OF DUNSTABLE. COMPILED FROM HER DIARY AND CORRESPONDENCE. Henry Fish. London: Printed for the Author, and sold by John Mason and A. Heylin, 1855.

937. Cooper, Susan Fenimore, 1813-1894. American naturalist and daughter of James Fenimore Cooper. RURAL HOURS. New York: G.P. Putnam's American Agency, 1850. 521p. New and revised edition, Boston and New York: Houghton Mifflin, 1887. 337p. Reprinted, Syracuse, N.Y.: Syracuse University Press, 1968. 337p.

Nature diary, 1848-1850.

938. ------. JOURNAL OF A NATURALIST IN THE UNITED STATES. London: R. Bentley, 1855. 2 vols.

939. Copeland, Estella M. American. OVERLAND BY AUTO IN 1913: DIARY OF A FAMILY TOUR FROM CALIFORNIA TO INDIANA. Indianapolis: Indiana Historical Society, 1981. 87p. (Indiana Hist. Soc. Publications Vol. 26, No. 2)

940. Coppola, Eleanor. American wife of film director Francis Ford Coppola. NOTES. New York: Simon & Schuster, 1979. 288p.

Journal March, 1976--November, 1978, made in the Philippines during the filming of APOCALYPSE NOW.

941. Cormany, Rachel Bowman. American diarist. THE CORMANY DIARIES: A NORTHERN FAMILY IN THE CIVIL WAR. Edited by James C. Mohr. Associate editor: Richard E. Winslow III. Pittsburgh, Penn.: University of Pittsburgh Press, 1982. 597p.

Extracts from the diaries of Rachel Cormany, née Bowman, and Samuel Cormany, 1858-1865, begining before they met, continuing through their courtship, marriage, and honeymoon trip to Canada on the eve of the Civil War. After two years of exile there, they return to the U.S.; Samuel to join the Union Forces. Rachel records life with their children on the home front in Chambersburg, twice occupied and burned by the Confederate Army. Their diaries end when the couple is reunited in 1865.

942. Cornwallis, Jane Meautys, later Bacon, Lady, ca. 1581-1659. THE PRIVATE CORRESPONDENCE OF JANE, LADY CORNWALLIS, 1613-1644. Edited from the originals in the possession of the family by Lord Brabrooke. London: Printed by S.&J. Bentley, Wilson & Fley, 1842. 314p.

943. Cortlandt, Catharine Ogden Van. American colonial. "A Loyalist's Wife: Letters of Mrs. Philip van Cortlandt, December 1776--February 1777. The Experiences of a Family of New Amsterdam Stock During the Early Months of the American Revolutionary War." H.O. Vernon-Jackson. HISTORY TODAY 14:8 (1964), 574-580.

Discussion of and excerpts from four letters of the wife of a Lieutenant-Colonel in the New Jersey Brigade, which reveal the background of the period as it affected an anxious wife and mother.

944. Cowan, Liza and Penny House. American Lesbians. "California Diary." DYKES: A QUARTERLY 1:1 (Winter, 1975-1976), 70.

945. Cowell, Emilie Marguerite Ebsworth, b. 1818. Wife of actor Samuel Houghton Cowell. THE COWELLS IN AMERICA: BEING THE DIARY OF MRS. SAM COWELL DURING HER HUSBAND'S CONCERT TOUR IN THE YEARS 1860-1861. Edited by M. Wilson Disher. London: Oxford University Press, Humphrey Milford, 1934. 426p.

946. Cowles, Julia, 1785-1803. American. THE DIARIES OF JULIA COWLES: A CONNECTICUT RECORD, 1797-1803. Edited from the original manuscripts in the possession of

of Anna Roosevelt Cowles by Laura Hadley Mosely. New Haven, Conn.: Yale University Press, 1931. 94p.

School diary, describing studies at Sarah Pierce's school for girls in Connecticut, and the daily life of a "young lady of quality."

947. Cowper, Mary Clavering Cowper, Countess, 1685-1724. English Lady-In-Waiting. THE DIARY OF MARY, COUNTESS COWPER, LADY OF THE BEDCHAMBER TO THE PRINCESS OF WALES, 1714-1720. Edited by Spencer Cowper. London: John Murray, 1864. 207p.

948. Cox, Kathleen. "A Journal of the Unconscious." LAMP IN THE SPINE 9 (Spring/Fall, 1974), 58-77.

Extracts from a diary kept as therapy.

Craigie, Pearl Mary Teresa Richards. See Hobbs, John Oliver.

949. Cranch, Elizabeth, b. 1743. American niece of Abigail Adams. "The Journal of Elizabeth Cranch." With an introductory note by Lizzie Norton Mason and James Duncan Phillips. ESSEX INSTITUTE HISTORICAL COLLECTIONS 80:1 (January, 1944), 1-36.

Diary for 1785 gives a picture of Haverhill, Massachusetts, just after the American Revolution.

950. Crapsey, Adelaide, 1878-1914. American poet. COMPLETE POEMS AND SELECTED LETTERS OF ADELAIDE CRAPSEY. Edited, and with an introduction and notes by Susan Sutton Smith. Albany, N.Y.: State University of New York Press, 1977. 288p.

Letters are divided into three parts; those to her family, 1893-1897, those to family and friends, 1908-1813; and those to Esther Lowenthal, 1913-1914 from a sanatorium where Crapsey was being treated for tuberculosis.

951. Craven, Charlotte Georgina Harriet Smythe, Lady,

later Duchesse de La Force, 1814-1867. THE PRETTIEST GIRL IN ENGLAND: THE LOVE STORY OF MRS. FITZHERBERT'S NIECE. From journals edited by Richard Buckle. London: John Murray, 1958. 241p.

Social diary. Includes extracts from the diary of Lady Craven's older sister, Louisa Mary Smythe, later Lady Hervey-Bathurst (1809-1836), 1827-1831.

Craven, Elizabeth Berkeley, Baroness Craven, afterwards Margravine of Anspach. See: Anspach, Elizabeth Berkeley, Baroness Craven, Margravine of.

952. Craven, Pauline Marie Armande Aglae Ferron de la Ferronays, b. 1808. French author and daughter-in-law of Elizabeth Berkeley, Margravine of Anspach. A MEMOIR OF MRS. AUGUSTUS CRAVEN (PAULINE DE LA FERRONAYS). WITH EXTRACTS FROM HER DIARIES AND CORRESPONDENCE. Maria Catherine Bishop. London: Richard Bentley & Son, 1894. 2 vols.

Biography drawing upon extracts from her diary and letters, describing life in the diplomatic and social circles of nineteenth century Europe.

953. Crawford, Dorothy Painter, b. 1892. American politician and first woman Mayor in Mississippi. STAY WITH IT VAN: FROM THE DIARY OF MISSISSIPPI'S FIRST LADY MAYOR. New York: Exposition Press, 1958. 312p.

Diary of her term of office as Mayor of Madison, Mississippi, 1951-1953.

954. Creevey, Caroline A. Stickney. American. A DAUGHTER OF THE PURITANS: AN AUTOBIOGRAPHY. New York and London: G.P. Putnam's Sons, 1916. 272p.

Contains three chapters of extracts from a childhood diary, describing growing up in the Church and in New England society, 1853-1854.

955. Crombie, Helen Elizabeth. American teacher.

"Account of the Pennsylvania Railroad Riots from a Young Girl's Diary, Helen Crombie." Edited by John Newell Crombie. WESTERN PENNSYLVANIA HISTORICAL MAGAZINE 54:4 (1971), 385-389.

Extracts from a diary written at age fifteen, describing railroad riots and labor unrest, July 1--August 8, 1887.

956. Crombrugghe, Ida Caroline Eugenie Ghislaine de Kerchova de Denterghem, Baronne de, 1820-1875. German translator and nurse during the Franco-German War. JOURNAL D'UNE INFIRMIÈRE PENDANT LA GUERRE DE 1870-1871. SARREBRUCK, METZ, CAMBRAI. Brussels: F. Claassen, 1871.

957. Crosley, Pauline S. American diplomat's Wife. INTIMATE LETTERS FROM PETROGRAD. New York: E.P. Dutton & Co., 1920. 332p.

Diplomatic diary, April 28, 1917--April 1, 1918. Crosley explains that much of political significance has been edited from the original letters, and more from the copies that were retained and used in this volume.

958. Cross, Eliza. English. DIARY OF THE LATE MISS ELIZA CROSS, OF WARLEY, ESSEX, WITH A PREFACE AND A BRIEF ACCOUNT OF HER LIFE. By the Reverend J. Atkinson, Hoxton. Embellished with a striking likeness of Miss Cross. London: Printed and Sold by the Author, 1807. 90p.

959. Crouter, Natalie, b. 1898. American woman interned in a civilian prison camp in the Philippines by the Japanese during World War II. "Courage is Grace Under Pressure: A Woman's Diary of Captivity." Edited by Lynn Z. Bloom. NEW AMERICA: A REVIEW (Fall, 1975/ Spring, 1976), 60-68.

Excerpts from Crouter's Philippine diary.

960. ------. FORBIDDEN DIARY: A RECORD OF WARTIME

INTERNMENT, 1941-1945. Edited and with an introduction by Lynn Z. Bloom. With drawings by Daphne Bird. New York: Burt Franklin & Co., 1980. 546p.

Secret diary kept while imprisoned by the Japanese at Baguio. Includes an epilogue by Bloom which covers Crouter's life from 1945 to 1980.

961. Crowninshield, Clara, (Clarissa), later Thies, 1811-1907. American friend of Henry Wadsworth Longfellow. THE DIARY OF CLARA CROWNINSHIELD: A EUROPEAN TOUR WITH LONGFELLOW, 1835-1836. Edited by Andrew Hilen. Seattle: University of Washington Press, 1956. 304p.

Travel diary of an eighteen-month stay in Europe; Crowninshield went as a companion to Longfellow's wife.

962. Cuca, Marian, 1939-1953. American. THE DIARY OF MARIAN CUCA. New York: Privately Printed, 1956.

Diary of a young girl living in New York City.

963. Culbertson, Manie. American schoolteacher. MAY I SPEAK? DIARY OF A CROSSOVER TEACHER. Edited with an introduction by Sue Eakin. Gretna, La.: Pelican Publishing Co., 1972. 156p.

Diary of a white schoolteacher in a racially integrated southern school.

964. Cullwick, Hannah, 1833-1909. English domestic worker and secret wife of Arthur Munby. THE DIARIES OF HANNAH CULLWICK, VICTORIAN MAIDSERVANT. Edited and introduced by Liz Stanley. New Brunswick, N.J.: Rutgers University Press, 1984. 327p.

Cullwick carried on an eighteen-year courtship with Arthur Munby, a barrister, poet and social worker obsessed with the lives of working class women. They married in 1873, keeping their marriage a secret at Hannah's insistence. Diary 1854-1873, kept at the request of Munby, to keep him informed of the details of her daily drudgery as maidservant and cook.

965. ------. "Class and Gender in Victorian England: The Diaries of Arthur J. Munby and Hannah Cullwick." Lenore Davidoff. FEMINIST STUDIES 5:1 (Spring, 1979), 86-141.

966. Cumming, Elizabeth Wells Randall, 1811-1867. American wife of the first non-Mormon Governor of Utah. THE GENTEEL GENTILE: LETTERS OF ELIZABETH CUMMING, 1857-1858. Edited and with an introduction and notes by Ray R. Canning and Beverly Beeton. Salt Lake City: University of Utah Press, 1977. 111p.

967. Cumming, Kate, 1828?-1909. American Confederate hospital administrator, nurse, and teacher. A JOURNAL OF HOSPITAL LIFE IN THE CONFEDERATE ARMY OF TENNESSEE FROM THE BATTLE OF SHILOH TO THE END OF THE WAR. WITH SKETCHES OF LIFE AND CHARACTER, AND BRIEF NOTICES OF CURRENT EVENTS DURING THAT PERIOD. Louisville, Ky.: John P. Morton & Co.; and New Orleans: William Evelyn, 1866. 199p.

Diary of hospital work in Mississippi and Georgia, 1863-1865. This is the first edition; a later expurgated edition, in which her anti-Northern sentiments were edited out, was published as GLEANINGS FROM SOUTHLAND, (Birmingham, Ala., 1895).

968. ------. KATE: THE JOURNAL OF A CONFEDERATE NURSE (1862-1865). Edited by Richard B. Harwell. Baton Rouge, La.: Louisiana University Press, 1959. 321p.

Edition based on the 1886 version, with a few deletions.

969. Cumming, Katherine Hubbell, 1838-1921. American. A NORTHERN DAUGHTER AND A SOUTHERN WIFE: THE CIVIL WAR REMINISCENCES AND LETTERS OF KATHERINE HUBBELL CUMMING, 1860-1865. Edited by W. Kirk Wood. With a foreword by Joseph B. Cumming. Augusta, Ga.: Richmond County Historical Society, 1976. 126p.

Letters 1861-1865 to family members, and a reminiscence based on the letters, written thirty years later. Simultaneously presents a Northern and Southern view of the coming of the Civil War, and gives personal reactions to conflicting family and sectional loyalties.

970. Curd, Sam, 1835?-1919. American merchant's wife. SAM CURD'S DIARY. Edited by Susan S. Arpad. Athens, Ohio: Ohio University Press, 1984. 172p.

Domestic and social diary, 1860-1863.

971. Curie, Marie [Marja Sklodowska Curie], 1867-1934. Polish-French chemist and physicist, and wife of Pierre Curie, with whom she worked until his death in 1906. MADAME CURIE. Eve Curie. Paris: Gallimard, 1938.

Biography written by her daughter; contains extracts from Curie's journal.

972. ------. MARIE CURIE: CORRESPONDANCE. CHOIX DES LETTRES (1905-1934) [DE] MARIE [ET] IRENE CURIE. Présentation par Gilette Ziegler. Paris: Les Editeurs Français Réunis, 1974. 348p.

973. Curtis, Louise Peelor. American housewife. "I AM SO SICK": THE DIARY OF A NINETEENTH CENTURY HOUSE-WIFE. Edited by Tawni Hileman. San Jose, Calif.: Sourisseau Academy for State and Local History, 1983. 180 leaves.

974. Curtiss, Mina Stein. American professor, editor and biographer of Marcel Proust. OTHER PEOPLE'S LETTERS: A MEMOIR BY MINA CURTISS. Boston: Houghton Mifflin, 1978. 243p.

Account of her research into the life of Proust during the 1940's, based on and including extracts from her journal and correspondence. Includes extracts from letters of the people she came to know as a result of her research, including Celeste Albaret, Enid Bagnold, and others.

975. Cushman, Charlotte Saunders, 1816-1876. American

actress. CHARLOTTE CUSHMAN: HER LETTERS AND MEMOIRS OF HER LIFE. Edited by Emma Stebbins. Boston: Houghton Mifflin & Co., 1878, 1881.

976. Cushman, Mary Ames, b. 1864. American. SHE WROTE IT ALL DOWN. New York: Charles Scribner's Sons, 1936. 226p.

Diary of travel in Europe, 1876-1880.

977. Daibu, Lady [Kenreimonin Ukyo No Daibu], b. 1157? Japanese Lady-In-Waiting. THE POETIC MEMOIRS OF LADY DAIBU. Translated and introduced by Phillip Tudor Harries. Palo Alto, Calif.: Stanford University Press, 1980. 320p.

Japanese poetic diary, written at the end of the Heian period. Her lover, Sukemori, the focus of the diary, died in 1185.

978. Dall, Caroline Wells Healey, 1822-1912. American author, Transcendentalist and reformer. MY FIRST HOLIDAY: OR, LETTERS HOME FROM COLORADO, UTAH AND CALIFORNIA. Boston: Roberts Bros., 1881. 430p.

979. ------. "Caroline Dall's Reminiscences of Margaret Fuller." Joel Myerson. HARVARD LIBRARY BULLETIN 22:4 (October, 1974), 414-428.

Extracts from Dall's Journals.

980. Dallmer, Mary Joseph [Religious name: Sister Mary Frances Johnstom], 1852-1909. A LIGHT SHINING: THE LIFE AND LETTERS OF MOTHER MARY JOSEPH DALLMER, URSULINE OF THE ROMAN UNION. S.M. Johnston. Preface by Reverend Albert Muntsch. New York and Cincinnati: Benziger Brothers, 1937. 415p.

981. Daly, Maria Lydig, 1824-1894. American wife of New York Judge Charles P. Daly. DIARY OF A UNION LADY, 1861-1865. Edited by Harold Earl Hammond. Foreword by Allan Nevins. New York: Funk & Wagnalls, 1962. 396p.

Diary of a Unionist, anti-abolitionist,

anti-slavery, and anti-Lincoln Democrat, describing society life in Washington D.C. during the Civil War.

Dame Shirley. See: Clappe, Louise Amelia Knapp Smith.

982. Damer, Mary Georgiana Emma Seymour Dawson, The Hon. Mrs., d. 1848. English. DIARY OF A TOUR IN GREECE, TURKEY, EGYPT AND THE HOLY LAND. London: H. Colburn, 1841. 2 vols.

Travel diary, October 1839--February, 1840.

983. Darling, Flora Adams, 1840-1910. American author and founder of the Daughters of the American Revolution. MRS. DARLING'S LETTERS: OR, MEMORIES OF THE CIVIL WAR. New York: J.W. Lovell Co., 1883. 223p.

984. Daschkaw, Primcess [Ekaterina Romanovna Vorontsova Dashkova], 1743-1810. Russian Lady-In-Waiting, scholar, and author. MEMOIRS OF THE PRINCESS DASCHKAW, LADY OF HONOUR TO CATHERINE II, EMPRESS OF ALL RUSSIA. WRITTEN BY HERSELF, COMPRISING LETTERS OF THE EMPRESS AND OTHER CORRESPONDENCE. Edited from the originals by Mrs. W. Martha Bradford. London, 1840. 2 vols.

Contains extracts from the correspondence of Princess Daschkaw, from the correspondence of Catherine Wilmot and from the letters and journals of Martha Wilmot Bradford.

985. ------. MEMOIRES DE LA PRINCESSE DASCHKOFF, DAME D'HONNEUR DE CATHERINE II, IMPÉRATRICE DE TOUTES LES RUSSIES. Édition presentée et annotée par Pascal Pontremoli. Paris: Mercure de France, 1966. 376p.

986. David-Neel, Alexandra [Louise Eugenie Alexandra Marie David-Neel], 1868-1969. French Traveller, author, singer, and Orientalist. LETTRES À SON MARI. Avan-propos de Marie-Madéleine Peyrounet; avec notes numerotées et redigées par le Professeur Gabriel Monod-Herzen. Paris: Librarie Plon, 1975-1976. 2 vols.

Travel letters written from China, India and Tibet, on different journeys between 1904 and 1940.

987. Davies, Hannah. English missionary to China. AMONG HILLS AND VALLEYS IN WESTERN CHINA: INCIDENTS OF MISSIONARY WORK. With an introduction by Mrs. Isabella Bishop. London: S.W. Partridge & Co., 1901. 326p.

Extracts from letters and journals describe seven years of missionary work in China, 1893-1901.

988. Davies, Sarah Emily, 1830-1921. English advocate of women's education and founder of Girton College at Cambridge. EMILY DAVIES AND GIRTON COLLEGE. Barbara Stephen. London: Constable & Co., 1927. 387p.

Chronicles the lives and work of three women who founded Girton College: Emily Davies, Elizabeth Garrett, and Barbara Bodichon, through their correspondence with each other, 1857-1919.

989. Davis, Lavinia Riker, 1909-1961. American author. THE JOURNALS OF LAVINIA DAVIS RIKER. New York: Privately printed, 1964. 168p.

Writer's journal, 1930-1951.

990. Davis, Mary Elizabeth Moragne, 1815?-1903. American author. THE NEGLECTED THREAD: A JOURNAL FROM THE CALHOUN COMMUNITY, 1836-1842. Edited with a preface and background by Delle Mullen Craven. Columbia, S.C.: University of South Carolina Press, 1951. 256p.

Account of her early life, begining at age nineteen, in Abbeville County, South Carolina, on a small plantation close to the frontier.

991. Davis, Nell, 1800-1955. American frontier settler. THE WAY IT WAS: DIARY OF A PIONEER LAS VEGAS WOMAN. Edited by Georgia Lewis. Las Vegas, Nev.: The Las Vegas Sun, 1978, 1979. 198p.

Pioneer diary, November, 1904--March, 1955.

992. Davis, Varina Anne, b. 1864. American author and

daughter of Jefferson Davis. "The Daughter of the Confederacy." Leah Strong. MISSISSIPPI QUARTERLY 20:4 (1967), 234-239.

Letters by Varina Anne Davis and her mother, Varina Howell Davis, to American author Charles Dudley Warner, begining in 1883.

993. Dawson, Sarah Ida Fowler Morgan, 1842-1909. American author and journalist. A CONFEDERATE GIRL'S DIARY. With an introduction by Warrington Dawson. Edited with a foreword and notes by James I. Robertson, Jr. Bloomington: Indiana University Press, 1960. 437p.

Civil War diary, 1862-1865, written at Baton Rouge and New Orleans, Lousiana.

994. Day, Ingeborg. Austrian-American author. "A Diary of My Son's Dying." MS. MAGAZINE 4:8 (February, 1976), 54-56; 84-85.

995. Dayan, Yael, b.1939. Israeli linguist, journalist, novelist and daughter of General Moshe Dayan. ISRAEL JOURNAL: JUNE, 1967. New York, Toronto, Sydney and London: McGraw-Hill Book Co., 1967. 111p.

Account of the 1967 Arab-Israeli War, based on a diary she kept while attached to an Army division fighting at Sinai.

996. ------. A SOLDIER'S DIARY: SINAI, 1967. London: Weidenfeld & Nicolson, 1967. 127p.

997. Dearmer, Mabel White, 1872-1915. English novelist and playwright. LETTERS FROM A FIELD HOSPITAL. With a memoir of the author by Stephen Gwynn. London: Macmillan & Co., 1915. 182p.

Describes work as a hospital orderly with the Belgian Refugee Committee in the Stobart Field Hospital at Kragujevatz, Serbia. She died in the war.

Deffand, Marie de Vichy Champrond, Marquise du. See: Du

Deffand, Marie de Vichy Champrond, Marquise.

998. Delany, Mary Granville Pendarves, 1700-1788. English social figure. LETTERS FROM MRS. DELANY (WIDOW OF DOCTOR PATRICK DELANY) TO MRS. FRANCES HAMILTON, FROM THE YEAR 1779, TO THE YEAR 1788. COMPRISING MANY UNPUBLISHED AND INTERESTING ANECDOTES OF THEIR LATE MAJESTIES AND THE ROYAL FAMILY. Now first printed from the original manuscript. Second edition. London: Printed for Longman, Hurst, Rees, Orme, and Brown, 1820. 106p.

Letters to Dorothea Hamilton, written while Mrs. Delany was residing with the Duchess Dowager of Portland, where she was introduced to Queen Charlotte and King George III. Describes Court life, social affairs.

999. ------. THE AUTOBIOGRAPHY AND CORRESPONDENCE OF MARY GRANVILLE, MRS. DELANY. WITH INTERESTING REMINISCENCES OF KING GEORGE THE THIRD AND QUEEN CHARLOTTE. Edited by the Rt. Hon. Lady Llanover. London: Richard Bentley, 1861. 3 vols. Second Series, 1862. 3 vols.

Autobiographical fragments edited together with letters, 1740-1785.

1000. ------. THE AUTOBIOGRAPHY AND CORRESPONDENCE OF MRS. DELANY. Revised from Lady Llanover's edition by Sarah Chauncey Woolsey. Boston: Roberts Brothers, 1879. 2 vols.

Abridged version of Lady Llanover's edition.

1001. ------. MRS. DELANY: AT COURT AMONG THE WITS: BEING THE RECORD OF A GREAT LADY OF GENIUS ON THE ART OF LIVING. Arranged from "The Autobiography of Mrs. Delany, With Interesting Reminiscences of George III and Queen Charlotte," edited by Lady Llanover in 6 Volumes, 1861-1862. With an introduction by R. Brimley Johnson. London: Stanley Paul & Co., 1925. 292p.

Abridged version of Lady Llanover's edition.

1002. Deming, Barbara, b. 1917. American political activist, poet, and Lesbian. PRISON NOTES. New York: Grossman, 1966. 185p.

Account of a racially integrated peace march. Deming and others were arrested twice when they tried to march through the white business district of Albany, Georgia. Her journal covers two months spent in the Albany Jail in 1964.

1003. Deming, Sarah Winslow, 1722-1788. American colonist. "Journal of Sarah Winslow Deming." AMERICAN MONTHLY MAGAZINE 4 (1894), 45-49; and 5 (1894), 67-70.

Journal-letter to a niece describes a journey from Boston to Providence, Rhode Island, April 15-26, 1775.

1004. Demoriane, Hermine. English artist. LIFE STAR: A DIARY OF NINE MONTHS. New York: Coward McCann, 1970. 104p.

Diary of a first pregnancy, October-June of an unspecified year, by a young artist living in London in the mid-nineteen sixties. Illustrated with photographs of rock stars.

1005. Derby, Emma C. American niece of California Historian Hubert H. Bancroft. "Diary of Emma C. Derby: Bancroft's Niece Keeps Record of European Tour, March 25--August 6, 1867." CALIFORNIA HISTORICAL SOCIETY QUARTERLY 31:3 (1952), 219-228; 31:4 (1952), 355-374; and 32:1 (1952), 65-80.

1006. Désbordes-Valmore, Marceline Felicité Josephe, Dame Lanchantine, 1786-1859. French author and poet. MADAME DÉSBORDES-VALMORE: SA VIE ET SA CORRESPONDANCE. C.A. Sainte-Beuve. Paris: M. Levy Frères, 1870. 246p.

1007. ------. LA CORRESPONDANCE INTIME DE MARCELINE DÉSBORDES-VALMORE. Publiée par Benjamin Rivière. Paris: Chez Lemerre, 1896. 2 vols.

1008. ------. LA JEUNESSE DE MADAME DESBORDES-

VALMORE. Suivie des Lettres inédites. Arthur Pougin. Paris: Calmann-Lévy, 1898.

1009. ------. MADAME DÉSBORDES-VALMORE: LETTRES INÉDITES, 1812-1857. Récueilliés et annotées par son fils Hippolyte Valmore. Préface de Boyer d'Agen. Notes d'Arthur Pougin. Paris: Louis-Michaud, 1912? 351p.

1010. Devonshire, Elizabeth Hervey Cavendish, Duchess of, 1758-1824. English. DEAREST BESS: THE LIFE AND TIMES OF LADY ELIZABETH FOSTER, AFTERWARDS DUCHESS OF DEVONSHIRE, FROM HER UNPUBLISHED JOURNALS AND CORRESPONDENCE. Dorothy Margaret Stuart. London: Methuen & Co., 1955. 266p.

1011. Devonshire, Georgiana Spencer Cavendish, Duchess of, 1757-1806. English social figure. SHERIDAN: FROM NEW AND ORIGINAL MATERIAL, INCLUDING A MS. DIARY BY GEORGIANA, DUCHESS OF DEVONSHIRE. London: Constable & Co., 1909. 2 vols.

Her diary, November 20, 1778--January 12, 1789, appears in Volume 2.

1012. ------. GEORGIANA: EXTRACTS FROM THE CORRESPONDENCE OF GEORGIANA, DUCHESS OF DEVONSHIRE. Edited by the Earl of Bessborough. London: John Murray, 1955. 307p.

1013. Dewees, Mary Coburn. American colonist. "Mrs. Mary Dewees' Journal from Philadelphia to Kentucky." PENNSYLVANIA MAGAZINE OF HISTORY AND BIOGRAPHY 28 (1904), 182-198.

1014. ------. JOURNAL OF A TRIP FROM PHILADELPHIA TO LEXINGTON, IN KENTUCKY, KEPT BY MARY COBURN DEWEES IN 1787. Crawfordsville, Ind.: R.E. Banta, 1936. 16p.

Limited edition of 75 copies.

1015. ------. "Mrs. Mary Dewees' Journal from Philadelphia to Kentucky." Edited by John L. Blair. KENTUCKY HISTORICAL SOCIETY REGISTER 63:3 (1965), 195-217.

1016. Dickens, Marguerite. American wife of a U.S. Naval Officer. ALONG SHORE WITH A MAN-OF-WAR. Boston: Arena, 1893. 242p.

Letters home, describing her experiences sailing with her husband along the east coast of South America.

1017. Dickenson, Mary Hamilton, 1756-1816. English intellectual. MARY HAMILTON, AFTERWARDS MRS. JOHN DICKENSON, AT COURT AND AT HOME: FROM LETTERS AND DIARIES, 1756-1816. Edited by her great-granddaughters, Elizabeth and Florence Anson. London: John Murray, 1925. 342p.

Social diary and letters, describing life at the Court of King George III, and among the intellectual circles of Europe.

1018. Dickinson, Emily, 1830-1886. American poet. LETTERS OF EMILY DICKINSON. Edited by Mabel Loomis Todd. Boston, 1894. New and enlarged edition, New York and London: Harper & Bros., 1931. 457p.

Letters 1845-1886. Appendix One of the revised edition lists passages omitted from the first edition.

1019. ------. THE LIFE AND LETTERS OF EMILY DICKINSON. By her niece, Martha Dickinson Bianchi. Boston and New York: Houghton Mifflin; and Cambridge, England: The Riverside Press, 1924. 386p.

Previously unpublished letters, arranged chronologically.

1020. ------. EMILY DICKINSON FACE TO FACE: UNPUBLISHED LETTERS WITH NOTES AND REMINISCENCES. Martha Dickinson Bianchi. With a foreword by Alfred Leete Hampson. Boston: Houghton Mifflin, 1932. Reprinted in facsimile, New York: Archon Books, 1970. 290p.

Includes a chapter of previously unpublished letters.

1021. ------. ANCESTOR'S BROCADE: THE LITERARY DISCOVERY OF EMILY DICKINSON, THE EDITING AND PUBLISHING OF HER LETTERS AND POEMS. Millicent Todd Bingham. New York: Dover Publications, 1945. Second edition, 1976. 464p.

Account of the publication of Dickinson's works. Draws heavily on letters and journals of Mabel Loomis Todd which relate to the project.

1022. ------. EMILY DICKINSON'S LETTERS TO DR. AND MRS. JOSIAH GILBERT HOLLAND. Edited by their Granddaughter, Theodora Van Wagenen Ward. Cambridge, Mass.: Harvard University Press, 1951. 252p.

Ninety-three letters, 1853-1886. Holland was a publisher, teacher and lecturer who wrote on manners and morals.

1023. ------. THE LETTERS OF EMILY DICKINSON. Edited by Thomas H. Johnson. Associate editor, Theodora Ward. Cambridge, Mass.: The Belknap Press of Harvard University Press, 1958. 3 vols.

Definitive edition of 1045 letters, 1842-1886, to over eighty correspondents, including Susan Gilbert, Thomas Wentworth Higginson, Dr. and Mrs. Josiah Gilbert, Mabel Loomis Todd, and others.

1024. ------. SELECTED POEMS AND LETTERS OF EMILY DICKINSON, TOGETHER WITH THOMAS WENTWORTH HIGGINSON'S ACCOUNT OF HIS CORRESPONDENCE WITH THE POET AND HIS VISIT TO HER IN AMHERST. Edited, with an introduction by Robert N. Linscott. Garden City, New York: Anchor Press /Doubleday Books, 1959. 343p.

Introductory edition to Dickinson's works, designed for "readers who wish to have in one volume the best of her poetry and the most interesting of her letters."

1025. ------. PORTRAIT OF EMILY DICKINSON: THE POET AND HER PROSE. David Higgins. New Brunswick, N.J.:

Rutgers University Press, 1967. 266p.

Study of Dickinson's letters, discussing biographical and stylistic considerations, focusing on the relationship between the letters and her poetry.

1026. ------. EMILY DICKINSON: SELECTED LETTERS. Edited by Thomas H. Johnson. Cambridge, Mass.: The Belknap Press of Harvard University Press, 1971. 364p.

Selected from Thomas H. Johnson's 1958 edition.

1027. ------. "Emily Dickinson's Letters to Sue Gilbert." Lillian Faderman. THE MASSACHUSETTS REVIEW 18:2 (Summer, 1977), 197-225.

Makes a case for the homoeroticism of some of Dickinson's poems, and for her love of women, especially Sue Gilbert. Quotes passages from Dickinson's letters to Gilbert which show evidence of strong passion, and discusses Dickinson's biographers and editors who ignored or tried to explain away Dickinson's attachment to Gilbert. The heavily edited version of the letters by Martha Dickinson Bianchi (Gilbert's mother) is taken into special account.

1028. Dickson, Lillian. American missionary. CHUCKLES BEHIND THE DOOR: LILLIAN DICKSON'S PERSONAL LETTERS. Edited by Marilyn Dickson Tank. Taiwan: Lillian Dickson, 1977. 350p.

1029. Diebitsch-Peary, Josephine. American explorer and wife of Arctic Explorer Robert Edwin Peary. MY ARCTIC JOURNAL: A YEAR AMONG THE ICE-FIELDS AND ESKIMOS. WITH AN ACCOUNT OF THE GREAT WHITE JOURNEY ACROSS GREENLAND BY ROBERT E. PEARY. New York and Philadelphia: The Contemporary Publishing Co., 1894. 240p.

Diary of an Arctic expedition with her husband and a small party.

1030. Dillwyn, Sarah. American colonist. "Correspondence of George and Sarah Dillwyn." PENNSYLVANIA

MAGAZINE OF HISTORY AND BIOGRAPHY 17:1 (1893), 93-98.

Includes a letter dated August 17, 1777, to Hannah More.

1031. Dinesen, Isak, pseud. for Karen Dinesen, Baroness Blixen, 1885-1962. Danish author. BREVE FRA AFRIKA. Edited by Frans Lasson. Copenhagen: Gylendal, 1978. 2 vols.

Letters from Africa, 1914-1931.

1032. ------. LETTERS FROM AFRICA, 1914-1931: THE PRIVATE STORY BEHIND KAREN BLIXEN'S GREAT MEMOIR OUT OF AFRICA. Edited for the Rungstedlund Foundation by Frans Lasson. Translated by Anne Born. Chicago: University of Chicago Press, 1981. 474p.

1033. Dino, Dorothee, Duchesse de, afterwards Duchesse de Talleyrand et de Sagan, 1793-1862. MEMOIRS OF THE DUCHESSE DE DINO (AFTERWARDS DUCHESSE DE TALLEYRAND ET DE SAGAN). Edited, with notes and biographical index by the Princess Radziwill (nee Castellane). New York: Charles Scribner's Sons, and London: William Heinemann, 1909-1910. 3 vols.

Memoirs, 1831-1850, composed of notes made in England during the Embassy of the Prince de Talleyrand, and of fragments of letters the Duchesse de Dino wrote over a period of 30 years to M. Adolphe de Bacourt.

1034. Dix, Dorothea Lynde, 1802-1887. American activist on behalf of the mentally ill. THE LADY AND THE PRESIDENT: THE LETTERS OF DOROTHEA DIX AND MILLARD FILLMORE. Edited by Charles M. Snyder. Lexington, Ky.: University Press of Kentucky, 1975. 400p.

Political and friendship correspondence, 1850-1869. Dix and Fillmore worked together in her activism on behalf of the indigent insane; she wrote to him from all over the country while on her tours and campaigns, keeping him informed of her movements and her work, and reporting on the political climate.

1035. Dixon, Agnes Margaret Powell. English. THE CANTEENERS. London: John Murray, 1917. 175p.

Diary of relief work during World War I.

1036. Djerassi, Norma Lundholm. American. GLIMPSES OF CHINA FROM A GALLOPING HORSE. New York: Pergamon Press, 1974. 141p.

Travel diary, May-June, 1973. She travelled to China with her husband, Carl Djerassi, visiting lecturer in Zoology.

1037. Doane, Didama Kelley. American sea merchant's wife. THE CAP'N'S WIFE: THE DIARY OF DIDAMA KELLEY DOANE OF WEST HARWICH MASSACHUSETTS, WIFE OF CAP'N URIEL DOANE, ON A TWO-YEAR VOYAGE WITH HER HUSBAND ABOARD THE SHIP RIVAL, 1866-1868, AND THE LOG OF THE CLIPPER GRANGER, URIEL DOANE, MASTER, FROM LIVERPOOL, BOUND FOR MANILA, LOST ON SWALLOW ROCK, LATITUDE 7.21 S., LONGITUDE BY DEAD RECKONING 114.03, ON OCTOBER 24, 1877. Albert Joseph George. Syracuse, N.Y.: Syracuse University Press, 1946. 130p.

Sea diary, prefaced by a biography of Doane and her family. Meant to be entertaining, and the material is presented in a light tone.

1038. Donnell, Anne. Australian. LETTERS OF AN AUSTRALIAN ARMY SISTER. Sydney: Angus & Robertson, 1920. 291p.

Letters of a World War I nurse.

Doolittle, Hilda. See: H.D.

1039. Dostoëvsky, Anna [Anna Grigor'evna Snitkina Dostoëvskaia], 1846-1918. Russian wife of author Feodor Dostoevsky. DAS TAGEBÜCH DER GATTIN DOSTOJEWSKIS. Herausgegeben von Rene Fulöp-Miller und Friedrich Eckstein. Munich: R. Piper & Co., 1925. 523p.

1040. ------. DOSTÖEVSKY PORTRAYED BY HIS WIFE: THE

DIARY AND REMINISCENCES OF MME. DOSTOËVSKY. Edited and translated by S.S. Koteliansky. New York: E.P. Dutton, and London: Routledge, 1926. 272p.

Travel diary, April 14--August 24, 1867. Detailed account written for her mother of travel in Germany and Switzerland.

1041. ------. THE DIARY OF DOSTOËVSKY'S WIFE. Edited by Rene Fulop-Miller and Dr. Friedrich Eckstein. Translated by Madge Pemberton. London: Victor Gollancz, and New York: The Macmillan Co., 1928. 421p.

Extracts from a shorthand diary, 1867-1868, written while traveling in Germany and Switzerland just before the outbreak of the Franco-German War. A large portion of the diary remains in shorthand script, and some volumes have been lost.

1042. Dow, Dorothy, b. 1904. American secretary. ELEANOR ROOSEVELT, AN EAGER SPIRIT: THE LETTERS OF DOROTHY DOW, 1933-1945. Edited by Ruth K. McClure. New York: W.W. Norton, 1984. 252p.

Dow was assistant to Eleanor Roosevelt's private secretary. Letters to her mother and sister in Wisconsin describe Mrs. Roosevelt and social life at the White House, the Great Depression and the war years of the 1940's, and the life of a woman who came to Washington "seeking adventure."

1043. Dow, Peggy, 1780-1820. American Methodist and wife of poet and editor Lorenzo Dow. VICISSITUDES IN THE WILDERNESS: EXEMPLIFIED IN THE JOURNAL OF PEGGY DOW. Liverpool: W. Forshaw, 1818, 144p. Norwich, Conn.: Faulkner, 1833. 214p.

1044. Drake, Sylvia, 1784-1868. American seamstress. "Sylvia Drake, 1784-1868: The Self Portrait of a Seamstress of Weybridge." Donald M. Murray and Robert M. Rodney. VERMONT HISTORY 34:2 (1966), 125-135.

Drake was a sewing partner of Charity Bryant, aunt

of William Cullen Bryant. Extracts from and summary of the diary, discussing three topics as the diary treats them: religion, domestic life in Drake-Bryant household, and the household's social life and travels.

1045. Draper, Ruth, 1884-1956. American actress. THE LETTERS OF RUTH DRAPER, 1920-1956: A SELF-PORTRAIT OF A GREAT ACTRESS. Edited with narrative notes by Neilla Warren. Foreword by Sir John Gielgud. London: W. Hamilton; New York: Charles Scribner's Sons, 1979. 362p.

Letters 1915-1956, chiefly written to family and friends during European theatrical tours. Warren notes that the "selection" of Draper's letters was made primarily by her family and friends, who routinely disposed of many, as she did of theirs.

1046. Drew, Elizabeth, b. 1935. American journalist. WASHINGTON JOURNAL: THE EVENTS OF 1973-1974. New York: Random House, 1975. 428p.

Reporter's journal, kept while covering Washington D.C. during the last years of the Nixon Administration.

1047. ------. AMERICAN JOURNAL: THE EVENTS OF 1976. New York: Random House, 1977. 561p.

1048. ------. CAMPAIGN JOURNAL: THE POLITICAL EVENTS OF 1983-1984. New York: Macmillan Co., 1985. 783p.

1049. Drew, Mary Gladstone, 1847-1927. English daughter of William E. Gladstone. MARY GLADSTONE (MRS. DREW): HER DIARIES AND LETTERS. Edited by Lucy Masterman. New York: E.P. Dutton and Co., 1930. 492p.

Letters and diaries, 1853-1924, edited together chronologically. There exists a series of typescript volumes of extracts from the diaries Drew prepared for publication, but as much of the "raciness and individuality" had been edited from them, they have been disregarded wherever the original manuscript exists.

1050. Drinker, Elizabeth Sandwith, 1743-1807.

Irish-American Quaker colonist and Loyalist. "Extracts from the Journal of Mrs. Henry Drinker of Philadelphia, from September 25, 1777 to July 4, 1778." PENNSYLVANIA MAGAZINE OF HISTORY AND BIOGRAPHY 13:3 (1889), 298-308.

Chiefly accounts of battles, given in brief, concise entries.

1051. ------. EXTRACTS FROM THE JOURNAL OF ELIZABETH DRINKER FROM 1759-1807 A.D. Edited by Henry D. Biddle. Philadelphia: J.B. Lippincott Co., 1889. 423p.

1052. Drouét, Juliette, 1806-1883. French actress and mistress of Victor Hugo. JULIETTE DROUET'S LETTERS TO VICTOR HUGO. Edited by Louis Cuimbaud. Translated by Lady Theodora Davidson. London: Stanley Paul & Co., 1915.

1053. ------. AUTOUR DE "RUY BLAS": LETTRES INÉDITES DE JULIETTE DROUET À VICTOR HUGO. Publiée par Paul Souchon. Paris: A. Michel, 1939. 253p.

1054. ------. OLYMPIO ET JULIETTE: LETTRES INÉDITES DE JULIETTE DROUÉT À VICTOR HUGO. Publiée par Paul Souchon. Paris: A. Michel, 1940. 253p.

1055. ------. MILLE ET UNE LETTRES D'AMOUR A VICTOR HUGO. Choix, préface et notes par Paul Souchon. Paris: Gallimard, 1951. 830p.

1056. ------. JULIETTE DROUÉT AUX PYRÉNEÉS. JOURNAL INÉDIT DE SON VOYAGE EN 1843. Publiée et annotée par Pierre de Gorsse. Paris: Imprimière Marrimpouey Jeune, 1956. 38p.

1057. Du Châtelet, Gabrielle Émilie de Tonnelier de Breteuil, Marquise, 1706-1749. French author, scholar, and mistress of Voltaire. LETTRES DE LA MARQUISE DU CHÂTELET. Réunies pour le première fois, révues sur les autographes et les éditions originales augmentées de 37 lettres entierement inédits, de nombreuses notes, d'un index, et précédées d'une notice biographique par Eugene Assé. Paris: Charpentier, 1882.

1058. ------. LES LETTRES DE LA MARQUISE DU CHÂTELET. Publieés par Theodore Besterman. Geneve: Institut et Musée Voltaire, 1958. 2 vols.

Volume 1: 1733-1739. Volume 2: 1740-1749.

1059. Du Deffand, Marie de Vichy Champrond, Marquise, 1697. French poet, letter-writer and salonist. CORRESPONDANCE INÉDITE DE MADAME DU DEFFAND AVEC D'ALEMBERT, MONTESQUIEU, LE PRESIDENT HENAULT, LA DUCHESSE DU MAINE, MESDAMES DE CHOISEUL, DE STAAL; LE MARQUIS D'ARGENS, LE CHEVALIER D'AYDIE, ETC. SUIVIE DES LETTRES DE M. DE VOLTAIRE A MADAME DU DEFFAND. Paris: Leopold Collin,, 1809. 2 vols.

1060. ------. THE UNPUBLISHED CORRESPONDENCE OF MADAME DU DEFFAND WITH D'ALEMBERT, MONTESQUIEU, THE PRESIDENT HENAULT, THE DUCHESS DU MAINE, MESDAMES DE STAAL, DE CHOISEUL, THE MARQUIS D'ARGENS, THE CHEVALIER D'AYDIE, ETC., FOLLOWED BY THE LETTERS OF VOLTAIRE TO MADAME DU DEFFAND. Translated from the French by Mrs. Meeke. London: For A.K. Newman & Co., 1810. 2 vols.

1061. ------. LETTERS OF THE MARQUISE DU DEFFAND TO THE HON. HORACE WALPOLE, AFTERWARDS EARL OF ORFORD, FROM THE YEAR 1766 TO THE YEAR 1780. TO WHICH ARE ADDED, LETTERS OF MADAME DU DEFFAND TO VOLTAIRE FROM THE YEAR 1769 TO THE YEAR 1775. Published from the originals at Strawberry-Hill. London: Printed for Longman, Hurst, Rees, and Orme, 1810. 4 vols.

1062. ------. LETTRES DE LA MARQUISE DU DEFFAND À HORACE WALPOLE. Paris: Chez Truettel et Wurtz, 1812. 2 vols.

1063. ------. LETTRES DE LA MARQUISE DU DEFFAND À HORACE WALPOLE, DEPUIS COMTE D'ORFORD, ÉCRITES DANS LES ANNÉSS 1766 A 1780; AUXELLES SONT JOINTES DES LETTRES DE MADAME DU DEFFAND A VOLTAIRE, ÉCRITES DANS LES ANNEES 1769 A 1775. Publiées d'après les originaux deposés à Strawberry-Hill. Nouvelle édition augmentée des extraits des lettres d'Horace Walpole. Paris: Ponthieu et Cie., 1827. 4 vols. in 2.

1064. ------. CORRESPONDANCE INÉDITE DE MADAME DU DEFFAND. Précédeé d'une notice par le Marquis de Sainte-Aulaire. Paris: Michel Levy Frères, 1859. 2 vols.

1065. ------. CORRESPONDANCE COMPLETE DE LA MARQUISE DU DEFFAND AVEC SES AMIES: LE PRESIDENT HENAULT; MONTESQUIEU; D'ALEMBERT; VOLTAIRE; HORACE WALPOLE. Classé dans l'ordre chronologique et sans suppressions. Augmentée des lettres inédites au Chevalier de L'Isle. Précédé d'une Histoire de sa vie, de son salon, des ses amies. Suivie de ses oeuvres diverses et éclairie de nombreuses notes par M. de Lescure. Paris: Henri Plon, Imprimeur-Éditeur, 1865. 2 vols. Reprinted, Geneve: Slatkine Reprints, 1971. 2 vols.

1066. ------. CORRESPONDANCE COMPLETE DE MADAME DU DEFFAND AVEC LA DUCHESSE DE CHOISEUL, L'ABBE BARTHÈLEMY ET MONSIEUR CRAUFORT. Publiée avec un introduction par Mons. le Marquis de Sainte-Aulaire. Paris: Calmann-Lévy, 1877. 4 vols.

1067. ------. LETTRES À VOLTAIRE. Introduction et notes de Joseph Trabucco. Paris: Éditions Bossard, 1922. 273p.

1068. ------. LETTERS TO AND FROM MADAME DU DEFFAND AND JULIE DE LESPINASSE. Edited by Warren Huntington Smith. New Haven, Conn.: Yale University Press; and London: Humphrey Milford, Oxford University Press, 1938. 97p.

Letters, in the original French, which reveal the stormy relationship between the two women as it changed from intimacy to rivalry. Julie de Lespinasse was a salonist and protoge of Madame du Deffand.

1069. ------. HORACE WALPOLE'S CORRESPONDENCE WITH MADAME DU DEFFAND AND WIART. Edited by W.S. Lewis and Warren Huntington Smith. New Haven, Conn.: Yale University Press; and London: Humphrey Milford, Oxford University Press, 1939. 6 vols. (Yale edition of Horace Walpole's Correspondence, Vols. 3-8.)

1070. ------. MADAME LA MARQUISE DU DEFFAND: LETTRES

A HORACE WALPOLE, VOLTAIRE, ET QUELQUES AUTRES. Precedes d'invitations à lire la Marquise Du Deffand de Francoise Bott et Jean-Claude Renault. Paris: Plasma, 1979. 213p.

1071. Duberly, Frances Isabella Locke, 1829-1903. English soldier's wife. JOURNAL KEPT DURING THE RUSSIAN WAR, FROM THE DEPARTURE OF THE ARMY FROM ENGLAND IN APRIL, 1854 TO THE FALL OF SEBASTOPOL. London: Longman, Brown, Green and Longmans, 1855. 311p. Second edition, 1856.

Travel journal, April, 1854--September, 1855, while with her husband; and an eyewitness account of the seige of Sebastopol during the Crimean War.

1072. Dudley, Dorothy. American colonist. THEATRUM MAJORUM: THE CAMBRIDGE OF 1776, WHEREIN IS SET FORTH AN ACCOUNT OF THE TOWN, AND OF THE EVENTS IT WITNESSED. WITH WHICH IS INCORPORATED THE DIARY OF DOROTHY DUDLEY. Together with a historical sketch done by divers hands, and edited by A.G. [A. Gilman]. Cambridge, Mass., 1867. Reprinted, New York: Kennikat Press, 1970. 123p.

Dudley's diary is dated April 18, 1775--July 19, 1776.

1073. Duff-Gordon, Lucie or Lucy, Lady, 1821-1869. English author and literary figure. LETTERS FROM EGYPT, 1863-1865. London: Macmillan & Co., 1865. 371p.

Travel letters, 1862-1865, written "under the influence of dangerous disease, and in the dreariness of solitary exile, far from all the resources which civilized society offers to the suffering body and the weary and dejected spirit, above all, far from all objects of the dearest affections."

1074. ------. LAST LETTERS FROM EGYPT. TO WHICH ARE ADDED, LETTERS FROM THE CAPE. London: Macmillan, 1875. 346p.

Travel letters written from Egypt, 1865-1869, and letters from the Cape of Good Hope, July, 1862--May, 1863.

1075. ------. LADY DUFF GORDON'S LETTERS FROM EGYPT. Revised edition. Edited with a memoir by her daughter Janet Ross. New introduction by George Meredith. New York: McClure, Phillips & Co., and London: R. Brimley Johnson, 1904. 383p.

Letters 1862-1869. Ross notes the letters in her mother's original edition were heavily edited to omit "much that might have given offence and made my mother's life uncomfortable--to say the least--in Egypt."

1076. ------. LETTERS FROM THE CAPE. Edited by John Purves. London: Humphrey Milford, 1921. 180p.

1077. ------. LETTERS FROM EGYPT, 1862-1869. Enlarged Centeneray Edition. With an introduction by Gordon Waterfield. London: Routledge and Kegan Paul, 1969. 385p.

1078. ------. "The Mysterious Lady." Goldie Levy. AFRICANA NOTES AND NEWS 20:8 (1973), 287-289.

Theorizes that several letters published in a Capetown paper by an anonymous woman in 1870 were written by Lady Duff-Gordon, citing similarities between the letters and Duff-Gordon's LETTERS FROM THE CAPE.

1079. Dufferin and Ava, Hariot Georgina Hamilton Hamilton-Temple Blackwood, Marchioness of, 1843-1936. English wife of Diplomat Frederick Temple-Hamilton-Temple Blackwood, Marquis of Dufferin and Ava. OUR VICEREGAL LIFE IN INDIA: SELECTIONS FROM MY JOURNAL, 1884-1888. London: John Murray, 1889. 2 vols. New and cheaper edition, London: John Murray, 1893. 2 vols.

1080. ------. MY CANADIAN JOURNAL, 1872-1878. EXTRACTS FROM MY LETTERS HOME WHILE LORD DUFFERIN WAS GOVERNOR-GENERAL. New York: D. Appleton & Co., 1891. 457p.

Social and travel diary. Records the business of the Governor General only as it affected the couple's social life, "and then, I fear," she writes, "in a somewhat light and irresponsible manner."

1081. ------. MY RUSSIAN AND TURKISH JOURNALS. BY THE DOWAGER DUCHESS OF DUFFERIN AND AVA. London: John Murray, 1916, and New York: Charles Scribner's Sons, 1917. 350p.

Journal-letters February, 1879--September, 1884. Describes social life at the British Embassies in Russia and Turkey. Again, "This account of life in our Embassies is altogether one-sided; the business part of it is entirely left out."

1082. Dugdale, Blanche Elizabeth Campbell Balfour. BAFFY: THE DIARIES OF BLANCHE DUGDALE, 1936-1947. Edited by N.A. Rose. Foreword by Meyer Weisgal. London: Vallentine, Mitchell, 1973. 262p.

1083. Dunbar-Nelson, Alice, 1875-1935. American Black poet, author, journalist, and activist. GIVE US EACH DAY: THE DIARY OF ALICE DUNBAR-NELSON. Edited with a critical introduction and notes by Gloria T. Hull. New York and London: W.W. Norton & Co., 1984. 480p.

Diary 1921 and 1926-1931 by a writer of the Harlem Renaissance; one of the few book-length diaries by a Black woman.

1084. Duncairn, Elizabeth Carey Mordaunt, Viscountess, d.1679. THE PRIVATE DIARIE OF ELIZABETH VISCOUNTESS MORDAUNT DUNCAIRN. Edited with a preface by Lord Roden. Privately Printed (Copied from the original manuscript and printed at his private press by Edmund Macrory), 1856.

Records the important events of her life, as well as public occurances, 1656-1678. Sir Arthur Ponsonby notes she kept a daily religious confessional for seven or eight weeks but did not continue it; he suggests the strain may have been too great.

1085. Duncan, Elizabeth Caldwell Smith, b. 1808. American wife of Illinois Governor Joseph Duncan. "Diary of Mrs. Joseph Duncan (Elizabeth Caldwell Smith)." Edited by Elizabeth Duncan Putnam. JOURNAL OF THE ILLINOIS STATE HISTORICAL SOCIETY 21:1 (April, 1928), 1-91.

Fragmentary diary describing life in the early days of New York and of Jacksonville, Illinois. Begins with a school diary, with entries for three months in 1824-1825. Supplemented by reminiscences dictated to her daughter in 1875.

1086. Dunlap, Susan, 1850-1916. Canadian frontier settler. "Susan Dunlap: Her Diary." G.G. Campbell. DALHOUSIE REVIEW 46:2 (1966), 215-222.

Discussion of the diary, with extracts from the first two years, 1866-1868. Dunlap kept a diary for sixty years, recording "the timeless trivia of a woman's days, in volume after volume after volume..." Dunlap's family settled in the Stewiacke Valley of Nova Scotia.

1087. Du Pont, Gabrielle Josephine de la Fite de Pellepont, 1770-1837. French wife of Diplomat Victor Du Pont. "Of Muslins and Merveilleuses: Excerpts from the Letters of Josephine Du Pont and Margaret Mannigault." Betty-Bright P. Low. WINTERTHUR PORTFOLIO 9 (1974), 29-75.

Extracts from the correspondence of Du Pont in New York and Charleston, North Carolina, and Margaret Izard Mannigault (1768-1824), in Paris, 1796-1824, relating to French influences on American fashions. The two women were lifelong friends, and the letters printed here represent only a small fraction of their long correspondence.

1088. Durham, Louisa Elizabeth Grey, Countess of, 1797-1841. Wife of John George Lambdon, 1st Earl of Durham, Governor of Canada. LETTERS AND DIARIES OF LADY DURHAM. Edited by Patricia Godsell. Toronto: Oberon Press, 1979. 203p.

1089. Dutt, Toru, 1856-1877. Indian author, poet and translator. LIFE AND LETTERS OF TORU DUTT. Harihar Das. With a foreword by the Rt. Hon. H.A.L. Fisher, M.P. London and New York: Humphrey Milford, Oxford University Press, 1921. 364p.

1090. Dwight, Margaret van Horn, 1790-1834. American. A JOURNEY TO OHIO IN 1810, AS RECORDED IN THE JOURNAL OF MARGARET VAN HORN DWIGHT. Edited by Max Farrand. New Haven, Conn.: Yale University Press, 1912. 64p.

Describes a journey by wagon from New Haven, Connecticut, to Warren, Ohio.

1091. Dymond, Ann, 1768-1816. English Quaker. SOME ACCOUNT OF ANN DYMOND, LATE OF EXETER. York, England: W. Alexander, 1820. 124p.

Chiefly composed of extracts from a Quaker diary, 1798-1816.

1092. Dymond, Mary Sparkes, 1808-1855. English Quaker. MEMOIR OF MARY DYMOND. COMPILED CHIEFLY FROM HER LETTERS AND MEMORANDA. Henry Dymond. London: W. and F.G. Cash, 1857. 98p.

Contains extracts from letters and from a Quaker diary, 1828-1837.

1093. Earhart, Amelia, 1897-1937. American aviator. LETTERS FROM AMELIA, 1901-1937. Jean L. Backus. Boston: Beacon Press, 1982. 253p.

Letters from Earhart to her mother, begining with a note printed on her fourth birthday (to her grand-mother) and ending with a letter written just before leaving on her last flight.

1094. Eastlake, Elizabeth Rigby, Lady, 1809-1893. English author, translator, and wife of English painter Sir Charles Locke Eastlake. LETTERS FROM THE SHORES OF THE BALTIC. London: John Murray, 1842. 2 vols. Reprinted 1844, 160p.

1095. ------. JOURNALS AND CORRESPONDENCE OF LADY EASTLAKE. Edited by her nephew, Charles Eastlake Smith. With facsimiles of her drawings and a portrait. London: John Murray, 1895. 2 vols. Reprinted, New York: AMS Press, 1975.

Social diary, 1842-1849, describing life at the Court of Queen Victoria, and letters, 1840-1854. Includes travel letters written on yearly trips to Italy, correspondence with her mother and sister and with her friend Sir Henry Layard.

1096. Eccles, Sybil, 1904-1977. English wife of politician and diplomat David Eccles. BY SAFE HAND: LETTERS OF SYBIL AND DAVID ECCLES, 1939-1942. London, Sydney, and Toronto: The Bodley Head, 1983. 432p.

Wartime letters, November, 1939--August, 1942, during which time Sybil lived with their children in Chute, and David was almost continuously abroad on diplomatic missions in Europe, Africa and the United States. Selection taken from "five or six hundred" letters, with some sensitive material cut to avoid giving offense.

1097. Eden, Emily, 1797-1869. English author. MISS EDEN'S LETTERS. Edited by her great niece Violet Dickinson. London: Macmillan & Co., 1919. 414p.

Letters 1814-1863, chiefly to Theresa Villiers. Villiers' side of the correspondence has not survived.

1098. ------. UP THE COUNTRY: LETTERS WRITTEN TO HER SISTER FROM THE UPPER PROVINCES OF INDIA BY EMILY EDEN. Introduction and notes by Edward Thompson. London: Humphrey Milford, Oxford University Press, 1930. 410p.

Diary-letters, 1837-1840. Eden accompanied her eldest brother George Eden to India when he became Vice General in 1835.

1099. ------. "Emily Eden as a Letter-Writer." Prudence Henry. HISTORY TODAY 21 (July, 1971), 491-501.

1100. Edgarton, Sarah and Luella J.B. Case. Americans. "Two Kindred Spirits: Sorority and Family in New England, 1839-1846." William R. Taylor and Christopher Lasch. NEW ENGLAND QUARTERLY 36:1 (March, 1963), 23-41.

Contains extracts from their correspondence.

1101. ------. "Sarah Edgarton and Luella J.B. Case: 'You Are Kissing Away the Venom of Some Angry Hornet From My Lips.'" In GAY AMERICAN HISTORY: LESBIANS AND GAY MEN IN THE U.S.A. Jonathan Katz. New York: Thomas Y. Crowell Co., 1975. p. 494-498.

Extracts from a correspondence which began when Edgarton contacted Case asking for a contribution to the Universalist Church annual publication THE ROSE OF SHARON, and blossomed into an intimate friendship.

1102. Edgerton, Mary Wright, 1827-1884. American wife of Montana Territorial Governor Sidney Edgerton. "Love From All to All: The Governor's Lady Writes Home to Ohio." James L. Thane, Jr. MONTANA: MAGAZINE OF WESTERN HISTORY 24:3 (July, 1974), 12+.

Letters to her family written from Bannack, Montana, 1863-1865.

1103. ------. GOVERNOR'S WIFE ON THE MINING FRONTIER: LETTERS OF MARY EDGERTON FROM MONTANA, 1863-1865. Edited with an introduction by James L. Thane, Jr. Salt Lake City: University of Utah Library, 1976. 148p.

1104. Edgeworth, Maria, 1767-1849. Irish novelist and pedagogue. MARIA EDGEWORTH: CHOSEN LETTERS. With an introduction by F.V. Barry. Boston and New York: Houghton Mifflin Co., n.d. 468p.

Selected correspondence, 1791-1849.

1105. ------. THE LIFE AND LETTERS OF MARIA EDGEWORTH. Edited by Augustus J.C. Hare. Boston and New York: Houghton Mifflin Co., and Cambridge, England:

1106. ------. ROMILLY-EDGEWORTH LETTERS, 1813-1818. Edited, with an introduction and notes by Samuel Henry Romilly. London: John Murray, 1936. 194p.

Chiefly letters of Anne Romilly to Maria Edgeworth; Edgeworth's letters to Romilly have not survived.

1107. ------. THE LETTERS OF MARIA EDGEWORTH AND ANNA LAETITIA BARBAULD. Selected from the Lushington Papers by Walter Sidney Scott. Illustrated by Lettice Sandford. London: Golden Cockerell Press, 1953. 86p.

Correspondence with English poet and author Anna Laetitia Barbauld (1743-1825). Edition of 300 copies.

1108. ------. LETTERS FROM ENGLAND, 1813-1844. Edited by Christina Colvin. Oxford: The Clarendon Press, 1971. 649p.

Letters written to friends and family in Ireland while on various trips to England as a tourist. Gives a picture of English social and literary circles.

1109. ------. MARIA EDGEWORTH IN FRANCE AND SWITZERLAND: SELECTED FROM THE EDGEWORTH FAMILY LETTERS. Edited by Christina Colvin. New York: Oxford University Press, 1979. 309p.

Companion volume to LETTERS FROM ENGLAND; describes travels in France in 1802 and 1803, and in France and Switzerland, 1820.

1110. Edmonston, Catherine Ann Devereux. American diarist. THE JOURNAL OF A SECESH LADY: THE DIARY OF CATHERINE ANN DEVEREUX EDMONSTON, 1860-1866. Edited by Margaret M. Jones. N.P.: Privately printed, 1954. 111p.

Extracts from a Civil War diary written by a resident of Halifax County, North Carolina. "Secesh" is short for "secessionist."

1111. ------. "Diary of a Soldier's Wife on Looking Glass Plantation (Halifax County, North Carolina)." In TRUE TALES OF THE SOUTH AT WAR: HOW SOLDIERS FOUGHT AND FAMILIES LIVED, 1861-1865. Clarence Hamilton Poe. Chapel Hill, N.C.: University of North Carolina Press, 1961. p.101-140.

1112. ------. JOURNAL OF A SECESH LADY: THE DIARY OF CATHERINE ANN DEVEREUX EDMONSTON, 1860-1866. Edited by Beth G. Crabtree and James W. Patton. Raleigh, N.C.: Division of Archives and History, Department of Cultural Resources, 1977. 850p.

1113. Eells, Myra Fairbanks, 1805-1878. American frontier missionary. "Journal of Myra Fairbanks Eells Kept While Passing Through the United States and Over the Rocky Mountains in the Spring and Summer of 1838." TRANSACTIONS OF THE 17TH ANNUAL REUNION OF THE OREGON PIONEER ASSOCIATION (June 8, 1889), 55-88a.

Eells was a member of the Whitman Mission to the Spokane Indians in Oregon. Journal describes hardships of frontier life and missionary work and travels.

1114. Egerton, Harriet Catherine Greville, later Countess of Ellesmere. English author. JOURNAL OF A TOUR OF THE HOLY LAND, IN MAY AND JUNE. By Lady Francis Egerton. With lithographed views, from original drawings by Lord Francis Egerton. For private circulation only; for the benefit of the Ladies Hibernian School Society. London: Privately Printed by Harrison & Co., 1841. 141p.

Travel diary, April--June, 1840.

1115. Eisenmenger, Anna. Austrian wife of a Viennese Physician. BLOCKADE: THE DIARY OF AN AUSTRIAN MIDDLE-CLASS WOMAN, 1914-1924. Translated by Winifred Ray. London: Constable & Co.; Bombay, Calcutta and Madras: Oxford University Press; Toronto: The Macmillan Company of Canada; and New York: Ray Long and Richard R. Smith, 1932. 273p.

Describes life in Austria during World War I and

her family's increasingly difficult efforts to survive as food supplies dwindled. Prefaced by a retrospective of the events leading to the war, and of her family's life before the war.

1116. Elgin, Mary Nisbet, Countess of, later Ferguson, 1777-1855. THE LETTERS OF MARY NISBET OF DIRLETON, COUNTESS OF ELGIN. Arranged by Lieutenent-Colonel Nisbet Hamilton Grant. London: John Murray, 1926. 358p.

Letters written during the period of her marriage to the Earl of Elgin.

1117. Eliot, George, pseud. for Marian Evans, afterwards Cross, 1819-1880. English author and critic. GEORGE ELIOT'S LIFE AS RELATED IN HER LETTERS AND JOURNALS. Arranged and edited by her husband, J.W. Cross. Edinburgh and London: W. Blackwood, and New York: Harper & Bros., 1885. 3 vols. Reprinted, New York and Boston: T.Y. Crowell & Co., 1900. 763p.

Literary letters and Journals 1838-1880, prefaced by an introductory sketch of Eliot's early life.

1118. ------. LETTERS FROM GEORGE ELIOT TO ELMA STUART, 1872-1880. Edited by Roland Stuart. London: Simpkin, Marshall, Hamilton, Kent & Co., 1909. 179p.

Correspondence with Stuart, a woodcarver, fan and friend of Eliot. Includes an appendix of literary letters by others, including Charlotte Bronte and Percy Bysshe Shelley.

1119. ------. LETTERS OF GEORGE ELIOT. Selected with an introduction by R. Brimley Johnson. London: John Lane, 1926, and New York: Lincoln MacVeagh, The Dial Press, 1927. 219p.

Selection taken from the Cross edition, and meant as an introduction to Eliot's letters.

1120. ------. GEORGE ELIOT'S FAMILY LIFE AND LETTERS. Arthur Paterson. Boston and New York: Houghton Mifflin Co., 1928. 254p.

Letters to the Lewes children and grandchildren (George Henry, Charles, and Thornton Lewes), 1859-1878, plus further letters to 1880. Focuses on Eliot's domestic life.

1121. ------. THE GEORGE ELIOT LETTERS. Edited by Gordon S. Haight. New Haven, Conn.: Yale University Press, and London: Geoffrey Cumberlege, Oxford University Press, 1954-1955. 9 vols.

Definitive edition. Letters 1836-1881, and extracts from Eliot's Journal, 1864-1880.

1122. ------. GEORGE ELIOT'S "MIDDLEMARCH" NOTEBOOKS: A TRANSCRIPTION. Edited with an introduction and preface by John Clark Pratt and Victor A. Neufeldt. Berkeley, Calif.: University of California Press, 1979. 365p.

Two notebooks Eliot kept on her reading from 1868-1871, the period in her career which culminated in the publication of MIDDLEMARCH.

1123. ------. SELECTIONS FROM GEORGE ELIOT'S LETTERS. Edited by Gordon S. Haight. New Haven, Conn.: Yale University Press, 1985. 567p.

1124. ------. GEORGE ELIOT: A WRITER'S NOTEBOOK, 1854-1879, AND UNCOLLECTED WRITINGS. Edited by Joseph Wiesenforth. Charlottesville, Va.: Published for the Bibliographic Society of the University of Virginia by the University of Virginia Press, 1981. 301p.

1125. Elizabeth I, Queen of Great Britain, 1533-1603. LETTERS OF QUEEN ELIZABETH AND KING JAMES VI OF SCOTLAND. SOME OF THEM PRINTED FROM THE ORIGINALS IN THE POSSESSION OF THE REVEREND EDWARD RYDER, AND OTHERS FROM A MANUSCRIPT WHICH FORMERLY BELONGED TO SIR PETER THOMPSON, KT. Edited by John Bruce. London: The Camden Society, 1849. 180p. (Camden Soc. Publications No. 44).

Letters 1582-1603 which more or less touch upon every important public incident in Scotland for the period. Queen Elizabeth seldom dated her letters, and that she often wrote in a style so involved that it is sometimes difficult to penetrate to the exact person or event alluded to.

1126. ------. THE LETTERS OF QUEEN ELIZABETH. G.B. Harrison. London: Cassell & Co., 1935. 323p. Reprinted, New York: Funk & Wagnalls, 1968.

Edition designed as a portrait of Queen Elizabeth as a woman and a ruler, through a selection of her personal letters and of letters which demonstrate her statecraft, 1533-1603.

1127. Elisabeth of Bavaria, Consort of Francis Joseph I, Emperor of Austria, 1837-1898. ÉLISABETH DE BAVIÈRE, IMPÉRATRICE D'AUTRICHE: PAGES DE JOURNAL, IMPRESSIONS, CONVERSATIONS, SOUVENIRS. Constantin Christomanos. Traduction de Gabriel Syvetor. Préface de Maurice Barres. Paris: Mercure de France, 1933. 273p.

1128. ------. ÉLISABETH, "DIE SELTSAME FRAU": NACH DEM SCHRIFTLICHEN NACHLASS DER KAISERIN, DEN TAGE-BÜCHERN, IHRER TOCHTER UND SONSTIGEN UNVEROFFENTLICHTEN TAGEBÜCHERN UND DOKUMENTEN. Conte Egon Caesar Corti. Bildtalfein bisher meist unbekannter photos. Salzburg-Leipzig: A. Pustet, 1937. 542p.

1129. Elizabeth of England, Consort of Frederick I, King of Bohemia, 1596-1662. Daughter of James IV of Scotland and Anne of Denmark. BRIEFE DER ELISABETH STUART, KÖNIGIN VON BÖHMEN, AN IHREN SOHN, DER KURFÜR-STEN CARL LUDWIG VON PFALZ, 1650-1662. Nach dem im Königlichen Staatsarchiv zu Hannover befindlichen originalen herausgegeben von Anna Wendland. Tubingen: Litterarischer verein in Stuttgart, 1902. 224p.

Letters are in English.

1130. ------. THE LETTERS OF ELIZABETH, QUEEN OF BOHEMIA. Compiled by L.M. Baker. With an introduction by C.V. Wedgwood. London: The Bodley Head, 1953. 361p.

1131. Elizabeth, Princess of France, 1764-1794. Sister of King Louis XVI. THE LIFE AND LETTERS OF MADAME ELIZABETH DE FRANCE, FOLLOWED BY THE JOURNAL OF THE TEMPLE BY CLERY, AND THE NARRATIVE OF MARIE THERESE DE FRANCE, DUCHESSE D'ANGOULEME. Translated by Katharine Prescott Wormely. Unexpurgated rendition into English. New York: Versailles Historical Society, 1889. 329p.

1132. Elizabeth, Countess Palatine, Abbess of Herford, 1618-1680. DESCARTES, LA PRINCESS ELISABETH ET LA REINE CHRISTINE. D'Après des Lettres inedités par A. Foucher de Careil. Paris: Cermer-Ballière, 1879. 219p.

Letters of Princess Elisabeth and of Queen Christina of Sweden (1626-1689), to Rene Descartes.

1133. ------. DIE BRIEFE DER KINDER DES WINTERKÖNIGS. Herausgegeben und mit einer einleitung von Karl Hauck. Heidelberg: G. Koester, 1908.

1134. Elizabeth of England, Consort of Frederich VI, Landgrave of Hesse-Homburg, 1770-1840. LETTERS OF PRINCESS ELIZABETH OF ENGLAND, DAUGHTER OF KING GEORGE III AND LANDGRAVINE OF HESSE HOMBURG. WRITTEN FOR THE MOST PART TO MISS LOUISA SWINBURNE. Edited, with notes and an introductory chapter by Miss Swinburne's great nephew Phillip Charles Yorke. London: T. Fisher Unwin, 1898. 360p.

Swinburne was an author and the daughter of Henry Swinburne. The letters, according to Yorke, are of no historical value, contain no gossip of contemporaries or of the Royal family, and have no pretensions to literary perfection. But they have two important characteristics: they are simple, natural, and familiar, and they reveal Elizabeth's great affection towards her friends.

1135. Elizabeth, Queen Consort of Charles I, King of Romania, 1843-1916. BRIEFE DER KÖNIGNIN ELISABETH VON RUMANIEN (CARMEN SYLVA), AN EINEN DEUTSCHEN GELEHRTEN. Mitgeteilt von Arthur Kleinschmidt. Berlin: Westermanns Monatschefte, 1916. 400p.

1136. ------. LETTERS AND POEMS OF QUEEN ELISABETH (CARMEN SYLVA). With an introduction and notes by Henry Howard Harper. Boston: Printed for members only, The Bibliophile Society, 1920. 2 vols.

1137. Elizabeth de la Trinite, Sister, 1880-1906. French Carmelite nun. THE PRAISE OF GLORY: REMINISCENCES OF SISTER ELISABETH OF THE TRINITY, A CARMELITE NUN OF DIJON, 1901-1906. Authorized translation by the Benedictines of Stanbrook from the fifth French edition. With an introduction by Benedict Zimmerman. London: R.&T. Washbourne, and New York: Benzinger Press, 1913. 288p.

Translation of an edition of ÉCRITS SPIRITUELS.

1138. ------. ÉCRITS SPIRITUELS D'ÉLISABETH DE LA TRINITÉ. Lettres, retriats, et inédites présénteés par R.P. Philipon. Paris: Éditions du Seuil, 1949. 253p.

Contains letters and extracts from her _journal intime._

1139. ------. SPIRITUAL WRITINGS: LETTERS, RETREATS, AND UNPUBLISHED NOTES BY SISTER ELIZABETH OF THE TRINITY. Edited by M.M. Philipon. New York: P.J. Kennedy & Sons, 1962. 180p.

1140. ------. J'AI TROUVÉ DIEU: OUVRES COMPLETES. Édition du Centenaire (1880-1980). Realisée, présénteé, annoteé par Conrad de Meester. Paris: Cerf, 1979-1980. 2 vols. in 3.

Contents: Lettres du Carmel; Journal et notes intimes; Lettres de Jeunesse; Poesies.

1141. ------. I HAVE FOUND GOD: COMPLETE WORKS. Edition realized, presented, annotated by Conrad de Meester. Translated by Alethia Cane. Centenary edition. Washington, D.C.: ICS Publications, 1984--.

1142. Ella, Martha Cheney. Canadian frontier settler. "The Diary of Martha Cheney Ella, 1853-1856." Edited by James K. Nesbitt. BRITISH COLUMBIA HISTORICAL QUARTERLY 13 (1949), 91-112, 257-270.

Describes life in pre-provincial British Columbia.

1143. Ellice, Jane. Canadian wife of Lord Durham's private secretary. DIARY OF JANE ELLICE. Edited by Patricia Godsell. Toronto and Ottowa: Oberon Press, 1975. 211p.

Travel diary, 1838, written in Canada and the United States.

1144. Elliot, Frances Minto Dickinson, 1820-1898. Travel author. DIARY OF AN IDLE WOMAN IN ITALY. New York: Brentano's: Publishers, 187?. 2 vols. in one. London: Chapman & Hall, 1871. 2 vols. in one. Leipzig: B. Tauchnitz, 1872. 2 vols. in one. New edition, revised, London: Chapman & Hall, 1872. 368p.

1145. ------. DIARY OF AN IDLE WOMAN IN SICILY. London: Richard Bentley & Sons, 1881. 2 vols. Leipzig: B. Tauchnitz, 1882. 319p.

1146. ------. DIARY OF AN IDLE WOMAN IN SPAIN. New York: Brentano's: Publishers, n.d. 2 vols. Leipzig: B. Tauchnitz, 1884. 2 vols. in one. London: F.V. White & Co., 1897. Limited "Florentine" edition of one hundred, New York: Crosscup & Sterling Co., 1897.

1147. ------. DIARY OF AN IDLE WOMAN IN CONSTANTINOPLE. London: John Murray, 1892, 1893. 425p. Leipzig: B. Tauchnitz, 1893. 350p. New York: D. Appleton & Co., 1893. 425p.

1148. Elliot, Grace Dalrymple, 1754-1823. JOURNAL OF MY LIFE DURING THE FRENCH REVOLUTION. London: Richard Bentley & Sons, 1859. 206p. Reprinted, New York: Rodale Press, 1955. 153p.

1149. Elssler, Fanny, 1810-1884. Opera singer. THE LETTERS AND JOURNALS OF FANNY ELSSLER. WRITTEN BEFORE AND AFTER HER OPERATIC CAMPAIGN IN THE UNITED STATES.

INCLUDING HER LETTERS FROM NEW YORK, LONDON, PARIS, HAVANNA & ETC. New York: H.G. Daggers, 1845. 65p.

1150. Emerson, Ellen Louisa Tucker, 1809-1831. American first wife of Ralph Waldo Emerson. OUR FIRST LOVE: THE LETTERS OF ELLEN LOUISA TUCKER TO RALPH WALDO EMERSON. Edited by Edith E.W. Gregg. Cambridge, Mass.: The Belknap Press of Harvard University Press, 1962. 208p.

Love letters 1828-1831.

1151. Emerson, Ellen Tucker, 1839-1909. American daughter of Ralph Waldo Emerson. THE LETTERS OF ELLEN TUCKER EMERSON. Edith E.W. Gregg. Kent, Ohio: Kent State University Press, 1982. 2 vols.

The last substantial body of Emerson family papers previously unpublished, Ellen Tucker Emerson's letters describe in detail life in the Emerson household from 1846 to 1892, touching on the social life of Concord, the Civil War, and everyday occurances of the period. She began writing letters at the age of seven, and continued her voluminous correspondence until her death.

1152. Emerson, Lidian Jackson, 1802-1892. American second wife of Ralph Waldo Emerson. THE SELECTED LETTERS OF LIDIAN JACKSON EMERSON. Edited with an introduction by Delores Bird Carpenter. Columbia: University of Missouri Press, 1987. 343p.

Letters 1813-1885 chronicle the day to day comaraderie of the lives of Ralph Waldo and Lidian Jackson Emerson. About half of the extant letters are printed here, and the selection is for notable correspondents (Margaret Fuller, the Alcott family, Thomas and Jane Welsh Carlyle), historical events and issues (the Civil War, slavery, women's rights), and references to Ralph Waldo Emerson.

1153. Emma, Consort of Kamehameha IV, King of the Hawaiian Islands, 1836-1885. NEWS FROM MOLOKAI: LETTERS BETWEEN PETER KAEO AND QUEEN EMMA, 1873-1876.

Edited with an introduction and notes by Alfons L. Korn. Honolulu: University of Hawaii Press, 1976. 345p.

1154. English, Lydia E. American frontier settler. "By Wagon from Kansas to Arkansas: The Travel Diary of Lydia E. English." Edited by John W. Snell. KANSAS HISTORICAL QUARTERLY 36:4 (1970), 369-389.

Overland diary, September 20--December 6, 1875.

1155. Épinay, Louise Florence Petronille Tardieu d'Esclavelles, Marquise d', 1726-1783. French salonist noted for her connection with Jacques Rousseau. DERNIERES ANNÉES DE MADAME. D'ÉPINAY. SON SALON ET SES AMIS. D'APRÈS DES LETTRES ET DES DOCUMENTS INÉDITS. Lucien Perey et Gaston Maugras. Paris: Calmann Lévy, 1894.

1156. ------. LA JEUNESSE DE MADAME D'ÉPINAY. D'APRÈS DES LETTRES ET DES DOCUMENTS INÉDITES. Lucien Perey et Gaston Maugras. Paris: Calmann Lévy, 1898.

1157. ------. THE MEMOIRS AND CORRESPONDENCE OF MADAME D'ÉPINAY. Edited, translated, with an introduction and brief notes by J.H. Freese. London: H.S. Nichols, 1899. 3 vols.

1158. ------. MEMOIRS AND CORRESPONDENCE OF MADAME D'ÉPINAY. Translated with an introduction by E.G. Allingham. London: George Rutledge & Sons, 1930. 314p.

Includes her diary. There is some controversy over whether the diary is really a memoir in diary form, or a fictional sketch for a novel.

1159. Erickson, Anna and Ethel Erickson. American homesteaders. Ethel was a teacher. "They Had a Wonderful Time: The Homesteading Letters of Anna and Ethel Erickson." Edited by Enid Bern. NORTH DAKOTA HISTORY 45:4 (Fall, 1978), 4-31.

Letters 1909-1911 describe life on their homestead in North Dakota.

1160. Erickson, Hilda Andersson, 1859-1968. Swedish-born Mormon frontier settler. "Diary, 1880-1885." OUR PIONEER HERITAGE 6 (1963), 82-95, 98-100.

1161. Erix-Dotter, Christina Louisa. Swedish-American frontier settler. "An American Letter in 1854 from a Varmlanning." Edited by Gustav E. Johnson. SWEDISH PIONEER HISTORICAL QUARTERLY 18:2 (1967), 93-100.

Translation of a letter written by a young immigrant to her family in Sweden.

1162. Erwin, Margaret Johnson, 1821-1863. American Southern social figure. LIKE SOME GREEN LAUREL: LETTERS OF MARGARET JOHNSON ERWIN. John Seymour Erwin. Baton Rouge, La., and London: Louisiana State University Press, 1981. 154p.

Letters chiefly to Philadelphia architect Samuel Sloane, who built Erwin's home, Mount Holly. The originals have been lost, and this book consists of incomplete transcriptions the editor's nephew made in 1937. Erwin was a strong-willed, independent woman whose radical social views often brought her into conflict with her conservative family.

1163. Essig, Maude Francis, 1884-1981. American. "A Hoosier Nurse in France." Alma S. Wooley. INDIANA MAGAZINE OF HISTORY 82 (1986), 37-68.

Diary 1917-1919 of a Red Cross Nurse assigned to a Base Hospital in France.

1164. Eubank, Mary James. American frontier settler. "A Journal of Our Trip to Texas, October 6--December 4, 1853, by Mary James Eubank." Edited by W.C. Nunn. TEXANA 10:1 (1972), 30-44.

Overland diary of the journey from Kentucky to Texas.

1165. Eugénie, Consort of Napoleon III, "L'Impératrice Eugénie," 1826-1920. LETTRES FAMILIÈRES DE L'IMPÉRATRICE

EUGÉNIE CONSERVÉES DANS LES ARCHIVES DU PALAIS DE LIRIA. Publiées par les soins du Duc d'Albe, avec le concours de F. de Llanos y Torriglia et Pierre Josserand. Préface de Gabriel Hanotaux. Paris: Le Divan, 1935. 2 vols.

Contents: Lettres d'enfance, 1836-1838; Lettres de jeune fille, 1843-1853; Les annees heureuses, 1853-1860; Des cimes a l'abime, 1860-1870; Les tristesses de Camden Place, 1870-1876; Les années de decouragement, 1876-1879; Les mois tragiques, 1879-1880; Lettres de survivante (Farnborough, Villa Cyrus, le Thistle), 1881-1920.

1166. Evans, Mary Peacock, 1821-1912. American. THE JOURNALS OF MARY PEACOCK: LIFE A CENTURY AGO, AS SEEN IN BUFFALO AND CHAUTAUQUA COUNTY BY A SEVENTEEN YEAR OLD GIRL IN BOARDING SCHOOL AND ELSEWHERE. Buffalo, N.Y.: Privately Printed, 1938. 60p.

1167. Evans, Rosalie Caden, d. 1924. American wife of banker Harry Evans, and champion of the rights of foreigners in Mexico. THE ROSALIE EVANS LETTERS FROM MEXICO. Arranged with comment by Daisy Caden Pettus. Indianapolis, Ind.: Bobbs-Merrill Co., 1926. 472p.

Letters to Evans' sister, the editor, 1918-1924, from her hacienda in Mexico. She was killed in an anti-foreigner uprising in 1924.

1168. Eve, Sarah, 1749/50-1774. American daughter of a Philadelphia sea captain and shipping merchant. "Extracts from the Journal of Miss Sarah Eve, Written While Living Near the City of Philadelphia in 1772-1773." Mrs. Eva Eve Jones. PENNSYLVANIA MAGAZINE OF HISTORY AND BIOGRAPHY 5:1 (1881), 19-36; and 5:2 (1888), 191-205.

1169. Everett, Anne Gorham, 1823-1843. American daughter of Edward Everett, clergyman and Governor of Massachusetts. MEMOIR OF ANNE GORHAM EVERETT, WITH EXTRACTS FROM HER CORRESPONDENCE AND JOURNAL. Philippa Call Bush. Boston: Privately Printed, 1857. 320p.

Girlhood diary and letters written in the early 1840's. Everett died young of tuberculosis.

1170. Everettt, Sarah Maria Colegrove, 1830-1864. American abolitionist and frontier settler. "Letters of John and Sarah Everett, 1854-1864, Miami County Pioneers." Thomas C. Wells. KANSAS HISTORICAL QUARTERLY 8:1 (February, 1939), 3-34; 8:2 (May, 1939), 143-174; 8:3 (August, 1939), 279-310; and 8:4 (November, 1939), 350-383.

Everett and her husband settled in Kansas Territory in 1855. Her Letters offer a picture of a family struggling against the hazards of the frontier and the turmoil of the Civil War.

1171. Ewart, Audrey. American Lesbian-feminist writer. "Silence, Culture and Slow Awakening." CONDITIONS 5 (Autumn, 1979), 79-80.

Extracts from her journal.

1172. Ewing, Juliana Horatia Gatty, 1841-1885. English-Canadian novelist and children's author. CANADA HOME: JULIANA HORATIA EWING'S FREDERICTON LETTERS, 1867-1869. Edited by Margaret Howard Blom and Thomas E. Blom. Vancouver: University of Vancouver Press, 1983. 425p.

1173. Faessler-Spiro, Annie. Swiss Nurse. JOURNAL D'UNE INFIRMIÈRE, 1939-1940. Illustrations de D. Bugnon. Thonex, Switzerland: Editions du Vieux Piolet, 1984. 95p.

1174. Fairbrother, Nan. English. AN ENGLISH YEAR. New York: Alfred A. Knopf, 1954. 243p.

Wartime diary of a young English mother. Reflections on the changing seasons, childhood memories of a northern English slum, books read, movies seen, and unsentimental observations of the growth of children.

1175. Fairfax, Sally. American Colonist and Loyalist.

"Diary of a Little Colonial Girl." VIRGINIA MAGAZINE OF HISTORY AND BIOGRAPHY 11:1 (1903-1904), 212-214.

Extracts from a private, domestic diary, 1771-1772, and a letter to her father, a Loyalist who was contemplating a voyage to England.

1176. Falk, Ruth, b. 1942. American author. WOMAN LOVING: A JOURNEY TOWARD BECOMING AN INDEPENDENT WOMAN. Berkeley and New York: Bookworks/Random House, 1975. 550p.

Sets down in diary form the feelings and processes Falk experiences as she explores her love for other women and for herself. Made up of poetry, essays, interviews, journal entries, letters, and political statements.

1177. Fanshawe, Anne, Lady, 1625-1680. English diarist. MEMOIRS OF THE LADY FANSHAWE, WIFE OF THE RT. HON. SIR RICHARD FANSHAWE, BART., AMBASSADOR FROM CHARLES THE 2ND TO THE COURT OF MADRID IN 1665. WRITTEN BY HERSELF. TO WHICH ARE ADDED, EXTRACTS FROM THE CORRESPONDENCE OF SIR RICHARD FANSHAWE. London: H. Colburn, 1829. 395p.

1178. Farmar, Eliza. American colonist. "Letters to Her Nephew, 1774-1783." PENNSYLVANIA MAGAZINE OF HISTORY AND BIOGRAPHY 40:1 (1916), 199-207.

Letters contain news of the Continental Congress, battles fought during the Revolution, and an account of flight from the British Army, which plundered Farmar's home.

1179. Farmborough, Florence. English nurse. WITH THE ARMIES OF THE TSAR: A NURSE AT THE RUSSIAN FRONT, 1914-1918. New York: Stein & Day, 1975. 422p.

Farmborough traveled to Russia in 1908 as a companion/governess to a family in Kiev. In 1914 she volunteered for Red Cross work and was sent to Poland. The original diary ran to some 400,000 words. Some of it was written on scraps of paper and abbreviated to one word entries which Farmborough later expanded upon, causing abrupt changes in tense.

1180. Farnsworth, Martha. American teacher, photographer, and suffragist. PLAINS WOMAN: THE DIARY OF MARTHA FARNSWORTH, 1882-1922. Edited by Marlene Springer and Haskell Springer. Bloomington, Ind.: Indiana University Press, 1985. 352p.

1181. Fay, Amy, 1844-1928. American concert pianist, music critic and teacher. MUSIC-STUDY IN GERMANY: FROM THE HOME CORRESPONDENCE OF AMY FAY. Edited by Mrs. Fay Pierce. Chicago: Jansen, McClurg & Co., 1881. 348p. New edition, with a new introduction by Frances Dillon, New York: Dover Publications, 1965. 352p.

Letters from Germany to her family in America, 1869-1875, written while studying with Franz Liszt and Ludwig Deppe. The book was very popular, going through twenty-one printings in America, and is said to have inspired over 2,000 students who went abroad to study music in the years before World War I.

1182. ------. MORE LETTERS OF AMY FAY: THE AMERICAN YEARS, 1879-1916. Selected and edited by Margaret William McCarthy. Detroit, Mich.: Information Coordinators, 1986. 168p.

1183. Fay, Anna Maria, 1828-1921. American. VICTORIAN DAYS IN ENGLAND: LETTERS OF AN AMERICAN GIRL, 1851-1852, BY ANNA MARIA FAY. Boston and New York: Houghton Mifflin, 1923. 249p.

1184. Fay, Eliza, 1756-1816. English. ORIGINAL LETTERS FROM INDIA (1779-1815). With introductory and terminal notes by E.M. Forster. London: Leonard and Virginia Woolf at the Hogarth Press, 1925. 288p. New York: Harcourt Brace & Co., 1925. 307p.

Eliza Fay married Anthony Fay in 1799 and moved with him to Calcutta. They later separated, and she lived alternately in England, America and India for the rest of her life. Fay compiled a version of this book, using letters, but after her death, the administer of her estate, thinking the entire manuscript of insufficient interest, published a shortened version and destroyed the original manuscript. This version leaves out the last twenty years of her life.

1185. Fedde, Elizabeth, Sister, 1850-1921. Swedish-American Deaconess and missionary to Swedes in America. "Elizabeth Fedde's Diary, 1883-1888." Edited by Beulah Folkedahl. NORWEGIAN-AMERICAN STUDIES AND RECORDS 20 (1959), 170-196.

Reveals much about her missionary work and about conditions among poor Norwegian immigrants in America. Contains about half of the original diary entries.

1186. Fenwick, Eliza. English. THE FATE OF THE FENWICKS: LETTERS TO MARY HAYS (1797-1828). Edited by her great-great niece, Annie F. Wedd. London: Methuem & Co., 1927. 248p.

Chiefly letters written by Eliza Fenwick. Hays and Fenwick were probably introduced by Mary Wollstonecraft. They both administered to Wollstonecraft when she was dying, and remained close friends for thirty years.

1187. Ferland, Carol, b. 1936. American. THE LONG JOURNEY HOME. New York: Alfred A. Knopf, 1980. 294p.

Diary of a year spent in a mental hospital.

1188. Fern, Francis Hewitt. American. DIARY OF A REFUGEE. Edited by Frances Fern. Illustrated by Rosalie Urguhart. New York: Moffat, Yard & Co., 1910. 149p.

Edited from notes taken down by the author's mother. Diary of a wealthy Southern woman, 1862-1867. After the invasion by Northern troops of her family plantation, she and her husband took flight, ultimately to France, where they moved in aristocratic circles.

1189. Ferrier, Susan Edmonstone, 1782-1854. Scottish novelist. MEMOIR AND CORRESPONDENCE OF SUSAN FERRIER, 1782-1854. BASED ON HER PRIVATE CORRESPONDENCE IN THE POSSESSION OF, AND COLLECTED BY, HER GRAND-NEPHEW JOHN FERRIER. Edited by John A. Doyle. London: E. Nash & Grayson, 1898, 1929. 348p.

1190. Ferris, Anna M., 1815-1890. American Quaker. "The Civil War Diaries of Anna M. Ferris." Edited by Harold B. Hancock. DELAWARE HISTORY 9:3 (April), 221-264.

Diary November 2, 1860--December 31, 1865. Probably the most complete diary written during the Civil War by a resident of Delaware, Ferris' diary reflects the opinions of a middle-class Quaker family on the political and military events of the war.

1191. Ferry, Amanda White. American frontier missionary. "Frontier Mackinac Island, 1823-1834. Letters of William Montague and Amanda White Ferry." Edited by Charles A. Anderson. PRESBYTERIAN HISTORICAL SOCIETY JOURNAL (December, 1947), 192-222; (March, 1948), 101-127; and (September, 1948), 182-191.

1192. Feuerbach, Henriette Heydenreich, 1812-1892. German author. HENRIETTE FEUERBACH: IHR LEBEN IN IHREN BRIEFEN. Herausgegeben von Hermann Uhde-Bernays. Berlin: Meyer & Jessen, 1912. 490p. Munchen: Kurt Wolff, 1920. 490p.

1193. Few, Frances. American daughter of William Few, a signer of the Constitution. "The Diary of Frances Few, 1808-1809." Edited by Noble E. Cunningham, Jr. JOURNAL OF SOUTHERN HISTORY 29:3 (1963), 345-361.

Diary extracts relate a visit to Few's aunt in Washington, D.C.; describes social and political life at the Capitol.

1194. Field, Joanna, pseud. for Marion Blackett Milner. English psychoanalyst. A LIFE OF ONE'S OWN. London: Chatto & Windus, 1934. Harmondsworth,

Middlesex, England: Penguin Books, 1934, 1952, 1955. 252p. New edition with afterword, Boston: Houghton Mifflin Co., 1981. 226p.

Chronicles a self-analysis, based in part on her diary. Includes extracts.

1195. Field, Kate, pseud. for Mary Katherine Keemle Field, 1838-1896. American journalist and lecturer. KATE FIELD: A RECORD. Lillian Whiting. Boston: Little, Brown & Co., 1899, 1900. 610p.

Biography which draws heavily upon extracts from Field's letters and journal. Since most of her papers have not survived, this book remains the most important primary source for the study of her life.

1196. Field, Michael, pseud. for Katherine Bradley, 1848-1914 and Edith Cooper, 1862-1913. English poets. WORKS AND DAYS: FROM THE JOURNAL OF MICHAEL FIELD. Edited by T. and D.C. Sturge Moore. London: John Murray, 1933.

Includes letters between the two poets and Robert Browning, and extracts from their joint diary, 1883-1914. Wherever possible, who wrote which section of diary or letter is indicated in footnotes. Bradley was Cooper's aunt, and they lived as close companions all their adult lives. Almost all of their work was written in collaboration; individual works by either were also published under their pseudomym.

1197. ------. "Works and Days: The Journal of 'Michael Field.'" Henri Locard. JOURNAL OF THE EIGHTEEN NINETIES SOCIETY 10 (1979), 1-9.

1198. Fields, Annie Adams, 1834-1915. American author and literary hostess. MEMORIES OF A HOSTESS: A CHRONICLE OF EMINENT FRIENDSHIPS. DRAWN CHIEFLY FROM THE DIARIES OF MRS. JAMES T. FIELDS. Edited by M.A. DeWolfe Howe. Boston: The Atlantic Monthly Press, 1922. 312p.

Literary social diary and letters, 1863-1913.

Heavily edited, chiefly in order to erase "embarassing" displays of affection for Sarah Orne Jewett, with whom she lived for many years in a model "Boston Marriage."

1199. Fiennes, Celia, 1662-1741. English tradeswoman and traveler. THROUGH ENGLAND ON A SIDE SADDLE, IN THE TIME OF WILLIAM AND MARY. BEING THE DIARY OF CELIA FIENNES. Introduction by Mrs. Griffiths. London: Field and Tuer, 1888. 336p.

Travel diary, 1685-1698. Fiennes travelled on business through every county in England, and her journal provides the most comprehensive personal account of the upperclass and wealthy merchant class of the time.

1200. ------. THE JOURNEYS OF CELIA FIENNES. Edited with an introduction by Christopher Morris. With a foreword by G.M. Trevelyan. London: The Cresset Press, 1947. Revised edition, 1949. 573p.

Definitive edition, based on the original manuscript. Includes extensive notes and biographical and historical background.

1201. Finzi, Kate John. English nurse. EIGHTEEN MONTHS IN THE WAR ZONE: THE RECORD OF A WOMAN'S WORK ON THE WESTERN FRONT. With an introduction by Major-General Sir Alfred Turner. London and New York: Cassell & Co., 1916. 260p.

War diary, October, 1914--February, 1916, written at a base hospital in Bologne.

1202. Fisher, Sarah Logan, 1751?-1796. American Quaker. "A Diary of Trifling Occurrences: Philadelphia, 1776-1778." Edited by Nicholaus B. Wainwright. PENNSYLVANIA MAGAZINE OF HISTORY AND BIOGRAPHY 82:4 (1958), 411-465.

Extracts from a loyalist diary, describing the occupation of Philadelphia by the Revolutionary Forces, the evacuation of the city, and the arrest of Fisher's father and her husband, Thomas Fisher.

1203. Fitzgerald, Alice L.F. American nurse. THE EDITH CAVELL NURSE FROM MASSACHUSETTS: A RECORD OF ONE YEAR'S PERSONAL SERVICE WITH THE BRITISH EXPEDITIONARY FORCE IN FRANCE, BOLOGNE--THE SOMME, 1916-1917. WITH AN ACCOUNT OF THE IMPRISONMENT, TRIAL AND DEATH OF EDITH CAVELL. Boston: W.A. Butterfield, 1917. 65p.

Fitzgerald was sent by the Edith Cavell Committee to serve with the British Expeditionary Force for the duration of the war. Proceeds from the sale of this book were used to fund a second year of service. Journal-letters to friends and to members of the Committee.

1204. Fitzgerald, Emily McCorkle. American wife of U.S. Army Surgeon Dr. John A. Fitzgerald. AN ARMY DOCTOR'S WIFE ON THE FRONTIER. LETTERS FROM ALASKA AND THE FAR WEST, 1874-1878. Edited by Abe Laufe. Preliminary editing by the late Russell J. Ferguson. Pittsburgh, Penn.: University of Pittsburgh Press, 1962. 352p.

Letters describe the journey from New York to Sitka, Alaska, in 1874; life there from 1874 to 1875; life at Fort Lapwai in the Idaho Territory during the Nez Perce Indian Wars, 1876-1877; and life at Fort Boise, Idaho, 1877-1878.

1205. Fitzherbert, Maria Anne Smythe, 1756-1837. English secret wife of King George IV. THE LETTERS OF MRS. FITZHERBERT AND CONNECTED PAPERS. BEING THE SECOND VOLUME OF THE LIFE OF MRS. FITZHERBERT. Shane Leslie. London: Burns Oates, 1940. 343p.

Correspondence 1788-1837 and extracts from the correspondence of others, highlighting the controversy concerning her marriage and over the disposal of her papers.

1206. ------. LETTERS BETWEEN AN ILLUSTRIOUS PERSONAGE (GEORGE, PRINCE OF WALES, AFTERWARDS KING GEORGE IV) AND A LADY OF HONOUR (MRS. FITZHERBERT) AT BRIGHTON. London: J. Walter, 1789. 87p.

1207. Flanner, Janet, 1892-1978. American author, journalist and foreign correspondent who wrote under the name of Ganet. DARLINGHISSIMA: LETTERS TO A FRIEND. Edited and with commentary by Natalia Danesi Murray. New York: Random House, 1985. 507p.

Correspondence 1944--1975 between Flanner, a "Europeanized American" and Murray, an "Americanized European" reveals a passionate friendship begun during World War II. Flanner went to Europe as a War Correspondent, Murray as a Captain in Special Services in the Psychological Warfare Branch of the Office of War Information; their letters, are important "as a demonstration of how two women surmounted obstacles trying to lead their personal and professional lives."

1208. Fleet, Maria Louisa Wacker. American educator. GREEN MOUNTAIN AFTER THE WAR: THE CORRESPONDENCE OF MARIA LOUISA WACKER FLEET AND HER FAMILY, 1865-1900. University of Virginia Press, 1977. 276p.

School letters to friends and relatives. Gives a good picture of the educational priorities of the nineteenth century as well as of daily life in late nineteenth century Virginia.

1209. Fleet, Mary, b. 1729. American. "Extracts from the Diary of Miss Mary Fleet, Boston, 1755-1803." NEW ENGLAND HISTORICAL AND GENEALOGICAL REGISTER 19:1 (January, 1856), 59-61.

Extracts from a religious diary.

1210. Fleming, Marjorie (Margaret), 1803-1811. Scottish child prodigy. PET MARJORIE: THE STORY OF PET MARJORIE WITH HER PORTRAITS AND COMPLETE DIARIES. New York: G.P. Putnam's Sons, and London: The Knickerbocker Press, 1904. 203p. London: Simpkin, Marshall, Hamilton, Kent & Co., 1914. 128p.

Childhood diary, 1809-1811, of a girl who was reading Shakespeare at the age of four and composing poetry at seven.

1211. ------. MARJORIE FLEMING'S BOOK: THE STORY OF PET MARJORIE TOGETHER WITH HER JOURNALS AND HER LETTERS. TO WHICH HAS BEEN ADDED, MARJORIE FLEMING, A STORY OF CHILD-LIFE FIFTY YEARS AGO, BY JOHN BROWN, M.D. Introduction by Clifford Smyth. New York: Boni & Liveright, The Modern Library, n.d. 225p.

1212. ------. THE COMPLETE MARJORIE FLEMING: HER JOURNALS, LETTERS AND VERSES. Transcribed and edited by Frank Sidgwick. London: Sidgwick & Jackson, 1934. 208p.

Nine letters, and journals for 1810 and 1811.

1213. Fletcher, Ellen Gordon, b. 1841. American frontier settler. A BRIDE ON THE BOZEMAN TRAIL: THE LETTERS OF ELLEN GORDON FLETCHER, 1866. Edited by Francis D. Haines, Jr. Medford, Ore.: Grandee Printing Center, 1970. 139p.

1214. Fletcher, Sarah Hill. American wife of Lawyer and banker Calvin Fletcher. DIARY OF CALVIN FLETCHER, INCLUDING LETTERS OF CALVIN FLETCHER AND HIS WIFE, SARAH HILL FLETCHER. Edited by Gayle Thornbrough. Indianapolis: Indiana Historical Society, 1972. 2 vols.

Volume two contains letters between Calvin and Sarah Fletcher, 1838-1843.

1215. Fontaine, Margaret Elizabeth, 1862-1940. English traveler and collector of diurnal lepidoptera. LOVE AMONG THE BUTTERFLIES: THE TRAVELS AND ADVENTURES OF A VICTORIAN LADY, MARGARET FONTAINE. Edited by W.F. Cater. London: Collins, 1980. Boston: Little, Brown & Co., 1982. Harmondsworth, Middlesex, England, and N.Y.: Penguin Books, 1982. 203p.

Diaries 1878-1939 by a woman who left the respectable life of a clergyman's daughter to travel the world, making journeys to Turkey, the United States, Africa and India. She collected some 22,000 butterflies, which she willed to the Castle Museum in Norwich, England, along with her diaries.

1216. Foote, Katharine, b. 1881. American. 88 BIS AND V.I.H.: LETTERS FROM TWO HOSPITALS, BY AN AMERICAN V.A.D. Boston: The Atlantic Monthly Press, 1919. 104p.

War letters of a nurse serving in the English Voluntary Aid Detachment during World War I.

1217. Foote, Mary Wilder, 1810-1857. American wife of Reverend Caleb Foote. CALEB AND MARY WILDER FOOTE: REMINISCENCES AND LETTERS. Edited by Mary Wilder Tileston. Boston and New York: Houghton Mifflin Co., and Cambridge, England: The Riverside Press, 1918. 369p.

Biography followed by letters and extracts from Mary Foote's correspondence, 1824-1857.

1218. Forbes, Mrs. E.A. A WOMAN'S FIRST IMPRESSIONS OF EUROPE. BEING WAYSIDE SKETCHES MADE DURING A SHORT TOUR IN THE YEAR 1863. New York: Derby & Miller, 1865. 355p.

Diary of a European Tour, July 21--November 21, 1863.

1219. Ford, Ann Jeannette Tooker. American missionary. "Missionary's Bride in 1846." Ann Tooker Ford. LONG ISLAND FORUM 36:8 (1973), 156-160.

Biography and excerpts from a journal-letter, November--December, 1846, written on the voyage to India with her husband, Missionary George Ford.

1220. Foreman, Susan E. American schoolteacher. "Notes from the Diary of Susan E. Foreman." Linda Finley. CHRONICLES OF OKLAHOMA 47:4 (Winter, 1969-1970), 388-397.

Short, often one-line entries from the diary of a young teacher at the Cherokee Neighborhood School at Webbers Fall, Oklahoma, 1862-1863. Provides insight into the upheaval caused among the Cherokee by the Civil War.

1221. Forest, Eva (Genoeva). Spanish feminist imprisoned without trial in 1974 for her alleged complicity in the bombing of the Cafe Rolando and the murder of Prime Minister Carrero Blanco. FROM A SPANISH PRISON: DIARIO Y CARTAS DESDE LA CARCEL (DIARY AND LETTERS FROM PRISON). New York: Moon Books/Random House, 1976. 191p.

Journal written during seven days of solitary confinement, and letters from prison to her three children. Includes a letter from Maria Luz Fernandez, arrested with Forrest, to her lawyer after her release from a solitary confinement of 114 days.

1222. Former, Anita. RAINER MARIA RILKE, ANITA FORMER: BRIEFWECHSEL. Herausgegeben von Magda Kerenyi. Frankfurt Am Main: Insel Verlag, 1982.

1223. Forten, Charlotte, afterwards Grimke, 1837-1914. American Black educator and abolitionist. "A Social Experiment: The Port Royal Journal of Charlotte Forten, 1862-1863." Edited by Ray Allen Billington. JOURNAL OF NEGRO HISTORY 35:2 (April, 1950), 233-264.

Extracts from her journal relating to her work as a teacher of newly freed slaves at Port Royal, South Carolina.

1224. ------. THE JOURNAL OF CHARLOTTE FORTEN: FREE NEGRO IN THE SLAVE ERA. Edited by Ray Allen Billington. New York: Dryden Press, 1953. 248p. New York: Collier-Macmillan, 1961. 268p.

Forten was the daughter of a well-to-do Philadelphia merchant family, whose home was a station on the underground railroad, and married the mulatto nephew of the abolitionist sisters Angelina and Sarah Grimke. The first part of her journal was written during her student years and early years as a teacher in Massachusetts; the second concerns her work as a teacher of Freedmen at Port Royal, South Carolina.

1225. Foster, Emily (Mary Amelia Foster), 1804?-1885.

English poet, novelist and clergyman's wife. THE JOURNAL OF EMILY FOSTER. Edited by Stanley T. Williams and Leonard B. Beach. New York and London: Oxford University Press, 1938. 171p.

Court diary, 1821-1824, written at Dresden, Germany. Foster was a friend of Washington Irving, who proposed marriage to her.

1226. Foucault, Geneviéve Marie Pauline de Foucault, Marquise de. A CHÂTEAU AT THE FRONT, 1914-1918. Translated by George B. Ives. Boston and New York: Houghton Mifflin Co., 1931. 338p.

Foucalt moved to the Château of Pronleroy in Picardy in 1913, and had just settled in when war broke out in 1914. She decided to remain there, although the Chateau was for a time behind German lines. She opened her home to Allied Army staff, officers, and refugees.

1227. Fouché, Catharina Thérèse Lovisa Frederika Élisabeth von Stedingk Grey, Duchesse d'Otrante, 1837-1901. JOURNAL OF A VISIT TO EGYPT, CONSTANTINOPLE, THE CRIMEA, GREECE & ETC., IN THE SUITE OF THE PRINCE AND PRINCESS OF WALES. BY THE HON. MRS. WILLIAM GREY. London: Smith, Elder & Co., 1869. 203p. New York: Harper & Bros., 1870. 209p.

1228. ------. DAGBOK UNDER EN RESA TILL EGYPTEN, KONSTANTINOPEL, KRIM OCH GREKLAND, I PRINSENS OCH PRINSESSANS AF WALES SUITE. THE HON. MRS. WILLIAM GREY. Ofversattnig. Stockholm: P.A. Norstedt & Soner, 1870. 162p.

1229. Fox, Caroline, 1819-1871. English Quaker. MEMOIRS OF OLD FRIENDS. BEING EXTRACTS FROM THE JOURNALS AND LETTERS OF CAROLINE FOX, OF PENJERRICK, CORNWALL, FROM 1835 TO 1871. TO WHICH ARE ADDED FOURTEEN ORIGINAL LETTERS FROM J.S. MILL NEVER BEFORE PUBLISHED. Edited by Horace N. Pym. London: Smith, Elder and Philadelphia: J.B. Lippincott, 1882. 2 vols.

A Quaker from a wealthy family, Fox moved in circles with Thomas and Jane Welsh Carlyle and John

Mill and Harriet Taylor. Sir Arthur Ponsonby has a high opinion of her diary; with its intimate portraits of leading intellectuals of her time, it is a valuable source-book for the period. This edition is heavily edited and contains excerpts only.

1230. ------. THE JOURNALS OF CAROLINE FOX, 1835-1871: A SELECTION. Edited by Wendy Monk. London: Elek, 1972. 250p.

1231. Fox, Margaret Askew Fell, 1614-1702. English Quaker and author. THE LIFE OF MARGARET FOX, WIFE OF GEORGE FOX. COMPILED FROM HER OWN NARRATIVE, AND OTHER SOURCES. WITH A SELECTION FROM HER EPISTLES, ETC. Philadelphia: Association of Friends for the Diffusion of Religious and Useful Knowledge, 1859. 112p. Philadelphia: Philadelphia Book Association of Friends, 1885. 112p.

1232. ------. "Margaret Fox to Her Grandchildren Bethina Rous and David English, 1699." JOURNAL OF FRIENDS HISTORICAL SOCIETY 12:3 (1915), 146-147.

Letter written from Swarthmore, September 17, 1699, sending family tidings and requesting her grandchildren write their mother more often, so that she may receive news of them.

1233. Fox, Maria Middleton, 1793-1884. English Quaker. MEMOIRS OF THE LATE MARIA FOX OF TOTTENHAM, CONSISTING CHIEFLY OF EXTRACTS FROM HER JOURNALS AND CORRESPONDENCE. Philadelphia: H. Longstreth, 1847. 491p. London: C. Gilpin, 1846. 493p.

1234. ------. A BRIEF MEMOIR OF MARIA FOX, LATE OF TOTTENHAM. Philadelphia: Association of Friends for the Diffusion of Religious and Useful Knowledge, 1858, 1859. 157p. Philadelphia: Book Association of Friends, 1885. 157p.

Abridged version of the 1846 edition.

1235. Frampton, Mary, 1773-1846. English. THE

JOURNAL OF MARY FRAMPTON FROM THE YEAR 1779 UNTIL THE YEAR 1846. INCLUDING VARIOUS INTERESTING AND CURIOUS LETTERS, ANECDOTES &TC, RELATING TO EVENTS WHICH OCCURED DURING THAT PERIOD. Edited, with notes, by Harriot Georgiana Mundy. London: Sampson Low, Marston, Searle & Rivington, 1885. 425p.

Social and domestic diary, with accounts of trips to London from Dorset, written as short summaries of the years events. The "Various Interesting and Curious Letters" make up most of the book, including letters by Mary Frampton, Lady Susan O'Brien, Lady Mary Talbot, Julia, Lady Sheffield, Maria, Countess of Ilchester, Lady Elizabeth Fielding, H.R.H Princess Elizabeth, Lady Harriot Acland, the Marchioness of Landsdowne, Caroline, Countess of Mount-Edcumbe, Lady Caroline Fox Strangways, and others. Also includes brief extracts from the journals of Miss Ann Agnes Porter and Lady Susan O'Brien.

1236. Francis, Harriet Elizabeth Tucker, 1828-1889. American. ACROSS THE MERIDIANS; AND FRAGMENTARY LETTERS. New York: The De Vinne Press, 1887. 300p.

Letters to friends, June 17, 1875--May 23, 1876, describe a world tour undertaken by a wealthy American family. "Fragmentary letters," July 19, 1882--October 19, 1885 describe travel in Europe.

1237. Frank, Anne (Annelies Marie), 1929-1945. Dutch Jew, who with her family and others hid from the Nazis for two years during the German occupation of Holland in World War II. Her diary of the experience is an international classic. She died in a Nazi death camp. HET ACHTERHUIS: DOGBOEKBRIEVEN VAN 12 JUNI 1942--1 AUGUSTUS 1944. Met een woord voaf door Annie Romein-Vershoor. Amsterdam: Contact, 1947. 258p.

1238. ------. ANNE FRANK'S DIARY. Translated from the Dutch by B.M. Mooyaart-Doubleday. With a foreword by Storm Jameson. London: Vallentine, Mitchell, 1954. 228p. Also published under the title: DIARY OF A YOUNG GIRL. London: Constellation Books, 1952.

1239. ------. ANNE FRANK: THE DIARY OF A YOUNG GIRL. Translated from the Dutch by B.M. Mooyaart-Doubleday. With an introduction by Eleanor Roosevelt. Preface by George Stevens. New York: Doubleday, 1952. 285p.

1240. ------. WORKS. Translated by B.M. Mooyart-Doubleday and Michel Mok. Introduction by Ann Birsetein and Alfred Kazin. Garden City, N.Y.: Doubleday, 1959. 332p.

1241. Franklin, Deborah. American colonist. "Deborah Franklin Correspondence." Edward M. Riley. AMERICAN PHILOSOPHICAL SOCIETY PROCEEDINGS 95 (1951), 239-245.

1242. Franklin, Jane Griffin, Lady, 1792-1875. English reformer and wife of explorer Sir John Franklin, Governor of Tasmania from 1837 to 1848. THE LIFE, DIARIES AND CORRESPONDENCE OF JANE, LADY FRANKLIN, 1792-1875. Edited by Willingham Franklin Rawnsley. London: E. MacDonald, 1923. 242p.

Biography incorporating extracts from her letters and diary, covering her life before her marriage, 1792-1828; as well as her travels with her husband in the Mediterranean and Tasmania, 1830-1875. Lady Franklin travelled or lived abroad almost continually from the time of her marriage to her death.

1243. ------. SOME CORRESPONDENCE OF SIR JOHN AND LADY JANE FRANKLIN. George Mackaness. Sydney: Privately Printed by George Mackaness, 1947.

1244. Franks, Rebecca, later Johnson. American Colonist. "A Letter of Rebecca Franks, 1778." Henry F. Thompson. PENNSYLVANIA MAGAZINE OF HISTORY AND BIOGRAPHY 16:2 (1829), 216-218.

Letter to Anne Harrison Paca, second wife of William Paca, a delegate to Congress; describes social life in Philadelphia the winter preceeding the evacuation of the city by the British.

1245. ------. "Letter of Miss Rebecca Franks."

PENNSYLVANIA MAGAZINE OF HISTORY AND BIOGRAPHY 23:3 (1899), 303-309.

"Vivacious and gossipy" letter to her sister Abigail, wife of Andrew Hamilton, August 10, 1781, relating family news and community affairs.

1246. Franqueville, Sophia Matilda Palmer, Comtesse de, 1852-1915. SOPHIA MATILDA PALMER, COMTESSE DE FRANQUEVILLE, 1852-1915: A MEMOIR. By her sister, Lady Laura Ridding. London: John Murray, 1919. 381p.

Biography comprised of extracts from letters.

1247. ------. A POLITICAL CORRESPONDENCE OF THE GLADSTONE ERA: THE LETTERS OF LADY SOPHIA PALMER AND SIR ARTHUR GORDON, 1884-1889. Edited by J.K. Chapman. Transactions of the American Philosophical Society, 1971.

1248. Fraser, Mary Crawford. English wife of British Ambassador Hugh Fraser A DIPLOMAT'S WIFE IN JAPAN: SKETCHES AT THE TURN OF THE CENTURY. Edited by Hugh Cortazzi. Weatherhill, 1982. 351p.

Letters 1889-1894, written home from Japan, where her husband served as Ambassdor.

1249. Fraser, Siri and Ebba Pederson. Americans. WITH LOVE, SIRI AND EBBA. New York: Times Change Press, 1974. 128p.

Letters describe a backpacking trip across North Africa in the early 1970's.

1250. Freeman, Ann Mason, 1797-1826. English Quaker. A MEMOIR OF THE LIFE AND MINISTRY OF ANN FREEMAN, A FAITHFUL SERVANT OF JESUS CHRIST. WRITTEN BY HERSELF. AND AN ACCOUNT OF HER DEATH, BY HER HUSBAND, HENRY FREEMAN. London: Printed for the Author, and sold by Harvey and Darton, 1826. 246p. Second edition, 1828, 195p. Exeter, N.H.: Published by Nancy Towle, L.F. Shepard, 1831. 216p.

1251. Freeman, Mary Eleanor Wilkins, 1852-1930. American author. THE INFANT SPHINX: COLLECTED LETTERS OF MARY E. WILKINS FREEMAN. Edited with biographical and critical introductions and annotations by Brent L. Kendrick. Metuchen, N.J.: The Scarecrow Press, 1985. 587p.

First collection of Freeman's letters, 1875-1930. Much of her correspondence with her family and friends has been lost, and those which remain--517 were found--are chiefly concerned with her work.

1252. Freidenberg, Olga Mikhailovna, 1890-1955. Russian scholar and cousin of Boris Pasternak. THE CORRESPONDENCE OF BORIS PASTERNAK AND OLGA FREIDENBERG, 1910-1954. Compiled and edited, with an introduction by Elliott Mossman. Translated by Elliott Mossman and Margaret Wettlin. A Helen and Kurt Wolf Book. London and New York: Harcourt Brace Jovanovich, 1982. 365p.

"Loving correspondence" between cousins who rarely met in person, but who shared a life in letters. Contains excerpts from Freidenberg's retrospective "diary" of her life, composed in her last years.

1253. Freke, Elizabeth. Irish wife of Percy Freke of County Cork. "Mrs. Elizabeth Freke, Her Diary." Edited by Mary Carberry. JOURNAL OF THE CORK HISTORICAL AND ARCHAEOLOGICAL SOCIETY, Second Series, vol. 16 (No. 88, October--December, 1910), 149-167; Vol. 17 (No. 89, January-March, 1911), 1-16, 45-58, 93-113, 142-154; Vol. 18 (No. 93, January-March, 1912), 39-47, 88-97, 151-159, 203-210; Vol. 19 (No. 97, January-March, 1913), 42-47, 84-90, 134-147.

Private diary, 1671-1714. The first installment contains a biography and a history of the Freke family.

1254. French, Emily, b. c.1843. American frontier settler. EMILY: THE DIARY OF A HARD-WORKED WOMAN. Edited by Janet LeCompte Lincoln. Lincoln, Nebr.: University of Nebraska Press, 1987. 166p.

1255. Freycinet, Rose Marie Pinon de Saulces de,

1794-1832. French traveler, and wife of Frigate Captain Louis-Claude de Freycinet. CAMPAGNE DE L'"URANIE" (1817-1820). JOURNAL DE MADAME ROSE DE SAULCES DE FREYCINET D'APRÈS LE MANUSCRIT ORIGINAL. Accompagnée de notes par Charles Duplomb. Paris: Société d'Éditions Geographiques, Maritimes, et Coloniales, 1927. 190p. Cover title: JOURNAL DU VOYAGE AUTOUR DE MONDE.

Freycinet was the first French woman to sail around the world.

1256. ------. REALMS AND ISLANDS: THE WORLD VOYAGE OF ROSE DE FREYCINET IN THE CORVETTE URANIE, 1817-1820: FROM HER JOURNALS AND LETTERS AND THE REPORTS OF LOUIS DE SAULCES DE FREYCINET, CAPTAINE DE CORVETTE. Edited by Marnie Bassett. London and New York: Oxford University Press, 1962.

1257. Frink, Margaret Ann Alsip. American frontier settler. A JOURNAL OF A PARTY OF CALIFORNIA GOLD SEEKERS, UNDER THE GUIDANCE OF MR. LEDYARD FRINK, DURING A JOURNEY ACROSS THE PLAINS FROM MARTINSVILLE, INDIANA, TO SACRAMENTO, CALIFORNIA, FROM MARCH 30, 1850 TO SEPTEMBER 7, 1850. FROM THE ORIGINAL DIARY OF THE TRIP KEPT BY MRS. MARGARET FRINK. Oakland, Calif.: No Publisher, 1897. 131p.

1258. Frizzell, Lodisa. American frontier settler. ACROSS THE PLAINS TO CALIFORNIA IN 1852. Edited by Victor H. Paltsits. New York: The New York Public Library, 1915.

Overland diary, 1852.

1259. Fromm, Bella. German journalist. BLOOD AND BANQUETS: A BERLIN SOCIAL DIARY. Introduction by Frederick T. Birchall. New York and London: Harper, in Association with Cooperation Publishing Co., 1942. 332p. London: G. Bles, 1943. 256p. Garden City, N.Y.: Garden City Publishing Co., 1944. 332p.

Diplomatic and social diary. Describes Germany

before World War II, 1930-1938. Fromm was the diplomatic columnist for VOSSICHE ZEITUNG.

1260. Frost, Elinor. American wife of poet Robert Frost. FAMILY LETTERS OF ROBERT AND ELINOR FROST. Edited by Arnold Grade. Foreword by Lesley Frost. Albany, N.Y.: State University of New York Press, 1972. 293p.

Nearly 200 letters, 1914-1963, written by Robert and Elinor Frost to their children, grandchildren and other members of the family. Most are addressed to Lesley Frost. Only about fifty of Elinor's letters are included, or about two-thirds of those made available.

1261. Frost, Lesley, b. 1900. American daughter of poet Robert Frost. NEW HAMPSHIRE'S CHILD: THE DERRY JOURNALS OF LESLEY FROST. With notes and index by Lawrence Thompson and Arnold Grade. Albany, N.Y.: State University of New York Press, 1969. unpaginated.

Facsimile reproductions of a childhood journal, 1905-1909, written between the age of five and ten.

1262. Frost, Sarah Scofield. KINGSTON AND THE LOYALISTS OF THE "SPRING FLEET" OF A.D. 1783. TO WHICH IS APPENDED A DIARY WRITTEN BY SARAH FROST ON HER VOYAGE TO St. JOHN, NEW BRUNSWICK WITH THE LOYALISTS OF 1783. Walter Bates. Edited with notes by W.O. Raymond. Saint John: Barnes, 1889. 30p.

1263. Frothingham, Helen Losanitch. Serbian Red Cross Delegate during World War I. MISSION FOR SERBIA: LETTERS FROM AMERICA AND CANADA. Edited by Matilda Spence Rowland. New York: Walker & Co., 1970. 326p.

Letters to her mother and sister, 1915-1920, written while traveling in the U.S. and Canada on a speaking tour to raise money and enlist help for Serbia.

1264. Fry, Elizabeth Gurney, 1780-1845. English Quaker, philanthropist and prison reformer. MEMOIR OF

THE LIFE OF ELIZABETH FRY. WITH EXTRACTS FROM HER JOURNAL AND LETTERS. Edited by two of her daughters (Katherine Fry and Rachel Elizabeth Fry Cresswell). London: C. Gilpin, J. Hatchard & Son, 1847. 2 vols. Philadelphia: H. Longstreth, 1847. 2 vols. Philadelphia: J.W. Moore, 1847-1848. 2 vols.

1265. ------. A MEMOIR OF ELIZABETH FRY. By Her Daughter, Mrs. Francis Cresswell. Abridged from the larger edition, with alterations and additions. London: Piper, Stephenson & Spence, 1856. 583p. London: James Nisbet & Co., 1868. 338p.

1266. ------. ELIZABETH FRY: LIFE AND LABORS OF THE EMINENT PHILANTHROPIST, PREACHER AND PRISON REFORMER. COMPILED FROM HER JOURNAL AND OTHER SOURCES. Edward Ryder. New York: E. Walker's Sons, 1883. 381p.

Quaker diary. Sir Arthur Ponsonby, in his review of Fry's journal (See item 94) considers her journal a cut above the usual Quaker diary.

1267. ------. THE DIARIES OF ELIZABETH FRY, 1797-1845. FROM THE LIBRARY OF THE SOCIETY OF FRIENDS, SPECIAL COLLECTIONS. List of contents and index to reels. London: World Microfilms Publications, 1979. 7 reels (35mm).

1268. Fujiwara no Nagako. Japanese diarist and Lady-In- Waiting. THE EMPEROR HORIKAWA DIARY (SANUKE NO SUKE NIKKI). Translated with an introduction by Jennifer Brewster. Honolulu: The University Press of Hawaii, 1977. 155p.

Japanese poetic diary. Fujiwara no Nagako was Lady-In-Waiting to the Emperor Horikawa who died in 1107, and later to his son, Emperor Toba, who reigned from 1107 to 1123. The first book of the diary relates the events of Horikawa's death; the second is more personal and reflective. The literary merit of this diary is not as great as those of Lady Sarashina or Lady Murasaki, but it contains the fullest description of the court of the Emperor Horikawa.

1269. Fuller, Elizabeth, 1775-1856. American daughter of a Massachusetts Minister. "Diary." In HISTORY OF THE TOWN OF PRINCETON, IN THE COUNTY OF WORCESTER AND THE COMMONWEALTH OF MASSACHUSETTS, 1759-1915. Francis Everett Blake. Princeton: Published by the Town, 1915. 2 vols.

Private diary October 4, 1790--December, 1792, describes the domestic life of a religious New England family.

1270. Fuller, Jan (pseud.). American. SPACE: THE SCRAPBOOK OF MY DIVORCE. New York: Arthur Fields Books, 1973. Unpaginated.

1271. Fuller, Margaret (Sarah Margaret Fuller, later Marchesa d'Ossoli), 1810-1850. American author, critic, teacher, feminist, and transcendentalist. MEMOIRS OF MARGARET FULLER OSSOLI. Edited by Ralph Waldo Emerson, William H. Channing and James Freeman Clarke. Boston: Phillips, Sampson, 1851-1852. 2 vols. Reprinted, New York: Burt Franklin, 1972.

The editors write of their relationships with Fuller in separate introductions and around her writings, and have arranged the different aspects of Fuller's writing into sections: her correspondence with them and with others; her journals; and her essays and articles. According to Robert Hudspeth, this volume was heavily edited, and much of the original material mutilated or destroyed.

1272. ------. LOVE LETTERS OF MARGARET FULLER, 1845-1846. With an introduction by Julia Ward Howe. To Which are Added the Reminiscences of Ralph Waldo Emerson, Horace Greeley and Charles T. Congdon. New York: D. Appleton & Co., 1903. 228p. Reprinted, Westport, Conn.: Greenwood Press, 1969.

Letters to James Nathan Hale, written while traveling in Europe. Fuller met Hale in the Fall of 1844 at "The Farm," where she was staying with Horace Greeley and his family. They struck up an "enthusiastic friendship" which came to an end unexpectedly and was never renewed. Fuller dismisses it from her thoughts in a few sentences in her diary.

1273. ------. "Margaret Fuller's Roman Diary." Leona Rostenberg. JOURNAL OF MODERN HISTORY 12:2 (June, 1940), 209-220.

Record and impressions of Italian life and public events during the months January-May, 1849, possibly the basis for her letters to the NEW YORK DAILY TRIBUNE.

1274. ------. MARGARET FULLER, AMERICAN ROMANTIC: A SELECTION FROM HER WRITINGS AND CORRESPONDENCE. Edited by Perry Miller. Garden City, N.Y.: Doubleday, 1963. Reprinted, Ithaca, N.Y.: Cornell University Press, 1970. 319p.

Essays, literary criticism and selections from her correspondence with Ralph Waldo Emerson and others.

1275. ------. "Margaret Fuller's 1842 Journal: At Concord with the Emersons." Joel Myerson. HARVARD LIBRARY BULLETIN 21 (July, 1973), 320-340.

1276. ------. "Margaret Fuller's 1839 Journal: Trip to Bristol." Robert N. Hudspeth. HARVARD LIBRARY BULLETIN 27:4 (1979), 445-470.

1277. ------. "Margaret Fuller: 'A Woman May Be In Love With A Woman.'" In GAY AMERICAN HISTORY: LESBIANS AND GAY MEN IN THE U.S.A. Jonathan Katz. New York: Thomas Y. Crowell Co., 1976. p.461-467.

Excerpts, with commentary, from Fuller's writings which deal with her love for women. Katz mentions the heavy-handed editing of the MEMOIRS and feels that in light of what remains, it would be interesting to know about the sort of material eliminated, suggesting some passages may have been too expressive of her love for women.

1278. ------. THE LETTERS OF MARGARET FULLER. Edited

by Robert N. Hudspeth. Ithaca and New York: Cornell University Press, 1983. 2 vols.

Brings together for the first time all of the known extant letters, 1817-1841. Provides illumination on the earlier editions of Fuller's letters, notably the MEMOIRS (1851/52). The editors of the MEMOIRS, according to Hudspeth, "so bowdlerized and manipulated their evidence to ruin a splendid book," in their attempt to "make Fuller intellectually safer and sexually acceptable, her marriage normal, her son legitimate."

1279. Gag, Wanda Hazel, 1893-1946. American artist and children's author. GROWING PAINS. DIARIES AND DRAWINGS FOR THE YEARS 1908-1917. New York: Coward McCann, 1940. 479p.

Diary of her school and college years, focusing on her maturation as a woman and an artist through extracts written from age 15 to 24.

1280. Gale, Anna D. American. "Glimpses of Margaret Fuller: The Green Street School." Edward A. Hoyt and Loriman S. Brigham. NEW ENGLAND QUARTERLY 29 (March, 1956), 87-98.

Excerpts from Gale's diary written while a student at Fuller's school.

1281. Galloway, Grace Growden, d. 1782. American colonist and Loyalist. DIARY OF GRACE GROWDEN GALLOWAY: JOURNAL KEPT JUNE 17, 1778 THROUGH SEPTEMBER 30, 1779. With an introduction and notes by Raymond C. Werner. New York: Arno Press, 1971. 189p. (Eyewitness Account of the American Revolution Series, No. 3.) Reprinted from the PENNSYLVANIA MAGAZINE OF HISTORY AND BIOGRAPHY 55:1 (1931), 32-94.

Diary written after her husband (Philadelphia businessman Joseph Galloway) and her daughter had sailed for England after the evacuation of Philadelphia by the British. She remained behind, hoping to reclaim property confiscated by the Revolutionary forces.

1282. ------. "Grace Growden Galloway: Survival of a Loyalist, 1778-1779." Beverly Baxter. FRONTIERS: A JOURNAL OF WOMEN'S STUDIES 3:1 (1978), 62-67.

Excerpts from the diary chronicling the loss of her wealth and social status during the American Revolution.

1283. Gardiner, Margaret, 1822-1857. American. LEAVES FROM A YOUNG GIRL'S DIARY: THE JOURNAL OF MARGARET GARDINER, 1840. New Haven, Conn.: Tuttle, Morehouse & Taylor, 1925. 69p.

Diary of travel in Europe, May 5--July 16, 1840.

1284. Gardner, Isabella Stewart, 1840-1924. American art collector and patron. She opened Fenway Court Museum in Boston in 1903. ISABELLA STEWART GARDNER AND FENWAY COURT. Morris Carter. With illustrations. Boston and New York: Houghton Mifflin Co., and Cambridge, England: The Riverside Press, 1925. 255p.

Biography comprised of Gardner family letters and Gardner's letters, written during art-collecting trips to Europe.

1285. Gaskell, Elizabeth Cleghorn Stevenson, 1810-1865. English author and biographer of Charlotte Bronte. MY DIARY: THE EARLY YEARS OF MY DAUGHTER MARIANNE. London: Privately Printed by Clement Shorter, 1923. 40p.

Reflections on the early years of Marianne and of her second child, Meta.

1286. ------. LETTERS OF MRS. GASKELL AND CHARLES ELIOT NORTON, 1855-1865. Edited, with an introduction by Jane Whitehill. London: Oxford University Press, Humphrey Milford, 1932. 131p.

Norton was an "educated gentleman," journalist, author and teacher. Mrs. Gaskell met him in Rome, and they remained friends until her death.

1287. ------. THE LETTERS OF MRS. GASKELL. Edited by Arthur Pollard and John A.V. Chapple. Manchester, England: Manchester University Press, 1966; and Cambridge, Mass: Harvard University Press, 1967. 1010p.

Definitive edition. Her travels provided much material for her letters, and she wrote a great deal about her work; a series of letters to George Smith gives an in-depth account of the publication of Gaskell's LIFE OF CHARLOTTE BRONTE.

1288. ------. "Some Unpublished Gaskell Letters." Miriam J. Benn. NOTES AND QUERIES (Great Britain), 27:6 (1980), 507-514.

Series of letters, 1863-1866, to James Malcolm Forbes, co-editor of THE READER: A REVIEW OF CURRENT LITERATURE.

1289. ------. ELIZABETH GASKELL: A PORTRAIT IN LETTERS. J.A.V. Chapple. Assisted by John Geoffry Sharpes. Manchester, England: Manchester University Press, 1980. 172p.

1290. Gay, Mary Ann Harris, b. 1827. American. LIFE IN DIXIE DURING THE WAR, 1861-1862-1863-1864-1865. Atlanta, Ga.: C.P. Byrd, 1897. Fifth edition, Atlanta, Ga.: Dekalb Historical Society, 1978. 448p.

1291. Gebhard, Anna Laura Munro, b. 1914. American minister's wife. RURAL PARISH: A YEAR FROM THE JOURNAL OF ANNA LAURA GEBHARD. New York: Abingdon-Cokesbury Press, 1947. 121p.

Diary of church life in rural Minnesota.

1292. Geer, Elizabeth Dixon Smith. American frontier settler. "Elizabeth Dixon Geer: Diary Written on the Oregon Trail in 1847." TRANSACTIONS OF THE OREGON PIONEER ASSOCIATION 35(June, 1907), 153-176.

Overland diary, April, 1847--February, 1848, written on the journey from Indiana to Oregon.

1293. Géoffrin, Marie Thérèse Rodet, Madame, 1699-1777. French social and literary figure. LA CORRESPONDANCE INÉDITE DU ROI STANISLAUS-AUGUSTE PONIATOWSKI ET MADAME GÉOFFRIN (1764-1777). Précédée d'une étude sur Stanislaus-Auguste et Madame Géoffrin et accompagnée de nombreuses notes par Charles de Mouy. Genève: Slatkine Reprints, 1970. 529p.

1294. Gibbons, Abigail Hopper, 1801-1893. American Abolitionist, prison reformer, nurse and welfare worker. LIFE OF ABBY HOPPER GIBBONS. TOLD CHIEFLY THROUGH HER CORRESPONDENCE. Edited by her daughter, Sarah Hopper Emerson. New York: G.P. Putnam's Sons, 1896-1897. 2 vols.

1295. Giffard, Martha Temple, Lady, 1638-1722. English sister of Sir William Temple and sister-in-law of Dorothy Osborne Temple. MARTHA, LADY GIFFARD, HER LIFE AND CORRESPONDENCE (1644-1722). A SEQUEL TO THE LETTERS OF DOROTHY OSBORNE. Edited by Julia G. Longe, with a preface by His Honour Judge Parry. London: George Allen & Sons, 1911. 370p.

Includes, in addition to Lady Giffard's correspondence, letters of Elizabeth, Countess of Chesterfield, 1664-1665; of Dorothy, Lady Sunderland and William Godwin, 1666-1669; of Elizabeth Joceline Percy Ogle, Duchess of Somerset, 1719-1922; and of Dorothy Osborne Temple, 1664-1665.

1296. Gilbert, Mary, 1751-1768. English Methodist. EXTRACT OF MARY GILBERT'S JOURNAL. WITH SOME ACCOUNT OF LADY ELIZABETH HASTINGS &TC. London: Privately Printed, 1763. 66p. Reprinted and sold by David Hall and William Sellers, 1769. 66p.

Religious diary.

1297. ------. AN EXTRACT OF MISS MARY GILBERT'S JOURNAL. [Edited by John Wesley]. Chester, England: Printed by J. Harvie, 1768. 94p. Fourth edition, London: Printed by J. Paramore and at the Reverend Mr. Wesley's Preaching-Houses, 1787. 176p.

1298. Gilchrist, Anne Burrows, 1828-1885. American. LETTERS OF ANNE GILCHRIST AND WALT WHITMAN. Edited with an introduction by Thomas B. Harned. Garden City, N.Y.: Doubleday, Page & Co., 1918. 241p.

Love letters, most of them from Gilchrist to Whitman, 1871-1885. Contains several letters by Gilchrist's children, Beatrice C. and Herbert H. Gilchrist.

1299. Gillespie, Angela, Mother, 1824-1887. American founder of the Sisters of the Holy Cross. FLAME IN THE WILDERNESS: LIFE AND LETTERS OF MOTHER ANGELA GILLESPIE, C.S.C., 1824-1887, AMERICAN FOUNDRESS OF THE SISTERS OF THE HOLY CROSS. Anna Shannon McAllister. With a foreword by the Most Reverend John T. McNicholas. Paterson, N.J.: St. Anthony Guild Press, 1944. 358p. (Centenary Chronicles of the Sisters of the Holy Cross, Vol. 6).

1300. Gillespie, Emily Hawley. American. "My Only Confidant: The Life and Diary of Emily Hawley Gillespie." Judy Nolte Lensink, Christine M. Kirkham, and Karen Pauba Witzke. ANNALS OF IOWA 45:4 (Spring, 1980), 288-312.

Discussion of and extracts from Gillespie's detailed thirty-year account of rural Iowa Life, 1858-1888.

1301. Gilman, Caroline Howard, 1794-1888. American author and editor of one of the earliest children's publications, THE ROSEBUD. "Letters of a Confederate Mother: Charleston in the Sixties." ATLANTIC MONTHLY (April, 1926), 503-515.

Extracts 1861-1865 from a voluminous correspondence of over seventy years.

1302. Gilmore, Mary Jean Cameron, Dame, 1865-1962. Australian poet, teacher, reformer, and advocate for the rights of Australian Aborigines. LETTERS OF MARY GILMORE. Selected and edited by W.H. Wilde and T. Inglis Moore. Melbourne: Melbourne University Press, 1980. 427p.

Letters 1896-1962 give a picture of life in William Lane's Cosme Settlement, a Socialist utopian community in Paraguay, and of her life in South America, where she traveled and worked as a governess and sheep-shearer after Cosme dissolved.

1303. Gisborne, Maria, 1770-1826. English literary figure. MARIA GISBORNE AND EDWARD E. WILLIAMS, SHELLEY'S FRIENDS: THEIR JOURNALS AND LETTERS. Edited by Frederick L. Jones. Norman, Okla.: University of Oklahoma Press, 1951. 189p.

Includes a journal written by Gisborne during a trip to England from Italy, kept for the Shelleys, May 2--September 26, 1820; and letters, 1818-1823.

Gladstone, Mary. See: Drew, Mary Gladstone.

1304. Glasgow, Ellen Anderson Gholson, 1873-1945. American author. THE LETTERS OF ELLEN GLASGOW. Edited, with an introduction and commentaries by Blair Rouse. New York: Harcourt Brace & Co., 1958. 384p.

Literary letters, 1897-1945 to Van Wyck Brooks, Maxwell Perkins, Carl Van Vechten, and others.

1305. ------. "Agent and Author: Ellen Glasgow's Letters to Paul Revere Reynolds." James B. Colvert. VIRGINIA UNIVERSITY BIBLIOGRAPHICAL SOCIETY STUDIES IN BIBLIOGRAPHY 14 (1961), 177-196.

1306. ------. "Ellen Glasgow's Letters to the Saxtons." Douglas T. Day. AMERICAN LITERATURE 35:2 (1963), 230-236.

Discussion of Glasgow's letters to Eugene F. Saxton, an editor at Doubleday, Page & Co., and his wife, 1925-1937. Reproduces five letters.

1307. ------. "A Farewell Exchange of Letters Between Hunter Stagg and Ellen Glasgow." Edited by Edgar E. MacDonald. ELLEN GLASGOW NEWSLETTER 7 (October, 1977), 4-12.

1308. Gobineau, Mere Benedicte (Marie-Caroline Hippolyte), 1820-1884. LE COMTE DE GOBINEAU ET MERE BENEDICTE DE GOBINEAU, CORRESPONDANCE (1872-1882). Publiée et annotée par A.B. Duff. Paris: Le Mercure de France, 1958. 2 vols.

Letters between Mere Benedicte de Gobineau and her brother, Joseph Arthur de Gobineau.

1309. Godley, Charlotte Wynne, 1821-1907. English immigrant to New Zealand. LETTERS FROM EARLY NEW ZEALAND, 1850-1853. Edited with notes by John R. Godley. Christchurch: Whitcombe & Toombs, 1951. 387p.

Account of a three-year sojourn in New Zealand during her husband's (John Rupert Godley) administration of the Canterbury Association Settlement, a group dedicated to seeing "a complete segment of English society" established in New Canterbury.

Godolphin, Mary. See: Aiken, Lucy.

1310. Goethe, Johanna Christina Sophia Vulpius von, 1765-1818. BRIEFE VON GOETHES FRAU AN NICHOLAUS MEYER. Mit einleitung facsimiles, einer lebensskizze Nicolaus Meyers und portraits. Strassburg: K.J. Trubner, 1887.

1311. Goethe, Katharina Elisabeth Textor, 1731-1808. German mother of Johann Wolfgang von Goethe. GOETHE'S MOTHER: CORRESPONDENCE OF CATHERINE ELIZABETH GOETHE WITH GOETHE, LAVATER, WIELAND, DUCHESS ANNA AMELIA OF SAXE-WEIMAR, FRIEDRICH VON STEIN, AND OTHERS. Translated with biographical sketches and notes by A.S. Gibbs. With an introductory note by Clarence Cook. New York: Dodd, Mead, & Co., 1880. 265p. Reprinted, New York: AMS Press, 1965. 265p.

1312. ------. BRIEFE VON GOETHE'S MUTTER AN IRHEN SOHN, CHRISTIAME UND AUGUST VON GOETHE. Weimar: Goethe- Gesellschaft, 1889. 416p.

1313. ------. DIE BRIEFE DER FRAU RATH GOETHE. Gesammelt und herausgegeben von Albert Koster. Leipzig: C.E. Poeschel, 1904. 2 vols.

1314. ------. BRIEF VON GOETHE'S MUTTER. Ausgewählt und eingeleitet von Albert Koster. Leipzig: Insel-Verlag, 1907. 243p.

1315. ------. FRAU AJA: GOETHE'S MUTTER IN IHREN BRIEFEN UND IN DEN ERZAHLUNGEN DER BETTINA BRENTANO. Herausgegeben von Kate Tischendorf, mit zeichnüngen von J. Bergmann. Ebenhausen bei München: W. Langewiesche-Brandt, 1914. 377p.

1316. ------. BRIEFE DER FRAU GOETHE. Ausgewählt und herausgegeben von Rudolf Bach. Wiesbaden: Insel-Verlag, 1960. 90p.

1317. Goethe, Ottile von Pogwisch von, 1796-1872. TAGEBÜCHER UND BRIEFE AN OTTILE VON GOETHE. Herausgegeben und eingeleitet von Heinz Bluhm. Wein: Bergland Verlag, 1962-1979. 5 vols.

Volume 1: Tagebücher 1839-1841. Volume 2: Briefe 1842-1849 von Henriette von Powisch (1766-1851). Volume 3: Tagebücher 1852-1854. Volume 4: Tagebücher 1854-1856. Volume 5: Tagebücher 1856-1857.

1318. Goldman, Emma, 1869-1940. Russian-born American anarchist and sexual rights activist. NOWHERE AT HOME: LETTERS FROM EXILE OF EMMA GOLDMAN AND ALEXANDER BERKMAN. Edited by Richard Drinnon and Anna Maria. New York: Schocken Books, 1975. 282p.

Correspondence with friend and fellow activist Alexander Berkman, 1919-1938, arranged by subject ("Communism and the Intellectuals," "Women and Men").

1319. Gollock, Georgina Anne, 1861-1940. English missionary and religious author. A WINTER'S MAILS FROM CEYLON, INDIA AND EGYPT: BEING JOURNAL LETTERS WRITTEN HOME. London: Church Missionary society, 1895. 189p.

1320. Goltra, Elizabeth Julia Ellison. American frontier settler. JOURNAL OF TRAVEL ACROSS THE PLAINS, 1853. Eugene, Oreg.: Lane County Historical Society, 1970.

1321. Goméz de Avellaneda y Arteaga, Gertrudis, 1814-1873. Spanish author and poet. DIÁRIO DE AMOR, OBRA INEDITA. Prológo, ordenacíon y notas de Alberto Ghiraldo. Madrid: M. Aguilar, 1928. 222p.

1322. ------. GERTRUDIS GOMÉZ DE AVELLANEDA. BIOGRAFÍA, BIBLIOGRAFÍA E ICONOGRAFÍA, INCLYENDO MUCHAS CARTAS, INEDITAS O PUBLICADAS, ESCRITAS POR LA GRAN POETISA O DIRIGIDAS A ELLA, Y SUS MEMORIAS. Domingo Figarola-Caneda. Notas ordenadas y publicadas por Dona Emilia Boxhorn. Madrid: Sociedad General Espanola de Libreria, 1929. 292p.

Biography, bibliography, and extracts from correspondence.

1323. ------. DIÁRIO INTIMO. Compilacíon de Lorenzo Cruz de Fuentes. Buenos Aires: Ediciones Universal, 1945. 156p.

Diary 1839-1850.

1324. Gordon, Caroline, b. 1895. American novelist and short story writer. THE SOUTHERN MANDARINS: LETTERS OF CAROLINE GORDON TO SALLY WOOD, 1924-1937. Edited by Sally Wood. Foreword by Andrew Lytle. Baton Rouge and London: Louisiana State University Press, 1984. 218p.

Literary letters. Gives a picture of a group of young writers "trying to do good work and make money enough to live on:" Gordon, her husband Allen Tate, Robert Penn Warren, Andrew Lytle, Katherine Ann Porter, Malcolm Cowley, Hart Crane, E.E. Cummings, and Ford Maddox Ford.

1325. Gordon, Julia Weber, b. 1911. American teacher. MY COUNTRY SCHOOL DIARY: AN ADVENTURE IN CREATIVE TEACHING. Foreword by Frank W. Cry. Illustrated by John R. Kollmar. New York and London: Harper & Bros., 1946. 270p. Reprinted with an introduction by John Holt, New York: Dell Publishing Co., 1974. 270p.

Diary June, 1936--December, 1939, kept while

teaching in a rural school in an isolated mountain neighborhood. The diary has been edited by Weber to one-fourth the length of the original, and the extracts primarily concern her teaching and her pupils.

1326. Gordon, Rebecca. American. LETTERS FROM NICARAGUA. Foreword by Barbara Smith. San Francisco: Spinsters/Aunt Lute, 1986. 244p.

1327. Görres, Ida Friederike Coudenhove, b.1901. German. NOCTURNEN: TAGEBÜCH UND AUFZEICHNÜNGEN. Frankfurt Am Main: J. Knecht, 1949. 306p.

1328. ------. ZWISCHEN DEN ZEITEN: AUS MEINEN TAGEBÜCHERN. 1951 BIS 1959. Olten: Walter-Verlag, 1960. 488p.

1329. ------. BROKEN LIGHTS: DIARIES AND LETTERS, 1951- 1959. Translated by Barbara Waldstein-Wartenburg. With a preface by Alan Pryce-Jones. Westminster, Md.: Newman Press, 1964. 308p.

Translation of ZWISCHEN DEN ZEITEN.

1330. Graham, Helen, later Tovey-Tennant. Scottish gentlewoman. PARTIES AND PLEASURES: THE DIARIES OF HELEN GRAHAM, 1823-1826. Edited by James Irvine. Introduction by Marion Lochhead. London: Paterson, 1957. 271p.

Society Diary.

1331. Graham, Isabella Marshall, 1742-1814. Scottish-American teacher and charitable worker. THE POWER OF FAITH: EXEMPLIFIED IN THE LIFE AND WRITINGS OF THE LATE MRS. ISABELLA GRAHAM, OF NEW YORK. New York: J. Seymour, 1816. 411p.

Biography by Divie Bethune, followed by extracts from Graham's letters and diary.

1332. ------. THE UNPUBLISHED LETTERS AND CORRESPONDENCE OF MRS. ISABELLA GRAHAM, FROM THE YEAR 1767

TO 1814; EXHIBITING HER RELIGIOUS CHARACTER IN THE DIFFERENT RELATIONS OF LIFE. Selected and arranged by her daughter, Joanna Graham Bethune. New York: J.S. Taylor, 1838. 314p.

1333. ------. THE LIFE OF MRS. ISABELLA GRAHAM. By Her daughter, Mrs. Joanna Bethune. New York: J.S. Taylor, 1839. 144p.

Abridged version of the 1838 edition.

1334. Granlund, Jan, and Diane Rusnak. American artists. MEXICAN COLLAGE. Berkeley, Calif.: Privately Printed, 1978. 61p.

Joint diary of a trip to Mexico by two California artists. Contains their journal of the trip, poetry, drawings, and reproductions of paintings by Rusnak.

1335. Grant, Anne McVicar ("Of Laggan"), 1755-1838. Scottish poet, essayist and biographer. LETTERS FROM THE MOUNTAINS: BEING THE REAL CORRESPONDENCE OF A LADY, BETWEEN THE YEARS 1773 AND 1803. London: Longman, Hurst, Rees, and Orme, 1806. 3 vols. Boston: Printed by Greenough and Stebbins, 1809. 2 vols.

1336. ------. MEMOIR AND CORRESPONDENCE OF MRS. GRANT OF LAGGAN. Edited by her son, J.P. Grant. London: Longman, Brown, Green & Longman, 1844. 3 vols.

1337. Grant, Nellie, 1885-1977. English-Kenyan immigrant farmer, and mother of author Elspeth Huxley. NELLIE: LETTERS FROM AFRICA. With a Memoir by Elspeth Huxley. London: Weidenfeld and Nicolson, 1973. 326p. Published under the title NELLIE'S STORY, New York: William Morrow & Co., 1981. 326p.

Extracts from Grant's letters to Elspeth Huxley from 1933-1977. The aim of the selection is to depict life on a Kenyan farm and to reveal the character of a "courageous, amusing and observant individual." Comments on political or world events are for the most part omitted.

1338. Granville, Harriet Elizabeth Cavendish Leveson-Gower, Countess, 1785-1862. English social figure. THE LETTERS OF HARRIET, COUNTESS GRANVILLE, 1810-1845. Edited by her son, the Hon. F. Leveson-Gower. London and New York: Longmans, Green & Co., 1894. 2 vols.

1339. ------. HARY-O: THE LETTERS OF LADY HARRIET CAVENDISH, 1796-1809. Edited by her Grandson, Sir George Leveson-Gower and his daughter, Iris Palmer. London: John Murray, 1940. 345p.

Social letters, 1796-1809, begining when Lady Granville was age eleven, ending with the announcement of her marriage.

1340. Gratz, Rebecca, 1781-1869. American Jewish charitable worker and Sunday-school founder. THE LETTERS OF REBECCA GRATZ. Edited with an introduction and notes by Rabbi David Philipson. Philadelphia: The Jewish Publication Society of America, 1929. 454p.

Letters to family, 1808-1866.

1341. Gray, Kathie (pseud.), b. 1864. American diarist. KATHIE'S DIARY: LEAVES FROM AN OLD, OLD DIARY. Edited by Margaret Eggleston. New York: George H. Doran Co., 1926.

Diary of a young girl living in Ohio; she began her diary at age twelve. It was edited by the diarist in her later years and published as a "book for young girls."

1342. Gray, Mildred Richards Stone, 1800-1851. American wife of Colonel William Fairfax Gray. THE DIARY OF MILLIE GRAY, 1832-1840. RECORDING HER FAMILY LIFE BEFORE, DURING, AND AFTER COLONEL WILLIAM F. GRAY'S JOURNEY TO TEXAS IN 1835; AND THE SMALL JOURNAL, GIVING PARTICULARS OF ALL THAT OCCURRED DURING THE FAMILY'S VOYAGE TO TEXAS IN 1838. Houston, Tex.: Printed in the Name of Rosenburg Library Press, Galveston, Texas, by the F. Young Publishing Co., 1967. 158p.

Diary of a journey from Fredericksburg, Virginia to Texas.

1343. Gray, Virginia Davis, b. 1834. American. "Life in Confederate Arkansas: The Diary of Virginia Davis Gray, 1863-1865." Edited by Carl H. Moneyhon. ARKANSAS HISTORICAL QUARTERLY 42:1 (Spring, 1983), 45-85 and 42:2 (Summer, 1983), 134-169.

Diary of daily life in Princeton, Virginia, during the Civil War. Describes working for the Confederate war effort, sewing clothes, working as a nurse. Her husband, Oliver C. Gray, joined the Confederate Army in the summer of 1861 and was gone for the duration of the war.

1344. Green, Lenamay, b. 1870. American. A GIRL'S JOURNEY THROUGH EUROPE, EGYPT AND THE HOLY LAND. Nashville, Tenn.: Printed for the author, 1889. 400p.

Travel diary of an 18-year-old girl.

1345. Greene, Catherine Ray. American friend of Benjamin Franklin. BENJAMIN FRANKLIN AND CATHERINE RAY GREEN: THEIR CORRESPONDENCE. Edited and annotated by William Greene Roelker. Philadelphia: American Philosophical Society, 1949. 147p. (Memoirs of the American Philosophical Society vol. 26.)

1346. Greene, Louisa Dickinson, 1830-1881. American. FORESHADOWINGS OF SMITH COLLEGE: SELECTIONS FROM THE LETTERS OF LOUISA DICKINSON TO JOHN MORTON GREENE, 1856-1857. Prepared by their daughter, Helen French Greene. Portland, Maine: Privately printed, the Southworth Press, 1928. 43p.

Letters written during Greene's senior year at Mt. Holyoke Seminary.

1347. Greenleaf, Mary Coombs, 1800-1857. American missionary to the Chickasaw Indians. LIFE AND LETTERS OF MISS MARY C. GREENLEAF. Boston: Massachusetts Sabbath School Society, 1858. 446p.

Contains letters and extracts from a diary, 1819-1857.

1348. Gregory, Isabella Augusta Persse, lady, 1852-1932. Irish author, playwright, a founder of the Abbey Theatre. LADY GREGORY'S JOURNALS, 1916-1930. Edited by Lennox Robinson. London and Dublin: Putnam & Co., 1946. 344p. New York: The Macmillan Co., 1947. 342p.

Private journal, arranged by subject: Coole, her family's estate; the Abbey Theatre; Politics; Persons and Books; and The Lane Pictures Controversy.

1349. ------. SEVENTY YEARS. BEING THE AUTOBIOGRAPHY OF LADY GREGORY. Edited with a foreword by Colin Smythe. New York: Macmillan Publishing Co., 1974. 583p.

Paraphrases her letters and journals, and incorporates extracts into a retrospective autobiography. Chronicles a life in the Theatre.

1350. ------. LADY GREGORY'S JOURNALS. Edited by Daniel J. Murphy. Gerrards Cross, England: Colin Smythe, and New York: Oxford University Press, 1978.

Journal October 10, 1916--February 24, 1925.

1351. ------. THEATRE BUSINESS: CORRESPONDENCE OF THE FIRST ABBEY THEATRE DIRECTORS: WILLIAM BUTLER YEATS, LADY GREGORY AND J.M. SYNGE. Selected and edited by Ann Saddlemyer. University Park, Penn., and London: The Pennsylvania State University Press, 1982. 330p.

Chronicles the first four years of the Abbey Theatre, from its opening in 1904 to Synge's death in March, 1909.

1352. Grenfell, Lydia, 1775-1829. English. EXTRACTS FROM THE DIARY OF MISS LYDIA GRENFELL. Edited by H.M. Jefferey. Fallmouth, England: Lake & Co., 1890. 142p.

Diary 1801-1821.

1353. Grierson, M.H. Scottish. IN SCOTLAND NOW:

LETTERS FROM M.H. GRIERSON, 1940-1941. New York: Privately Printed for the Cosmopolitan Club War Relief, 1941. 33p.

Excerpts from letters to Grierson's sister, from a small country town on the North coast of Scotland portray life in a comparatively quiet corner of Britain during World War II.

1354. Groth, Doris, 1830-1878. German wife of author Klaus Groth. WOHIN DAS HERZ UNS TREIBT: DIE TAGEBÜCHER DER DORIS GROTH GEB. FINKE. Unter Mitwirkung von Joachim Hartig. Herausgegeben und erlautert von Elvira Hartig. Heide in Holstein: Westholsteininische Verlagssanstalt Boyens, 1985. 234p.

1355. Groult, Benoite and Flora. French sisters. JOURNAL À QUATRE MAINS. Paris: Éditions Denoel, 1962.

1356. ------. DIARY IN DUO. Translated from the French by Humphrey Hare. London: Barrie and Rockliff, 1965. 350p. New York: Appleton-Century Co., 1965. 407p.

Diary 1940-1945. Sisters describe life and love during the German Occupation and after the Liberation of France during World war II.

1357. Grove, Harriet, later Helyer. English lover of Percy Bysshe Shelley. THE JOURNAL OF HARRIET GROVE FOR THE YEARS 1809-1810. Edited by Roger Ingpen. London: Privately printed, 1932. 87p.

1358. Guedalla, Mrs. Hayyim. English Jew and friend of Sir Moses and Lady Judith Montefiore. DIARY OF A TOUR TO JERUSALEM AND ALEXANDRIA IN 1855, WITH SIR MOSES AND LADY MONTEFIORE. London: Darling, printed for private circulation, 1890. 73p.

1359. Guerard, Maria Lucia Bull. American colonist. "A Woman's Letters in 1779 and 1782." SOUTH CAROLINA HISTORICAL AND GENEALOGICAL MAGAZINE 10:1 (January, 1909), 125-128.

Letters written during General Provost's

expedition against Charleston describe the "tribulations and dangers of a young 'Rebel' lady during the Revolutionary War."

1360. Guérin, Eugénie de, 1805-1848. French devout, diarist, and sister of religious philosopher Maurice de Guérin. JOURNAL OF EUGÉNIE DE GUÉRIN. Edited by G.S. Trebutien. New York: Dodd, Mead & Co., 1893. 2 vols.

Religious and domestic diary, 1834-1840, written for her brother in the form of journal-letters, informing him of family matters, visits, social affairs, and sharing her religious and philosophical musings.

1361. ------. LETTERS. Edited by G.S. Trebutien. London and New York: A. Strahan, 1866. 453p.

1362. ------. EUGÉNIE DE GUÉRIN: LETTRES À LOUISE DE BAYNE, 1830-1834. Textes inédits precedées d'un historique et litteraire par Émile Barthes. Paris: J. Gabalda, 1924. 466p.

Letters to Louise de Bayne (1812-1846).

1363. ------. EUGÉNIE DE GUÉRIN: LETTRES À SON FRÈRE MAURICE, 1824-1839. Textes en majorite inédits precedées d'un avant-propos litteraire et suivis d'une table analytique par Émile Barthes. Paris: Librairie Lecoffre, 1929. 116p.

1364. ------. THE IDOL AND THE SHRINE: BEING THE STORY OF MAURICE DE GUÉRIN. TOGETHER WITH TRANSLATED EXTRACTS FROM THE JOURNAL OF EUGÉNIE DE GUÉRIN. Presented by Naomi Royde Smith. London: Hollis & Carter, 1949. 301p.

1365. ------. MAURICE ET EUGÉNIE DE GUÉRIN. Préface de François Mauriac. Textes choisis, Présentées et annotées par Pierre Moreau. Paris: Mercure de France, 1965. 254p.

Extracts from the correspondence and journal of Eugénie de Guérin from 1831 to the death of her brother in 1838, and after his death, 1839-1841.

1366. Guerin, Mother Theodore. American founder of the Sisters of Providence. JOURNALS AND LETTERS OF MOTHER THEODORE GUERIN, FOUNDRESS OF THE SISTERS OF PROVIDENCE OF SAINT-MARY-OF-THE-WOODS, INDIANA. Edited, with notes by Sister Mary Theodosia Mug. Saint-Mary-of-the-Woods, Ind.: Sisters of Providence, 1937. 433p.

1367. Guiney, Louise Imogen, 1861-1920. American Catholic poet, essayist and scholar. LETTERS OF LOUISE IMOGEN GUINEY. Edited by Grace Guiney. With a preface by Agnes Repplier. New York and London: Harper & Bros., 1926. 2 vols.

Literary letters, 1872-1920, to Clement Shorter, Gelett Burgess, Edmund Gosse, and others.

1368. Gunn, Elizabeth LeBreton, 1811-1906. American frontier settler. RECORDS OF A CALIFORNIA FAMILY: JOURNALS AND LETTERS OF LEWIS C. GUNN AND ELIZABETH LEBRETON GUNN. Edited by Anna Lee Marston. San Francisco: Privately printed by Johnck & Seeger, 1928. 279p. Reprinted, San Diego, Calif.: Donald I. Segerstrom Memorial Fund, 1974. 279p.

Includes letters and journal describing the voyage around the Cape to California, February- August, 1851, where Gunn and her three small children joined her husband; and letters 1851-1861, describing life in Sonora, California.

1369. Gunnerson, Esther, 1893-1972. American teacher. "Esther Gunnerson: A Nebraskan at Oxford, 1920-1921." Edited by Dolores Gunnerson. NEBRASKA HISTORY 59:1 (1978), 1-30.

Extracts from a diary and letters, November 5, 1920--July 17, 1921, describe her year at Oxford University.

1370. Gurney, Eliza Paul Kirkbride, 1801-1881. American Quaker minister. MEMOIR AND CORRESPONDENCE OF ELIZA PAUL KIRKBRIDE GURNEY. Edited by Richard F. Mott. Philadelphia: J.B. Lippincott, 1884. 377p.

1371. Gurney, Elizabeth. English Quaker and niece of Elizabeth Fry. ELIZABETH FRY'S JOURNEYS ON THE CONTINENT, 1840-1841. FROM A DIARY KEPT BY HER NIECE ELIZABETH GURNEY. Edited with an introduction by R. Brimley Johnson. Foreword by the Rt. Hon. Sir Maurice de Bunsen. London: John Lane, the Bodley Head, 1931. 208p.

Journal accounts of two missionary journeys to the Continent: to Holland, Belgium and Germany in 1840, and to Holland, Germamy, and Denmark in 1841.

1372. Gurney, Emelia Batten, 1823-1896. Author. LETTERS OF EMELIA RUSSELL GURNEY. Edited by her niece, Ellen Mary Gurney. London: J. Nisbet & Co., 1902. 380p.

Includes a diary of travels in Sicily, March--May, 1889.

1373. Haardt, Sarah, 1898-1935. American wife of H.L. Mencken. MENCKEN AND SARAH: A LIFE IN LETTERS. THE PRIVATE CORRESPONDENCE OF H.L. MENCKEN AND SARA HAARDT. Edited by Marion Elizabeth Rodgers. New York: McGraw-Hill, 1987. 551p.

1374. Habersham, Anna Wylly. American Civil War diarist. THE JOURNAL OF ANNA WYLLY HABERSHAM. Darien, Ga.: The Ashantilly Press, 1961. 23p. (Ashantilly Leaflets. Series II, Regional History, No. 2.)

Civil War diary of a fifteen-year-old girl, August 20--October 16, 1864.

1375. Habersham, Josephine Clay Habersham, 1821-1893. American Civil War diarist. EBB TIDE: AS SEEN THROUGH THE DIARY OF JOSEPHINE CLAY HABERSHAM, 1863. Spencer Bidwell King, Jr. Illustrated by William Etsel Snowden, Jr. Athens, Ga.: University of Georgia Press, 1958. 129p.

1376. Hadley, Martha E., 1852-1915. American Quaker missionary. ALASKAN DIARY OF A PIONEER QUAKER MISSIONARY. Mt. Dora, Fla.: Loren S. Hadley, 1969. 210p.

Diary 1899-1903.

1377. Hagger, Mary Knight, ca.1758-1840. English Quaker. EXTRACTS FROM THE MEMORANDA OF MARY KNIGHT HAGGER. ASHFORD, KENT. London: Harvey and Darton, 1841. 108p.

Quaker diary, 1814-1839.

1378. Hahn-Hahn, Ida Maria Luise Sophie Friederike Gustava, Grafin von, 1805-1880. German author. LETTERS OF A GERMAN COUNTESS: WRITTEN DURING HER TRAVELS IN TURKEY, EGYPT, THE HOLY LAND, SYRIA, NUBIA, ETC., IN 1843-1844. London: H. Colburn, 1845. 3 vols.

1379. Hale, Betty May. American. MY TRIP TO EUROPE, 1837. San Francisco: Wallace Kibbel & Son, 1938.

Travel diary by a thirteen-year-old describes a family trip to England to see the Coronation of King George VI, and travels in Europe.

1380. Hale, Sarah. American missionary. DIARIES OF MISS SARAH HALE, MISSIONARY FOR MANY YEARS TO MEXICO. Nashville, Tenn.: The Historical Commission, Southern Baptist Convention, n.d. One reel microfilm (35mm).

1381. Hale, Susan, 1833-1910. American author and artist. LETTERS OF SUSAN HALE. Edited by Caroline Atkinson. Introduction by Edward E. Hale. Boston: Marshall Jones Co., 1918. 481p.

Letters to friends and relatives 1848-1910 describe early life in Boston and Brookline; teaching; studying art in Europe; traveling in Europe and various trips to Mexico, Jamaica and Egypt.

1382. Hall, Calista Marsh, b. 1816. American. "The Letters of Calista Hall." Edited by Carol Kammen. NEW YORK HISTORY 63:2 (April, 1982), 208-234.

Letters to her husband, Pliny Hall, who had left their farm in Lansing, New York to take a position as a prison guard to supplement their income. Hall's letters reveal facets of life in rural New York in the mid nineteenth century, and are particularly interesting for their references to physical love and birth control.

1383. Hall, Emily Mary, 1819-1901; and Ellen Augusta Hall, 1822-1911. English sisters. TWO VICTORIAN GIRLS. O.A. Sherrard. With extracts from the Hall Diaries, edited and with an introduction by Anthony Reginald Mills. London: Frederick Muller, 1966. 309p.

Biography 1838-1863, which draws heavily on the diaries of Emily and Ellen Hall, followed by extracts from their diaries, 1860-1863. They kept domestic and social diaries for nearly sixty years, in which they "discussed and deplored, pronounced and praised, assessing everyone and everything."

1384. ------. TWO VICTORIAN LADIES: MORE PAGES FROM THE JOURNALS OF EMILY AND ELLEN HALL. Anthony Reginald Mills. London: Frederick Muller, 1969. 220p.

1385. Hall, Margaret Hunter, 1799-1876. THE ARISTOCRATIC JOURNEY: BEING THE OUTSPOKEN LETTERS OF MRS. BASIL HALL WRITTEN DURING A FOURTEEN MONTH'S SOJOURN IN AMERICA, 1827-1828. Edited by Una Pope-Hennessy. London and New York: G.P. Putnam's Sons, 1931. 308p.

Account of a tour of the United States, which Hall compared unfavorably to Spain, where she had also traveled. She liked meeting society people rather than intellectuals; thus the title.

1386. Hall, Melinda, later Aylesworth. American. "Letters Home: An Illinois Coed in the 1850's." James M. Kedro. JOURNAL OF THE ILLINOIS STATE HISTORICAL SOCIETY 70:3 (1977), 196-200.

Letters written to her brother from Berean College in Jacksonville, Illinois, 1855-1857. Provides an intriguing picture of a college town at mid-century, as well as Hall's own perspective on life at school.

1387. Hall, Sharlot Mabridth, 1870-1943. American author, historian, politician and pioneer Arizona rancher. SHARLOT HALL ON THE ARIZONA STRIP: A DIARY THROUGH NORTHERN ARIZONA IN 1911. Edited by C. Gregory Crampton. Flagstaff, Ariz.: Northland Press, 1975. 97p.

While serving as Territorial Historian of Arizona, Hall traveled by wagon through the Arizona Strip, a region north of the Colorado River, to survey the people, resources, and history of the area.

1388. Hall, Susan Mitchell. American frontier settler and wife of Dr. Obed Harvey, founder of the City of Galt in Sacramento County, California. "The Diary of a Trip from Ione to Nevada in 1859, by Susan Mitchell Hall." CALIFORNIA HISTORICAL SOCIETY QUARTERLY 17:1 (March, 1938), 75-80.

Describes a vacation trip from her parent's home in Ione, California, to Carson City, Nevada.

1389. Halstead, Jenny. American. "The Washington Visits of Jenny Halstead, 1879-1881, From Her Letters." Edited by Watt. P. Marchman. OHIO HISTORICAL AND PHILOSOPHICAL SOCIETY BULLETIN (July, 1954), 179-193.

1390. Hamilton, Emma Lyon, Lady, c.1765-1815. English wife of Sir William Hamilton, Ambassador at Naples; best known as the mistress of Lord Nelson. THE LIFE AND LETTERS OF EMMA HAMILTON. Edited by Hugh Tours. London: Victor Gollancz, 1963. 288p.

Attempts to provide a more balanced picture of a life "over-glamorised, sometimes unnecessarily maligned," noting that Lady Hamilton was Nelson's mistress for only seven years. To this end, as many as possible of Lady Hamilton's letters are printed in full.

1391. Hamilton, Gail, pseud. for Mary Abigail Dodge, 1833-1896. American author and teacher. GAIL HAMILTON'S LIFE IN LETTERS. Edited by H. Augusta Dodge. Biographical sketch by Harriet Prescott Spofford. Boston: Lee and Shepard, 1901. 2 vols.

Letters, 1845-1896, and autobiographical fragments.

1392. ------. "Last Years of Gail Hamilton's Life,

With Extracts from Letters Written by Her During that Time." Edited by Max Bennett Thrasher. ARENA 17 (December, 1896), 112-119.

1393. Hampton, Sally Baxter, 1833-1862. American. A DIVIDED HEART: LETTERS OF SALLY BAXTER HAMPTON, 1853-1862. Edited with an introduction by Ann Fripp Hampton. Spartanburg, S.C.: The Reprint Co., 1980. 146p.

Describes life on a South Carolina plantation, and events during the Civil War. Hampton suffered from Tuberculosis.

1394. Hancock, Cornelia, 1840-1926. American Quaker nurse, hospital administrator and educator. SOUTH AFTER GETTYSBURG: LETTERS FROM THE ARMY OF THE POTOMAC, 1863-1868. Edited by Henrietta Stratton Jaquett. Philadelphia: University of Philadelphia Press, 1937. 173p. Second edition, with a foreword by Bruce Catton, New York: T.Y. Crowell Co., 1956. 288p.

Diary of a Civil War nurse. Hancock established a Quaker school for Black students in South Carolina after the War; the second edition contains additional letters giving an account of this school.

1395. Hanff, Helen. American author. 84, CHARING CROSS ROAD. New York: Grossman Publishers, 1970. 97p.

Letters between Hanff in New York and Frank Doel of Marks & Co., Booksellers, in London, October 5, 1949--October, 1969. Begins with a simple want list from Hanff and grows into a trans-Atlantic friendship.

1396. Hanna, Wanda Muir. American daughter of naturalist John Muir. DEAR PAPA: LETTERS BETWEEN JOHN MUIR AND HIS DAUGHTER WANDA. Edited and documented by Jean Hanna Clark and Shirley Sargent. Fresno, Calif.: Panorama West Books in cooperation with Flying Spur Press, Yosemite, Calif., 1985. 100p.

1397. Hansberry, Lorraine, 1930-1965. Black American author and dramatist. TO BE YOUNG, GIFTED, AND BLACK.

Adapted, forewarded and postcripted by Robert Nemiroff. Introduction by James Baldwin. Englewood Cliffs, N.J.: Prentice-Hall, 1969. 266p.

Collection of diary entries, letters, autobiographical fragments, and dramatic pieces.

1398. Hansen, Effie. American farmer. "The Letters of Effie Hansen, 1917-1923: Farm Life in Troubled Times." Edited by Frances M. Wold. NORTH DAKOTA HISTORY 48 (Winter, 1981), 20-43.

1399. Hanson, June. American. "Going Solo." MS. MAGAZINE 1:10 (April, 1973), 71-73, 104.

Journal of a three-day Outward-Bound Solo journey by a mother of three.

1400. Harcourt, Mary, Lady. Lady-In-Waiting at the Court of King George III. MRS. HARCOURT'S DIARY. Miscellanies of the Philobiblon Society 13 (1871-1872), 57p.

Court diary, February, 1789--March, 1791.

1401. Hardin, Elizabeth Pendleton, 1839-1895. American. THE PRIVATE WAR OF LIZZIE HARDIN: A KENTUCKY CONFEDERATE GIRL'S DIARY OF THE CIVIL WAR IN KENTUCKY, VIRGINIA, TENNESSEE, ALABAMA AND GEORGIA. Edited by G. Glenn Clift. Frankfort: Kentucky Historical Society, 1963. 306p.

Record of refugee life during the Civil War, written from day-by-day notes.

1402. Hardon, Anne Frances. American. 43 BIS: WAR LETTERS OF AN AMERICAN V.A.D. New York: Privately Printed, 1927. 330p.

Letters written during World War I by an American member of England's Voluntary Aid Detachment.

1403. Hardy, Emma Lavinia Gifford, 1840-1912. English

wife of Thomas Hardy. EMMA HARDY DIARIES. Edited by Richard H. Taylor. Ashington, England: Mid Northumberland Arts Group, and New York: Carcanet, 1985. 216p.

Chiefly travel diaries, 1874-1897, written in France, September-October, 1874; Holland, the Rhine and the Black Forest, May-June, 1876; Italy, March-April, 1887; and Switzerland, June-July, 1897. The diaries are reprinted in facsimile with the text printed below.

1404. Hardy, Mary Raven, 1733-1809. English wife of William Hardy. MARY HARDY'S DIARY. With an introduction by B. Cozens-Hardy. Norfolk, England: Norfolk Record Society, 1968. 148p.

Domestic diary, 1773-1809.

1405. Hargrave, Letitia Mactavish, 1813-1854. Scottish immigrant to Canada. THE LETTERS OF LETITIA HARGRAVE. Edited with an introduction and notes by Margaret Arnett Macleod. Toronto: Champlain Society, 1947. 310p.

1406. Harker, Mary Haines. American Quaker. "Diary of a Quaker Maid, 1853." VIRGINIA QUARTERLY REVIEW 2:1 (January, 1935), 61-81.

Social diary.

1407. Harley, Brilliana Conway, Lady, 1600?-1643. English Puritan. She withstood a seige laid by Royalists against Brampton Bryan Castle in 1643. THE LETTERS OF LADY BRILLIANA HARLEY, WIFE OF SIR ROBERT HARLEY, OF BRAMPTON BRYAN, KNIGHT OF THE BATH. Edited with notes by Thomas Taylor Lewis. London: Printed for the Camden Society, 1854. 275p. Reprinted, New York: AMS Press, 1968. 275p.

1408. Harper, Elizabeth Tuck, 1734-1768. English Methodist. AN EXTRACT FROM THE JOURNAL OF MRS. ELIZABETH HARPER. London, 1796. 47p.

Religious diary, 1765-1768.

1409. Harriman, Florence Jaffray Hurst, b. 1870. American politician. FROM PINNAFORES TO POLITICS. New York: Henry Holt & Co., 1923. 359p.

Includes a chapter of letters written from the Republican Convention of 1912.

1410. Harris, Isabella Tindall, 1791-1868. English? Quaker. FAMILY MEMORIALS. CHIEFLY THE MEMORIALS LEFT BY ISABELLA HARRIS. WITH SOME EXTRACTS FROM THE JOURNAL OF HER MOTHER, ETC. Edited by M.A. Harris. "Not published." London: R. Barrett & Sons, Printers, 1869. 291p.

Quaker diary, 1808-1868 by Isabella Harris, and extracts from the journal of her mother, Isabella Mackiver Tindall (1761-1836).

1411. Harris, Katherine. A LADY'S DIARY OF THE SEIGE OF LUCKNOW. London: John Murray, 1858. 208p.

Describes the Indian Mutiny of 1857-1858.

1412. Harris, Lucy Hamilton. EACH DAY'S DOINGS: OR, A TRIP TO EUROPE IN THE SUMMER OF 1875. JOURNAL OF LUCY HAMILTON HARRIS. Albany, N.Y.: Weed Parsons & Co., 1875. 123p.

Travel journal, June 23--September 28, 1875.

1413. Harrison, Anna Symmes, 1775-1864. American wife of U.S. President William Henry Harrison. THE INTIMATE LETTERS OF JOHN CLEVES SYMMES AND HIS FAMILY, INCLUDING THOSE OF HIS DAUGHTER, MRS. WILLIAM HENRY HARRISON, WIFE OF THE NINTH PRESIDENT OF THE UNITED STATES. Edited by Beverly W. Bond, Jr. Cincinnati: Historical and Philosophical Society of Ohio, 1956. 174p.

1414. Harrison, Constance Cary, 1843-1920. American author and Southern Belle. RECOLLECTIONS GRAVE AND GAY. New York: Charles Scribner's Sons, 1911. 386p.

Civil War diary.

1415. Harrison, Jane Ellen, 1850-1928. English scholar and archeologist. JANE ELLEN HARRISON: A PORTRAIT FROM LETTERS. Edited by Jessie G. Stewart. London: Merlin Press, 1959. 216p.

Short biography and study of her works, followed by a selection of her letters, 1900-1928, focusing on her work and her intellectual friendships.

Harrison, Jemima Condict. See: Condict, Jemima.

1416. Harrison, Juanita. Black American traveler. MY GREAT, WIDE, BEAUTIFUL WORLD. Arranged and prefaced by Mildred Morris. New York: Macmillan, 1936. 318p.

Travel diary, June 25, 1927--April, 1935, by a Mississippi woman who worked her way through France, Syria, Israel, Egypt, Ceylon, India, Spain, Russia, Japan and China.

1417. Harrison, Michelle, M.D. American gynecologist. A WOMAN IN RESIDENCE. New York: Random House, 1982. Harmondsworth, New York, Victoria, Ontario and Auckland: Penguin Books, 1983. 264p.

Diary describes Harrison's residency, during the 1970's, at an unnamed but prestigious American hospital, and her disillusionment with the medical system, particularly the ways in which women patients are denied dignity.

1418. Harvard, Elizabeth. English missionary and wife of missionary William Martin Harvard. MEMOIRS OF MRS. ELIZABETH HARVARD, LATE OF THE WESLEYAN MISSION TO CEYLON AND INDIA. WITH EXTRACTS FROM HER DIARY AND CORRESPONDENCE. London: John Mason, 1833. 130p.

1419. Harvey, Margaret Boyle, 1786-1832. American Quaker and wife of Irish merchant Edward Harvey. A JOURNAL OF A VOYAGE FROM PHILADELPHIA TO CORK IN THE YEAR OF OUR LORD 1809. TOGETHER WITH A DESCRIPTION OF A SOJOURN IN IRELAND. With a supplement by her granddaughter, Dora Harvey Develin. Philadelphia: West Park Publishing Co., 1915. 78p.

1420. ------. "Journal of Margaret B. Harvey, 1809." JOURNAL OF THE FRIEND'S HISTORICAL SOCIETY 24:1 (1927), 3-20.

Extracts from the 1915 edition.

1421. Haskell, Mary Elizabeth, 1873-1964. American teacher and lover of Lebanese-American Mystic Kahlil Gibran. BELOVED PROPHET: THE LOVE LETTERS OF KAHLIL GIBRAN AND MARY HASKELL, AND HER PRIVATE JOURNAL. Edited and arranged by Virginia Hilu. New York: Alfred A. Knopf, 1972. 464p.

Love letters, 1908-1931, and extracts from her journal, 1910-1924 dealing with her relationship with Gibran and with his death.

1422. Haskell, Rachel. American frontier settler. "A Literate Woman in the Mines: The Diary of Rachel Haskell." Edited by Richard G. Lillard. THE MISSISSIPPI VALLEY HISTORICAL REVIEW 21:1 (June, 1944), 81-98.

Short diary, March, 1867, describing life in Aurora, a Nevada mining town.

1423. Hatch, Olivia Stokes. American philanthropist. OLIVIA'S AFRICAN DIARY: CAPE TOWN TO CAIRO, 1932. Photographs by Mary Marvin Breckinridge Patterson. Washington, D.C.: Privately Printed by the Monotype Composition Co., Baltimore, Md., and New Haven, Conn.: Eastern Press, 1980. 162p.

Travel diary, July 15--December 19, 1932, describes a trip with her father, a visiting lecturer on Race Relations to the Universities of the Union of South Africa. The photographer, Mary Marvin Breckinridge Patterson, was a life-long friend of Hatch.

1424. Hathaway, Katharine Butler, 1890-1942. American author and artist. THE JOURNALS AND LETTERS OF THE LITTLE LOCKSMITH. Illustrated by the author. New York: Coward McCann, 1946. 395p.

Collected writings of a disabled woman (childhood

tuberculosis left her with a small stature and severe respiratory problems) of great sensitivity and passion for life. Includes undated fragments from her journals, and letters, 1909-1942.

1425. Haven, Charlotte. American. "A Girl's Letters from Nauvoo." OVERLAND MONTHLY, Series 2 (December, 1890).

Letters January 3--October 15, 1843 by a resident of Nauvoo, Massachusetts describe the Mormon settlement there and the political events which led to their expulsion from the city.

1426. Haven, Martha Hall, b. 1819. American Mormon. "Death of a Mormon Dictator: Letters of Massachusetts Mormons, 1843-1848." Edited by George F. Partridge. NEW ENGLAND QUARTERLY 9:4 (December, 1936), 583-617.

Letters of Martha Hall Haven and her sister, Sarah Hall Scott (b.1843) describe anti-Mormon unrest in Nauvoo, Massachusetts, which led to the lynching of John and Hyrum Smith in 1844, and the dissolution of the Mormon Community there.

1427. Havens, Catherine Elizabeth, 1840-1939. American. DIARY OF A LITTLE GIRL IN OLD NEW YORK. New York: H.C. Browne, 1919. 101p.

Childhood diary, begun in 1849 at age ten, describes school days and life in New York City.

1428. Hawks, Esther Hill, 1833-1906. American doctor. A WOMAN DOCTOR'S CIVIL WAR: ESTHER HILL HAWKS' DIARY. Edited with a foreword by Gerald Schwartz. Columbia, S.C.: University of South Carolina Press, 1984. 301p.

1429. Hawthorne, Elizabeth Manning, 1802-1883. American sister of Nathaniel Hawthorne. "Aunt Ebe: Some Letters of Elizabeth Manning Hawthorne." NEW ENGLAND QUARTERLY (June, 1947), 209-231.

Letters written to her Manning cousins, 1816-1882.

1430. Hawthorne, Sophia Amelia Peabody, 1811-1872. American artist, writer, and wife of Nathaniel Hawthorne. NOTES IN ENGLAND AND ITALY. New York: G.P. Putnam's Sons, 1869. 549p. London: G.S. Low, 1872. 549p. Illustrated edition, New York: G.P. Putnam's Sons, and London: G.S. Low, 1875. 549p.

Travel diary, April-July, 1857.

1431. Hayes, Marie Elizabeth, 1874?-1908. English missionary physician. AT WORK: LETTERS OF MARIE ELIZABETH HAYES, M.D, MISSIONARY DOCTOR, DELHI, 1905-1908. Edited by her mother. Introduction by the Venerable G.R. Wynne. London: Marshall Bros., 1909. 263p.

1432. Hays, Mary, 1759/60-1843. English feminist and friend of Mary Wollstonecraft. THE LOVE-LETTERS OF MARY HAYS, 1779-1780. Edited by her Great-great niece, A.F. Wedd. London: Methuen & Co., 1925. 250p.

Letters to John Eccles, February 12, 1779--August 23, 1781. The correspondence is considerably abridged. Includes some letters of Mary Wollstonecraft and Mary Shelley.

1433. Hazard, Sarah Condon. American sea Captain's wife. "Around the Horn: Journal of the Captain's Wife." NEWPORT HISTORY 38:4 (1965), 131-149.

Sea diary July--December, 1863, written aboard the ship Lancashire enroute from New York to San Francisco.

1434. Hazlitt, Sarah Stoddart. THE JOURNALS OF SARAH AND WILLIAM HAZLITT, 1822-1831. Edited by Willard Hallam Bonner. Buffalo: University of Buffalo Press, 1959. 172-281p.

1435. Head, Caroline Hanbury, 1852-1904. THE LIFE OF MRS. ALBERT HEAD. By her sister, Charlotte Hanbury. London: Marshall Bros., 1905. 286p.

Includes extracts from a religious diary, 1871-1893.

1436. Hecox, Margaret M. American frontier settler. CALIFORNIA CARAVAN: THE 1846 OVERLAND TRAIL. MEMOIR OF MARGARET M. HECOX. Edited by Richard Dillon. San Jose, Calif.: Harlan-Young Press, 1966. 70p.

1437. Hedvig Elisabeth Charlotte, Consort of Karl XIII, King of Sweden and Norway, 1759-1818. LA FIN D'UNE DYNASTIE, D'APRÈS LES MEMOIRS ET LA CORRESPONDANCE D'UNE REINE DE SUÈDE, HEDVIG-ÉLISABETH-CHARLOTTE (1774-1818). Oscar Gustaf von Hedenstam. Paris: Plon-Nourrit et Cie., 1911. 514p.

1438. Hegermann-Lindencrone, Lillie Greenough de. Danish diplomat's wife. THE SUNNY SIDE OF DIPLOMATIC LIFE, 1875-1912. New York and London: Harper Bros., 1914. 336p.

Social letters, from Washington, D.C., 1875-1880; from Rome, 1880-1890; from Stockholm, 1890-1897; from Paris, 1897-1902; and from Berlin, 1902-1912.

1439. Heloise, 1101-1164. French nun, Abbess, and letter writer. LETTERS OF ABELARD AND HELOISE. TO WHICH IS PREFIXED, A PARTICULAR ACCOUNT OF THEIR LIVES, AMOURS, AND MISFORTUNES. Extracted chiefly from Monsieur Bayle. Translated from the French by the late John Hughes. London: Printed for J. Watts, 1713. Sixth edition, corrected, London: Printed for F. Watts and sold by J. Osborn, 1736. 228p.

1440. ------. THE LETTERS OF ABELARD AND HELOISE. Translated from the Latin by C.K. Scott Moncrieff. With a prefatory letter by George Moore. London: G. Chapman, 1925. 211p. New York: Alfred A. Knopf, 1926. 264p. New York: Cooper Square Publishers, 1974. 264p.

Personal letters of Heloise, Letters of Direction by Abelard, and the love letters of Heloise and Abelard. After an ill-fated love affair and secret marriage to her tutor, Peter Abelard, they both took religious orders. Heloise eventually became the Abbess of the paraclete founded by Abelard. Their letters have gone through hundreds of editions in many languages.

1441. ------. LA LETTERE DI ABELARDO ED ELOISA. Nella Traduzione di Jean de Meun. A cura di Fabrizio Beggiato. Modena: S.T.E.M. Mucchi, 1977. 2 vols. [Studi, testi, e manuali / Instituto di Filologia Romanza dell'Universita di Roma, 5].

Text of letters is in Old French.

1442. ------. LETTRES PAR HELOISE ET ABELARD. SUIVIES DE QUELQUES TEXTES CONTEMPORAINES. Textes choisies, présentées et partiellement établis par Louis Stouff. Paris: Union Général d'Éditions, 1964. 310p.

1443. ------. CORRESPONDANCE: ABELARD ET HELOISE. Texte traduit [du Latin] et presentée par Paul Zumthor. Paris: Union Générale d'Éditions, 1979. 203p.

1444. ------. LETTERE ABELARDO ED ELOISA. A cura di Nada Cappelletti Truci. Torino: G. Einaudi, 1979. 412p. Second edition, 1982. 412p.

1445. Hemans, Felicia Dorothea Browne, 1793-1835. English poet. MEMORIALS OF MRS. HEMANS. WITH ILLUSTRATIONS OF HER LITERARY CHARACTER FROM HER PRIVATE CORRESPONDENCE. Henry F. Chorley. London: Saunders and Otley, 1837. 2 vols.

Consists chiefly of her literary correspondence, 1808-1835.

1446. Henderson, Caroline A. American farmer. "Letters from the Dust Bowl." In OKLAHOMA MEMORIES. Edited by Anne Hodges Morgan and Rennard Strickland. Norman, Okla.: University of Oklahoma Press, 1981. pp.223-244. Reprinted from the ATLANTIC MONTHLY 157 (May, 1936), 540-551.

Letters June 30, 1935--March 13, 1936, by a farm woman of Eva, Oklahoma describe disaster in the heart of the Dust Bowl. While others migrated West, Henderson and her husband elected to remain on their farm.

1447. Hendricks, Cecilia Hennel, 1883-1969. American

frontier settler. LETTERS FROM HONEYHILL: A WOMAN'S VIEW OF HOMESTEADING, 1914-1931. Cecilia Hennel Hendricks. Compiled and edited by Cecilia Hendricks Wahl. Boulder, Colo.: Pruett Co., 1986. 704p.

Describes homesteading in the Shoshone River Valley of Wyoming.

1448. Henning, Rachel, later Taylor, 1826-1914. Australian frontier settler. THE LETTERS OF RACHEL HENNING. Edited by David Adams. Foreword and pen-drawings by Norman Lindsay. Sydney: Angus & Robertson, 1966. 292p. Ringwood, Victoria: Penguin Books, 1969.

Letters 1853-1882 to family in England. Henning emigrated to Australia with her younger brother and two sisters Amy and Annie; her letters are "chatty, day by day, observant and often downright" in their description of life in frontier Australia.

1449. Henriette-Anne d'Angleterre, Duchess D'Orléans. HENRIETTE-ANNE D'ANGLETERRE, DUCHESSE D'ORLÉANS: SA VIE ET SA CORRESPONDANCE AVEC SON FRÈRE CHARLES II. Le Comte de Baillon. Paris: Perrin et Cie., 1887. 463p.

1450. Herbert, Muriel Katherine, Lady, b. 1833. English. SERBIA AND THE SERBIANS: LETTERS FROM LADY MURIEL HERBERT WHO WAS WITH THE SECOND SERBIAN RELIEF FUND UNIT. London: Waifs and Strays Society, 1915. 113p.

Account of relief work during World War I.

1451. Herndon, Sarah Raymond, b. 1840. American frontier settler. DAYS ON THE ROAD: CROSSING THE PLAINS IN 1865. By Sarah Raymond Herndon. New York: Burr Printing House, 1902. 270p.

1452. ------. OVERLAND DAYS TO MONTANA IN 1865: THE DIARY OF SARAH RAYMOND AND JOURNAL OF DR. WAID HOWARD. Edited by Raymond W. Settle and Mary Lund Settle. Glendale, Calif.: The Arthur H. Clark Co., 1971. 232p.

Overland diary of a 25-year-old schoolteacher,

written on the journey from Missouri to Virginia City, Montana.

1453. Herschel, Caroline. English astronomer. MEMOIR AND CORRESPONDENCE OF CAROLINE HERSCHEL. Mrs. John Herschel. London: John Murray, 1879. 355p.

1454. Hervey, Mary Lepel, Lady. LETTERS OF MARY LEPEL, LADY HERVEY. WITH A MEMOIR AND ILLUSTRATIVE NOTES. Edited by John Wilson Croker. 1821.

Letters to the Reverend Edmund Morris, 1742-1868 describe life at the English Court.

1455. Herzen, Natalie, 1844-1936. Russian daughter of revolutionary Alexander Herzen. DAUGHTER OF A REVOLUTIONARY: NATALIE HERZEN AND THE BAKUNIN-NECHAYEV CIRCLE. Michael Confino. Translated by Hilary Sternberg and Lydia Bott. LaSalle, Ill.: Library Press, 1974. 416p.

Letters and extracts from a diary, 1869-1870. Documents Herzen's life among the Russian émigrés in Western Europe.

1456. Hesketh, Harriet Cowper, Lady, 1733-1807. English friend of poet William Cowper and one of his chief correspondents. LETTERS OF LADY HESKETH TO THE REVEREND JOHN JOHNSON, LL.D., CONCERNING THEIR KINSMAN, WILLIAM COWPER THE POET. Edited by Catharine Bodham Johnson (née Donne). London: Jarrold, 188?. 128p.

Letters 1790-1806.

1457. Hesse, Marie, 1842-1902. German. MARIE HESSE. EIN LEBENSBILD IN BRIEFEN UND TAGEBÜCHERN. Adele Gundert. Stuttgart: D. Gundert Verlag, 1953. 283p.

Letters and diary, 1857-1902.

1458. Heyking, Elisabeth von Fleming, Baroness von, 1861-1925. German author. ELISABETH VON HEYKING: TAGEBÜCHER AS VIER WELTTEILEN 1886-1904. Herausgegeben von Grete Litzmann. Leipzig: Koëhler & Amelang, 1926. 413p.

1459. Heyman, Eva, 1931-1944. Transylvanian Jew, executed by the Nazis in a death camp. THE DIARY OF EVA HEYMAN. Edited with an introduction and notes by Judah Marton. Translated from the Hebrew into English by Moshe M. Kohn. Jerusalem: Yad Vashem, 1974. 124p.

Death camp diary of a thirteen-year-old girl.

1460. Heywood, Martha Spence. American Mormon. Third plural wife of Utah Merchant Joseph Heywood. NOT BY BREAD ALONE: THE JOURNAL OF MARTHA SPENCE HEYWOOD, 1850-1856. Salt Lake City: Utah State Historical Society, 1978. 141p.

Overland diary and diary of life in early Salt Lake City, where she lived in a wagon box set off its running gears. Gives insight into the major events of the first decade of Salt Lake City society, the loneliness of plural marriage, dissentions in the Church, and the social and domestic life of Mormon women.

1461. Higbee, Lucy Ann. American. THE DIARY OF LUCY ANN HIGBEE, 1837. Edited by Mrs. Fanny Southard Hay Hall. Cleveland, Ohio: Privately printed, 1924. 57p.

Travel diary. Describes a journey, partly by canal boat, from Trenton, New Jersey to Ohio, returning via Niagra Falls and Saratoga.

1462. Higginson, Louisa S. American mother of Thomas Wentworth Higginson. "Cambridge Eighty Years Since: Letters in the Form of a Diary by Louisa Higginson, 1827- 1828." CAMBRIDGE HISTORICAL PUBLICATIONS 2 (1906-1907), 20-32.

Excerpts from diary-letters, October, 1827--March, 1828 describe social life at Cambridge, Massachusetts.

1463. Higginson, Mehitabel, d. 1818. American colonial teacher and Loyalist. "Letters of Mehitabel Higginson." Charles C. Smith. PROCEEDINGS OF THE MASSACHUSETTS HISTORICAL SOCIETY, 2nd. Ser., Vol. 10 (1896), 455-466.

Six letters, 1775-1783.

1464. Hill, Emma Shepard. American frontier settler. A DANGEROUS CROSSING AND WHAT HAPPENED ON THE OTHER SIDE. With illustrations by Jane Porter Robertson. Denver: Smith-Brooks, 1914. 117p.

Contents: A dangerous crossing of the plains among Indians in the summer of 1864--what happened on the other side; being events recorded by the author in an old diary, begun at the age of fourteen and covering a period of years.

1465. Hill, Frances Baylor. American daughter of a land-holding Virginia family. "The Diary of Frances Baylor Hill of 'Hillsborough'; King and Queen County, Virginia, 1797." Edited by William K. Bottorff and Roy C. Flannagan. EARLY AMERICAN LITERATURE 2 (Winter, 1967), 4+.

Domestic diary; describes family and social duties, town affairs and charitable nursing work.

1466. Hill, Hanna Lloyd, 1666-1726? NANCY LLOYD: THE JOURNAL OF A QUAKER PIONEER. Edited by Anna Lloyd Thomas. New York: Frank-Maurice, 1927. 192p.

1467. Hill, Octavia, 1838-1912. English housing reformer and open space activist. LIFE OF OCTAVIA HILL AS TOLD IN HER LETTERS. Edited by C. Edmund Maurice. London: Macmillan & Co., 1913. 591p.

Letters 1852-1912, plus a few childhood letters.

1468. ------. OCTAVIA HILL: EARLY IDEALS. From letters edited by Emily S. Maurice. London: George Allen & Unwin, 1928. 239p.

Early letters, 1856-1874, written between the age of seventeen and twenty; chiefly to Mary Harris, a Quaker, and to author John Ruskin. Letters were chosen to throw light on Hill's early struggles and aspirations as an activist for social reform.

1469. Hillard, Harriet Low, 1809-1877. American

daughter of a China shipping merchant. MY MOTHER'S JOURNAL: A YOUNG LADY'S DIARY OF FIVE YEARS SPENT IN MANILA, MACAO, AND THE CAPE OF GOOD HOPE, FROM 1829 TO 1834. Edited by Katharine Hillard. Boston: George H. Ellis, 1900. 320p.

Describes a sea voyage from Salem, Massachusetts to China, and life there under the auspices of the East India Company, by whom her father was employed. She lived in "all the luxury and formality of English society at that time," which began to pall for Hillard after only a short time.

1470. Hillesum, Etty, 1914-1943. Dutch Jew who died at Auschwitz. AN INTERRUPTED LIFE: THE DIARIES OF ETTY HILLESUM, 1941-1943. Translated from the Dutch by Arno Pomerans. Introduction by J.G. Gaarlandt. New York: Pantheon Books, 1983. 226p.

Prison diary kept at Westerbork, the halfway camp for prisoners eventually transferred to Auschwitz.

1471. ------. ETTY: A DIARY, 1941-1943. Translated by Arnold J. Pomerans. Toronto: Lester & Orphen Dennys, 1983.

1472. ------. LETTERS FROM WESTERBORK. Translated from the Dutch by Arnold J. Pomerans. Introduction and notes by Jan G. Gaarlandt. New York: Pantheon Books, 1986. 156p.

Letters 1942-1943, most of them from Westerbork, a transit camp near Assen in northeast Netherlands, the last stop before Auschwitz for more than one hundred thousand Dutch Jews, and where Hillesum spent the last months of her life. Her letters reveal a woman of courage and humanity, with strong spirit and a great faith in life that was never broken.

1473. Hilton, Ruth Naomi Savage, b. 1891. American Mormon missionary. "...AND HER NAME SHALL BE RUTH NAOMI..." Edited by Eugene Hilton. Oakland, Calif.: The Hilton Family, 1969.

Includes a diary of missionary work in the Eastern States Mission, 1914-1916; excerpts from a diary 1951-1953 of work with the British Mission; and excerpts from a diary 1958-1961 describing travel in Hawaii and New Zealand.

1474. Hinde, Catherine Antonia Hegwill. English. JOURNAL OF A TOUR MADE IN ITALY IN THE WINTER OF THE YEARS 1819 AND 1820. Edited with an introduction by M. Merlini. Geneve: Editions Slatkine, 1982. 120p.

Travel diary. Merlini asserts it was general practice at the time Hinde's journal was written to compile travel "diaries" at home from notes taken during the trip, and argues that this was the case with Hinde's journal. It was originally published anonymously, and Merlini details his discovery of its author.

1475. Hinderer, Anna Martin, 1827-1870. SEVENTEEN YEARS IN THE YORUBA COUNTY: MEMORIALS OF ANNA HINDERER. GATHERED FROM HER JOURNALS AND LETTERS. With an introduction by Richard B. Hone. Third edition. London: Seeley, Jackson and Halliday, 1873. 343p.

1476. Hines, Celinda E. American frontier settler. "Diary of Celinda E. Hines." TRANSACTIONS OF THE OREGON PIONEER ASSOCIATION 46 (1918), 69-125.

Overland diary, February--September, 1853, written on the journey from New York to Oregon by railroad, steamboat and wagon.

1477. Hippius (or Gippius), Zinaida Nikolayevna, 1869-1945. Russian poet, author and salonist; wife of poet Dmitry Merezhkovsky. INTELLECT AND IDEAS IN ACTION: SELECTED CORRESPONDENCE OF ZINAIDA HIPPIUS. Translated and edited by Temira Pachmuss. Munich: Wilhelm Fink Verlag, 1972.

1478. ------. BETWEEN PARIS AND St. PETERSBURG: SELECTED DIARIES OF ZINAIDA HIPPIUS. Edited, translated, and with an introduction by Temira Pachmuss. Urbana: University of Illinois Press, 1975. 329p.

Extracts 1893-1930 give a picture of the spiritual atmosphere of St. Petersburg at the begining of the twentieth century; of Poland after the October Revolution; and of the activities of Émigré Russians in Paris in the 1930's and 1940's. Hippius considered the writing of letters and diaries to be the same creative art as the composing of poetry.

1479. ------. "IZ Arkiva Merezhkovskih Pis'ma Z.N. Hippius K M.V. Vishniaku." CAHIERS DU MONDE RUSSE ET SOVIETIQUE 23:3-4 (1982), 417-467.

Excerpts from the Merezhkovsky Archives: Letters of Zinaida Hippius to M.V. Vishniak. Vishniak was the editor and publisher of an influential Russian Émigré publication. Letters give a picture of Russian Émigré circles in Paris.

1480. ------. PETERSBURGSKIE DNEVNIKI (1914-1919). New York: Orfei, 1982. 285p.

1481. Hirsh, Charlotte Teller, b. 1876. American author. THE DIARY OF AN EXPECTANT MOTHER. With illustrations by Clara Elsene Peck. Chicago: A.C. McClurg & Co., 1917. 209p.

1482. Hitchcock, Mary E. American. TWO WOMEN IN THE KLONDIKE: THE STORY OF A JOURNEY TO THE GOLD-FIELDS OF ALASKA. New York and London: G.P. Putnam's Sons, The Knickerbocker Press, 1899. 485p.

Travel diary, June 16--October 11, 1898 describes the adventures of two women, Hitchcock and her friend Edith Van Buren, on the Alaskan frontier.

1483. Hitchener, Elizabeth. English lover of Percy Bysshe Shelley. LETTERS OF ELIZABETH HITCHENER TO PERCY BYSSHE SHELLEY. Edited by Walter E. Peck. New

York: Privately printed for Carl H. Pforzheimer and his friends by the Pynson Printers, 1926. Reprinted, Folcroft Library Editions, 1977.

1484. Hixon, Adrietta Applegate, d. 1935. American frontier settler. "ON TO OREGON! A TRUE STORY OF A YOUNG GIRL'S JOURNEY INTO THE WEST. Edited by Waldo Taylor. Weiser, Idaho: Signal-American Printers, 1947. 48p.

Overland diary.

1485. Hobbs, John Oliver, pseud. for Pearl Mary Teresa Richards Craigie, 1867-1906. English-American novelist and dramatist. Born Pearl Richards, she converted to Catholicism in 1892 and added Mary and Teresa to her name. THE LIFE OF JOHN OLIVER HOBBS TOLD IN HER CORRESPONDENCE WITH NUMEROUS FRIENDS. With a biographical sketch by her father John Morgan Richards, and an introduction by the Right Reverend Bishop Welldon. London: John Murray, and New York: E.P. Dutton, 1911. 381p.

1486. Hobbs, Mary Mendenhall, 1852-1930. American Quaker. LETTERS TO GERTRUDE, 1910-1913. Edited by Mary I. Shamburger. Philadelphia: The John C. Winston Co., 1936. 175p.

Letters by Hobbs and her husband, Lewis Lyndon Hobbs, to their daughter, Gertrude Mendenhall Hobbs (later Korner) who was attending a boarding school near Philadelphia.

1487. Hoby, Margaret Dakins Devereux Sidney, 1571-1633. Earliest known European woman diarist. THE DIARY OF LADY MARGARET HOBY, 1599-1605. Edited by Dorothy M. Meads. London: George Routledge & Sons, 1930. 289p.

Religious diary consisting of short daily entries; a record of religious thoughts and lapses, and daily household activities.

1488. ------. "The Diary of an Elizabethan Gentlewoman." Evelyn Fox. TRANSACTIONS OF THE ROYAL HISTORICAL SOCIETY, 3rd Ser., Vol. 3 (1908), 153-174.

Study of the diary of Lady Hoby.

1489. Hocker, Karla, b. 1901. German author. BESCHREIBUNG EINES JAHRES: BERLINER NOTIZEN 1945. Mit einer einfuhrung von Ingebord Drewitz und Berichton von Boleslaw Barlog. Berlin: Arani, 1984. 156p.

1490. Hoffman, Anita. American leftist activist and wife of activist Abbie Hoffman. TO AMERICA WITH LOVE: LETTERS FROM THE UNDERGROUND. Abbie and Anita Hoffman. New York: Stonehill Co./George Braziller, 1976. 206p.

Letters April, 1974--March, 1975 describe Abbie's life as a fugitive and Anita's as a destitute mother on welfare.

1491. Hofmanowa, Klementyna Tanska, "Countess Krasinska," 1798-1845. Polish consort of Charles, Duke of Courland. THE JOURNAL OF COUNTESS FRANÇOISE KRASINSKA: GREAT GRANDMOTHER OF VICTOR EMMANUEL. Translated from the Polish by Kasimir Dziekonska. Chicago: A.C. McClurg & Co., 1896. 182p.

Extracts from her adolescent diary and from her journal dealing with her love affair with and secret marriage to the Duke of Courland.

1492. ------. A GIRL WHO WOULD BE QUEEN: THE STORY AND THE DIARY OF THE YOUNG COUNTESS KRASINSKA. Eric Philbrook Kelley and Clara Hofmanowa. Decorations by Vera Bock. Chicago: A.C. McClurg & Co., 1939.

1493. Holden, Edith, 1871-1920. THE COUNTRY DIARY OF AN EDWARDIAN LADY, 1906. A FACSIMILE REPRODUCTION OF A NATURALIST'S DIARY. New York: Holt, Rinehart and Winston, 1977. 176p.

1494. Holder, Maryse. American. GIVE SORROW WORDS: MARYSE HOLDER'S LETTERS FROM MEXICO. With an introduction by Kate Millet. New York: Grove Press/Random House, 1979. 302p.

1495. Holland, Elizabeth Vassall Fox, Lady, 1770-1845. English social and political leader. THE JOURNAL OF ELIZABETH, LADY HOLLAND, 1791-1811. Edited by the Earl of Ilchester. London: Longmans, Green, 1908. 2 vols.

Private diary, 1785-1788. Describes society life, travel, and an unhappy first marriage to Sir Godfrey Webster.

1496. ------. THE SPANISH JOURNAL OF ELIZABETH, LADY HOLLAND. Edited by the Earl of Ilchester. London: Longmans, Green, 1910. 437p.

Accounts of two journeys to Spain, 1802-1805 and 1808-1809. The first is a travel diary; the second describes the early part of the Peninsular War. Lady Holland wrote down daily reports received from the Front.

1497. Holland, Mary Sibylla, b. 1836. English Vicar's wife. LETTERS OF MARY SIBYLLA HOLLAND. Selected and edited by her son, Bernard Holland. Second edition. London: Edward Arnold, 1898. 315p.

The second edition includes an appendix of letters that came to light after the first edition was published. Letters begin in 1861 when Holland was twenty-five and continue to 1891, with the greater number written in the last years of her life. Describes travels and parish duties in St. Dunstan Parish, a suburb of Canterbury.

1498. Holley, Mary Phelps Austin, 1784-1846. American author and land speculator. Her book on Texas was the first on its subject in English. TEXAS: OBSERVATIONS, HISTORICAL, GEOGRAPHICAL, AND DESCRIPTIVE, IN A SERIES OF LETTERS, WRITTEN DURING A VISIT TO AUSTIN'S COLONY, WITH A VIEW OF PERMANENT SETTLEMENT IN THAT COUNTRY, IN THE AUTUMN OF 1831. WITH AN APPENDIX CONTAINING SPECIFIC ANSWERS TO CERTAIN QUESTIONS, RELATIVE TO COLONIZATION IN TEXAS, ISSUED SOME TIME SINCE BY THE LONDON GEOGRAPHICAL SOCIETY. ALSO, SOME NOTICE OF THE RECENT POLITICAL EVENTS IN THAT QUARTER. Baltimore: Armstrong and Plaskitt, 1833. 167p.

1499. ------. LETTERS OF AN EARLY AMERICAN TRAVELLER: MARY AUSTIN HOLLEY, HER LIFE AND WORKS, 1784-1846. Mattie Austin Hatcher. Dallas: Southwest Press, 1933. 216p.

Biography based on and including long extracts from Holley's personal letters to her family, 1808-1846. Portrays her as a tireless traveller, a pioneer settler, and a cultured, witty, enterprising and indomitable woman.

1500. ------. MARY AUSTIN HOLLEY: THE TEXAS DIARY, 1835-1838. Edited with an introduction by J.P. Bryan. Austin, Tex.: University of Texas Press, 1965. 120p.

Diary April 30, 1835--June 22, 1838, written during a second trip to Texas, after the publication of TEXAS (1833).

1501. Holley, Sallie, 1818-1893. American abolitionist and educator of Freedmen. A LIFE FOR LIBERTY: ANTISLAVERY AND OTHER LETTERS OF SALLIE HOLLEY. Edited with introductory chapters by John White Chadwick. New York and London: G.P. Putnam's Sons, 1899. 202p.

Includes, in somewhat edited form, many extracts from her correspondence.

1502. Holmes, Emma E., 1838-1910. American Civil War diarist. THE DIARY OF MISS EMMA HOLMES, 1861-1866. Edited by John F. Marszalek. Baton Rouge, La.: Louisiana State University Press, 1979. 496p.

Civil War diary by an invalid woman living in Charleston, Virginia.

1503. ------. "The Charleston fire of 1861 as Described in the Emma E. Holmes Diary." John F. Marszalek. SOUTH CAROLINA HISTORY MAGAZINE 76:2 (1975), 60-67.

1504. ------. "A Civil War Sermon as Recounted in the

Emma E. Holmes Diary." John F. Marszalek. HISTORICAL MAGAZINE OF THE PROTESTANT EPISCOPAL CHURCH 46 (March, 1977), 57-62.

Describes a sermon by the Reverend John H. Elliott.

1505. Holmes, Sarah Katherine Stone, 1841-1907. American Civil War diarist. BROKENBURN: THE JOURNAL OF KATE STONE, 1861-1868. Edited by John Q. Anderson. Baton Rouge: Louisiana State University Press, 1955. 400p.

Civil war diary.

1506. Holtby, Winifred, 1898-1935. English author, political activist, and companion of Vera Brittain. LETTERS TO A FRIEND. Edited by Alice Holtby and Jean McWilliam. New York: The Macmillan Co., 1938. 463p.

Letters 1920-1935 to "Rosalind," a woman Holtby met while serving in the W.A.A.C.s. Deals with writing, activism on behalf of the League of Nations and other causes, and social life.

1507. ------. SELECTED LETTERS OF WINIFRED HOLTBY AND VERA BRITTAIN, 1920-1935. Edited by Vera Brittain and Geoffrey Handley-Taylor. London: A. Brown & Son, 1960. 384p.

Brittain and Holtby were intimate friends and lived together from 1922 to 1925.

1508. Hooker, Isabella Beecher, 1822-1907. American suffragist. THE ISABELLA BEECHER HOOKER PROJECT: A MICROFICHE EDITION OF HER PAPERS AND SUFFRAGE-RELATED CORRESPONDENCE OWNED BY THE STOWE-DAY FOUNDATION. Edited, with an introductory essay by Anne Thorne Margolis. Hartford, Conn.: The Stowe-Day Foundation and Kraus Microform, 1979. 145 microfiches and clothbound guide/index.

One thousand seven hundred items, focusing on Hooker's participation in the Suffrage Movement.

Includes diaries, manuscripts of Suffrage essays, and correspondence with over one hundred people on the subject of Woman Suffrage, including Elizabeth Cady Stanton, Susan B. Anthony, Victoria Woodhull, Lucy Stone, and Henry Brown Blackwell.

1509. Hooper, Alice Forbes Perkins, b. 1867. American daughter of Charles Elliot and Edith Forbes Perkins. DEAR LADY: THE LETTERS OF FREDERICK JACKSON TURNER AND ALICE FORBES PERKINS HOOPER, 1910-1932. Edited by Ray Allen Billington, with the collaboration of Walter Muir Whitehill. San Marino, Calif.: The Huntington Library, 1970. 487p.

Correspondence between Hooper and Western historian Frederick Jackson Turner reveals an intellectual companionship that lasted a quarter of a century.

1510. Horner, Joyce Mary, 1903-1980. American novelist, poet, and teacher. THAT TIME OF YEAR: A CHRONICLE OF LIFE IN A NURSING HOME. Amherst: University of Massachusetts Press, 1982. 207p.

Journal March 11, 1975--June 27, 1977, by a woman who, disabled by arthritis, entered a nursing home and kept a journal of her life there for the next three years. Reveals her resilence of spirit in the face of increasing physical disability and her growing realization of mortality.

1511. Horney, Karen Danielsen, 1885-1952. German-born psychiatrist and psychoanalyst. THE ADOLESCENT DIARIES OF KAREN HORNEY. Foreword by Marianne Horney Eckardt, M.D. New York: Basic Books, 1980. 271p.

Early diaries, 1899-1911, begining when Horney was thirteen; and letters to her husband, Oskar Horney, 1906-1907.

1512. Hosmer, Harriet Goodhue, 1830-1908. American sculptor and intimate of actress Charlotte Cushman. HARRIET HOSMER, LETTERS AND MEMORIES. Edited by Cornelia Carr. New York: Moffit, Yard & Co., 1912; and London: John Lane, 1913. 386p.

1513. Hosmer, Lucy Barnes, 1742-1818. American colonist. "Journal of Lucy Barnes Hosmer: Tuesday 18 April--Wednesday 19 April, 1755, Concord, Massachusetts." Mary Hosmer Lupton. DAUGHTERS OF THE AMERICAN REVOLUTION MAGAZINE 114 (1980), 14-17.

1514. Hotchkis, Katharine Bixby. American. TRIP WITH FATHER. California Historical Society, 1971. (Serial Publications No. 48). 43p.

Diary of a five hundred mile horseback trip from San Francisco to Los Angeles in 1916.

1515. Houdetot, Élisabeth Françoise Sophie de la Live de Bellegarde, Comtesse de', 1730-1813. French. LES AMITIES AMERICAINES DE MADAME D'HOUDETOT D'APRÈS SA CORRESPONDANCE INÉDITE AVEC BENJAMIN FRANKLIN ET THOMAS JEFFERSON. Publiée par Gilbert Chinard. Paris: E. Champion, 1924. 62p.

1516. Houghton, Adelaide Louise Wellington, b. 1867. American wife of U.S. Ambassador Allen B. Houghton. THE LONDON YEARS: THE DIARY OF ADELAIDE WELLINGTON HOUGHTON, 1925-1929. Washington, D.C.: Privately printed at the Spiral Press, New York, 1963. 274p.

Social diary of diplomatic life at the U.S. Embassy in London.

1517. Houghton, Mary. English. IN THE ENEMY'S COUNTRY: BEING THE DIARY OF A LITTLE TOUR IN GERMANY AND ELSEWHERE DURING THE EARLY DAYS OF THE WAR. With a Foreword by Edward Garnett. London: Chatto & Windus, 1915. 280p.

Travel diary, July 20--September 29, 1914. Despite the title, this is not a war diary; Houghton "recognized early the futility of her pen," and cut from the diary nearly all references to the war, leaving only the "lighter aspects as seen by the wanderer."

1518. Howe, Julia Ward, 1819-1910. American women's club and suffrage leader, poet and author of "The

Battle Hymn of the Republic." JULIA WARD HOWE. Laura E. Richards and Maud Howe Elliott. Assisted by Florence Howe Hall. Boston and New York: Houghton Mifflin Co., and Cambridge, England: The Riverside Press, 1916. 2 vols.

Biography comprised of letters and journal entries, with commentary. Volume 1 covers her life; Volume 2 covers the years 1877-1910 in depth.

1519. ------. THE WALK WITH GOD. EXTRACTS FROM MRS. HOWE'S PRIVATE JOURNALS. TOGETHER WITH SOME VERSES HITHERTO (WITH A FEW EXCEPTIONS) UNPUBLISHED; AND AN ESSAY ON IMMORTALITY ENTITLED "BEYOND THE VEIL." Edited by her daughter, Laura E. Richards. New York: E.P. Dutton & Co., 1919. 161p.

Extracts 1864-1910 from those portions of her journals concerning her religion.

1520. Howe, Maude, later Elliott, 1854-1948. Author, art critic, travel writer, and daughter of Julia Ward Howe. ROMA BETA: LETTERS FROM THE ETERNAL CITY. With illustrations from drawings by John Elliott and from photographs. Boston: Little, Brown & Co., 1905. 362p.

Letters 1894-1900 describe travels in Italy and life in Rome with her husband, artist John Elliott.

1521. Howell, Elizabeth Lloyd, b. 1811. American. ELIZABETH LLOYD AND THE WHITTIERS: A BUDGET OF LETTERS. Edited by Thomas Franklin Currier. Cambridge, Mass.: Harvard University Press, 1939. 146p.

Lloyd's letters to the Whittier family. Includes some letters of John Greenleaf Whittier to her, and an extract from a letter by Hannah Lloyd Neal.

1522. Howitt, Mary, 1799-1888. English poet and children's author; wife of poet William Howitt. MARY HOWITT: An AUTOBIOGRAPHY. Edited by her daughter, Margaret Howitt. London: William Ibister, 1889. 2 vols.

Chiefly letters and autobiographical fragments written at various times in her life, with an introductory biographical essay.

1523. Hsieh Pingying, b. 1903. Chinese author and soldier. LETTERS OF A CHINESE AMAZON AND WAR ESSAYS. Shanghai, China: The Commercial Press, 1930, 1933. 211p.

Includes letters written at the front during the Japanese invasion of China, translated by Lin Yutang.

1524. ------. HSIEH PINGYING: GIRL REBEL. THE AUTOBIOGRAPHY OF HSIEH PINGYING. WITH EXTRACTS FROM HER NEW WAR DIARIES. Translated by Adet and Anor Lin. Introduction by Lin Yutang. New York: The John Day Co., 1940. 270p.

Diary September-November, 1937, written at the front during the Japanese Invasion of China. She was still fighting at Shensi at the time this book was being translated into English.

1525. Hug-Helmuth, H.A. A YOUNG GIRL'S DIARY. Prefaced with a letter by Sigmund Freud. Translated by Eden and Cedar Paul. New York: T. Seltzer, 1921. 284p.

1526. Hughes, Emmy, 1863-1934. English social worker among the unemployed in Tennessee. DISSIPATIONS AT UFFINGTON HOUSE: THE LETTERS OF EMMY HUGHES, RUGBY, TENNESSEE, 1881-1887. Introduction by John R. Debruyn. Memphis, Tenn: Memphis State University Press, 1976. 80p.

1527. Hughes, Margaret. French. LES LAURIERS SONT COUPÉS...JOURNAL D'UNE VOLONTAIRE AMERICAINE EN FRANCE (AVRIL-SEPTEMBRE, 1940). New York: Brentano's: Publishers, 1941. 251p.

Chapters: Drôle de Guerre, Avril-Mai, 1940; Blitzkrieg, Mai-Juin, 1940; Armistice, Juin-Septembre, 1940.

1528. Hugo, Adélé, 1830-1915. French daughter of poet

Victor Hugo. LE JOURNAL D'ADÉLÉ HUGO. Introduction et notes par Frances Vernor Guille. Paris: Lettres Modernes, 1968-1971. 2 vols.

Journal and family letters describe life of the Hugo family on the Island of Jersey, 1852-1853.

1529. Hulton, Ann. American colonist and Loyalist. LETTERS OF A LOYALIST LADY: BEING THE LETTERS OF ANN HULTON, SISTER OF HENRY HULTON, COMMISSIONER OF CUSTOMS AT BOSTON, 1767-1776. Cambridge, Mass.: Harvard University Press, 1927. 106p. Reprinted, New York: Arno Press, 1970.

Loyalist and social letters, written to Mrs. Adam Lightbody, the wife of a Liverpool merchant. Chiefly concerned with town gossip, household expenses, domestic matters, and to a lesser degree, public events.

1530. Humbolt, Karoline Fredericke Dacheroden von, 1766-1829. German wife of Guillaume de Humbolt. KAROLINE VON HUMBOLT IN IHREN BRIEFEN AN ALEXANDER VON RENNENKAMPFF. Nebst einer charakteristik beider als einleitung und eniem anhange von Albrecht Stauffer. Berlin: Ernst Siegfried Mittler und Sohn, 1804. 242p.

1531. ------. BRIEFWECHSEL ZWISCHEN KAROLINE VON HUMBOLT, RAHEL UND VARNHAGEN. Herausgegeben von Albert Leitzmann. Weimar: Hermann Bohlaus Nachfolger, 1896. 221p.

Letters 1795-1818.

1532. Hunolstein, Aglaé de. French lover of the Marquis de Lafayette. LADY IN WAITING: THE ROMANCE OF LAFAYETTE AND AGLAÉ DE HUNOLSTEIN. Louis Gottschalk. Baltimore: Institut Francais de Washington and Johns Hopkins Press, 1939. 137p.

Study of their brief affair, based on their correspondence. Includes de Hunolstein's letters to the Comte Schouvalow (or Shuvalov), 1778-1782; her letters to John Paul Jones, 1780; and a letter from Lafayette to de Hunolstein, reprinted in facsimile.

1533. Hunt, Ellen Elizabeth Kellog, 1835-1880. American wife of Alexander Cameron Hunt, Territorial Governor of Colorado. "Diary of Mrs. A.C. Hunt., 1859." With an introduction and notes by LeRoy R. Hafen. COLORADO MAGAZINE 21:5 (1944), 160-170.

Diary April 25--September 15, 1859 describes travel overland from Michigan to the Colorado gold rush region of Pike's Peak, and hardships of life in the mining towns.

1534. Hunt, Violet, 1866-1942. THE RETURN OF THE GOOD SOLDIER: FORD MADDOX FORD AND VIOLET HUNT'S 1917 DIARY. Robert Secor and Marie Secor. Victoria, B.C.: English Literary Studies, Dept. of English, University of Victoria, 1983. 85p.

Hunt's diary for February 24, 1917--January 24, 1918 traces the disintegration of her relationship with Ford (they had been living together) and gives a picture of the social and literary circles in England during World War I.

1535. Huntingdon, Selina Shirley Hastings, Countess of, 1707-1791. English founder of the Methodist branch known as Lady Huntingdon's Connexion. LIFE AND TIMES OF SELINA, COUNTESS OF HUNTINGDON. By a member of the Houses of Shirley and Hastings. London: William and Edward Painter, 1839. 2 vols.

Biography; includes letters and extracts from her correspondence.

1536. Huntington, Annie Oaks, 1875-1940. American botanical and gardening author. TESTAMENT OF HAPPINESS: LETTERS. Edited by Nancy Byrd Turner. With an introduction by Mark Anthony DeWolfe Howe. Portland, Maine: Anthoensen Press, 1947. 235p.

Early letters, 1885-1896, written from Hong Kong, where her father was employed by American China Merchants Russell & Co., to family and friends in Boston; and later letters, 1898-1940 focusing on her botanical writings, her longtime friendship with

Jeannette Payson, with whom she lived for many years, and the long illness that ended in her death in 1940.

1537. Huntington, Susan Mansfield, 1791-1823. American. MEMOIRS OF THE LATE SUSAN HUNTINGTON, OF BOSTON, MASSACHUSETTS, CONSISTING PRINCIPALLY OF EXTRACTS FROM HER JOURNAL AND LETTERS. WITH THE SERMON OCCASIONED BY HER DEATH. Second edition. Boston: Crocker & Brewster, 1826. 392p.

1538. Hurnscot, Loran, pseud. for Gay Stuart Taylor, d. 1970. A PRISON, A PARADISE. Introduction by Kathleen Raine. New York: The Viking Press, 1959. 320p.

Extracts from a diary, 1922-1958, focusing on a painful love affair with author A.E. Coppard (the prison) and religious study and enlightenment (the paradise).

1539. Huston, Nancy, b. 1953. A L'AMOUR COMME A LA GUERRE: CORRESPONDANCE / NANCY HUSTON, SAM KINSER. Paris: Editions Seuil, 1984. 329p.

1540. Hutchinson, Sara, 1775-1835. English sister-in-law of William Wordsworth. LETTERS OF SARA HUTCHINSON FROM 1800-1835. Edited by Kathleen Coburn. London: Routledge & Kegan Paul; and Toronto: University of Toronto Press, 1954. 474p.

Letters to her family, from her early days at Yorkshire to within a few weeks of her death at Rydal Mount. She was a member of the Wordsworth circle, and an intimate friend of Samuel Coleridge, who wrote many poems to her as "Asra."

1541. Hutchison, Susan Nye, b. 1790. American. "Extracts from the Journal of Susan Nye Hutchison While She Was Living at Augusta, Georgia." Virginia E. Treville. RICHMOND COUNTY HISTORY 11 (1979), 216-233.

Extracts from her journal, 1826-1833.

1542. Hutton, Catherine, 1756-1846. English novelist,

biographer and historian. REMINISCENCES OF A GENTLE-WOMAN OF THE LAST CENTURY: LETTERS OF CATHERINE HUTTON. Edited by her cousin, Mrs. Catherine Hutton Beale. Birmingham, England: Cornish Bros., 1891. 250p.

1543. ------. CATHERINE HUTTON AND HER FRIENDS. Edited by her cousin Mrs. Catherine Hutton Beale. Birmingham, England: Cornish Bros., 1895. 264p.

Chiefly Hutton's correspondence.

1544. Hutton, Mrs. Mary. American. LIVING CHRISTIANITY DELINEATED, IN THE DIARIES AND LETTERS OF TWO EMINENTLY PIOUS PERSONS LATELY DECEASED; VIZ., MR. HUGH BRYAN AND MRS. MARY HUTTON, BOTH OF SOUTH CAROLINA. With a preface by the Reverend Mr. John Conder, and the Reverend Mr. Thomas Gibbons. London: J. Buckland, 1760.

1545. Huxley, Elspeth Joscelin Grant, b. 1907. English-Kenyan author and daughter of Nellie Grant. RACE AND POLITICS IN KENYA: A CORRESPONDENCE BETWEEN ELSPETH HUXLEY AND MARGERY PERHAM. With an introduction by Lord Lugard. New and Revised edition. London: Faber and Faber, 1956. 302p.

1546. ------. WITH FORKS AND HOPE: AN AFRICAN NOTEBOOK. Illustrated by Jonathan Kingdon. New York: William Morrow, 1964. 398p. London: Chatto & Windus, 1964. 272p.

Political diary, reporting on the rapid and critical changes in Tanganyika, Uganda and Zanzibar. Written as a diary during a visit to Africa, February-May, 1963, but not dated.

1547. Hyde, Nancy Maria, 1792-1816. American teacher. THE WRITINGS OF NANCY MARIA HYDE OF NORWICH, CONNECTICUT, CONNECTED WITH A SKETCH OF HER LIFE. Edited by Mrs. Lydia Sigourney. Norwich, Conn.: Russell Hubbard, 1816. 252p.

Includes extracts from diaries and letters. Hyde taught at a girl's school in Norwich, Connecticut.

1548. Hynes, Maureen. Canadian teacher, communist, activist and feminist. LETTERS FROM CHINA. Toronto: The Women's Educational Press, 1981. 255p.

Diary entries and letters, April 27-- September 24, 1980 describe work and experiences as a teacher of English at Sichuan University in Chengdu.

1549. Ide, Lucy A. American frontier settler. "Mrs. Lucy A. Ide's Diary: In a Prairie Schooner, 1878." Edited by J. Orin Oliphant. WASHINGTON HISTORICAL QUARTERLY 18:2 (April, 1927), 122-131; 18:3 (July, 1927), 191-198; and 18:4 (October,1927), 277-288.

Diary of a trip overland from Wisconsin to Washington Territory; a contribution to the study of the later period of immigration to the Pacific Northwest.

1550. Inber, Vera Mikhailovna, b. 1890. Russian poet. LENINGRAD DIARY. Translated from the Russian by Serge M. Wolff and Rachel Grieve; with an introduction by Edward Crankshaw. London: Hutchinson & Co., and New York: St. Martin's Press, 1971. 207p.

Firsthand account of the Siege of Leningrad during World War II.

1551. Inchbald, Elizabeth Simpson, 1753-1821. English novelist and actress. MEMOIRS OF MRS. INCHBALD, INCLUDING HER FAMILIAR CORRESPONDENCE WITH THE MOST DISTINGUISHED PERSONS OF HER TIME. Edited by J. Boaden. London: R. Bentley, 1833.

1552. Inderwick, Mary E. Canadian rancher. "A Lady and Her Ranch." ALBERTA HISTORICAL REVIEW 15:4 (1967), 1-9.

Extracts from the letters of a cattle rancher's wife living in Alberta, Canada.

1553. Inglis, Julia Selina Thesiger, Lady, 1833-1904. English. THE SEIGE OF LUCKNOW: A DIARY. New York:

Charles Scribner's Sons, 1892. 240p. Leipzig: B. Tauchnitz, 1892. 255p. London: James R. Osgood, McIlvaine & Co., 1893. 224p.

Diary account of the Indian Mutiny of 1857-1858.

1554. Ingraham, Elizabeth Mary Meade, b. 1806. American Civil War diarist. "The Vicksburg Diary of Mrs. Alfred Ingraham, May 2-June 13, 1863." Edited by Maury W. Darst. JOURNAL OF MISSISSIPPI HISTORY 44:2 (May, 1982), 148-179.

Diary account of General Grant's seige of Vicksburg, Mississippi, written by the sister of Confederate General Meade; contains information on wartime events intermingled with personal accounts and observations.

1555. Isherwood, Kathleen Machell Smith, 1868-1960. English mother of author Christopher Isherwood. KATHLEEN AND FRANK. Christopher Isherwood. New York: Simon & Schuster, 1971. 570p.

Biography of the author's parents, including extracts from Kathleen Isherwood's diary.

1556. Izard, Alice DeLancey. American; wife of Ralph Izard, U.S. Senator and a member of the Continental Congress. "Letters of Mrs. Ralph Izard to Mrs. William Lee." VIRGINIA MAGAZINE OF HISTORY AND BIOGRAPHY 8 (1901), 16-28.

Letters from Paris, 1781-1782.

1557. Izumi Shikibu, b. 974. Japanese Lady-In-Waiting to the Empress Akiko. THE IZUMI SHIKIBU DIARY: A ROMANCE OF THE HEIAN COURT. Translated with an introduction by Edwin A. Cranston. Cambridge, Mass.: Harvard University Press, 1969. 332p.

Japanese poetic diary, chronicling the beginning of her affair with Prince Atsumichi. Izumi Shikibu was a contemporary of Sei Shonagon and Lady Murasaki.

1558. Jackson, Eleanor Hardin. American. "Selected Social Correspondence of Miss Eleanor Hardin Jackson of Rutherford County (1860-1865)." TENNESSEE FOLKLORE SOCIETY BULLETIN 41:1 (1975), 9-18.

Social correspondence of a young lady of Tennessee during the Civil War "serves to confirm that life was still composed of trivialities within the framework of what was momentous for society and the nation."

1559. Jackson, Nannie Stillwell. American farmer. VINEGAR PIE AND CHICKEN BREAD: A WOMAN'S DIARY OF LIFE IN THE RURAL SOUTH, 1890-1891. Edited with an introduction by Margaret Jones Bolsterli. Fayetteville: University of Arkansas Press, 1982. (Distributed by the University of Missouri Press.) 108p.

Strict copy of the daily record of domestic affairs kept by an Arkansas farm wife. The value of the diary lies in its tedium, through which is revealed a segment of the "underside" of history: the "stifling, intellectually empty, mind deadening quality of life in nineteenth-century rural America."

1560. Jackson, Rebecca Cox, 1795-1871. American Black Shaker. GIFTS OF POWER: THE WRITINGS OF REBECCA COX JACKSON, BLACK VISIONARY, SHAKER ELDRESS. Edited by Jean M. Humez. Amherst, Mass.: University of Massachusetts Press, 1981. 368p.

Autobiography based on and including extracts from a journal, 1863-1864.

1561. Jackson, Sara. English musician and actress. DARK WITH NO SORROW. New York: Harcourt Brace & World, 1968. 116p.

Daily letters exchanged between Jackson and her husband, Stephen Thomas, written when he was dying of cancer. The letters were written after Jackson's daily visits to the hospital, July 3, 1960-March 1, 1961.

1562. Jacobi, Mary Putnam, 1842-1906. American

physician and women's rights activist. LIFE AND LETTERS OF MARY PUTNAM JACOBI, 1842-1906. Edited by Ruth Putnam. Foreword by George Haven Putnam. New York and London: G.P. Putnam's Sons, 1925. 381p.

1563. Jacobs, Zina Diantha Huntington. American Mormon and plural wife of Mormon leader Brigham Young. "All Things Move in Order in the City: The Nauvoo Diary of Zina Diantha Huntington Jacobs." Edited by Maureen U. Beecher. BRIGHAM YOUNG UNIVERSITY STUDIES 19:3 (1979), 285-320.

Extracts from a diary, 1844-1845, describe the tumultuous year among the Mormons after the martyrdom of Joseph and Hyrum Smith and the persecution of the Mormons in Nauvoo, Illinois; as well as events in Jacobs' private life.

1564. Jacquet, Eliane. French student. 4 SAISONS EN U.R.S.S. Éditions Pierre Horay, 1959.

1565. ------. HIGH HEELS IN RED SQUARE. New York: Holt, Rinehart and Winston, 1961. 209p.

Diary of a Parisian student's year in Russia. Translation of 4 SAISONS EN U.R.S.S.

1566. Jacquier, Ivy. French-English artist. THE DIARY OF IVY JACQUIER. With an introduction by Sir Francis Meynell. London: Victor Gollancz, 1960. 223p.

Literary diary, 1907-1926.

1567. James, Alice, 1848-1892. American diarist and invalid sister of novelist Henry James and philosopher William James. ALICE JAMES: HER BROTHERS, HER JOURNAL. Edited with an introduction by Anna Robeson Burr. New York: Dodd, Mead & Co., 1934. 253p.

First published edition, heavily edited. Includes family correspondence.

1568. ------. THE DIARY OF ALICE JAMES. Edited by

Leon Edel. New York: Dodd, Mead & Co., 1934. 241p.

1569. ------. THE DEATH AND LETTERS OF ALICE JAMES: SELECTED CORRESPONDENCE. Edited and with a biographical essay by Ruth Bernard Yeazell. Berkeley, Calif.: University of California Press, 1981. 214p.

Letters 1860-1892 to family and friends, including Frances Rollins Morse and Sara Sedgwick Darwin. Letters are heavily annotated and Yeazell provides a very thorough essay on James' invalidism and death.

1570. James, Winifred. OUT OF THE SHADOWS. London: Chapman and Hall, 1924. 280p.

Travel diary, 1915-1918. Describes travel and life in Panama, London, and New York.

1571. Jameson, Anna Brownell (Murphy), 1794-1860. Irish-born author who lived most of her life in Canada. She wrote a fictional diary, DIARY OF AN ENNUYEE (1826). WINTER STUDIES AND SUMMER RAMBLES IN CANADA. Toronto: McClelland & Stewart, 1838. Reprinted and abridged, 1965.

Diary 1836-1837 describes eight months spent in Canada with her husband, Vice Chancellor of Upper Canada.

1572. ------. ANNA JAMESON: LETTERS AND FRIENDSHIPS (1812-1860). Edited by Mrs. Steuart Erskine [Beatrice Strong Erskine]. London: T. Fisher Unwin, 1915. 350p.

Letters to her family, and to Lady Noel Byron, Ottilie Van Goethe, Harriet Martineau and others. Contains letters from Martineau, Mary Russell Mitford, Harriet Grote, and others.

1573. ------. LETTERS OF MRS. ANNA JAMESON TO OTTILIE VON GOETHE. Edited by G.H. Needler. Published with the permission of the Goethe and Schiller Archives in Weimar. London and New York: Oxford University Press, 1939. 247p.

Letters 1833-1860. The friendship of Jameson and Ottilie von Goethe was passionate--Needler suggests it was the supreme interest of Jameson's life--and although for most of their lives they lived apart, in different countries (Jameson in Canada, Goethe in Germany), their friendship lasted until Jameson's death. Goethe's letters to Jameson have not survived.

1574. Jay, Cornelia, 1839-1907. American. THE DIARY OF CORNELIA JAY, 1861-1873. Rye, N.Y.: Privately Printed, 1924. 228p.

Deals with the Civil War, and with travels in Europe.

1575. Jebb, Caroline Lane Reynolds Slemmer, 1840-1930. American society belle and hostess who lived in England. WITH DEAREST LOVE TO ALL: THE LIFE AND LETTERS OF LADY JEBB. Edited by Mary Reed Bobbitt. Chicago: Henry Regnery Co., 1960. 277p.

Biography comprised of letters and journal extracts, 1858-1924, edited together, annotated and supplemented. Lively and intelligent description of society life in the United States and England.

1576. Jefferson, Lara (pseud.). THESE ARE MY SISTERS: A JOURNAL FROM THE INSIDE OF INSANITY. Tulsa, Okla.: Vickers Publishing Co., 1948. Reprinted, Garden City, New York: Doubleday & Co., 1974. 238p.

1577. Jenner, Delia. English teacher. LETTERS FROM PEKING. New York, Toronto, London: Oxford University Press, 1967. 105p.

Extracts from letters to her family comprising a daily account of two years in China, July, 1963--August, 1965. Her husband worked as a translator at the Foreign Languages Press, and she taught English at the Peking Broadcasting Institute.

1578. Jephson, Harriet Julia Campbell, Lady, b. 1854. English. CANADIAN SCRAP-BOOK. London, 1897. 183p.

1579. ------. A WAR-TIME JOURNAL: GERMANY 1914 AND GERMAN TRAVEL NOTES. London: Elkin Matthews, 1915. 99p.

Diary August--September, 1914, by an Englishwoman detained at Altheim at the begining of World War I. She is eventually released and travels to France and England. The "Travel Notes" deteriorate into a rather mundane tourist travel diary.

1580. Jernegan, Laura, b. 1862. American daughter of a New England whaling family. "A Child's Diary of a Whaling Voyage." Edited by Marcus Wilson Jernegan. NEW ENGLAND QUARTERLY 2:1 (1929), 130-139.

Extracts from a diary 1868-1871 beginning when Jernegan was six, on board her father's ship, sailing with her family from New Bedford around Cape Horn to California.

1581. Jerningham, Frances Dillon, Lady, d. 1825. Irish Catholic gentlewoman. THE JERNINGHAM LETTERS (1780-1843). BEING EXCERPTS FROM THE CORRESPONDENCE AND DIARIES OF THE HONORABLE LADY JERNINGHAM AND HER DAUGHTER, LADY BEDINGFELD. Edited with notes by Egerton Castle. London: R. Bentley & Son, 1896. 2 vols.

Extracts from the personal writings of Lady Jerningham and Charlotte, Lady Bedingfeld (d.1854).

1582. Jervey, Susan Ravenel, b.1840, and Charlotte St. Julien Ravenel, d.1880, Americans. TWO DIARIES FROM MIDDLE ST. JOHN'S, BERKELEY, SOUTH CAROLINA, February--May, 1865. JOURNALS KEPT BY MISS SUSAN R. JERVEY AND MISS CHARLOTTE ST. JULIEN RAVENEL, AT NORTHAMPTON AND POOSHEE PLANTATIONS, AND REMINISCENCES OF MRS. WARING HENEGAN. WITH TWO CONTEMPORARY REPORTS FROM FEDERAL OFFICIALS. Pinopolis, S.C.: St. John's Hunting Club, 1921.

Civil War diaries, kept by Charlotte Ravenel at Pooshee Plantation and Susan Jervey at Northampton Plantation, both in Berkeley County, South Carolina.

1583. Jesus, Carolina Maria de, b. 1913. Portuguese-Brazilian slum-dweller. CASA DE ALVENARIA: DIARIO DE UMA EX-FAVELADA. Apresentaco de Audalio Dantos: Capa de Cyro del Nero. Rio De Janeiro: Ediciones P. de Azevedo, 1961. 183p.

1584. ------. CHILD OF THE DARK: THE DIARY OF CAROLINA MARIA DE JESUS. Translated by David St. Clair. New York: E.P. Dutton Co., 1962. 159p.

Diary of a poor woman struggling to make a living and feed her children in the "Favela" or slums.

1585. ------. QUARTO DE DESPEJO: DIARIO DE UMA FAVELADA. Rio de Janeiro: Livraria Francisco Alves Editoria, 1983. 213p.

1586. Jeune, Margaret Dyne Symons, 1818-1891. English wife of a Master of Pembroke College, Oxford. PAGES FROM THE DIARY OF AN OXFORD LADY, 1843-1862. Edited by Margaret Jeune Gifford. Oxford: Printed at the Shakespeare Head and sold by B. Blackwell, 1932. 141p.

Describes social life at Oxford University.

1587. Jewett, Sarah Orne, 1849-1909. American author. LETTERS OF SARAH ORNE JEWETT. Edited by Annie Fields. Boston and New York: Houghton Mifflin Co., 1911. 259p.

Correspondence 1880-1909.

1588. ------. LETTERS OF SARAH ORNE JEWETT NOW IN THE COLBY COLLEGE LIBRARY. With explanatory notes by Carl J. Weber. Waterville, Maine: Colby College Press, 1947. 75p.

1589. ------. SARAH ORNE JEWETT: LETTERS. Edited with an introduction and notes by Richard Cary. Waterville, Maine: Colby College Press, 1956. 117p. Revised edition, 1967. 186p.

Prints 94 letters in the Colby College Library, to Jewetts's editors, publishers, and friends, 1868-1908.

1590. ------. "Yours Always Lovingly: Sarah Orne Jewett to John Greenleaf Whittier." Edited by Richard Cary. ESSEX INSTITUTE HISTORICAL COLLECTIONS 107:4 (October, 1971), 412-450.

Twenty-eight extant letters to Whittier, 1877-1890, reveal a father-daughter relationship between them that lasted more than fifteen years. The letters also contain the fullest account of Jewett's developing attachment to Annie Adams Fields.

1591. Jewsbury, Geraldine Endsor, 1812-1880. English novelist and intimate of Jane Welsh Carlyle. SELECTIONS FROM THE LETTERS OF GERALDINE ENDSOR JEWSBURY TO JANE WELSH CARLYLE. Edited by Mrs. Alexander Ireland. Prefaced by a monograph of Miss Jewsbury, by the editor. London and New York: Longmans, Green and Co., 1892. 443p.

Intimate letters of friendship, 1841-1852. Carlyle's side of the correspondence was destroyed by Jewsbury after Carlyle's death, according to her wishes.

1592. Johnson, Claudia Alta Taylor, "Lady Bird," b. 1912. American wife of U.S. President Lyndon B. Johnson. A WHITE HOUSE DIARY. New York: Holt, Rinehart and Winston, 1970. 806p.

Diary of life in the White house during the Johnson Administration, 1963-1969.

1593. Johnson, Edith Eugenie, M.D., b. 1872. American obstetrician. LEAVES FROM A DOCTOR'S DIARY. With a Foreword by Alvin Johnson. Palo Alto, Calif.: Pacific Books, 1954. 279p.

Diary 1927-1953 by an obstetrician who practiced in Palo Alto, California among the Chinese and Japanese immigrants. The diary was sent in weekly installments to family in New England.

1594. Johnson, Elizabeth. Irish Methodist. AN ACCOUNT

OF MRS. ELIZABETH JOHNSON, WELL KNOWN IN THE CITY OF BRISTOL FOR HER PIETY AND BENEVOLENCE. TO WHICH IS ADDED, AN EXTRACT FROM HER DIARY. Dublin: B. Dugdale, 1799. 46 [58]p.

Extracts from a Methodist diary, November, 1750-July, 1784.

1595. Johnson, Mary Oppel. American Missionary to Burma. BURMA DIARY, 1938-1942. New York: Carlton Press (A Hearthstone Book), 1981. 96p.

Diary of work in a Methodist Chinese School for Girls in Rangoon, and of her "mandatory vacations" during which she travelled in Burma and neighboring countries.

1596. Johnson, Rebekah Baines, d. 1958. American mother of U.S. President Lyndon B. Johnson. LETTERS FROM THE HILL COUNTRY: THE CORRESPONDENCE BETWEEN REBEKAH AND LYNDON BAINES JOHNSON. Edited by Philip R. Rulon. Austin, Tex.: Thorp Springs Press, 1982. 202p.

Letters 1922-1958 reveal a close mother-son relationship. Rebekah Baines was also the family historian, and with Lady Bird Johnson compiled A FAMILY ALBUM (1954).

1597. Johnston, Eliza Griffen. American wife of Confederate General Albert Sidney Johnston. "The Diary of Eliza (Mrs. Albert Sidney), Johnston: The Second Cavalry Comes to Texas." Edited by Charles P. Roland and Richard C. Robbins. SOUTHWESTERN HISTORICAL QUARTERLY 60:4 (1957), 463-500.

Letters and Brief diary 1855-1856, written while traveling cross-country from Missouri to Texas with her husband. Describes weather, terrain, marching conditions, inhabitants along the route, disease and injuries, births and deaths, and her personal reactions to her comrades, the Second Calvary.

1598. Johnston, Jill. American Lesbian activist and

political columnist. LESBIAN NATION: THE FEMINIST SOLUTION. New York: Simon & Schuster, 1973. 283p.

Two sections, "Slouching Towards Consciousness," and "Record Book Entries (March 1971-December 1971)" are excerpted from Johnston's journals, with commentary. Excerpts deal with coming to terms with feminism, her theories of Lesbian separatism, and her activities in the Left and Feminist movements.

1599. Johnston, Priscilla Buxton, 1808-1852. English Quaker. EXTRACTS FROM PRISCILLA JOHNSTON'S JOURNAL; AND LETTERS. Collected by her daughter, E. MacInnes. Carlisle: Charles Thurnam and Sons, 1862. 203p.

Extracts from a Quaker diary, 1820-1850.

1600. Jones, Mary Sharpe, 1808-1869, and Mary Mallard Jones, 1835-1889. Americans. YANKEES A'COMING: ONE MONTH'S EXPERIENCE DURING THE INVASION OF LIBERTY COUNTY, GEORGIA, 1864-1865. Edited by Haskell Monroe. Tuscaloosa: Confederate Publishing Co., 1959. 102p.

Journal kept by Mary S. Jones and her daughter, December 13, 1864--January 27, 1865, during the invasion of Liberty County by Northern Calvary troops. Heavily documented and annotated.

1601. Jones, Mother, 1843(?)-1930. Irish-American labor activist. THE CORRESPONDENCE OF MOTHER JONES. Edited by Edward M. Steele. Pittsburgh, Penn.: University of Pittsburgh Press, 1985. 360p.

Fragmentary correspondence November 30, 1900--October 18, 1930. Much of her correspondence has been lost, as Mother Jones had no fixed home, traveled light, and saved few papers. Her letters "carry the reader headlong into protest rallies, confrontations in the streets, the inner circles of national labor unions, and the tent colonies where strikers fought their battles for recognition."

1602. Jordon, Dora, b. 1762? Welsh-Irish actress.

THE LIFE OF MRS. JORDON. INCLUDING ORIGINAL PRIVATE CORRESPONDENCE AND NUMEROUS ANECDOTES OF HER CONTEMPORARIES. James Boaden. London: Edward Bull, 1831. 2 vols.

Biography based on and including letters and extracts from her correspondence.

1603. Josephine, Empress Consort of Napleon I, 1763-1814. CONFIDENTIAL CORRESPONDENCE OF THE EMPEROR NAPLEON AND THE EMPRESS JOSEPHINE. INCLUDING LETTERS FROM THE TIME OF THEIR MARRIAGE UNTIL THE DEATH OF JOSEPHINE, AND ALSO SEVERAL PRIVATE LETTERS FROM THE EMPEROR TO HIS BROTHER, JOSEPH, AND OTHER IMPORTANT PERSONAGES. John S.C. Abbott. New York: Mason Brothers, 1856. 404p.

1604. Judd, Laura Fish, d. 1873. American Missionary. HONOLULU: SKETCHES OF LIFE, SOCIAL, POLITICAL AND RELIGIOUS, IN THE HAWAIIAN ISLANDS FROM 1828 TO 1861. New York: Randolph, 1880. 258p.

Missionary journal and correspondence.

1605. Judson, Ann Hasseltine, b. 1789. American missionary and first wife of missionary Adoniram Judson. MEMOIR OF MRS. JUDSON. WIFE OF THE REVEREND ADONIRAM JUDSON, MISSIONARY TO BURMA. INCLUDING A HISTORY OF THE AMERICAN BAPTIST MISSION IN THE BURMAN EMPIRE. James D. Knowles. London: Wightman & Cramp, 1829. 324p.

Memoir taken chiefly from her journals and letters, 1806-1827. A large part of the journal was destroyed by Judson in 1824.

1606. Judson, Emily Chubbuck, 1817-1854. American missionary, author and third wife of missionary Adoniram Judson. THE LIFE AND LETTERS OF MRS. EMILY C. JUDSON. Edited by Asahel Clark Kendrick. New York: Sheldon and Co., and Boston: Gould and Lincoln, 1861.

1607. Kardoff, Ursula von. German. BERLINER AUFZEICHNÜNGEN AUS DEN JAHREN 1942 BIS 1945. München: Biederstein Verlag, 1962. 323p.

1608. ------. DIARY OF A NIGHTMARE: BERLIN, 1942-1945. Translated from the German by Ewan Butler. New York: The John Day Co., 1966. 256p.

Account by a young woman living in Berlin during World War II, with two brothers fighting on the front. Assembled from diary entries, notebook jottings and letters.

1609. Kartini, Raden Adjeng, 1879-1904. Javanese daughter of the Regent, feminist, and founder of schools for women. DOOR DUISTERNIS TOT LICHT; GEDACHTEN OVER EN VOOR HET JAVAANSCHE VOLK VAN WIJLEN RADEN ADGENG KARTINI. Tweede Druk. S'Gravenhage: N.V. Eliectrische Drukkerij, "Luctor et Emergo," 1912. 371p.

1610. ------. LETTERS OF A JAVANESE PRINCESS. Translated from the original Dutch by Agnes Louise Symmers. With a foreword by Louis Couperus. New York: Alfred A. Knopf, 1920 and London: Duckworth, 1921. 310p.

Letters 1899-1904 written to her friends in the Netherlands on a variety of subjects, including women's rights and education. Contains only about two thirds of the letters printed in the original edition.

1611. ------. LETTERS OF A JAVANESE PRINCESS: RADEN ADJENG KARTINI. Translated from the Dutch by Agnes Louise Symmers. Edited by Hildred Geertz. Preface by Eleanor Roosevelt. New York: W.W. Norton & Co., 1964. 246p.

Includes expanded biographical information.

1612. ------. "Kartini: Letters from a Javanese Feminist, 1899-1902." Translated by E.M. Beekman. MASSACHUSETTS REVIEW 25:4 (Winter, 1984), 579-616.

1613. Kays, Melanie. American lesbian writer. "Scrambled Eggs: Feminist Notes and Musings." SINISTER WISDOM 7 (Fall, 1978), 51-56; 8 (Winter, 1979), 26-29; and 9 (Spring, 1979), 75-79.

Journal extracts.

Keats, Frances, afterwards Llanos. See: Brawne, Frances.

1614. Keays, Elizabeth Parke, 1890-1922. American frontier settler. THE SAGA OF "AUNTIE" STONE AND HER CABIN; ELIZABETH HICKOCK ROBBINS STONE (1801-1895) A PIONEER WOMAN WHO BUILT AND OWNED THE FIRST DWELLING, OPERATED THE FIRST HOTEL, BUILT THE FIRST FLOUR MILL AND ERECTED THE FIRST BRICK KILN IN THE CITY OF FORT COLLINS, COLORADO. WITH THE OVERLAND DIARY OF ELIZABETH PARKE KEAYS. Edited by Nolie Mumie. Centenary edition. Boulder, Colo: Johnson Publishing Co., 1964. 128p.

1615. Keller, Helen Adams, 1880-1968. American deaf-blind writer and advocate for the blind. HELEN KELLER'S JOURNAL, 1936-1937. Foreword by Nella Braddy. New York: Doubleday Doran, 1938. 313p.

Begins after the death of Anne Sullivan Macy, Keller's teacher, interpreter and companion. Record of a journey to Scotland she made with Polly Thompson, to find a quiet place in which to come to terms with grief and to adjust her life.

1616. ------. THE STORY OF MY LIFE. WITH HER LETTERS (1887-1901) AND A SUPPLEMENTARY ACCOUNT OF HER EDUCATION, INCLUDING PASSAGES FROM THE REPORTS AND LETTERS OF HER TEACHER, ANNIE MANSFIELD SULLIVAN. John Macy. Garden City, New York: Doubleday & Co., 1954. 382p.

Includes letters to a variety of people, including correspondence 1887-1891 with Anne Sullivan. Begins with a letter to a cousin written three months after the beginning of her instruction with Sullivan.

1617. Kelley-Wischnewetzky, Florence. American socialist and wife of Lazare Wischnewetzky. DEAR MR. ENGELS: UNPUBLISHED LETTERS, 1884-1894 OF FLORENCE KELLEY (WISCHNEWETZKY) TO FRIEDRICH ENGELS. Dorothy Rose Blumberg. New York: Tamiment Institute, 1964. 102-133p. Reprinted from LABOR HISTORY 5:2 (Spring, 1964), 103-133.

Contains quotations from forty of her letters.

1618. Kellog, Doris. American. CANTEENING UNDER TWO FLAGS: LETTERS OF DORIS KELLOG. East Aurora, N.Y.: The Roycrofters, 1920. 198p.

Account of volunteer work during World War I.

1619. Kemble, Frances Anne, 1809-1893. English-American actress, and wife of Georgia plantation owner Pierce Butler. JOURNAL OF FRANCES ANNE BUTLER. Philadelphia: Carey, Lee & Blanchard, 1835. 2 vols.

Journal August 1, 1832--July 17,1833, written during a theatrical tour of the U.S.

1620. ------. JOURNAL OF A RESIDENCE IN AMERICA. Paris: A. and W. Galignani and Co., (printed by Bourgogne and Martinet, Rue de Colombier) 1835. 326p.

Personal journal, written daily after "the fatigues of a laborious evening's duty at the Theatre." Describes a theatrical tour of the Atlantic Seaboard.

1621. ------. A YEAR OF CONSOLATION. London: Edward Moxon, 1847. 2 vols.

Diary of a year spent in Italy.

1622. ------. JOURNAL OF A RESIDENCE ON A GEORGIA PLANTATION IN 1838-1839. New York: Harper & Bros., 1863. 337p. London: Longmans, Green, Longman, Roberts and Green, 1863. (Printed by Spottiswoode & Co.) 434p.

Diary of life on a Southern plantation; particularly concerned with the living conditions of her husband's slaves. She vigorously and publicly denounced slavery, and her strongly held views on the subject eventually led to a separation from her husband.

1623. ------. RECORDS OF A GIRLHOOD. London: Beccles, 1878. New York, 1884. 605p.

Autobiography including extracts from her diary, 1831-1832 and letters to 1834.

1624. ------. RECORDS OF A LATER LIFE. London: R. Bentley, and New York: Henry Holt, 1882. 3 vols.

Letters written to "Harriet" or "H", 1834-1848.

1625. ------. FURTHER RECORDS, 1848-1883. A SERIES OF LETTERS, FORMING A SEQUEL TO "RECORDS OF A GIRLHOOD" AND "RECORDS OF A LATER LIFE." New York: Henry Holt & Co., 1891. 380p.

Letters to her daughter and friends, written at York Farm on the Butler Estate in Philadelphia, and during travels in Europe.

1626. ------. JOURNAL OF A RESIDENCE ON A GEORGIA PLANTATION IN 1838-1839. Edited by John Scott. New York: Alfred A. Knopf, 1961. 415p.

1627. ------. JOURNAL OF A RESIDENCE ON A GEORGIA PLANTATION IN 1838-1839. Foreword by Jean-Louis Brindamour. Chicago: Afro-American Press, 1969. 337p.

Reprint of the 1863 edition, with a new preface by Brindamour.

1628. ------. "On the Authenticity of Fanny Kemble's JOURNAL OF A RESIDENCE ON A GEORGIA PLANTATION IN 1838-1839." John A. Scott. JOURNAL OF NEGRO HISTORY (October, 1961), 233-242.

1629. ------. FANNY: THE AMERICAN KEMBLE: HER JOURNALS AND UNPUBLISHED LETTERS. Edited with annotations by Fanny Kemble Wister. Tallahassee: South Pass Press, 1972. 227p.

1630. ------. "Fanny Kemble's 'Vulgar' Journal." Clifford Ashby. PENNSYLVANIA MAGAZINE OF HISTORY AND BIOGRAPHY 98:1 (January, 1974), 58-66.

Discussion of the pre-publication rumours of the "scandalous" content of Kemble's Plantation journal, citing contemporary reviews denouncing the journal as vulgar and unladylike.

1631. Kennard, Dorothy Katharine Barclay, Lady. English. A ROUMANIAN DIARY, 1915, 1916, 1917. London: William Heinemann, 1917. 191p.

Short summary of Lady Kennard's impressions of Roumania several months previous to its entry into World War I, supplemented by letters from friends who remained in Roumania to work for the relief efforts.

1632. Kennedy, Margaret. English novelist. WHERE STANDS A WINGED SENTRY. New Haven, Conn.: Yale University Press, 1941. 251p.

Journal describes conditions in England during World War II, May, 1940--Fall, 1940. Not dated entry.

1633. Kennedy, Margaret, Lady, Later Lady Burnet, 1630-1685. LETTERS FROM LADY MARGARET KENNEDY TO JOHN, DUKE OF LAUDERDALE. Edinburgh: 1828. 107p. (Bannatyne Club Publications No. 24)

Correspondence with John, Duke of Lauderdale, 1661-1669. An appendix includes letters of Mary Pyeres or Peris, Margaret Kirkaldy, Mary Maitland, Anne Carnegie, Countess of Southesk, Lady Katherine, Viscountess Ranelaugh, Lady Anne Makenzie, Countess of Balcarres, Amelia Sophia, Marchioness of Athole, and Lady Margaret Lesley, Countess of Wemyss.

Kenreimonin Ukyo no Daibu. See: Daibu, Lady.

1634. Ketcham, Rebecca. American frontier settler. "From Ithaca to Clatsop Plains: Miss Ketcham's Journal of Travel." Edited by Leo M. Kaiser and Priscilla Knuth. OREGON HISTORICAL QUARTERLY 62:3 (September, 1961), 237-287 and 62:4 (December, 1961), 337-402.

1635. Kidder, Harriette Smith, 1816-1916. American teacher and wife of a Methodist Minister. "Reminiscences of Winchester, Connecticut, 1825: From the Diary of Harriette Smith Kidder." Edited by William J. Chute. CONNECTICUT HISTORICAL SOCIETY BULLETIN 29:1 (1964), 9-16.

1636. Kidder, Mary Bigelow, b. 1914. American wife of archeologist Dr. Alfred Kidder III. LEAVES FROM MY DIARY. Boston: Harvard University Press, 1932. 127p.

Diary of a Carribean cruise, through the Panama Canal to Acapulco and Baja California, May-June, 1931.

1637. ------. NO LIMITS BUT THE SKY: THE JOURNAL OF AN ARCHEOLOGIST'S WIFE IN PERU. Cambridge, Mass.: Harvard University Press, 1942. 233p.

A diary account of two archeological trips to Peru in 1937 and 1939, the second to excavate at a pre-Incaic site in the Andean highlands.

1638. Kilham, Hannah Spurr, 1774-1832. English Quaker. MEMOIR OF THE LATE HANNAH KILHAM, CHIEFLY COMPILED FROM HER JOURNAL. Edited by her daughter-in-law, Sarah Biller. London: Darton & Harvey, 1837. 506p.

Quaker diary, 1796-1832, including an account of missionary work in Sierra Leone.

1639. King, E. Augusta, "Mrs. Robert Moss King." English. THE DIARY OF A CIVILIAN'S WIFE IN INDIA, 1877-1882. London: Richard Bentley & Son, 1884.

Daily record of the life led by most Englishwomen in north India, written in the hope it may "interest those who have a sister or a daughter whose married life is cast, as mine was, in India."

1640. King, Harriet Lethbridge. Australian frontier pioneer. THE ADMIRAL'S WIFE: MRS. PHILLIP PARKER KING: A SELECTION OF LETTERS, 1817-1856. Edited by Dorothy Walsh. Melbourne: Hawthorne Press, 1967.

1641. Kingsbury, Electa May. American second wife of missionary Cyrus Kingsbury. "Two Letters from Pine Ridge Mission." Elizabeth H. Hunt. CHRONICLES OF OKLAHOMA 50:2 (Summer, 1972), 219-225.

Two letters to Mrs. Eliza Albert Wright, a friend

from the Mayhew Mission in Mississippi, dated February 28, 1842, and August 26, 1844.

1642. Kingsbury, Sallie D. Smith, ca. 1847-1871. American wife of Robert Taylor Kingsbury. "The Journal of Sallie D. Smith." Dan O. Jensen. MISSOURI HISTORICAL SOCIETY BULLETIN 20 (January, 1964), 124-145.

Diary of a trip from Howard County, Missouri, to Southern Kentucky, June-October, 1868.

1643. Kingsford, Anna Bonus, 1846-1888. English Christian Scientist and religious author. ANNA KINGSFORD: HER LIFE, LETTERS, DIARY AND WORK. By her collaborator, E. Maitland. London: G. Redway, 1896. 2 vols.

Religious diary, 1881-1887.

1644. Kinsman, Rebecca Chase. American Quaker and wife of Nathaniel Kinsman, a Salem merchant with connections in China. "Life in Macao in the 1840's: Letters of Rebecca Chase Kinsman to Her Family in Salem." From the Collection of Mrs. Rebecca Kinsman Munroe. ESSEX INSTITUTE HISTORICAL COLLECTIONS 86:1 (January, 1950), 15-40 and 86:2 (April, 1950), 106-107.

Letters home from China, November 4--December 16, 1843.

1645. ------. "The American Mission to China: Letters and Diary of Rebecca Kinsman of Salem." ESSEX INSTITUTE HISTORICAL COLLECTIONS 86:2 (April, 1950), 108-143.

Letters and diary extracts February 26--September, 1844 describe the first Diplomatic Mission of Caleb Cushing, which resulted in the Treaty of 1844.

1646. ------. "The Daily Life of Rebecca Chase Kinsman." Edited by Mrs. Frederick C. Monroe. ESSEX INSTITUTE HISTORICAL COLLECTIONS 86:3 (July, 1950), 257-284 and 86:4 (October, 1950), 311-330.

Letters January 18--August 20, 1844 and October 7, 1844--January 21,1845 describe daily life in China.

1647. ------. "The Daily Life of Mrs. Nathaniel Kinsman in Macao, China: Excerpts from Letters of 1845." Contributed by Mrs. Frederick Monroe. ESSEX INSTITUTE HISTORICAL COLLECTIONS 87:2 (April, 1951), 114-149.

Letters from China continued, February 2--October 26, 1845.

1648. ------. "The Daily Life of Mrs. Nathaniel Kinsman on a Trip to Manila." Contributed by Mrs. Frederick Monroe. ESSEX HISTORICAL COLLECTIONS 87:3 (July, 1951), 269-305.

Letters from the Orient continued, November 1, 1845--February 15, 1846.

1649. ------. "The Daily Life of Mrs. Nathaniel Kinsman in China, 1846." Contributed by Mrs. Frederick Monroe. ESSEX INSTITUTE HISTORICAL COLLECTIONS 87:4 (October, 1951), 388-409 and 88:1 (January, 1952), 48-99.

Letters from China continued, February 24--August 24, 1846 and September 19, 1846--May 16, 1847, including an account of the death of her husband and the return voyage to Salem.

1650. Kirchner, Adelaide Rosalind. American. A FLAG FOR CUBA: PEN SKETCHES OF A RECENT TRIP ACROSS THE GULF OF MEXICO TO THE ISLAND OF CUBA. New York: Mershon, 1897. 177p.

Travel Diary, March 6--16, 1897.

1651. Kirk, Lydia Chapin. American wife of Alan Goodrich Kirk, Ambassador to Russia. POSTMARKED MOSCOW. New York: Charles Scribner's Sons, 1952. 278p.

Social letters of a diplomat's wife, dated 1949-1951, describe life in Moscow.

1652. Kitman, Suzy. American. "Diary of a Mad 12-Year-Old, 1972." MS. MAGAZINE 1:3 (September, 1972), 62-63, 123. Also in SEXISM AND YOUTH, Compiled by

Diane Gersoni. New York: R.R. Bowker, 1974. p.78-82.

Extracts from the diary of a young feminist.

1653. Klarsfeld, Beate. German political activist. PARTOUT OU ILS SERONT! Paris: J.C. Lattes--Editions Speciale, 1972.

1654. ------. WHEREVER THEY MAY BE! New York: The Vanguard Press, 1975.

An autobiographical record of her work, containing excerpts from her journals. With her husband Serge Klarsfeld, she has worked to prevent former Nazi leaders from obtaining positions in the French and German governments, and to bring Nazi war criminals to trial.

1655. Knapp, Augusta Murray Spring, 1822-1885. American frontier settler. GIDEON LEE KNAPP AND AUGUSTA MURRAY SPRING HIS WIFE: EXTRACTS FROM LETTERS AND JOURNAL. Edited by one of their Grandsons. New York: privately printed, 1909. 66p.

1656. Knight, Amelia Stewart. American frontier settler. "Diary of Mrs. Amelia Stewart Knight, an Oregon Pioneer of 1853." TRANSACTIONS OF THE OREGON PIONEER ASSOCIATION 56 (1928), 38-53.

Overland diary of the journey from Iowa to Oregon, 1853. When she began the journey, she was in the first trimester of pregnancy with her eighth child; she gave birth in Oregon, still en route to her destination. William Matthews considers this is one of the best among pioneer diaries written by women.

1657. Knight, Sarah Kemble, 1666-1727. American colonial businesswoman. THE JOURNALS OF SARAH KNIGHT AND REVEREND MR. BUCKINGHAM. FROM THE ORIGINAL MANUSCRIPTS. Edited by Theodore Dwight, Jr. New York: Wilder and Campbell, 1825. 129p.

Diary October 2, 1704--January 6, 1705 describes a trip from Boston to Connecticut and back. Harriet

Forbes calls Madame Knight "a woman of superior intelligence and an acute observer."

1658. ------. "Travelling in America." BLACKWOOD'S EDINBURGH MAGAZINE 18 (October, 1825), 422-432. Reprinted in THE MUSEUM OF FOREIGN LITERATURE AND SCIENCE 8 (1826), 30-38.

Extracts from Madame Knight's journal.

1659. ------. "Madame Knight: Her Diary and Times." Edited by Anson Titus. BOSTON: SOCIETY PUBLICATIONS 9: (1912), 99-126.

1660. ------. "The Editing and Publishing of the JOURNAL OF MADAME KNIGHT." Alan Margolies. PAPERS OF THE BIBLIOGRAPHIC SOCIETY OF AMERICA 58:1 (January, 1964), 25-32.

Corrects many errors concerning the early history of the publication of the JOURNAL. Notes that the text of the first edition, published by Theodore Dwight, Jr., is the earliest surviving form of the journal; the original manuscript was destroyed sometime prior to 1846.

1661. ------. THE JOURNAL OF MADAME KNIGHT. Introduction by Malcolm Freiberg. Boston: David R. Godine, 1972. 39p.

1662. Knight, Sophia, or Sofka. WINDOW ON SHANGHAI: LETTERS FROM CHINA, 1965-1967. With a foreword by Dr. Joseph Needham. London: Andre Deutsch, 1967. 256p.

Letters to her mother. Knight taught English for two years in Shanghai.

1663. Knightley, Louisa Mary Bawater Knightley, Baroness, 1842-1913. English reformer,suffragist, and Lady-In-Waiting to Queen Victoria. THE JOURNALS OF LADY KNIGHTLEY OF FAWSLEY, 1856-1884. Edited by Julia Cartwright (Mrs. Ady). London: John Murray, 1916. 403p.

Describes life at court and her work in the woman

suffrage and other reform movements. Edited from a journal Lady Knightley began at age fourteen comprising over sixty volumes covering fifty-seven years, 1856-1913. She wrote with at least half an eye towards publication; she mentions studying the diaries of Marie Bashkirtseff and the letters of Lady Lyttleton with the object of improving her journal.

1664. Koller, Alice. American. AN UNKNOWN WOMAN: A JOURNEY TO SELF DISCOVERY. New York: Holt, Rinehart and Winston, 1981. 258p.

Diary of self-discovery, written during three months of self-exile on the island of Nantucket.

1665. Köllwitz, Kathë Schmidt, 1867-1945. German graphic artist and sculptor. KATHE KÖLLWITZ: TAGEBUCHBLÄTTER UND BRIEFE. Herausgegeben von Hans Köllwitz. Berlin: Gebr. Mann Verlag, 1948. 192p.

Diary September 18, 1909--May, 1943; letters May, 1907--April 16, 1945.

1666. ------. THE DIARY AND LETTERS OF KATHË KÖLLWITZ. Edited by Hans Kollwitz. Translated from the German by Richard and Clara Winston. Chicago: Henry Regnery, 1955. 200p.

1667. ------. "Kathë Köllwitz: Role Model for the Older Woman." Elizabeth R. Curry. CHRYSALIS: A MAGAZINE OF WOMEN'S CULTURE 7 (1979), 55-69.

Critical study of Köllwitz's life and work, focusing on the relationship between her later self-portraits and her diary, begun in 1909 at the age of forty-two.

1668. Koren, Else Elisabeth Hysing, 1832-1918. Norwegian- American frontier settler and minister's wife. THE DIARY OF ELISABETH KOREN, 1853-1855. Translated and edited by David T. Nelson. Northfield: Minn.: Norwegian-American Historical Association, 1955. 381p. Reprinted, New York: Arno Press, 1979.

Diary of a voyage across the Atlantic, the journey to Iowa, and life there with her husband the Reverend Ulrik Vilhelm Koren, a Minister to Norwegian immigrants. Provides a portrait of the Norwegian mission and community, and of life on the frontier.

1669. Kosterina, Nina Alekseevna, 1921-1941. Russian student who fought as a soldier against the Nazis in World War II. She was killed in action. THE DIARY OF NINA KOSTERINA. Translated from the Russian by Mirra Ginsburg. New York: Crown Publishers, 1968. 188p.

Begins in 1936 as a school diary; Kosterina confides her feelings about friends, falling in love, arguments with her parents. Takes a more serious turn as her family is threatened by the Stalinists and her father and an uncle are imprisoned. Diary ends November 14, 1941, on the eve of her departure to the front.

1670. Kraft, Barbara. American. THE RESTLESS SPIRIT: JOURNAL OF A GEMINI. Preface by Anais Nin. Millbrae, Calif.: Les Femmes Publications, 1976. 204p.

1671. Krieger, Susan. American lesbian writer. "Trip to the Amza-Borrego Desert: March 19-28." CONDITIONS 1 (April, 1977), 82-89.

Journal excerpt.

1672. Kristina, Queen of Sweden, 1626-1689. LETTRES CHOISIES DE CHRISTINE, REINE DE SUÈDE. À DESCARTES, GASSENDI, GROTIUS, PASCAL, BAYLE, AU PRINCE DE CONDÉ, AU DUC D'ORLÉANS, REGENT, À LOUIS XIV, À LA COMTESSE DE SPARRE, À LA COMTESSE DE BROGI, &tc. AVEC LA MORT TRAGIQUE DE MONADESKI, SON GRAND-ECUYER. M.L.A. Villefranche. Chez Hardi Filocrate, 1759. 2 vols. in One.

1673. ------. CHRISTINE DE SUÈDE ET LE CARDINAL AZZOLINO: LETTRES INÉDITES (1666-1668). Avec une inroduction et des notes par le Baron de Bildt. Paris: Éditions Plon, Nourrit, 1899. 514p.

Letters to Cardinal Decio Azzolini.

1674. Kroenenberg, Susan. American lesbian writer. "Seripbos: Based on a Journal Kept in 1975." CONDITIONS 2 (April, 1977), 82-89.

1675. Kyger, Joanne. American poet. THE JAPAN AND INDIA JOURNALS, 1960-1964. Bolinas, Calif.: Timbouctou Books, 1981. 280p.

1676. L.M., pseud. for Ida Constance Baker, b.1888. English. KATHERINE MANSFIELD: THE MEMORIES OF L.M. New York: Taplinger Press, 1972. 240p.

Includes correspondence with Mansfield, 1916-1923, and extracts from L.M.'s diary of Mansfield's last illness and death, 1923.

1677. Labadie, Cecilia, 1839-1873. American. "Cecilia Labadie, Diary Fragment, January 29, 1863--February 5, 1863." Edited by Marjorie Logan Williams. TEXANA 10:3 (1972), 273-283.

1678. Ladron de Guevara, Matilde. Chilean author. ADIOS AL CANAVERAL: DIARIO DE UNA MUJER EN CUBA. 2nd ed. Buenos Aires: Editorial Goyanarte, 1962. 290p.

Diary April 5--September, 1961, describes the U.S. invasion of Cuba.

1679. La Fayette, Madame de (Marie Madeleine Pioche de la Vergne, Comtesse de La Fayette), 1634-1693. French author and friend of Madame de Sévigné. LETTRES DE MARIE-MADELEINE PIOCHE DE LA VERGNE, COMTESSE DE LA FAYETTE ET DE GILLES MENAGE. Publiées, d'après les originaux, avec une introduction, des notes et un index par H. Ashton. Liverpool: The University Press of Liverpool, and London: Hodder & Stoughton, 1924. 200p.

1680. ------. CORRESPONDANCE. Editée d'après les travaux de Andre Beaunier. Paris: Gallimard, 1942. 2 vols.

1681. Lagerlöf, Selma Ottiliana Lovisa, 1858-1940. Swedish author. THE DIARY OF SELMA LAGERLÖF.

Translated by Velma Swanston Howard. Illustrated by Johan Bull. New York: Doubleday Doran & Co., 1936. 240p. Reprinted by Kraus Reprint, 1975.

Diary of a trip to Stockholm undertaken at age fifteen in order to be treated for a disabling ailment of the hip. Dated January 20--May 13, 1873.

1682. ------. BREV. I Urval Utg. av Ying Toijer-Nilsson. Lund: Gleerup, 1967-1969. 2 vols.

Correspondence, 1871-1940.

1683. La Grange, Clementine de Chaumont-Quitry, Baronne de, b. 1864. French patriot. OPEN HOUSE IN FLANDERS, 1914-1918: CHÂTEAU DE LA MOTTE AU BOIS. Baroness Ernest de la Grange. Translated from the unpublished French by Melanie Lind. With an introduction by Field-Marshal the Viscount Allenby, G.C.B., etc. New York: Frederick A. Stokes Co., 1930. 399p.

Baroness la Grange kept her historical chateau in the Forest of Neippe open to French and British soldiers during World War I. Lively and intelligent diary dated July, 1914--July 1918 describes the progress of the War, everyday life at the Chateau, and the visitors there.

1684. Lainer Von Lainsheim, Grete (Gretchen). Viennese. TAGEBÜCH EINES HALBWUCHSIGEN MADCHENS. Herausgegeben von Dr. Hermine Hug-Helmuth. Leipzig: Dritte Auflage, Quellenschriften zur Seelischen Entwicklung, No. 1. 1919.

1685. ------. A YOUNG GIRL'S DIARY. Prefaced with a letter by Sigmund Freud. New York: Barnes & Noble/ Unwin Books, 1961. 176p.

1686. Laing, Caroline Hyde Butler, 1804-1892. American. A FAMILY HERITAGE: LETTERS AND JOURNALS OF CAROLINE HYDE BUTLER LAING, 1804-1892. Edited by Edith Nevill Smythe Ward. East Orange, N.J.: Abbey Printers, 1957. 161p.

1687. Lamartine, Alix de Roys de, 1766-1829. French. LE JOURNAL DE MADAME DE LAMARTINE (MÈRE D'ALPHONSE DE LAMARTINE) 1801-1829. Présentée et annotée par Michel Domange. Paris: Lettres Modernes, 1983.

Volume 1: 1801-1809.

1688. Lamb, Mary Ann, 1764-1847. English literary figure and sister of English historian Charles Lamb. MARY AND CHARLES LAMB: POEMS, LETTERS AND REMAINS. Now first collected, with reminiscences and notes by W. Carew Hazlitt. London: Chatto & Windus, 1874. 51, 307, 31p.

Chapter One contains letters and poems of Mary Lamb.

1689. ------. THE LETTERS OF CHARLES LAMB, TO WHICH ARE ADDED, THOSE OF HIS SISTER MARY LAMB. Edited by E.V. Lucas. New Haven, Conn.: Yale University Press, and London: J.M. Dent & Sons, 1935. 3 vols.

Correspondence of Mary Lamb covers the period 1803-1842, and includes letters to Sarah Stoddart, Dorothy Wordsworth, Sarah Hazlitt, and others. The editor is chiefly concerned with the correspondence of Charles Lamb; Mary Lamb is not mentioned in the introduction.

1690. ------. THE LETTERS OF CHARLES AND MARY LAMB. VOLUME TWO: 1801-1809. Edited with an introduction by Edwin W. Marrs, Jr. Ithaca, N.Y.: Cornell University Press, 1976.

Definitive edition. Volume One contains the letters of Charles Lamb only. Volume Two contains letters of Mary Lamb.

1691. Lamb, Patricia Frazer and Kathryn Joyce Hohlwein. Americans. TOUCHSTONES: LETTERS BETWEEN TWO WOMEN, 1953-1964. New York: Harper & Row, 1983. 330p.

Letters between two women who met at the

University of Utah in the early 1950's. Lamb married a specialist in tropical medicine and followed him to Tanganyika; Hohlwein, a poet, married a German artist and lived in Beirut, Scotland and the U.S. As their lives diverged, their appoaches to life also changed, and the correspondence ended in 1964.

1692. Lamballe, Marie Thérèse Louise de Savoie de Carignan, Princesse de, 1749-1792. MEMOIRS RELATIFS A LA FAMILLE ROYALE DE FRANCE PENDANT LA REVOLUTION, PUBLIÉES D'APRÈS LE JOURNAL, LES LETTRES ET LES ENTRETIENS DE LA PRINCESSE DE LAMBALLE. Paris, 1826. 2 vols.

1693. ------. SECRET MEMOIRS OF PRINCESS LAMBALLE: BEING HER JOURNALS, LETTERS, AND CONVERSATIONS DURING HER CONFIDENTIAL RELATIONS WITH MARIE ANTOINETTE. Edited and annotated by Catherine Hyde, Marquise de Gouvion Broglie Scolari. With a special introduction by Oliver H.G. Leigh. Washington: M.W. Dunne, 1901. 356p.

1694. Lambert, Anne Thérèse de Marguenat de Courcelles, Marquise de, 1647-1733. French intellectual. MEMOIRS ET CORRESPONDANCE. Publiées d'après les manuscrits, avec une notice des notes et les pieces justificatives par M. Paul Pougin. Paris: P. Jannet, 1855. 233p.

1695. Lamson, Mary Swift, 1822-1909. American educator. THE FIRST STATE NORMAL SCHOOL IN AMERICA: THE JOURNALS OF CYRUS PIERCE AND MARY SWIFT. With an introduction by Arthur O. Norton. Cambridge, Mass.: Harvard University Press, and London: Humphrey Milford, Oxford University Press, 1926.

1696. Lane, Emma Durant, 1852-1922. American diarist. EMMA LANE DURANT: HER DIARIES AND MEMOIRS, 1852-1922. ST. CHARLES, ILLINOIS, 1870-1922. Edited by Alexander G. Rose, with biographical notes and annotations. Compiled with the assistance of Constance Dutton Heacox Mikiska, Lorraine E. Miller and Norma C. Shearer. Baltimore: Rose, 1978. 163p.

1697. Lane, Rose Wilder, 1866-1968. American author

and daughter of Laura Ingalls Wilder. THE LADY AND THE TYCOON: LETTERS OF ROSE WILDER LANE AND JASPER CRANE. Edited by Roger Lea MacBride. Caldwell, Idaho: The Caxton Printers, 1973. 401p.

Correspondence spanning twenty years with scholar and Du Pont executive Jasper Crane.

1698. ------. TRAVELS WITH ZENOBIA: PARIS TO ALBANIA BY MODEL T. FORD. A JOURNAL. Edited by William Holtz. Columbia: University of Missouri Press, 1983. 128p.

Journal of a 1926 automobile trip taken with her friend Helen Dore Boylston.

1699. Langgasser, Elisabeth, 1899-1950. German author. SOVIEL BERAUSCHENDE VERGANGLICHKEIT. BRIEFE, 1926-1950. Hamburg: Claussen Verlag, 1954. 251p. Reprinted, Frankfurt: Ullstein, 1981. 251p.

1700. Langton, Anne, 1804-1893. English-born settler in Canada. LANGTON RECORDS. JOURNALS AND LETTERS FROM CANADA, 1837-1846. [BY ANNE LANGTON AND OTHERS]. Preface by Ellen Josephine Philips. Edinburgh: Clark, 1904. 369p. Printed for private circulation only.

1701. ------. A GENTLEWOMAN IN UPPER CANADA: THE JOURNALS OF ANNE LANGTON. Edited by H.H. Langton. Toronto: Clarke Irwin, 1950. 249p. 2nd edition, 1964. 207p.

1702. Lapinski, Susan. IN A FAMILY WAY: A HUSBAND AND WIFE'S DIARY OF A PREGNANCY, BIRTH, AND THE FIRST YEAR OF PARENTHOOD. Susan Lapinski and Michael de Courcy Hinds. Boston: Little, Brown & Co., 1982. 229p.

1703. Larcom, Lucy, 1824-1893. American millworker, author, teacher, editor and poet. LUCY LARCOM: HER LIFE, LETTERS AND DIARY. Daniel Dulany Addison. Boston and New York: Houghton Mifflin Co., and Cambridge, England: The Riverside Press, 1894. 295p.

Diary fragments which, owing to their sporadic

nature, "have not the value of a continuous life-history, but are interesting as records of phases of her thoughts and...reflect vividly the conditions in which she lived"; and letters from 1846 on, which trace her life as a teacher and author.

1704. ------. LETTERS OF LUCY LARCOM TO THE WHITTIERS. Edited by Grace F. Shepard. Baltimore: The Southworth Press, 1930. 20p. Reprinted from THE NEW ENGLAND QUARTERLY 3:3 (1930).

1705. ------. "Lucy Larcom Letters. Extracts from the Collection in the Library of the Essex Institute." ESSEX INSTITUTE HISTORICAL COLLECTIONS 68 (1932), 257-279.

1706. Lathrop, Abigail Alexander Pomeroy, 1815-1861. American resident of Northampton, Massachusetts. THE LETTERS OF JOSEPH STODDARD LATHROP AND ABIGAIL ALEXANDER POMEROY, 1837-1838. No Place: Privately Printed for Lucy Whitelaw Rexford, 1959.

1707. La Touche, Maria, b.1824. Irish poet and mother of Rose La Touche. THE LETTERS OF A NOBLE WOMAN (MRS. LA TOUCHE OF HARRISTOWN). Edited by Margaret Ferrier Young. London: George Allen & Sons, 1908. 251p.

Correspondence 1858-1906 with Rose La Touche, John Ruskin, and others.

1708. La Touche, Rose Lucy, d. 1875. Irish fiancee of John Ruskin; she died before they could be married. JOHN RUSKIN AND ROSE LA TOUCHE: HER UNPUBLISHED DIARIES OF 1861 AND 1867. Introduced and edited by Van Akin Burd. London: Oxford University Press, 1979. 192p.

Journal of travel in France and Italy, March 7--April 1, 1861, and autobiography and diary for January 1--February 24, 1867. Prefaced by an essay concerning the background of the La Touche- Ruskin papers. According to Burd, Ruskin's first editor, his biographer, his executors, and his later editors deliberately suppressed information about Ruskin's relationship with La Touche.

1709. Laurens, Caroline Olivia. American. "Journal of a Visit to Greenville from Charleston in the Summer of 1825." Edited by Louise C. King. SOUTH CAROLINA HISTORICAL MAGAZINE 72:3 (1971), 164-173, and 72:4 (1971), 220-223.

Travel diary, May 23--November 11, 1825.

1710. Lauterbach, Judith, 1926-1950. JUDITH LAUTERBACH'S LETTERS TO HER FATHER. Selected by Leo Lauterbach. Jerusalem, 1957. 161p.

1711. Lavergne, Julie Dzaneaux, 1823-1886. CORRESPONDANCE DE MADAME JULIE LAVERGNE. Recueillie par son fils Joseph Lavergne. Paris: Tafflin-Lefort, 1924. 2 vols.

Letters 1832-1886.

1712. Lawrence, Frieda Emma Johanna, Freiin von Richthofen, 1879-1956. German-English literary figure and wife of D.H. Lawrence. NOT I BUT THE WIND. Santa Fe, N. Mex.: Privately printed by The Rydal Press, 1934. 311p. New York: Viking Press/Curtis Brown, 1934. 297p.

Memoirs and letters.

1713. ------. THE MEMOIRS AND CORRESPONDENCE. Edited by E.W. Tedlock, Jr. London: William Heinemann, 1961. 436p. New York: Alfred A. Knopf, 1964. 481p.

Unfinished Memoir, supplemented with extracts from her correspondence.

1714. ------. FRIEDA LAWRENCE AND HER CIRCLE. LETTERS FROM, TO, AND ABOUT FRIEDA LAWRENCE. Edited by Harry T. Moore and Dale B. Montague. London and Basingstoke: The Macmillan Press, 1981. 145p.

Letters between Frieda Lawrence and Edward W. Titus, 1930-1932; between Lawrence and Caresse Crosby, 1929-1930; to Martha Gordon Crotch, 1930-1935; between Lawrence and Richard Aldington, 1932-1956; and to Mrs. Hazel Guggenheim McKinley, 1951.

1715. Lawrence, Honoria Marshall, Lady, 1808-1854. English wife of Soldier-Statesman and philanthropist Henry Lawrence of Lucknow. THE JOURNALS OF HONORIA LAWRENCE: INDIA OBSERVED, 1837-1854. Edited by Lawrence and Audrey Woodiwiss. London: Hodder & Stoughton, 1980. 253p.

Describes life in British India.

1716. Lawrence, Love, 1754-1803. American. "Letters of An American Woman Sailing for England in 1784." Edith W. Linn. JOURNAL OF AMERICAN HISTORY 3 (1909), 441-446.

1717. Lawrence, Mary Chipman, 1827-1906. American wife of a whaling merchant. THE CAPTAIN'S BEST MATE: THE JOURNAL OF MARY CHIPMAN LAWRENCE ON THE WHALER ADDISON, 1856-1860. Edited by Stanton Garner. Providence, R.I.: Brown University Press, 1966. 311p.

Sea diary.

1718. Lazarus, Emma, 1849-1887. American Jewish author and poet, best known as the author of "The New Colossus," inscribed on the pedestal of the Statue of Liberty. THE LETTERS OF EMMA LAZARUS, 1868-1885. Edited with an introduction by Morris U. Schappes. New York: New York Public Library, 1949. 68p.

1719. Lazarus, Rachel Mordecai, 1788-1838. American Jewish educator. THE EDUCATION OF THE HEART: THE CORRESPONDENCE OF RACHEL MORDECAI LAZARUS AND MARIA EDGEWORTH. Edited and introduction by Edgar E. MacDonald. Chapel Hill, N.C.: University of North Carolina Press, 1977. 341p.

Correspondence 1815-1838. The correspondence began with a letter from Lazarus to Edgeworth, respectfully but firmly criticizing Edgeworth's use of a derogatory Jewish stereotype--an evil character named Mordecai--in her novel THE ABSENTEE (1812). Their literary exchange grew into a friendship which lasted until Lazarus's death, but they never met.

1720. Leach, Christina. German-American colonist. "Selections from the Diary of Christina Leach, of Kingsessing, 1765-1796." Edited by Robert H. Hinckley. PENNSYLVANIA MAGAZINE OF HISTORY AND BIOGRAPHY 35:3 (1911), 343-349.

Short extracts describe domestic affairs, family business, community gossip, and news of battles. She had sons fighting in the Revolution; her house was plundered by the British, and her father taken prisoner (later parolled).

1721. Leadbeater, Mary Shackelton, 1758-1826. Irish Quaker, related to most of the leading Quaker families of Ireland. "A Tour Through Part of England, by Mary Shackleton, in the Year 1784." PENNSYLVANIA MAGAZINE OF HISTORY AND BIOGRAPHY 40:2 (1916), 129-160.

Diary of a trip from Ireland to England, with her father, Abraham Shackleton, to visit Edmund Burke, a former pupil and lifetime friend of her father.

1722. ------. "Journal." JOURNAL OF THE FRIENDS HISTORICAL SOCIETY 37 (1940), 25-28.

1723. Le Broq, Elisabeth. French. CAPTIVE: JOURNAL D'UNE FRANÇAISE EN ALLEMAGNE PENDANT LA GUERRE, 1914-1918. Paris: C. Bohrer, 1921. 481p.

1724. Le Conte, Caroline Eaton, 1863-1945. American. YO SEMITE 1878: ADVENTURES OF N.&C. JOURNAL AND DRAWINGS BY CARRIE E. LE CONTE. Introduction to "C." by Susanna B. Dakin. San Francisco: The Book Club of California, 1964. 98p. Limited edition of 450 copies.

1725. LeConte, Emma, later Furman, b. 1847. American farmer. WHEN THE WORLD ENDED: THE DIARY OF EMMA LECONTE. Edited by Earl Schenck Miers. New York: Oxford University Press, 1957.

1726. ------. "A Righteous Aim: Emma LeConte Furman's 1918 Diary." Edited by Lester D. Stephens. GEORGIA HISTORICAL QUARTERLY 62:3 (Fall, 1978), 213-224.

Extracts January--August, 1918, from the diary of an astute observer, describing her work in the Red Cross, and giving her observations on military events, the Germans, and affairs on the home front, including the effect of war propaganda on Americans.

1727. Lécouvreur, Adrienne, 1692-1730. French actress. ADRIENNE LECOUVREUR, D'APRÈS SA CORRESPONDANCE. Gustave Larroumet. Paris: Chamerot et Renouard, 1892. 82p.

1728. ------. LETTRES DE ADRIENNE LÉCOUVREUR. Réunies pour la première fois et publiées avec notes, étude biographique, des documents inédites tires des archives de la Comedie. Des minutiers de notaires et des papiers de la Bastille, portrait et fac-similé par Georges Monval. Paris: Éditions Plon, Nourrit, 1892. 302p.

1729. ------. ADRIENNE LÉCOUVREUR ET MAURICE DE SAXE, LEURS LETTRES D'AMOUR. Marquis d'Argenson [Maurice Charles Marc René de Voyer de Paulmy, Marquis d'Argenson]. Paris: A. Messein, 1926. 334p.

1730. Lee, Andrea. American. RUSSIAN JOURNAL. New York: Random House, 1981. 239p.

Lee went to Russia in 1978 with her husband, Tom Lee, then a Harvard doctoral candidate in Russian history. Half of the entries were written during the ten months she lived in Russia, 1978-1979, and half were written later in America, from notes and fragments.

1731. Lee, Anna Maria Pittman, 1803-1838. American missionary. LIFE AND LETTERS OF MRS. JASON LEE, FIRST WIFE OF REVEREND JASON LEE OF THE OREGON MISSION. Theressa Gay. Portland, Ore.: Metropolitan Press, 1936. 224p.

1732. Lee, Laurel. American. LAUREL LEE'S JOURNAL (COMBINING "WALKING THROUGH THE FIRE" AND "SIGNS OF SPRING"). Chappaqua, New York: Christian Herald Books, 1980. 118p.

Combines two journals previously published

separately. Lee was diagnosed with Hodgkins' disease while pregnant with her third child; journal describes treatment, the birth of a healthy child and the remission of the disease.

1733. Lee, Lucinda, later Orr. American. JOURNAL OF A YOUNG LADY OF VIRGINIA. Edited by Emily V. Mason. Baltimore: Published for the Benefit of the Lee Memorial Association of Richmond by J. Murphy & Co., 1871. 56p.

1734. Lee, Margaret Cabot, 1866-1920. American kindergarten teacher and charitable worker. LETTERS AND DIARIES OF MARGARET CABOT LEE. Extracts selected by her sisters, Marian C. Putnam and Amy W. Cabot, with a biographical sketch by her husband, Joseph Lee. No Place: Privately Printed, 1923. 401p.

Extracts from letters and diaries 1881-1920 describe travel and social life. Begins with an adolescent diary.

1735. Lee, Mary Charlton. American. "An Extract from the Journal of Mrs. Hugh Holmes Lee of Winchester, Virginia, May 23-31, 1862." Edited by Porter C.A. Hopkins. MARYLAND HISTORY MAGAZINE (December, 1958), 380-393.

Civil War diary.

1736. Lee, Mary Jackson, 1783-1860. American. HENRY AND MARY LEE: LETTERS AND JOURNALS. WITH OTHER FAMILY LETTERS. Prepared by their granddaughter (Frances Rollins Morse). Boston: T. Todd Co., Printers, 1926. 423p.

Diary January, 1813--April, 1816.

1737. Le Fanu, Elizabeth Sheridan, 1758-1837. Irish sister of Thomas Sheridan. BETSY SHERIDAN'S JOURNAL: LETTERS FROM SHERIDAN'S SISTER, 1784-1786 AND 1788-1790. Edited by William Le Fanu. New Brunswick, N.J.: Rutgers University Press, 1960. 223p

Journal sent as weekly letters from England to her sister Alicia in Dublin.

1738. Le Grand, Julia Ellen, later Waitz, 1829-1875. American Civil War diarist. THE JOURNAL OF JULIA LE GRAND: NEW ORLEANS, 1862-1863. Edited by Kate M. Rowland and Mrs. M.L. Croxall. Richmond, Va.: Everett Waddey, 1911. 318p.

Diary December 1, 1861--April 8, 1863, recording her family's flight from New Orleans after the fall of the city; refugee existence in Mississippi, Georgia, Alabama, and Florida; and ultimate settlement in Galveston, Texas, where other members of the family lived.

1739. Le Guiner, Jeanne. French. LETTERS FROM FRANCE. Translated by H.M.C. Boston: Houghton Mifflin, and Cambridge, England: The Riverside Press, 1916. 100p.

Letters September 23, 1914--December 31, 1915. Le Guiner was studying at the Sorbonne when war broke out, and would have liked to devote all her time to war work, but her parents insisted she continue her studies. Letters describe study and, during her vacations, nursing and relief work.

1740. Leitch, Mary, and Margaret W. Leitch. American missionaries to Ceylon. SEVEN YEARS IN CEYLON: STORIES OF MISSIONARY LIFE. New York: American Tract Society, 1890. 170p.

Selection of letters, February, 1880--April, 1886, followed by stories of missionary life, pleas for aid, and sermons.

1741. Lenclos or L'Enclos, Anne de, called Ninon de, b. 1615. French author, courtesan and salonist. CORRESPONDANCE AUTHENTIQUE DE NINON DE LENCLOS, COMPRENANT UN GRAND NOMBRE DE LETTRES INÉDITES, ET SUIVIE DE LA COQUETTE VENGÉE. Avec une introduction et des notes, par Emile Colombey (pseud.). Paris: Éditions Dentu, 1886. 332p.

1742. ------. NINON DE LENCLOS: ÉDITION DÉFINITIVE. Portraits et documents inédits. Emile Magné. Émile-Paul, 1948. 367p.

1743. Léneru, Marie, 1875-1918. French composer; she became deaf. JOURNAL DE MARIE LÉNERU. Avec une Préface de François de Curel. Paris: G. Cres, 1921. 2 vols.

1744. ------. JOURNAL OF MARIE LÉNERU. Translated by William Aspenwall Bradley. Introduction by François de Curel. New York: Macmillan, 1923. 295p.

1745. ------. MARIE LÉNERU. SA VIE, SON JOURNAL, SON OEUVRE. These pour le Doctorat d'Université. Paris: Société Française d'Éditions Litteraires et Techniques, 1932. 281p.

1746. ------. JOURNAL. PRÉCÉDÉ DU JOURNAL D'ENFANCE. Éditions complete établie par Fernande Dauriac. Paris: Grasset, 1945. 401p.

Includes her childhood diary, 1886-1890, and her later journal, 1893-1918.

Lennox, Sarah, Lady: See Napier, Sarah Lennox Bunbury.

1747. Lensing, Elise, 1804-1854. German author. BRIEFE AN FRIEDRICH UND CHRISTINE HEBBEL. Herausgegeben in auftrage des Hebbel-Museums in Wesselburen von Rudolf Kardel. Berlin and Leipzig: B. Behr/F. Feddersen, 1928. 214p.

1748. Lerner, Gerda, b. 1920. Austrian-American historian. A DEATH OF ONE'S OWN. New York: Simon & Schuster, 1978. New York: Harper & Row/Harper Colophon Books, 1980. 269p.

Lerner writes of her husband's death, caused by a malignant brain tumor, through reflective narrative, poetry, and journal entries.

1749. Lesley, Susan Inches Lyman, 1823-1904. American abolitionist. RECOLLECTIONS OF MY MOTHER. Anne Jean Lyman. Boston: Privately printed by the Press of Geo. H. Ellis, 1886.

Biography followed by extracts from her

correspondence with Ralph Waldo Emerson, John Greenleaf Whittier, and other reformers. Reprint of an earlier edition, (1876) with some letters omitted and new ones added.

1750. ------. LIFE AND LETTERS OF PETER AND SUSAN LESLEY. Edited by their daughter, Mary Lesley Ames. New York: G.P. Putnam's Sons, 1909. 2 vols.

Biography based on and including extensive extracts from letters, arranged chronologically with commentary.

1751. Lespinasse, Julie Jeanne Eléonore de, 1732-1776. French salonist and intimate of Madame du Deffand. LETTRES DE MADEMOISELLE DE LESPINASSE. Suivies de ses autres Oevres et de Lettres de Madame du Deffand, de Turgot, de Bernardin de Saint-Pierre, revues sur les éditions originales, augmentées des variantes, des nombreuses notes, d'un appendice comprenant les écrites de d'Alembert, de Guibert, de Voltaire, de Frédéric II, sur Mlle. de Lespinasse, d'un index, et précedées d'une notice biographique et litteraire par Eugene Asse. Édition ornee du fac-simile d'une lettre inédite du Mlle. de Lespinasse. Paris: Bibliotheque Charpentier, 1876. 409p.

1752. ------. LETTRES INÉDITES DE MADEMOISELLE DE LESPINASSE A CONDORCET, A D'ALEMBERT, A GUIBERT, AU COMTE DE CRILLON. Publiées avec des lettres de ses amis, des documents nouveaux et une étude par Charles Henry. Paris: Éditions Dentu, 1887. 408p.

1753. ------. LETTERS OF MADEMOISELLE DE LESPINASSE WITH NOTES ON HER LIFE AND CHARACTER BY D'ALEMBERT, MARMONTEL, DE GUIBERT, ETC., AND AN INTRODUCTION BY C.A. SAINTE-BEUVE. Unexpurgated rendition into English. Translated by Katharine Prescott Wormeley. New York: Versailles Historical Society, 1899. 342p. Boston: Hardy, Pratt & Co., 1902. 342p.

Letters to the Comte Hippolyte de Guibert, 1773-1776.

1754. ------. CORRESPONDANCE ENTRE MADEMOISELLE DE LESPINASSE ET LE COMTE DE GUIBERT. Par le Comte de Villeneuve-Guibert. Paris: Calmann-Lévy, 1906.

1755. ------. LOVE LETTERS OF MADEMOISELLE DE LESPINASSE TO AND FROM THE COMTE DE GUIBERT. Translated with an introduction and biographical index by E.H.F. Mills. London: George Routledge and Sons, 1929. 553p.

1756. Le Sueur, Meridel, b. 1900. American short story writer and poet. "Meridel Le Sueur: Voice of the Prairie." Patricia Hampl. MS. MAGAZINE 4:2 (August, 1975), 62-66, 96.

Includes extracts from her journal, mainly from the 1960's, originally published in the LAMP IN THE SPINE 9.

1757. ------. RIPENING: SELECTED WORK, 1927-1980. Edited with an introduction by Elaine Hedges. Old Westbury, New York: The Feminist Press, 1981. 384p.

Includes excerpts from her journal.

1758. Le Vert, Octavia Celeste Walton, 1810/1811-1877. American Southern author and social leader. SOUVENIRS OF TRAVEL. Mobile, Ala. and New York: S.H. Goetzel & Co., 1857. 2 vols. New York: Derby & Jackson, 1859.

Compiled from letters and journals written during two trips to Europe in 1853 and 1855. She moved in high social and literary circles; she was received by Queen Victoria, presented to Napoleon III, and escorted in Paris by Robert and Elizabeth Barrett Browning. Le Vert "carefully revised" the original manuscript, omitting much she considered "personal and egoistic;" the excerpts are dated, but no distinction is made between letters and journal entries.

1759. ------. "Madame Le Vert's Diary." Mrs. Thaddeus Horton. ALABAMA HISTORY QUARTERLY (Spring, 1941), 31-54.

1760. Levy, Hanna. Early Jewish feminist and radio

announcer. "Notes From the Camp of the Dead." In WOMEN IN THE RESISTANCE AND IN THE HOLOCAUST: THE VOICES OF EYEWITNESSES. Edited with an introduction by Vera Laska. Westport, Conn.: Greenwood Press, 1983. p.248-257.

Extracts from a diary kept at Bergen-Belsen, describe "not merely physical deprivations but also the wounds to the soul inflicted on those condemned to Bergen-Belsen."

1761. Lewald-Stahr, Fanny, 1811-1889. German author. ENGLAND UND SCHOTTLAND: REISETAGEBÜCH VON FANNY LEWALD. Berlin: Otto Janke, 1864. 2 vols.

Travel diary.

1762. ------. SOMMER UND WINTER AM GENFERSEE. EINE TAGEBÜCH VON FANNY LEWALD. Berlin: Otto Janke, 1869. 490p.

1763. ------. ROMISCHES TAGEBÜCH, 1845/46. Herausgegeben von Heinrich Spiero. Leipzig: Klinkhardt Biermann, 1927. 308p.

1764. ------. GROSSHERZOG CARL ALEXANDER UND FANNY LEWALD-STAHR IN IRHEN BRIEFEN, 1848-1889. Eingeleitet und herausgegeben von Rudolf Gohler. Berlin: Verlag von E.S. Mittler & Sohn, 1932.

1765. Lewis, Abigail, pseud. American. AN INTERESTING CONDITION: THE DIARY OF A PREGNANT WOMAN. Garden City, N.Y.: Doubleday & Co., 1950. 256p.

Lieven, Princess. See: Liven, Dar'ia Khristovorovna Benckendorff, Kniaginia, 1785-1857.

1766. Liew, Elizabeth van, 1790-1873. "Jottings from An Old Journal." SOMERSET COUNTY HISTORICAL QUARTERLY 7 (1918), 55-61.

Diary 1821--1856.

1767. Lightner, Mary Elizabeth Rollins, 1818-1913.

American Mormon frontier settler. THE LIFE AND TESTIMONY OF MARY ELIZABETH LIGHTNER. Compiled and published by N.B. Lundwall. No place: no date. 44p.

Includes extracts from a Mormon diary, 1863.

1768. Lincoln, Mary Todd, 1818-1882. American wife of U.S. President Abraham Lincoln. "The Mary Lincoln Letters to Mrs. Felician Slataper." Justin G. Turner. ILLINOIS STATE HISTORICAL SOCIETY JOURNAL 49:1 (Spring, 1956), 7-33.

Background and text of eleven letters to Eliza Jane Slataper of Pittsburgh, Pennsylvania, September 21--October 4, 1871. The first five were written in various places in the U.S. while Lincoln was contemplating a trip to Europe; four were written in Europe; and two after the death of her youngest son. Eight of the letters were written on mourning stationery.

1769. ------. MARY TODD LINCOLN: HER LIFE AND LETTERS. Edited by Justin G. Turner and Linda Levitt Turner. With an introduction by Fawn M. Brodie. New York: Alfred A. Knopf, 1972. 750p.

1770. ------. "'My Dear W.': Mary Lincoln Writes to Alexander Williamson." Edited by Gerald Steffens Cowden. ILLINOIS STATE HISTORICAL SOCIETY JOURNAL 76:1 (Spring, 1983), 71-74.

Discussion and excerpts from letters. Lincoln had engaged the services of Williamson after the death of Abraham Lincoln, to act as intermediary for her and to straighten out her debts. These letters do not appear in MARY TODD LINCOLN: HER LIFE AND LETTERS (1972).

1771. Lind, Jenny (Jenny Maria Lind-Goldschmidt), 1820-1887. Swedish opera singer and wife of composer Otto Goldschmidt. THE LOST LETTERS OF JENNY LIND. Translated from the German and edited with commentaries. W. Porter Ware and Thaddeus C. Lockhard, Jr. London: Victor Gollancz, 1966. 159p.

Thirty-nine letters, written in German, to Frau

Amalia Weichman, 1845-1876, furnish information on Lind's opinion of her abilities as a singer, on her relationship with her husband and the years they worked together, and on their retirement in England.

1772. ------. P.T. BARNUM PRESENTS JENNY LIND: THE AMERICAN TOUR OF THE SWEDISH NIGHTINGALE. W. Porter Ware and Thaddeus C. Lockhard, Jr. Baton Rouge and London: Louisiana University Press, 1980. 204p.

The story of Lind's American tour, based on contemporary newspaper accounts, correspondence, and contracts. Appendix I presents thirty-four letters, March, 1845--August, 1849, from Lind to Charlotte Birch-Pfeiffer, her language teacher in Berlin. Appendix II presents four letters to Otto Goldschmidt, 1849-1850.

1773. Lindbergh, Anne Spencer Morrow, b. 1906. American aviator, diarist, poet, and wife of aviator Charles Lindbergh. BRING ME A UNICORN: DIARIES AND LETTERS, 1922-1928. New York: Harcourt Brace Jovanovich, 1971. 259p.

Covers her school days (she began her diary at age sixteen), college, the family life of the Morrows, trips abroad, and the beginning of her courtship with Charles Lindbergh.

1774. ------. HOUR OF GOLD, HOUR OF LEAD: DIARIES AND LETTERS, 1929-1932. New York: Harcourt Brace Jovanovich, 1973. 340p.

Covers her early married life, becoming a pilot, the trials of living a public life, and the kidnapping and murder of her first child.

1775. ------. LOCKED ROOMS AND OPEN DOORS: DIARIES AND LETTERS, 1933-1935. New York: Harcourt Brace Jovanovich, 1974. 352p.

Describes the long Atlantic air-route survey flight on which Charles Lindbergh studied the geographical terrain, weather conditions, and possible landing sites for air service stations in America and Europe; the kidnap trial and attendant publicity; recovering from the death of her son. Ends on the Lindberghs' sea-voyage to England in 1935, to start a new life there.

1776. ------. THE FLOWER AND THE NETTLE: DIARIES AND LETTERS, 1936-1939. New York: Harcourt Brace Jovanovich, 1976. 605p.

The Lindberghs seek privacy and a secluded life in pre-war Europe; describes Charles Lindbergh's flights and trips to Germany, and the European social scene.

1777. ------. WAR WITHIN AND WITHOUT: DIARIES AND LETTERS OF ANNE MORROW LINDBERGH, 1939-1944. New York: Harcourt Brace Jovanovich, 1980. 471p.

Diary of the war years; details the Lindbergh's social and domestic lives, and the anguish they felt as they became targets for public hostility because of Charles Lindbergh's pre-war anti-intervention stance.

1778. Lindgren, Ida Nibelius. Swedish-American homesteader. "A Swedish Woman Views Her Home in Kansas, 1870-1881: The Letters and Diary of Ida Nibelius Lindgren." Emory Lindquist. SWEDISH PIONEER HISTORICAL QUARTERLY 16:1 (1965), 3-17.

Diary and letters to her mother and sister describe life on a frontier farm in Kansas. The Lindgren family returned to Sweden in 1881.

1779. Lindsay, Anna Suzanne O'Dwyer, 1764-1820. CORRESPONDANCE DE BENJAMIN CONSTANT ET D'ANNA LINDSAY. Publiée par la Baronne Constant de Rebeque. Préface de Fernand Baldensperger. Paris: Libraries Plon, 1933. 240p.

1780. Lindsay, Elizabeth Dick, 1792-1845. American. DIARY OF ELIZABETH DICK LINDSAY. With an introduction by Jo White Linn. Salisbury, N.Y.: Salisbury Publishing Co., 1975. unpaged.

Diary 1837-1861 of life on a North Carolina plantation.

1781. Lindsay, Elizabeth Sherman Hoyt, 1885-1954. American. THE LETTERS OF ELIZABETH SHERMAN HOYT LINDSAY, 1911-1954. Edited by Olivia James. New York: Privately printed at the Marchbanks Press, 1960. 246p.

1782. Lindsey, Sarah Crosland, d. 1876. English Quaker missionary and wife of missionary Robert Lindsey. "English Quakers Tour Kansas in 1858: From the Journal of Sarah Lindsey." Edited by Sheldon Jackson. KANSAS HISTORICAL QUARTERLY 13 (1944), 36-52.

1783. ------. "Willamette Valley in 1859: The Diary of a Tour." Edited by H.S. Nedry. OREGON HISTORICAL QUARTERLY 46:3 (September, 1945), 235-254.

Describes her first tour of the American frontier.

1784. ------. "An English Quaker Tours California: The Journal of Sarah Lindsey, 1859-1860." Edited by Sheldon G. Jackson. SOUTHERN CALIFORNIA QUARTERLY 51:1 (1969), 1-33; 51:2 (1969), 153-175; and 51:3 (1969), 221-246.

Describes a journey with her husband to California in 1859-1860 to minister to California gold miners.

1785. Lindsley, Margaret Lawrence, 1840-1922. American. "MAGGIE!" MAGGIE LINDSLEY'S JOURNAL, NASHVILLE, TENNESSEE, 1864: WASHINGTON, D.C., 1865. Southbury, Conn.: Privately printed by Muriel Davies Mackenzie, 1977. 129p.

1786. Lines, Amelia Jane Akehurst, 1827-1886. English-American teacher. TO RAISE MYSELF A LITTLE: THE DIARIES AND LETTERS OF JENNIE, A GEORGIA SCHOOLTEACHER, 1851-1886. Edited by Thomas Dyer. Athens, Ga.: University of Georgia Press, 1982. 284p.

Writings of a nineteenth-century schoolteacher. Sheds light on a variety of social history topics: education in the North and the South from a teacher's viewpoint; family relationships, childbearing, and life styles among middle class Southerners before and after the Civil War; the development of radical ideas in a migrant from the North; and the attitudes of Northerners towards seccession and the Civil War.

1787. Linsingen, Caroline von, 1768-1815. CAROLINE VON LINSINGEN, DIE GATTIN EINES ENGLISCHER PRINZEN. Ungedruckte Briefe und Abhandlungen aus dem nachlasse des Freiherr K. von Reichenbach. Herausgegeben und mit einer einleitung von Freiherr K. von Reichenbach. Leipzig: Duncker & Humbolt, 1880. 154p.

1788. ------. CAROLINE VON LINSINGEN AND KING WILLIAM THE FOURTH: UNPUBLISHED LOVE LETTERS DISCOVERED AMONG THE LITERARY REMAINS OF BARON REICHENBACH. Translated, with the German editor's introduction and Baron Reichenbach's account of the letters, by Theophilus G. Arundel. London: W.S. Sonnenschein & Allen, 1880. 183p.

1789. Linton, Elizabeth Lynn, 1822-1898. English novelist, journalist, and women's rights activist. MRS. ELIZABETH LYNN LINTON: HER LIFE, LETTERS AND OPINIONS. London: Methuen, 1901. 387p.

1790. Lippincott, Sara Jane Clarke, 1823-1904. American popular author and journalist. HAPS AND MISHAPS OF A TOUR IN EUROPE. By Grace Greenwood (pseud.). Boston: Ticknor, Reed & Fields, 1854. 437p.

Travel diary written on a fifteen-month tour of Europe, 1852-1853.

1791. Little, Alicia Helen Neva Bewicke, "Mrs. Archibald Little." English? MY DIARY IN A CHINESE FARM. Shanghai, Hongkong, Singapore and Yokohama: Kelly & Walsh, 1894?

Diary July 6, 1893--August 3, 1894 by a woman who apparently accompanied her husband who traveled to China on business. She was "shut up in the one farm house sitting room," and started a diary to pass the time as she had "often observed people do so on a sea voyage."

1792. Liven, Dar'ia Khristovorovna Benckendorff,

Kniaginia, "Princess Lieven," 1785-1857. Russian social figure, spy, wife of Count Christopher Lieven, Russian Ambassador to England, and mistress of Prince Metternich. THE CORRESPONDENCE OF LORD ABERDEEN AND PRINCESS LIEVEN, 1832-1854. Edited for the Royal Historical Society by E. Jones Parry. London: Offices of the Royal Historical Society, 1938-1939. 2 vols. (Royal Historical Society, London, Publications, Camden Third Series, Vol. 60, 62).

Correspondence with George John James Hamilton Gordon, Earl of Aberdeen.

1793. ------. CORRESPONDENCE OF PRINCESS LIEVEN AND EARL GREY. Edited and translated by Guy Le Strange. London: R. Bentley & Son, 1890. 3 vols.

Correspondence 1824-1841.

1794. ------. LETTERS OF DOROTHEA, PRINCESS LIEVEN, DURING HER RESIDENCE IN LONDON, 1812-1834. Edited by Lionel G. Robinson. London and New York: Longmans, Green & Co., 1902. 414p.

Letters to her brother, General Alexander Benckendorf, written from London during Prince Lieven's term as Ambassador to England.

1795. ------. THE UNPUBLISHED DIARY AND POLITICAL SKETCHES OF PRINCESS LIEVEN, TOGETHER WITH SOME OF HER LETTERS. Edited with elucidations by Harold Temperley. London: Jonathan Cape, 1925. 283p.

Life of Princess Lieven to 1825 followed by extracts from her diary, 1825-1830. Details European politics for the period, including her mission as a spy for Austria, and includes political sketches of the Grand Duchess Anne, Queen of the Netherlands, Lord Palmerston, Francois Guizot, and others.

1796. ------. THE PRIVATE LETTERS OF PRINCESS LIEVEN TO PRINCE METTERNICH, 1820-1826. Edited with a biographical foreword by Peter Quennell, assisted in translation by Dilys Powell. London: John Murray, 1937. 386p.

Letters from England, written during Prince Lieven's embassy, keeping Prince Metternich informed of the English political situation. The originals were love letters as well; this manuscript was edited from a journal-book of fair copies of the originals, from which Princess Lieven had cut passages that were too revealing of her affair with Metternich.

1797. ------. THE LIEVEN-PALMERSTON CORRESPONDENCE, 1828-1856. Translated and edited by Lord Sutley, with a preface by Sir John Squire. London: John Murray, 1943. 244p.

Correspondence with Emily, Countess Cowper, Lady Palmerston. Both had a great deal of power and influence in European politics, sometimes on opposite sides. How far they trusted each other is uncertain, but their friendship and their correspondence lasted many years.

1798. ------. LETTERS OF PRINCESS LIEVEN TO LADY HOLLAND, 1847-1857. Edited by A.E. Smith. Presented by Viscount Esher. Introduction by Mary Augusta, Lady Holland. London: Oxford University Press for presentation to the members of the Roxburghe Club (Printed by Charles Batey), 1956. 86p.

Letters, in French, to Mary Augusta Coventry Fox, Baroness Holland.

1799. ------. LETTRES DE FRANCOIS GUIZOT ET DE LA PRINCESSE DE LIEVEN. Préface de Jean Schlumberger. Edition annotée par Jacques Naville. Paris: Mercure de France, 1963-1964. 3 vols.

Correspondence with Francois Pierre Guillaume Guizot.

1800. Livingston, Alida Schuyler, b.1656. American Colonial businesswoman. "Business Letters of Alida

Schuyler Livingston, 1680-1726." NEW YORK HISTORY 63:2 (April, 1982), 183-207.

Letters between Livingston and her husband, Albany businessman and politician Robert Livingston indicate theirs was a marriage of equals. She shared the management of their properties and business, and influenced his economic and political decisions.

1801. Lloyd-George, Frances Louise Stevenson, Countess, 1888-1972. English private secretary, mistress, and later wife of British Prime Minister David Lloyd-George. LLOYD-GEORGE: A DIARY BY FRANCES STEVENSON. Edited by A.J.P. Taylor. New York: Harper & Row, 1971. 338p.

Diary 1914-1944. Much of the diary is transcribed from David Lloyd-George's conversations and thus is more of a reflection of his personality than of hers.

1802. ------. MY DARLING PUSSY: THE LETTERS OF LLOYD GEORGE AND FRANCES STEVENSON. Edited by A.J.P. Taylor. London: Weidenfeld and Nicolson, 1975. 258p.

Letters 1912-1945, and brief extracts from her diary which illuminate the letters. Intimate correspondence which, Taylor says, "reads like a romantic novel." "Pussy" was David Lloyd-George's nickname for Frances.

1803. Lockwood, Casandra Sawyer. American. "Letters of Casandra Sawyer Lockwood: Dwight Mission of 1834." Edited by Joseph B. Thoburn. CHRONICLES OF OKLAHOMA 33 (1955), 202-237.

1804. Logan, Martha Daniell, 1704-1779. American colonial businesswoman and horticulturist. "Letters of Martha Logan to John Bartram, 1760-1763." Edited by Mary Barbot Prior. SOUTH CAROLINA HISTORICAL AND GENEALOGICAL MAGAZINE 59 (January, 1958), 38-46.

Correspondence with Philadelphia botanist John Bartram.

1805. Lomax, Elizabeth Lindsay, b. 1796. American. LEAVES FROM AN OLD WASHINGTON DIARY, 1854-1863: A CLEAR CUT AND ENLIGHTENING PICTURE OF THE CIVIL WAR PERIOD. Edited by Lindsay Lomax Wood. Supplemented by Virginia Lomax. New York: Books, Inc./E.P. Dutton, 1943. 256p.

Social diary describes events in and around Washington, D.C., 1854-1863.

1806. Long, Margaret, b. 1873. American physician. THE SHADOW OF THE ARROW. Caldwell, Idaho: The Caxton Printers, 1941. 310p. Revised and enlarged edition, 1950. 354p.

Diary October, 1921, of an automobile trip through Death Valley with her friend Anne Marton.

1807. Longfellow, Fanny (Frances Elizabeth) Appleton, 1817-1861. American society belle and wife of poet Henry Wadsworth Longfellow. MRS. LONGFELLOW: SELECTED LETTERS AND JOURNALS. Edited by Edward Wagenknecht. New York and London: Longmans, Green, 1956. 255p.

Selections from Fanny Longfellow's extensive social and literary journals and correspondence.

1808. Lord, Louisa. American companion to a Sea Captain's Wife. MISS LOUISA LORD'S DIARY OF A VOYAGE ON THE SHIP ST. PETERSBURG. New York: Ivy Press, 1975. 49p.

Sea diary, May--September, 1840.

1809. Lorde, Audre. American Black feminist lesbian poet. "Breast Cancer: A Black Lesbian Feminist Experience." SINISTER WISDOM 10 (Summer, 1979), 44-61.

Includes extracts from her journal written during her illness.

1810. ------. THE CANCER JOURNALS. Argyle, N.Y.: Spinsters Ink, 1981. 77p.

Journal extracts, 1978-1980, with commentary,

written during her illness with breast cancer which led to a modified radical masectomy. Explores her feelings about death and disability, applying a feminist ethic.

1811. Loughborough, Mary Ann Webster, 1836-1887. American Southern magazine editor. MY CAVE LIFE IN VICKSBURGH, WITH LETTERS OF TRIAL AND TRAVEL. BY A LADY. New York: D. Appleton & Co., 1864. 196p.

Account of refugee during the Civil War life by the wife of Confederate officer James M. Loughborough.

1812. Louise von Coburg, Princess of Belgium, 1858-1924. Daughter of King Leopold II of Poland. THE LIAISON. Maria Matray and Answald Kruger. Translated by Richard Sharp. New York: William Morrow, 1976. 346p.

Extracts from the diaries of Princess von Coburg and her lover, Lieutenant Geza von Mattachich, interwoven together to form an account of their love affair.

1813. Louise de Coligny, Consort of William I, Prince of Orange, 1555-1620. LETTRES DE LOUISE DE COLIGNY, PRINCESSE D'ORANGE À SA BELLE-FILLE CHARLOTTE-BRABANTINE DE NASSAU, DUCHESSE DE TREMOILLE. Publiées d'après les originaux par Paul Marchegay. Les Roches-Baritaud (Vendee), 1872. 112p.

1814. ------. LOUISE DE COLIGNY: LETTRES À HENRI DE LA TOUR, VICOMTE DE TURENNE. Publiées d'après les originaux conserves aux Archives Nationales par Auguste Laugel. Paris: Sandoz et Fischbacher, 1877. 61p.

Letters to Henri de La Tour d'Auvergne, Vicomte de Turenne, duc de Bouillon.

1815. ------. CORRESPONDANCE DE LOUISE DE COLIGNY, PRINCESSE D'ORANGE, 1555-1620. Recueille par Paul Marchegay. Publiée avec une introduction biographique et notes par Léon Marlet. Paris: O. Doin, 1887. 379p. Reprinted, Genève: Slatkine Reprints, 1970. 382p.

1816. Louise Marie de Orléans, consort of Leopold I, King of the Belgians, 1812-1850. LA COUR DE BELGIQUE ET LA COUR DE FRANCE DE 1832-1850: LETTRES INTIMES DE LOUISE MARIE D'ORLÉANS, PREMIÈRE REINE DE BELGES, AU ROI LOUIS PHILIPPE ET LA REINE MARIE AMELIE. Publiées par le Comte Hippolyte d'Ursel. Paris: Librarie Plon, 1933. 323p.

1817. Louise Auguste of Prussia, Queen Consort of Frederic Guillaume IV, King of Prussia, 1776-1806. LUISE KONIGIN VON PREUSSEN IN IHREN BRIEFEN. Berlin, 1888.

1818. ------. BRIEFWECHSEL KONIG FRIEDRICH WILLHELM IV UN DER KONIGIN LUISE MIT KAISER ALEXANDER I. Nebst erganzenden furstlichen korrespondenzen herausgegeben von Paul Bailleu. Veranlasst und unterstutzt durch die K. Archiv-Verwaltung. Leipzig: S. Hirzel, 1900. 564p.

1819. Low, Ann Marie, b. 1912. American farmer. DUST BOWL DIARY. Lincoln, Nebr. and London: University of Nebraska Press, 1984. 188p.

Diary entries April 30, 1928--June 4, 1937, followed by commentary. An account of the effects of the drought, Depression, and government programs upon Low's family and neighbors; of coming of age during the Depression; and of her frustration with the restrictions society placed upon young women.

1820. Low, Mary Porter. American. "Hard Cash: A Salem Housewife in the 1820's." Edited by Elma Loines. ESSEX INSTITUTE HISTORICAL COLLECTIONS 91 (July, 1955).

1821. Lowell, Amy, 1874-1925. American poet. See item 507. AMY LOWELL, A CHRONICLE, WITH EXTRACTS FROM HER CORRESPONDENCE. Samuel Foster Damon. Boston and New York: Houghton Mifflin Co., and Cambridge, England: The Riverside Press, 1935. 773p.

1822. ------. "The Correspondence of Amy Lowell and Barrett Wendell, 1915-1919." Robert T. Self. NEW ENGLAND QUARTERLY 47:1 (March, 1974), 65-86.

Twenty-two letters from Lowell on the subject of

poetry and literature. None of Wendell's letters have survived.

1823. ------. "A Musical Apprentice: Amy Lowell to Carl Engel." William C. Bedford. MUSICAL QUARTERLY 58:4 (October, 1972), 519-542.

Discusses the correspondence between Lowell and her "musical mentor," 1909-1925 and presents eleven letters by Lowell.

1824. ------. THE LETTERS OF D.H. LAWRENCE AND AMY LOWELL, 1914-1925. Edited by E. Claire Healey and Keith Cushman. Santa Barbara: Black Sparrow Press, 1985. 143p.

1825. Lowell, Maria White, 1821-1853. American poet, temperance worker, abolitionist, and wife of poet James Russell Lowell. THE POEMS OF MARIA LOWELL, WITH UNPUBLISHED LETTERS AND A BIOGRAPHY. Hope Jillson Vernon. Introduction by S. Foster Damon. Providence, R.I.: Brown University, 1936. 187p.

Includes almost all of Lowell's letters, and all of her published poetry.

1826. Lowndes, Marie Adelaide Belloc, 1868-1947. English author, sister of Hillaire Belloc and daughter of Bessie Parkes Belloc. DIARIES AND LETTERS OF MARIE BELLOC LOWNDES, 1911-1947. Edited by Susan Lowndes. London: Chatto & Windus, 1971. 291p.

Autobiography followed by letters and diary extracts edited together chronologically. Gives a picture of the political and literary circles of her day, including a personal account of World War II England.

1827. Lucas, Bertha June Richardson. American Red Cross Volunteer. THE CHILDREN OF FRANCE AND THE RED CROSS. New York: Frederick A. Stokes Co., 1918. 193p.

Journal-letters, September 28, 1917--April 27, 1918. Her husband, William Palmer Lucas, was Chief of the Children's Bureau of the Department of Civil Affairs under the Red Cross in France during World War I. Lucas accompanied him to France and for ten months worked organizing Red Cross hospital services for children.

1828. Lunt, Dolly Sumner (later Burge), b. 1818. American Confederate diarist. A WOMAN'S WARTIME JOURNAL: AN ACCOUNT OF THE PASSAGE OVER A GEORGIA PLANTATION OF SHERMAN'S ARMY ON THE MARCH TO THE SEA, AS RECORDED IN THE DIARY OF DOLLY SUMNER LUNT. With an introduction and notes by Julian Street. New York: The Century Co., 1918. 54p.

1829. ------. DIARY. Edited by James I. Robertson, Jr. Athens: University of Georgia Press, 1962. 141p.

Excerpts from the 1918 editon.

1830. Luxemburg, Rosa, 1870-1919. Polish Communist, revolutionary and poltical theorist. LETTERS FROM PRISON. Translated from the German by Eden and Cedar Paul. Berlin: Publishing House of the Young International, 1921. 82p. London: The Socialist Book Center, 1946. 48p.

1831. ------. ROSA LUXEMBURG: BRIEFE AUS DEM GEFANGNIS. Berlin: Verlag der Jugend-Internationale, 1922. 75p.

1832. ------. ROSA LUXEMBURG: BRIEF AN KARL UND LUISE KAUTSKY, 1896-1918. Herausgegeben von Luise Kautsky. Berlin: E. Laub, 1923. 234p.

1833. ------. ROSA LUXEMBURG: LETTERS TO KARL AND LUISE KAUTSKY FROM 1896 TO 1918. Edited by Luise Kautsky and translated from the German by Louis P. Lochner. New York: R.M. McBride & Co., 1925. 238p.

1834. ------. ROZA LUKSEMBURG, LISTY DO LEONA JOGICHESA-TYSZKI, 1893-1914. Edited and annotated by Professor Feliks Tych. Warsaw: Ksiazka i Wiedza, 1968-1971. 3 vols.

1835. ------. J'ÉTAIS, JE SUIS, JE SERAI: CORRESPONDANCE, 1914-1919. Paris: Francois Maspero (Bibliotheque Socialiste), 1977.

1836. ------. THE LETTERS OF ROSA LUXEMBURG. Edited with an introduction by Stephen Eric Bronner. With a foreword by Henry Pachter. Boulder, Colo.: Westview Press, 1978. 259p.

Letters 1894-1919, selected to reveal the "human face of this great revolutionary, the woman, the lover, the companion, the friend of nature and poetry, the prisoner who charms her jailer, the employer, the cook, and of course, the political activist."

1837. ------. COMRADE AND LOVER: ROSA LUXEMBURG'S LETTERS TO LEO JOGICHES. Edited and translated by Elzbieta Ettinger. Cambridge, Mass., and London: The MIT Press, 1979. 206p.

Letters 1893-1897. Considerably edited version of the Polish edition (1968-1971). Letters are selected to show Luxemburg's personal side, to reveal a woman "whose sex did not diminish her political stature and whose politics did not interfere with her private life."

1838. ------. GESAMMELTE BRIEFE: ROSA LUXEMBURG. Herausgegeben von Institut fur Marxismus- Leninismus beim ZK der SED. Redaktion George Adler...ubersetzung aus dem Polnschen, Hildegard Bamberger, Edward Ulmann unter Mitarbeit von Ines Mietkowska-Kaiser. Berlin: Dietz, 1982. 4 vols.

1839. Lyman, Ellen Bancroft Lowell, 1837-1894. American. ARTHUR THEODORE LYMAN AND ELLA LYMAN: LETTERS AND JOURNALS. WITH AN ACCOUNT OF THOSE THEY LOVED AND WERE DESCENDED FROM. Prepared by their daughter, Ella Lyman Cabot. Menasha, Wis.: Privately printed by George Banta Publishing Co., 1932. 3 vols.

1840. Lyman, Sarah Joiner, 1805-1885. American missionary. SARAH JOINER LYMAN OF HAWAII: HER OWN

STORY. Compiled from the Journals and Letters by Margaret Greer Martin. Hilo, Hawaii: Lyman House Memorial Museum, 1970. 201p.

Missionary diary, 1830-1841.

1841. Lyon, Mary, 1797-1849. American teacher and founder of Mount Holyoke Female Seminary. MARY LYON THROUGH HER LETTERS. As edited by Marion Lansing. Boston: Books, Inc., 1937. 317p.

1842. Lyttleton, Sarah Spencer Lyttleton, Baroness, 1787-1870. English wife of William, Lord Lyttleton; later Royal Governess and Lady-In-Waiting to Queen Victoria. CORRESPONDENCE OF SARAH SPENCER, LADY LYTTLETON, 1787-1870. Edited by her great-granddaughter the Hon. Mrs. Hugh Wynham. New York: Charles Scribner's Sons, 1912. 444p.

Social and political letters 1804-1870, beginning with letters to her grandmother when she was seventeen. Describes life at Court.

1843. Lytton, Constance Georgina, Lady, 1867-1923. English suffragist. LETTERS OF CONSTANCE LYTTON. Selected and arranged by Betty Balfour. London: William Heinemann, 1925. 272p.

Letters 1887-1923. After 1902 her letters become increasingly political and concerned with the suffrage movement. She caused herself to be imprisoned four times in order to expose the abuses of the prison system and the treatment of suffragists. She suffered a stroke in 1912 as a result of force-feeding, but continued her activism until her death.

1844. Lytton, Edith, 1841-1936. English? Lady-In-Waiting to Queen Victoria and to Queen Alexandra. LADY LYTTON'S COURT DIARY, 1895-1899. Edited by Mary Lutyens. London: Rupert Hart-Davis, 1961. 192p.

Court diary. Includes a few extracts from the JOURNAL of Queen Victoria, and from the correspondence of Tsaritsa Alexandra.

Lytton, Rosina Doyle Wheeler Bulwer-Lytton, Baroness. See: Bulwer-Lytton, Rosina Doyle Wheeler, Baroness Lytton.

1845. Mabuce, Ethel Lincy, b. 1886. American Missionary. I ALWAYS WORE MY TOPI: THE BURMA LETTERS OF ETHEL MABUCE, 1916-1921. Edited with an introduction by Lucille Griffith. University of Alabama Press, 1974. 336p.

Missionary letters, which her mother preserved as a "kind of diary" of Mabuce's experiences in Burma.

1846. Macaulay, Rose, Dame, 1881-1958. British novelist. LETTERS TO A FRIEND, 1950-1958. Edited by Constance Babington-Smith. New York: Atheneum, 1962. 381p.

Letters to her cousin, the Reverend John Hamilton Cowper Johnson, of the Society of St. John the Evangelist.

1847. ------. LAST LETTERS TO A FRIEND, 1952-1958. Edited by Constance Babington-Smith. London: Collins, 1962. New York: Atheneum, 1963. 288p.

Further letters to the Reverend John Hamilton Cowper Johnson.

1848. ------. LETTERS TO A SISTER. Edited by Constance Babington-Smith. London: Collins, 1964. 352p. New York: Atheneum, 1964. 352p.

Letters to her sister Jean, 1926-1958. Jean's half of the correspondence was destroyed, since according to Macaulay's wishes, all personal papers at her apartment were destroyed after her death. Jean also destroyed many of Macaulay's letters, and parts of others, before turning them over for publication.

1849. McBeth, Sue. American missionary. "The Diary of Sue McBeth, A Missionary to the Choctaws, 1860-1861." Edited by Anna Lewis. CHRONICLES OF OKLAHOMA 17 (1939), 428-447 and 21 (1943), 186-195.

1850. McCalla, Margaret. American Confederate refugee during the Civil War. "The Wartime Experiences of Margaret McCalla: Confederate Refugee from East Tennessee." Edited by Robert Partin. TENNESSEE HISTORICAL QUARTERLY 24:1 (1965), 29-53.

Excerpts from letters to her husband written in 1863 after she fled Tennessee to South Carolina.

1851. McCaughey, Anne, b. 1915. American journalist and Red Cross volunteer. "Anne McCaughey." In AMERICAN DIARIES OF WORLD WAR II. Edited with introductions by Donald Vining. New York: Pepys Press, 1982. p.82-106.

McCaughey served in the American Red Cross with the assimilated rank of Second Lieutenant; her duties were to provide recreational and social service needs to patients of the U.S. Army 50th General Hospital. Diary extracts December 15, 1943--June 15, 1945, written during basic training in Camp Carson, Colorado and on duty in London, Glasgow, and Paris.

1852. McClatchey, Minerva Leah Rowles. American plantation owner. "A Georgia Woman's Civil War Diary: The Journal of Minerva Leah Rowles McClatchey, 1864-1865." Edited by Bryan T. Conn. GEORGIA HISTORICAL QUARTERLY 51 (June, 1967), 197-216.

Describes life on a northwest Georgia plantation in the last years of the Confederacy.

1853. McCrae, Georgiana Huntly Gordon. English-Australian frontier settler. GEORGIANA'S JOURNAL: MELBOURNE A HUNDRED YEARS AGO. Edited by Hugh McCrae, grandson of the diarist. Melbourne: Angus & Robertson, 1934. 314p.

1854. ------. GEORGIANA'S JOURNAL: MELBOURNE, 1841-1865. Edited by Hugh McCrae, grandson of the diarist. Sydney, London, and Melbourne: Angus & Robertson, 1966. 262p.

Diary 1838-1845, with fragments until 1865, and

with "supplements" written in her later years. She kept a diary from 1909, but her early diary is not included here, save for some brief excerpts from her "English Note Book," written before her emigration. Diary describes life on the Australian frontier, and chronicles the growth of Melbourne.

1855. McDonald, Cornelia Peake, 1822-1909. American daughter of a wealthy plantation owner and wife of a Virginia Lawyer. A DIARY WITH REMINISCENCES OF THE WAR AND REFUGEE LIFE IN THE SHENANDOAH VALLEY, 1860-1865. Annotated and supplemented by Hunter McDonald. Nashville, Tenn.: Cullum & Ghertner, 1934. 540p.

Recollections of the years 1860-1862; a diary with reminiscences of the Civil War, March, 1862--August, 1863, written for her husband, who had left their home town of Winchester in 1862 to join the Stonewall Brigade; and a narrative of refugee life from 1863 to 1865. The Recollections and the Narrative appear to be rewritten from a diary.

1856. McDougall, Jane. American frontier settler. "A Woman's Log of 1849, from the Diary of Mrs. John McDougall." William H. McDougall. OVERLAND MONTHLY, 2nd Series, 16 (September, 1890), 273-280.

Diary of a California settler.

1857. McGary, Ellen Pratt, 1832-1895, and Ellen Spencer Clawson, 1832-1895. American Mormons. "DEAR ELLEN": A UTAH-CALIFORNIA CORRESPONDENCE, 1856-1857. Edited by S. George Ellsworth. Salt Lake City: privately published, 1959. 219p.

1858. ------. DEAR ELLEN: TWO MORMON WOMEN AND THEIR LETTERS. Edited by S. George Ellsworth. Salt Lake City: Tanner Trust Fund, University of Utah Library, 1974. 92p.

1859. McGuire, Judith White Brockenbrough, b. 1813. American wife of a Southern school teacher. DIARY OF A SOUTHERN REFUGEE DURING THE WAR, BY A LADY OF VIRGINIA.

New York: E.J. Hale & Sons, 1867. 360p. Third edition, with corrections and additions. Richmond, Va.: J.W. Randolph & English, 1889. 372p.

Civil War diary.

1860. McKnown, Bethia Pyatt Donaldson, b. 1798? American. "The Civil War Letters of Bethia Pyatt McKnown." Edited by James W. Goodrich. MISSOURI HISTORICAL REVIEW 67:2 (January, 1973), 227-252.

McKnown had sons fighting on both sides of the Civil War, and one son was first a Confederate and later a Unionist. Excerpts from her letters shed light on the divisive effects of political beliefs within families during the Civil War, as well as on how elderly people with small incomes managed at mid-nineteenth century.

1861. Maclehose or M'Lehose, Agnes Craig, 1759-1841. Scottish beauty, and the "Clarinda" of Robert Burns's poem. SYLVANDER AND CLARINDA: THE LOVE LETTERS OF ROBERT BURNS AND AGNES M'LEHOSE. Edited by Amelia Josephine Burr. New York: Doran Co., 1917.

Covers their love affair to 1791 and their correspondence to 1794.

1862. McLeod, Ellen, 1813-1888. English immigrant to Natal. DEAR LOUISA: HISTORY OF A PIONEER FAMILY IN NATAL, 1850-1888: ELLEN MCLEOD'S LETTERS TO HER SISTER IN ENGLAND FROM THE BRYNE VALLEY. Edited by R.E. Gordon. Cape Town: A.A. Balkema, 1970. 280p.

1863. McNab, Sophia Mary, 1832-1917. THE DIARY OF SOPHIA MACNAB. Edited by Charles Ambrose Carter and Thomas Melville Bailey. Second revised edition. Hamilton, Ontario: W.L. Griffith, 1974. 88p.

On cover: The Diary of Sophia MacNab written at Dundurn Castle, Hamilton, 1846, age 13.

1864. MacNaughton, Sarah Broom, d.1916. English

novelist. A WOMAN'S DIARY OF THE WAR. London and New York: Thomas Nelson & Sons, 1915. 168p.

1865. ------. MY WAR EXPERIENCE IN TWO CONTINENTS. Edited by Mrs. Lionel Salmon (Betty Keays-Young). London: John Murray, 1919. 286p.

Compiled from her diary of hospital work in Antwerp, in the trenches of Flanders, and in Russia.

1866. McNeeley, Sylvia, b. 1919. American. DIARY OF SYLVIA MCNEELEY. New York and Toronto: Longmans, Green, 1931. 121p.

Childhood diary, written at age ten.

1867. McPherson, Sarah M. American. "The Brazeau, Missouri Scene, 1852-1856: Excerpts from the Diary of Sarah M. McPherson." Mary Alice Bull Cody. CONCORDIA HISTORICAL INSTITUTE QUARTERLY 47:1 (1974), 3-6.

1868. Macqueen, Katherine Stuart, 1867-1917. Scottish. RECORDS OF A SCOTSWOMAN: KATHERINE STUART MACQUEEN, A MEMOIR AND ACCOUNT OF HER WORK. INCLUDING LETTERS AND DIARY OF HER TRAVELS IN THE BALKANS, 1912-1914. Olive Maclehose. Glasgow: Maclehose, Jackson & Co., 1920. 182p.

1869. Macy, Henrietta Gardner, b. 1854. American sculptor who lived most of her life in Venice. THE NUN OF CA'FROLLO: THE LIFE AND LETTERS OF HENRIETTA GARDNER MACY. Clementine Bacheler and Jessie Orr White. New York: William Farquhar Payson, 1931. 321p.

Biography told in letters, with connecting commentary. Covers her childhood, study at Vassar College, travels, life in Venice, work and friendship with Eleanora Duse, and her experiences during World War I.

1870. Madison, Dorothy ("Dolly") Payne Todd, 1768-1849. American wife of U.S. President James Madison. MEMOIRS AND LETTERS OF DOLLY MADISON, WIFE OF

JAMES MADISON, PRESIDENT OF THE UNITED STATES. Edited by her grand-niece (Lucia B. Cutts). Boston and New York: Houghton, Mifflin and Co., and Cambridge, England: The Riverside Press, 1886. 210p.

Biography, consisting chiefly of letters, with connecting biographical narrative.

1871. Maglin, Nan Bauer. American. "Journal of a Women's Course." UNIVERSITY OF MICHIGAN PAPERS IN WOMEN'S STUDIES 2:2 (1974), 249-259.

1872. ------. "Awaiting Quintana: A Journal of Adoption, November 19, 1976--August 23, 1977." FRONTIERS: A JOURNAL OF WOMEN STUDIES 3:2 (Summer, 1978), 49-53

Maglin muses on the decision to adopt, on family and motherhood, on waiting through the adoption process and the enormous changes Quintana will make in her life.

1873. Magoffin, Susan Shelby, 1827-1855. American frontier settler. DOWN THE SANTA FE TRAIL AND INTO MEXICO: THE DIARY OF SUSAN MAGOFFIN, 1846-1847. Edited by Stella M. Drumm. New Haven, Conn.: Yale University Press, and London: Humphrey Milford, 1926. Paperback edition With a foreword by Howard R. Lamar, New Haven and London: Yale University Press, 1962.

Overland diary, written on the Santa Fe trail during it's busiest years of trade and travel.

1874. Maheux-Forcier, Louise. French-Canadian author. LE SABLIER: JOURNAL INTIME, 1981-1984. Louise Maheux-Forcier. Montreal: P. Tisseyre, and Ottowa: Le Cercle du Livre de France, 1984. 291p.

1875. Mahoney, Mary. American. "End of an Era: The Travel Journal of Mary Mahoney." Edited by Donald Mahoney. NEBRASKA HISTORY 47:3 (September, 1966), 329-333.

Diary in the form of daily reports to her parents

in Alliance, Nebraska, Spring-Summer, 1901. Describes travel in one of the last covered wagon journeys from Nebraska to Colorado at the turn of the century.

1876. Maintenon, Françoise d'Augigne, Marquise de, 1635-1729. French educator and secret second wife of Louis XIV. LETTRES INÉDITE DE MADAME DE MAINTENON ET DE LA PRINCESSE DES URSINS. Paris: Bossange Frères, 1826. 4 vols.

Letters to Anne Marie de la Tremoille Noirmoustier, Duchessa di Bracciano.

1877. ------. THE SECRET CORRESPONDENCE OF MADAME DE MAINTENON, WITH THE PRINCESS DES URSINS; FROM THE ORIGINAL MANUSCRIPTS IN THE POSSSESSION OF THE DUKE DE CHOISEUL. Translated from the French. London: Geo. B. Whittaker, 1827. 3 vols.

1878. ------. QUELQUES LETTRES DE MADAME DE MAINTENON, 1708-1716. Victor Glachant. Versailles: Bernard, 1927. 64p. Originally published in RÉVUE DE L'HISTOIRE DE VERSAILLES ET DE SEINE-ET-OISE 27 (1925), 5-65.

Scholarly edition of thirty-three letters, thirty of them previously unpublished.

1879. ------. LETTRES. Publiée par Marcel Langlois. Letouzey & Ane, 1935-1939. 4 vols.

Letters 1655-1701. Definitive edition.

1880. Malcolm, Clementina Elphinstone, Lady, d. 1830. A DIARY OF ST. HELENA: THE JOURNAL OF LADY MALCOLM, CONTAINING THE CONVERSATIONS OF NAPOLEON WITH SIR PULTENEY MALCOLM. Edited by Sir Arthur Wilson. London: A.D. Innes & Co., 1899. 168p. New edition with an introduction by Muriel Kent. New York and London: Harper & Bros., 1929. 160p.

Public diary, June, 1816--July, 1817. According to Sir Arthur Ponsonby (item 94), "the diary is written with great restraint in the third person in almost an official tone, and contains hardly any feminine touches." The oldest extant copy is in Sir Pulteney's handwriting.

1881. Malina, Judith. American actress and activist. With her husband Julian Beck, she is a founder of the avant-garde theatre group The Living Theatre. THE ENORMOUS DESPAIR: THE DIARY OF JUDITH MALINA, AUGUST 1968 TO APRIL 1969. New York: Random House, 1972. 249p.

Diary of an eight-month tour of the U.S. undertaken by the Living Theatre at the height of the social unrest of the 1960's. Preaching anarchy and political resistance, the troupe was repeatedly arrested, turned out of hotels and banned from performing.

1882. ------. "From the Brazilian Diaries." Edited by Karen Malpede. HERESIES 9 (Vol. 3:1, 1980), 18-21.

In 1970 the Living Theatre went to Brazil, where they began to work on a cycle of plays called "The Legacy of Cain," to be performed for and with the poor in the streets; they were arrested on charges of subversion and possession of marijuana. Malina, Beck, and other members served three-month jail sentences. Excerpts from her diary, April 28--May 14, 1971.

1883. ------. THE DIARIES OF JUDITH MALINA, 1947-1957. New York: Grove Press, 1984. 485p.

1884. Mallet, Marie, Lady, 1862-1934. English. LIFE WITH QUEEN VICTORIA: MARIE MALLET'S LETTERS FROM COURT, 1887-1901. Edited by Victor Mallet. Boston: Houghton Mifflin, 1968. 245p.

1885. Mallon, Catherine, Sister. American nun. "Sister Catherine Mallon's Journal." Edited by Thomas Richter. NEW MEXICO HISTORICAL REVIEW 52:2 (1977), 135-155 and 52:3 (1977), 237-250.

Sister Catherine went from Cincinnati to Santa Fe in 1865 to work in a Catholic hospital there.

1886. Mallory, Mary Alice Shutes, 1849-1939. American frontier settler. DIARY: EIGHT HUNDRED MILES IN THIRTY-SIX DAYS BY COVERED WAGON: 1862 FROM WYANDOTT COUNTY OHIO TO CARROLL COUNTY IOWA. Bloomington, Ill.: L.L. Shutes, 1967. 45p.

Overland diary May-June, 1862, written when Mallory was thirteen.

1887. Mannigault, Ann, 1703-1782. American colonist. "Extracts from the Journal of Mrs. Ann Mannigault, 1754-1781." Edited by Mabel L. Webber. SOUTH CAROLINA HISTORICAL AND GENEALOGICAL MAGAZINE 20:1 (1919), 57-63; 20:2 (1919), 128-141; 20:3 (1919), 204-212; 20:4 (1919), 256-259; 21:1 (1920), 10-23; 21:2 (1920), 59-72; and 21:3 (1920), 112-120.

1888. Mansfield, Katherine, 1888-1923. New Zealand short story writer. THE JOURNAL OF KATHERINE MANSFIELD. Edited by John Middleton Murray. New York: Alfred A. Knopf, 1927. 256p.

Compiled and edited from four diaries and thirty notebooks, and about one hundred loose sheets of miscellaneous writing covering the years 1907-1923. The journals and notebooks did not exist as such, but were the editorial creation of John Middleton Murray.

1889. ------. THE LETTERS OF KATHERINE MANSFIELD. Edited by John Middleton Murray. London: Constable, 1928. 2 vols. New York: Alfred A. Knopf, 1929. 2 vols. Reprinted by Alfred A. Knopf, 1941, 2 vols. in one. 517p.

Letters 1913-1922 arranged to form, when read together with the Journal, a complete autobiography for the last ten years of Mansfield's life.

1890. ------. PASSIONATE PILGRIMAGE: A LOVE AFFAIR IN LETTERS. KATHERINE MANSFIELD'S LETTERS TO JOHN MIDDLETON MURRAY FROM THE SOUTH OF FRANCE, 1915-1920. In an edition by Helen McNeish. London: Joseph, 1976. 143p.

1891. Maraise, Madame de, 1737-1822. French businesswoman. UNE FEMME D'AFFAIRES AU XVIIIe SIECLE: LA CORRESPONDANCE DE MADAME DE MARAISE, COLLABORATRICE D'OBERKAMPF. Presentée par Serge Chassagne. Toulouse: Editions Privat, 1981. 158p.

Personal and business correspondence, 1769-1815.

1892. Marchmann, Mrs. George. American. "Six Weeks to Texas." Maury Darst. TEXANA 6:2 (1968), 140-152.

Diary kept in 1861 on a trip from New York to LaGrange, Texas.

1893. Marette, Fanny. French actress. J'ÉTAIS LE NUMERO 47.177: JOURNAL D'UNE COMEDIENNE DEPORTÉ. Préface de Remy Roure. Paris: Robert Laffont, 1954. 256p.

Concentration camp diary, January 27--April 27, 1944 written at Sarresbruck and Ravensbruck.

1894. ------. I WAS NUMBER 47.177. FANNY MARETTE. Geneva: Ferni Publishing House, dist. by Pleasant Valley Press, 1979. 262p.

1895. Margaret d'Angoulême, Queen of Navarre, 1492-1549. French politician, poet, scholar, and religious reformer. LETTRES DE MARGARET D'ANGOULÊME, QUEEN OF NAVARRE, SOUER DE FRANÇOIS I, REINE DE NAVARRE. Publiées d'après les manuscrits de la Bibliothèque du Roi par François Genin. Paris: J. Renouard et Cie., 1841. 485p.

1896. ------. NOUVELLES LETTRES DE LA REINE DE NAVARRE, ADDRESSÉES AU ROI FRANCOIS I, SON FRÈRE. Publiées d'après le manuscrit de la Bibliothèque du Roi. Francois Genin. Paris: J. Renouard, 1842. 303p.

1897. ------. LETTRES DE MARGUERITE DE VALOIS-ANGOULÊME. Publiées par Raymond Ritter. Paris: E. Champion, 1927. 9, 38p. 175 copies printed.

1898. ------. MARGUERITE DE NAVARRE: REPERTOIRE

ANALYTIQUE ET CHRONOLOGIQUE DE LA CORRESPONDANCE DE MARGUERITE D'ANGOULÊME, DUCHESSE D'ALENÇON, REINE DE NAVARRE. Pierre Jourda. Paris: Champion, 1930. 265p.

1899. ------. CORRESPONDANCE, 1521-1524. GUILLAUM BRICONNET, MARGUERITE D'ANGOULÊME. Édition du texte et annotations par Christine Martineau et Michel Veissière, avec le councours de Henry Heller. Genève: Librarie Droz, 1975-1979. 2 vols.

1900. ------. "Marguerite de Navarre aux Temps de Briconnet: Étude de la Correspondance Generale (1521-1522)." V.L. Saulner. BIBLIOTHÈQUE D'HUMANISME ET RENAISSANCE [Switzerland] 39:3 (1977), 437-478; 40:1 (1978), 7-47; and 40:2 (1978), 193-231.

1901. Margaret d'Anjou, Queen Consort of Henry VI, 1430-1482. English Queen and military heroine. LETTERS OF QUEEN MARGARET OF ANJOU AND BISHOP BECKINGTON AND OTHERS WRITTEN IN THE REIGNS OF HENRY V AND HENRY VI. Edited by Cecil Monro. From a manuscript found at Emral in Flintshire. Westminster: Printed for the Camden Society, 1863. 177p.

1902. Maria de la Paz, Consort of Louis Ferdinand, Prince of Bavaria, b. 1862. THROUGH FOUR REVOLUTIONS, 1862-1933. By H.R.H. Princess Ludwig Ferdinand of Bavaria, Infanta of Spain. Set Forth from her diaries and correspondence by her son H.R.H. Prince Adalbert of Bavaria. Edited with a preface and notes by Major Desmond Chapman-Huston. London: John Murray, 1933. 407p.

Personal, first-hand accounts of the Spanish Revolution of 1868, the French Revolution of 1870, the German Revolution of 1918, and the Spanish Revolution of 1931, by a woman closely related to all the royal houses of Europe.

1903. Maria Feodorovna, Empress Consort of Paul I, Emperor of Russia, 1759-1828. CORRESPONDANCE DE SA MAJESTE L'IMPÉRATRICE MARIE FEODOROVNA AVEC MADEMOISELLE DE NELIDOFF, SA DEMOISELLE D'HONNEUR (1797-1801). SUIVIE DES LETTRES DE MADEMOISELLE DE NELIDOFF

AU PRINCE A.-B. KOURAKINE. Publiée par la princesse Lise Troubetzkoi. Paris: Éditions Leroux, 1896. 372p.

1904. Mariia Feodoronva, Empress Consort of Alexander II, Emperor of Russia, 1847-1928. THE LETTERS OF TSAR NICHOLAUS AND EMPRESS MARIA, BEING THE CONFIDENTIAL CORRESPONDENCE BETWEEN NICHOLAUS II, LAST OF THE TSARS, AND HIS MOTHER, DOWAGER EMPRESS MARIA FEODOROVNA. Edited by Edward J. Bing. London: I. Nicholson and Watson, 1937. 311p. Also published under the title THE SECRET LETTERS OF THE TSAR: BEING THE SECRET CORRESPONDENCE BETWEEN NICHOLAUS II AND HIS MOTHER EMPRESS MARIA FEDOROVNA. New York and Toronto: Longmans, Green & Co., 1938.

Personal correspondence reveals the daily events in the life of two Imperial households. Some of the letters are abridged.

1905. Maria Louisa, Queen Consort of Philip V, King of Spain, 1688-1714. CORRESPONDANCE INÉDITE DE LA DUCHESSE DE BOUGOGNE ET DE LA REINE D'ESPAGNE, PETITE-FILLES DE LOUIS XIV. Publiée par Madame la Comtesse della Rocca (Irene Verasis de Castiglione, Comtesse Morozzo della Rocca). Paris: Michel Lévy Frères, 1865. 262p.

Correspondence with Marie-Adelaide de Savoie, Duchess of Burgandy (1685-1712).

1906. Marie Amélie, Consort of Louis Philippe, King of France, 1782-1866. JOURNAL DE MARIE-AMÉLIE. Publiée par S.A.R. la Duchesse de Vendôme, Princesse Henriette de Belgique. Paris: Librarie Plon, 1935-1938. 2 vols.

1907. Marie Antoinette, Josephe Jeanne d'Autriche, Queen Consort of Louis XVI, King of France, 1755-1793. MARIE-ANTOINETTE, JOSEPH II UND LEOPOLD II, IHRE BRIEFWECHSEL. Herausgegeben von Alfred ritter Von Arneth. Leipzig: K.F. Kohler, 1866. 300p.

1908. ------. CORRESPONDANCE INEDITE DE MARIE ANTOINETTE. Publiée sur les Documents originaux par le Comte Paul Vogt d'Hunolstein. Fourth edition. Paris: Éditions Dentu, 1868. 333p.

1909. ------. LETTRES INÉDITES DE MARIE-ANTOINETTE ET DE MARIE-CLOTHILDE DE FRANCE (SOEUR DE LOUIS IVI) REINE DE SARDAIGNE. Publiées et annotées par le Comte de Reiset. Paris: Firmin-Didot Frères, Fils, et cie., 1876.

Letters to Maria Clothilda, Consort of Charles Emmanuel IV, King of Sardinia (1759-1802).

1910. ------. LETTRES DE MARIE ANTOINETTE RECUEIL DES LETTRES AUTHENTIQUES DE LA REINE. Publiée pour le Société d'Histoire Contemporaine par Maxime de la Rocheterie & le Marquise de Beaucourt. Paris: Picard et Fils, 1895-1896. 2 vols. (Société d'Histoire Contemporaine, Paris, Publications Volume 9, 12.)

1911. ------. THE LETTERS OF MARIE ANTOINETTE, FERSEN AND BARNAVE. Edited, with a foreword by O.-G. de Heidenstam and translated from the French by Winifred Stephens and Mrs. Wilfred Jackson. London: John Lane, 1926. 244p.

Correspondence with Hans Axel, Comte von Fersen, and with Antoine Pierre Joseph Marie Barnave.

1912. ------. MARIE ANTOINETTE ET BARNAVE, CORRES-PONDANCE SECRÈTE (JULLIET 1791-JANVIER 1792). Première édition complete établie d'après les originaux, par Alma Soderhjelm. Paris: A. Colin, 1934. 257p.

1913. Marie Christine, Consort of Albrecht Kasimir, Duke of Saxe-Teschen, 1742-1798. BRIEFE DER ERZHERZOGIN MARIE CHRISTINE, STAAT HATERIN DER NIEDERLANDE AN LEOPOLD II. Nebst einer einleitung: Zur geschicte der franzosischen politick Leopolds II. Herausgegeben von Dr. Hanns Schlitter. Wien: C. Gerold's Sohn, 1896. 360p.

1914. Marie de Lorraine (Or Mary of Guise), Queen of Scotland, 1515-1560. Queen Consort of James V of Scotland and mother of Mary, Queen of Scots. THE SCOTTISH CORRESPONDENCE OF MARY OF LORRAINE: INCLUDING SOME THREE HUNDRED LETTERS FROM 20TH FEBRUARY 1542-3 TO 15TH MAY 1560. Edited by Annie I. Cameron. Edinburgh:

Printed at the University Press by T.& A. Constable for the Scottish History Society, 1927. 476p. (Publications of the Scottish History Society, 3rd Ser., Vol. 10).

1915. Marie Louise, Empress Consort of Napoléon I, 1791-1847. CORRESPONDANCE DE MARIE LOUISE AVEC LA COMTESSE DE COLLOREDO ET MADEMOISELLE DE POUTET (1799-1847). Vienne, 1887.

1916. ------. THE PRIVATE DIARIES OF THE EMPRESS MARIE-LOUISE, WIFE OF NAPOLEON I. With an introduction and commentary by Frederic Masson. New York and London: D. Appleton & Co., 1922. 245p.

Diaries 1810-1814, kept on journeys to Belgium, Holland and the Rhenish Provinces (1811); to Dresden (1812); to Prague, Wurzburg, Mayence and Cherbourg (1813); and the trip to Blois in 1814 which indicated abdication.

1917. ------. MY DEAREST LOUISE: MARIE-LOUISE AND NAPOLEON, 1813-1814. UNPUBLISHED LETTERS FROM THE EMPRESS WITH PREVIOUSLY PUBLISHED REPLIES FROM NAPOLEON. Collected and annotated by C.F. Palmstierna. Translated by E.M. Wilkinson. London: Methuen, 1958. 267p.

1918. Marie d'Orléans, Duchess of Wurtemberg, 1813-1839. Italian artist and sculptor. UNE CORRESPONDANCE INÉDITE DE LA PRINCESSE MARIE D'ORLÉANS, DUCHESSE DE WURTEMBERG. Publiée avec une introduction et des notes par Marthe Kolb. Paris: Boivin, 1937. 289p.

Most of the letters are addressed to Louis Charles d'Orleans, Duc de Nemours.

1919. Marie of Roumania (Marie Alexandra Victoria Saxe- Coburg, Consort of Ferdinand, King of Roumania). 1875-1938. ORDEAL: THE STORY OF MY LIFE. New York: Charles Scribner's Sons, 1935. 429p.

Second volume of her reminiscences. Chiefly extracts from her diary and letters, covering the war years in Roumania from the time she took the throne in 1915 to December, 1918. Deals with politics, diplomatic matters, and life at Court.

1920. Marie Adelaide de Savoie, Duchesse de Bougogne, Dauphine de France, 1685-1712. MARIE-ADELAIDE DE SAVOIE: LETTRES ET CORRESPONDANCES. A. Gagnière. Paris: P. Ollendorf, 1897. 373p.

1921. Marie Thérèse, Archduchess of Austria, Queen of Hungary and Bohemia, Empress of Germany, 1717-1780. MARIE THÉRÈSE UND MARIE ANTOINETTE: IHREN BRIEFWESCHSEL. Herausgegeben von Alfred ritter von Arneth. Mit Briefen des Abbe de Vermond an dem Grafen Mercy. Leipzig: K.F. Kohler, 1866. 415p.

1922. ------. CORRESPONDANCE SECRÈTE ENTRE MARIE-THÉRÈSE ET LE COMTE DE MERCY-ARGENTEAU, AVEC LES LETTRES DE MARIE-THÉRÈSE ET DE MARIE ANTOINETTE. Publiée avec une introduction et des notes par M. Le Chevalier Alfred d'Arneth et de M.A. Geffroy. Paris: Firmin Didot Frères, Fils, et Cie., 1874. 3 vols.

1923. ------. BRIEFE DER KAISERIN MARIA THERESIA AN IHRE KINDER UND FREUNDE. Herausgegeben von Alfred Ritter von Arneth. Wien: W. Braumuller, 1881. 4 vols.

1924. ------. BRIEFE DER KAISERIN MARIE THERESIA. Asgewählt, herausgegeben und eingeleitet von W. Fred. In deutscher ubertragung von Hedwig Kubin. München und Leipzig: G. Miller, 1914. 2 vols.

1925. ------. LETTERS OF AN EMPRESS: A COLLECTION OF INTIMATE LETTERS FROM MARIA THERESIA TO HER CHILDREN AND FRIENDS. Edited by G. Pusch. Translated by Eileen R. Taylor. London: Massie Publishing Co., 1939. 184p.

1926. Maritain, Raïssa Oumansoff, 1833-1960. French religious philosopher and wife of Jacques Maritain. JOURNAL DE RAÏSSA. Publiée par Jacques Maritain. Préface par René Voillaume. Paris: Desclée de Brouwer, 1963, 1965. 383p.

1927. ------. RAÏSSA'S JOURNAL. Presented by Jacques Maritain. Preface by René Voillaume. Albany, N.Y.: Magi Books, 1975. 426p.

Religious diary, 1906-1960.

1928. Markievicz, Constance Georgina Gore-Booth de, 1868-1927. Irish patriot and politician; first woman to be elected to the British Parliament. PRISON LETTERS OF COUNTESS MARKIEVICZ (CONSTANCE GORE-BOOTH). Also Poems and Articles Relating to Easter Week by Eva Gore-Booth, and a Biographical Sketch by Esther Roper. With a preface by President De Valera. London, New York, Etc.: Longmans, Green & Co., 1934. 315p.

Markievicz was a leader of the Irish Worker's Strike in 1913 and second in command of the Easter Rebellion of 1916, for which she was tried and found guilty of treason. Letters from Aylesbury prison, 1916-1917; "on the run," during the 1920's; from Cork Jail, 1919; from Montjoy Prison, 1920-1921; and letters after her imprisonment up to 1926. Most of the letters are to her sister, Eva Gore-Booth.

1929. Marlborough, Sarah Jennings Churchill, Duchess of, 1660-1744. English society leader and intimate of Queen Anne. PRIVATE CORRESPONDENCE OF SARAH, DUCHESS OF MARLBOROUGH, ILLUSTRATIVE OF THE TIME OF QUEEN ANNE; WITH HER SKETCHES AND OPINIONS OF HER CONTEMPORARIES; AND THE SELECT CORRESPONDENCE OF HER HUSBAND, JOHN, DUKE OF MARLBOROUGH. London: H. Colburn, 1838. 2 vols.

1930. ------. LETTERS OF SARAH, DUCHESS OF MARLBOROUGH. Now first published from the original manuscripts at Madresfield Court. With an introduction. London: John Murray, 1875. 174p.

Letters 1710-1725, relating to Queen Anne's reign and the fall of the Whig ministry, in which the Duke of Marlborough took a leading role.

1931. ------. LETTERS OF A GRANDMOTHER, 1732-1735: BEING THE CORRESPONDENCE OF SARAH, DUCHESS OF

MARLBOROUGH, WITH HER GRANDDAUGHTER DIANA, DUCHESS OF BEDFORD. Edited by Gladys Scott Thomson. London: Jonathan Cape, 1943. 184p.

Letters concern family affairs, relate experiences abroad, and discuss public affairs, books read, and architecture.

1932. Marquard, Margaret Murray, b. 1862. LETTERS FROM A BOER PARSONAGE: LETTERS OF MARGARET MARQUARD DURING THE BOER WAR. Edited by Leo Marquard. Cape Town, Johannesburg: Purnell, 1967. 140p.

1933. Marr, Margaret. American. "A Visit to Mount Vernon--1850." MT. VERNON LADIES ASSOCIATION OF THE UNION ANNUAL REPORT, October 1964-October, 1965 (1965), 27-28.

Letter to her brother, dated June 8, 1850, describing Mt. Vernon, New York.

1934. Marshall, Lenore, b. 1897. American author. INVENTED A PERSON: THE PERSONAL RECORD OF A LIFE. Edited with an introduction by Janice Thaddeus. Foreword by Muriel Rukeyser. New York: Horizon Books, 1979. 264p.

Writer's diary. Knowing she was dying of cancer, Marshall had begun to assemble some of her papers into notebooks in 1971; she died before the task was finished. Except for her travel diaries (she went on various European trips, including an aborted tour at the outbreak of World War I) the entries are not dated, but are arranged by theme.

1935. Martin, Martha (pseud. for Helen Bolyan), d. 1959. American. O RUGGED LAND OF GOLD. New York: The Macmillan Co., 1953. 233p.

Highly suspenseful account by a woman six months pregnant, injured in a landslide, and stranded alone for a winter in a mountain cabin on the Alaskan shore.

1936. Martineau, Harriet, 1802-1876. English author,

social reformer, economist and philanthropist. HARRIET MARTINEAU'S LETTERS TO FANNY WEDGWOOD. Edited by Elisabeth Sanders Arbuckle. Stanford, Calif.: Stanford University Press, 1983. 329p.

More than 120 letters, "meant for burning," to Fanny Wedgwood (1800-1889) and her family reveals a friendship between two intelligent and socially aware Victorian women, and affords glimpses into the literary, social, and political circles of the day.

1937. Martinez de Nisser, Maria. Columbian author and soldier. MARIA MARTINEZ DE NISSER Y LA REVOLUTION DE LOS SUPREMOS. Roberto Maria Tisnes Jimenez. Bogota, Columbia: Banco Popular, 1983. 383p.

Includes extracts from her diary account of her experience as a soldier during the Revolution in Antioquia in 1840-1841.

1938. Mary II, Queen of Great Britain, 1662-1694. THE THIRD MARY STUART, MARY OF YORK, ORANGE, AND ENGLAND: BEING A CHARACTER STUDY WITH MEMOIRS AND LETTERS OF QUEEN MARY II OF ENGLAND, 1662-1694. Marjorie Bowen. London: John Lane, 1929. 319p.

1939. Mary Stuart, Queen of Scots, 1542-1587. LETTERS OF MARY, QUEEN OF SCOTS, AND DOCUMENTS CONNECTED WITH HER PERSONAL HISTORY. Introduction by Agnes Strickland. London: H. Colburn, 1842. 2 vols.

1940. ------. LETTRES, INSTRUCTIONS ET MEMOIRES DE MARIE STUART, REINE D'ÉCOSSE. Publiées sur les originaux de les manuscrits du State Paper Office de Londres et des principales archives et bibliothèques de l'Europe, et accompagne d'un resumé chronologique par le Prince Labanoff. London: C. Dolman, 1844. 7 vols.

1941. ------. LETTRES DE MARIE STUART. Publiées avec sommaires, traductions, et notes par A. Teulet. Paris: Firmin Didot Frères, Fils et Cie., 1859. 448p.

Letters to the Earl of Bothwell and others.

1942. ------. A LETTER FROM MARY QUEEN OF SCOTS TO THE DUKE OF GUISE, JANUARY 1562. Reprinted in facsimile from the original manuscript in the possession of the late John Scott, of Halkshill. Edited, with translation, historical introduction and appendix of original documents, by John Hungerford Pollen. Edinburgh: Printed at The University Press by T. and A. Constable, for the Scottish History Society, 1904. 81p. (Publications of the Scottish History Society, Vol. 43.)

1943. ------. LETTERS, TRANSCRIPTS AND PAPERS. Foster Collection, Victoria and Albert Museum, London. West Yorkshire, England: Microform, Ltd. 1 reel (35mm).

1944. Mary Adelaide Wilhelmina Elizabeth, Duchess of Teck, Princess, 1833-1897. A MEMOIR OF PRINCESS ADELAIDE, DUCHESS OF TECK, BASED ON HER PRIVATE DIARIES AND LETTERS. Sir Clement Kinloch-Cooke. New York: Charles Scribner's Sons; London: John Murray, 1900. 2 vols.

1945. Masterson, Jenny Gove, pseud. LETTERS FROM JENNY. Edited and interpreted by Gordon W. Allport. New York: Harcourt Brace & World, 1965. 223p.

Letters 1926-1937 reveal a destructive mother-son relationship. Allport presents various psychological analyses of the letters (existential, depth approaches, Jungian, Adlerian, and Freudian) as well as a structural-dyanmic approach and a discussion of normality and abnormality using "Jenny's" letters as a base.

1946. Matheson, Eleanor Shepphird. Canadian missionary. "Documents of Western History: The Journal of Eleanor Shepphird Matheson, 1920." Edited by Ruth Matheson Buck. SASKATCHEWAN HISTORY 22:2 (1969), 66-72 and 22:3 (1969), 109-117.

1947. May, Anna (pseud.). American. JOURNAL OF ANNA MAY. Edited by George W. Robinson. Cambridge, Mass.: Privately Printed, 1941. 100p.

Diary of a senior student at New Hampton Institution in the second half of the academic year, 1856-1857.

1948. Mayo, Abigail de Hart, 1761-1843. American. AN AMERICAN LADY IN PARIS, 1828-1829: THE DIARY OF MRS. JOHN MAYO. Edited by Mary Mayo Crenshaw. Boston and New York: Houghton Mifflin Co., 1927. 144p.

Social diary.

1949. Mead, Margaret, 1901-1978. American anthropologist. LETTERS FROM THE FIELD, 1925-1975. New York: Harper & Row, 1977. 343p.

Letters, selected by Mead, spanning a fifty-year career of anthropological fieldwork, begining with her first assignment in Samoa.

1950. Meakin, Annette M. British traveler and travel author. WHAT AMERICA IS DOING: LETTERS FROM THE NEW WORLD. Edinburgh and London: William Blackwood and Sons, 1911. 346p.

Travel letters of a British woman touring the United States at the turn of the century, containing extensive and detailed observations on American culture.

1951. Meath, Mary Jane Maitland Brabazon, Countess of, d. 1918. English philanthropist. THE DIARIES OF MARY, COUNTESS OF MEATH. Edited by her husband, (Reginald Brabazon, 12th Earl of Meath). London: Hutchinson, 1928-1929. 2 vols.

Diary 1880-1918 describes philanthropic work.

1952. Mecom, Jane Franklin, 1712-1794. American sister of Benjamin Franklin. THE LETTERS OF BENJAMIN FRANKLIN AND JANE MECOM. Edited with an introduction by Carl Van Doren. Princeton, N.J.: Published for the American Philosophical Society by Princeton University Press; and London: Geoffry Cumberledge, Oxford University Press, 1950. 380p.

Correspondence between Franklin and Mecom, 1726-1790, with letters from Mecom to relatives to

1793. Franklin's favorite sister, Mecom is, according to Van Doren, the only one of the many Franklins who can be compared with him.

1953. Mecquier, Mary Jane. American frontier settler. APRON FULL OF GOLD: THE LETTERS OF MARY JANE MECQUIER FROM SAN FRANCISCO, 1849-1856. Edited by Robert Glass Cleland. San Marino, Calif.: The Huntington Library, 1949.

1954. Melbourne, Elizabeth Milbanke Lamb, Viscountess, 1752-1818, and Emily Mary Lamb Temple, Viscountess Palmerston, 1787-1869. IN WHIG SOCIETY, 1775-1818: COMPILED FROM THE HITHERTO UNPUBLISHED CORRESPONDENCE OF ELIZABETH, VISCOUNTESS MELBOURNE AND EMILY LAMB, COUNTESS COWPER, AFTERWARDS VISCOUNTESS PALMERSTON. Edited by Countess Airlie (Mabel Frances Elizabeth Gore Ogilvy, Countess of Airlie). London and New York: Hodder and Stoughton, 1921. 205p.

1955. Mendenhall, Abby Grant (Swift). American? SOME EXTRACTS FROM THE PERSONAL DIARY OF MRS. R.J. MENDENHALL; ALSO PRESS NOTICES AND SOME EARLY AND LATER CORRESPONDENCE TO HER, BY HER, ETC. [Minneapolis? 1900?] 542p.

Mere Agnes. See: Arnauld, Jeanne Catherine Agnes.

Mere Angelique. See: Arnauld, Jacqueline Marie Angelique.

1956. Meredith, Emily Robertson Sorin, 1836-1913. American frontier settler. "Bannack and Gallatin City in 1862-1863: A Letter by Mrs. Emily R. Meredith." Edited by Clyde McLemore. FRONTIER AND MIDLAND 17:4 (Summer, 1937), 282-290.

Lengthy letter to her father in Minnesota, written in installments during an overland journey to Idaho in 1862.

1957. Merlin, Maria de Los Mercédés Santa Cruz y Montalvo, Condese de. Cuban aristocrat. VIAJE A LA

HABAÑA, POR LA CONDESA DE MERLIN. Precidido de Una Biografía de esta Ilustre Cubana por la Senorita D. A. Gertrudis Goméz de Avellaneda. Madrid: Imprenta de la Sociedad Literaría y Tipografica, 1844. 109p.

1958. Merrill, Catharine, 1824-1900. American educator, biographer and historian. CATHARINE MERRILL: LIFE AND LETTERS. Collected and arranged by Katherine Merrill Graydon. Greenfield, Ind.: Mitchell, 1934. 483p.

1959. Mesnil-Amar, Jacqueline. French. CEUX QUI NE DORMAIENT PAS (1944-1946: FRAGMENTS DE JOURNAL). Paris: Les Editions de Minuit, 1957. 190p.

World War II diary.

1960. Meysenbug, Malwida von, 1816-1903. German author and social reformer. Friend of Wagner, Nietzsche, Herzen, and Mazzini. IM ANFANG WAR DIE LIEBE: BRIEFE AN IHRE PFLEGETOCHTER. Herausgegeben von Berta Schleicher. Munchen: C.H. Beck, 1926. 327p.

1961. ------. LETTERS OF ROMAINE ROLLAND AND MALWIDA VON MEYSENBUG, 1890-1891. Translated from the French by Thomas J. Wilson. New York: Henry Holt and Co., 1933. 274p.

Letters between Meysenbug and Rolland, a young French artist, tells the story of their passionate, intellectual, platonic friendship.

1962. ------. MALWIDA VON MEYSENBUG: BRIEFE AN JOHANNA UND GOTTFRIED KINKEL, 1849-1885. Herausgegeben von Stefania Rossi, unter Mitarbeit von Yoko Kikuchi. Bonn: Rohrscheid, 1982. 269p.

Includes correspondence with Johanna Kinkel (1810-1858).

1963. Michaelis, Karin (Katharina Marie Bech Brodum), 1872-1950. Danish author. THE DANGEROUS AGE: LETTERS AND FRAGMENTS FROM A WOMAN'S DIARY. New York: John Lane, 1911. 215p.

1964. Middleton, Harriet, and Susan Middleton. American Confederate letter-writers. "Middleton Correspondence, 1861-1865." Edited by Isabella Middleton Leland. SOUTH CAROLINA HISTORICAL MAGAZINE 63: 1 (1962), 33-41; 63:2 (1962), 61-70; 63:3 (1962), 164-174; 63:4 (1962), 204-210; 64:1 (1963), 28-38; 64:2 (1963), 95-104; 64:3 (1963), 158-168; 64:4 (1963), 212-220; 65:1 (1964), 33-44; and 65:2 (1964), 98-109.

Civil war letters between sisters, Susan in Flat Rock, North Carolina, and Harriet in Columbia, South Carolina.

1965. Milburn, Clara. English. MRS. MILBURN'S DIARIES: AN ENGLISHWOMAN'S DAY-TO-DAY REFLECTIONS, 1939-1945. Edited, with an introduction by Peter Donnelly. Afterword by Judy Milburn. New York: Schocken Books, 1980. 304p.

World War II diary, describing blackouts, bombings, and anxiety about a son who fought and was captured at Dunkirk.

1966. Mill, Harriet Taylor, 1807-1858. English philosopher and feminist, wife of John Stuart Mill. JOHN STUART MILL AND HARRIET TAYLOR: THEIR FRIENDSHIP AND SUBSEQUENT MARRIAGE. F.A. Hayek. London: Routledge & Kegan Paul, 1951. 320p.

Contains practically "every scrap" of correspondence written during their eighteen years of friendship prior to their marriage, and a selection thereafter. Letters span the years 1829- 1858, and give a good overview of Taylor's life and philosophy.

1967. Millard, Shirley. American. I SAW THEM DIE: DIARY AND RECOLLECTIONS OF MRS. SHIRLEY MILLARD. Edited by Adele Comandini. London: George G. Harp & Co., and New York: Harcourt Brace & Co., 1936. 115p.

Diary March 16--November 10, 1918, and reminiscences of an American working as a nurse with a volunteer unit in France.

1968. Millay, Edna St. Vincent, 1892-1950. American poet. THE LETTERS OF EDNA ST. VINCENT MILLAY. Edited by Allan Ross Macdougall. New York: Harper & Bros., 1952. 384p.

Letters 1900-1950 to the Millay family, and to Arthur Davidson Ficke, Louis Untermeyer, Charlotte Babcock Sills, Edmund Wilson, and others. Macdougall notes that Millay's husband, Eugene Boissevain, assumed much of her correspondence in order to leave her free to work.

1969. Millin, Sara Gertrude Liebson, b.1889. English. THE REELING EARTH. London: Faber & Faber, 1945. 305p.

World War II diary, September 3, 1940--August 31, 1941.

1970. ------. THE PIT OF THE ABYSS. London: Faber & Faber, 1946. 304p.

World War II diary, September 1, 1941--September 1, 1942.

1971. ------. THE SOUND OF THE TRUMPET. London: Faber & Faber, 1947. 269p.

World War II diary, September, 1942--September, 1943.

1972. ------. FIRE OUT OF HEAVEN. London: Faber & Faber, 1947. 316p.

World War II diary, September 1, 1943--September 1, 1944.

1973. ------. THE SEVEN THUNDERS. London: Faber & Faber, 1948. 335p.

World War II diary, September 1, 1944--October 14, 1946.

1974. Millington, Ada, later Jones, 1849-1930. American journalist, religious writer and frontier settler. "Journal Kept While Crossing the Plains, by Ada Millington." Edited and annotated by Charles G. Clarke. SOUTHERN CALIFORNIA QUARTERLY 59 (Spring, 1977), 13-48; 59:2 (Summer, 1977), 139-184; and 59:3 (Fall, 1977), 251-270.

Journal April 29--September 6, 1862, kept while traveling on the overland route from Nebraska City to Santa Rosa, California. The journal is significant for two reasons: because it describes a new route across central Nevada, and because it was written by a young girl: she was twelve when she made the journey. The journal was rewritten by Millington from the original, but retains the diary form.

1975. Mist, Augusta Ultenhage de. DIARY OF A JOURNEY TO THE CAPE OF GOOD HOPE AND THE INTERIOR OF AFRICA IN 1802 AND 1808. Capetown: A.A. Balkema, 1954. 57p.

1976. Mistral, Gabriela (pseud. for Lucila Godoy Alcayaga), 1889-1957. Chilean poet, teacher, author, diplomat and traveler. EPISTOLARIO: CARTAS A EUGENIO LABARCA, 1915-1916. Introduccion y notas de Raul Silva Castro. Santiago: Ediciones de la Annales de la Universidad de Chile, 1947, 1957. 58p.

1977. ------. GABRIELA MISTRAL, REBELDE MAGNIFICA. Biblioteca Contemporanea. Buenos Aires: Editions Losada, 1962. 189p.

Correspondence between Mistral and Chilean author Matilde Ladron de Guevara.

1978. ------. CARTAS DE AMOR DE GABRIELA MISTRAL. Introduccion, recopilacion, iconografia ye notas de Sergio Fernandez Larrain. Santiago: Editorias Andres Bello, 1978. 243p.

1979. Mitchell, Clara. American. "In Society." MISSOURI HISTORICAL SOCIETY BULLETIN 22:2 (1965), 115-132.

Diary extracts describe social life in St. Louis in 1887.

1980. Mitchell, Margaret, 1900-1949. American newspaper reporter and author. MARGARET MITCHELL'S "GONE WITH THE WIND" LETTERS, 1936-1949. Edited by Richard Harwell. New York: Macmillan Publishing Co., and London: Collier-Macmillan Publishers, 1976. 441p.

Correspondence regarding her novel GONE WITH THE WIND, including letters to friends, fans, her publishers, historians, authors, and people connected with the film version of the novel.

1981. Mitchell, Maria, 1818-1889. American astronomer, educator, novelist and poet. MARIA MITCHELL: LIFE, LETTERS, AND JOURNALS. Compiled by Phoebe Mitchell Kendall. Boston: Lee & Shepard, 1896. 293p.

Extracts from letters and journals 1847-1889, with commentary by the editor.

1982. Mitchell, Maria Hay Flyter, d. 1907. American missionary. IN SOUTHERN INDIA: MISSION STATIONS IN MADRAS. London: Religious Tract Society, 1885. 372p.

Diary January-March, 1882, written while visiting Mission stations in India.

1983. ------. A MISSIONARY'S WIFE AMONG THE WILD TRIBES OF SOUTHERN BENGAL: EXTRACTS FROM THE JOURNAL OF MRS. MURRY MITCHELL. George Smith. Edinburgh: John MacLaren, 1871. 70p.

1984. ------. IN INDIA: SKETCHES OF INDIAN LIFE AND TRAVEL FROM LETTERS AND JOURNALS. London and New York: T. Nelson and Sons, 1876. 319p.

Diary of travel in Bengal and Madras.

1985. Mitchell, Suzanne, pseud. American psychotherapist. MY OWN WOMAN: THE DIARY OF AN ANALYSIS. New York: Horizon Press, 1973. 269p.

Diary account of psychoanalysis.

1986. Mitchill, Catharine Akerly Cocks. American wife of Congressman Lathan Mitchill of New York. "Catharine Mitchill's Letters From Washington, 1806-1812." Carolyn Hoover Sung. QUARTERLY JOURNAL OF THE LIBRARY OF CONGRESS 34:3 (1977), 171-189.

Discussion and summary of letters, giving an account of the developing Capital city during the eighteen hundreds, and Mitchill's life in politics as the wife of a Congressman.

1987. Mitchison, Naomi Margaret Haldane, b. 1897. Irish- American journalist, novelist and poet. NAOMI MITCHISON'S VIENNA DIARY. New York: Harrison Smith and Robert Haas, 1934. 287p.

Diary February 23--April 10, 1934 of a socialist writer who traveled to Vienna to obtain information about the Socialist-Democrats there after the counter-revolution of 1934.

1988. ------. AMONG YOU TAKING NOTES: The WARTIME DIARY OF NAOMI MITCHISON, 1939-1945. Edited by Dorothy Sheridan. London: Victor Gollancz, 1985. 352p.

1989. Mitford, Mary Russell, 1786-1855. English poet, playwright, novelist and essayist. THE LIFE OF MARY RUSSELL MITFORD, RELATED IN A SELECTION FROM HER LETTERS TO HER FRIENDS. Edited by the Reverend A.G. L'Estrange. London: Richard Bentley, 1870. 3 vols. New York: Harper & Bros., 1870. 2 vols.

1990. ------. LETTERS OF MARY RUSSELL MITFORD, SECOND SERIES. Edited by Henry Chorley. London: Richard Bentley, 1872. 2 vols.

1991. ------. MARY RUSSELL MITFORD: CORRESPONDENCE WITH CHARLES BONER AND JOHN RUSKIN. Edited by Elizabeth Lee. Chicago: Rand McNally & Co., 1914. 323p.

Letters to Boner, 1845-1855 and to Ruskin, 1852-1854. The difference in tone in her letters to Boner and those to Ruskin is very noticeable. To

Ruskin she wrote with complete abandonment; to Boner she wrote as a "sort of English correspondent."

1992. ------. THE LETTERS OF MARY RUSSELL MITFORD. Selected, with an introduction by R. Brimley Johnson. London: John Lane, and New York: Lincoln Macveagh, the Dial Press, 1925. 236p.

Selection of letters intended for the popular audience, as an introduction to her life and letters.

1993. Modersohn-Becker, Paula, 1876-1907. German artist and pioneer of modern art. EINE KUNSTLERIN: BRIEFE UND TAGEBÜCHBLATTER / PAULA MODERSOHN-BECKER. Bremen: F. Leuwer, 1918. 159p.

1994. ------. DIE BRIEFE UND TAGEBÜCHBLATTER VON PAULA MODERSOHN-BECKER. Herausgegeben von Sophie Dorothee Gallwitz. Berlin: Kurt Wolff Verlag, 1920. München: Paul List Verlag, 1957. 240p.

1995. ------. PAULA MODERSOHN-BECKER. 8 FARBBILDER, 24 SWARZWEISSBILDER UND 7 ABBILDUNGEN IM TEXT. Min einer einfuhrung von Harald Seiler. München: Verlag F. Bruckmann, 1959. 32p.

Color and black & white reproductions of a selection of her works, accompanied by extracts from her letters and diary.

1996. ------. PAULA MODERSOHN-BECKER: IN BRIEFEN UND TAGEBÜCHERN. Herausgegeben von Gunter Busch und Liselotte von Reinken. Frankfurt am Main: S. Fischer, 1979. 621p.

Diaries and letters, 1892-1907.

1997. ------. LETTERS AND JOURNALS OF PAULA MODERSOHN- BECKER. Translated and annotated by J. Diane Radycki. Introduction by Alessandra Comini. Epilogue by Adrienne Rich and Lily Engler. Metuchen, N.J.: Scarecrow Press, 1980. 344p.

Letters and journals are edited together

chronologically to compare her public statements in her letters with her private writings and admissions in her diary.

1998. ------. PAULA MODERSOHN-BECKER: THE LETTERS AND JOURNALS. Edited by Gunther Busch and Liselotte von Reinken. Translated by Arthur S. Wensinger and Carole Clew Hoey. New York: Taplinger Publishing, 1983. 576p.

1999. Moffat, Mary. English missionary. APPRENTICESHIP AT KURUMAN: BEING THE JOURNALS AND LETTERS OF ROBERT AND MARY MOFFAT, 1820-1828. Edited by I. Schapera. London: Chatto & Windus, 1951. 308p.

Official journal by Robert Moffat required by the London Missionary Society of Missionaries in the Field. Letters by Mary Moffat, describing missionary work in South Africa. Most of the letters are severely pruned, especially of personal matter ("such as news and gossip about relatives and friends") in favor of the more public material the editor sees as more valuable for a study of the mission at Kuruman.

2000. Mohl, Mary Elizabeth Clarke, 1793-1883. French salonist and wife of German orientalist Julius Mohl. LETTERS AND RECOLLECTIONS OF JULIUS AND MARY MOHL. Mary Charlotte Mair Simpson. London: Paul and Trench Co., 1887. 398p.

2001. ------. CORRESPONDANCE DE FAURIEL ET MARY CLARKE. Publiée par Ottmar de Mohl; avec trois portraits. Paris: Plon-Nourrit et Cie., 1911.

Correspondence with Claude Charles Fauriel.

2002. Molloy, Alice. American Lesbian feminist. IN OTHER WORDS: NOTES ON THE POLITICS AND MORALE OF SURVIVAL. FROM MY NOTEBOOKS OF 1971 THROUGH 1973 WITH COMMENTS AND WORD TRIPS AND EXCERPTS FROM THINGS I WAS READING. Berkeley, Calif.: The Women's Press Collective, 1977. 131p.

Chronicles three years of feminist growth and the

amassing of knowledge to form her "feminist-anarchist-lesbian-witch" philosophy.

2003. Monkswell, Mary Josephine Hardcastle Collier, Baroness, 1849-1930. English diarist. A VICTORIAN DIARIST: EXTRACTS FROM THE JOURNALS OF MARY, LADY MONKSWELL. Edited by the Hon. E.C.F. Collier. London: John Murray, 1944-1946. 2 vols.

Diaries 1873-1909.

2004. Monnier, Adrienne, 1892-1955. English author and bookseller. THE VERY RICH HOURS OF ADRIENNE MONNIER. AN INTIMATE PORTRAIT OF THE LITERARY AND ARTISTIC LIFE IN PARIS BETWEEN THE WARS. Translated, with an introduction and commentaries by Richard Mc-Dougall. New York: Charles Scribner's Sons, 1976. 536p.

Literary autobiography, containing autobiographical essays, letters, and extracts from her journals.

2005. Montagu, Elizabeth Robinson, 1720-1800. English intellectual, author, letter writer and Bluestocking. THE LETTERS OF ELIZABETH MONTAGU, WITH SOME OF THE LETTERS OF HER CORRESPONDENTS. PART THE FIRST, CONTAINING HER LETTERS FROM AN EARLY AGE TO THE AGE OF TWENTY-THREE. Published by Matthew Montagu. London: printed for T. Cadell and W. Davies by W. Bulmer & Co., 1809-1813. 4 vols. Reprinted, New York: AMS Press, 1974. 4 vols.

2006. ------. A LADY OF THE LAST CENTURY (MRS. ELIZABETH MONTAGU) ILLUSTRATED IN HER UNPUBLISHED LETTERS. Collected and arranged, with a biographical sketch and a chapter on Blue Stockings by Dr. Doran [John Doran]. London: R. Bentley and Son, 1873. 372p.

2007. ------. ELIZABETH MONTAGU: QUEEN OF THE BLUE-STOCKINGS. HER CORRESPONDENCE FROM 1720 TO 1761. Edited by her great-great niece, Emily J. Climenson. London: John Murray, 1906. 2 vols. New York: E.P. Dutton, 1906. 2 vols.

Selection of Montagu's letters, intended for the

general reader, to her most notable correspondents, including Dr. Johnson, Lawrence Sterne, Hannah More, Elizabeth Carter, Mrs. Delany, Mrs. Thrale, Edmund Burke, and Fanny Burney.

2008. ------. MRS. MONTAGU, "QUEEN OF THE BLUES": HER LETTERS AND FRIENDSHIPS FROM 1762 TO 1800. Edited by Reginald Blunt from material left to him by her Great-great-niece Emily J. Climenson. London: Constable & Co., 1923. 2 vols. Boston: Houghton Mifflin, 1923. 2 vols.

Continuation of the Climenson volumes.

2009. ------. "A Blue-Stocking Friendship: The Letters of Elizabeth Montagu and Frances Reynolds in the Princeton Collection." Richard Wendorf and Charles Ryskamp. PRINCETON UNIVERSITY LIBRARY CHRONICLE 41:3 (1980), 173-207.

2010. Montagu, Mary Pierrepont Wortley, Lady, 1689-1762. English poet, political essayist, and advocate of smallpox innoculation in England. LETTERS OF THE RIGHT HONORABLE M--Y W-----Y M------E; WRITTEN DURING HER TRAVELS IN EUROPE, ASIA AND AFRICA, TO PERSONS OF DISTINCTION, MEN OF LETTERS, ETC., IN DIFFERENT PARTS OF EUROPE. WHICH CONTAIN, AMONG OTHER CURIOUS RELATIONS, ACCOUNTS OF THE POLICY AND MANNERS OF THE TURKS; DRAWN FROM SOURCES THAT HAVE BEEN INACCESSIBLE TO OTHER TRAVELLERS. London: Printed for T. Becket and P.A. De Hondt, in the Strand, 1763. 3 vols.

First unauthorized edition of her letters, based on a copy of the "Embassy Letters," a compilation of fifty-two pseudo-letters derived from actual letters to friends Lady Montagu had rearranged and edited to form a travelogue/essay.

2011. ------. AN ADDITIONAL VOLUME TO THE LETTERS OF THE RIGHT HONORABLE LADY M--Y W-----Y M------E. London: Printed for T. Becket and P.A. De Hondt, in the Strand, 1767.

Published as a supplementary volume to the first

edition. According to Robert Halsband, it contains five spurious letters, and the events surrounding both editions are mysterious.

2012. ------. THE WORKS OF THE RIGHT HONORABLE LADY MARY WORTLEY MONTAGU, INCLUDING HER CORRESPONDENCE, POEMS, AND ESSAYS. Published by permission from her genuine papers. (Edited by James Dallaway). London: Printed for Richard Phillips, No. 71, St. Paul's Churchyard, 1803. 5 vols.

2013. ------. THE LETTERS AND WORKS OF LADY MARY WORTLEY MONTAGU. Edited by Her Great Grandson Lord Wharncliffe. London: Richard Bentley, 1837. 3 vols. Third edition, with additions and corrections derived from the original manuscripts, illustrative notes and a new memoir by W. Moy Thomas. London: Henry G. Bohn, 1861. 2 vols.

Includes anecdotes by Lady Louisa Stuart, Lady Mary's grandmother, and letters to Lady Pomfret, Lady Oxford, and Sir James and Lady Frances Steuart. The third edition contains no new letters, but the text of some letters is different, as this edition is drawn from the original manuscripts wherever possible.

2014. ------. THE BEST LETTERS OF LADY MARY WORTLEY MONTAGU. Edited with a dedicatory letter to Lady Montagu by Octave Thanet. Chicago: A.C. McClurg & Co., 1890. 302p.

A selection from the 1861 edition (item 2013).

2015. ------. LADY MARY WORTLEY MONTAGU: SELECT PASSAGES FROM HER LETTERS. Edited by Arthur R. Ropes. New York, 1892? 308p.

2016. ------. LETTERS FROM CONSTANTINOPLE, BY LADY MARY WORTLEY MONTAGU. Selected and edited with an introduction and notes by Hilda Chatwin. London: Methuen and Co., 1921. 95p.

2017. ------. THE COMPLETE LETTERS OF LADY MARY

WORTLEY MONTAGU. Edited by Robert Halsband. Oxford: The Oxford University Press at the Clarendon Press, 1965-1967. 3 vols.

Definitive edition. Letters 1708-1762, including one hundred letters _to_ Lady Montagu, and a childhood correspondence with Philippa Mundy.

2018. ------. THE SELECTED LETTERS OF LADY MARY WORTLEY MONTAGU. Edited by Robert Halsband. London and New York: Longmans, 1970. 310p.

Abridged version of the 1965-1967 edition.

2019. Montcalm-Gozon, Armande Marie Antoinette du Plessis, Marquise de, 1777-1832. UN SALON POLITIQUE SOUS LA RESTORATION: CORRESPONDANCE DE LA MARQUISE DE MONTCALM, NÉE RICHELIEU, SOEUR DU LIBERATEUR DU TERRITOIRE. Préface de J. Fouques Dupark. Publiée par Emmanuel de Levis Mierpoix. Paris: Éditions du Grand Siècle, 1949. 293p.

2020. ------. LA MARQUISE DE MONTCALM: MON JOURNAL, 1815-1818, PENDANT LE PRÉMIER MINISTERE DE MON FRÈRE. Publiée par Sebastien Charlety. Paris: Éditions Bernard Grasset, 1936. 368p.

2021. Montefiore, Judith Cohen, Lady, 1784-1862. English Jewish traveler and philanthropist; wife of Sir Moses Montefiore. NOTES FROM A PRIVATE JOURNAL OF A VISIT TO EGYPT AND PALESTINE BY WAY OF ITALY AND THE MEDITERRANEAN. London: Printed by J. Rickerby, 1836, 1844. 322p. "Not published." Second edition, London: Printed by Wertheimer, Lea, 1885. 410p.

2022. ------. DIARIES OF SIR MOSES HAIM AND LADY MONTEFIORE, COMPRISING THEIR LIFE AND WORKS AS RECORDED IN THEIR DIARIES FROM 1812 TO 1883. Edited by L. Loewe, assisted by his son. Chicago: Belford-Clarke, 1890. 2 vols.

Memoirs written from some eighty-five diaries by Sir Montefiore and five by Lady Montefiore. The entries are much abridged and often rewritten in the third person.

2023. Montgomery, L.M. (Lucy Maud), 1874-1942. Canadian-American novelist and children's author. "L.M. Montgomery as a Letter-Writer." Ephraim Weber. DALHOUSIE REVIEW 22:3 (October, 1942), 300-310.

Personal, intimate essay on the correspondence between Weber and Montgomery; contains extracts from her letters.

2024. ------. THE GREEN GABLES LETTERS: FROM L.M. MONTGOMERY TO EPHRAIM WEBER, 1905-1909. Edited by Wilfred Eggleston. Toronto: Ryerson, 1960. 102p.

2025. ------. "MY DEAR M.": LETTERS TO G.B. MACMILLAN. Edited by F.W.P. Bolger and Elizabeth Epperly. Toronto and New York: McGraw-Hill Ryerson, 1980. 212p.

2026. ------. THE SELECTED JOURNALS OF L.M. MONTGOMERY. Edited by Mary Rubio and Elizabeth Waterston. Toronto: Oxford University Press, 1985.

Volume 1: 1889-1910.

2027. Moodie, Susana Strickland, 1803-1885. English-Canadian author; sister of Agnes Strickland and Catharine Parr Strickland. LETTERS OF A LIFETIME. Edited by Carl Ballstadt, Elizabeth Hopkins and Michael Peterman. Toronto and Buffalo, N.Y.: University of Toronto Press, 1985. 390p.

Literary letters, 1826-1832 to editors, publishers and other London literary figures; and letters from Canada to her family, 1833-1885, touching on Canadian social and political life, domestic and family affairs, and literary matters.

Moore, Alice: See Sawyer, Alice Moore.

2028. Moore, Jessie Fremont, b. 1857. English

missionary and wife of P.H. Moore, missionary to India. TWENTY YEARS IN ASSAM: OR, LEAVES FROM MY JOURNAL. Nowgong: Privately printed by Mrs. P.H. Moore, 1901. 222p.

2029. ------. FURTHER LEAVES FROM ASSAM: A CONTINUATION OF MY JOURNAL "TWENTY YEARS IN ASSAM." Nowgong: Privately printed by Mrs. P.H. Moore, 1907. 191p.

Missionary diary, 1900-1907.

2030. ------. AUTUMN LEAVES FROM ASSAM: A CONTINUATION OF MY JOURNAL "TWENTY YEARS IN ASSAM AND "FURTHER LEAVES FROM ASSAM." Nowgong: Privately printed by Mrs. P.H. Moore, 1910. 96p.

2031. ------. STRAY LEAVES FROM ASSAM: A CONTINUATION OF MY JOURNAL "TWENTY YEARS IN ASSAM," "FURTHER LEAVES FROM ASSAM," AND "AUTUMN LEAVES FROM ASSAM." Rochester: Privately printed by Mrs. P.H. Moore, 1916. 128p.

2032. Moore, Nancy E., 1807-1899. American Shaker. THE JOURNAL OF ELDRESS NANCY, KEPT AT SOUTH UNION, KENTUCKY, SHAKER COLONY, AUGUST 15, 1861-- SEPTEMBER 4, 1864. Edited with an introduction and glossary by Mary Julia Neal. Nashville, Ky.: Parthenon Press, sold by the Shaker Museum, Auburn, Kentucky, 1963. 256p.

Shaker diary, 1861-1864, kept during the Civil War, "apparently an official record of the Colony at South Union, Kentucky" (cf. AMERICAN DIARIES, 1983)

Mordaunt, Elizabeth Cary, Viscountess Duncairn. See: Duncairn, Elizabeth Carey Mordaunt, Viscountess.

2033. More, Hannah, 1745-1833. English intellectual, educator, and Bluestocking. THE LETTERS OF HANNAH MORE TO ZACHARY MACAULAY. CONTAINING NOTICES OF LORD MACAULAY'S YOUTH. Edited by Arthur Roberts. London: J. Nisbet, and New York: Carter & Brother, 1860. 215p.

2034. ------. MEMOIRS OF THE LIFE AND CORRESPONDENCE OF MRS. HANNAH MORE. Edited by William Roberts. New York: Harper & Brothers, 1855. 2 vols.

2035. ------. THE LETTERS OF HANNAH MORE. Selected, with an introduction by R. Brimley Johnson. London: John Lane, 1925. 212p.

2036. Morely, Helena [pseud. for Senhora Alice Dayrell Brant Caldeira], b. 1881. Brazilian diarist. THE DIARY OF "HELENA MORELY." Translated by Elizabeth Bishop. New York: Farrar, Straus & Cudahy, 1957. 281p.

Diary of a young girl living in the Brazilian mining town of Diamantina, 1893-1895. First published privately in an edition of 2,000 copies, it has become a Brazilian classic.

2037. ------. MINA VIDA DE MENINA: CADERNOS DE UMA MENINA PROVINCIANA NOS FINS DO SECULO. HELENA MORELY. Rio de Janeiro: Livraria Jose Olympio, 1971. 271p.

2038. Morgan, Emily Malbone, 1862-1937. LETTERS TO HER COMPANIONS. Edited by Vida Dutton Scudder. With a biographical sketch by Emily Sophie Brown. Adelynrood, South Byfield, Mass.: Privately printed by the Society of the Companions of the Holy Cross, 1944. 314p.

2039. Morgan, Sydney Owenson, Lady, 1783-1859. Irish novelist and songwriter. LADY MORGAN'S MEMOIRS, AUTOBIOGRAPHY, DIARY AND CORRESPONDENCE. Edited by Iris Origo. Preface by William Hepworth Dixon. London: William H. Allen & Co., 1862. 2 vols.

2040. ------. AN ODD VOLUME: EXTRACTED FROM THE AUTOBIOGRAPHY. (RUNNING TITLE: DIARY OF LADY MORGAN.) London: R. Bentley, 1859. 339p.

2041. ------. LADY MORGAN'S MEMOIRS: AUTOBIOGRAPHY, DIARIES, CORRESPONDENCE. Edited by W.H. Dixon and J. Jewsbury. London: W.H. Allen & Co., 1863. 3 vols. in 1. Second revised edition, 1863. 2 vols.

2042. Moriarty, Donna. American. "The Right to Mourn." MS. MAGAZINE 11:5 (November, 1982), 79-84.

Diary notes kept by a pregnant mother who discovers her child has died in the womb.

2043. Morisot, Berthe Marie Pauline Manet, 1841-1895. French impressionist painter. CORRESPONDANCE DE BERTHE MORISOT AVEC SA FAMILLE ET SES AMIS MANET, PUVIS DE CHAVANNES, DEGAS, MONET, RENOIR ET MALLARMÉ. Documents réunis et présentées par Denis Rouart. Paris: Quatre Chemins-Éditart, 1950. 184p.

2044. ------. THE CORRESPONDENCE OF BERTHE MORISOT WITH HER FAMILY AND FRIENDS MANET, PUVIS DE CHAVANNES, DEGAS, MONET, RENOIR AND MALLARMÉ. Compiled and edited by Denis Rouart. Translated by Betty W. Hubbard. New York: George Wittenborn, 1957. 187p.

Letters arranged in a loose chronological format, with connecting biographical commentary. Describes exhibitions, events in Paris during the Siege and the Commune, travel impressions, and society life.

2045. Morrell, Ottoline Violet Anne Cavendish-Bentinck, Lady, 1873-1938. English literary figure connected with the Bloomsbury Group. OTTOLINE: THE EARLY MEMOIRS OF LADY OTTOLINE MORRELL. Edited with an introduction by Robert Gathorne-Hardy. London: Faber & Faber, 1963.

Autobiography through World War I, based on and including lengthy extracts from her journals.

2046. ------. OTTOLINE AT GARSINGTON: MEMOIRS OF LADY OTTOLINE MORRELL, 1915-1918. Edited by Robert Gathorne-Hardy. New York: Alfred A. Knopf, 1974. 304p.

Autobiography and extracts from her journals. An appendix deals with her relationship with Bertrand Russell, 1910-1913, also drawing upon her journals.

2047. Morris, Jane Burden, 1840-1914. English artist's model, lover of Dante Gabriel Rossetti and wife of William Morris. DANTE GABRIEL ROSSETTI AND JANE MORRIS: THEIR CORRESPONDENCE. Edited by John Bryson in association with Janet Camp Troxell. Oxford: The Clarendon Press, 1976. 219p.

Correspondence March, 1868--October, 1881 reveals

a love affair that in later years cooled to friendship, especially on Morris' part; the chief interest of the letters is in what they tell of the everyday life and pursuits of their authors.

2048. ------. JANE MORRIS TO WILFRED SCAWEN BLUNT: THE LETTERS OF JANE MORRIS TO WILFRED SCAWEN BLUNT, TOGETHER WITH EXTRACTS FROM BLUNT'S DIARIES. Edited by Peter Faulkner. Exeter, Devon: University of Exeter, 1986. 135p.

Jane Morris was a lover of Wilfred Scawen Blunt; love letters and later, letters of friendship, 1884-1913.

2049. Morris, Margaret Hill, 1737-1816. American author, Quaker, and patriot. PRIVATE JOURNAL, KEPT DURING A PORTION OF THE REVOLUTIONARY WAR FOR THE AMUSEMENT OF A SISTER. BY MARGARET MORRIS OF BURLINGTON, NEW JERSEY. Philadelphia: privately printed, 1836. 31p. Reprinted, New York: Arno Press, 1969.

Quaker diary, December 1776--June 1778, describes her experiences during the American Revolution.

2050. ------. MARGARET MORRIS: HER JOURNAL. Edited with biographical sketch and notes by John W. Jackson. Philadelphia: George S. MacManus, 1949. 132p.

Entries are dated December 1776--June 1977.

2051. Morrison, Anna R., b. 1820. "Diary of Anna R. Morrison, Wife of Issac L. Morrison." Edited by Miriam Morrison Worthington. ILLINOIS HISTORICAL JOURNAL 7:1 (1914), 34-50.

Travel diary, 1840-1841.

2052. Morrow, Elizabeth Cutter, 1873-1955. American author and educator; wife of a U.S. Ambassador to Mexico. THE MEXICAN YEARS: LEAVES FROM THE DIARY OF ELIZABETH MORROW CUTTER. New York: Elizabeth Cutter Morrow, the Spiral Press, 1953. 272p.

2053. Morse, Katherine D. THE UNCENSORED LETTERS OF A CANTEEN GIRL. New York: Henry Holt and Co., 1920. 265p.

War letters written 1917-1919, but not sent due to wartime censorship. Records a young woman's experience with the American Expeditionary Forces in France.

2054. Mott, Lucretia, 1793-1880. American Quaker, feminist and social reformer. THE WOMAN QUESTION: LUCRETIA MOTT'S DIARY OF HER VISIT TO GREAT BRITAIN TO ATTEND THE WORLD'S ANTI-SLAVERY CONVENTION OF 1840. Edited by F. Tolles. Haverford, Penn.: Friends Historical Association, 1952. 86p.

2055. ------. JAMES AND LUCRETIA MOTT: LIFE AND LETTERS. Edited by their granddaughter, Anna Hallowell. Boston: Houghton Mifflin, 1884. 566p. Reprinted in microfilm, Princeton: American Theological Library Association, Board of Microtext. (105x148mm).

Munby, Hannah Cullwick. See: Cullwick, Hannah.

2056. Munger, Eliza. American pioneer settler. "Diary of Asahel Munger and Wife." OREGON HISTORICAL QUARTERLY 8 (December, 1907), 387-405.

Journal letters written on the overland journey from Ohio to Oregon in 1839.

2057. Murasaki Shikibu. Japanese author and Lady-In-Waiting. MURASAKI SHIKIBU: HER DIARY AND POETIC MEMOIRS. Translation and study by Richard Bowring. Princeton: Princeton University Press, 1982. 437p.

Heian-period Japanese poetic diary.

2058. Murray, Amelia Matilda, Hon., 1795-1884. English reformer. LETTERS FROM THE UNITED STATES, CUBA AND CANADA. New York: G.P. Putnam's Sons, and London: J.W. Parker & Son, 1856. 2 vols.

Travel diary, 1854-1855. She traveled to North America in order to observe slavery firsthand.

2059. ------. "An English View of Slavery." Communicated by L.B. Howry. TYLER'S QUARTERLY 12 (1931), 156-160.

Discussion of, and extracts from Murray's LETTERS FROM THE UNITED STATES, CUBA AND CANADA (1856). Her views on slavery presented here were written on a tour of the Southern states.

2060. Murray, Emma Rutherfoord. English. YOUNG MRS. MURRAY GOES TO BLOEMFONTEIN, 1856-1860: LETTERS. Edited by Joyce Murray. Cape Town: A.A. Balkema, 1954. 156p.

2061. Murtaugh, Mary G. SNATCHES FROM A DIARY. Boston: The Four Seas Co., 1918. 64p.

World War I diary.

2062. Musser, Elise Furer, 1877-1967. Swiss-American politician. "Utah's Peace Advocate, the 'Mormona': Elise Furer Musser." Edited by Juanita Brooks and Janet G. Butler. UTAH HISTORICAL QUARTERLY 46:2 (1978), 151-166.

Extracts from her writings, diaries, and letters.

2063. Myers, Elizabeth, 1912-1947. Author. THE LETTERS OF ELIZABETH MYERS. With a biographical introduction and some comments on her books by her husband, Littleton C. Powys. London: Chapman & Hall, 1951. 338p.

Literary letters, 1932-1947, to Walter de la Mare, Eleanor Farjeon, John Cowper Powys, and others.

2064. Nadolny, Isabella. German. SEEHAMER TAGEBUCH. Munchen: P. List, 1962. 179p.

2065. Napear, Peggy. American. BRAIN CHILD: A MOTHER'S DIARY. New York: Harper & Row, 1970. 503p.

Napear's daughter had been diagnosed as retarded, cerebral palsied, and autistic, with an I.Q. of 40.

Unconvinced that her child was only "trainable," Napear took her to the controversial Institutes for the Achievement of Human Potential, where her daughter made much more progress than had been predicted.

2066. Napier, Sarah Lennox Bunbury, 1745-1826. English hostess and friend of King George III. THE LIFE AND LETTERS OF LADY SARAH LENNOX, 1745-1826. DAUGHTER OF CHARLES, SECOND DUKE OF RICHMOND AND SUCCESSIVELY THE WIFE OF SIR THOMAS CHARLES BUNBURY, BART, AND OF THE HON. GEORGE NAPIER. ALSO A SHORT POLITICAL SKETCH OF THE YEARS 1760 TO 1763 BY HENRY FOX, 1ST LORD HOLLAND. Edited by the Countess of Ilchester and Lord Stavordale. London: John Murray, 1901. 2 vols.

Letters, chiefly written to Lady Susan Fox Strangways O'Brien, 1761-1817, describe life at Court.

2067. Neal or Neall, Hannah Lloyd. American Quaker poet and author. "Hannah Lloyd Neal: A Literary Philadelphian in Post 1853 California." Marie Denervaud Dun. CALIFORNIA HISTORICAL SOCIETY QUARTERLY 31:3 (1952), 240-252.

Background of a trip from New York to California, via the Isthmus of Panama, to join her husband. Reproduces letters home to family, 1855-1862 and includes some letters written to her by family and friends, among them John Greenleaf Whittier.

2068. Neutra, Dione, b. 1901. American wife of architect Richard Joseph Neutra. RICHARD NEUTRA, PROMISE AND FULFILLMENT, 1919-1932: SELECTIONS FROM THE LETTERS AND DIARIES OF RICHARD AND DIONE NEUTRA. Carbondale, Ill.: Southern Illinois University Press, 1986. 240p.

2069. Nevill, Dorothy Fanny Walpole, Lady, 1826-1913. English social leader, hostess and author. THE LIFE AND LETTERS OF LADY DOROTHY NEVILL. By her son Ralph Nevill. London: Macmillan & Co., 1907. 357p. London: Methuen & Co., 1917. 307p.

Letters 1905-1907 describe social life and

politics of the English aristocracy. Most of the letters included here are to her; few of her letters are printed in their entirety, but are liberally quoted.

2070. Newberry, Julia, 1854-1876. American heiress and diarist. JULIA NEWBERRY'S DIARY. With an introduction by Margaret Ayer Barnes and Janet Ayer Fairbank. New York: W.W. Norton & Co., 1933. 176p.

Diary of a European tour, 1869-1871 undertaken when Newberry was fifteen to seventeen years old.

2071. Newcastle, Margaret Cavendish, Duchess of, 1624-1673/4. English author and intellectual. LETTERS OF MARGARET LUCAS TO HER FUTURE HUSBAND. Edited by Richard William Goulding. London: John Murray, 1909.

2072. Newdigate-Newdegate, Anne Emily Garnier, Lady, 1574-1618. GOSSIP FROM A MUNIMENT-ROOM: PASSAGES FROM THE LIVES OF ANNE AND MARY FYTTON, 1574 TO 1618. London: D. Nutt, 1797. 156p.

Extracts from letters and papers of Lady Newdigate and her sister, Lady Mary Fytton (1578?-1647), found in the Muniment Room at Arbury, the Newdigate estate in Warwickshire. Mary Fitton, Maid of Honour to Queen Elizabeth, was once argued to be the "dark lady" of Shakespeare's sonnets; Anne married an impoverished aristocrat, John Newdigate (Newdegate).

2073. ------. THE CHEVERELS OF CHEVEREL MANOR: BEING THE CORRESPONDENCE OF SIR ROGER AND LADY NEWDIGATE. Edited by Lady Newdigate-Newdegate [Lady Hester Margaretta Mundy Newdigate]. London and New York: Longmans, Green & Co., 1898. 231p.

Sir Roger and Lady Newdigate were the models for Sir Christopher and Lady Cheverel of George Eliot's SCENES OF CLERICAL LIFE.

2074. Newman, Frances, 1883-1928. American librarian and author. FRANCES NEWMAN'S LETTERS. Edited by

Hansell Baugh. With a prefatory note by James Branch Cabell. New York: Horace Liveright, 1929. 372p.

Letters 1914-1928, and extracts from a brief journal kept on her travels in Europe. Includes letters from James Branch Cabell.

2075. Newton, Esther, and Shirley Walton. Americans. WOMENFRIENDS: OUR JOURNAL. New York: Friends Press, 1976. 210p.

Joint diary of two women, one heterosexual and married, the other Lesbian, bound together by their feminism and a long friendship which began in college.

2076. Nichols, Clarinda Irene Howard, 1810-1885. American suffragist, temperance worker, abolitionist, and author. "The Forgotten Feminist of Kansas: The Papers of Clarinda I.H. Nichols, 1854-1885." Edited by Joseph G. Gambone. KANSAS HISTORICAL QUARTERLY 39:1 (1973), 12-57 and 39:2 (1973), 220-261.

Part I is a biography; Part II contains her letters to editors and friends, 1855-1856.

2077. Nightingale, Florence, 1820-1910. English nurse, hospital administrator, and social reformer. LETTERS OF FLORENCE NIGHTINGALE IN THE HISTORY OF NURSING ARCHIVE SPECIAL COLLECTIONS, BOSTON UNIVERSITY LIBRARIES. Edited by Lois A. Monteiro. Boston: Boston University, Mugar Memorial Library Nursing Archive, 1974. 69p.

2078. ------. "Florence Nightingale and John Stuart Mill Debate Women's Rights." Evelyn L. Pugh. JOURNAL OF BRITISH STUDIES 12:2 (1982), 118-138.

Correspondence between Mill and Nightingale, 1860-1867, that was not made public during their lives.

2079. ------. A CALENDAR OF THE LETTERS OF FLORENCE NIGHTINGALE. Edited by S. Goldie for the Wellcome Institute. Oxford, England: Oxford Microform Publications. Microfiche (105x148).

2080. ------. LETTERS AND PAPERS. West Yorkshire, England: Microform, Ltd. Reel microfilm (35mm).

2081. Nijo, Lady, 1257-13? Japanese Imperial Concubine and diarist. LADY NIJO'S OWN STORY. TOWAZUGATARI: THE CANDID DIARY OF A THIRTEENTH-CENTURY JAPANESE IMPERIAL CONCUBINE. Translated by Wilfred Whitehouse and Eizo Yanagisawa. Rutland, Vt., and Tokyo: Charles E. Tuttle Co., 1974. 397p.

Japanese poetic diary, 1271-1306.

2082. Nin, Anaïs, 1903-1977. American novelist, critic and diarist. THE DIARY OF ANAÏS NIN. Edited with introductions by Gunther Stuhlmann. New York: Harcourt Brace & World (Volumes 3-7 Harcourt Brace Jovanovich), 1966-1980. 7 vols. Published in Great Britain under the title THE JOURNALS OF ANAÏS NIN. London: P. Owen, 1966-1980.

Volume 1: 1931-1934. Volume 2: 1934-1939. Volume 3: 1939-1944. Volume 4: 1944-1947. Volume 5: 1947-1955. Volume 6: 1955-1966. Volume 7: 1966-1974. Nin is perhaps the most famous diarist of this century; her diary is the chief model for the modern literary, introspective diary. Nin and Stuhlman edited these volumes from the originals; they are much abridged. (Volume 1, for example, is edited from 15,000 manuscript pages to 600.) Each volume is meant to stand alone as a self contained unit, bounded by external events and internal changes that mark significant phases of Nin's life and work.

2083. ------. "Portrait of Anaïs Nin as a Bodisattva: Reflections on the Diary, 1934-1939." Wayne McEvilly. STUDIES IN THE TWENTIETH CENTURY 1 (Fall, 1968), 51-60.

2084. ------. "The Diary of Anaïs Nin." Daniel Stern. STUDIES IN THE TWENTIETH CENTURY 1 (Fall, 1968), 39-43.

2085. ------. ANAÏS NIN: UNPUBLISHED SELECTIONS FROM

THE DIARY. Athens, Ohio: Hand set and hand pressed at the Duane Schneider Press, 1968. Limited edition of 140 copies.

Excerpts May, 1932--August, 1938, selected from unpublished portions of the typescript copy of Nin's diary, intended to present a coherent diary in miniature which focuses on Henry Miller, Dr. Rene Allendy, and others who figured in Nin's life in Paris during the 1930's.

2086. ------. "Thoughts on the Diary of Anaïs Nin." Marianne Hauser. JOURNAL OF THE OTTO RANK ASSOCIATION 5 (June, 1970), 61-67.

2087. ------. "The Bread of Tradition: Reflections on the Diary of Anaïs Nin." Wayne McEvilly. PRAIRIE SCHOONER 45 (Summer, 1971), 161-167.

2088. ------. PARIS REVISITED. Santa Barbara: Capra Press, 1972. (Yes Capra Chapbook No. 3).

Chapbook edition of extracts from the Diary, Volume 5, 1947-1955.

2089. ------. "The Personal Life Deeply Lived." Anaïs Nin. In ANAÏS NIN: A WOMAN SPEAKS. THE LECTURES, SEMINARS AND INTERVIEWS OF ANAÏS NIN. Edited, with an introduction by Evelyn J. Hinz. Chicago: The Swallow Press, 1975. p.148-180.

Discusses the connection between the DIARY and life.

2090. ------. "Anaïs: Her Book." Sharon Spencer. In COLLAGE OF DREAMS: THE WRITINGS OF ANAÏS NIN. Sharon Spencer. New York: The Swallow Press, 1977. p.117-141.

Discusses the growth and history of the DIARY, its problems and its relationship to Nin's novels.

2091. ------. LINOTTE: THE EARLY DIARY OF ANAÏS NIN, 1914-1920. Translated from the French by Jean L.

Sherman. Preface by Joaquin Nin-Culmell. New York and London: Harcourt, Brace, Jovanovich, 1978. 518p.

Nin's adolescent diary, begun when she and her mother moved from Barcelona to New York in 1914. This is the first volume of the DIARY to be published essentially in the form in which it was written, unlike the previous volumes, which Nin consciously shaped. It has, however, been cut somewhat to avoid repetitions and redundancies.

2092. ------. JOURNAL D'ENFANCE. Preface par Joaquin Nin-Culmell. Presente par Marie-Claire Van der Elst. Paris: Editions Stock, 1979. 2 vols.

Volume 1: 1914-1919. Volume 2: 1919-1920. Uncut version of Nin's adolescent diary in the original French.

2093. ------. THE EARLY DIARY OF ANAÏS NIN, VOLUME II, 1920-1923. Preface by Joaquin Nin-Culmell. New York and London: Harcourt Brace Jovanovich, 1982. 541p.

This volume and two yet to be published bridge the gap between LINOTTE and the diary volumes published during Nin's lifetime.

2094. ------. "Truth and Artistry in the Diary of Anaïs Nin." Joan Bobbit. JOURNAL OF MODERN LITERATURE 9:2 (May, 1982), 267-276.

2095. ------. JOURNAL OF A WIFE: THE EARLY DIARY OF ANAÏS NIN, 1923-1927. With a preface by Joaquin Nin-Culmell. London and Washington, D.C.: Peter Owen Publishers, 1984.

Dwells on the first years of her marriage to Hugh Guiler and her return to Paris as a married woman; she gave this part of her diary the title "Le Journal d'une Spouse." Deals with her rediscovery of her idealized father, her disillusionment with life in Paris; the culture shock of a Europe she'd forgotten, and her discovery, with Guiler, of modern tendencies in art.

2096. ------. HENRY AND JUNE: FROM THE UNEXPURGATED DIARY OF ANAÏS NIN. San Diego, Calif.: Harcourt Brace Jovanovich, 1986. 274p.

2097. Nithsdale, Winifrede Herbert Maxwell, Countess of, d.1749. English Royalist. LADY NITHSDALE AND HER FAMILY. Henrietta Tayler. London: Lindsay Drummond 1939. 288p.

Biography and extracts from letters. Lady Nithsdale was of a Royalist family and helped her husband, Lord Nithsdale, escape from the Tower on the eve of his execution for his part in the Jacobite rising of 1715.

2098. Nivedita, Sister [Margaret Elizabeth Noble], 1867-1911. Irish teacher, reformer, and mystic. LETTERS OF SISTER NIVEDITA. Collected and edited by Sankari Prasad Basu. Assisted by Bimal Kumar Ghosh. Calcutta: Nababharat Publishers, 1982. 2 vols.

Letters 1898-1911. Noble met and became a follower of Swami Vivekanada in 1895, and founded the Vedanta Movement in London. In 1898 she went to India, where she became involved in reform work, helping to found a school for girls in Baghbazar.

2099. Noel, Marie, pseud. for Marie-Melanie Rouget, 1883-1967. French Catholic poet. NOTES INTIMES. Suivies de Souvenirs sur l'Abbé Bremond. Paris: Librarie Stock, 1959. 357p.

2100. ------. NOTES FOR MYSELF. Translated by Howard Sutton. Foreword by Francois Mauriac. Ithaca, N.Y.: Cornell University Press, 1968. 280p.

2101. Nordica, Lillian, 1857-1914. American opera singer. LILLIAN NORDICA'S HINTS TO SINGERS, TOGETHER WITH AN ACCOUNT OF LILLIAN NORDICA'S TRAINING FOR THE OPERA, AS TOLD IN THE LETTERS OF THE SINGER AND HER MOTHER, AMANDA ALLEN NORTON. New York: E.P. Dutton & Co., 1923. 167p.

2102. Norris, Mary Ann, 1801-1880. Canadian. "The

Diary of Mary Ann Norris, 1818-1838." Edited by Susan Flewelling. THE DALHOUSIE REVIEW 29 (1949-1950), 439-450 and 30 (1950-1951), 90-103.

2103. North, Marianne, 1830-1890. English naturalist and painter. SOME FURTHER RECOLLECTIONS OF A HAPPY LIFE. SELECTED FROM THE JOURNALS OF MARIANNE NORTH, CHIEFLY BETWEEN THE YEARS 1859 AND 1869. Edited by her sister, Mrs. J.A. Symonds. London: Macmillan, 1893. 316p.

Companion volume to her autobiography, RECOLLECTIONS OF A HAPPY LIFE, (1892).

2104. Northumberland, Elizabeth Seymour Percy, Duchess of, 1716-1776. English. THE DIARIES OF A DUCHESS. EXTRACTS FROM THE DIARIES OF THE FIRST DUCHESS OF NORTHUMBERLAND (1716-1776). Edited by James Greig. With a foreword by the Duke of Northumberland (Alan Ivan Percy, 8th Duke of Northumberland). London: Hodder & Stoughton, 1926 and New York: Doran Co., 1927. 229p.

Public diary, 1752-1774, detailing life at Court. William Matthews calls this "a good diary."

2105. Norton, Caroline Elizabeth Sarah Sheridan, Hon. Mrs., later Lady Stirling-Maxwell, 1808-1877. English poet, historian, novelist, composer and women's rights activist. SOME UNRECORDED LETTERS OF CAROLINE NORTON IN THE ALTSCHUL COLLECTION OF THE YALE UNIVERSITY LIBRARY. Bertha Coolidge. Boston: privately printed by D. Updike, the Merrymount Press, 1934. 25p. Seventy-five copies printed.

2106. ------. A RESIDENCE AT SIERRA LEONE. DESCRIBED FROM A JOURNAL KEPT ON THE SPOT AND FROM LETTERS WRITTEN TO FRIENDS AT HOME. London: John Murray, 1849. 335p.

2107. ------. THE LETTERS OF CAROLINE NORTON TO LORD MELBOURNE. Edited by James O. Hoge and Clark Olney. Columbus, Ohio: Ohio State University Press, 1974. 182p.

Lord Melbourne was implicated in the divorce

proceedings of Caroline Norton and George Chappel Norton; in 1836, Lord Norton brought action of criminal conversation against Lord Melbourne, but the Court rejected it.

2108. Nowell, Elizabeth. Literary agent and editor of Thomas Wolfe. BEYOND LOVE AND LOYALTY: THE LETTERS OF THOMAS WOLFE AND ELIZABETH NOWELL. TOGETHER WITH "NO MORE RIVERS," A STORY BY THOMAS WOLFE. Edited by Richard Kennedy. Chapel Hill, N.C.: University of North Carolina Press, 1983. 164p.

2109. Nowell, Nancy F., b. 1805. American Mormon Frontier Settler. TESTIMONY OF NANCY NOWELL: MY COPY OF MY JOURNALS. COMMENCED IN LAPEE, MICHIGAN. A DAILY ACCOUNT OF THE DEVOTIONAL AND DEVOUT EXCERCISES OF MY HEART AND THE TESTIMONY OF THE TRUTH. Salt Lake City: George Q. Cannon & Sons, 1892. 355p.

Religious diary, 1840-1892.

2110. Noyer, Anne Marguerite Petit, Madame du, 1663-1719. French. THE CORRESPONDENCE OF MADAME DU NOYER. Translated and edited by Florence L. Layard. London: Richard Bentley & Son, 1890. 2 vols.

Letters by a woman adopted into a wealthy French family describe travels in Europe and social and historical events during the reign of Louis IV. Layard notes that a heavily edited and "untrustworthy" translation of the letters was published around 1728, which caused so much anger among the families of persons mentioned in the letters, that the book was suppressed.

2111. Nugent, Maria Skinner, Lady, d. 1834. English wife of Sir George Nugent, appointed Lieutenant-Governor and Commander in Chief of Jamaica in 1801. A JOURNAL FROM THE YEAR 1801 TO THE YEAR 1805, INCLUDING A VOYAGE TO, AND RESIDENCE IN, INDIA, WITH A TOUR TO THE NORTH-WESTERN PARTS OF THE BRITISH POSSESSIONS IN THAT COUNTRY, UNDER THE BENGAL GOVERNMENT. London: 1839. 2 vols.

2112. ------. LADY NUGENT'S JOURNAL: JAMAICA ONE HUNDRED YEARS AGO. REPRINTED FROM A JOURNAL KEPT BY MARIA, LADY NUGENT, FROM 1801 TO 1805. Edited by F. Cundall. London: Published for the Institute of Jamaica, by A. and C. Black, 1907. 404p.

2113. Nunez, Bonita Wa Wa Calachaw, 1888-1972. Native American artist and Indian rights activist. SPIRIT WOMAN: THE DIARIES AND PAINTINGS OF BONITA WA WA CALACHAW NUNEZ. Edited by Stan Steiner. San Francisco: Harper & Row, 1980. 243p.

Arranged by the editor from thirty-eight notebooks. Not dated entry, instead, the entries are titled. Describes the life of a poor Native American woman adopted at birth by a well-to-do white woman, through meditations on her roots, her philosophy, her art, and her activism in the Native American and women's rights movements.

2114. Oakley, Deborah. JOURNAL OF A TRIP TO CHINA, AUGUST 17--SEPTEMBER 16, 1977. Ann Arbor, Mich.: Department of Community Health Programs, School of Public Health, University of Michigan, 1977. 104p.

2115. O'Brian, Alice Lord. American nurse and hospital administrator. NO GLORY: LETTERS FROM FRANCE, 1917-1919. Buffalo: Printed by Airport Publishers, 1936. 184p.

Letters written to members of her family while serving with the Red Cross in France. O'Brian founded La Cantine Americaine de St. Germain-Des Fosses and received two French Decorations, the Medaille d'Honneur and the Medaille de la Reconnaissance Francaise.

2116. O'Brien, Margaret Angela Maxine, b.1937. American Actress. MY DIARY. With Drawings by the author and a foreword by Lionel Barrymore. Philadelphia: J.B. Lippincott, 1948. 117p.

Diary of a Hollywood child star, 1947.

2117. O'Brien, Mary Sophia Gapper. English Immigrant

to Canada. THE JOURNALS OF MARY O'BRIEN, 1828-1838. Edited by Audrey Saunders Miller. Toronto: Macmillan of Canada, 1968. 314p.

Diary, written as letters to family in England, describes pioneer farm life in newly settled Thornhill, Upper Canada, and contains a wealth of information about social, political, and family life in Upper Canada.

2118. O'Connor, Flannery (Mary Flannery O'Connor), 1925-1964. American author. THE HABIT OF BEING: LETTERS OF FLANNERY O'CONNOR. Edited by Sally Fitzgerald. New York: Farrar, Straus, Giroux, 1979. 596p.

2119. ------. "Six Unpublished Letters of Flannery O'Connor." James F. Farnham. THE FLANNERY O'CONNOR BULLETIN 12 (Autumn, 1983), 60-66.

Six letters and two brief Christmas greetings written to Farnham while he was writing a critical thesis of O'Connor's work at Case-Western Reserve Library.

2120. ------. "Flannery O'Connor and Rebekah Poller: A Correspondence." Louise Westling. THE FLANNERY O'CONNOR BULLETIN 12 (Autumn, 1983), 68-76.

Eleven letters, 1958-1964, recording a friendship that began after Poller attended a lecture given by O'Connor at Georgia State College for Women.

2121. ------. THE CORRESPONDENCE OF FLANNERY O'CONNOR AND THE BRAINARD CHENEYS. Edited by C. Ralph Stephens. Jackson, Miss.: University Press of Mississippi, 1986. 200p.

Correspondence with Brainard and Frances Neel Cheney (b.1906).

2122. O'Connor, Rachel Swayze, 1744-1846. American plantation owner and businesswoman. MISTRESS OF EVERGREEN PLANTATION: RACHEL O'CONNOR'S LEGACY OF LETTERS, 1823-1845. Edited by Allie Bayne and Windham

Webb. Albany, N.Y.: State University of New York Press, 1983. 304p.

Letters of a successful woman planter, owner of a plantation in Feliciana County, Louisiana, who faced and overcame epidemics, lawsuits, hazards of travel, and threatened slave uprisings.

2123. O'Hara, Mary, pseud. for Mary Alsop Sture-Vasa, 1885- 1980. American children's author. NOVEL IN THE MAKING. New York: David McKay Co., 1954. 244p.

Based on the diary she kept while writing MY FRIEND FLICKA.

2124. O'Hare, Kate Richards, 1877-1948. American Socialist party leader and activist. KATE RICHARDS O'HARE: SELECTED WRITINGS AND SPEECHES. Edited with an introduction and notes by Philip S. Foner and Sally M. Miller. Baton Rouge and London: Louisiana State University Press, 1982. 363p.

Includes "Letters from Prison," p.203-304.

2125. Older, Cora Miranda Baggerly, 1875-1968. American historical author and wife of editor Fremont Older. DIARIES OF MRS. CORA BAGGERLY OLDER, 1916-1923. Edited by Donna R. Harris. Santa Clara Valley: Local History Studies, Foothill College District, Winter, 1971. 32p. (Local History Studies No. 7).

Short diary describing life in the Santa Clara Valley, California.

2126. Oliphant, Margaret Oliphant Wilson, 1828-1897, better known as Mrs. Oliphant. Scottish author. THE AUTOBIOGRAPHY OF MRS. M.O.W. OLIPHANT. Arranged and edited by Mrs. Harry Coghill. New York: Dodd, Mead and Co., 1899. 450p.

Includes letters 1850 to 1897, chiefly to the Blackwoods' of Blackwoods Magazine and publishing Company.

2127. Olnhausen, Mary Phinney, Baroness von, 1818-1902. American author and nurse during the Civil War. ADVENTURES OF AN ARMY NURSE IN TWO WARS. EDITED FROM THE DIARY AND CORRESPONDENCE OF MARY PHINNEY, BARONESS VON OLNHAUSEN. James Phinney Monroe. Boston: Little, Brown, & Co., 1904. 355p.

Account edited from correspondence, a diary, and autobiography, covering Olhnhausen's work in America during the Civil War, 1862-1865 and in France during the Franco-American War, 1870-1871, as well as travels in Europe and a visit to her husband's family in Germany, 1871-1873.

2128. Opie, Amelia Alderson, 1769-1853. English novelist and poet. MEMORIALS OF THE LIFE OF AMELIA OPIE. SELECTED AND ARRANGED FROM HER LETTERS, DIARIES AND OTHER MANUSCRIPTS. Edited by Cecelia Lucy Brightwell. Norwich: Fletcher and Alexander, 1854.

2129. Origo, Iris. English-American. WAR IN VAL D'ORCIA: AN ITALIAN WAR DIARY, 1943-1944. Boston: Godine, 1984. 239p.

Origo married an Italian, Antonio Origo, in the 1920's, and lived with him on a farm in Val D'Orcia, an area occupied by the Germans during World War II.

2130. Orléans, Elisabeth Charlotte, Duchesse d', Princess Palatine, called "Madame," and "Liselotte," 1652-1722. French letter-writer and second wife of Philippe I of Orleans, brother of King Louis XIV. BRIEFE DER HERZOGIN ELISABETH CHARLOTTE VON ORLEANS. Herausgegeben von Dr. Wilhelm Ludwig Holland. Stuttgart, 1867-1881. 6 vols.

2131. ------. LIFE AND LETTERS OF CHARLOTTE ELIZABETH, PRINCESS PALATINE AND MOTHER OF PHILIPPE D'ORLEANS, REGENT OF FRANCE, 1652-1722. Compiled, translated and gathered from various published and unpublished sources, comprising the Archives of the French Foreign Office, the Archives of the House of France, and the manuscripts in the Bibliotheque

Nationale, by Frederick L. Jones. London: Chapman & Hall, 1889. 341p.

2132. ------. AUS DEN BRIEFEN DER HERZOGIN ELISABETH CHARLOTTE VON ORLEANS AN DIE KURFURSTIN SOPHIE VON HANNOVER. Herausgegebn von Ed. Bodemann. Hannover: Hahn, 1891. 2 vols.

Correspondence with Sophie, Consort of Ernest Augustus, Elector of Hanover (1630-1714).

2133. ------. BRIEFE DER HERZOGIN ELISABETH CHARLOTTE VON ORLEANS AN IHRE FRUHERE HOFMEISTERIN A.K. VON HARLING, UND DEREN GEMAHL, GEB RATH FR. VON HARLING ZU HANNOVER. Herausgegeben von Dr. Ed. Bodemann. Hannover: Hahn, 1895. 234p.

2134. ------. AUS DEN BRIEFEN DER HERZOGIN ELISABETH CHARLOTTE VON ORLEANS AN ETIENNE POLIER DU BOTTENS. Herausgegeben von S. Hellmann. Tubingen: Litterarischer Verein in Stuttgart, 1903. 131p.

2135. ------. ELISABETH CHARLOTTENS BRIEFE AN KAROLINE VON WALLES UND ANTON ULRICH VON BRAUNSCHWEIG-WOLFENBUTTEL. Besorgt und erlautert von Hans F. Helmolt. Annaberg in Sachsen: Grasser, 1909. 446p.

2136. ------. DIE BRIEFE DER LISELOTTE. Ausgewahlt und biographilch verbunden von C. Kunzel. Munchen: Wilhelm Langewiesch, 1912. 480p.

2137. ------. THE LETTERS OF MADAME: THE CORRESPONDENCE OF ELIZABETH CHARLOTTE OF BAVARIA, PRINCESS PALATINE, DUCHESS OF ORLEANS, CALLED "MADAME" AT THE COURT OF KING LOUIS XIV, 1661-1708. Translated and edited by Gertrude Scott Stevenson, M.A. New York: D. Appleton & Co., 1924. 287p.

Her chief correspondents were her aunt, the Electress Sophia of Hanover; her two half sisters the Raugravines Louisa and Amelia Elizabeth; her two step daughters, the Queens of Spain and Sicily; and her daughter, the Duchess of Lorraine (later Caroline,

Princess of Wales). The correspondence is edited from manuscript letters, but omits much that is repetitious.

2138. ------. LETTERS FROM LISELOTTE: ELISABETH CHARLOTTE, PRINCESS PALATINE AND DUCHESS OF ORLEANS, "MADAME," 1652-1722. Edited by Maria Kroll. New York: The McCall Publishing Co., 1971. 269p.

Letters 1672-1722. Kroll describes "Liselotte" as "spontaneous, bawdy, outspoken, extremely biased, a compulsive letter-writer for over half a century."

2139. ------. BRIEFE DER HERZOGIN ELISABETH CHARLOTTE VON ORLEANS AN IHRE GESCHWISTER [VON] LISELOTTE VON DER PFALZ. Herausgegeben von Heinz Herz. Leipzig: Koehler und Amelang, 1972. 471p.

2140. ------. A WOMAN'S LIFE AT THE COURT OF THE SUN KING: LETTERS OF LISELOTTE VON DE PFALZ, 1652-1722, ELISABETH CHARLOTTE, DUCHESSE D'ORLÉANS. Translated and introduced by Elborg Forster. Baltimore: Johns Hopkins University Press, 1984. 287p.

2141. Orléans, Henrietta Anne, Duchesse d', 1644-1670. French sister of Charles II of France. CHARLES II AND MADAME. Cyril Hughes Harmann. London: W. Heinemann, 1934.

Study of the lives of King Charles II and his sister, based upon and including all extant correspondence between them, 1659-1669. Much of it has been lost; what remains contains some court gossip and family news, but chiefly concerns the projected alliance between Charles II and Louis XIV that came into being under the Treaty of Dover in 1670.

2142. Ormerod, Eleanor, LL.D., 1828-1901. English entomologist. ELEANOR ORMEROD, ECONOMIC ENTOMOLOGIST: AUTOBIOGRAPHY AND CORRESPONDENCE. Edited by Robert Wallace. London: John Murray, 1904. 348p.

Correspondence 1887-1901 with colleagues, profusely illustrated with figures of insects. The letters, except in a few cases, have been "pruned" of personal matter.

2143. Orrery, Harriet Hamilton, Lady. THE ORRERY PAPERS. Edited by the Countess of Cork and Orrery. London: Duckworth & Co., 1903. 2 vols.

Correspondence between Lady Orrery and her husband, John, Fifth Earl of Orrery; her letters are printed in Volume Two.

2144. Orsini, Anne Marie de la Tremoille Noirmoustier, Duchesse di Bracciano, d. 1722. French political figure. LETTRES INÉDITES DE MADAME LA PRINCESSE DES URSINS A M. LE MARECHAL DE VELLEROI, SUIVIES DE SA CORRESPONDANCE AVEC MADAME DE MAINTENON, ET PRÉCÉDÉES D'UNE NOTICE BIOGRAPHIQUE SUR LA VIE DE MADAME DES URSINS. Paris: Chez Leopold-Collin, 1806.

2145. ------. LETTRES INÉDITES DE LA PRINCESSE DES URSINS. Recueillies et publiées avec une introduction et des notes, par M.A. Geffroy. Paris: Didier et Cie., 1859. 495p.

2146. ------. MADAME DES URSINS ET LA SUCCESSION D'ESPAGNE: FRAGMENTS DE CORRESPONDANCE. Nantes: Imprimèrie E. Grimaud et Fils, 1902-1907. 6 vols.

2147. Orsini, Felice Maria, 1819-1858. Italian revolutionary. FELICE ORSINI ED EMMA HERWEGH. Nuovi documenti con introduzione e note di Alessandro Luzio. Firenze: F. Le Monnier, 1937. 156p.

Letters of Orsini, Emma Herwegh (1816-1904), George Herwegh, J. Mazzini, and others.

2148. Orvis, Marianne Dwight, 1816-1901. American teacher. LETTERS FROM BROOK FARM, 1844-1847. Edited by Amy L. Reed, with a note on Anna Q.T. Parsons by Helen Dwight Orvis. Poughkeepsie, N.Y.: Vassar College, 1928. 191p.

In 1844 Orvis moved with her family to the Utopian

Brook Farm Community. Her letters form a strong feminist document and an enthusiastic first-hand description of Brook Farm.

2149. Osborn, Sarah Byng, 1693-1775. English businesswoman. POLITICAL AND SOCIAL LETTERS OF A LADY OF THE EIGHTEENTH CENTURY, 1721-1771. Edited by Emily F.D. Osborn. London and Sydney: Printed for Griffith, Farran, Okeden & Welsh, 1890. New York: Dodd, Mead & Co., 1891. 190p.

Personal and business letters 1721-1773 reflect the political and social life of the British upperclass. Osborn was widowed at the age of 24 and undertook the management of her husband's large estate, later of her son's affairs, and still later those of her grandson.

2150. ------. LETTERS OF SARAH BYNG OSBORN, 1721-1773. From the Collection of the Hon. Mrs. McDonnell. Introduction and further notes by John McClelland. London: Humphrey Milford, Oxford University Press, and Stanford: Stanford University Press, 1930. 148p.

Selection from the original edition (1890).

2151. Osborn, Sarah Haggar, 1714-1796. American colonist noted for her piety and as a teacher of religion. MEMOIRS OF THE LIFE OF MRS. OSBORN, WHO DIED AT NEWPORT ON THE SECOND DAY OF AUGUST, 1796 IN THE EIGHTY-THIRD YEAR OF HER AGE. Edited by Samuel Hopkins. Printed at Worcester, Mass., by Leonard Worcester, 1799. 380p. Second edition, Catskill: N. Elliot, 1814. 359p.

Includes a religious diary, 1744-1768.

2152. Osborne, Catherine, Lady. English-Irish wife of Sir Thomas Osborne, Bart. MEMORIALS OF THE LIFE AND CHARACTER OF LADY OSBORNE AND SOME OF HER FRIENDS. Edited by her daughter, Mrs. Osborne. Dublin: Hodges, Foster & Co., 1870. 2 vols.

Volume 1: Letters of Lady Osborne, 1816-1856.

Volume 2: Letters of her friends Mary Stanley, Miss M.R. Wade, A. Riall and Alicia Hill, for the same period.

2153. O'Shaughnessy, Edith Louise Coues. American wife of U.S. Ambassador Nelson O'Shaughnessy. A DIPLOMAT'S WIFE IN MEXICO. LETTERS FROM THE AMERICAN EMBASSY AT MEXICO CITY COVERING THE DRAMATIC PERIOD BETWEEN OCTOBER 8, 1913 AND THE BREAKING OFF OF DIPLOMATIC RELATIONS ON APRIL 23RD, 1914, TOGETHER WITH AN ACCOUNT OF THE OCCUPATION OF VERA CRUZ. New York and London: Harper & Bros., 1916. 355p.

2154. ------. DIPLOMATIC DAYS. New York and London: Harper & Bros., 1917. 337p.

Letters May, 1911--October, 1912 describe social life and travel in Mexico.

2155. ------. MY LORRAINE JOURNAL. New York and London: Harper & Bros., 1918. 195p.

World War I diary, written in France.

2156. ------. ALSACE IN RUST AND GOLD. New York and London: Harper & Bros., 1920. 183p.

Diary of war work at Alsace, which the French recaptured from the Germans in 1914.

2157. Osler, Grace Revere Gross, Lady. Canadian wife of Sir William Osler (1849-1919). THE TWILIGHT YEARS OF LADY OSLER: LETTERS OF A DOCTOR'S WIFE. Frederick B. Wagner, Jr. Canton, Mass.: Science History Publications, U.S.A., 1985. 144p.

2158. Otis, Sally Foster. American wife of U.S. Representative Harrison Gray Otis. "A Visit to Mount Vernon: 1801." THE MOUNT VERNON LADIES ASSOCIATION OF THE UNION ANNUAL REPORT October, 1960--October, 1961 (1961), 34-36.

Letter dated January 13, 1801, describes a trip to Mount Vernon, New York.

2159. Ouvry, M.H. English wife of a British Colonial Officer stationed in India. A LADY'S DIARY BEFORE AND AFTER THE INDIAN MUTINY. Lymington: C.T. King, 1892. 166p.

Concerns the Indian Mutiny of 1857-1858.

2160. Owen, Maggie, later Wadelton, b. 1896. Irish emigrant to the United States. THE BOOK OF MAGGIE OWEN. New York and Indiana: Bobbs-Merrill, 1941. 262p.

Adolescent diary, begun in 1908 in Castle Rea, Ireland and ending on the ship to America with the words, "Tomorrow 'tis a United States book you'll be."

2161. Page, Charlotte A. American daughter of Seaman Alvin R. Page. UNDER SAIL AND IN PORT IN THE GLORIOUS 1850's. BEING THE JOURNAL FROM 1 MAY TO 3 OCTOBER, 1852, KEPT BY CHARLOTTE A. PAGE. ALSO EXCERPTS FROM JOURNAL AND LETTERS WRITTEN SEPTEMBER 20, 1856 TO JANUARY 30, 1857, BY ALVIN R. PAGE, JR. Introduction and notes by Alvin Page Johnson. Salem: Peabody Museum, 1950. 88p.

Account of a sea journey, undertaken at sixteen years of age for health reasons.

2162. Paget, Georgiana Theodosia Fitzmoor-Halsey, d. 1919. Wife of British Colonial Officer Major Leopold Paget. CAMP AND CANTONMENT: A JOURNAL OF LIFE IN INDIA IN 1857-1859. WITH SOME ACCOUNT OF THE WAY THITHER; TO WHICH IS ADDED A SHORT ACCOUNT OF THE PURSUIT OF THE REBELS IN CENTRAL INDIA BY MAJOR PAGET. London: Longman, Green, Longman, Roberts, and Green, 1865. 469p.

Concerns the Indian Mutiny of 1857-1858.

2163. Paige, Harriet Story White, 1809-1863. American. DANIEL WEBSTER IN ENGLAND: JOURNAL OF HARRIET STORY PAIGE, 1839. Edited by Edward Gray. Boston and New York: Houghton Mifflin, 1917. 370p.

Travel diary, written in 1839 while on a tour of the British Isles with Daniel Webster and his wife.

2164. Painter, Charlotte. American author and poet. WHO MADE THE LAMB. New York: McGraw-Hill, 1965. 196p.

Based on a journal kept while pregnant with her first child.

2165. ------. CONFESSIONS FROM THE MALAGA MADHOUSE: A CHRISTMAS DIARY. New York: The Dial Press, 1971. 212p.

Part of this diary was written in a mental hospital, combined with a later diary, and revised.

2166. Palmer, Alice Elvira Freeman, 1855-1902. American educator and second president of Wellesley College. AN ACADEMIC COURTSHIP: LETTERS OF ALICE FREEMAN AND GEORGE HERBERT PALMER, 1886-1887. With an introduction by Caroline Hazard. Cambridge, Mass.: Harvard University Press, 1940. 259p.

Courtship letters of Freeman and George Herbert Palmer, a Professor at Harvard College, reveals much about the social life of educated people of the time, from the point of view of teachers living and working at Wellesley and Harvard.

2167. Palmer, Ann, 1806-1834. English. EXTRACTS FROM THE DIARY OF ANN PALMER. A CHRISTIAN IN HUMBLE LIFE. With a short Memoir by G.P. Richards. Exeter, 1838.

Extracts from a religious diary, 1827-1834.

2168. Palmer, Esther, d. 1714. American Quaker. "The Journal of Susanna Freeborn and Esther Palmer." FRIENDS HISTORICAL SOCIETY JOURNAL 6 (1909), 38-40.

Travel diary, 1704.

2169. ------. "The Journal of Esther Palmer and Mary Lawson." FRIENDS HISTORICAL SOCIETY JOURNAL 6 (1909), 63-71.

Travel diary, 1705.

2170. ------. "The Journal of Mary Banister and Esther Palmer's Travells." FRIENDS HISTORICAL SOCIETY JOURNAL 6 (1909), 133-139.

Travel diary, 1705.

Palmerston, Emily Lamb Cowper, Viscountess. See: Melbourne, Elizabeth Milbanke Lamb, Viscountess.

2171. Palmerston, Emily Mary Lamb Temple, Viscountess, 1787-1869. English wife of statesman Henry John Temple, Viscount Palmerston. LADY PALMERSTON AND HER TIMES. By Mabell, Countess of Airlie. London and New York: Hodder & Stoughton, 1922. 2 vols.

Letters between Viscountess Palmerston and her brother, Frederick James Lamb, Third Viscount Melbourne.

2172. ------. THE LETTERS OF LADY PALMERSTON. Selected and edited from the originals at Broadlands and elsewhere by Tresham Lever. London: John Murray, 1975. 376p.

2173. Pardo Bazan, Emilia, Condessa de, 1852-1921. Spanish author and novelist. CARTAS A BENITO PERÈZ GALDOS (1889-1890). EMILIA PARDO BAZAN. Prológo y edicíon, Carmen Bravo Villasante. Madrid: Ediciones Turner, 1975?. 125p.

2174. Pardoe, Julia, 1806-1862. "A Victorian Correspondence: Letters from Julia Pardoe to Sir John Philippart, 1841-1860." Lola L. Szladits. BULLETIN OF THE NEW YORK PUBLIC LIBRARY (July, 1955), 367-378.

2175. Parkerson, Julia Etta. American. ETTA'S JOURNAL, JANUARY 2, 1874--JULY 25, 1875. Edited by Ellen Payne Paullin. Canton, Conn.: Lithographers, Inc., 1981. 60p. Reprinted from KANSAS HISTORY 3 (Autumn, 1980), 201-219; and 4 (Winter, 1980), 255-278.

2176. Parkes, Menie, 1839-1915. LETTERS FROM MENIE: SIR HENRY PARKES AND HIS DAUGHTER. Edited by A.W.

Martin. Carlton, Victoria, Australia: Melbourne University Press, dist. by Beaverton, Ore.: International Scholarly Book Services, 1983. 192p.

2177. Parlby, Fanny Parks. Wife of an East India employee stationed in India. WANDERINGS OF A PILGRIM, IN SEARCH OF THE PICTURESQUE, DURING FOUR-AND-TWENTY YEARS IN THE EAST. WITH REVELATIONS OF LIFE IN ZENANA. London: Pelham Richardson, 1850. 2 vols. Reprinted with an introduction and notes by Esther Chawner. Karachi: Oxford University Press, 1975. 2 vols.

Travel and social diary describes life in British India.

2178. Parra, Teresa de la, 1895-1936. Venezuelan novelist and distant relative of Simon Bolivar. CARTAS. Prologo de Mariano Piconsalas. Caracas: Libreria Cruz del Sur, 1951. 133p.

2179. ------. TERESA DE LA PARRA: CLAVE PARA UNA INTERPRETACION. Glosas de cartas, fotografías, conferencias y fragmentes del diarío de la éscritoria, desde su revelacion literaria en Caracas, 1922, hasa su muerte en Madrid, 1936...Finaliza con un elogio epistolar por Gabriel Mistral y una nota postrera de Tierra de Jugo. Sancho Ramon Díaz. Caracas: Édiciones Garrido, 1954. 201p.

2180. ------. ÉPISTOLARIO INTIMO. Prefacio de Rafael Carias. Diarío di uma Senorita que se Fastida (la lectura Semanal No. 12, Junio de 1922). Caracas, Venezuela: Linea Aeoropostal Venezolana, 1953. 261p.

2181. Parrish, Helen. American Quaker and reformer. "Reform and Uplift Among Philadelphia Negroes: The Diary of Helen Parrish, 1888." Allen F. Davis and John F. Sutherland. PENNSYLVANIA MAGAZINE OF HISTORY AND BIOGRAPHY 94 (October, 1970), 496-517.

Extracts from a diary, July 3--October 4, 1888, written while working in a settlement house in Philadelphia, reveals living conditions in the Philadelphia slums as well as the maternalistic attitudes of some white reformers towards Blacks.

2182. Parsons, Anna Quincy Thaxter. American. "A Newburyport Wedding One Hundred and Thirty Years Ago." ESSEX INSTITUTE HISTORICAL COLLECTIONS 87 (October, 1951), 309+.

Journal May 6--27, 1821 describes the wedding preparations, wedding, and early days of marriage of Parsons's half-sister, Elizabeth Margaret Carter, daughter of a a wealthy Newburyport merchant.

2183. Partridge, Frances, b. 1900. English pacifist, editor, and translator. A PACIFIST'S WAR. New York: Universe Books, and London: Hogarth Press, 1978. 215p.

Extracts from a World War II diary, 1939-1945, written at Partridge's estate, Ham Spray. Although the war was distant, Partridge and her circle "thought, felt and talked about it endlessly." The book is meant to stand as a testimony to her pacifist beliefs.

2184. ------. EVERTHING TO LOSE. London: Victor Gollancz, and Boston: Little, Brown Co., 1985. 383p.

Diary continued. Describes life and work (her writing) at Ham Spray, her "enduring partnership" with her husband, Ralph Partridge, and the people--refugee friends--who come to stay with them.

2185. Paston, Katherine Knyvet, Lady, 1578-1629. THE CORRESPONDENCE OF LADY KATHERINE PASTON, 1603-1627. Edited, with an introduction and notes by Ruth Hughey. Norfolk, England: Norfolk Record Society, 1941. 152p.

Chiefly letters to or concerning her son, Sir William Paston.

2186. Paton, Rita, b. 1906. Scottish. "An Edwardian Childhood." BRITISH HERITAGE 3:2 (1982), 52-55; 3:4 (1982), 71-72; and 3:5 (1982), 44-47.

Diary of a girl of Leith, Scotland, 1909-1911.

2187. Patterson, Cornelia Bell, 1755-1783. American wife of Attorney General William Patterson. "The Cornelia Bell Patterson Letters." J. Lawrence Boggs. NEW JERSEY HISTORICAL SOCIETY PROCEEDINGS, New Series, 15:4 (1930), 508-517; 16:1 (1931), 56-57; and 16:2 (1931), 186-201.

Letters beginning January 30, 1777 between a brother and sister who fell on opposite sides during the Revolutionary War; she a Revolutionary, he a Royalist fighting in the British lines at New York. Their relationship remained affectionate.

2188. Paxson, Mary Scarborough. MARY PAXSON: HER BOOK, 1880-1884. Introduction by Agnes Sleigh Turnbull. Illustrated by Pelagie Doane. New York: Doubleday Doran & Co., 1936. 98p.

Childhood diary, in an edition intended for young readers.

2189. Peabody, Elizabeth Palmer, 1804-1894. American educator, reformer and intellectual. LETTERS OF ELIZABETH PALMER PEABODY: AMERICAN RENAISSANCE WOMAN. Edited, with an introduction by Bruce A. Ronda. Middletown, Conn.: Wesleyan University Press, and Scranton, Penn., dist. by Harper & Row, 1984. 477p.

2190. Peabody, Josephine Preston, 1874-1922. American poet, dramatist, and songwriter. DIARY AND LETTERS OF JOSEPHINE PRESTON PEABODY. Selected and edited by Christina Hopkinson Baker. Boston and New York: Houghton Mifflin Co., and Cambridge: The Riverside Press, 1925. 346p.

Literary diary and letters, 1891-1922, edited together chronologically.

2191. Peabody, Marian Lawrence, b. 1875. American daughter of an Episcopal Bishop of Massachusetts. TO BE YOUNG WAS VERY HEAVEN. Boston: Houghton Mifflin Co., 1967. 366p.

Diary 1888-1906 describes childhood in Cambridge,

Massachusetts, her studies at art school, a trip to Europe, and ends with her marriage. Gives a picture of the life of an educated, well-to-do American family before World War I. Condensed version of the original eighteen manuscript volumes.

2192. Pearl, Louisa Brown, 1801-1886. American. "The Civil War Diary of Louisa Brown Pearl." Edited by James A. Hoobler. TENNESSEE HISTORICAL QUARTERLY 38:3 (1979), 308-321.

Civil War diary, September 1861--March 1862. Pearl was a Union sympathizer.

Peary, Josephine Diebitsch. See: Diebitsch-Peary, Josephine.

2193. Pease, Louisa, 1833-1861. English Quaker. SELECTIONS FROM THE PRIVATE MEMORANDA AND LETTERS OF LOUISA PEASE. London: Printed by E. Barrett, 1862. 75p.

Extracts from letters and diary.

2194. Pember, Phoebe Yates. American. A SOUTHERN WOMAN'S STORY. Edited by Bell I. Wiley. New York: G.W. Carleton & Co., 1879.

Reminiscences of the Civil War. Contains nine of her wartime letters.

Pembroke, Anne Clifford Herbert, Countess of, 1590-1676. See Clifford, Anne, Lady.

2195. Pennington, Patience, pseud. for Elizabeth Watris Allston, also known as Elizabeth Allston Pringle, 1845-1921. American plantation owner. A WOMAN RICE PLANTER. Edited by Cornelius O. Cathey. Cambridge, Mass.: The Belknap Press of Harvard University Press, 1961. 446p.

Diary 1903-1906 describes an unsuccessful attempt to carry on a family tradition of rice-planting, using tenant-farm labor (her family's former slaves).

2196. Pepin, Yvonne. American artist. THREE SUMMERS: A JOURNAL. Illustrated by the author. Berkeley, Calif.: Shameless Hussy Press, 1986. 175p.

2197. Perkins, Edith Forbes, 1843-1925. American. LETTERS AND JOURNALS OF MRS. EDITH FORBES PERKINS, 1908-1925. Edited by her daughter, Edith Perkins Cunningham. Cambridge, Mass.: Printed at the Riverside Press for private distribution, 1931. 4 vols.

2198. Peter, Sarah Worthington King, 1800-1877. American Catholic charitable worker and patron of the arts and education. IN WINTER WE FLOURISH: LIFE AND LETTERS OF SARAH WORTHINGTON KING PETER, 1800-1877. Anna Shannon McAllister. New York, Philadelphia and Toronto: Longmans, Green & Co., 1939. 398p.

2199. Phelps, Elizabeth Porter, 1747-1817. American colonist. "Diary." In UNDER A COLONIAL ROOF-TREE: FIRESIDE CHRONICLES OF EARLY NEW ENGLAND. Arria S. Huntington. Boston and New York: Houghton Mifflin, 1891. p.26-105.

2200. ------. "The Diary of Elizabeth Porter Phelps." NEW ENGLAND HISTORICAL AND GENEALOGICAL REGISTER 118:1 (1964), 3-30; 118:2 (1964), 108-127; 118:3 (1964), 207-236; 118:4 (1964), 297-308; 119:1 (1965), 43-59; 119:2 (1965), 127-140; 119:3 (1965), 205-223; 119:4 (1965), 289-307; 120:1 (1966), 57-63; 120:2 (1966), 123-135; 120:3 (1966), 203-214; 120:4 (1966), 293-304; 121:1 (1967), 57-69; 121:2 (1967), 95-100; 121:4 (1967), 296-303; 122:1 (1968), 62-70; 122:2 (1968), 115-123; 122:3 (1968), 220-227; and 122:4 (1968), 302-309.

Social and religious diary.

2201. Phifer, Louisa Jane. American farmer. "Letters from an Illinois Farm, 1864-1865." Edited by Carol Benson Pye. JOURNAL OF THE ILLINOIS STATE HISTORICAL SOCIETY 66:4 (1973), 387-403.

Civil War letters to her husband George Brown Phifer, a soldier in the Union Army.

2202. Phillips, Daisy, d. 1960. Canadian frontier settler. LETTERS FROM WINDERMERE, 1912-1914. Edited by R. Cole Harris and Elizabeth Phillips. Vancouver: University of British Columbia Press, 1984. 243p.

Pioneer letters, chiefly by Daisy Phillips, describe frontier life in the Windermere Lake Region of British Columbia.

2203. Pierce, Ruth Phinney. TRAPPED IN "BLACK RUSSIA": LETTERS, JUNE-- NOVEMBER 1915. Boston and New York: Houghton Mifflin Co., 1918. 149p.

World War I letters to family form a vivid account of wartime Russia.

2204. Pigot, Sophia, 1804-1881. South African pioneer settler. THE JOURNALS OF SOPHIA PIGOT, 1819-1821. Edited by Margaret Rainier. Cape Town: Rhodes University, Grahamstown / A.A. Balkema, 1974. 172p.

2205. Pinckney, Elizabeth, "Eliza" Lucas, 1722-1793. American agronomist and wife of South Carolina Chief Justice Charles Pinckney. JOURNAL AND LETTERS OF ELIZA LUCAS. Harriot Pinckney Holbrook. Wormsloe, Ga.: Wormsloe Quartos, No. 3, 1850. 30p.

Edition of nineteen copies.

2206. ------. ELIZA PINCKNEY. Harriott Horry Ravenel. New York: Charles Scribner's Sons, 1896. 331p.

Biography based on and including a large number of letters, 1737-1786.

2207. ------. "Eliza Lucas Pinckney: Portrait of an Eighteenth Century American." S.S. Baskett. SOUTH CAROLINA HISTORY MAGAZINE 72 (October, 1971), 207-219.

Quotations from and discussion of several excerpts from the LETTERBOOK.

2208. ------. THE LETTERBOOK OF ELIZA LUCAS PINCKNEY

1739-1762. Edited by Elise Pinckney with the editorial assistance of Marvin R. Zahniser and an introduction by Walter Muir Whitehill. Chapel Hill, N.C.: The University of North Carolina Press, 1972. 195p.

Complete text of the letters taken from Pinckney's letterbook, or copy book, in which she drafted her correspondence. Such books were common in her day.

2209. ------. "Letters of Eliza Lucas Pinckney, 1768-1782." Edited by Elise Pinckney. SOUTH CAROLINA HISTORICAL MAGAZINE 76:3 (1975), 143-170.

Collection of miscellaneous letters held by the South Carolina Historical Society.

2210. Pinzer, Maimie. American Jewish prostitute and social reformer. THE MAIMIE PAPERS. Edited by Ruth Rosen and Sue Davidson. Old Westbury, N.Y.: The Feminist Press, 1977. 437p.

Letters between Pinzer and Fanny Quincy Howe, an upperclass social reformer, chiefly concerning the story of Pinzer's life, and the two women's ideas on social reform. Pinzer founded a halfway house for young prostitutes, at which women received an early form of peer-group counseling, as opposed to the then-current methods of Christian "salvation."

Piozzi, Hester Lynch Salusbury Thrale. See: Thrale, Hester Lynch Salusbury.

2211. Plath, Sylvia, 1932-1963. American poet and novelist; wife of poet Ted Hughes. LETTERS HOME: Correspondence, 1950-1963. Edited by Aurelia Schober Plath. New York: Harper & Row, 1975. 502p.

Letters written to her family from the time she entered Smith College until her suicide in 1963, edited by her mother. Also includes her correspondence with Olive Higgins Prouty.

2212. ------. JOHNNY PANIC AND THE BIBLE OF DREAMS:

SHORT STORIES, PROSE AND DIARY EXCERPTS. Introduction by Ted Hughes. New York, Hagerstown, San Francisco and London: Harper & Row, 1978. 313p.

Includes excerpts from her journals for 1956 and for 1961-1962.

2213. ------. THE JOURNALS OF SYLVIA PLATH. Edited by Frances McCullough. Ted Hughes, consulting editor. With a foreword by Ted Hughes. New York: The Dial Press, 1982. 370p.

According to Hughes, Plath set down in her journals, for her eyes only, the "day to day struggle with her warring selves." Because some of the people mentioned in her journals are still alive, some of the material has been cut, and names have been changed. Hughes also notes that he destoyed two notebooks that continued up to within three days of her death because he did not want her children to have to read them. This book represents about a third of an assortment of notebooks and loose sheets left among Plath's papers.

2214. Platt, Jeanette Hulme, 1816-1877. American mother of social worker Martha Platt Falconer. LIFE AND LETTERS OF MRS. JEANETTE H. PLATT. Compiled by her husband (Cyrus Platt). Philadelphia: E. Claxton & Co., 1882. 17, 363p.

2215. Pless, Mary Theresa Olivia Cornwallis-West, "Daisy", Furstin von, b. 1873. DAISY, PRINCESS OF PLESS, BY HERSELF. Edited with an introduction by Major Desmond Chapman-Huston. London: John Murray, 1928, 1929; and New York: E.P. Dutton & Co., 1929, 1931. 529p.

Diary to 1918. Presents a picture of life in the highest social and political circles of pre-World War I Europe, and an inside account of life in Germany during the war. Princess Pless was nonpartisan, with family at the English Court and many friends and relatives by marriage at the German.

2216. ------. FROM MY PRIVATE DIARY, BY DAISY,

PRINCESS OF PLESS. Edited, with an introduction and notes by Major Desmond Chapman-Huston. London: John Murray, 1931. 346p. Also published under the title BETTER LEFT UNSAID, BY DAISY, PRINCESS OF PLESS. New York: E.P. Dutton & Co., 1931. 356p.

A more personal chronicle than the previous volume. Consists of excerpts from a manuscript diary of over 600,000 words.

2217. ------. WHAT I LEFT UNSAID, BY DAISY, PRINCESS OF PLESS. Edited, with an introduction and notes by Major Desmond Chapman-Huston. New York: E.P. Dutton Co., 1936. 302p.

Memoir, diary extracts, and letters written during World War I to friends and relatives fighting at the Front, including her brother Prince Clary, Prince Eitel Friedrich of Prussia, and others.

2218. Podlipska, Sofie Rottova, 1833-1897. Czech author. DOPISY JAROSLAVA VRCHLICKEHO SE SOFII PODLIPSKOU Z LET 1875-1876. S uvodni studii F.X. Saldy a s literarne historickymi poznamkami V. Brtnika V Praze: F. Borovy, 1917. 441p.

2219. Poitiers, Diane de, or Diana of Poiters, Comtesse de Breze, Duchesse de Valentinois, 1499-1566. French political figure and mistress of Henry II of France. LETTRES INEDITE DE DIANE DE POYTIERS. Publiée après les manuscrits de la Bibliotheque Imperiale avec une introduction et des notes par Georges Guiffrey. Paris: J. Renouard, 1866. 274p.

2220. Pollock, Elizabeth R. American W.A.A.C. YES, MA'AM! THE PERSONAL PAPERS OF A WAAC PRIVATE. By Auxillary Elizabeth R. Pollock. Arranged and edited by Page Cary. Philadelphia and New York: J.B. Lippincott Co., 1943.

Sprightly, patriotic letters to her family describe life as a WAAC during World War II. Letters are not fully dated, but were written in the early 1940's.

2221. Pompadour, Jeanne-Antoinette Poisson, Madame le Normand d'Etoiles, Marquise de, 1721-1764. French politician and chief mistress of Louis XV. A series of fictitious letters supposedly by Mme. Pompadour, later attributed to François, Marquis de Barbe-Marbois, were published in London and Paris, 1771-1774. LETTRES DE MADAME LA MARQUISE DE POMPADOUR, ÉCRITES À PLUSIERS PERSONNAGES ILLUSTRES DU XVIIIe SIÈCLE. Nouvelle édition, augmentée d'une notice sur la vie de cette femme célèbre. Paris, 1811. 2 vols.

2222. ------. CORRESPONDANCE DE MADAME POMPADOUR AVEC SON PÈRE M. POISSON, SON FRÈRE M. DE VANDIÈRES. Publiée pour la première fois par A. Poulet-Malassis, suivie de lettres de cette Dame a la Comtesse de Lutzelbourg... etc. Paris: J. Baur 1878. 261p.

2223. Ponsonby, Mary Elizabeth Bulteel, Lady, 1832-1916. English politician and Maid of Honor to Queen Victoria. MARY PONSONBY: A MEMOIR, SOME LETTERS AND A JOURNAL. Edited by her daughter, Magdalen Ponsonby. London: John Murray, 1927. Also published under the title A LADY IN WAITING TO QUEEN VICTORIA, New York: J.H. Sears & Co., 1927. 304p.

Letters and journals edited together chronologically, covering her years as Maid of Honor, her marriage, and a visit to Germany. Contains correspondence with George Eliot and letters to the Empress Frederick.

2224. Porter, Ann Eliza Bacon, 1821-1890. American. CHOICE SEED IN THE WILDERNESS: FROM THE DIARY OF ANN ELIZA BACON PORTER, COOKSVILLE, WISCONSIN, 1845-1890. Edited by Lillian Russell Porter. Rockland, Maine: Seth Low Press, 1964. 207p.

2225. Porter, Katherine Anne, b. 1894. American novelist and short story writer. THE COLLECTED ESSAYS AND OCCASIONAL WRITINGS OF KATHERINE ANNE PORTER. New York: Delacorte Press, 1970. 496p.

Includes "From the Notebooks: Yeats, Joyce, Eliot,

Pound,"; "Notes on Writing," "Ole Woman River: a Correspondence with Katherine Anne Porter" (by Donald Sutherland); "Letters to a Nephew,"; and "A Letter to Sylvia Beach" (on the death of Adrienne Monnier).

2226. Porter, Lavinia Honeyman. American pioneer settler. BY OX TEAM TO CALIFORNIA: A NARRATIVE OF CROSSING THE PLAINS IN 1860. Oakland, Calif.: Oakland Enquirer Publishing Co., 1910. 139p.

2227. Portes, Marie Felice de Budos de, 1628-1693. LA CORRESPONDANCE DE MARIE FELICE DE BUDOS, MARQUISE DE PORTES, AVEC LE GRANDE CONDÉ. Jean-Bernard Elziere. Nimes: Renaissance du Château de Portes, 1975. 95p.

Correspondence with Prince Louis II de Bourbon-Conde.

Post, Lydia Minturn. See Barclay, Grace.

2228. Potter, Beatrix, 1866-1943. English illustrator and children's author. BEATRIX POTTER: LETTERS TO CHILDREN. New York: Harvard College Library, Dept. of Printing and Graphic Arts, and Walker & Co., 1966. 48p.

Facsimile reproductions, followed by transcriptions, of nine letters, 1896-1902, to her young friends Noel, Eric, and Freda Moore, children of her former governess.

2229. ------. JOURNAL OF BEATRIX POTTER FROM 1881-1897. Transcribed from her code writing by Leslie Linder, with an appreciation by H.L. Cox. London and New York: Frederick Warne & Co., 1966. 448p.

Covers her adolescence and life to age thirty.

2230. ------. BEATRIX POTTER'S AMERICANS: SELECTED LETTERS. Edited by Jane Crowell Morse. Boston, Mass.: Horn Book, 1982. 216p.

2231. Pougy, Liane de (Princess Anne-Marie Chassaigne Ghika), 1869-1950. French courtesan and Lesbian, later princess and nun. MES CAHIERS BLEUS. Préface du R.P. Rzewuski. Paris: Librarie Plon, 1977. 327p.

2232. ------. MY BLUE NOTEBOOKS. Preface by R.P. Rzewuski. Translated from the French by Diana Athill. New York: Harper & Row; and London: A. Deutsch, 1979. 288p. London: Century Publisher, 1986. 288p.

Frank and intimate journal, 1919-1941 about her life in the demi-monde, her marriage to the Prince Georges Ghika, and her religious conversion. De Pougy was a member of Natalie Barney's circle; among her women lovers were Barney, Emilienne d'Alencon and Louise Bathy ("Polaire"). Later in life she converted to Catholicism and died a nun.

2233. Poutiatine, Olga, Countess, [Ol'ga Even'evna Putiatina] 1891-1940. Russian artist. WAR AND REVOLUTION: EXCERPTS FROM THE LETTERS AND DIARIES OF COUNTESS POUTIATINE. Edited and translated by G.A. Lensen. Tallahassee, Fla.: Diplomatic Press, n.d.

Account of the conditions in World War I field hospitals.

2234. Powell, Anne, b. 1769. Canadian. "Journal of Miss Powell on a Tour from Montreal to Detroit." MAGAZINE OF AMERICAN HISTORY 5 (1880), 34-47.

Travel diary.

2236. Powell, Maude, b. 1889. American Quaker. ETERNALLY YOURS: RALPH AND MAUDE POWELL'S LEGACY OF LETTERS. With an introduction and postscript by Rose Lewis. Burnsville, N.C.: Celo Press, 1979. 325p.

Courtship letters, 1912-1914, between two midwestern Quakers, beginning in the early days of their courtship following an acquaintanceship at Michigan Agricultural College, and ending with their wedding.

2235. Powell, Mildred Elizabeth. American Civil War diarist and activist. "Journal of Mildred Elizabeth

Powell." Mary Stella Hereford Ball. In REMINISCENCES OF THE WOMEN OF MISSOURI DURING THE SIXTIES. Gathered, compiled and published by Missouri Division, United Daughters of the Confederacy, n.d. p.148-182.

Journal of a Palmyra, Missouri Belle. An ardent Confederate, her influence in the community was so great she was imprisoned by Union Forces and later banished to Nevada. An account of the journey to Nevada and exile there, September 29, 1862--February 13, 1863.

2237. Powers, Elvira J. American. HOSPITAL PENCILLINGS: BEING A DIARY WHILE IN JEFFERSON GENERAL HOSPITAL, JEFFERSONVILLE, INDIANA AND OTHERS AT NASHVILLE, TENNESSEE, AS MATRON AND VISITER. Boston: Edward L. Mitchell, 1866. 211p.

Civil War diary April-October, 1864. Partly an account of hospital conditions, partly a travel diary.

2238. Powers, Mary Rockwood, d.1858. American frontier settler. A WOMAN'S OVERLAND JOURNAL TO CALIFORNIA, BY MARY ROCKWOOD POWERS. Edited with an introduction by W.B. Thorsen. Fairfield, Wash.: Ye Galleon Press, 1985. 73p.

2239. Powys, Caroline Girle, 1738-1817. MRS. POWYS: PASSAGES FROM THE DIARIES OF MRS. PHILIP LYBBE POWYS, OF HARDWICK HOUSE, OXON, A.D. 1756-1808. Edited by Emily J. Climenson. London, New York and Bombay: Longmans, Green & Co., 1899. 399p.

According to Sir Arthur Ponsonby, her diary describes social affairs, travels, scenery, notes on weather, comments on plays seen and "as many references as possible to the Royal Family."

2240. Preble, Harriet, 1795-1854. American intellectual and proponent of women's education. MEMOIR OF THE LIFE OF HARRIET PREBLE, CONTAINING PORTIONS OF HER CORRESPONDENCE, JOURNAL AND OTHER WRITINGS, LITERARY AND RELIGIOUS. Professor Richard Henry Lee. New York: G.P. Putnam's Sons, 1856. 409p.

2241. Prentiss, Elizabeth Payson, 1818-1878. American hymnist, poet and novelist. LIFE AND LETTERS OF ELIZABETH PRENTISS. By the Reverend G.L. Prentiss. London: Hodder & Stoughton; and New York: Anson D.F. Randolph, 1882. 573p. Reprinted in microform, Princeton, N.J.: American Theological Library Association Board of Microtext. Microfiche (105x148 mm.)

Early letters to her sister and to other friends and relatives, and extracts from journals and diaries.

2242. Preston, Madge [Margaret Smith Preston], b. 1815. American. A PRIVATE WAR: LETTERS AND DIARIES OF MADGE PRESTON, 1862-1867. Edited by Virginia Walcott Beauchamp. New Brunswick, N.J.: Rutgers University Press, 1987. 374p.

Two voices emerge from Preston's writings: the voice of the letters is sociable, conversational, and through them we move through the ordered world of mother, devoted wife, and kindly mistress of the household. The voice of the diary is unstudied, private, and reveals the torment of a battered wife.

2243. Preston, Margaret Junkin, 1820-1897. American Confederate poet. LIFE AND LETTERS OF MARGARET JUNKIN PRESTON. Edited by Elizabeth Preston Allen. Boston and New York: Houghton Mifflin, 1903.

Extracts from her letters and journals, 1840-1897, including a Civil War Diary, 1862-1865.

2244. Preus, Caroline Dorthea Margrethe Keyser, 1829-1880. Norwegian-American Immigrant and wife of Lutheran Minister Herman Preus. LINKA'S DIARY, ON LAND AND SEA. Translated and edited by Johan C.K. and Diderikke M. Preus. Minneapolis: Augsburg Publishing House, 1952. 288p.

Diary 1845-1864 describes the life of a pioneer Norwegian immigrant family living in Wisconsin.

2245. Price, Elizabeth Lees Moffat, 1839-1919.

English missionary. JOURNALS WRITTEN IN BECHUANALAND, SOUTH AFRICA, 1854-1883, WITH AN EPILOGUE, 1889 AND 1900. Edited with an introduction, annotations, etc., by Una Long for Rhodes University, Grahamstown, South Africa. London: E. Arnold, 1956. 564p.

Journal letters written to relatives and friends while doing missionary work with her husband, Reverend Robert Price, in South Africa. The journal has been much abridged from the original.

2246. Price, Eugenia. American novelist and inspirational author. DIARY OF A NOVEL. New York: Lippincott & Crowell, 1980.

Diary September 13, 1978--September 6, 1979, chronicles the writing of her novel MARGARET'S STORY.

2247. Primrose, Olive Clare. Canadian wife of author John Coulter. PRELUDE TO A MARRIAGE: LETTERS AND DIARIES OF JOHN COULTER AND OLIVE CLARE PRIMROSE. Ottowa: Oberon Press, 1979. 145p.

2248. Pringle, Catherine Sager. American frontier settler. "Letter of Catherine Sager Pringle." OREGON HISTORICAL QUARTERLY 37:4 (December, 1936), 354-360.

Letter dated September 21, 1854. She was the oldest child of Henry and Naomi Sager, who started across the plains in 1844, but who died before the journey's end. Sager and six brothers and sisters were taken in by the Whitman Mission, where they lived until the massacre of 1847. The letter gives news of herself and a vivid account of the Whitman massacre.

Pringle, Elizabeth Allston. See: Pennington, Patience.

2249. Pruyn, Mary. American missionary to Japan. GRANDMAMA'S LETTERS FROM JAPAN. Boston: J.H. Earle, 1877. 219p.

Letters sent from Japan to her grandchildren and others. Intended for young readers, in hopes they will feel called to missionary work; however, the letters were not originally written for publication.

2250. Ptaschkina, Nellie L'ovna, 1903-1920. Russian. DIARY OF NELLIE PTASCHKINA. Translated by Pauline D. Chary. Edited by J. Jacques Povolotsky. London: Jonathan Cape, 1923. 316p.

Diary of a young aristocrat written during the Russian Revolution, 1917-1918. Her early diary, begun in 1908 at the age of ten, is not reproduced here.

2251. Pugh, Sarah, 1800-1884. American abolitionist and suffragist. THE MEMORIAL OF SARAH PUGH: A TRIBUTE OF RESPECT FROM HER COUSINS. Philadelphia: J.B. Lippincott, 1888. 136p.

Journals and letters, 1828-1882.

2252. Putnam, Roselle, 1832-1861. American frontier settler, journalist, publisher and printer. "The Letters of Roselle Putnam." Transcript and notes by Sheba Hargreaves. OREGON HISTORICAL QUARTERLY 29 (September, 1928), 242-264.

Letters dated September, 18, 1849--February 5, 1852, describe life in Oregon Territory. The wife of Oregon publisher Charles Putnam, she was the first woman to set type in Oregon.

2253. Pym, Barbara, 1913-1980. English novelist. A VERY PRIVATE EYE: THE DIARIES, LETTERS AND NOTEBOOKS OF BARBARA PYM. Edited by Hazel Holt and Hilary Pym. London: Macmillan, 1984. 358p.

Literary diary, 1931-1948, written as finished pieces; notebook entries 1948-1980; and letters to close personal friends. Letters were chosen to fill gaps in the narrative provided by the diaries and to illuminate various aspects of her work. The selection is meant to stand as a "kind of autobiography," to show the development of Pym's style, and to reveal her idiosyncratic view of life.

2254. Radclyffe, Ann Ward, 1764-1823. English novelist. THE POSTHUMOUS WORKS OF ANN RADCLYFFE. COMPRISING GASTON DE BLONDEVILLE, A ROMANCE; ST. ALBAN'S ABBEY, A METRICAL TALE, WITH VARIOUS POETICAL PIECES; TO WHICH IS PREFIXED A MEMOIR OF THE AUTHORESS, WITH EXTRACTS FROM HER PRIVATE JOURNALS. London: Published for Henry Colburn by Richard Bentley, 1833. 4 vols.

Volume 1 contains extracts from a journal kept on various tours of England: along the coast of Kent, Autumn, 1797; along the coast from Portsmouth to Dover, 1798; and visits to Leicester and Warwick, returning by Woodstock and Oxford, 1802, including descriptions of Warwick and Blenheim Castles.

2255. Radziwill, Marie Dorothea Elisabeth de Castellane, Furstin von, 1840-1915. French Princess. UNE GRANDE DAME D'AVANT GUERRE: LETTRES DE LA PRINCESSE RADZIWILL AU GENERAL DE ROBILANT, 1889-1914. [Publiee par Irene de Robilant]. Bologna: N. Zanichelli, 1933-1934. 4 vols.

Correspondence with Mario Antonio Nicolis di Robilant (b.1855).

2256. ------. THIS WAS GERMANY: AN OBSERVER AT THE COURT OF BERLIN. LETTERS OF PRINCESS MARIE RADZIWILL TO GENERAL DI ROBILANT, ONE TIME MILITARY ATTACHÉ AT BERLIN (1908-1915). Edited and translated, with an introduction and notes explaining events by Cyril Spencer Fox. London: John Murray, 1937. 403p.

Translation of Volume 4 of UNE GRANDE DAME D'AVANT GUERRE. Princess Radziwill occupied a leading position in European society which enabled her to meet most of the important political and social figures of Europe in the years just before World War I.

2257. Rahel (Rahel Antoine Fredericke Levin Varnhagen von Ense), 1771-1833. German literary figure. AUS DEM NACHLASS VARNHAGEN'S VON ENSE. BRIEFWECHSEL ZWISCHEN RAHEL UND DAVID VEIT. Leipzig: F.A. Brockhaus, 1861. 2 vols. in one.

2258. ------. RAHEL: HER LIFE AND LETTERS. Mrs. Vaughn Jennings. London: H.S. King & Co., 1876. 268p.

2259. ------. AUS RAHEL'S HERZENSLEBEN, BRIEFE UND TAGEBÜCHBLATTER. Herausgegeben von Ludmilla Assing. Leipzig: F.A. Brockhaus, 1877. 256p.

2260. ------. RAHEL VARNHAGEN, EINE FRAUENLEBEN IN BRIEFEN. Ausgewahlt und mit einer einleitung versehen von Augusta Weldler-Steinberg. Potsdam: G. Kiepenheuer, 1917, 1925. 545p.

2261. ------. DIE RAHEL: BRIEFE UND TAGEBÜCHBLATTER. Ausgewahlt und eingeleitet von Agathe Weigelt. Berlin: Allstein, 1921. 191p.

2262. ------. RAHEL UND ALEXANDER VON DER MARWITZ IN IHREN BRIEFEN. Ein bild aus der zeit der romantiker. Nach den originalen herausgegegen von Heinrich Meisner. Gotha-Stuttgart: F.A. Perthes, 1925. 310p.

2263. ------. RAHEL VARNHAGEN, LEBENSGESCHICHTE EINER DEUTSCHEN JUDIN AUS DER ROMANTIK. Mit einer auswahl von Rahel. Briefen un Zeitg enossischen Abbildüngen. Hannah Arendt. München: R. Piper, 1959. 297p.

Includes extracts from letters and diary.

2264. ------. BRIEFWECHSEL VON RAHEL VARNHAGEN. Herausgegeben von Friedhelm Kemp. Münic: Kosel, 1966-1968. 4 vols.

Volume 1: correspondence with Alexander von der Marwitz, Karl von Finckenstein, Wilhelm Bokelmann, and Raphael d'Urquijo. Volume 2: Correspondence with August Varnhagen von Ense. Volume 3: Correspondence 1793-1833. Volume 4: Correspondence 1800-1833.

2265. Ramsay, Martha Laurens, 1759-1811. American colonial horticulturist. MEMOIRS OF THE LIFE OF MARTHA LAURENS RAMSAY, WHO DIED IN CHARLESTON, SOUTH CAROLINA, ON THE TENTH OF JUNE, 1811 IN THE FIFTY-SECOND YEAR OF HER AGE. CONTAINING EXTRACTS FROM HER DIARY, LETTERS,

AND OTHER PRIVATE PAPERS, AND ALSO FROM LETTERS WRITTEN TO HER BY HER FATHER, HENRY LAURENS, 1771-1776. David Ramsay. Philadelphia: James Maxwell, Printer, 1811. 308p. Second edition, Charlestown, Mass.: Printed and Sold by Samuel Etheridge, Jr., 1812. Third edition, Boston: S.T. Armstrong, 1812. 280p.

Biography, including extracts from her diary, 1791-1808 and her letters, 1792-1811.

2266. Randall, Margaret, b. 1936. American poet, editor, translator, and political activist self-exiled to Cuba. PART OF THE SOLUTION: PORTRAIT OF A REVOLUTIONARY. New York: New Directions Press, 1973. 192p.

Contains a chapter of diary extracts, "Notes from a Diary, 1970-1972: From a Society of Consumers to a Society of Workers...Fragments of First Two Years in Cuba."

2267. Ranous, Dora Knowlton Thompson, 1859-1916. American actress. DIARY OF A DALY DEBUTANTE. BEING PASSAGES FROM THE JOURNAL OF A MEMBER OF AUGUSTIN DALY'S FAMOUS COMPANY OF PLAYERS. New York: Duffield, 1910. 249p. Reprinted by B. Blom, New York, 1972.

Theatre diary, 1879-1880.

2268. Ratcliff, Mildred, 1773-1847. American Quaker. MEMORANDA AND CORRESPONDENCE OF MILDRED RATCLIFF. Philadelphia: Friend's Bookstore, 1890. 210p.

Contains extracts from her journals and letters.

2269. Rawle, Anna. American. "A Loyalist's Account of Certain Occurances in Philadelphia After Cornwallis' Surrender at Yorktown. Extracted from the Diary of Miss Anna Rawle." PENNSYLVANIA MAGAZINE OF HISTORY AND BIOGRAPHY 16:1 (1892), 103-110.

Rawle was the stepdaughter of Philadelphia Loyalist Samuel Shoemaker. The family was in New York just before the evacuation of Philadelphia by British Troops; Rawle kept her diary "for entertainment."

2270. Rawlings, Marjorie Kinnan, 1896-1953. American author. SELECTED LETTERS OF MARJORIE KINNAN RAWLINGS. Edited by Gordon E. Bigelow and Laura V. Monti. Gainesville, Fla.: University Presses of Florida, 1983. 414p.

Letters written from New York and Cross Creek, Florida, 1918-1953, selected from a collection of over 1,000 letters in the Rawlings Collection at the University of Florida at Gainesville. Letters were chosen that best represent the many facets of her character, that convey a good idea of her literary theory and practice, and that give a picture of her acquaintance with celebrated people of her time and with the people of rural Florida.

2271. Read, Jenny, 1935-1976. American artist and sculptor. JENNY READ: IN PURSUIT OF ART AND LIFE. THE JOURNALS AND LETTERS OF A YOUNG SCULPTOR, SAN FRANCISCO, 1970-1976. Arranged with commentary by Dallas Johnson. Edited by Kathleen Doyle. Burnsville, N.C.: Antioch University with Celo Press, 1982. 173p.

2272. Reading, Alice Isaacs, Countess of. Wife of Rufus Reading, Viceroy of India. THE VICEROY'S WIFE: LETTERS OF ALICE ISAACS, COUNTESS OF READING, FROM INDIA, 1921-1925. Edited by Iris Butler. London: Hodder & Stoughton, 1969. 190p.

2273. Récamier, Jeanne Françoise Julie Adelaide Bernard, 1777-1849. French intellectual, salonist, politician and social leader. SOUVENIRS ET CORRESPONDANCE. TIÈRES DES PAPIERS DE MADAME RÉCAMIER. Publiée par Amelie Cyvoct Lenormant. Paris: Michel Lévy, Frères, 1859. 2 vols.

Biography and extracts from her MEMOIRS, followed by letters, chiefly from her correspondents.

2274. ------. MEMOIRS AND CORRESPONDENCE OF MADAME RÉCAMIER. Translated from the French and edited by Isaphene M. Luyster. Second edition. Boston: Roberts Brothers, 1867. 408p.

Correspondence consists of letters to her; only

seven of her own letters are included. Women correspondents represented include Madame de Stael, Madame Krudner, Lady Charlotte Sutton, Madame de Chateaubriand, Queen Hortense and Madame Salvage.

2275. ------. LETTRES INÉDITES ET SOUVENIRS BIOGRAPHIQUES DE MADAME DE RÉCAMIER ET DE MADAME DE STAËL. Paris: J. Renouard, 1868. 89p.

2276. ------. MADAME RÉCAMIER: LES AMIS DE SA JEUNESSE ET SA CORRESPONDANCE INTIME. Par l'Auteur des Souvenirs de Madame de Récamier (Amelie Cyvoct Lenormant). Paris: Michel Lévy, Frères, 1872. 406p.

2277. Recke, Elisa (Elizabeth) Charlotte Constanzia Reichsgrafin von Medem, Baronin von der, 1754-1833. TAGEBUCH EINER REISE DURCH EINEN THEIL DEUTSCHLAND UND DURCH ITALIEN, IN DEN JAHREN 1804 BIS 1806. Herausgegeben von Hofrath Bottiger. Berlin: In der Nicolaischen Buchhandlung, 1815. 4 vols.

Travel diary.

2278. ------. ELISA VON DER RECKE. AUFZEICHNÜNGEN UND BRIEFE AUS IHREN JUGENTAGEN. Herausgegeben von Paul Rachel. Leipzig: Dieterich, 1900. 487p. Second edition 1902, 2 vols.

Volume 1: Aufzeichnüngen und briefe aus ihren Jugentagen. Volume 2: Tagebucher und brief aus ihren Wanderjahren.

2279. ------. BRIEFE AN ELISA VON DER RECKE. AUS DEN ORIGINALEN IN DER MUSEUMSBIBLIOTHEK IN MITAU. Herausgegeben von Otto Clemen. Berlin: Steglitz, F. Wurtz, 1907(?). 80p.

2280. ------. MEIN JOURNAL: ELISAS NEU AUFGEFUNDENE TAGEBÜCHER AS DEN JAHREN 1791 UND 1793/95. Herausgegeben von Johannes Werner. Leipzig: Koehler & Ameland, 1927. 272p.

2281. ------. TAGEBÜCHER UND SELBSTZEUGNISSE.

Herausgegeben und mit einem vorwort versehen von Christine Trager. München: C.H. Beck, 1984. 475p.

2282. Regnier, Paule, 1890-1950. French author. JOURNAL. Préface de Jacques Madaule. Paris: Librarie Plon, 1953. 296p.

2283. ------. LETTRES. Préface du R.P. Louis Barjon. Paris: Desclée, De Brouwer, 1955. 240p.

2284. Reiman, Brigitte, 1933-1973. German author. DIE GELIEBT, DIE VERFLUCHTE HOFFNUG: TAGEBÜCHER UND BRIEFE, 1947-1972. Herausgegeben von Elisabeth Elten-Krause und Walter Lewerenz. Darmstadt und Neuwied: Luchterhand, 1984. 359p.

2285. Rémusat, Claire Élisabeth Jeanne Gravier de Vergennes, Comtesse de, 1780-1821. French author and politician, lady-in-waiting to Empress Josephine, and wife of the Comte de Rémusat, Chamberlain to Napoléon. LETTRES DE MADAME REMUSAT, 1804-1814. Publiées par son petit-fils Paul de Rémusat. Paris: Calmann-Lévy, Frères, 1881. 2 vols.

2286. ------. A SELECTION FROM THE LETTERS OF MADAME RÉMUSAT TO HER HUSBAND AND SON, FROM 1804 TO 1813. Translated from the French by Mrs. Cashel Hoey and Mr. John Lillie. New York: D. Appleton & Co., 1881. 324p. London: Sampson Low, Marston, Searle & Rivington, 1881. 434p.

Selection taken from the 1881 edition.

2287. Renan, Henriette, 1811-1861. French sister of philologist and historian Ernest Renan. ERNEST RENAN--HENRIETTE RENAN: LETTRES INTIMES, 1842-1845. Paris: Calmann-Lévy, Frères, 1896. 408p.

2288. ------. BROTHER AND SISTER: A MEMOIR AND THE LETTERS OF ERNEST AND HENRIETTE RENAN. Translated by Lady Mary Lloyd. New York: Macmillan, 1896. 323p.

Translation of LETTRES INTIMES (1896).

2289. ------. ERNEST RENAN--HENRIETTE RENAN: NOUVELLES LETTRES INTIMES, 1846-1850. Paris: Calmann-Lévy, Frères, 1923. 517p.

2290. Rennert, Maggie. American journalist. SHELANU: AN ISRAEL JOURNAL. Englewood Cliffs, N.J.: Prentice Hall, 1979. 446p.

Autobiography of a woman who went to live in the Israeli frontier city of Beersheba in the 1970's. Includes extracts from her journal.

2291. Reventlow, Franziska, Grafin zu, 1871-1918. German author. BRIEF DER GRAFIN FRANZISKA ZU REVENTLOW. Herausgegeben von Else Reventlow. Min vier bildbeilagen. München: A. Langen, 1929. 229p.

2292. ------. TAGEBUCHER, 1895-1910. Herausgegeben von Else Reventlow. München: Langen Müller, 1971. 495p. Frankfurt Am Main: Fischer Taschenbüch, 1976. 493p.

2293. ------. BRIEF, 1890-1917. (Achtzehnhundertnewnzig bis neunzehnnhundersiebzehn). Herausgegeben von Else Reventlow. Munchen, Wein: Langen Muller, 1975. Frankfort am Main: Fischer Taschenbuch, 1977. 598p.

2294. Reynolds, Hannah Darby, d. 1762. English Quaker. REYNOLDS-RATHBONE DIARIES. Edited by Mrs. E. Greg. London: Privately printed, 1905. 203p.

Quaker diary, January, 1761--May, 1762.

2295. Rhys, Jean. American author. THE LETTERS OF JEAN RHYS. Selected and edited by Francis Wynham and Diana Melly. New York: Viking Penguin/Edith Sifton Books, 1984.

2296. Ribblesdale, Emma, Lady, 1833-1911. LETTERS AND DIARIES. Collected by Beatrix Lister. Privately Published, 1930.

Society diary, 1870-1907.

2297. Rice, Ruth Kessler, 1883-1942. American frontier settler. LETTERS FROM NEW MEXICO, 1899-1904, BY RUTH KESSLER RICE. Edited by Margaret W. Reid. Wichita Falls, Tex.: M.W. Reid, and Albuquerque, N.Mex.: Adobe Press, 1981. 82p.

2298. Rice, Sally. American mill worker. "I Can Never Be So Happy There In Among So Many Mountains: The Letters of Sally Rice." Edited by Nell W. Kull. VERMONT HISTORY 38 (Winter, 1970), 49-57.

Biographical background and brief extracts from letters. Rice left Vermont to work in the textile mills of Connecticut to provide herself with a dowry.

2299. Richards, Caroline Cowles, later Clarke, 1842-1913. American Civil War diarist. DIARY OF CAROLINE COWLES RICHARDS, 1852-1872. Canandigua, New York: 1908. 162p.

2300. ------. VILLAGE LIFE IN AMERICA, 1852-1872, INCLUDING THE PERIOD OF AMERICAN CIVIL WAR AS TOLD IN THE DIARY OF A SCHOOL-GIRL, BY CAROLINE COWLES RICHARDS. With an introduction by Margaret E. Sangster. New and enlarged edition. London: T. Fisher Unwin, 1912. New York: Henry Holt & Co., 1913. 225p.

2301. Richards, Eva Alvey. American teacher. ARCTIC MOOD: A NARRATIVE OF ARCTIC ADVENTURES. Caldwell, Idaho: The Caxton Printers, 1949. 282p.

Account, with extracts from a journal, of teaching Eskimo children in Alaska, 1924-1926.

2302. Richmond, Rebecca. American first cousin to Elizabeth Bacon Custer. "Rebecca Visits Kansas and the Custers: The Diary of Rebecca Richmond." Edited by Minnie Dubbs Millbrook. KANSAS HISTORICAL QUARTERLY 42:4 (1976), 366-402.

Diary extracts January 1--April 24, 1868 and February 19--March 23, 1870, describe visits to the Custer family at Fort Leavenworth, Texas.

2303. Ricketson, Annie Holmes, b. 1841. American. THE JOURNAL OF ANNIE HOLMES RICKETSON ON THE WHALESHIP A.R. TUCKER, 1871-1874. New Bedford, Mass.: Old Dartsmouth Historical Society, 1958. 79p.

2304. Ricketts, Frances (Fanny) Lawrence. American Army wife. "Fanny Ricketts: Nurse, Diarist, Devoted Wife." L. Vanloan Naisawald. VIRGINIA CAVALCADE 21 (Winter, 1972), 14-21.

Story of Fanny Ricketts, who journeyed to Manassas in 1861 to care for her wounded husband, a Captain in the United States Army. Based on her diary.

2305. Ridgely, Anna, later Hudson, 1842-1926. American. "A Girl in the Sixties: Excerpts From the Journal of Anna Ridgely." Edited by her niece, Octavia Roberts Corneau. ILLINOIS STATE HISTORICAL SOCIETY JOURNAL 22 (October, 1929), 401-446.

Social diary written by the daughter of a prominent family of Springfield, Illinois.

Ridley, Rebeccah Crosthwaite. See: Blackmore, Rebeccah Crosthwaite Ridley.

2306. Riedesel, Frederika Charlotte Louise von Massow, Baroness von, 1746-1808. German wife of Baron von Riedesel, Commanding General of the Brunswick Troops serving with the British Army during the American Revolution. LETTERS AND JOURNALS RELATING TO THE WAR OF THE AMERICAN REVOLUTION, AND THE CAPTURE OF THE GERMAN TROOPS AT SARATOGA. BY MRS. GENERAL RIEDESEL. Translated from the original German by William L. Stone. Albany, N.Y.: Joel Munsell, 1867. 235p.

2307. ------. BARONESS VON RIEDESEL AND THE AMERICAN REVOLUTION: JOURNAL AND CORRESPONDENCE OF A TOUR OF DUTY, 1776-1783. A revised translation. With an introduction and notes by Marvin L. Brown, Jr., with the assistance of Marta Huth. Chapel Hill, N.C.: Published for the Institute of Early American History and Culture at Williamsburg, Virginia, at the University of North Carolina Press, 1965. 222p.

2308. Riedmatten, Marie de, 1862-1924. JOURNAL INTIME, 1882-1896. Marie de Riedmatten. Édition integrale publiée sous les auspices de la Bourgeoisie de Sion. Texte établi, annotée et présentée par André Donnet. Preface de Bernard de Torrente. Martigny: Bibliotheca Vallesiana Lausanne: Diffusion Payout, 1975. 2 vols.

2309. Ringo, Mary, 1826-1876. American pioneer settler. THE JOURNAL OF MRS. MARY RINGO: A DIARY OF HER TRIP ACROSS THE GREAT PLAINS IN 1864. With a foreword and conclusion by her daughter, Mattie Bell Cushing. Santa Anna, Calif.: Privately Printed, 1956. 38p. Edition of 45 copies.

2310. Rinser, Luise, b. 1911. German author. GEFANGNISTAGEBÜCH. München: Zinnen-Verlag, 1946. 234p.

2311. ------. GRENZUBERGANGE: TAGEBÜCH-NOTIZEN. Frankfort am Main: S. Fischer, 1972. 348p.

2312. ------. BAUSTELLE: EINE ART TAGEBÜCH, 1967-1970. Frankfort am Main: S. Fischer, 1970. 300p.

2313. ------. KRIEGSSPIELZEUG: TAGEBÜCH 1972 BIS 1978. Frankfort Am Main: S. Fischer, 1978. 267p.

2314. Ritchie, Anne Isabelle Thackeray, 1837-1919. English author and daughter of William Makepeace Thackeray. THE LETTERS OF ANNE THACKERAY RITCHIE. WITH FORTY-TWO ADDITIONAL LETTERS FROM HER FATHER, WILLIAM MAKEPEACE THACKERAY. Selected and edited by her daughter, Hester Ritchie. New York and London: John Murray, 1924. 314p.

Letters begining in 1852, and journals 1854-1882 edited together. Includes a few letters written by her mother, Isabella Gethen Creagh Shawe Thackeray.

2315. Rittenhouse, Isabella Maud. American. MAUD. Edited by Richard Lee Strout. New York: The Macmillan Co., 1939. 593p.

Social diary of a typical, bright, middle class

girl of nineteenth-century Chicago. She kept a journal from 1881 to 1895, from age twelve to age thirty.

2316. Rizzi, Marcia Salo. American feminist. SOME PICTURES FROM MY LIFE. Times Change Press, 1972. Unpaged.

An assemblage of diary entries, dreams, drawings and photographs chronicles Rizzi's movement towards a feminist consciousness.

2317. Robbins, Margaret Dreier. American sociologist. MARGARET DREIER ROBBINS: HER LIFE, LETTERS AND WORK. Mary E. Dreier. New York: Island Press, 1950. 278p.

2318. Roberts, Phoebe McCarty, b. 1776? American Quaker. "Phoebe Roberts' Diary of a Quaker Missionary Journey to Upper Canada." Edited by Leslie R. Gray. ONTARIO HISTORICAL SOCIETY PAPERS AND RECORDS 42 (1950), 7-46.

2319. Roberts, Rachel, 1927-1980. Welsh-American actress and fourth wife of Rex Harrison. NO BELLS ON SUNDAY: THE RACHEL ROBERTS JOURNALS. Edited with a documentary biography by Alexander Walker. New York: Harper & Row, 1984. 246p.

2320. Robertson, Emma. American ranch manager. "The Ranch Letters of Emma Robertson, 1891-1892." James E. Potter. NEBRASKA HISTORY 56:2 (Summer, 1975), 221-229.

With her husband, James E. Robertson, Emma Robertson managed the Hershey Stock Ranch located near North Bend, Dodge County, Nebraska.

2321. Robertson, Martha Wayles, 1812-1867. American. "A Prayer for the Spirit of Acceptance: The Journal of Martha Wayles Robertson, 1860-1866." HISTORICAL MAGAZINE OF THE PROTESTANT EPISCOPAL CHURCH 46:4 (December, 1977), 397-408.

2322. Robeson, Eslanda Goode, 1896-1965. American Black activist, author, and anthropologist. AFRICAN

JOURNEY. New York: John Day Co., 1945.

Diary of an anthropological trip to Africa undertaken in 1936.

2323. Robinson, Ione, b.1910. American artist. A WALL TO PAINT ON. New York: E.P. Dutton Co., 1946. 451p.

Autobiography in a diary and letters to Robinson's family, 1927-1939.

2324. Robinson, Sophie Michau. L'ODYSSÉE AMERICAIN D'UNE FAMILLE FRANCAISE. LE DOCTEUR ANTON SAUGRAIN. ÉTUDE DE SUIVIE DE MANUSCRITS INEDITS ET DE LA CORRESPONDANCE DE SOPHIE MICHAU ROBINSON. Par H. Foure Selter. Institut Francais de Washington. Baltimore: The Johns Hopkins Press; London: Humphrey Milford; and Paris: Librarie Droz, 1936. 123p.

The family lived in Gallipolis, in the Ohio Valley. Includes a life of Robinson, followed by her letters, October 8, 1817--October 23, 1828, chiefly written to relatives in France.

2325. Roderick, Mary Louise Rochester, b. 1889. American singer. A NIGHTINGALE IN THE TRENCHES. New York: Vantage Press, 1966. 289p.

World War I diary, 1918-1919. Signed on by the YMCA National War Work Council, she worked on ships, in front-line trenches, in camps and field stations, and in French villages, entertaining troops of wounded soldiers.

2326. Roe, A.S. English missionary to China. CHINA AS I SAW IT: A WOMAN'S LETTERS FROM THE CELESTIAL EMPIRE. London: Hutchinson & Co., 1910. 330p.

Missionary travel letters, 1907-1909.

2327. Roe, Frances Marie Antoinette Mack. American Army wife. ARMY LETTERS FROM AN OFFICER'S WIFE,

1871-1888. Illustrated by I.W. Taber from contemporary photographs. New York and London: D. Appleton & Co., 1909. Reprinted, with an introduction by Sandra L. Myres. Lincoln, Nebr.: University of Nebraska Press, 1981. 387p.

Describes life with the U.S. Infantry; her husband was stationed at Fort Lyon, Colorado, a frontier post, shortly after they were married.

2328. Roe, Marion Precilla Hooker, 1827-1863. American teacher. HOME-SCENES AND HEART-TINTS: A MEMORIAL OF MRS. MARION H. ROE. New York: John F. Grow, 1865. 208p.

Letters 1843-1863 describe life as a student and later as a teacher.

2329. Roedel, Josephine Forney, 1825-1904. American wife of Reverend William D. Roedel. "Diary of Josephine Forney Roedel." Elsie Singmaster. PENNSYLVANIA MAGAZINE OF HISTORY AND BIOGRAPHY 67:4 (October, 1943), 390-411.

Civil War diary, October, 1863--March, 1864, describes travel in 1863 to visit her family in Gettysburg. Her diary suggests some of the problems which arose in families whose loyalties were divided between the North and South.

2330. Rogers, Clara Kathleen (Clara Doria), 1844-1931. English-American composer. JOURNAL LETTERS FROM THE ORIENT. Edited, with introductory letters and supplementary notes by Henry Munroe Rogers. Privately Printed at the Plimpton Press, 1934. 420p.

Travel letters, written as a journal and sent in batches to her sister in London and to her sister-in-law in Boston, describing a trip to Asia and the Middle East, 1903-1904.

2331. Rogers, Dale Evans. American actress, religious author and wife of actor Roy Rogers. MY SPIRITUAL

DIARY. Westwood, Los Angeles, London and Glasgow: Fleming H. Revell Co., 1955. 144p.

Undated daily religious reflections, and some extracts from letters.

2332. Rogers, Emma Winner. American. THE JOURNAL OF A COUNTRY WOMAN. New York: Eaton & Mains; and Cincinnati: Jennings & Graham, 1912. 116p.

Journal of a city bred woman who decided to live the greater part of each year in her family's homestead in New Jersey's Hudson Valley. Journal covers March 1--October 8 of an unspecified year.

2333. Rohde, Ruth Owen, 1885-1954. American legislator and diplomat. LEAVES FROM A GREENLAND DIARY. New York: Dodd, Mead & Co., 1935. 166p.

Rohde served as U.S. Minister to Denmark from 1933-1936.

2334. Rolleston, Charlotte Emma Maud Dalzell, Lady. YEOMAN SERVICE: BEING THE DIARY OF THE WIFE OF AN IMPERIAL YEOMANRY OFFICER DURING THE BOER WAR, BY LADY MAUD ROLLESTON. London: Smith, Elder & Co., 1901. 310p.

2335. Romig, Emily Craig. American frontier traveler. A PIONEER WOMAN IN ALASKA. Caldwell, Idaho: The Caxton Printers, 1948. 140p.

Account based on a diary, with copious extracts, of a woman who traveled with her husband to the Alaskan gold-fields. The main diary entries cover 1897-1899, with recollections and some diary entries to 1944.

2336. Roos, Rosalie Ulrika, 1823-1898. Swedish editor and reformer. "Rosalie Ulrika Roos in South Carolina." Edited and translated by Nils William Olsson. SWEDISH PIONEER HISTORICAL SOCIETY 10:4 (October, 1959), 127-140.

Roos came to America to work as a governess on a

Virginia plantation. Extracts from letters to her brother-in-law, 1851-1855.

2337. ------. RESA TILL AMERIKA, 1851-1855. Stockholm: Alquist & Wiksell, 1969.

Travels and work in America, described in letters.

2338. ------. TRAVELS IN AMERICA, 1851-1855. BASED ON RESA TILL AMERIKA, 1851-1855. Edited by Sigrid Laurell. Translated and edited by Carl L. Anderson. Carbondale and Edwardsville, Ill.: Published for the Swedish Historical Society by Southern Illinois University Press, 1982. 152p.

Contains her girlhood diary, and letters to 1850 depicting the life of a middle class family in Sweden, and letters to her family from Charleston, Virginia, where she worked as a governess. This version is edited from the Swedish edition; it omits a brief account of an excursion on Gota Canal taken before the journey to the United States, and abridges her travel notes after she left Charleston. The diary and letters are excerpted from the originals, with running commentary edited in.

2339. Roosevelt, Eleanor, 1884-1962. American politician, lecturer and author; wife of U.S. President Franklin Delano Roosevelt and niece of President Theodore Roosevelt. "Letters from Mrs. Roosevelt." Louis Fischer. JOURNAL OF HISTORY STUDIES 1:1 (1967), 24-30.

Four letters written to Louis Fischer.

2340. ------. LOVE, ELEANOR: ELEANOR ROOSEVELT AND HER FRIENDS. Joseph P. Lash. Foreword by Franklin Delano Roosevelt, Jr. Garden City, N.Y.: Doubleday & Co., 1982. 534p.

Biography which relies heavily on Roosevelt's letters, chiefly extracts, although the book is referred to as a "collection." This is the first of two volumes, covering the years up to 1943.

2341. ------. MOTHER AND DAUGHTER: THE LETTERS OF

ELEANOR AND ANNA ROOSEVELT. Edited by Bernard Asbell. New York: Coward, McCann & Geoghegan, 1982. 366p.

Letters between Roosevelt and her only daughter, Anna (1906-1975), 1916-1962.

2342. ------. A WORLD OF LOVE: ELEANOR ROOSEVELT AND HER FRIENDS, 1943-1962. Joseph P. Lash. Foreword by Franklin D. Roosevelt, Jr. Garden City, N.Y.: Doubleday & Co., 1984. 610p.

Continues LOVE, ELEANOR.

2343. Root, Esther Sayles and Marjorie Crocker. Americans. OVER PERISCOPE POND: LETTERS FROM TWO AMERICAN GIRLS IN PARIS, OCTOBER 1916-JANUARY 1918. Boston and New York: Houghton Mifflin Co., 1918. 295p.

Letters of two young volunteers describe their experiences as relief-workers among French refugees during World War I.

2344. Ropes, Hanna. American nurse. CIVIL WAR NURSE: THE DIARY AND LETTERS OF HANNAH ROPES. Edited, with an introduction and commentary by John R. Brumgardt. Knoxville, Tenn.: The University of Tennessee Press, 1980.

An articulate Northern reformer, feminist, and abolitionist, Ropes is best known through Louisa May Alcott's HOSPITAL SKETCHES. She supervised Alcott from December, 1862 to 1863.

2345. Rosas, Manuelita, afterwards Terrero, 1817-1898. Argentine daughter of dictator Juan Manuel de Rosas. MANUELITA ROSAS. Edicion definitiva. Buenos Aires: Libreria y Edit. "La Facultdad" de Juan Roldan y Cia. 1933. 172p.

Biography, with letters, 1852-1875.

2346. Rosenberg, Ethel Greenglass, 1915-1933. American political activist and communist. With her husband, Julius Rosenberg, she was convicted of conspiracy to commit espionage and publicly executed. THE ROSENBERG

LETTERS. London: D. Dobson, 1953. 191p.

Selected letters of the Rosenbergs, written to each other during their two years on Death Row.

2347. ------. DEATH HOUSE LETTERS OF ETHEL AND JULIUS ROSENBERG. New York: Jero Publishing Co., 1953. 148p.

2348. ------. THE TESTAMENT OF ETHEL AND JULIUS ROSENBERG. New York: Cameron & Kahn, 1954. 222p.

Enlarged and revised edition of DEATH HOUSE LETTERS.

2349. ------. WE ARE YOUR SONS: THE LEGACY OF ETHEL AND JULIUS ROSENBERG. Written by their children, Robert and Michael Meeropol. Boston: Houghton Mifflin, 1975. 419p.

Much expanded version of DEATH HOUSE LETTERS; prints all extant letters between the Rosenbergs written while in prison, 1951-1953.

2350. Rosser, Phyllis. American housewife. "Making Time: A Housewife's Log." MS. MAGAZINE 4:9 (March, 1976), 54-56, 87-88.

Minute-by-minute diary kept during one week in Summer describes the daily routine of an American housewife.

2351. Rothschild, Louisa Montefiore, Lady de, 1821-1910. English Jewish philanthropist from the prominent banking family. LADY DE ROTHSCHILD: EXTRACTS FROM HER NOTEBOOKS. With a preface by her daughter, Constance Battersea. London: A.L. Humphreys, 1912. 111p.

2352. Routh, Martha Winter, 1743-1817. English Quaker. MEMOIR OF THE LIFE, TRAVELS AND RELIGIOUS EXPERIENCE OF MARTHA ROUTH. WRITTEN BY HERSELF, OR COMPILED FROM HER OWN NARRATIVE. York: W. Alexander & Son, 1822. 317p. Second edition, 1824. 307p.

2353. ------. "Memoir of the Life, Travels and Religious Experiences of Martha Routh, a Minister in the Religious Society of Friends." FRIENDS LIBRARY 12 (1848), 413-477.

Extracts from her diary cover two visits to America, and describes her ministry in New England, Pennsylvania, and the Southern states, 1794-1805.

2354. Rowe, Elizabeth Singer, 1674-1737. English author and poet. THE MISCELLANEOUS WORKS IN PROSE AND VERSE OF MRS. ELIZABETH ROWE. BY MRS. THEOPHILUS ROWE, TO WHICH ARE ADDED, POEMS ON SEVERAL OCCASIONS BY MR. THOMAS ROWE. AND TO THE WHOLE IS PREFIXED AN ACCOUNT OF THE LIVES AND WRITINGS OF THE AUTHORS. London: Printed for R. Hett, 1739. 2 vols.

Contains correspondence, including fictional letters written under pseudonyms. The letters are dated from 1697 and were written to Thomas Rowe, to "several of his relations," and to various unamed correspondents.

2355. Ruskin, Euphemia Chalmers Gray, later Millais, 1828-1897. She was married to John Ruskin for six years. The marriage was annulled. YOUNG MRS. RUSKIN IN VENICE. UNPUBLISHED LETTERS OF MRS. JOHN RUSKIN WRITTEN FROM VENICE BETWEEN 1849-1852. Edited by Mary Lutyens. New York: The Vanguard Press, 1965. 354p.

Weekly letters to her family during two long sojourns in Venice. The book also contains much biographical material on "Effie," who has been, according to Lutyens, for the most part ignored or expunged from Ruskin's biographies.

2356. ------. "Effie Ruskin and Pauline Trevelyan: Letters to Ruskin's 'Monitress-Friend.'" Raleigh Trevelyan. BULLETIN OF THE JOHN RYLANDS UNIVERSITY LIBRARY OF MANCHESTER 62:1 (1979), 232-258.

Seventeen letters from Euphemia Ruskin to Pauline Trevelyan, 1848-1855.

2357. Russell, Frances Anna Maria Elliot, Countess, 1815-1898. English patriot and wife of Lord John Russell. LADY JOHN RUSSELL: A MEMOIR, WITH SELECTIONS FROM HER DIARIES AND CORRESPONDENCE. Edited by Desmond MacCarthy and Agatha Russell. London: Methuen & Co., 1910; and New York: John Lane Co., 1911. 325p.

Contains extracts from her letters and diary, 1830-1893, describing travels, politics and life at Court in England and Scotland. William Matthews calls her diary "a valuable picture of the times."

2358. Russell, Rachel Wriothesley Vaughn, Lady, 1636-1723. English author and wife of William, Lord Russell, who was arrested on charges of treason for his participation in the Rye House Plot and executed in 1683. LETTERS OF LADY RACHEL RUSSELL FROM THE MANUSCRIPTS IN THE LIBRARY AT WOBURN ABBEY. TO WHICH IS PREFIXED: AN INTRODUCTION VINDICATING THE CHARACTER OF LORD RUSSELL AGAINST SIR JOHN DALRYMPLE & ETC. London: Printed for E. and C. Dilly, 1773. 216p.

Letters 1679-1718, prefaced with a background of the treason charges levelled against Lord Russell.

2359. ------. SOME ACCOUNT OF THE LIFE OF RACHEL WRIOTHESLEY, LADY RUSSELL. BY THE EDITOR OF MADAME DU DEFFAND'S LETTERS [MARY BERRY]. FOLLOWED BY A SERIES OF LETTERS FROM LADY RUSSELL TO HER HUSBAND, WILLIAM LORD RUSSELL; FROM 1672 TO 1682; TOGETHER WITH SOME MISCELLANEOUS LETTERS TO AND FROM LADY RUSSELL. TO WHICH ARE ADDED: ELEVEN LETTERS FROM DOROTHY SIDNEY, COUNTESS OF SUNDERLAND, TO GEORGE SAVILLE, MARQUIS OF HALLIFAX, IN THE YEAR 1680. Published from the originals in the possession of His Grace the Duke of Devonshire. London: Printed by Strahan and Spottiswoode for Longman, Hurst, Rees, Orme and Brown, 1819. 150p.

Lauditory biography followed by letters to Lord Russell 1672-1716. Letters of Dorothy Sidney Spencer, Countess of Sunderland, written in 1680, shed light on Lady Russell's correspondence, as the views and principles of the two women were in direct opposition.

2360. ------. THE LETTERS OF RACHEL, LADY RUSSELL. London: Longman, Brown, Green and Longmans, 1853. 2 vols.

New edition, containing previously unpublished letters. Correspondence 1670-1723 chiefly concerned with politics and the events leading up to Lord Russell's execution.

2361. Sackville-West, Victoria Sackville, Lady, 1862-1936. English daughter of English diplomat Lionel Sackville-West and mother of author Vita Sackville-West. LADY SACKVILLE: A BIOGRAPHY. Susan Mary Alsop. Garden City, N.Y.: Doubleday & Co., and London: Weidenfeld and Nicolson, 1978. 273p.

Biography based on and including dated extracts from the diaries of Lady Sackville-West.

2362. Sackville-West, Vita [Victoria Mary], 1892-1962. English author and poet; wife of British politician Harold Nicolson. COUNTRY NOTES IN WARTIME. New York: Doubleday, Doran & Co., 1941. 85p.

World War II diary.

2363. ------. PORTRAIT OF A MARRIAGE. Nigel Nicolson. New York: Atheneum, 1973. 272p.

Biographical portrait of Nicolson's parents, based upon and reproducing lengthy extracts from their letters and diaries.

2364. ------. DEAREST ANDREW: LETTERS FROM V. SACKVILLE-WEST TO ANDREW REIBER, 1951-1962. Edited by Nancy MacKnight. New York: Charles Scribner's Sons, 1979. 127p.

Correspondence chiefly centers around her garden in Kent and gardening matters; Reiber developed something of a "crush" on Sackville-West and his letters (described but not reproduced here) are playfully affectionate.

2365. ------. THE LETTERS OF VITA SACKVILLE-WEST TO VIRGINIA WOOLF. Edited by Louise De Salvo and Mitchell A. Leaska. Introduction by Mitchell A. Leaska. London: Hutchinson, 1984. 473p. New York: William Morrow, 1985. 448p.

2366. St. John, Mary. American frontier settler. "A Prairie Diary." Edited by Glenda Riley. ANNALS OF IOWA 44:2 (Fall, 1977), 103-117.

Diary of a woman who moved with her family from New York to Iowa in 1858. Also contains some extracts from a diary written by her sister Esther.

2367. Saint-Joseph, Mere, 1786-1858. French nun and abbess; founder of the Soeurs Maristes. CORRESPONDANCE DE MERE SAINT JOSEPH, FOUNDATRICE DES SOEURS MARISTES, 1786-1858. Rome: Comités Historiques des Pères et des Soeurs Maristes, 1965. 441p.

2368. Salinger, Sylvia. American. JUST A VERY PRETTY GIRL FROM THE COUNTRY: SYLVIA SALINGER'S LETTERS FROM FRANCE, 1912-1913. Edited, with a foreword and afterword by Albert S. Bennett. Carbondale: Southern Illinois University Press, 1987. 166p.

2369. Salisbury, Charlotte Y. American travel author and wife of Harrison E. Salisbury. ASIAN DIARY. New York: Charles Scribner's Sons, 1967. 158p.

Diary of travel in Asia, 1966.

2370. ------. CHINA DIARY. Introduction by Harrison E. Salisbury. New York: Walker & Co., 1973. 210p.

2371. ------. RUSSIAN DIARY. New York: Walker & Co., 1975. 179p.

2372. ------. CHINA DIARY: AFTER MAO. New York: Walker & Co., 1979. 214p.

2373. ------. TIBETAN DIARY. New York: Walker & Co., 1981. 164p.

2374. ------. THE LONG MARCH DIARY. New York: Walker & Co., 1986. 190p.

Diary February 29, 1984--June 19, 1984 describes a journey made with her husband following the route of the original Long March in China. Salisbury celebrated her seventieth birthday en route.

2375. Salisbury, Frances Mary Gascoyne-Cecil, Marchioness of, 1802-1839. English. THE GASCOYNE HEIRESS: THE LIFE AND DIARIES OF FRANCES MARY GASCOYNE-CECIL, 1802-1839. Carola Oman. London: Hodder & Stoughton, 1968. 320p.

2376. Salisbury, Harriet Hutchinson. American. "The Girl He Left Behind: The Letters of Harriet Hutchinson Salisbury." Allen F. Davis. VERMONT HISTORY 33:1 (January, 1965), 274-282.

Letters of a young woman who stayed behind in East Braintree, Vermont, when her fiancé, Lucius Salisbury, went west to seek his fortune in Missouri. Summary of and extracts from their correspondence, 1843-1847.

2377. Sanchez de Mendeville, Maria, 1786-1868. Argentine philanthropist and salonist. CARTAS DE MARIQUITA SANCHEZ, BIOGRAFIA DE UNA EPOCA. Compilation, prologue and notes by C. Vilaseca. Buenos Aires: Ediciones Peuser, 1952. 426p.

Letters 1804-1868, and an appendix including extracts from her diary, 1839-1840.

2378. Sand, George, pseud. for Amaudine Aurore Lucie Dupin, Baronne Dudevant, 1804-1875. French author. JOURNAL D'UN VOYAGEUR PENDANT LA GUERRE. Paris: Michel Lévy Frères, 1871. 310p.

Diary written during the Franco-Prussian War, 1870-1871.

2379. ------. NOUVELLES LETTRES D'UN VOYAGEUR. George Sand. Paris: Calmann-Lévy Frères, 1877. 354p.

Reprinted, with a presentation by Georges Lubin, Paris: Éditions d'Aujourd'hui, 1976. 209p.

2380. ------. CORRESPONDANCE, 1812-1876. Paris: Calmann Lévy Frères, 1882-1884. 6 vols.

Complete correspondence, 1812-1876.

2381. ------. LETTERS OF GEORGE SAND. Translated and edited by Raphael Ledos de Beaufort. With a preface and biographical sketch by the translator. London: Ward and Downey, 1886. 3 vols.

Selected letters, 1812-1876.

2382. ------. LETTRES À ALFRED DE MUSSET ET À SAINTE-BEUVE. Introduction de S. Rocheblave. Third edition. Paris: Calmann-Lévy, Frères, 1897. 269p.

2383. ------. CORRESPONDANCE DE GEORGE SAND ET D'ALFRED DE MUSSET. Publiée integralment et pour le première fois d'apres les documents originaux par Felix Decori. Nouvelle édition. Brussels: E. Deman, 1904. 242p. Limited edition of sixty copies.

2384. ------. UNE AMITIE ROMANTIQUE: LETTRES INÉDITE DE GEORGE SAND ET FRANÇOIS ROLLINAT. Jules Bertaut. Paris: Renaissance du Livre, 1921. 157p.

2385. ------. THE GEORGE SAND--GUSTAVE FLAUBERT LETTERS. Translated by Aimée L. McKenzie. Introduction by Stuart P. Sherman. New York: Boni & Liveright, 1921. London: Duckworth & Co., 1922. 382p.

Letters 1863-1880 between two "natural antagonists," she temperamental, lyrical, sanguine, imaginative, optimistic and sympathetic, he dramatic, melancholy, observing, cynical and satirical. Correspondence covers their later years, when both were established authors.

2386. ------. FLAUBERT AND GEORGE SAND IN THEIR CORRESPONDENCE. Henri Charles Edouard David. Chicago: The Chicago Literary Club, 1924. 31p.

2387. ------. JOURNAL INTIME (POSTHUME). Publiée par Aurore Sand. Paris: Calmann-Lévy Frères, 1926. 232p.

2388. ------. THE INTIMATE JOURNAL OF GEORGE SAND. Preface by Aurore Sand. Translated with notes by Marie Jenney Howe. London: Williams & Norgate; and New York: John Day Co., 1929. 198p. Reprinted, Chicago: Cassandra Editions, 1977.

2389. ------. LETTERS OF GEORGE SAND. Selected and translated by Veronica Lucas. With an introduction by Elizabeth Drew. London: George Routledge & Sons; and Boston: Houghton Mifflin Co., 1930. 426p.

Selected letters, 1815-1876.

2390. ------. CORRESPONDANCE INÉDITE DE GEORGE SAND ET MARIE DORVAL. Publiée avec une introduction et des notes par Simone Andre-Maurois. Préface d'Andre Maurois. Paris: Gallimard, 1953. 405p.

History of the correspondence between Sand and Dorval (1798-1849) followed by the letters, 1832-1840. Also includes letters between Dorval and Caroline Dorval-Luguet, and between George Sand and Caroline and Rene Luguet, Marie Laurent, Eugene Taillefert, and others.

2391. ------. LETTRES INÉDITE DE GEORGE SAND ET DE PAULINE VIARDOT, 1839-1849. Recueillies, annotées et precedées d'une introduction par Thérèse Marix-Spire. Paris: Nouvelles Éditions Latines, 1959. 316p.

Correspondence between Sand and French-Spanish opera singer Pauline Viardot-Garcia (1821-1910).

2392. ------. RÉPERTOIRE DES LETTRES PUBLIÉES DE GEORGE SAND. Publiée par la Révue d'Histoire Litteraire de la France. Marie Cordroc'tt. Paris: Armand Colin, 1962. 210p.

A list of the publication dates and places of Sand's letters in the CORRESPONDANCE GENERALE, in other volumes, and in periodicals and journals.

2393. ------. LES LETTRES DE GEORGE SAND À SAINTE-BEUVE. Texte établi, presentée et annotée par Osten Sodergard. Genève: Librarie Droz, 1964. 179p.

2394. ------. CORRESPONDANCE INÉDITE AVEC GEORGE SAND ET SES AMIS. Lettres choisies et commentees avec une introduction par Jean Briquet. Paris: C. Klincksieck, 1966. 152p.

Also includes letters of Lise Perdiguier.

2395. ------. HISTOIRE D'UNE AMITIE (D'APRÈS UNE CORRESPONDANCE INÉDITE, 1836-1866: PIERRE LEROUX ET GEORGE SAND. Texte établi, présentée et commentée par Jean-Pierre Lacassagne. Paris: Klincksieck, 1973. 368p.

2396. ------. CORRESPONDANCE. Textes réunis, classeés et annotées par Georges Lubin. Paris: Éditions Garnier Frères, 1964-1983. 21 vols.

New edition of the correspondence, revised and annotated. Volumes published to date cover the years 1812-1870.

2397. ------. SAND ET MUSSET: LETTRES D'AMOUR. Presentée par Françoise Sagan. Avec quatre portraits de George Sand par Alfred de Musset. Paris: Hermann, 1985. 169p.

2398. ------. GEORGE SAND ET ALFRED DE MUSSET: CORRESPONDANCE. JOURNAL INTIME DE GEORGE SAND (1834). Nombreux Documents annexes et Lettres Inédites. Text établie, annotée et presentée par Louis Evard. Monaco: Éditions du Rocher, n.d. 335p.

Correspondence with Musset and extracts from her journal for the same period. Includes correspondence with others concerning her relationship with Musset, and appendices relating to the correspondence and her journal.

2399. Sand, Julia. American. "The President's Dwarf:

The Letters of Julia Sand to Chester A. Arthur." Thomas C. Reeves. NEW YORK HISTORY 52:1 (1971), 73-83.

Sand, an invalid, wrote twenty-three letters to President Arthur between 1881 and 1883, advising him and exhorting him to become a great president.

2400. Sanders, Tobi Gillian and Joan Frances Bennett. Americans. MEMBERS OF THE CLASS WILL KEEP DAILY JOURNALS: THE BARNARD JOURNALS OF TOBI GILLIAN SANDERS AND JOAN FRANCES BENNET, SPRING, 1968. New York: Winter House, 1970. 153p.

College diaries of two Barnard students, Sanders from a wealthy Jewish family and Bennett from a Black South Carolina family.

2401. Sanford, Mollie Dorsey, 1838-1915. American pioneer settler. MOLLIE: THE JOURNAL OF MOLLIE DORSEY SANFORD IN NEBRASKA AND COLORADO TERRITORIES, 1857-1866. With an introduction and notes by Donald F. Danker. Lincoln, Nebr.: University of Nebraska Press, 1959. 199p.

Sanford's family homesteaded in the Nebraska and Colorado territories. In 1895, Sanford made a holograph copy of her journal, and destroyed the original, which had been damaged in a flood and was almost unreadable.

2402. Santamaria, Frances Karlen. American. JOSHUA: FIRSTBORN. New York: The Dial Press, 1970. 194p.

Based on a diary kept during her first pregnancy, March, 1964--February, 1965.

2403. Sarashina, Lady, also known as Sugawara no Takasue no Musume, b.1058. Japanese lady-in-waiting at the Heian Court. Her real name is unknown, but she is referred to as Takasue no Musume--Takasue's daughter. Takasue was made Governor of Kazusa in 1017. THE SARASHINA DIARY. Translated by Annie Shepley Omori and Kochi Doi. Japan: San Kaku Sha, 192?. 68p.

2404. ------. AS I CROSSED THE BRIDGE OF DREAMS: RECOLLECTIONS OF A WOMAN IN ELEVENTH CENTURY JAPAN. Translated by Ivan Morris. New York: The Dial Press, 1971. 159p.

Japanese poetic diary, chronicling Lady Sarashina's life from age twelve to age fifty.

2405. Sarton, Eleanor Mabel, 1878-1950. American artist and designer. LETTERS TO MAY. BY ELEANOR MABEL SARTON, 1878-1950. Selected, edited, and with an introduction by May Sarton. Orono, Maine: Puckerbush Press, 1986.

2406. Sarton, May (Eleanore Marie), b. 1912. Belgian-American novelist, poet, and diarist. THE HOUSE BY THE SEA: A JOURNAL. Photographs by Beverly Hallam. New York: W.W. Norton & Co., 1977. 387p.

Diary of change, November 13, 1974--August 17, 1976; in 1973, Sarton moved from her home of fifteen years in New Hampshire to a house on the coast of Maine.

2407. ------. JOURNAL OF A SOLITUDE: THE INTIMATE DIARY OF A CREATIVE WOMAN. New York: W.W. Norton & Co., 1977. 208p.

Journal written during a period of self-imposed solitude.

2408. ------. RECOVERING: A JOURNAL. New York and London: W.W. Norton & Co.; and Toronto: George J. McLeod, 1980. 246p.

Journal December 28, 1978--1979. Sarton writes of recovering from her mother's death, from a mastectomy, and of dealing with a lover and friend of thirty-five years becoming senile and ill. More outspokenly Lesbian than her earlier journals.

2409. ------. "As We Shall Be: May Sarton and Aging." Marlene Springer. FRONTIERS: A JOURNAL OF WOMEN'S

STUDIES 5:3 (Fall, 1980), 46-49.

Discusses Sarton's treatment of aging in her journals.

2410. ------. AT SEVENTY: A JOURNAL. New York: W.W. Norton & Co., 1984. 335p.

2411. Saunders, Eleanor, d. 1895, and Elizabeth Saunders, d. 1895. Australian missionaries to China. THE SISTER MARTYRS OF KU CHEN. MEMOIR AND LETTERS OF ELEANOR AND ELIZABETH SAUNDERS ("NELLIE" AND "TOPSY") OF MELBOURNE. Second edition. London: J. Nisbet, 1896? 308p.

Letters of missionary sisters to their mother, 1893-1895. They were killed in an anti-Western, anti-missionary uprising.

2412. Saunders, Margaret Marshall, 1861-1947. Canadian author. "Margaret Marshall Saunders: Edinburgh Diary, 1876." ATLANTIS [Canada] 6:1 (1980), 68-82.

Brief biography, followed by a diary written in Scotland, where she had been sent to finishing school.

2413. Savage, Eliza Mary Anne, 1836-1885. English friend and literary confidante of Samuel Butler. LETTERS BETWEEN SAMUEL BUTLER AND MISS ELIZA MARY ANNE SAVAGE, 1871-1885. Edited by Geoffry Keynes and Brian Hill. London: Jonathan Cape, 1935. 380p.

2414. Sawyer, Alice Moore, b. 1896. American. THE LAST EDEN: THE DIARY OF ALICE MOORE AT THE XX RANCH. Edited by Austin L. Moore. Kalamazoo, Mich.: Sequoia Press, 1968. 37p. Reprinted from ANNALS OF WYOMING 41:1 (1961), 63-81. Limited edition of 125 copies.

Account by a teenage girl of a 1912 camping outing with her family on the XX Ranch in Wyoming.

2415. Sawyer, Harriet Newell Williams, d. 1841. American frontier settler. REMINISCENCES OF A DECEASED

SISTER: A BRIEF MEMOIR OF MRS. HARRIET N.W. SAWYER, WHO DIED AT HUNTINGTON, INDIANA, JUNE 16, 1841. Newberry, VT: Hayes & Co., 1843. 123p.

Letters to her family in Maine describe life in Indiana, where Sawyer settled with her husband in 1840; she died in childbirth a year later.

2416. Scales, Cordelia Lewis. American. "The Civil War Letters of Cordelia Scales." Edited by Percy L. Rainwater. JOURNAL OF MISSISSIPPI HISTORY 1 (July, 1939), 170-181.

2417. Schaffer, Doris, 1938-1963. American activist. DEAR DEEDEE: FROM THE DIARIES OF DORI SCHAFFER. Edited and annotated by Anne Schaffer. Seacaucus, N.J.: Lyle Stuart, 1978. 222p.

Excerpts from the diary of a bright but troubled middle-class Jewish woman who committed suicide in 1963. One chapter of the diary, dealing with her experiences with marijuana, is reproduced in her own hand. The diary is edited by her mother.

2418. Schaw, Janet. Scottish. JOURNAL OF A LADY OF QUALITY: BEING THE NARRATIVE OF A JOURNEY FROM SCOTLAND TO THE WEST INDIES, NORTH CAROLINA AND PORTUGAL, IN THE YEARS 1774-1776. Edited by Evangeline Andrews, in collaboration with Charles M. Andrews. New Haven, Conn.: Yale University Press; and London: Humphrey Milford, the Oxford University Press, 1921, 1939. 341p.

Describes a voyage from Scotland to the West Indies and life there at Antigua and St. Kitts; a voyage from St. Kitts to South Carolina and life there just before the American Revolution; and various adventures on the way back to Scotland. Little is known about the author.

2419. Schenck, Annie B. American. "Camping Vacation, 1871." COLORADO MAGAZINE 42:3 (1965), 185-215.

Diary of an Eastern woman on a camping trip in the Colorado Rockies, August, 1871.

2420. Schluter, Auguste, 1850-1917. English maid to the daughters of Sir William Gladstone. A LADY'S MAID IN DOWNING STREET. Edited by Mabel Duncan. Foreword by Sir Basil Thomson, K.C.B. London: T. Fisher Unwin, 1922; and Boston: Small, Maynard & Co., 1922. 178p.

Domestic diary, October, 1877--August, 1890.

2421. Schneider, Eliza Cheney Abbot, 1809-1856. American missionary to Turkey. LETTERS FROM BROOSA, ASIA MINOR. WITH AN ESSAY ON THE PROSPECTS OF THE HEATHENS AND OUR DUTIES TO THEM. Chambersburg, Penn.: German Reformed Church, 1846. 210p.

Describes missionary work in the 1830's and 1840's.

2422. Schotz, Myra Glazer. American author and poet. "THE JOURNAL OF SANTA CATERINA." Illustrated by Shirley Faktor. CHRYSALIS: A MAGAZINE OF WOMAN'S CULTURE 7 (1979), 73-81.

Extracts from a journal written in the desert near Mt. Sinai; deals with her feelings about her companions, her writing, and what she sees as the primordial femaleness of the desert landscape.

2423. Schreiber, Charlotte Elizabeth Bertie Guest, Lady, 1812-1895. English businesswoman and connoisseur and collector of antique china. LADY CHARLOTTE SCHREIBER'S JOURNALS. CONFIDENCES OF A COLLECTOR OF CERAMICS AND ANTIQUES THROUGHOUT BRITAIN, FRANCE, HOLLAND, BELGIUM, SPAIN, TURKEY, AUSTRIA AND GERMANY FROM THE YEAR 1869 TO 1885. Edited by her son Montague J. Guest. Annotations by Egan Mew. London: John Lane, the Bodely Head, and New York: John Lane, 1911. 2 vols.

Travel journal; a record of places visited and pieces seen and purchased.

2424. ------. LADY CHARLOTTE GUEST: EXTRACTS FROM HER JOURNAL. Edited by the Earl of Bessborough. London: John Murray, 1952. 212p.

Extracts from her journal, 1853-1891.

2425. Schreiner, Olive, 1855-1920. South African-English author and feminist. LETTERS OF OLIVE SCHREINER, 1876-1920. Edited by S.C. Cronwright-Schreiner. London: T. Fisher Unwin, 1924. 410p. Reprinted, Westport, Conn.: Hyperion Press, 1976. 410p.

Selection from some 6,000 written letters from South Africa, England, and the European continent, chiefly to Havelock Ellis.

2426. ------. UNTIL THE HEART CHANGES: A GARLAND FOR OLIVE SCHREINER. Edited by Zelda Friedlander. Tafelberg-Uitgewers, 1967. 158p.

Contains two essays which discuss her correspondence. "Letters and Pets," by May Murray Parker discusses the correspondence between Schreiner and her parents. "A Critical Review of S.C. Cronwright-Schreiner's LETTERS and LIFE of His Wife" by R.S.A criticizes Cronwright- Schriener's edition of the letters as "mutilated."

2427. ------. OLIVE SCHREINER: A SHORT GUIDE TO HER WRITINGS. Ridley Beeton. Cape Town: Howard Timmins, 1974. 118p.

In an essay on her correspondence (p.76-82) Beeton notes the character of her letters to Havelock Ellis is not literary but personal, and that she never intended them to be published. She asked Ellis to destroy her letters to him, and he did reluctantly destroy a number of them. An essay on manuscript sources (p.83-87) describes the Havelock Ellis-Olive Schreiner Manuscript Collection at the Humanities Research Center, University of Texas at Austin, and stresses the differences between the published versions of her letters and the originals.

2428. Schultze, Emma Wegscheider. German physician's wife. LETTERS FROM MEIJI JAPAN: CORRESPONDENCE OF A GERMAN SURGEON'S WIFE, 1878-1881. Edited by Charlotte T. Marshall and John Z. Bowers, M.D. New York: Josiah Macy, Jr. Foundation, 1980. 160p.

Letters to family and friends in Germany during a

three year residence at the Tokyo Imperial University Faculty of Medicine, where her husband taught. Schultze learned Japanese, observed Japan's customs with interest, and wrote at length on her experiences.

2429. Schumann, Clara Josephine Wieck, 1819-1896. German pianist, composer, and wife of Robert Schumann. CLARA SCHUMANN: AN ARTIST'S LIFE BASED ON MATERIAL FOUND IN DIARIES AND LETTERS. Berthold Litzman. Translated and abridged from the fourth edition by Grace E. Hadow. With a Preface by W.H. Hadow. 1913. 2 vols.

2430. ------. CLARA SCHUMANN, JOHANNES BRAHMS: BRIEFE AUS DEN JAHREN 1853-1896. Im auftrage von Marie Schumann. Herausgegeben von Berthold Litzmann. Leipzig: Drud un Verlag von Breitthopf & Hartel, 1927. 2 vols.

Correspondence 1853-1896.

2431. ------. LETTERS OF CLARA SCHUMANN AND JOHANNES BRAHMS, 1853-1896. Edited by Berthold Litzmann. New York: Longmans, Green & Co.; and London: E. Arnold & Co., 1927. 2 vols.

Translation and abridgement of the German edition of 1927.

2432. ------. A PASSIONATE FRIENDSHIP: CLARA SCHUMANN AND BRAHMS. Marguerite and Jean Alley. Translated by Mervyn Savill. London: Staples Press, 1956. 214p.

2433. ------. LETTERS OF CLARA SCHUMANN AND JOHANNES BRAHMS, 1853-1896. Edited by Dr. Berthold Litzmann. New York: Vienna House, 1972. 2 vols.

Abridged version of the editions published by Longmans, Green & Co. (1927) and of the German collection published by Breitthopf & Hartel (1927). Does not include letters which appear in the English version of CLARA SCHUMANN: AN ARTIST'S LIFE. Letters cover the entire period of their deep and intimate friendship; however, Schumann's correspondence begins in 1858, because she had begun to destroy her letters when her daughter, Marie, persuaded her to save them.

2434. ------. BRIEFWECHSEL: KRITISCHE GESAMTAUSGABE. CLARA UND ROBERT SCHUMANN. Volume 1: 1832-1838. Herausgegeben von Eva Weissweiller. Basel; Frankfurt Am Main: Stroemfeld/ Roter Stern, 1984.

2435. Scott, Evelyn, pseud. for Elsie Dunn Wellman Metcalfe, 1893-1963. American poet and novelist. ESCAPADE. New York: Thomas Seltzer, 1923. 286p. Saint Clair Shores, Mich.: Scholarly Press, 1971. 286p.

2436. Scott, Kathleen, Lady Kennet (Edith Agnes Kathleen Scott, Lady Kennet), 1878-1947. English sculptor. SELF-PORTRAIT OF AN ARTIST. FROM THE DIARIES AND MEMOIRS OF LADY KENNET, KATHLEEN, LADY SCOTT. London: John Murray, 1949. 368p.

Diary 1911-1945 describes European society circles, and the life of an artist in England.

2437. Scott-Maxwell, Florida Pier, b. 1883. American-born actress, writer, suffragist, playwright and psychologist. THE MEASURE OF MY DAYS. New York: Alfred A. Knopf, 1968, 1975. 150p.

Undated notebook of musings on aging and reflections on life from the vantage point of eighty years; the frustrations of disability and feeling at variance with the times.

2438. Scott-Russell, Rachel. Lover of composer Arthur Sullivan. ARTHUR, DARLING: THE ROMANCE OF ARTHUR SULLIVAN AND RACHEL SCOTT RUSSELL (FROM HER LOVE LETTERS). George S. Emerson. London, Ontario: Galt House, 1980. 139p.

2439. ------. SULLIVAN AND THE SCOTT RUSSELLS: A VICTORIAN LOVE AFFAIR TOLD THROUGH THE LETTERS OF RACHEL AND LOUISE SCOTT RUSSELL TO ARTHUR SULLIVAN, 1864-1870. John Wolfson. Chichester, West Sussex: Packard Publishing, 1984. 130p.

2440. Scriabine, Helene (Elena Skrjabina), b.1906. Russian-American professor. SIEGE AND SURVIVAL: THE

ODYSSEY OF A LENINGRADER. By Elena Skrjabina. Foreword by Harrison E. Salisbury. Translated, edited and with an afterword by Norman Luxenburg. Carbondale, Ill.: Southern Illinois University Press, 1971. 174p.

2441. ------. AFTER LENINGRAD: FROM THE CAUCASUS TO THE RHINE, AUGUST 9, 1942--MARCH 25, 1945: A DIARY OF SURVIVAL DURING WORLD WAR II. By Elena Skrjabina. Translated, edited, and with an introduction by Norman Luxenburg. Carbondale, Ill.: Southern Illinois University Press, 1978. 190p.

Continuation of her diary, written after the evacuation of Leningrad. An eyewitness account of the retreat of 1843. She had gone to Pyatigorsk with her children, but the Russians forced the refugees to evacuate Pyatigorsk before the advancing Geman army arrived there.

2442. ------. THE ALLIES ON THE RHINE, 1945-1950. Elena Skrjabina. Translated, edited, and with a preface by Norman Luxenburg. Foreword by Harrison E. Salisbury. Carbondale, Ill.: Southern Illinois University Press and London: Feffer & Sons, 1980. 158p.

Continuation of her diary, written at Bendorf, where she worked at the Konkordia Works, a stove factory turned over to military production. Describes the coming of the allies, the occupation, and the first signs of post-war recovery in Germany.

2443. Scrivener, Jane, pseud. American. INSIDE ROME WITH THE GERMANS. New York: Macmillan Co., 1945. 204p.

Diary of an American woman in Rome during World War II, September 8, 1943--June 5, 1944.

2444. Scudery, Madeleine de, 1607-1701. French novelist, poet, and salonist. MADEMOISELLE DE SCUDERY, SA VIE ET SA CORRESPONDANCE. AVEC UN CHOIX DE SES POÉSIES. Ratherey et Boutron. Paris: Leon Techener, 1873. 540p.

2445. Sears, Mary. American. "A Young Woman in the Midwest: The Journal of Mary Sears." Edited by Daryl E. Jones and James W. Pickering. OHIO HISTORY 82: 3/4 (1973), 215-234.

2446. Sears, Mary Pratt, 1864-1928. American. MARY PRATT SEARS, 1864-1928: LETTERS TO HER FRIENDS. Edited by Annie Lyman Sears. With an introduction by Ella Lyman Cabot. Boston: Privately printed, 1932. 429p.

2447. Secor, Lella, 1887-1966. American journalist, peace worker and feminist. LELLA SECOR: A DIARY IN LETTERS, 1915-1922. Edited, with a preface by Barbara Moench Florence. Foreword by Eleanor Flexner. New York: Artemis Books/Burt Franklin, 1978. 295p.

Letters written from England to her mother and sisters during World War I dealing chiefly with peace work; after her marriage in 1917 her letters deal more with the details of life as a conventional housewife and mother.

2448. Sedgwick, Anne Douglas, 1873-1935. English novelist. ANNE DOUGLAS SEDGWICK: A PORTRAIT IN LETTERS. Chosen and edited by Basil de Selincourt. London: Constable and Co., 1936. 319p. New York and Boston: Houghton Mifflin Co., and Cambridge, England: The Riverside Press, 1936. 260p.

Literary letters 1898-1935.

2449. Sedgwick, Catharine Maria, 1789-1867. American author. LETTERS FROM ABROAD TO KINDRED AT HOME. BY THE AUTHOR OF "HOPE LESLIE." New York: Harper & Bros., 1841. 2 vols.

Letters written on a tour of Europe, 1839-1840.

2450. ------. LIFE AND LETTERS OF CATHERINE MARIA SEDGWICK. Edited by Mary E. Dewey. New York: Harper & Bros., 1872. 446p.

Includes extracts from a journal.

2451. ------. "Miss Sedgwick Observes Harriet Martineau." NEW ENGLAND QUARTERLY 7 (1934), 533-541.

Extracts from previously unpublished journals, 1837-1849.

2452. Seebohm, Wilhelmina, 1863-1895. English Quaker. A SUPPRESSED CRY: LIFE AND DEATH OF A QUAKER DAUGHTER. Victoria Glendinning. London: Routledge and Kegan Paul, 1969. 120p.

Includes extracts from a childhood diary and letters written during her last illness. She died young of asthma.

2453. Seghers, Anna, b. 1900. German author. ANNA SEGHERS, WIELAND HERZFELD: GEWOHNLICHES UND GEFAHRLICHES LEBEN. EIN BRIEFWECHSEL AUS DER ZEIT DES EXILES, 1939-1946. Mit faksimiles, fotos, un dem Aufsatz "Frauen und Kinder in der Emigration" von Anna Seghers im Anhang. Darmstadt, Neuwied: Luchterhand, 1985, 1986. 204p.

2454. Sei Shonagon, b. ca. 965. Japanese Lady-in-Waiting to Empress Sadako at the Heian Court, and later to Empress Akiko. THE PILLOW BOOK OF SEI SHONAGON. Translated and edited by Arthur Waley. Boston: Houghton Mifflin Co., 1920. 162p.

Japanese poetic diary. Covers her years at Court, 990-1000. She had many lovers and much of her book is devoted to romantic reminiscences.

2455. ------. THE PILLOW BOOK OF SEI SHONAGON. Translated and edited by Ivan Morris. New York: Columbia University Press, 1967. 2 vols.

2456. Seltzer, Adele Szold, b. 1876. American publisher. D.H. LAWRENCE: LETTERS TO THOMAS AND ADELE SELTZER. Edited by Gerald M. Lacy. Santa Barbara, Calif.: Black Sparrow Press, 1976. 284p.

Letters between Lawrence and the Seltzers during

the period the Seltzers were his publishers. Contains letters of Adele Seltzer to Lawrence and to her friend Dorothy Hoskins.

2457. Selwyn, Elizabeth. JOURNAL OF EXCURSIONS THROUGH THE MOST INTERESTING PARTS OF ENGLAND, WALES AND SCOTLAND, DURING THE SUMMER AND AUTUMNS OF 1819, 1820, 1821, 1822 AND 1823. London: Printed by Plummer and Brewis, 1824. 256p.

2458. ------. CONTINUATION OF JOURNALS THROUGH THE YEARS 1824, 1825, 1826, 1827, 1828 AND 1829. Printed at the request of friends, and for private distribution only. Kensington: Printed by W. Birch, 1830. 194p.

Travel diary, written on a summer journey through England, Wales, and Scotland.

2459. Senesh, Hannah, 1921-1944. Hungarian Jewish soldier and heroine. HANNAH SENESH, HAYAH, SHELIHOTAH U-MOTAH. Tel Aviv: Ha-Kibuts ha-Me'Ukhad, 1966. 378p.

2460. ------. HANNAH SENESH: HER LIFE AND DIARY. Introduction by Abba Eban. Translated by Marta Cohn. New York: Schocken Books, 1972. 257p.

Diary 1934-1944, beginning at age thirteen. Describes her adolescence in Hungary, her emigration to Israel, life in a Kibbutz and her decision to volunteer for a parachute rescue mission to help Jews escape from the occupied countries of Rumania, Hungary and Czechoslovakia. Also includes letters, written to her family in Hungary, from 1939 to the eve of her departure with the rescue mission in 1944. Senesh was captured and executed by the Nazis.

2461. Sergeant, Elizabeth Shepley. American. SHADOW-SHAPES: THE JOURNAL OF A WOUNDED WOMAN, OCTOBER, 1918--MAY, 1919. Boston and New York: Houghton Mifflin Co., 1920. 236p.

War diary of a woman wounded by a hand-grenade explosion; describes war in France, treatment in a field hospital, and convalescence in a Paris hospital.

2462. Seton, Elizabeth Ann Bayley, 1744-1821. American Saint and founder of the Sisters of Charity. MEMOIR, LETTERS AND JOURNAL OF ELIZABETH SETON, CONVERT TO THE CATHOLIC FAITH, AND SISTER OF CHARITY. Edited by the Right Reverend Robert Seton. New York: O'Shea, 1869. 2 vols.

2463. ------. LETTERS OF MOTHER SETON TO MRS. JULIANNA SCOTT. Edited by Reverend Joseph B. Code. Emitsburgh, Md.: Daughters of Charity of St. Vincent de Paul, 1935. 459p.

Letters to Julianna Sitgreaves Scott, 1798-1821.

2464. ------. ELIZABETH ANN SETON: SELECTED WRITINGS. Edited by Ellin Kelley and Annabelle Melville. New York: Paulist Press, 1987. 377p.

Includes excerpts from her diaries and letters.

2465. Sévigné, Marie de Rabutin-Chantal, Marquise de, 1626-1696. French intellectual. LETTRES CHOISIES... QUI CONTIENNENT BEAUCOUP DE PARTICULARITÉS DE L'HISTOIRE DE LOUIS XIV. 1725. 75p.

2466. ------. RECUEIL DES LETTRES DE MADAME DE SÉVIGNÉ. Nouvelle Édition, Augmentée d'un Prècis de la Vie de Cette Femme Célèbre, de Rèflexions sur les Lettres. Par S.J.B. de Vauxcelles, et ornée de portraits graves d'après les meilleurs modèles. Paris: Bossange, Masson et Besson, 1801. 10 vols.

2467. ------. LETTRES DE MADAME DE SÉVIGNÉ, DE SA FAMILLE, ET DE SES AMIS. Par M. Gault-de-Saint-German. Paris: Dalibon, 1823. 12 vols.

2468. ------. LETTRES DE MADAME DE SÉVIGNÉ. Précedées d'une Notice sur sa Vie et du Traits Sur le Style Épistolaire de Madame de Sévigné. Par M. Suard. Paris: Librarie Firmin Didot, 1858. 651p.

2469. ------. LETTRES DE MARIE DE RABUTIN-CHANTAL, MARQUISE DE SÉVIGNE À SA FILLE ET À SES AMIS. Édition révue et publiée par Monsieur U. Silvestre de Sacy. Paris: J. Techener, 1861. 11 vols.

2470. ------. LETTRES CHOISIES DE MADAME DE SÉVIGNÉ. Précedeés d'une notice par Grouvelle, d'observations Litteraires par Suard, accompagnés de notes éxplicatives sur le faits et sur les personnages du temps, ornées d'une galèrie de portraits historiques dessines par Staal; graves au burin par Massard. Paris: Garnier-Frères, 1862. 702p.

2471. ------. LETTRES DE MADAME DE SÉVIGNÉ DE SA FAMILLE ET DE SES AMIS. Nouvelle édition revisée sur les autographes, les copies les plus authentiques et les plus anciennes impressions, et augmentée de lettres inédites, d'une nouvelle notice, d'un lèxique des mots et locutions remarquable, de portraits et facsimile, etc. Recueillies et annotées par L.J.N. Monmerque. Notice biographique de P. Mesnard. Paris: Hachette et Cie., 1862-1868. 14 vols.

Standard edition of her letters up to 1868.

2472. ------. LETTERS OF MADAME DE SÉVIGNÉ TO HER DAUGHTER AND FRIENDS. Edited by Mrs. Hale. Revised edition. Boston: Little, 1869. 438p.

2473. ------. LETTRES INÉDITES. Publiées par Charles Capmas. Paris: Hachette et Cie., 1876. 2 vols.

Letters which came to light in 1872.

2474. ------. LE PRÉMIER TEXTE DES LETTRES DE MADAME DE SÉVIGNÉ. Réimpression de l'Édition de 1725. Publiée par le Marquis de Queux de Saint-Hilaire. Librarie des Bibliophiles, 1880. 109p.

2475. ------. THE BEST LETTERS OF MADAME DE SÉVIGNÉ. Edited with an introduction by Edward Playfair Anderson. Chicago: A.C. McClurg and Co., 1890, 1898. 318p.

2476. ------. LETTERS OF MADAME DE SÉVIGNÉ TO HER DAUGHTER AND HER FRIENDS. Selected with an introductory essay by Richard Aldington. With an appendix of biographical and historical information, and an index. New York: Brentano's: Publishers, 1927. London: George Routledge & Sons, 1937. 2 vols.

Letters Primarily to Her Daughter, Comtesse Françoise Marguerite de Sévigné Grignan; also Letters to Count de Bussy Rabutin, M. de Pompone, M. de Moucea, and M. de Coulanges.

2477. ------. THE LETTERS OF MADAME DE SÉVIGNÉ. Carnavalet Edition, newly re-edited, revised and corrected, including over three hundred letters not previously translated into English. Introduction by A. Edward Newton. Philadelphia: J.P. Horn & Co., 1927. 7 vols.

Letters 1647-1696.

2478. ------. LETTERS FROM THE MARCHIONESS DE SÉVIGNÉ TO HER DAUGHTER THE COUNTESS DE GRIGNAN. With an introductory essay by Madame Duclaux. London: Spurr & Swift, 1927. 10 vols.

2479. ------. "La Litterature Épistolaire: Madame de Sévigné." In HISTOIRE DE LA LITTERATURE FRANÇAISE CLASSIQUE (1660-1700): SES CARACTERES VERITABLES, SES ASPECTS INCONNUS. Troisième edition. Daniel Mornet. Paris: Colin, 1947. p.318-329.

Places Madame de Sévigné in the trends and styles of seventeenth-century letter-writing.

2480. ------. LETTRES. Publiée par Emile Gerard-Gailly. Paris: Gallimard, 1853-1860. Reprinted 1953-1960. 3 vols.

New edition of selected letters, incorporating additions and revisions to the text.

2481. ------. LETTERS FROM MADAME LE MARQUISE DE SÉVIGNÉ. Selected, translated, and introduced by Violet Hammersley. With a preface by W. Somerset Maugham. London: Secker & Warburg, 1955. 389p.

2482. ------. LETTRES DE MADAME DE SÉVIGNÉ. Choix, notes et préface de Marcel Jouhandeau. Paris: Le Club Français du Livre, 1967. 484p.

2483. ------. MADAME DE SÉVIGNÉ ET LA LETTRE D'AMOUR. Roger Duchene. Paris: Bordas, 1970. 417p.

2484. ------. PETIT GLOSSAIRE DES LETTRES DE MADAME DE SÉVIGNÉ. Edouard Pilastre. Genève: Slatkine Reprints, 1971. 90p.

2485. ------. MADAME DE SÉVIGNÉ: LETTRES. Introduction, chronologie, notes par Bernard Raffali. Paris: Garnier-Flammarion, 1976. 448p.

2486. ------. CORRESPONDANCE. Texte établi, presentée, et annotée par Roger Duchene. Paris: Gallimard, 1972-1978. 3 vols.

Definitive edition. Volume 1: March, 1646--July, 1675. Volume 2: July, 1675--September, 1680. Volume 3: September, 1680--April, 1696.

2487. ------. "Life as Theatre in the Letters of Madame de Sévigné." Robert N. Nicolich. ROMANCE NOTES 16 (Winter, 1975), 376-382.

2488. ------. ÉCRIRE DU TEMPS DE MADAME DE SÉVIGNÉ: LETTRES ET TEXTE LITTERAIRE. Roger Duchene. Paris: Librarie Philosophique J. Vrin, 1981. 224p.

2489. ------. MARIE DE RABUTIN CHANTAL, MARQUISE DE SÉVIGNÉ: LETTRES CHOISIES. Illustrations d'Auguste Sandoz et de Jean Antoine Valentin Foulquier. Paris: Jean de Bonnot, 1981. 411p.

2490. ------. MADAME DE SÉVIGNÉ: SELECTED LETTERS. Translated with an introduction by Leonard Tancock. Harmondsworth, Middlesex, England, and New York: Penguin Books, 1982. 319p.

2491. ------. MADAME DE SÉVIGNÉ: A LIFE AND LETTERS. Frances Mossiker. New York: Alfred A. Knopf, 1983. 538p.

2492. Seward, Anna, 1742-1809. English poet, author and literary figure. LETTERS OF ANNA SEWARD WRITTEN BETWEEN THE YEARS 1784 AND 1807. Edited by Sir Walter Scott. Edinburgh: Constable & Co., 1811. 6 vols.

2493. ------. THE SWAN OF LICHFIELD: BEING A SELECTION FROM THE CORRESPONDENCE OF ANNA SEWARD. Edited, with a short biography and preface by Hesketh Pearson. London: H. Hamilton, 1936. 315p.

2494. Seward, Anna, b. 1862. American frontier teacher and missionary to China. "California in the Eighties: As Pictured in the Letters of Anna Seward." CALIFORNIA HISTORICAL QUARTERLY 16:4 (December, 1937), 291-303; and 17:1 (March, 1938), 28-39.

Letters 1883-1887 sets down in a vivid and entertaining manner a "true picture of the time when California below the Tehachapi was filling up with mid-western settlers."

2495. Sewell, Elizabeth Missing, 1815-1906. English author and educator. A JOURNAL KEPT DURING A SUMMER TOUR, FOR THE CHILDREN OF A VILLAGE SCHOOL. New York: D. Appleton & Co., 1852. 3 vols. in one.

Travel diary. Contents: Part 1: From Ostend to the Lake of Constance. Part 2: From the Lake of Constance to Simplon. Part 3: From the Simplon through Part of the Tyrol to Genon.

2496. Sexton, Anne, 1928-1974. American poet. ANNE SEXTON: A SELF-PORTRAIT IN LETTERS. Edited by Linda Gray Sexton and Lois Ames. Illustrated with photographs. Boston: Houghton Mifflin Co., 1977. 433p.

Selection from over 50,000 letters, written to family and friends, to her publishers, magazine editors, readers of her work, and to writers W.D. Snodgrass, Tillie Olsen, Robert Lowell and others. Begins with childhood letters and ends with a "goodbye" letter written shortly before her suicide to her daughter Linda Gray Sexton.

2497. Shackelton, Elizabeth Carleton, 1726-1804. Irish. MEMOIRS AND LETTERS OF RICHARD AND ELIZABETH SHACKELTON, LATE OF BALLITORE, IRELAND. Compiled by their daughter, Mary Leadbeater. Including a concise biographical sketch, and some letters, of her grandfather, Abraham Shackelton. London: Harvey and Darton, 1822. 221p. New York: S. Wood, and Baltimore, S.S. Wood, 1823. 318p.

2498. Shannon, Elizabeth. American journalist and wife of William Shannon, Ambassador to Ireland under President Carter. UP IN THE PARK: THE DIARY OF THE WIFE OF THE AMERICAN AMBASSADOR TO IRELAND, 1977-1981. New York: Atheneum, 1983. 358p.

2499. Sharp, Cornelia A. American frontier settler. "Crossing the Plains from Missouri to Oregon in 1852." TRANSACTIONS OF THE OREGON PIONEER ASSOCIATION 31 (1903), 171-188.

Overland diary, May-October, 1852, written on the Oregon trail.

2500. Shaw, Anna Howard, 1847-1919. American minister, lecturer, and suffragist. LETTERS FROM DR. ANNA HOWARD SHAW TO DR. ALETTA JACOBS. Leiden: E.J. Brill, 1938. 71,134p.

Aletta Henriette Jacobs Gerritsen (b.1854) was a Dutch physician who opened the first birth control clinic in Holland.

2501. Shelley, Frances Winckley, Lady, 1787-1873. THE DIARY OF FRANCES, LADY SHELLEY. Edited by Richard Edgcumbe. London: John Murray, 1912-1913. 2 vols. New York: Charles Scribner's Sons, 1912. 406p.

Autobiography-diary 1804-1873. Sir Arthur Ponsonby calls this a "periodic memoir" that barely comes under the category of a diary. Entries are very occasionally dated, and very seldom recorded on the day itself. A large part of the memoir is taken up with descriptions of travels in Switzerland, Italy, and Vienna.

2502. Shelley, Harriet Westbrook, d. 1816. English. HARRIET SHELLEY'S LETTERS TO CATHERINE NUGENT. London: Printed for Private Distribution, 1889. 64p.

2503. Shelley, Mary Wollstonecraft, 1797-1851. English novelist, daughter of Mary Wollstonecraft and wife of Percy Bysshe Shelley. THE LIFE AND LETTERS OF MARY WOLLSTONECRAFT SHELLEY. Mrs. Julian Marshall. London: R. Bentley & Son, 1889. 2 vols.

First publication of extracts from her journal and correspondence, woven together to form a biography.

2504. ------. LETTERS OF MARY WOLLSTONECRAFT SHELLEY (MOSTLY UNPUBLISHED). Edited by Henry Howard Harper. Boston: Printed only for members of the Bibliophile Society. Norwood, Mass.: The Plimpton Press, 1918. 191p. Reprinted, Folcroft, Penn.: Folcroft Library Editions, 1972. 191p., and Norwood, Penn.: Norwood Editions, 1976. 191p.

Letters to Leigh and Marianne Hunt, 1817- 1844, and journal extracts, 1838.

2505. ------. "The Letters of Mary Shelley in the Bodleian Collection." Introductory note by R.H. Hill. THE BODLEIAN QUARTERLY RECORD 6:3 (1929), 51-59; 6:4 (1929), 79-86; 8:1 (Spring, 1937), 297-310, 360-371; and 8:3 (Autumn, 1937), 412-420.

Letters to John and Maria Gisborne, Emilia Curran, Amelia Curran, Leigh Hunt, and others.

2506. ------. SHELLEY AT OXFORD: THE EARLY CORRESPONDENCE OF PERCY BYSSHE SHELLEY WITH HIS FRIEND THOMAS JEFFERSON HOGG. TOGETHER WITH LETTERS OF MARY SHELLEY AND THOMAS LOVE PEACOCK, AND WITH AN HITHERTO UNPUBLISHED PROSE FRAGMENT BY SHELLEY. Edited by Walter Sidney Scott. London: The Golden Cockerel Press, 1944.

2507. ------. HARRIET AND MARY: BEING THE RELATIONS BETWEEN PERCY BYSSHE SHELLEY, HARRIET SHELLEY, MARY SHELLEY AND THOMAS JEFFERSON HOGG, AS SHOWN IN LETTERS

BETWEEN THEM. Now published for the first time. Edited by Walter Sidney Scott. London: The Golden Cockerel Press, 1944. 84p.

2508. ------. THE LETTERS OF MARY WOLLSTONECRAFT SHELLEY. Collected and edited by Frederick L. Jones. Norman,: University of Oklahoma Press, 1946. 2 vols.

All correspondence available at the time this edition was prepared. Jones notes that some existing letters were unavailable, and gives information about these in an appendix. Correspondence 1814-1828.

2509. ------. MARY SHELLEY'S JOURNAL. Edited by Frederick L. Jones. Norman, Okla.: University of Oklahoma Press, 1947. 257p.

Diary 1814-1840, covering the period from her elopement with Shelley in 1814 to his death in 1822, with sporadic entries written until her death in 1851.

2510. ------. "Eight Letters by Mary Wollstonecraft Shelley." Elizabeth Nitchie. KEATS-SHELLEY MEMORIAL BULLETIN 3 (1950), 23-34.

Extracts from and summary of eight letters, presented with commentary and physical descriptions.

2511. ------. MY BEST MARY: THE SELECTED LETTERS OF MARY WOLLSTONECRAFT SHELLEY. Edited and with an introduction by Muriel Spark and Derek Stanford. London: A. Wingate, 1953. 240p. Reprinted, Folcroft, Penn.: Folcroft Library Editions, 1972. 246p.

Selected correspondence with Maria Gisborne, Leigh and Marianne Hunt, Percy Bysshe Shelley, Edward John Trelawny and others, 1814-1850.

2512. ------. "Mary Shelley to Maria Gisborne: New Letters, 1818-1822." Frederick L. Jones. STUDIES IN PHILOLOGY 52 (January, 1955), 39-74.

Twenty-seven letters, 1818-1822.

2513. ------. THE LETTERS OF MARY WOLLSTONECRAFT SHELLEY. Edited with an introduction by Betty T. Bennett. Baltimore, Md.: The Johns Hopkins University Press, 1980-1983. 2 vols.

Letters October, 1814--August, 1827. The most complete edition to date, it focuses on Mary Shelley in her own right rather than an adjunct to Percy Shelley and the Romantics; Mary Shelley's letters add a different and equally important perspective to the understanding of the Romantic period.

2514. ------. THE JOURNALS OF MARY WOLLSTONECRAFT SHELLEY, 1814-1844. Edited by Paula R. Feldman and Diana Scott-Kilvert. Oxford: The Clarendon Press, and New York: Oxford University Press, 1987. 2 vols.

Volume 1: 1814-1822. Volume 2: 1822-1844.

2515. Sheridan, Clare Consuelo Frewen, 1855-1970. American sculptor. RUSSIAN PORTRAITS. London: Jonathan Cape, 1921. 202p. Also published under the title MAYFAIR TO MOSCOW: CLARE SHERIDAN'S DIARY. New York: Boni & Liveright, 1921. 239p.

Diary August 14--November 23, 1920, chiefly concerned with travel in Russia and with her work sculpting busts of Krassin, Kameneff, Zinoviev, Dzhirjinsky, Trotsky, and Lenin.

2516. ------. MY AMERICAN DIARY. New York: Boni & Liveright, 1922. 359p.

Diary February 2, 1921--January 9, 1922; describes travel in America following the publication of MAYFAIR TO MOSCOW. She visted American intellectuals and artists, and toured farms and factories, reporting on conditions there from a socialist point of view.

2517. Sherman, Jane. American dancer. SOARING: THE DIARIES AND LETTERS OF A DENISHAWN DANCER IN THE FAR EAST, 1925-1926. Middletown, Conn.: Wesleyan University Press, 1976. 288p.

2518. Sherwood, Mary Martha Butt, 1775-1851. English author. THE LIFE AND TIMES OF MRS. SHERWOOD: FROM THE DIARIES OF CAPTAIN AND MRS. SHERWOOD. Edited by F.J. Harvey Darton. London: Wells Gardner, Darton & Co., 1910. 519p.

2519. Shimada Sachiko, pseud. Composite of the younger sisters of Japanese photographer Chie Nishio, wife of James Trager. LETTERS FROM SACHIKO: A JAPANESE WOMAN'S VIEW OF LIFE IN THE LAND OF ECONOMIC MIRACLE. James Trager. New York: Atheneum, 1982. 218p.

Letters are adapted from letters by several sisters, living in Omiya City on the outskirts of Tokyo. Describes daily life as well as social and economic aspects of Japan, with emphasis on women's lives.

2520. Shinn, Julia Tyler. American. "Forgotten Mother of the Sierra: Letters of Julia Tyler Shinn." Grace Tompkins Sargent. CALIFORNIA HISTORICAL SOCIETY QUARTERLY 38 (1959), 157-228.

2521. Shippen, Nancy (Anne Home Shippen Livingston), 1763-1841. American colonial belle. NANCY SHIPPEN: HER JOURNAL BOOK: THE INTERNATIONAL ROMANCE OF A YOUNG LADY OF FASHION OF COLONIAL PHILADELPHIA, WITH LETTERS TO AND ABOUT HER. Compiled and edited by Ethel Armes. Philadelphia and London: J.B. Lippincott Co., 1935. 349p.

Biography followed by Shippen's journal, which includes copies of letters received and sent, 1783-1800. Records daily life in Philadelphia society, her wedding, and unhappy marriage to a man chosen by her family.

2522. Shore, Emily Margaret, 1819-1839. English child prodigy and diarist. THE JOURNAL OF EMILY SHORE. London: Kegan Paul, Trench, Trubner & Co., 1891. 373p.

Diary 1831-1839. By the age of nineteen, Shore had mastered four languages, had a profound knowledge of history, botany and natural history, and had written a diary of over 2,000 pages. According to Sir Arthur

Ponsonby, Shore's diary examines the psychology of diary-writing, the problems of honesty of introspection, the question of motive, and the eventual fate of a diary.

2523. Shortall, Katherine. A "Y" GIRL IN FRANCE: LETTERS OF KATHERINE SHORTALL. Boston: R.G. Badger, 1919. 80p.

Letters of a woman serving with the YMCA in France during World War I.

2524. Shortt, Elizabeth Smith, 1859-1949. Canadian physician. ELIZABETH SMITH: A WOMAN WITH A PURPOSE. THE DIARIES OF ELIZABETH SMITH, 1872-1884. Edited, with an introduction by Veronica Strong-Boag. Toronto, Buffalo, and London: University of Toronto Press, 1980. 298p.

Diary from age thirteen to twenty-five, beginning with life on her parent's farm and continuing through her college years.

2525. Shrode, Maria Hargrave. American frontier settler. "Overland by Ox-Train in 1870: The Diary of Maria Hargrave Shrode." QUARTERLY OF THE HISTORICAL SOCIETY OF SOUTHERN CALIFORNIA 26 (March, 1944), 9-37.

2526. Shunk, Caroline Saxe Merrill. American Army wife. AN ARMY WOMAN IN THE PHILIPPINES: EXTRACTS FROM THE LETTERS OF AN ARMY OFFICER'S WIFE, DESCRIBING HER PERSONAL EXPERIENCES IN THE PHILIPPINE ISLANDS. Kansas City, Mo.: Franklin Hudson, 1914. 183p.

2527. Shutes, Mary Alice, 1849-1939. American frontier settler. "Pioneer Migration: The Diary of Mary Alice Shutes." Edited by Glenda Riley. ANNALS OF IOWA 43:7 (Winter, 1977), 487-514; and 43:8 (Spring, 1977), 567-592.

Diary of a thirteen-year-old written on the month-long journey from Wyandott County, Ohio, to Carroll County, Iowa, in 1862.

2528. Sibbald, Susan Mein, 1783-1866. English wife of a Colonial Officer in the British Navy. THE MEMOIRS OF SUSAN SIBBALD (1783-1812). Edited by her great-grandson, Francis Paget Hett. London: John Lane, 1926. 339p.

Extracts from letters written by Sibbald to her sons during the last ten years of her life, when her husband, Colonel Sibbald, was Envoi to Canada. Touches on the Crimean War, the Fenian Raids in Canada, and the American Civil War.

2529. Siddons, Sarah Kemble, popularly known as "Mrs. Siddons," 1775-1831. English actress. AN ARTIST'S LOVE STORY. TOLD IN THE LETTERS OF SIR THOMAS LAWRENCE, MRS. SIDDONS, AND HER DAUGHTER. Edited by Oswald G. Knapp. London: G. Allen, 1905. 238p. Second edition.

Letters 1797-1803 by Sarah Siddons and her daughters Sally and Maria give an account of a disastrous double-courtship carried on by Sir Thomas Lawrence with Mrs. Siddons' daughters.

2530. ------. "The Siddons Letters." In LEAVES FROM A BEECH TREE. Gwendolyn Beaufoy. Oxford: Printed for the author by Basil Blackford, 1930. p.241-288.

Letters of Sarah Siddons to her youngest son George, from 1803, when he sailed to India, until her death.

2531. Simcoe, Elizabeth Posthuma Gwillim, 1766-1850. English immigrant to Canada and wife of John Graves Simcoe, first Lieutenant-Governor of the Province of Upper Canada. A SIMCOE RELIC AMONG THE THOUSAND ISLES IN 1796. FRAGMENT OF A MANUSCRIPT JOURNAL OF MRS. SIMCOE. Edited by Rev. H. Scadding. Toronto, 1896. 7p.

2532. ------. THE DIARY OF MRS. JOHN GRAVES SIMCOE, WIFE OF THE FIRST LIEUTENANT-GOVERNOR OF THE PROVINCE OF UPPER CANADA, 1792-1796. With notes and a biography by J. Ross Robertson, and two hundred and thirty-seven illustrations, including ninety reproductions of interesting sketches made by Mrs. Simcoe. Toronto: W. Briggs, 1911. 440p. Toronto: Coles Publishing Co., 1973. 439p.

2533. ------. MRS. SIMCOE'S DIARY. Edited by Mary Quayle Innis. With illustrations from the original manuscript. Toronto: Macmillan of Canada, and New York: St. Martin's Press, 1965, 1978. 223p.

2534. ------. "Portrait of Elizabeth Simcoe." ONTARIO HISTORY 69:2 (1977), 79-100.

Biography of Simcoe, illustrated with extracts from her letters and diary.

2535. Simkin, Margaret Timberlake. American Quaker missionary to China. LETTERS FROM SZECHWAN, 1923-1944: MARGARET TIMBERLAKE SIMKIN. [Pasadena, Calif.]: Friend in the Orient Committee, Pacific Yearly Meeting, 1978. 273p.

2536. Sims, Mary Ann Owen, 1830-1861. American. "Private Journal of Mary Ann Owen Sims." Edited by Clifford Dale Whitman. ARKANSAS HISTORICAL QUARTERLY 35:2 (1976), 142-187; 3 (1976), 261-291

Extracts from a journal, 1855-1861.

2537. Sinclair, May, c.1865-1946. English novelist. A JOURNAL OF IMPRESSIONS IN BELGIUM. London: Hutchinson & Co., 1915. 332p. New York: The Macmillan Co., 1915. 294p.

Diary September 15, 1914--July 15, 1915 describes hospital work in Belgium. Not a daily journal, but written from notes and from memory. Sinclair writes that circumstances seldom allowed regular journal-keeping.

2538. Singers-Bigger, Gladys, d. 1970. English novelist and feminist. DARLING MADAME: SARAH GRAND AND DEVOTED FRIEND. Gillian Kersley. London: Virago Press, 1983. 364p.

Includes extracts from the diaries of Gladys Singers-Bigger.

2539. Sitwell, Constance Talbot, b. 1887. English

author. BOUNTEOUS DAYS. With an introduction by James Pope-Hennessy. London: C. Woolf, 1976. 73p.

Social diary, 1920-1925, covering her life in a Northumbrian castle near the sea, at her London house near the Thames, and a stay in florence with her husband's cousins, Sir George and Lady Ida Sitwell.

2540. Sitwell, Edith. EDITH SITWELL: SELECTED LETTERS, 1919-1964. Edited by John Lehmann and Derek Parker. London: Macmillan, 1970, and New York: Vanguard Press, 1971. 264p.

Selection from the correspondence of an "uninhibited and energetic" letter writer. No family letters and none of the large number written to Pavel Tchelitchew can be published until the year 2000.

2541. Sitwell, Florence Alice, 1858-1930. English. TWO GENERATIONS. Edited by Osbert Sitwell. London and New York: Macmillan Co., 1940. 308p.

Includes a diary 1873-1877, begun when Sitwell was fifteen. Describes the life of an Englishwoman of good family; religious and social affairs, and travels.

2542. Sjoborg, Sofia Charlotta. Swedish Lutheran immigrant to the United States. "Journey to Florida, 1871." Translated by Wesley M. Westerberg. SWEDISH PIONEER HISTORICAL QUARTERLY 26:1 (1975), 24-25.

Diary of a journey from Sweden to New York, then to Florida, where her family settled.

2543. Skilbeck, Sarah Midgley, 1832-1893. English immigrant to Australia. THE DIARIES OF SARAH MIDGLEY AND RICHARD SKILBECK: A STORY OF AUSTRALIAN SETTLERS, 1851- 1864. Edited by H.A. McCorkell. Melbourne: Cassell Australia, 1967. 208p.

Her diary covers 1851-1861, from the time she emigrated to Australia with her family to her marriage to Richard Skilbeck. Describes travel in Australia and life in the early days of Victoria.

2544. Skinner, Mary Louise. LETTERS OF A V.A.D. London: A. Melrose, 1918. 313p.

World War I letters by a member of England's Voluntary Aid Detachment.

2545. Slayden, Ellen Maury, 1860-1926. American Washington hostess and wife of Congressman James Luther Slayden. WASHINGTON WIFE: THE JOURNAL OF ELLEN MAURY SLAYDEN FROM 1897-1919. Preface by Terrell D. Webb. Introduction by Walter Prescott Webb. Foreword by Ellen Maury Slayden. New York: Harper & Row, 1963. 385p.

Detailed and personal society diary, describes life in Washington between the Spanish-American War and World War I. Edited from a manuscript prepared by Slayden, who intended it to be published.

2546. ------. "Washington Wife: From the Journal of Ellen Maury Slayden." Edited by Walter Prescott Webb. SOUTHWEST REVIEW 48 (Winter, 1963), 1-14.

2547. Sloane, Florence Adele, 1873-1960. American society belle. MAVERICK IN MAUVE: THE DIARY OF A ROMANTIC AGE. Commentary by Louis Auchincloss. Garden City, N.Y.: Doubleday Co., 1983.

Excerpts from a diary 1893-1896 by a wealthy young woman of New York. Records a life of beaux, dances, and European travel during the "Gilded Age."

2548. Smith, Abigail Adams, 1765-1813. American daughter of John and Abigail Adams. JOURNAL AND CORRESPONDENCE OF MISS ADAMS, DAUGHTER OF JOHN ADAMS, SECOND PRESIDENT OF THE UNITED STATES. WRITTEN IN FRANCE AND ENGLAND, 1785. Edited by her daughter (Caroline Amelia Smith de Windt). New York: Wiley & Putnam, 1841. 217p.

2549. Smith, Amy Grinnell, 1807-1875, and Mary Ermina Smith, 1840-1912. LETTERS FROM EUROPE, 1865-1866, BY AMY GRINNELL SMITH AND MARY ERMINA SMITH. Edited by David Saunders Clark. Washington, 1948. 140p.

Travel letters.

2550. Smith, Elizabeth, d. 1885. Irish. THE IRISH JOURNALS OF ELIZABETH SMITH, 1840-1850. A selection edited by David Thomson and Moyra McGusty. Oxford: Clarendon Press, and New York: Oxford University Press, 1980. 326p.

2551. Smith, Hannah Whitall, 1832-1911. American Quaker author. A RELIGIOUS REBEL: THE LETTERS OF "H.W.S." (MRS. PEARSALL SMITH). Edited by her son, Logan Pearsall Smith. With a preface and memoir by Robert Gathorne-Hardy. London: Nisbet, 1949. 232p. Published in the United States as PHILADELPHIA QUAKER: THE LETTERS OF HANNAH WHITALL SMITH. New York: Harcourt, Brace, 1950. 234p.

2552. Smith, Julia M. LEAVES FROM A JOURNAL IN THE EAST, DECEMBER, 1899--NOVEMBER, 1900. London: W.R. Russell & Co., 1901. 197p.

Travel diary, describing a journey through Ceylon, Burma, and India.

2553. Smith, Lydia. American. "Journal, 1805-1806." MASSACHUSETTS HISTORICAL SOCIETY PROCEEDINGS 48 (1914-1915), 508-534.

Fragment of a social and travel diary, December, 1805--January, 1806; and letters to her friend Miss Anna Lothrop.

2554. Smith, Margaret Bayard, 1778-1844. American author and letter writer. THE FIRST FORTY YEARS OF WASHINGTON SOCIETY IN THE FAMILY LETTERS OF MARGARET BAYARD SMITH. Edited by Gaillard Hunt. New York: Charles Scribner's Sons, 1906. 424p. Reprinted, New York: Frederick Ungar Publishing Co., 1965.

Smith wrote essays, novels, stories and verse based on her life in Washington as the wife of journalist Samuel Harrison Smith, founder of THE NATIONAL INTELLIGENCER. However, she is most well known for her letters and notebooks, published after her death.

2555. Smith, Sadie B., later Trail, 1873-1942. American frontier school teacher. "A Nebraska High School Teacher in the 1890's: The Letters of Sadie B. Smith." Rosalie Trail Fuller. NEBRASKA HISTORY 58:4 (Summer, 1977), 447-473.

Brief biography followed by a selection of letters to her future husband, Rollin A. Trail, September 13, 1896--November 3, 1899. Describes her experience teaching in a small Nebraska high school.

2556. Smith, Sarah Foote, b. 1829. American frontier settler. A JOURNAL KEPT BY MISS SARAH FOOTE (MRS. SARAH FOOTE SMITH) WHILE JOURNEYING WITH HER PEOPLE FROM WELLINGTON, OHIO, TO FOOTEVILLE, TOWN OF NEPEUSKUN, WINNEBAGO COUNTY, WISCONSIN, APRIL 15 TO May 10, 1846. No Place: Privately printed, 1925?

2557. Smith, Sarah Gilbert White, 1813/14-1855. American frontier missionary. THE JOURNAL OF MRS. SARAH WHITE SMITH, WIFE OF REVEREND ASA SMITH, WRITTEN ON THEIR JOURNEY TO OREGON UNDER APPOINTMENT OF THE A.B.C.-F.M., AS MISSIONARIES TO THE INDIANS. COPIED BY HER NIECE ALICE WHITE. MARCH 10, 1838--SEPTEMBER 14, 1839. Denver: Dakota Microfilm Service, 1964. 1 reel (35mm).

Filmed from the original manuscript in the Western History Department of the Denver Public Library.

2558. Smith, Sarah Hathaway (Bixby) b. 1871. American Frontier Settler. ADOBE DAYS. THE TRUTHFUL NARRATIVE OF EVENTS IN THE LIFE OF A CALIFORNIA GIRL ON A SHEEP FARM IN EL PUEBLO DE NESTRA SENORA DE LOS ANGELES, WITH AN ACCOUNT OF HOW THREE MAINE MEN (1853) DROVE SHEEP AND CATTLE ACROSS THE UNITED STATES TO THE PACIFIC COAST, AND THE STRANGE PROPHECY OF ADMIRAL THATCHER ABOUT SAN PEDRO HARBOR. Revised edition. Cedar Rapids, Iowa: Torch Press, 1926. 217p.

2559. Smith, Stevie, 1902-1971. English poet and author. ME AGAIN: UNCOLLECTED WRITINGS OF STEVIE SMITH. Illustrated by herself. Edited by Jack Barbera and William McBrien. With a preface by James MacGibbon. London: Virago Press, 1981. 360p.

2560. Smith, Virginia Cox. American secretary. WOMAN ALONE AROUND THE WORLD. New York: Exposition Press, 1955. 282p.

Letters May 8--December 20 of an unspecified year, written on a world tour. The letters were written for her employer, "Mr. A.," and for people, especially women, who would like to know what it is like to travel alone around the world but who might be afraid to travel on their own.

2561. Snow, Eliza R. American Mormon. "Eliza Snow's Nauvoo Journal." Edited by Maureen Ursenbach. BRIGHAM YOUNG UNIVERSITY STUDIES 15:4 (1975), 387-391.

Diary excerpts 1842-1844 describe the Mormon community in Nauvoo, Illinois.

2562. Snow, Leslie, and Susan Snow. Americans. "North Central Kansas in 1887-1889: From the Letters of Leslie Snow and Susan Snow of Junction City." Edited by Lela Barnes. KANSAS HISTORICAL QUARTERLY 29 (Autumn, 1963), 267-323, and 29 (Winter, 1963), 372-428.

2563. Somerhausen, Anne, b. 1903. Belgian. WRITTEN IN DARKNESS: A BELGIAN WOMAN'S ACCOUNT OF THE OCCUPATION, 1940-1944. New York: Alfred A. Knopf, 1946. 339p.

Diary May 10, 1940--May 12, 1945 gives a first-hand account of the German invasion and occupation of Belgium during World War II.

2564. Somerset, Frances Thynne Seymour, Duchess of, 1699-1754. English Lady In Waiting to Queen Caroline. CORRESPONDENCE BETWEEN FRANCES, COUNTESS OF HARTFORD (AFTERWARDS DUCHESS OF SOMERSET) AND HENRIETTA LOUISA, COUNTESS OF POMFRET, BETWEEN THE YEARS 1738 AND 1741. Edited by William Bingley. London: R. Phillips, 1805. 3 vols. Second edition, 1806. 3 vols.

Correspondence with Henrietta Louisa Jeffreys Fermor, Countess of Pomfret (1700?-1761). Both women had been Ladies-In-Waiting to Queen Caroline.

2565. Somerville, Mary Fairfax, 1780-1879. English scientific writer. PERSONAL RECOLLECTIONS, FROM EARLY LIFE TO OLD AGE, OF MARY FAIRFAX SOMERVILLE. WITH SELECTIONS FROM HER CORRESPONDENCE. By her daughter, Martha Somerville. Boston: Roberts Bros., 1874. 377p.

2566. Sonnenthal-Scherer, Maria, 1884-1916. EIN FRAUENSCHICKSAL IM KRIEGE: BRIEFE UND TAGEBÜCH AUF ZEICHNÜNGEN VON SCHWESTER MARIA SONNENTHAL-SCHERER. Eingeleitet und nach den handschriften von Hermine von Sonnenthal. Berlin: Ullstein & Co., 1918. 253p.

Personal account of World War I.

2567. Sophie Dorothea, Consort of George I, King of Great Britain, 1666-1726. THE LOVE OF AN UNCROWNED QUEEN, SOPHIE DOROTHEA, CONSORT OF GEORGE I, AND HER CORRESPONDENCE WITH PHILIP CHRISTOPHER, COUNT KONIGS-MARK. W.H. Wilkins. Chicago and New York: H.S. Stone & Co., 1901. New York: Duffield, 1906. 578p.

2568. Sophie, Consort of Ernest Augustus, Elector of Hannover, 1630-1714. DIE MUTTER DER KONIGE VON PREUSSEN UND ENGLAND: MEMORIEN UND BRIEFEN DER KURFÜRSTIN SOPHIE VON HANNOVER. Herausgegeben von Robert Geerds. Ebenhausen-München und Leipzig: W. Langewiesche-Brandt, 1913. 447p.

2569. Southall, Elizabeth Allen, 1823-1851. English Quaker. PORTIONS OF THE DIARY, LETTERS, AND OTHER REMAINS, OF ELIZA SOUTHALL, LATE OF BIRMINGHAM, ENGLAND. Edited by William Southall. For private circulation Birmingham, England: White and Pike, 1855. 191p. Philadelphia: Association of Friends for the Diffusion of Religious and Useful Knowledge, 1861. 195p.

Includes a Quaker diary, 1837-1851.

2570. Sparrow, Jane. English social worker. DIARY OF A DELINQUENT EPISODE. London and Boston: Routledge & Kegan Paul, 1976. 130p.

Diary of social work among delinquent girls.

2571. ------. DIARY OF A STUDENT SOCIAL WORKER. London: Henley, and Boston: Routledge and Kegan Paul, 1978. 148p.

Consists of two diaries. The first was written towards the end of a five-year period of residential work in a farm-centered institution for adolescent girls, and has been "drastically pruned." The second was required of her as a student during the final five months of a training course for professional social work and is presented as written. No years are given for either, but the second was written before the Children and Young Persons Act of 1968.

2572. Spencer, Cornelia Phillips, 1825-1908. American author and historian of the Chapel Hill, N.C. area. OLD DAYS IN CHAPEL HILL: BEING THE LIFE AND LETTERS OF CORNELIA PHILLIPS SPENCER. Chapel Hill: University of North Carolina Press, 1926. 325p.

2573. Spender, Dale. Australian feminist scholar and author. SCRIBBLING SISTERS: DALE AND LYNNE SPENDER. Sydney, N.S.W.: Hale & Iremonger, 1984. 173p.

Correspondence between sisters Dale and Lynne Spender.

2574. Sperry, Almeda, b. 1879. American anarchist. "Almeda Sperry to Emma Goldman." In GAY AMERICAN HISTORY: LESBIANS AND GAY MEN IN THE U.S.A. A DOCUMENTARY. Jonathan Katz. New York: Thomas Y. Crowell Co., 1976. p.523-530.

Letters written in 1912 reveal, strongly and unambiguously, Sperry's passion for Goldman.

2575. Staël-Holstein, Anne Louise Germaine Necker, Baronne de, 1766-1817. French political and social figure, author and intellectual. MADAME DE STAËL AND THE GRAND-DUCHESS LOUISE. A SELECTION FROM THE UNPUBLISHED CORRESPONDENCE OF MADAME DE STAËL AND THE GRAND DUCHESS LOUISE OF SAXE-WEIMAR, FROM 1800 TO 1817, TOGETHER WITH A LETTER TO BONAPARTE, FIRST CONSUL, AND

ANOTHER TO NAPOLEON, EMPEROR. By the author of "Souvenirs of Madame Récamier." [Amelie Cyvoct Lenormant]. London: Saunders, Otley, 1862. 223p.

2576. ------. LETTRES INÉDITES DE MADAME DE STAËL À HENRI MEISTER. Publiées par M.M. Paul Usteri et Eugene Ritter. Paris: Hachette et Cie., 1903. 284p.

2577. ------. MADAME DE STAËL AND BENJAMIN CONSTANT: UNPUBLISHED LETTERS. TOGETHER WITH OTHER MEMENTOS FROM THE PAPERS LEFT BY MADAME CHARLOTTE DE CONSTANT. Edited by Madame de Constant's great granddaughter, Baroness Elisabeth de Nolde. Translated from the French by Charlotte Harwood. New York and London: G.P. Putnam's Sons, the Knickerbocker Press, 1907. 298p.

Correspondence between Madame de Staël and her protégé; author, political orator and politician Henri Constant de Rebeque.

2578. ------. "La Correspondance de Madame de Staël avec Jefferson." G. Chinard. RÉVUE DE LITTERATURE COMPARÉE 2 (1922), 621-640.

2579. ------. MADAME DE STAËL ET M. NECKER, D'APRÈS LEUR CORRESPONDANCE INÉDITE. Paris: Calmann-Lévy, 1925. 413p.

2580. ------. LETTRES DE MADAME DE STAËL AU COMTE MAURICE O'DONNELL. Publiée par Jean Mistler. Paris: Calmann-Lévy, 1926.

2581. ------. LETTRES DE MADAME DE STAËL À BENJAMIN CONSTANT. Publiée pour la prémière fois en original par Madame la Baronne de Nolde (Baroness Élisabeth de Nolde) avec un introduction et des notes par Paul L. Leon. Avant-propos de Gustave Rudler. Paris: Kra, 1928. 164p.

2582. ------. MADAME DE STAËL AND THE UNITED STATES. Richmond Laurin Hawkins. Cambridge, Mass.: Harvard University Press, 1930. 81p.

Includes letters by de Staël, Jacques Necker,

Camille Jordan, Governor William Morris, Thomas Jefferson, and others.

2583. ------. MADAME DE STAËL: LETTRES INÉDITES À JUSTE CONSTANT DE REBEQUE, 1795-1812. Publiées par Gustave Rudler. Lusanne: F. Roth et Cie., 1937. 48p.

2584. ------. MADAME DE STAËL: LETTRES INÉDITES À MADAME ODIER. Publiées par Paul-Émile Schazmann. Berne: Société de Bibliophiles, 1940. 20p.

Letters to Madame Andrienne Lecointe Odier.

2585. ------. LETTRES À UN AMI: BENJAMIN CONSTANT ET MADAME DE STAËL; CENT ONZE LETTRES INÉDITES À CLAUDE HOCHET. Publiée avec une introduction et des notes par Jean Mistler. Neuchatel: A La Baconnière, 1949. 253p.

2586. ------. LETTRES DE MADAME DE STAËL À MADAME RÉCAMIER. Présentées et annotées par E. Beau de Loumenie. Paris: Domat, 1952. 275p.

2587. ------. UNE AMITIÉ AMOUREUSE: MADAME DE STAËL ET MADAME DE RÉCAMIER. LETTRES ET DOCUMENTS INÉDITS. Paris: Hachette, 1956. 383p.

Correspondence with intimate friend Jeanne Francoise Julie Adelaide Bernard Récamier, (1777-1849).

2588. ------. MADAME DE STAËL: LETTRES À NARBONNE. Préface de la Comtesse Jean de Pange. Introduction, notes et commentaires par Georges Solovieff. Paris: Gallimard, 1960. 559p.

Letters to Louis Narbonne, August, 1792--May, 1794. Appendices contain additional letters to others.

2589. ------. MADAME DE STAËL: LETTRES À RIBBING. Préface de la Comtesse Jean de Pange. Établissement du Texte, introduction et notes par Simone Balaye. Paris: Gallimard, 1960. 462p.

Letters to Grefve Adolf Ludwig Ribbing, 1793-1797.

2590. ------. CORRESPONDANCE GÉNÉRALE. Texte établie et presentée par Beatrice W. Jasinski. Paris: J.J. Pauvert, 1960-1978. 5 vols. (Each volume in two books).

Definitive edition. Letters 1777-1804 to Louis Narbonne, Alexandre Chevassu, Edward Gibbon, Lord Grenville, Fanny Burney, Henri Meister, Rosalie Constant, Aldolphe-Louis Ribbing, Alexandre d'Arblay, Madame de Gouvernet, Madame Necker de Saussure, Mary Berry, Joseph Bonaparte, Pierre-Samuel Du Pont de Nemours, and others.

2591. ------. MADAME DE STAËL ET LE DUC DE WELLINGTON: CORRESPONDANCE INÉDITE, 1815-1817. Victor de la Pange. Paris: Gallimard, 1962. 161p.

Correspondence with Arthur Wellesley, Duke of Wellington (1769-1852).

2592. ------. THE UNPUBLISHED CORRESPONDENCE OF MADAME DE STAËL AND THE DUKE OF WELLINGTON. Victor de Pange. Translated by Harold Kurtz. With a foreword by Comtesse Jean de Pange. London: Cassell & Co., 1965. 90p. New York: Humanities Press, 1966. 90p.

2593. ------. DE STAËL-DU PONT LETTERS: CORRESPONDENCE OF MADAME DE STAËL AND PIERRE SAMUEL DU PONT DE NEMOURS AND OTHER MEMBERS OF THE NECKER AND DU PONT FAMILIES. Edited and translated by James F. Marshall. Madison and London: University of Wisconsin Press, 1968. 400p.

Letters 1778-1818 reveals the friendship between Madame de Staël and Du Pont, and the involvement of the Necker family in the early history of the Du Pont enterprises in the United States. Much of the correspondence is concerned with financial matters, revealing Mme. de Stael in her role as a business woman.

2594. ------. MADAME DE STAËL ET J.-B.-A. SUARD: CORRESPONDANCE INÉDITE (1786-1817). Robert de Luppé. Geneve: Droz, 1970. 126p.

Correspondence with Jean-Baptiste-Antoine Suard.

2595. ------. MADAME DE STAËL, SES AMIS, SES CORRESPONDANTS. CHOIX DE LETTRES (1778-1817). Presentée et commentée par Georges Solovieff. Préface de la Comtesse Jean de Pange. Paris: Klincksieck, 1970. 586p.

2596. ------. MADAME DE STAËL, DON PEDRO DE SOUZA: CORRESPONDANCE. Préface, introduction, commentaires et notes par Beatrix d'Andlau. Paris: Gallimard, 1980. 136p.

2597. ------. LE PLUS BEAU DE TOUTES LES FÊTES: MADAME DE STAËL ET ÉLISABETH HERVEY, DUCHESSE DE DEVONSHIRE, D'APRÈS LEUR CORRESPONDANCE INÉDITE, 1804-1817. Victor de Pange. Paris: Klincksieck, 1980. 266p.

2598. Stanhope, Hester Lucy, Lady, 1776-1839. English traveler. THE NUN OF LEBANON: THE LOVE AFFAIR OF LADY HESTER STANHOPE AND MICHAEL BRUCE: THEIR NEWLY DISCOVERED LETTERS. Edited by Ian Bruce. London: Collins, 1951. 415p.

Chiefly letters, with connecting biographical material, covering the years 1810-1815, with a postscript covering the last twenty years of her life. Stanhope settled in a castle at Djoun on Mt. Lebanon in 1814, and cared for Druse refugees during periods of Ottoman oppression. Because of her generosity, she was revered as a queen by neighboring tribes.

2599. Stanley, Augusta Frederica Elizabeth Bruce, Lady, 1822-1876. English Lady in Waiting to the Duchess of Kent, later to Queen Victoria. LETTERS OF LADY AUGUSTA STANLEY: A YOUNG LADY AT COURT, 1849-1863. Edited by the Dean of Windsor and Hector Bolitho. London: Gerald Howe, and New York: George H. Doran Co., 1927. 334p.

Letters written during her life at court, chiefly to her sister, Lady Frances Baillie; no letters after her marriage in 1863 are included.

2600. ------. LATER LETTERS OF LADY AUGUSTA STANLEY, 1864-1876, INCLUDING MANY UNPUBLISHED LETTERS TO AND FROM QUEEN VICTORIA AND CORRESPONDENCE WITH DEAN STANLEY, HER SISTER, LADY FRANCES BAILLIE, AND OTHERS.

Edited by the Dean of Windsor and Hector Bolitho. London: Jonathan Cape, and New York: Jonathan Cape & Harrison Smith, 1929. 288p.

2601. Stanley, Catherine Leycester, 1792-1862. English wife of Edward Stanley, Bishop of Norwich. MEMOIRS OF EDWARD AND CATHERINE STANLEY. Edited by their son, Arthur Penrhyn Stanley. London: John Murray, 1879. 337p.

Includes extracts from Stanley's diary, 1809-1862.

2602. Stanley, Eleanor Julian, later the Hon. Mrs. Long, 1821-1903. Extra Honorary Maid of Honour to Queen Victoria. TWENTY YEARS AT COURT: FROM THE CORRESPONDENCE OF THE HON. ELEANOR STANLEY, MAID OF HONOUR TO HER LATE MAJESTY QUEEN VICTORIA, 1842-1862. Edited by Mrs. Steuart Erskine. London: Nisbet & Co., 1916. 404p.

2603. Stanley, Maria Josepha Holroyd Stanley, Baroness, 1771-1863. THE GIRLHOOD OF MARIA JOSEPHA HOLROYD (LADY STANLEY OF ALDERLY) RECORDED IN LETTERS OF A HUNDRED YEARS AGO: FROM 1776-1796. Edited by J. H. Adeane. London and New York: Longmans, Green & Co., 1896. 420p.

Literary letters, 1782-1796. Lady Stanley's father, a Peer, was fond of literature and entertained the leading intellectuals of the day. At the age of twelve, Lady Stanley was writing letters on easy terms of equality to her older relatives and was sometimes given letter-writing duty by her family.

2604. ------. THE EARLY MARRIED LIFE OF MARIA JOSEPHA, LADY STANLEY. WITH EXTRACTS FROM SIR JOHN STANLEY'S "PRAETERITA." Edited by one of their grandchildren, Jane H. Adeane. London and New York: Longmans, Green & Co., 1899. 461p.

Extracts from her correspondence tells the story of the early years of her marriage. Also contains letters of Sara (Serena) Martha Holroyd with whom Lady Stanley carried on a long correspondence, and letters and extracts from the journal of Lady Stanley's sister-in-law, Louisa Margaret Anne Stanley.

2605. ------. THE LADIES OF ALDERLY: BEING THE LETTERS BETWEEN MARIA JOSEPHA, LADY STANLEY OF ALDERLY AND HER DAUGHTER-IN-LAW HENRIETTA MARIA STANLEY DURING THE YEARS 1841-1850. Edited by Nancy Mitford. Foreword by Lord Stanley of Alderly. London: Chapman & Hall, 1938. 315p.

Henrietta Maria, Lady Stanley of Alderly (1807-1895) married Edward John Stanley, Second Baron of Alderly. She was a promoter of education for women.

2606. Stanley, Monica M. English nurse. MY DIARY IN SERBIA, APRIL 1, 1915-NOVEMBER 1, 1915. ATTACHED TO THE STOBART FIELD HOSPITAL IN SERBIA. London: Simpkin, Marshall, Hamilton, Kent & Co., 1916. 128p.

Diary of hospital work under Mrs. St. Clair Stobart, under the aegis of the Serbian Relief Fund, at Kragujevatz, Serbia.

2607. Stanton, Elizabeth Cady, 1815-1902. American suffragist, feminist and historian. ELIZABETH CADY STANTON AS REVEALED IN HER LETTERS, DIARY AND REMINISCENCES. Edited by Theodore Stanton and Harriet Stanton Blatch. New York: Harper & Row, 1922. 2 vols.

Volume 1 is her autobiography, published elsewhere as EIGHTY YEARS AND MORE. Volume 2 contains letters 1839-1880, and a diary of her later years, 1880-1902.

2608. ------. "Elizabeth Cady Stanton and Gerrit Smith." W. Freeman Galpin. NEW YORK HISTORY 16 (1935), 321-328.

Excerpts from correspondence 1856-1875 pertaining to woman suffrage.

2609. Stark, Flora, d. 1942. English businesswoman and mother of Freya Stark. AN ITALIAN DIARY. With a Foreword by Freya Stark. Edited by Sydney Cockerell. London: John Murray, 1945. 50p.

Wartime and prison diary, June 10--September 2, 1940. Stark was imprisoned by the Fascists in June, released, and allowed to return to her home in Asolo (near Venice), which had been taken over by the Gestapo. She lived there in three rooms on the upper floor for another eight months (not covered by the diary) until friends arranged for her to leave Italy for the United States.

2610. Stark, Freya, Dame, b. 1892. English traveler, chiefly in the Middle East. LETTERS FROM SYRIA. London: John Murray, 1942. 194p.

Letters 1927-1929 to her parents, and to friends in Canada and the United States, written while traveling in the Middle East.

2611. ------. LETTERS. Edited by Lucy Moorehead and Caroline Moorehead. Salisbury, Wiltshire: Compton Russell, 1974-1982. 8 vols.

Volume 1: THE FURNACE AND THE CUP, 1914-1930. Volume 2: THE OPEN DOOR, 1930-1935. Volume 3: THE GROWTH OF DANGER, 1935-1939. Volume 4: BRIDGE OF THE LEVANT, 1940-1943. Volume 5: NEW WORLDS FOR OLD, 1943-1946. Volume 6: THE BROKEN ROAD, 1946- 1952. Volume 7: SOME TALK OF ALEXANDER, 1952-1959. Volume 8: TRAVELLER'S EPILOGUE, 1960-1980.

2612. Steele, Harriet. English. "Gold Rush Letters Copied From an Old Letter Book." PACIFIC HISTORIAN 8:1 (1964), 43-52.

Steele traveled across the United States in 1852.

2613. Steele, Millicent Pollock, afterwards Henderson. English. "Diary of a Voyage from London to Upper Canada in 1833 by Millicent Pollock Steele and Ellen Francis Steele." ONTARIO HISTORICAL SOCIETY PAPERS AND RECORDS 23 (1926), 483-510.

Travel letter-diary, April 27--August 8, 1833 by Steele and her sister, Ellen Frances Steele, daughters of Captain Elmes Yelverton Steele, to friends in England.

2614. Stein, Gertrude, 1874-1946. American author, salonist, and art patron. SHERWOOD ANDERSON/GERTRUDE STEIN: CORRESPONDENCE AND PERSONAL ESSAYS. Edited by Ray Lewis White. Chapel Hill, N.C.: University of North Carolina Press, 1972. 130p.

2615. ------. DEAR SAMMY: LETTERS FROM GERTRUDE STEIN AND ALICE B. TOKLAS. Edited with a memoir by Samuel M. Steward. Boston: Houghton Mifflin Co., 1977. 260p.

Literary letters, written to Steward from Stein, 1933-1946, and from Toklas, 1946-1963.

2616. ------. THE LETTERS OF GERTRUDE STEIN AND CARL VAN VECHTEN, 1913-1946. Edited by Edward Burns. New York: Columbia University Press, 1986. 2 vols.

Collects all extant letters between Stein and Van Vechten, as well as letters written to or from Alice Toklas and Fania Marinoff Van Vechten during the years covered by the correspondence. Letters reveal the devotion Stein and Van Vechten had for each other, and Stein's character as a letter-writer. Writing was a lonely and emotionally draining experience for her, and correspondence with Van Vechten and others gave her support and offered a respite from the tension of formal composition.

2617. Stein, Judith Beck, b. 1925. American mental patient. THE JOURNAL OF JUDITH BECK STEIN. Washington, D.C.: The Columbia Journal, 1973. 170p.

2618. Stephens, Octavia, 1841-1908. "Children of Honor: Letters of Winston and Octavia Stephens, 1861-1862." Edited by Ellen E. Hodges and Stephen Kerber. FLORIDA HISTORICAL SOCIETY 56:1 (1977), 45-74.

Letters exchanged by a Florida couple during the Civil War.

2619. ------. "Rogues and Black-Hearted Scamps: Civil War Letters of Winston and Octavia Stephens, 1862-1863."

Edited by Ellen E. Hodges and Stephen Kerber. FLORIDA HISTORICAL QUARTERLY 57:1 (1978), 54-82.

2620. Stern, Susan, b. 1943. American member of the revolutionary group the Weathermen. WITH THE WEATHERMEN: THE PERSONAL JOURNAL OF A REVOLUTIONARY WOMAN. Garden City, N.Y.: Doubleday & Co., 1975. 374p.

Autobiography 1966-1972; much of it is re-written from her journal into a narrative.

2621. Stevens, Harriet F. American frontier settler. "One of the Mercer Girls.: A Journal of Life on the Steamer Continental." ANNALS OF WYOMING 35:2 (1963), 214-228.

The "Mercer Girls" were single girls living in the eastern United States whom Asa Shinn Mercer persuaded to emigrate to the Washington Territory in 1866.

2622. Stevenson, Fanny Van de Grift Osbourne, 1840-1914. Scottish Wife of author Robert Louis Stevenson. THE CRUISE OF THE "JANET NICHOL" AMONG THE SOUTH SEA ISLANDS. A DIARY KEPT BY MRS. ROBERT LOUIS STEVENSON. New York: Charles Scribner's Sons, 1914. 189p.

Diary of a cruise, April-July, 1890. The diary has been severely pruned. Intended to aid Robert Stevenson's memory when his own diary had fallen into arrears, incidents recorded in her diary were amplified, rewritten, and used in his. These passages have been deleted, as well as passages containing "things pertaining to private affairs of others, and naturally, our own."

Stevenson, Frances. See: Lloyd-George, Frances Stevenson, Countess.

2623. Stevenson, Margaret Isabella Balfour, 1829-1897. FROM THE SARANAC TO THE MARQUESAS AND BEYOND: BEING LETTERS WRITTEN TO HER SISTER, JANE WHYTE BALFOUR. With a short introduction by George W. Balfour. Edited and arranged by Marie Clothilde Balfour. London: Methuen & Co., 1903. 313p.

2624. Stewart, Agnes. American frontier settler. "The Journey to Oregon: A Pioneer Girl's Diary." Introduction and editing by Claire Warner Churchill. OREGON HISTORICAL QUARTERLY 29:1 (March, 1928), 76-97.

Overland diary March-September, 1853.

2625. Stewart, Catherine. American frontier settler. NEW HOMES IN THE WEST. Nashville: Cameron and Fall, Deaderick Street, 1843. 198p. Reprinted, Ann Arbor, Mich.: University Microfilms, Inc. (A Subsidiary of Xerox Corp.) 1966.

Letters 1832-1836, plus undated letters, description and poetry. Bright, optimistic descriptions of life and travels in Michigan, Illinois, Missouri and Indiana.

2626. Stewart, Elinore Pruitt, b. 1878. American frontier settler. LETTERS OF A WOMAN HOMESTEADER. With illustrations by N.C. Wyeth. Boston and New York: Houghton Mifflin Co., 1914. 281p. Reprinted with a foreword by Jessamyn West. Lincoln, Nebr.: University of Nebraska Press, 1961. 282p.

Lively and vivid letters of a woman with a young daughter homesteaded in Wyoming. The letters, April, 1909--November, 1931, were written to a former employer in Detroit.

2627. ------. LETTERS ON AN ELK HUNT. Boston and New York: Houghton Mifflin Co., 1915. 161p. Reprinted with a foreword by Elizabeth Fuller Ferris. Lincoln, Nebr.: University of Nebraska Press, 1970. 162p.

Letters from Wyoming, July 8--October 15, 1914, written on an Elk-hunting trip.

2628. Stewart, Frances Browne, 1794-1872. Irish emigrant to Canada. OUR FOREST HOME: BEING EXTRACTS FROM THE CORRESPONDENCE OF THE LATE FRANCES STEWART. Compiled and edited by her daughter, E.S. Dunlop. Toronto: Printed by the Presbyterian Printing and

Publishing Co., 1889. 210p. Montreal: The Gazette Printing and Publishing Co., 1902. 300p.

Autobiography comprised of extracts from letters and journals, 1822-1872, of an Irish settler who lived with her family near Peterborough, Quebec. Describes conditions of travel and of pioneer settlement, and the growth of communities and social life in Upper Canada.

2629. Stieglitz, Charlotte Sophie Willhoft, 1806-1834. CHARLOTTE STIEGLITZ, EIN DENKMAL. Herausgegeben von Theodore Mundt. Berlin: Veit & Comp., 1835. 314p.

Letters and diary, 1827-1834.

2630. Stimson, Julia Catherine, b. 1881. American nurse. FINDING THEMSELVES: THE LETTERS OF AN AMERICAN ARMY CHIEF NURSE IN A BRITISH HOSPITAL IN FRANCE. New York: Macmillan Co., 1918. 231p.

War letters, May 4, 1917--April 12, 1918.

Stock, Nellie Weeton. See: Weeton, Nellie.

Stone, Kate. See: Holmes, Katherine Stone.

2631. Stone, Lucy, 1818-1893. American suffragist, abolitionist, and feminist. LOVING WARRIORS: SELECTED LETTERS OF LUCY STONE AND HENRY B. BLACKWELL, 1853-1893. Edited and introduced by Leslie Wheeler. New York: The Dial Press, 1981. 406p.

Letters selected to illuminate the various facets of both correspondents, their relationship with each other, and the times in which they lived. Since Stone's activities in the Suffrage Movement are not always well documented in her letters to Blackwell, these are supplemented with letters to Susan B. Anthony and others. Letters are divided into three sections: Courtship, 1853-1855; A Model Couple, 1855-1864; and Gray-Haired Champions, 1866-1893.

2632. ------. SOUL MATES: THE OBERLIN CORRESPONDENCE

OF LUCY STONE AND ANTOINETTE BROWN, 1846-1850. Edited by Carol Lesser and Marlene Merrill. Oberlin, Ohio: Oberlin College, 1983. 100p.

Correspondence with Antoinette Brown Blackwell (1825-1921).

2633. ------. FRIENDS AND SISTERS: LETTERS BETWEEN LUCY STONE AND ANTOINETTE BROWN BLACKWELL, 1846-1893. Edited by Carol Lasser and Marlene Deahl Merrill. Urbana: University of Illinois Press, 1987. 278p.

2634. Stopes, Marie C., 1880-1958. English birth control advocate. JOURNAL FROM JAPAN: A DAILY RECORD OF LIFE AS SEEN BY A SCIENTIST. London, Glasgow, etc.: Blackie & Son, 1910. 280p.

Stopes traveled to Japan because of a scientific interest in coal mines and the fossils they contain. She learned enough Japanese to get by, and kept a daily record of impressions of the people and culture of Japan, August 6, 1907--January 24, 1909.

2635. Storrow, Ann Gillam, b. 1784. American intellectual. LETTERS OF ANN GILLAM STORROW TO JARED SPARKS. Edited by Frances Bradshaw Blanshard. Northampton, Mass.: Department of History and Government of Smith College, 1921. 252p. (Smith College Studies in History Vol. 1, No. 3.)

Letters 1820-1857 to American minister, editor, and historian Jared Sparks, touching on literary and philosophical matters, gossip about the Cambridge and Boston social scenes, and Sparks' work.

2636. Storrs, Monica. English missionary to Canada. GOD'S GALLOPING GIRL: THE PEACE RIVER DIARIES OF MONICA STORRS, 1929-1931. Edited by W.L. Morton. Vancouver: University of British Columbia Press, 1979. 370p.

Presents only the first two years of Storrs's extensive diary; it was thought better to provide the complete text of a portion rather than extracts from the whole. Describes work in frontier Sunday Schools and other Church activities, and gives a detailed and vivid picture of life in pioneer British Columbia.

2637. Stowe, Harriet Beecher, 1811-1896. American author and reformer. SUNNY MEMORIES OF FOREIGN LANDS. Boston: Sampson, 1854. 2 vols.

Letters to friends written during a European tour, 1853-1854.

2638. ------. LIFE OF HARRIET BEECHER STOWE. COMPILED FROM HER LETTERS AND JOURNALS. By her son, Charles Edward Stowe. Boston: Houghton Mifflin, 1880, 1889. 530p. London: Sampson, Low, Marston, Searle & Rivington, 1889. 530p. Reprinted, Detroit: Gale Research Co., 1967.

2639. ------. LIFE AND LETTERS OF HARRIET BEECHER STOWE. Annie Adams Fields. Boston: Houghton Mifflin Co., 1897. 406p.

2640. ------. "Correspondence of Harriet Beecher Stowe and Elizabeth Barrett Browning." Hazel Harrod. UNIVERSITY OF TEXAS STUDIES IN ENGLISH 27:1 (June, 1948), 28-34.

Short essay points out the mutual interests of the two women, which ranged from anti-slavery to Spiritualism, and reprints a letter from Stowe to Browning, dated November 20, 1860.

2641. Straiton, Mrs. M. American. TWO LADY TRAMPS ABROAD. A COMPILATION OF LETTERS DESCRIPTIVE OF NEARLY A YEAR'S TRAVEL IN INDIA, ASIA MINOR, EGYPT, THE HOLY LAND, TURKEY, GREECE, ITALY, AUSTRIA, SWITZERLAND, FRANCE, ENGLAND, IRELAND AND SCOTLAND. BY TWO AMERICAN LADIES. Flushing, N.Y.: Evening Journal Press, 1881. 335p.

The two "lady tramps" are Mrs. Straighton and her daughter. Travel letters, January-November, 1880, describe a world tour.

2642. Strang, Ellen. American frontier settler. "Diary of a Young Girl: Grundy County to Correctionville, 1862." ANNALS OF IOWA 36 (Fall, 1962), 437-457

Quaker diary, November, 1862--April, 1863.

2643. Stravinsky, Vera. DEAREST BUBUSHKIN: THE CORRESPONDENCE OF IGOR AND VERA STRAVINSKY, 1921-1954, WITH EXCERPTS FROM VERA STRAVINSKY'S DIARIES, 1922-1971. Edited by Robert Craft. Translated from the Russian by Lucia Davidora. New York: Thames and Hudson, 1985. 239p.

2644. Stritecky, Marie. Czech Immigrant to South Dakota. "Life Anew for Czech Immigrants: The Letters of Marie and Vavrin Stritecky, 1913-1934." SOUTH DAKOTA HISTORY 11 (Fall/Winter, 1981), 253-304.

2645. Strong, Julia Barbard. American missionary. "A Missionary's Wife Looks at Missouri: Letters of Julia Barbard Strong. MISSOURI HISTORICAL REVIEW 47 (July, 1953), 329-346.

2646. Stuart, Louisa, Lady, 1757-1851. British letter writer and correspondent of Sir Walter Scott. (See item 294). LADY LOUISA STUART: SELECTIONS FROM HER MANUSCRIPTS. Edited by the Hon. James A. Home. Edinburgh: David Douglas, 1889. 308p. New York, London: Harper & Bros., 1899. 310p.

Includes correspondence with Sir Walter Scott, 1826-1830, Mrs. Lockhart, 1831, and Lady Mary Wortley Montagu, 1835 and 1837.

2647. ------. LETTERS OF LADY LOUISA STUART TO MISS LOUISA CLINTON. Edinburgh, D. Douglas, 1901-1903. 2 vols.

Letters 1817-1834.

2648. ------. THE LETTERS OF LADY LOUISA STUART. Selected, with an introduction, by R. Brimley Johnson. London: John Lane, n.d. [1926], and New York: Lincoln MacVeagh, the Dial Press, 1926. 274p.

2649. Suffolk, Henrietta Howard, Countess of, 1681-1767. English Lady In Waiting to Queen Caroline and secret mistress of George III. LETTERS TO AND FROM THE COUNTESS OF SUFFOLK AND HER SECOND HUSBAND THE HON. GEORGE BERKELEY, FROM 1712-1767. With historical, biographical and explanatory notes. London: John Murray, 1824. 2 vols.

2650. Sulzberger, Marina Ladas, 1919-1976. Greek wife of journalist C.L. Sulzberger. MARINA: LETTERS AND DIARIES OF MARINA SULZBERGER. Edited by C.L. Sulzberger. New York: Crown, 1978. 530p.

Describes travel, and of life in diplomatic, social and artistic circles around the world.

2651. Summers, Eliza Ann, 1844-1900. American teacher. "DEAR SISTER": LETTERS WRITTEN ON HILTON HEAD ISLAND, 1867. Edited by Josephine W. Martin. Beaufort, S.C.: Beaufort Book Co., 1977. 133p.

Account of work among freed slaves in "contraband" camps during the Civil War.

2652. Sumter, Nathalie de Delage, 1782-1841. American friend of Theodosia Burr. FIFTEEN LETTERS OF NATHALIE SUMTER. Edited, with an introduction and notations by Mary Virginia Saunders White. Columbia, S.C.: Printed for Gittman's Book Shop by R.L. Bryan Co., 1942. 124p.

2653. Sundon, Charlotte Clayton, Viscountess, d. 1742. English political figure and Lady In Waiting to Queen Caroline. MEMOIRS OF THE VISCOUNTESS SUNDON, MISTRESS OF THE ROBES TO QUEEN CAROLINE, CONSORT OF GEORGE III. INCLUDING LETTERS FROM THE MOST CELEBRATED PERSONS OF HER TIME. Mrs. Katherine Thomson. London: Henry Colburn, 1847. 2 vols.

Includes letters of the Viscountess Sundon, Sarah, Duchess of Marlborough, Henrietta Louisa, Countess of Pomfret, Lady Mary Lepel, and others.

2654. Suslova, Apollinariia Prokof'evna, 1840-1918.

Russian lover of Fyodor Dostoevsky. THE GAMBLER, WITH POLINA SUSLOVA'S DIARY. Feodor Dostoevsky. Edited by Edward Wasiolek. Translated by Victor Terras. Chicago: University of Chicago Press, 1972. 366p.

"The Gambler," a fictional account of Dostoevksy's obssession with gambling and of the turbulent and destructive affair with Suslova; followed by extracts from Suslova's diary, 1826-1866, chronicling their affair, and her fictional treatment of it, "The Stranger and Her Lover." Also includes selected correspondence, reproducing two of Suslova's letters.

2655. Sutherland, Millicent Fanny St. Clair-Erskine Sutherland-Levenson-Gower, Duchess of, b. 1867. SIX WEEKS AT THE WAR. Chicago: A.C. McClurg, 1915. 116p.

Account of relief work in Belgium during World War I. She joined a branch of the Red Cross, and set up the Millicent Sutherland Ambulance with the funding of women friends in England. Written from a diary and includes extracts from the original.

2656. Svendson, Gro Nilsdatter, 1840/41-1878. Norwegian-American frontier settler. FRONTIER MOTHER: THE LETTERS OF GRO SVENDSEN. Translated and edited by Pauline Farseth and Theodore C. Blegen. Northfield, Minn.: Norwegian-American Historical Association, 1950. 153p.

Svendson's letters from Iowa to relatives in Norway, 1861-1878. Describes frontier life and rural agriculture, and adjustment to new customs and language.

2657. Swain, Clara A., Dr., 1835-1910. American physician and missionary. A GLIMPSE OF INDIA: BEING A COLLECTION OF EXTRACTS FROM THE LETTERS OF DR. CLARA A. SWAIN, FIRST MEDICAL MISSIONARY TO INDIA OF THE WOMAN'S FOREIGN MISSIONARY SOCIETY OF THE METHODIST EPISCOPAL CHURCH IN AMERICA. New York: J. Pott & Co., 1909. 366p.

Describes thirty years of missionary work in India, helping to build hospitals, teaching nurses, training midwives, and other Church work.

2658. Swan, Annie S., 1859-1943. Scottish novelist, religious poet and journalist. THE LETTERS OF ANNIE S. SWAN. Edited by Mildred Robertson Nicoll. London: Hodder & Stoughton, 1945. 397p.

Letters 1894-1943.

2659. Swetchine, Sophia, Madame [Sofia Petrovna Soimonova Sviechina], 1782-1857. Russian author and Parisian salonist. LETTRES DE MADAME SWETCHINE. Publiée par le Comte de Falloux. Paris: Librarie Academique, Didier et Cie., Libraires-Editeurs, 1862. 2 vols.

Letters 1814-1856 to Madame Roxandre Stourdza, Comtesse Edling, Madame la Comtesse de Nesselrode, Madame la Princesse Alexis Galitzin, Madame la Duchesse de la Rochefoucauld, Madame la Comtesse de Mesnard, Madame Craven, and others.

2660. ------. CORRESPONDANCE DU R.P. LACORDAIRE ET DE MADAME SWETCHINE. Publiée par le Comte de Falloux. Paris: Didier et Cie., 1865. 584p. Paris: Perrin, 1886. Thirteenth edition, 1914. 576p.

Correspondence with Jean Baptiste Henri Dominique de Lacordaire.

2661. Swisshelm, Jane Grey Cannon, 1815-1844. American journalist and reformer. CRUSADER AND FEMINIST: LETTERS OF JANE GREY SWISSHELM. Edited by Arthur Larsen. St. Paul: Minnesota Historical Society, 1934. Reprinted by Hyperion Press, 1976. 327p.

Public letters, written to the ST. CLOUD DEMOCRAT, 1858-1865, dealing with conditions in Military base hospitals in and around Washington, D.C., where she worked as a nurse until the end of the Civil War.

2662. Szold, Henrietta, 1860-1945. American Zionist leader. LIFE AND LETTERS. Marvin Lowenthal. New York: The Viking Press, 1942. 350p.

Letters 1887-1941 deal with family life, a

European tour, Jewish community work and scholarship, work in Palestine with the American Zionist Medical Unit, her worry over the rise of Adolf Hitler, the formation of Youth Ailya and the "Children's Migration" from Germany to Palestine, and the Arab-Jewish War of 1936-1939.

2663. Tabbara, Lina Mikdadi. Lebanese. SURVIVRE DANS BEYROUTH. Avec la collaboration de Jean-Dominque Bauby. Paris: O. Orban, 1977. 286p.

Diary of an upperclass half-Palestinian woman caught in the Civil war in Beirut, 1977.

2664. ------. SURVIVAL IN BEIRUT: A DIARY OF CIVIL WAR. Translated from the French by Nadia Hijab. London: Onyx Press, 1979. 186p.

2665. Talma, Julie Carreau, 1756-1805. French. LETTRES DE JULIE TALMA À BENJAMIN CONSTANT. Publiées avec une introduction biographique et des notes par the Baronne Constant de Rebeque. Paris: Librarie Plon, 1933. 254p.

2666. Tallman, Cornelia Augusta, 1838?-1866?. American. "1860: The Last Year of Peace: Augusta Tallman's Diary." Rachel Salisbury. WISCONSIN MAGAZINE OF HISTORY 44 (Winter, 1961), 85-94.

2667. Taylor, Eliza Pierce, d. 1776. English heiress. THE LETTERS OF ELIZA PIERCE, 1751-1775, WITH LETTERS FROM HER SON, A SCHOOLBOY AT ETON. Edited by Violet M. MacDonald. London: F. Etchelle and H. MacDonald, 1927. 124p.

Letters to her son, and to Thomas Taylor, Esq., before their marriage, 1751-1752, and after their marriage to 1775.

2668. Taylor, Elizabeth, b. 1932. English actress. NIBBLES AND ME. Illustrated by the author. New York: Duell, Sloan and Pierce, 1946. 77p.

Diary written at age 13, about her pet chipmunk.

2669. Taylor, Hannah, ca.1784-1812. Irish Quaker. MEMOIR OF HANNAH TAYLOR. EXTRACTED FROM HER OWN MEMORANDUMS. York: W. Alexander, 1820. 168p.

Quaker diary, 1799-1810.

2670. Taylor, Jane, 1783-1824. English poet and children's hymnist. MEMOIRS, CORRESPONDENCE AND POETICAL REMAINS OF JANE TAYLOR. Edited by Isaac Taylor. London: Jackson & Walford, 1841. 329p.

2671. Taylor, Katherine Kressman. DIARY OF FLORENCE IN FLOOD. New York: Simon & Schuster, 1967. 192p.

Diary written during the 1966 flood that devastated the city of Florence and damaged or destroyed many of its art treasures. Includes a description of a Christmas celebration, presided over by the Pope, and of the slow work of cleaning and rebuilding.

2672. Taylor, Laurette, b. 1887. American actress. "THE GREATEST OF THESE": A DIARY WITH PORTRAITS OF THE PATRIOTIC ALL-STAR TOUR OF "OUT THERE." New York: George H. Doran Co., 1918. 61p.

Diary May-June, 1918, of an actress on tour to raise funds for Red Cross work.

2673. Taylor, Mary, 1817-1893. English author. MARY TAYLOR, FRIEND OF CHARLOTTE BRONTË: LETTERS FROM NEW ZEALAND AND ELSEWHERE. Edited, with narrative, notes and appendices by Joan Stevens. Dunedin: Auckland University Press and Oxford University Press, 1972. 192p.

Letters from school in Brussels and Germany, 1841-1845, and from New Zealand, 1845-1863. Includes a few letters to Ellen Nussey and to Mrs. Gaskell, with an appendix of Taylor's letters about Brontë written to Mrs. Gaskell, 1856-1857, reconstructed from Gaskell's LIFE OF CHARLOTTE BRONTË. Also includes letters from Taylor's sister, Martha Taylor, to Ellen Nussey, 1832.

2674. Taylor, Mary Geraldine Guinness. English

missionary to China. IN THE FAR EAST: LETTERS FROM GERALDINE GUINNESS IN CHINA. FROM THE MEDITERRANEAN TO THE PO YANG LAKE, CHINA, 1888-1889. Edited by her sister. London: Morgan & Scott, 1889. Third edition, re-cast and freshly illustrated, London: Morgan & Scott, 1901. 180p.

Account of missionary work in China by a daughter and wife of missionaries; religious reflections and exhortations. Profusely illustrated.

Taylor, Rachel Henning. See: Henning, Rachel.

2675. Tellier, Sarah Biddle. American. "Extracts from the Letters of Randolph and Sarah Biddle Tellier, 1789." Mrs. Clement A. Griscom. PENNSYLVANIA MAGAZINE OF HISTORY AND BIOGRAPHY 38:1 (1914), 100-109.

Extracts from letters written to family in America while traveling in Europe, January- October, 1789.

2676. Temple, Dorothy Osborne, Lady, 1627-1694. English letter writer and wife of British statesman Sir William Temple. LETTERS FROM DOROTHY OSBORNE TO SIR WILLIAM TEMPLE, 1652-1654. Edited by Edward Abbot Parry. London: Griffith Farran O'Keden & Welsh, 1888. 332p.

2677. ------. THE LOVE LETTERS OF DOROTHY OSBORNE TO SIR WILLIAM TEMPLE. Newly edited from the original manuscript by Israel Gollancz. London: A. Moring, the De La More Press, 1903. 364p.

2678. ------. THE LETTERS OF DOROTHY OSBORNE TO WILLIAM TEMPLE. Edited by permission of Sir Edward Parry and of his publishers Messrs. Sherrat and Hughes, Ltd., and Messrs. J.M. Dent and Sons, Ltd., by G.C. Moore Smith. London: Oxford at the Clarendon Press, 1928, 1929. 331p.

Includes a diary written by Osborne during their courtship, 1652-1654. William Temple's half of the correspondence was destroyed.

2679. Ten Boom, Corrie. CORRIE TEN BOOM'S PRISON

LETTERS. Old Tappan, N.J.: F. H. Revell Co., 1975. 90p.

Letters written from Scheveningen Prison, February 29--June 5, 1944, with commentary. Ten Boom's family was imprisoned during World War II for hiding Jewish refugees.

2680. Tennyson, Audrey Georgina Florence Boyle, 1854-1916. English wife of a Colonial Governor of Australia. AUDREY TENNYSON'S VICEREGAL DAYS: THE AUSTRALIAN LETTERS OF AUDREY, LADY TENNYSON TO HER MOTHER ZACYNTHA BOYLE, 1899-1903. Edited by Alexandra Hasluck. Canberra: National Library of Australia, 1978. 333p.

2681. Tennyson, Emily Sellwood Tennyson, Baroness, 1813-1896. English wife of Alfred, Lord Tennyson. THE LETTERS OF EMILY LADY TENNYSON. Edited, with an introduction by James O. Hoge. University Park: Pennsylvania State University Press, 1974. 404p.

Letters 1844-1896, from shortly before her marriage to a week before her death. Chiefly correspondence with her family, chosen to illuminate the Tennyson circle and the larger social and literary world of the period.

2682. ------. LADY TENNYSON'S JOURNAL. Edited, with an introduction by James O. Hoge. Charlottesville, Va.: The University Press of Virginia, 1981. 401p.

Diary 1850-1896. This version was condensed by Lady Tennyson from a number of earlier diaries and journals, of which none of the originals have survived. She compiled the Journal for her son Hallam for his biography of Sir William Tennyson, and it chiefly concerns him.

2683. Teresa of Avila, Saint, 1515-1582. THE LETTERS OF SAINT TERESA OF AVILA. Translated from the Spanish by Reverend John Dalton. London: T. Jones, 1853. Embellished with a facsimile of the Saint's handwriting. London: Catholic Publishing and Bookselling Co., 1860. 289p.

2684. ------. THE LETTERS OF SAINT TERESA OF AVILA. Complete edition. Translated from the Spanish and annotated by the Benedictines of Stanbrook. With an introduction by Cardinal Gasquet. London: Baker, 1912-1914. 4 vols.

2685. Teresa of Lisieux, Saint, 1873-1897. LETTRES DE SAINT THÉRÈSE DE L'ENFANT JESUS. Lisieux (Office Central de Lisieux) 1948. 472p.

2686. ------. COLLECTED LETTERS. Edited by the Abbe Combes. Translated by F.J. Sheed. Foreword by Father Vernon Johnson. New York: Sheed & Ward, 1949. 394p.

2687. Terry, Ellen, Dame, 1848-1928. English actress. ELLEN TERRY AND BERNARD SHAW: A CORRESPONDENCE. Edited by Christopher St. John. London: Constable, and New York: G.P. Putnam's Sons/Knickerbocker Press, 1931. 334p.

Letters 1892-1922 chronicle their careers in the theatre and their friendship, which was chiefly carried on through correspondence. Throws much light on the inner history of the London stage during their heydey.

2688. Thaxter, Celia Laighton, 1835-1894. American poet and hostess. LETTERS OF CELIA THAXTER. Edited by her friends A.F. and R.L. Boston and New York: Houghton Mifflin & Co., 1895. 232p.

Edited by Annie F. Fields and Rose Lamb.

2689. Therriault, Selma Crow, b. 1904? American. SOUTH-WEST RAMBLIN'S. Philadelphia: Dorrance & Co., 1978.

Travel diary written on trips to the American West and Southwest.

2690. Thilman, Elisa. American Negro slave and emmigrant to Liberia. "Letter from Liberia, 1848." Terry L. Alford. MISSISSIPPI QUARTERLY 22:2 (Spring, 1969), 150-151.

Letter dated May 11, 1848, by a slave emancipated

by Edward Brett Randolph of Columbus, Mississippi, who had converted to Methodism and decided slavery was against the tenets of Christianity. Makes references to her family, who were still living under slavery in the United States (they were not owned by Randolph); the death of a sister; her children; and religion.

2691. Thomas, Anna Hasell. American. "The Diary of Anna Hasell Thomas (July 1864--May 1865)." Edited by Charles E. Thomas. SOUTH CAROLINA HISTORICAL MAGAZINE 74:3 (July, 1973), 128-143.

Civil War diary of a native of South Carolina living in New York at the outbreak of the Civil War; she was granted presidential permission to visit South Carolina.

2692. Thomas, Martha Carey, 1857-1935. American educator; first Dean and second President of Bryn Mawr. THE MAKING OF A FEMINIST: EARLY JOURNALS AND LETTERS OF M. CAREY THOMAS. Marjorie Housepian Dobkin. With a foreword by Millicent Cary McIntosh. Kent, Ohio: The Kent State University Press, 1979. 314p.

Contains her childhood diary, her adult diary and letters written up to her appointment at Bryn Mawr, and an appendix of miscellaneous autobiographical writings.

2693. ------. THE PAPERS OF M. CAREY THOMAS IN THE BRYN MAWR COLLEGE ARCHIVES: REEL GUIDE AND INDEX TO THE MICROFILM. Compiled by Lucy Fisher West. Woodbridge, Conn.: Research Publications, 1982. Hard copy index, 359p.

2694. Thomas, Mary. English emigrant to Australia. THE DIARY AND LETTERS OF MARY THOMAS: BEING A RECORD OF THE EARLY DAYS OF SOUTH AUSTRALIA. 3rd ed. Edited by Evan Kyffin Thomas. Adelaide: W.K. Thomas & Son, 1925.

Diary and letters to her family in England describe life in South Australia, 1836-1866.

2695. Thompson, Dorothy, 1893-1961. American

journalist. DOROTHY AND RED. Vincent Sheean. Boston: Houghton Mifflin Co., 1973. 363p.

Biography based upon long extracts from Thompson's personal writing, including a diary of her struggle to come to terms with lesbian feelings for Christa Winsloe (p.207-242).

2696. Thompson, Harriet Jane Parsons, 1836-1897. American army wife. "Civil War Life: The Letters of Harriet Jane Parsons Thompson." Glenda Riley. ANNALS OF IOWA 44:3 (1978), 214-231; and 44:4 (1978), 296-314.

Letters to her husband, Union Major William G. Thompson, 1862. Riley notes that while William Thompson's letters were published, "Jane's poignant letters to him relating the trials and vicissitudes of a childless young wife" were almost forgotten.

2697. Thomson, Hannah. American colonist. "Letters of Hannah Thomson, 1785-1788." PENNSYLVANIA MAGAZINE OF HISTORY AND BIOGRAPHY 14:1 (1890), 28-40.

Letters by the wife of Charles Thomson, Secretary of Congress, addressed to John Mifflin of Philadelphia.

2698. Thoreau, Sophie E., d. 1876. SOME UNPUBLISHED LETTERS OF HENRY DAVID AND SOPHIE THOREAU: A CHAPTER IN THE HISTORY OF A STILL-BORN BOOK. Edited by Samuel Arthur Jones. Jamaica, Queensborough, N.Y.: Marion Press, 1899. 86p. Reprinted, New York: AMS Press, 1985. 86p.

2699. Thornton, Anna Maria Brodeau, 1775?-1805. American colonist and wife of architect William Thornton. "Diary of Mrs. William Thornton, 1800-1863." COLUMBIA HISTORICAL SOCIETY RECORDS 10 (1907), 88-226.

Extracts from her diary, 1800-1863. More of a record of her husband's activities than of her own.

2700. ------. "Diary of Mrs. William Thornton: Capture of Washington by the British." COLUMBIA HISTORICAL SOCIETY RECORDS 19 (1916), 172-182.

2701. Thrale, Hester Lynch Salusbury, later Piozzi, 1741-1821. English intellectual and literary figure. MRS. THRALE, AFTERWARDS MRS. PIOZZI: A SKETCH OF HER LIFE AND PASSAGES FROM HER DIARIES, LETTERS AND OTHER WRITINGS. Edited by L.B. Seeley. New York: 1891. 336p.

Biography and extracts from Thrale's private writings. Includes excerpts from the diary of Fanny Burney.

2702. ------. DOCTOR JOHNSON AND MRS. THRALE: INCLUDING MRS. THRALE'S UNPUBLISHED JOURNAL OF THE WELSH TOUR MADE IN 1774 AND MUCH HITHERTO UNPUBLISHED CORRESPONDENCE OF THE STREATHAM COTERIE. Alexander Meyrick Broadley. With an inroductory essay by Thomas Seccombe. London: John Lane, 1910. 338p.

2703. ------. MRS. PIOZZI'S THRALIANA, WITH NUMEROUS EXTRACTS HITHERTO UNPUBLISHED. London: Simpkin, 1913. 63p.

2704. ------. THE INTIMATE LETTERS OF HESTER PIOZZI AND PENELOPE PENNINGTON, 1788-1821. Edited by Oswald G. Knapp. London: John Lane, the Bodley Head; New York: John Lane Co.; and Toronto: Bell & Cockburn, 1914. 396p.

Penelope Sophia Weston Pennington was the leading spirit of "a knot of ingenious and charming females of Ludlow in Shropshire"; a Bluestocking, and friend of Anna Seward, Mrs. Siddons, and Fanny Burney. The letters date from just after Mrs. Thrale's second marriage to just before her death.

2705. ------. THE TRUE STORY OF THE SO-CALLED LOVE LETTERS OF MRS. PIOZZI. IN DEFENCE OF AN ELDERLY LADY. Percival Merritt. Cambridge, Mass.: Harvard University Press, 1927. 85p.

Discusses the letters of the eighty-year-old Piozzi to William Augustus Conway, a young actor who committed suicide in 1828. Merritt argues that the two were close friends, but that Piozzi was not infatuated with Conway.

2706. ------. THE LETTERS OF MRS. THRALE. Selected, with an introduction by R. Brimley Johnson. London: John Lane, 1926. 218p.

Selection from Thrale's correspondence, meant as an introduction to her work.

2707. ------. THE FRENCH JOURNALS OF MRS. THRALE AND DOCTOR JOHNSON. Edited from original manuscripts in the John Rylands Library in the British Museum, with an introduction and notes by Moses Tyson and Henry Guppy. Manchester, England: Manchester University Press, 1932. 274p.

2708. ------. THRALIANA: THE DIARY OF MRS. HESTER LYNCH THRALE, LATER MRS. PIOZZI, 1776-1809. Edited by Katherine C. Balderston. Published in cooperation with the Huntington Library. Oxford: The Clarendon Press, 1942. 2 vols.

2709. ------. THE LETTERS OF SAMUEL JOHNSON WITH MRS. THRALE'S GENUINE LETTERS TO HIM. Collected and edited by R.W. Chapman. Oxford: The Clarendon Press, 1952. 3 vols.

Volume 1: 1719-1774. Volume 2: 1775-1782. Volume 3: 1783-1784.

2710. ------. "Scrapbook of a Self: Mrs. Piozzi's Later Journals." Patricia Ann Meyer Spacks. HARVARD LITERARY BULLETIN 18 (1970), 221-247.

2711. ------. THE THRALES OF STREATHAM PARK. Edited by Mary Hyde. Cambridge, Mass.: Harvard University Press, 1977. 373p.

2712. ------. "Portrait of a Georgian Lady: The Letters of Hester Lynch Thrale Piozzi, 1784-1821." Edward A. Bloom, Lillian D. Bloom and Joan Klingel. JOHN RYLANDS UNIVERSITY LIBRARY OF MANCHESTER BULLETIN 60 (September, 1978), 303-338.

2713. Thurston, Lucy Goodale, 1795-1876. American

missionary to Hawaii. LIFE AND TIMES OF MRS. LUCY GOODALE THURSTON, WIFE OF REVEREND ASA THURSTON, PIONEER MISSIONARY TO THE SANDWICH ISLANDS. GATHERED FROM LETTERS AND JOURNALS EXTENDING OVER A PERIOD OF MORE THAN FIFTY YEARS. Selected and arranged by herself. Ann Arbor, Mich.: S.C. Andrews, 1934. 307p.

Thurston was called "The Mother" of Hawaiian missionaries. She went to Kailua with her husband, the Rev. Asa G. Thurston in 1820, and with him worked as a missionary there for forty-eight years.

2714. Tiernan, Lynn Carson. American rancher. "Journal of a Ranch Wife, 1932-1935." Edited by Helen Crosby Glenn. FRONTIER AND MIDLAND 19:4 (Summer, 1939), 258-276.

Records the daily life of a western couple, she from North Dakota, he from Montana, who married during the Depression.

2715. Tillich, Hannah. Wife of religious philosopher Paul Tillich. FROM TIME TO TIME. New York: Moffat, Yard and Co., 1912. New York: Stein and Day, 1973. 252p.

Autobiography comprised of journal extracts, poems, fragments, memoirs, parables and plays. Includes two chapters of extensive extracts from her journal: "Diary of a Witch," and "Trip to Italy (Excerpts)."

2716. ------. FROM PLACE TO PLACE. TRAVELS WITH PAUL TILLICH. TRAVELS WITHOUT PAUL TILLICH. New York: Stein and Day, 1976. 223p.

Autobiography comprised of poems, essays, plays, dreams, fantasies, and extracts from journals written in Egypt and Israel in 1963 with Paul Tillich; with Tillich in Japan in 1960; and alone in India and Southeast Asia, 1966; the Carribean Islands, 1967; Mexico, 1968; and Germany, 1971.

2717. Timms, Mary, 1808-1834. English Methodist. MEMOIRS OF THE LATE-MRS. MARY TIMMS. EXTRACTED FROM

HER DIARY AND LETTERS. Edited by Elija Morgan. Watchet, 1835.

Methodist diary and letters, 1818-1834.

2718. Tivy, Anna. Canadian frontier settler. YOUR LOVING ANNA: LETTERS FROM THE ONTARIO FRONTIER. Toronto: University of Toronto Press, 1972. 172p.

Letters to her family in England by a woman married to a man barely making a living as a logger and a railway builder.

2719. Todd, Mabel Loomis, 1856-1932. American biographer and relative of Emily Dickinson. AUSTIN AND MABEL: THE AMHERST AFFAIR AND LOVE LETTERS OF AUSTIN DICKINSON AND MABEL LOOMIS TODD. Polly Longsworth. New York: Farrar, Straus & Giroux, 1984. 499p.

2720. Todd, Martha Gaddis, 1873-1932. American author and Christian Scientist. LIFE AND LETTERS OF MARTHA GADDIS TODD. Written and edited by Arthur James Todd. Chicago: School of the Art Institute, 1940. 248p.

2721. Toklas, Alice Babette, 1877-1967. American author and intimate of Gertrude Stein. STAYING ON ALONE: LETTERS OF ALICE B. TOKLAS. Edited by Edward Burns. With an introduction by Gilbert A. Harrison. New York: Liveright Publishing Corp, 1973. 426p.

Selection concentrates on the last twenty years of her life, 1946-1966, chiefly because large portions of her earlier correspondence has been lost or destroyed. Letters were chosen for their biographical, literary, and artistic significance to Stein and her circle; that illustrate the catholicity of Toklas's friendships; that reveal the quality of her sensibility; and that delight for their description of everyday living.

2722. Tolstoy, Sophia (Sofia Andreevna Bers, Grafina Tolstaia), 1844-1919. Russian wife of author Leo Tolstoy. THE DIARY OF TOLSTOY'S WIFE, 1860-1891. Translated from the Russian by Alexander Werth. London: Victor Gollancz, 1928. 272p.

2723. ------. THE COUNTESS TOLSTOY'S LATER DIARIES, 1891-1897. Authorized translation from the Russian, with an introduction by Alexander Werth. London: Victor Gollancz, 1929. 267p. Reprinted, Freeport, N.Y.: Books for Libraries Press, 1971. 267p.

2724. ------. LA TRAGEDIE DE TOLSTOI ET DE SA FEMME, D'APRES LEUR CORRESPONDANCE ET LEURS "JOURNAL INTIME" INEDITS. E. Halperine-Kaminsky. Paris: A. Fayard et Cie., 1931. 365p.

2725. ------. THE FINAL STRUGGLE: BEING COUNTESS TOLSTOY'S DIARY FOR 1910. WITH EXTRACTS FROM LEO TOLSTOY'S DIARY FOR THE SAME PERIOD. Preface by S.L. Tolstoy, editor of the Russian edition. Translated, with an introduction by Aylmer Maude. New York: Oxford University Press, and London: Allen & Unwin, 1936. 407p.

2726. ------. THE DIARIES OF SOFIA TOLSTOY. Edited by O.A. Golinenko. Translated by Cathy Porter. With an introduction by R.F. Christian. London: Jonathan Cape, 1985. 1043p.

2727. Tolstoy, Tatyana [Tatiana L'ovna Tolstoia, later Sukhotina], 1864-1949. Russian daughter of Leo Tolstoy. THE TOLSTOY HOME: DIARIES OF TATYANA TOLSTOY. Translated by Alec Brown. London: Harvill Press, 1950, and New York: Columbia University Press, 1951. 352p.

2728. Tomlinson, Lucia Ruggles Holman, 1793-1886. American missionary to Hawaii. JOURNAL OF LUCIA RUGGLES HOLMAN. Honolulu, Hawaii: The Museum, 1931. 40p. (Bernice P. Bishop Museum Special Publication, 17).

Missionary diary.

2729. Tompkins, Ellen Wilkins. American. "The Colonel's Lady: Some Letters of Ellen Wilkins Tompkins, July-December, 1861." Edited by Ellen Wilkins Tompkins. VIRGINIA MAGAZINE OF HISTORY AND BIOGRAPHY 69:4 (1961), 387-419.

Civil War letters.

2730. Tompkins, Sarah Haight. American. THE RALSTON-FRY WEDDING; AND THE WEDDING JOURNEY TO YOSEMITE, MAY 20, 1858. FROM THE DIARY OF MISS SARAH HAIGHT (MRS. EDWARD TOMPKINS). Edited by Francis P. Farquhar. Berkeley, Calif.: Friends of the Bancroft Library, University of California, 1961. 24p.

2731. Torr, Maria Jackson, 1815-1846. English wife of John Smale Torr, a Managing Clerk to a firm of solicitors. LETTERS OF COURTSHIP BETWEEN JOHN TORR AND MARIA JACKSON, 1838-1843. Edited by E.F. Carritt. London: Oxford University Press, Humphrey Milford, 1933. 289p.

Love letters. The letters dated November 14, 1838--March 17, 1841, had been copied out in note books and nearly all the originals destroyed. However, they appear to be accurate transcriptions. The letters dated after 1841 are reprinted from originals.

2732. Towne, Laura Mathilda, 1825-1901. American educator of slaves freed after the Civil War. LETTERS AND DIARY OF LAURA M. TOWNE. WRITTEN FROM THE SEA ISLANDS OF SOUTH CAROLINA 1862-1884. Cambridge, Mass: The Riverside Press, 1912. 310p.

Towne volunteered as a teacher under the auspices of the Port Royal Relief Committee of Philadelphia. She later founded the Penn school, one of the earliest and long lived of Freedmen's schools, and one which followed an academic rather than a vocational curriculumn.

2733. Tracy, Eleanor Ethel, b. 1880. American teacher. SCHOOLMA'AM: STONE LAGOON, CALIFORNIA, 1903-1904. THE LETTERS OF ELEANOR ETHEL TRACY. Compiled and arranged by Harriet Tracy DeLong. Seattle: Artcraft Print Co., 1978. 77p.

2734. Trail, Florence, b. 1854. American novelist and critic. MY JOURNAL IN FOREIGN LANDS. Baltimore: Stork, 1884. 103p.

Journal of a European Tour undertaken in 1883.

2735. Traill, Catherine Parr Strickland, 1802-1899. English-Canadian novelist and natural history writer. THE BACKWOODS OF CANADA: BEING LETTERS FROM THE WIFE OF AN EMIGRANT OFFICER, ILLUSTRATIVE OF THE DOMESTIC ECONOMY OF BRITISH AMERICA. London: Knight, 1836. 352p.

Traill's letters to her mother, July 18, 1832--November 28, 1834, were published as a guide and a warning to prospective female emigrants to Canada. Describes hardships and joys of backwoods life.

2736. Trant, Clarissa Sandford Bramston, 1800-1844. English. THE JOURNAL OF CLARISSA TRANT, 1800-1832. Edited by Clara Georgina Ward. London: John Lane, 1925. 335p.

Autobiography, partly re-written from her early journal, a social diary 1823-1832, and letters to her brother, Thomas Abercrombie Trant, June-December, 1923. Details of love affairs (she had 12 suitors), friends met, books read, sermons heard; of sojourns in the South of France and in Ireland, and of social life in London.

2737. Trask, Sarah E. American shoebinder and seaman's wife. "I Am Doom to Disappointment: The Diaries of a Beverly, Massachusetts, Shoebinder, Sarah E. Trask, 1849-1851." Mary H. Blewett. ESSEX INSTITUTE HISTORICAL COLLECTIONS 117:3 (July, 1981), 192-212.

Diary of a woman who made a living as a shoebinder in the absence of her husband, who sailed from Massachusetts in January, 1849. An introduction places the diary into the context of working class life of the time, and compares diary to the middle class diaries studied by feminist scholars Nancy Cott and Caroll Smith-Rosenberg.

2738. Trefusis, Violet, 1894-1972. English novelist and lover of Vita Sackville-West. THE OTHER WOMAN: A LIFE OF VIOLET TREFUSIS. Boston: Houghton Mifflin Co., 1976. 256p.

Biography which includes previously unpublished

correspondence with Vita Sackville-West, 1918-1921, written at the height of their romance. Includes original French versions of the letters Trefusis wrote from Ceylon, 1910-1911, at the age of sixteen.

2739. Trench, Melesina Chenivix St. George, 1768-1827. English author. THE REMAINS OF THE LATE MRS. RICHARD TRENCH. BEING SELECTIONS FROM HER JOURNALS, LETTERS, AND OTHER PAPERS. Edited by her son, the Dean of Westminster. London: Parker, 1860. 525p. Revised second edition: London: Parker, Son, and Bourn, 1862. 525p.

After the death of her first husband, Richard St. George, Trench went into seclusion for ten years, after which she began traveling in Germany. Contains letters written to her second husband, Richard Trench, and extracts from a journal she kept in Germany.

2740. ------. JOURNAL KEPT DURING A VISIT TO GERMANY IN 1799, 1800. Edited by the Dean of Westminster. London: Savill and Edwards, Printers, 1861. 97p.

Social and travel diary. She met most of the notable people of the day, including Lord Nelson and Lady Hamilton, Lucien Bonaparte, and John Quincy Adams, and describes them in her journal.

2741. Trevelyan, Mary. I'LL WALK BESIDE YOU: LETTERS FROM BELGIUM, SEPTEMBER 1944-May 1945. London and New York: Longmans, Green, 1946. 111p.

Describes relief work during World War II.

2742. Trimmer, Sarah Kirby, 1741-1801. English author and friend of Samuel Johnson. SOME ACCOUNT OF THE LIFE AND WRITINGS OF MRS. TRIMMER WITH ORIGINAL LETTERS AND MEDITATIONS AND PRAYERS, SELECTED FROM HER JOURNAL. London: Printed by C.& J. Rivington for Law and Gilbert, 1814. 2 vols.

Daily self-examination inspired by the example of Samuel Johnson.

2743. Tristan, Flora, 1803-1844. French feminist. LETTRES/FLORA TRISTAN. Réunies, presentées et annotées par Stephane Michaud. Paris: Editions Seuil, 1980. 261p.

2744. ------. UNION OUVRIERE. SUIVIE DE LETTRES DE FLORA TRISTAN. Édition preparée par Daniel Armogathe et Jacques Grandjonc. Publiée avec le Concourse de Central National des Lettres. Paris: Des Femmes, 1986. 366p.

2745. Truitt, Anne. American artist. DAYBOOK: THE JOURNAL OF AN ARTIST. New York: Pantheon, 1983. Harmondsworth, Middlesex, England: Penguin Books, 1984. 225p. New York: Viking Press, 1986. 225p.

Artist's diary, 1974-1981, by a sculptor.

2746. ------. TURN: THE JOURNAL OF AN ARTIST. Harmondsworth, Middlesex, England; New York; Victoria, Australia; Markham, Ontario; and Auckland, New Zealand: Penguin Books, 1986. 214p.

Artist's diary, July 14, 1982--December 22, 1983. In this second volume, Truitt discusses DAYBOOK and how it differs from her usual work, sculpture. In contrast to her sculptures, which are unique, a book is common; there are 6,500 DAYBOOKS in the world. English is a "legible language"; by contrast she realizes how few people can read meaning in the "visual syntax" of art.

2747. Tsvetayeva, Marina, 1892-1941. Russian poet. BORIS PASTERNAK, MARINA TSVETAYEVA, RAINER MARIA RILKE: LETTERS, SUMMER, 1926. Translated by Margaret Wettlin and Walter Arndt. Edited by Yevgen Pasternak, Yelena Pasternak, and Konstantin M.A. Zadovsky. San Diego, New York, and London: Harcourt Brace Jovanovich, 1985. 251p.

Literary correspondence, 1926.

2748. Tucker, Charlotte Maria, 1821-1893. English religious author and missionary who wrote under the pseudonym "A.L.O.E." (A Lady of England). A LADY OF ENGLAND: THE LIFE AND LETTERS OF CHARLOTTE MARIA TUCKER. A. Gilmore. New York: Armstrong, 1895.

2749. Tucker, Mary Orne, 1775-1806. "Diary of Mary Orne Tucker." ESSEX INSTITUTE HISTORICAL COLLECTIONS 77 (1941), 306-338.

Social and domestic diary, 1802.

2750. Turchin, Nadine [Nedezhda Lvova Turcheninov], b. 1826. Russian emigrant to the United States and wife of Union General John Basil Turchin. "A Monotony Full of Sadness: The Diary of Nadine Turchin, May 1863--April 1864." Edited by Mary Ellen McElligott. JOURNAL OF THE ILLINOIS STATE HISTORICAL SOCIETY 70:1 (1977), 27-89.

The Turchins were Liberal aristocrats who fled Russia in 1856 in search of political freedom. Once in the U.S., John Turchin joined the Union Army, and Nadine accompanied him on the field with the Army of the Cumberland.

2751. Turnbull, Agnes Sligh, b. 1888. American author. DEAR ME: LEAVES FROM THE DIARY OF AGNES SLIGH TURNBULL. New York: Macmillan, 1941. 170p.

2752. Turner, Ethel Sybil, 1872-1958. Australian author. THE DIARIES OF ETHEL SYBIL TURNER. Compiled by Philippa Poole. Edited by Peita Royle. Sydney, N.Y.: Ure Smith, 1979. 288p.

2753. Twisleton, Ellen Dwight, 1828-1862. American society belle. LETTERS OF THE HON. MRS. EDWARD TWISLETON, WRITTEN TO HER FAMILY, 1852-1862. London: John Murray, 1928. 329p.

Letters to her sisters from England, where she went to live with her husband, English scholar Edward Twisleton. Describes English society and literary circles.

2754. Twiss, Ruth M. American teacher. MORNING, NOON, AND NIGHT: A TEACHER'S DIARY. Smithtown, N.Y.: Exposition Press, 1982. 67p.

2755. Tyndall, Mary. THE DIARY OF MARY TYNDALL, ONE OF THE EARLY QUAKERS. London: Hall and Co., 1876. 174p.

2756. Tyler, Gertrude Elizabeth, b. 1835. American. "A Schoolgirl's Impressions of Paris Under the Second Empire: Correspondence Between Gertude Tyler and Her Family, 1852-1854." In AMERICAN BACKLOGS: THE STORY OF GERTRUDE TYLER AND HER FAMILY, 1600-1860. Compiled by her daughter and her grandson, Mrs. Theodore Roosevelt and Kermit Roosevelt. New York and London: Charles Scribner's Sons, 1928. p.81-196.

Letters home from a finishing school in Paris to her family in Norwich, Connecticut.

2757. Tyler, Mary Hunt Palmer, 1775-1866. GRANDMOTHER TYLER'S BOOK: THE RECOLLECTIONS OF MARY PALMER TYLER (MRS. ROYALL TYLER), 1775- 1866. Edited by Frederick Tyler and Helen Tyler Brown. New York: G.P. Putnam's Sons, 1925.

2758. Ulrich, Mabel S., M.D. American physician. "A Doctor's Diary, 1904-1932." MS. MAGAZINE 1:1 (July, 1972), 11-14.

2759. Underhill, Evelyn, 1875-1941. English writer on Catholic theology and mysticism. THE LETTERS OF EVELYN UNDERHILL. Edited with an introduction by Charles Williams. London and New York: Longmans, Green and Co., 1943. 344p.

Letters 1899-1941 to friends and other authors chiefly concern religion and mysticism.

2760. Underwood, Edna Worthley. LETTERS FROM A PRAIRIE GARDEN. Boston: Marshall Jones Co., 1919. 165p.

Letters to an unnamed "famous artist" who visited the country town in which she lived and became acquainted with her.

2761. Undset, Sigrid, 1822-1949. Norwegian novelist. SIGRID UNDSET SKRIVER HJEM: EN VANDRING GJENNON EMIGRANTARENE I AMERIKA. Arne Skouen. Oslo: Aschehoug, 1982. 149p.

2762. ------. "Sigrid Undset's Letters to Hope Emily

Allen." Marlene Ciklamini. JOURNAL OF THE RUTGERS UNIVERSITY LIBRARY 33:1 (1969), 20-27.

Discusses letters to Medievalist Hope Emily Allen, which date from February, 1941--December, 1948, and chiefly concerns their mutual interest in Medieval Scandinavian literature.

2763. Urbino, Levina Buoncuore. American author. AN AMERICAN WOMAN IN EUROPE. THE JOURNAL OF TWO YEARS AND A HALF SOJOURN IN GERMANY, SWITZERLAND, FRANCE AND ITALY. Boston: Lee & Shepard, 1869. 388p.

Account of travels in Europe, 1866-1868, partly taken from her journal.

Ursins, Princesse des. See: Orsini, Anne Marie de la Tremoille Noirmoustier, Duchessa de Bracciano.

2764. Vallon, Annette, 1766-1841. Lover of William Wordsworth and mother of his daughter, Anne Caroline Wordsworth. WILLIAM WORDSWORTH AND ANNETTE VALLON. Emile Legouis. London and Toronto: J.M. Dent & Sons, and New York: E.P. Dutton & Co., 1922. 146p. Revised and enlarged edition, Hamden, Conn.: Archon Books, 1967. 176p.

Includes letters to William and Dorothy Wordsworth, 1793.

2765. Vanhomrigh, Esther, "Vanessa." Friend of Jonathan Swift. VANESSA AND HER CORRESPONDENCE WITH JONATHAN SWIFT. The Letters edited for the first time from the originals. With an introduction by A. Martin Freeman. Boston and New York: Houghton Mifflin Co., 1921. 216p.

Letters 1712-1722 reveal friendship on his side, some passion on hers.

2766. Van Rensselaer, Maria van Courtlandt, 1645-1689. American colonist and political figure. CORRESPONDENCE OF MARIA VAN RENSSELAER, 1669-1689. Translated and edited by A.J.F. Van Laer. Albany, N.Y.: The State University of New York Press, 1935. 206p.

Van Rensselaer was the wife of Jeremias van Rensselaer, Administrator of the Dutch Patroonship of Rensselaerswyck in New York. She was the Administrator and Treasurer of Rensselaerswyck from her husband's death in 1674 to 1687. Chiefly correspondence with her husband's younger brother, Richard van Rensselaer, in regard to the administration of the Patroonship, with some letters to Stephanus van Courtlandt and other members of the van Courtlandt family.

2767. Van Vorst, Marie. American. WAR LETTERS OF AN AMERICAN WOMAN. New York: John Lane Co., 1916. 352p.

Letters July 15, 1914--November 3, 1915. She was in Italy when War was declared, and stayed, working with the American Ambulance at Neuilly.

2768. Vassilieff, Elizabeth Sutton. Australian peace worker. PEKING--MOSCOW LETTERS: ABOUT A FOUR MONTH'S JOURNEY, TO AND FROM VIENNA, BY WAY OF PEOPLE'S CHINA AND THE SOVIET UNION. Melbourne: Australasian Book Society, 1953. 295p.

Vasillieff attended the Congress of Peoples for Peace in Vienna as a delegate from the Australian Peace Council and as an observer for the Fellowship of Australian Writers. She traveled through China as a guest of the China Peace Committee and through the Soviet Union as a private tourist.

2769. Vaughn, Elizabeth, 1905-1957. American. THE ORDEAL OF ELIZABETH VAUGHN: A WARTIME DIARY OF THE PHILIPPINES. Edited by Carol M. Petillo. Athens, Ga.: University of Georgia Press, 1985. 312p.

2770. Vernon, Lorraine, b. 1921. Canadian poet. MASTECTOMY: AN APRIL JOURNAL. Sooke, British Columbia: Fireweed Press, 1980.

2771. Vichy, Diane de. UN HIVER EN PROVENCE: LETTRES

DE DIANE DE VICHY À SES ENFANTS, 1767-1787. Texte établi d'après les manuscrits originaux avec une introduction, un index, des annexes et des notes par Jean Noel Pascal. Saint-Étienne: Universite, 1980. 200p.

2772. Victoria, Queen of Great Britain, 1819-1901. LEAVES FROM THE JOURNAL OF OUR LIFE IN THE HIGHLANDS FROM 1848 TO 1861. TO WHICH ARE PREFIXED AND ADDED EXTRACTS FROM THE SAME JOURNAL GIVING AN ACCOUNT OF EARLIER VISITS TO SCOTLAND AND TOURS IN ENGLAND AND IRELAND AND YACHTING EXCURSIONS. Edited by Arthur Phelps. London: Smith, Elder; and New York: Harper & Row, 1868. 315p.

2773. ------. MORE LEAVES FROM THE JOURNAL IN THE HIGHLANDS, FROM 1862-1882. London: Smith, Elder, 1884. 404p. New York: N.Y.R. Worthington, 1884. 185p.

2774. ------. THE LETTERS OF QUEEN VICTORIA: A SELECTION OF HER MAJESTY'S CORRESPONDENCE BETWEEN THE YEARS 1837 AND 1861. Edited by Arthur Christopher Benson, M.A. and Viscount Esher. Published by Authority of His Majesty the King. London: John Murray, 1907. 3 vols.

2775. ------. THE GIRLHOOD OF QUEEN VICTORIA: A SELECTION FROM HER MAJESTY'S DIARIES, BETWEEN THE YEARS 1832 AND 1840. Edited by Viscount Esher. Published by authority of His Majesty the King. London: John Murray, 1912. 2 vols.

2776. ------. THE TRAINING OF A SOVEREIGN: AN ABRIDGED SELECTION FROM "THE GIRLHOOD OF QUEEN VICTORIA," BEING HER MAJESTY'S DIARIES BETWEEN THE YEARS 1832 AND 1840. Published by authority of His Majesty the King. Edited by Viscount Esher. New York: Longmans, Green & Co., and London: John Murray, 1914. 354p.

2777. ------. THE LETTERS OF QUEEN VICTORIA, SECOND SERIES. A SELECTION FROM HER MAJESTY'S CORRESPONDENCE AND JOURNAL BETWEEN THE YEARS 1862 AND 1878. Edited by George Earle Buckle. Published by authority of His Majesty the King. London: John Murray, 1926-1928. 3 vols.

2778. ------. THE LETTERS OF QUEEN VICTORIA, THIRD

SERIES. A SELECTION FROM HER MAJESTY'S CORRESPONDENCE AND JOURNAL BETWEEN 1886 AND 1901. Edited by George Earle Buckle. Published by authority of His Majesty the King. London: John Murray, 1930-1932. 3 vols.

2779. ------. THE QUEEN AND MR. GLADSTONE. Philip Guedalla. Garden City, N.Y.: Doubleday Doran and Co., 1934. 793p.

Selection of 1500 letters and telegrams exchanged between Queen Victoria and her Prime Minister, 1845-1897.

2780. ------. LETTERS OF QUEEN VICTORIA. FROM THE ARCHIVES OF THE HOUSE OF BRANDENBURG-PRUSSIA. Translated from the German by Mrs. J. Pudney and Lord Sudley. Edited by Hector Bolitho. New Haven, Conn.: Yale University Press, 1938. 203p.

Over two hundred previously unpublished letters preserved in the Charlottenburg Archives, by Queen Victoria to members of the Prussian Royal Family, 1841-1889.

2781. ------. REGINA VS. PALMERSTON: THE CORRESPONDENCE BETWEEN QUEEN VICTORIA AND HER FOREIGN AND PRIME MINISTER, 1837-1865. Edited by Brian Connell. Garden City, N.Y.: Doubleday & Co., 1961. 404p.

Correspondence with Henry John Temple, 3rd Viscount Palmerston.

2782. ------. QUEEN VICTORIA: EARLY LETTERS. Edited by John Raymond. Revised edition. New York: Macmillan Co., 1963. 310p.

2783. ------. DEAREST CHILD: LETTERS BETWEEN QUEEN VICTORIA AND THE PRINCESS ROYAL, 1858-1861. Edited by Roger Fulford. New York: Holt, Rinehart Winston, 1964. 401p.

Selection from the correspondence. The letters of both women are frank, even blunt, and deal with intimate matters concerning the Royal Family. The Empress

Frederick, along with the Queen's other children, was not happy with the publication of the Queen's journals, as she felt it revealed too much about them as children. Most of the letters in the Fulford volumes have not been previously published, although a few appear in editions of Queen Victoria's letters and some of the Empress Frederick's appeared in the Ponsonby editions.

2784. ------. DEAREST MAMA: LETTERS BETWEEN QUEEN VICTORIA AND THE CROWN PRINCESS OF PRUSSIA, 1861-1864. Edited by Roger Fulford. New York: Holt, Rinehart and Winston, 1968. 372p.

Further selections from the correspondence of Queen Victoria and the Empress Frederick.

2785. ------. DEAR AND HONORED LADY: THE CORRESPONDENCE BETWEEN QUEEN VICTORIA AND ALFRED TENNYSON. Edited by Hope Dyson and Charles Tennyson. London: Macmillan, 1969. 152p.

2786. ------. VICTORIA TRAVELS: JOURNEYS OF QUEEN VICTORIA BETWEEN 1830 AND 1900, WITH EXTRACTS FROM HER JOURNAL. London: Frederick Muller, 1970. 383p.

2787. ------. YOUR DEAR LETTER: PRIVATE CORRESPONDENCE OF QUEEN VICTORIA AND THE CROWN PRINCESS OF PRUSSIA, 1865-1871. Edited by Roger Fulford. New York: Charles Scribner's Sons, 1971. 346p.

2788. ------. ADVICE TO A GRANDDAUGHTER: LETTERS FROM QUEEN VICTORIA TO PRINCESS VICTORIA OF HESSE. Selected with a commentary by Richard Hough. With a foreword by the Princess's grand-daughter, the Lady Brabourne. London: Heinemann, 1975. 156p.

Letters 1870-1900 to Princess Victoria of Hesse (1863-1950).

2789. ------. DARLING CHILD: PRIVATE CORRESPONDENCE OF QUEEN VICTORIA AND THE CROWN PRINCESS OF PRUSSIA, 1871-1868. Edited by Roger Fulford. London, Evans, 1976. 307p.

2790. ------. VICTORIA IN THE HIGHLANDS: THE PERSONAL JOURNAL OF HER MAJESTY QUEEN VICTORIA. With notes, introductions and a description of the acquisition and rebuilding of Balmoral Castle, by David Duff. London: Frederick Muller, 1968. Revised edition, Exeter, Great Britain: Webb and Bower, 1981. 240p.

2791. ------. LIFE AT THE COURT OF QUEEN VICTORIA, 1861-1901. ILLUSTRATED FROM THE COLLECTION OF LORD EDWARD PELHAM-CLINTON, MASTER OF THE HOUSEHOLD; WITH SELECTIONS FROM THE JOURNALS OF QUEEN VICTORIA. Edited and with additional material by Barry St. John Nevill. Exeter, England: Webb & Bower, 1984. 224p.

2792. ------. QUEEN VICTORIA IN HER LETTERS AND JOURNALS. A selection by Christopher Hibbert. London: John Murray, 1984. 374p. New York: Viking Press, 1985. 374p.

2793. Victoria Adelaide Mary Louisa, Consort of Friedrich II, German Emperor, better known as the Empress Frederick, 1840-1901. First child of Queen Victoria and Prince Albert. LETTERS OF THE EMPRESS FREDERICK. Edited by the Right Honourable Sir Frederick Ponsonby. London: Macmillan & Co., 1929. 492p.

Biography comprised of letters, with accompanying commentary. The letters were written from Prussia, chiefly to Queen Victoria.

2794. ------. BRIEFE DER KAISERIN. Herausgegeben von Sir Frederick Ponsonby, eingeleitet von Wilhelm II. Berlin: Verlag fur Kulturpolitic, 1929. 516p.

2795. ------. THE EMPRESS FREDERICK WRITES TO SOPHIE, HER DAUGHTER, CROWN PRINCESS AND LATER QUEEN OF THE HELLENES: LETTERS, 1889-1901. Edited by Arthur Gold Lee, with an introduction by Her Majesty, Queen Helen, Queen Mother of Rumania. London: Faber & Faber, 1955. 360p.

Correspondence with Sophie, Consort of Constantine I, King of the Hellenes (1870-1932).

2796. Victoria, Princess of Prussia, 1866-1929. QUEEN VICTORIA AT WINDSOR AND BALMORAL: LETTERS FROM HER GRAND-DAUGHTER, PRINCESS VICTORIA OF PRUSSIA, JUNE, 1889. Edited by James Pope-Hennessy. Drawings by Lynton Lamb. London: Allen & Unwin, 1959. 103p.

Letters to the Empress Frederick.

2797. Vigdorova, Frida Abramovna. Russian teacher and pedagogue. DIARY OF A RUSSIAN SCHOOLTEACHER. Translated from the Russian by Rose Prokofieva. New York: The Grove Press, 1960. 256p.

Fictional diary of a composite teacher Vigdorova calls Marian Nikolayevna. Vigdorova taught in Magnitogorsk, and during the first years of teaching she kept a diary, upon which this work is based.

2798. Villars, Marie Gigault de Bellefonds, Marquise de, 1624-1706. LETTRES DE MADAME LA MARQUISE DE VILLARS, AMBASSADRICE EN ESPAGNE, DANS LE TEMPS DU MARRIAGE DE CHARLES II, ROI D'ESPAGNE, AVEC LA PRINCESSE MARIE-LOUISE D'ORLEANS. Amsterdam and Paris: Chez M. Lambert, 1759.

2799. Vining, Elizabeth Gray, b. 1902. American author. BEING SEVENTY: THE MEASURE OF A YEAR. New York: Viking Press, 1978. 194p.

2800. Viva. American actress and author, former Andy Warhol star. "Viva's Diary." MS. MAGAZINE 1:11 (May, 1973), 52-55, 104-105.

Diary of a trip to a suburban Midwest community to visit friends.

2801. Vodges, Ada Adams. American Army wife. "The Journal of Ada Vodges, 1868-1871." Donald K. Adams. MONTANA: THE MAGAZINE OF WESTERN HISTORY 13:3 (Summer, 1963), 2-17.

Wife of Anthony Wayne Vodges, a Lieutenent in the U.S. Army stationed at Fort Laramie and Fort Fetterman,

Wyoming. The subtitle on the contents page reads: "A sensitive young Army wife recorded her fears, feelings of desolation, wounded sensibilities, and growing fascination with life at Wyoming's frontier military posts, Laramie and Fetterman."

2802. Vulliez, Gabrielle, 1890-1970. LA TRISTESSE D'UN AUTOMNE SANS ÉTÉ: CORRESPONDANCE DE GABRIELLE VULLIEZ AVEC ANDRÉ GIDE ET PAUL CLAUDEL (1923-1931). Wanda Vulliez. Bron: Centre d'Études Gidiennes, Universite Lyon II, 1981. 74p.

2803. Waddington, Mary Alsop King, d. 1923. English wife of French diplomat and Premier William Henry Waddington. LETTERS OF A DIPLOMAT'S WIFE, 1883-1900. New York: Charles Scribner's Sons, 1904. 417p.

In 1883, her husband was appointed Ambassador Extraordinary to Russia, and she accompanied him to Moscow. Letters describe diplomatic and social circles in London and Moscow.

2804. ------. ITALIAN LETTERS OF A DIPLOMAT'S WIFE: JANUARY-MAY, 1880, FEBRUARY-APRIL, 1905. New York: Charles Scribner's Sons, 1905. 324p.

Describes two pleasure trips to Rome.

2805. ------. MY WAR DIARY. New York: Charles Scribner's Sons, 1917. 373p. London: John Murray, 1918. 364p.

Diary in the form of letters written during World War I, chiefly from Paris and Mareuil, August, 1914--February, 1916.

2806. Waerenskjold, Elise Amelie Trede, 1815-1895. Norwegian emigrant to the United States. LADY WITH THE PEN: ELISE WAERENSKJOLD IN TEXAS. Edited by C.A. Clavsen. Foreword by Theodore C. Blegen. Northfield, Minn.: Norwegian-American Historical Association, 1961. 183p.

Letters 1851-1895.

2807. Wagner, Cosima Liszt de Bulow, 1837-1930. German composer and wife of Richard Wagner. COSIMA WAGNERS BRIEFE AN IHRE TOCHTER DANIELA VON BULOW, 1866-1885, NEBST 5 BRIEFEN RICHARD WAGNERS. Herausgegeben von Max Freiherrn von Waldberg. Stuttgart und Berlin: Cotta, 1933. 376p.

Correspondence with Daniela Thode-von Bulow (b.1860).

2808. ------. COSIMA WAGNER UND HOUSTON STEWART CHAMBERLAIN IM BRIEFWECHSEL 1888-1908. Herausgegeben von Paul Pretzsch. Leipzig: P. Reclam jun., 1934. 713p.

2809. ------. BRIEFWECHSEL ZWISCHEN COSIMA WAGNER UN FURST ERNST ZU HOHENLOHE-LANGENBURG. Stuttgart: Cotta, 1937. 403p.

Letters 1891-1923.

2810. ------. COSIMA WAGNER: BRIEFE AN LUDWIG SCHEMANN. Herausgegeben von Bertha Schemann. Regensburgh: G. Bosse, 1937. 84p.

2811. ------. LETTRES À JUDITH GAUTIER PAR RICHARD AND COSIMA WAGNER. Presentées et annotées par Léon Guichard. Paris: Gallimard, 1964. 382p.

Correspondence with Judith Gautier (1846-1917).

2812. ------. DIE BRIEFE AN FRIEDRICH NIETZSCHE. Herausgegeben von Erhart Thierbach. Weimar: Nietzsche-Archiv, 1938-1942. 3 vols. Reprinted, Nendeln, Liechtenstein: Kraus Reprint, 1975. 3 vols. in 1.

2813. ------. DIE TAGEBÜCHER. Herausgegeben und kommentiert von Martin Gregor-Dellin und Dietrich Mack. Munchen und Zurich: Piper, 1976-1977. 2 vols.

Diary 1869-1883.

2814. ------. COSIMA WAGNER--RICHARD STRAUS: EIN BRIEFWECHSEL. Herausgegeben von Gabrielle Strauss. Tutzig: H. Schneider, 1978. 312p.

2815. ------. COSIMA WAGNER'S DIARIES. Edited and annotated by Martin Gregor-Dellin and Dietrich Mack. Translated and with an introduction by Geoffrey Skelton. New York: Harcourt Brace Jovanovich, 1978-1980. 2 vols.

Diaries 1869-1883.

2816. ------. DAS ZWEITE LEBEN: BRIEFE UND AUFZEICH-NÜNGEN, 1883-1930. Herausgegeben von Dietrich Mack. Munchen, Zurich: Piper, 1980. 897p.

2817. Walker, Dora M. WITH THE LOST GENERATION, 1915-1919: FROM A V.A.D.'S DIARY. Hull, England: A Brown & Sons, 1970. 36p.

World War I diary by a member of England's Voluntary Aid Detachment.

2818. Walker, Georgiana Freeman Gholson, 1833-1904. PRIVATE JOURNAL, 1862-1865, WITH SELECTIONS FROM THE POST-WAR YEARS, 1865-1876. Edited by Dwight Franklin Henderson. Tuscaloosa, Ala.: Confederate Publishing Co., 1963. 148p. Limited edition of 450 copies.

Confederate Civil War diary.

2819. Walker, Mary Richardson, 1811-1897. American frontier missionary and wife of missionary Elkanah Richardson. THE DIARY OF MARY RICHARDSON WALKER, JUNE 10--DECEMBER 21, 1838. Edited by Rufus A. Coleman. Missoula: State University of Montana, 1931. 19p.

2820. ------. ELKANAH AND MARY WALKER: PIONEERS AMONG THE SPOKANES. Clifford Merrill Drury. Caldwell, Idaho: The Caxton Printers, 1940. 283p.

2821. ------. MARY RICHARDSON WALKER: HER BOOK. THE THIRD WHITE WOMAN TO CROSS THE ROCKIES. Edited by Ruth Karr McKee. Caldwell, Idaho: Caxton Printers, 1945. 357p.

Diary 1833-1848, with added biographical information, later reminiscences, and letters.

2822. ------. THE OREGON MISSIONS AS SHOWN IN THE WALKER LETTERS, 1839-1851. Edited by Paul C. Phillips and W.S. Lewis. Missoula, Mont.: State University of Montana, n.d.? 18p.

2823. ------. "Wilderness Diaries: A Missionary Couple in the Pacific Northwest, 1839-1848." Clifford M. Drury. AMERICAN WEST 13:6 (1976), 4-9, 62-63.

Based on Drury's previous publication of Walker's diary.

2824. Walters, Madge Hardin Smith. American. EARLY DAYS AND INDIAN WAYS: THE JOURNAL OF MADGE HARDIN WALTERS. With an introduction by M.R. Harrington. Los Angeles: Westernlore Press, 1956. 254p. (Great West and Indian Series, 5.)

2825. Wander, Marie. Austrian author. TAGEBUCHER UND BRIEFE. Herausgegeben von Fred Wander. Berlin: Aufbau-Verlag, 1981. 244p.

2826. Ward, Frances Elizabeth, b. 1836. American frontier settler. FRANKIE'S JOURNAL, BY FRANCES ELIZABETH WARD, DAUGHTER OF THE PRAIRIE SCHOONER LADY. Presented by Florence Stark DeWitt. Los Angeles: Westernlore Press, 1960. 67p.

Overland diary.

2827. Ward, Harriet Sherrill, 1803-1865. American frontier settler. PRAIRIE SCHOONER LADY: THE JOURNAL OF HARRIET WARD, 1853. As Presented by Ward G. DeWitt and Florence Stark DeWitt. Los Angeles: Westernlore Press, 1959. 180p.

Overland diary, April 20--October 9, 1853, written on the journey from Ohio to California.

2828. Ward, Mrs. Humphrey [Mary Augusta Arnold], 1851-1920. English author. ENGLAND'S EFFORT: LETTERS TO AN AMERICAN FRIEND. With a preface by Joseph H. Choate. New York: Charles Scribner's Sons, 1916. 183p.

2829. ------. TOWARDS THE GOAL. With an introduction by the Hon. Theodore Roosevelt. London: John Murray, 1917. 246p. New York: Charles Scribner's Sons, 1918. 231p.

2830. Warder, Ann Head, 1758-1829. American Quaker colonist. "Extracts from the Diary of Mrs. Ann Warder." Edited by Sarah Cadbury. PENNSYLVANIA MAGAZINE OF HISTORY AND BIOGRAPHY 17 (1893), 444-461 and 18 (1894), 51-63.

She married Philadelphia Quaker and shipping merchant John Warder in London, 1776 and returned with him to the United States. Social and domestic diary June, 1776--October, 1778 describes life in Philadelphia.

2831. Waring, Malvina Black Gist. American. "A Confederate Girl's Diary." In SOUTH CAROLINA WOMEN IN THE CONFEDERACY. Records collected By Mrs. A.T. Smythe, Miss M.B. Poppenheim, and Mrs. Thomas Taylor. Edited and published by Mrs. Thomas Taylor, Mrs. A.T. Smythe, and Miss. M.B. Poppenheim. Columbia, S.C.: State Committee, Daughters of the Confederacy, Columbia, S.C. and The State Co., 1903-1907. 2 vols. Reprinted in microfiche, Ann Arbor: University Microfilms International, 1982. 8 fiches (11x15cm). Vol.1, p. 272-288.

2832. Waring, Mary, 1760-1805. English Quaker. A DIARY OF THE RELIGIOUS EXPERIENCE OF MARY WARING, DAUGHTER OF ELIJAH AND SARAH WARING, LATE OF GODALMING. London: Printed and Sold by W. Phillips, 1809. 275p.

Quaker diary, 1791-1805.

2833. Warner, Agnes. American. MY BELOVED POILUS. St. John, N.B.: Barnes, 1917. 123p. Reprinted in microfilm, Ann Arbor, Mich.: University Microfilms International, 1982. 2 fiches (11x15cm.)

Letters of an American nurse working with an Army ambulance in France during World War I, 1914, published without her knowledge by her friends in order to raise money to help her continue her work.

2834. Warner, Luna. E., later Lewis. American frontier settler. "The Diary of Luna E. Warner: A Kansas Teenager of the Early 1870's." Edited by Venola Lewis Bivans. KANSAS HISTORICAL QUARTERLY 35:3 (1969), 276-311; and 35:4 (1969), 411-441.

Extracts from a diary, February, 1871--December, 1872, written by a teenage girl living on the Kansas frontier.

2835. Warner, Susan Bogert, "Elizabeth Wetherell," 1819-1885. American author. SUSAN WARNER ("ELIZABETH WETHERELL"). By Anna B. Warner. New York and London: G.P. Putnam's Sons/Knickerbocker Press, 1909. 509p.

Biography comprised of letters and journal extracts.

2836. ------. LETTERS AND MEMORIES OF SUSAN AND ANNA BARTLETT WARNER. Edited by Olivia Eggleston Phelps Stokes. New York and London: G.P. Putnam's Sons, 1925. 229p.

Includes letters between Susan Warner and her sister, American author Anna B. Warner (1827-1915).

2837. Warner, Sylvia Townsend, b. 1893. English author, poet, and biographer. SYLVIA TOWNSEND WARNER: LETTERS. Edited by William Maxwell. New York: Viking: 1982. 311p.

Literary letters, 1921-1978 to David Garnett, William Maxwell, Jean Stair Untermeyer, Nancy Cunard, and others. Respecting Warner's wishes, her love letters to her lifelong companion, Valentine Ackland, have been omitted.

2838. Warren, Eliza Spaulding, 1837-1919. American missionary. MEMOIRS OF THE WEST: THE SPAULDINGS. By Eliza Spaulding Warren. Portland, Ore.: Press of the Marsh Printing Co., 1916(?). 153p.

Includes extracts from her diary.

2839. Warren, Mercy Otis, 1728-1815. American poet, political satirist and historian. CORRESPONDENCE BETWEEN JOHN ADAMS AND MERCY OTIS WARREN RELATING TO HER HISTORY OF THE AMERICAN REVOLUTION, JULY-AUGUST 1807. New York: Arno Press, 1972. 202p.

2840. ------. "THE WARREN-ADAMS LETTERS. Massachusetts Historical Society Collections 72 (1917), and 73 (1925). 2 vols.

Letters between Mercy Otis Warren and John and Abigail Adams. Includes letters of Martha Washington and Hannah Winthrop.

2841. Warwick, Mary Boyle Rich, Countess of, 1625-1678. Irish. MEMOIR OF LADY WARWICK. ALSO HER DIARY FROM A.D. 1666 TO 1672, NOW FIRST PUBLISHED, TO WHICH ARE ADDED: EXTRACTS FROM HER OTHER WRITINGS. London: Religious Tract Society, 1847. 320p.

Includes extracts from a religious diary, July, 1666--May, 1669, and November, 1669--March, 1673.

2842. Washington, Ella. American Civil War diarist. "An Army of Devils: The Diary of Ella Washington." Edited by James O. Hall. CIVIL WAR TIMES ILLUSTRATED 16:10 (1978), 18-25.

Confederate diary May 27--June 13, 1864, written at her family plantation in Hanover County, Virginia.

2843. Washington, Martha Dandridge Custus, 1731-1802. American wife of U.S. President George Washington. "A Martha Washington Letter." THE MOUNT VERNON LADIES ASSOCIATION OF THE UNION, ANNUAL REPORT (1944), 18-19.

Letter to Fanny Bassett Washington, June 2, 1793.

2844. ------. "Three Letters of Martha Washington." THE MOUNT VERNON LADIES ASSOCIATION OF THE UNION, ANNUAL REPORT (1950), 32-36.

One undated, unaddressed letter, probably to a

neighbor and written before the American Revolution; and two letters to her niece Fanny Bassett, August 7, 1784, and March 2, 1794.

2845. ------. "A Martha Washington Letter." THE MOUNT VERNON LADIES ASSOCIATION OF THE UNION, ANNUAL REPORT (1966), 17-18.

Letter dated June 22, 1784 to her sister-in-law, Hannah Bushrod Washington.

2846. ------. "A Martha Washington Letter." THE MOUNT VERNON LADIES ASSOCIATION OF THE UNION, ANNUAL REPORT (1972), 34-35.

Letter dated March 19, 1778, to her son, John Park Custis and his wife, Eleanor Custis, giving news and chiding them for not writing more often.

2847. ------. "My Dear Fanny." THE MOUNT VERNON LADIES ASSOCIATION OF THE UNION, ANNUAL REPORT (1978), 29+.

Two letters to Fanny Bassett dated February 3, 1793 and February 10, 1793.

2848. ------. "A Martha Washington Letter." THE MOUNT VERNON LADIES ASSOCIATION OF THE UNION, ANNUAL REPORT (1974), 18-20.

Letter to her sister, Anna Maria Dandridge Bassett. The editors note: "The Association has long had the policy of printing the texts of newly discovered letters of Martha Washington. There has been no other known systematic attempt to publish her writings which are so rich in the details of domestic life."

2849. ------. "Mrs. Washington Writes to Her Sister." THE MOUNT VERNON LADIES ASSOCIATION OF THE UNION, ANNUAL REPORT (1975), 24-25

Letter to Anna Maria Dandridge Bassett, dated April 6, 1762.

2850. Waters, Lydia Milner. American frontier settler. "A Trip Across the Plains in 1855." QUARTERLY OF THE SOCIETY OF CALIFORNIA PIONEERS 6 (June, 1929), 59-79.

2851. Waterston, Jane Elizabeth, 1843-1932. Scottish missionary to South Africa. THE LETTERS OF JANE ELIZABETH WATERSTON, 1866-1905. Edited by Lucy Bean and Elizabeth Van Heyningen. With an introduction by Elizabeth Van Heyningen. Cape Town: Van Riebeeck Society, 1983. 304p.

Letters to James Stewart, principal of Lovedale Institution in Cape Colony (South Africa) where Waterston taught during her first years in South Africa as a Scottish Free Church missionary. Gives a remarkably full picture of her early career as a mission teacher at Lovedale, her return to England to qualify as a doctor, and her return to Africa. A "rare reflection of a Victorian missionary and woman doctor in Africa."

2852. Watkins, Ann Kirkham, 1813-1885. English Quaker. EXCERPTS FROM THE MEMORANDA AND LETTERS OF ANN WATKINS, A MINISTER OF THE SOCIETY OF FRIENDS. Ipswich: S. And W.J. King, 1888. 159p.

Autobiography, letters, and extracts from a Quaker diary, 1844-1885.

2853. Webb, Beatrice Potter, 1858-1943. English socialist. MY APPRENTICESHIP. New York and London: Longmans, Green, 1926. 422p.

Autobiographical outline of her philosophy of work and life. Includes extensive excerpts from her diary.

2854. ------. OUR PARTNERSHIP. Edited by Barbara Drake and Margaret I. Cole. New York: Longmans, Green, 1948. 543p.

Sequel to MY APPRENTICESHIP, comprised of excerpts from her diary, 1892-1911. Deals with the early years of her marriage to Fabian theorist Sidney Webb.

2855. ------. BEATRICE WEBB'S DIARIES, 1912-1932. Edited by Margaret I. Cole. With an introduction by Lord Beveridge. London: Longmans, Green & Co., 1952-1956. 2 vols.

Third and fourth volumes of Webb's autobiography. Each subsequent volume has contained more extensive quotes from Webb's diaries; MY APPRENTICESHIP containing relatively few while OUR PARTNERSHIP consists mainly of short essays introducing diary material. This volume describes Webb's public social and political life, work with her husband, and labor activism.

2856. ------. THE WEBB'S AUSTRALIAN DIARY, 1898. Edited by A.G. Austin. Melbourne: I. Pitman, 1965. 139p.

Observations on Australian society and politics. Less a sociological document than a record of the impressions made on two highly intelligent and idiosyncratic travelers. One third of the material is written by Sidney Webb.

2857. ------. BEATRICE WEBB'S AMERICAN DIARY, 1898. Edited by David A. Shannon. Madison, Wis.: University of Wisconsin Press, 1963. 181p.

Diary March 29--July 25, 1898, of a visit to America on one lap of the tour that also included Australia and New Zealand. Observations on American government, particularly city government, social life, and public affairs.

2858. ------. THE WEBBS IN NEW ZEALAND. BEATRICE WEBB'S DIARY WITH ENTRIES BY SIDNEY WEBB. Edited by D.A. Hamer. Wellington, Australia: Price, Milburn, for Victoria University Press, 1974. 71p.

2859. ------. THE LETTERS OF SIDNEY AND BEATRICE WEBB. Edited by Norman MacKenzie. Cambridge and York: Cambridge University Press, 1978. 3 vols.

2860. ------. THE DIARY OF BEATRICE WEBB, VOLUMES

1-57. 1873-1943. Cambridge, England: Chadwyck-Healy, Ltd., 1978. Microfiche (105x148mm).

2861. ------. INDEX TO THE DIARY OF BEATRICE WEBB, 1873-1943. Compiled by Archive Arrangement Routledge Associates. With introductions by Dame Margaret Cole, Geoffrey Allen, and Norman MacKenzie, and a Chronology of the lives of the Webbs. Cambridge: Chadwyck-Healy; and Teaneck, N.J.: Somerset House, 1978. 157p.

2862. Webb, Deborah Brooks, 1830-1895. Quaker. DIARY AND LETTERS OF DEBORAH B. WEBB, A MINISTER OF THE GOSPEL IN THE RELIGIOUS SOCIETY OF FRIENDS. Compiled by Anna M. Townsend. Philadelphia: Friends Book Store, 1898. 199p.

Quaker diary.

2863. Webber, Anna, b. 1860. American teacher. "The Diary of Anna Webber: Early Day Teacher of Mitchell County." Edited by Lila Gravatt Scrimsher. KANSAS HISTORICAL QUARTERLY 38:3 (Autumn, 1972), 320-337.

Diary of one school term by a new teacher, May-July, 1881. She taught seventeen students, ages 7-13, in a district school located near the Settlement of Blue Hill, Center Township, Kansas.

2864. Weber, Nettie O., b. 1840. American farmer. "Not So Long Ago: Nettie O. Weber's Farm Venture." Edited by Mrs. Dana O. Jensen. MISSOURI HISTORICAL SOCIETY BULLETIN 18 (October, 1961), 20-32.

While visiting relatives, Weber purchased, without consulting her husband, a small farm near St. Louis, Missouri. She moved there with her four youngest sons; her husband visited on weekends and did not move there permanently until he was in his seventies. Includes extracts from her diary, 1891-1909.

2865. Webster, Caroline LeRoy, 1797-1882. MR. WEBSTER AND I: BEING THE AUTHENTIC DIARY OF CAROLINE WEBSTER, DURING A FAMOUS JOURNEY WITH THE HON. DANIEL WEBSTER TO

GREAT BRITAIN AND THE CONTINENT IN THE YEAR 1839. With an introduction by Claude M. Fuess. New York: I. Washburn, 1942. 264p.

Travel diary.

2866. Wedgewood, Julia, 1833-1913. English intellectual and friend of Robert Browning. ROBERT BROWNING AND JULIA WEDGEWOOD: A BROKEN FRIENDSHIP AS REVEALED BY THEIR LETTERS. Edited by Richard Curle. New York: Frederick A. Stokes Co., 1937. 199p.

Letters 1864-1870 document a passionate friendship, eventually broken off by Wedgewood. After 1865 their friendship was maintained entirely through correspondence.

2867. Weeton, Nellie, afterwards Stock, 1776-1844. English teacher and governess. MISS WEETON: THE JOURNAL OF A GOVERNESS. Edited by Edward Hall. London: Oxford University Press, Humphrey Milford, 1936, 1939. 2 vols.

Journals and letters 1807-1825 describe work as a governess, a brutal marriage and eventual separation from her husband.

2868. Weigall, Rose Sophia Mary Fane, b. 1834. LADY ROSE WEIGALL: A MEMOIR BASED ON HER CORRESPONDENCE AND THE RECOLLECTIONS OF FRIENDS. By her daughter Rachel Weigall. New York: D. Appleton & Co., 1923. 316p.

Letters 1846-1920 to Julian Fane, Priscilla Burghersh, Countess of Westmoreland, Louise, Grand Duchess of Baden, John Weigall, Admiral von Eisendecher, and others. Includes some letters of the Countess of Westmoreland and the Grand Duchess of Baden.

2869. Weil, Simone, 1909-1943. French mystic, philosopher and author. THE NOTEBOOKS OF SIMONE WEIL. Translated by Arthur Wills. New York: G.P. Putnam's Sons; and London: Routledge, 1956. 2 vols.

Notebooks 1940-1942.

2870. ------. SIMONE WEIL: SEVENTY LETTERS. SOME HITHERTO UNTRANSLATED TEXTS FROM PUBLISHED AND UNPUBLISHED SOURCES. Translated and arranged by Richard Rees. London: Oxford University Press, 1965. 207p.

Letters 1931-1943 concern science and literature, the psychology of manual labor, pacifism, front-line nurses, religion and other topics.

2871. ------. SIMONE WEIL: FIRST AND LAST NOTEBOOKS. Translated by Richard Rees. London: Oxford University Press, 1970. 368p.

Contains Weil's pre-war notebook, roughly 1933-1939; a transitional passage, probably written in France before she left for America in 1942; the New York Notebook, 1942; and the London Notebook, 1943. The Notebooks were kept with a view to future use in books, and explore questions of philosophy, ethics, and religion.

2872. ------. SIMONE WEIL, JOE BOUSQUET: CORRESPONDANCE. Lausanne: Éditions l'Age d'Homme, 1982. 49p.

2873. Weingarten, Violet Brown, 1915-1976. American novelist and sociologist. INTIMATIONS OF MORTALITY. New York: Alfred A. Knopf, 1978. 243p.

Journal February, 1975--April, 1976 by a cancer patient.

2874. Weir, Jeanne Elizabeth, 1870-1950. American local historian. DIARY (1908) OF JEANNE ELIZABETH WEIR. Reno, Nev., 1961. 23p. Reprinted from the QUARTERLY OF THE NEVADA HISTORICAL SOCIETY 4:1 (January-March, 1961).

Record of travels in Nevada, while studying the history of the area.

2875. Weissman, Debbie. Israeli. "A Woman's Diary of the Yom Kippur War." RESPONSE 7:4 (Winter, 1973-1974), 87-92.

A record of her impressions of war October, 1973--

January 6, 1974, and musings on the different roles of men and women.

2876. Weitbrecht, Martha Edwards. English missionary and wife of Reverend John James Weitbrecht, English missionary to Bengal. FEMALE MISSIONARIES IN INDIA: LETTERS FROM A MISSIONARY'S WIFE ABROAD TO A FRIEND IN ENGLAND. London: Nisbet, 1843.

2877. Welby-Gregory, Victoria Alexandrine Maria Louisa Stuart-Wortley, Hon. Lady, 1837-1912. English philosopher. SEMIOTIC AND SIGNIFICS: THE CORRESPONDENCE BETWEEN CHARLES S. PEIRCE AND VICTORIA LADY WELBY. Edited by Charles S. Hardwick with the assistance of James Cook. Bloomington: Indiana University Press, 1977. 201p.

Correspondence 1903-1911. Lady Welby, author of WHAT IS MEANING, initiated the correspondence after reading Peirce's articles on logic in Baldwin's DICTIONARY OF PHILOSOPHY AND PSYCHOLOGY, seeing in his work similarities to her own. The correspondence is chiefly concerned with their work.

2878. Weld, Angelina Grimke, 1805-1879, and Sarah Grimke, 1792-1873. American abolitionists and women's rights advocates. LETTERS OF THEODORE DWIGHT WELD, ANGELINA GRIMKE WELD AND SARAH GRIMKE, 1822-1844. Edited by Gilbert H. Barns and Dwight L. Dummond. New York and London: D. Appleton-Century Co., 1934. 2 vols.

Selections from the Weld and Grimke letters which have biographical significance or which throw light on the antislavery movement. Includes some letters of Elizabeth Cady Stanton, Lydia Maria Child and Abbey Kelley.

2879. Wernher, Hilda. MY INDIAN FAMILY. New York: The John Day Co.; and Toronto: Longmans, Green & Co., 1943. 298p.

Diary written sometime in the 1930's, by a woman who accompanied her daughter Mary Ann and her son-in-law, Rahsid, to India. After her daughter's death in an automobile accident, Wernher stays on, eventually to oversee the preparations of the Muslim wedding of Rahsid and his second wife, Maryam.

2880. West, Jessamyn, b. 1902. American author. TO SEE THE DREAM. New York: Harcourt Brace & Co., 1957. 314p.

Diary of the making of the film version of her novel THE FRIENDLY PERSUASION.

2881. ------. DOUBLE DISCOVERY: A JOURNEY. New York: Harcourt Brace Jovanovich, 1980.

Autobiography comprised of journal entries, letters to her parents and husband, retrospective analysis, and a description of her first trip abroad in 1929.

2882. Westminster, Elizabeth Mary Leveson-Gower Grosvenor, Marchioness of, 1797-1891. DIARY OF A TOUR IN SWEDEN, NORWAY, AND RUSSIA, IN 1827. WITH LETTERS. London: Hurst and Blackett, 1879. 297p.

Travel diary and letters, May 19--November 6, 1827.

2883. Westmoreland, Priscilla Anne Wellesly Pole, Countess of, b. 1793. English social and political figure and niece of the Duke of Wellington. THE CORRESPONDENCE OF PRISCILLA ANNE WELLESLY, COUNTESS OF WESTMORELAND. Edited by her daughter, Lady Rose Weigall. London: John Murray, 1909. 487p.

Letters to family members, 1812-1870, deal with English and German politics, the Sardianian War of 1859, and social life at the English and German Courts.

2884. Wharton, Edith Newbold Jones, 1862-1937. American novelist. FIGHTING FRANCE FROM DUNKERQUE TO BELFORT. New York: Charles Scribner's Sons, 1915.

Journal entries and reminiscences of travel through France during World War I. She organized an extensive refugee program during the War and in 1916 was awarded the French Legion of Honor.

2885. Wheatley, Phillis, 1755-1784. American Black poet. LETTERS OF PHILLIS WHEATLEY, THE NEGRO SLAVE-POET OF BOSTON. Boston: Privately Printed by J. Wilson & Son, 1864. 19p. Reprinted from the PROCEEDINGS OF THE MASSACHUSETTS HISTORICAL SOCIETY 7 (1863-1864), 267-279

Wheatley maintained a sizeable correspondence with Susannah Wheatley, Orbour (or Arbour) Tanner, and John Thornton. Few of her letters have survived; however, those that did indicate she cultivated the letter as a literary form. Letters to Orbour Tanner, 1772-1779.

2886. ------. POEMS AND LETTERS. First Collected edition. Edited by Charles Frederick Heartman. With an appreciation by Arthur A. Schomburg. London: A.C. McClurg & Co., 1911; and New York: C.F. Heartman, 1915. 111p. Reprinted, Miami, Fla: Mnemosyne Publishing, 1969.

2887. ------. LIFE AND WORKS OF PHILLIS WHEATLEY. CONTAINING HER COMPLETE POETICAL WORKS, NUMEROUS LETTERS, AND A COMPLETE BIOGRAPHY OF THIS FAMOUS POET OF A CENTURY AND A HALF AGO. G. Herbert Renfro. Washington, D.C., 1916. Reprinted, Miami, Fla.: Mnemosyne Publishing Co., 1969. 112p.

Includes Wheatley's correspondence with fellow slave and friend Orbour (or Arbour) Tanner, 1772-1779, and a letter to George Washington, October 26, 1775.

2888. ------. "Letters of Phillis Wheatley and Susanna Wheatley." Sarah Dunlap Jackson. JOURNAL OF NEGRO HISTORY 57:2 (April, 1972), 211-215.

Presents three previously unpublished letters to the Countess of Huntingdon, October 24, 1770; June 27, 1773; and July 17, 1773; and two letters of Susanna Wheatley, February 20, 1773 and April 30, 1773.

2889. ------. "Four New Letters by Phillis Wheatley." Edited by Kenneth Silverman. EARLY AMERICAN LITERATURE 8:3 (Winter, 1974), 257-271.

Letters span April 1772--October 1774, the period

when her poems are first published in English magazines, her first volume of poetry is published, and she is released from slavery.

2890. Wheaton, Ellen Douglas Birdseye, 1816-1858. American. DIARY OF ELLEN BIRDSEYE WHEATON, 1816-1858. With notes by Donald Gordon. Privately Printed by Louise Ayer Gordon. Boston: D.B. Updike, The Merrymount Press, 1923. 419p.

Diary 1850-1857, prefaced by four letters to her sister, Charlotte Amelia Birdseye. An appendix contains early letters of Ellen, James V., and Victor Birdseye. Describes daily social, domestic, and religious life of a middle class merchant family. Ellen Birdseye was the daughter of a magistrate, and married dry-goods merchant Charles Augustus Wheaton in 1834.

2891. Whetten, Harriet Douglas. American Civil War nurse. "A Volunteer Nurse in the Civil War: The Letters of Harriet Douglas Whetten." Edited by Paul H. Hass. WISCONSIN MAGAZINE OF HISTORY 48:2 (1964), 131-151; and 48:3 (1965), 205-221.

Describes daily activities of a Sanitary Commission nurse in hospital transport service during the Spring, Summer and Fall of 1862.

2892. White, Tryphena Ely, b. 1784. TRYPHENA ELY WHITE'S JOURNAL, 1805-1850. BEING A RECORD, WRITTEN ONE HUNDRED YEARS AGO, OF THE DAILY LIFE OF A YOUNG LADY OF PURITAN HERITAGE. Published by her granddaughter, Kellog Port Kent. New York, 1904. New York: Grafton Press, 1905.

2893. White, Viola Chittenden, 1890-1977. American feminist, pacifist, poet and nature writer. NOT FASTER THAN A WALK: A VERMONT NOTEBOOK. Preface by Walter Prichard Eaton. Illustrated by Edward Sanborn. Middlebury, Vt.: Middlebury College Press, 1939. 144p.

2894. ------. PARTRIDGE IN A SWAMP: THE JOURNALS OF VIOLA C. WHITE, 1918-1939. Edited by W. Storrs Lee.

Taftsville, Vt.: Countryman Press, 1979. 255p.

Selections from a diary of over 50,000 manuscript pages, covering a broader sampling of the diary than NOT FASTER THAN A WALK, which White edited in her lifetime. Chief concerns are nature, politics, and poetry.

2895. Whitely, Opal Stanley, b. ca. 1855. American orphan who grew up in the frontier lumber camps of Oregon. THE DIARY OF OPAL WHITELY. London: G.P. Putnam's Sons, 1920. 311p.

2896. ------. THE STORY OF OPAL: THE JOURNAL OF AN UNDERSTANDING HEART. Boston: Atlantic Monthly Press, 1920.

2897. ------. THE SINGING CREEK WHERE THE WILLOWS GROW: THE REDISCOVERED DIARY OF OPAL STANLEY. Presented by Benjamin Huff. New York: Ticknor & Fields, 1986. 367p.

2898. Whitford, Maria. American farmer. AND A WHITE VEST FOR SAM'L: AN ACCOUNT OF RURAL LIFE IN WESTERN NEW YORK. Edited by Helene C. Phelan. Almond, N.Y.: Privately Printed, 1976.

Farm diary, January 1, 1857--July 17, 1861.

2899. Whiting, Martha, 1795-1853. American teacher. THE TEACHER'S LAST LESSON. A MEMOIR OF MARTHA WHITING, LATE OF THE CHARLESTOWN FEMALE SEMINARY. CONSISTING CHIEFLY OF EXTRACTS FROM HER JOURNAL, INTERSPERSED WITH REMINISCENCES AND SUGGESTIVE REFLECTIONS. Catharine Naomi Badger. Boston: Gould & Lincoln; and New York: Sheldon, Lamport & Blackman, 1855. 284p.

2900. Whitman, Martha Mitchell, 1836-1873. American sister-in-law of poet Walt Whitman. MATTIE: THE LETTERS OF MARTHA MITCHELL WHITMAN. Edited by Randall H. Waldron. New York: New York University Press, 1977. 101p.

Letters 1863-1872, from the wife of Walt Whitman's

favorite brother. Next to his mother, Martha Whitman was the woman Whitman most respected and loved. His side of the correspondence has been lost; the one surviving letter from him is printed here.

2901. Whitman, Narcissa Prentiss, 1808-1847. American frontier missionary and wife of missionary Marcus Whitman. "A Journey Across the Plains in 1836: Journal of Mrs. Whitman." TRANSACTIONS OF THE 19TH ANNUAL REUNION OF THE OREGON PIONEER ASSOCIATION FOR 1891 (1893), 40-68.

Journal of the overland journey to Oregon June-September, 1836. Begins with a letter to Whitman's relatives, dated June 27-July 16, 1836.

2902. ------. "Letters Written by Mrs. Whitman from Oregon to Her Relatives in New York." TRANSACTIONS OF THE 19TH ANNUAL REUNION OF THE OREGON PIONEER ASSOCIATION FOR 1891 (1893), 79-179.

2903. ------. "Mrs. Whitman's letters (1843-1847)." TRANSACTIONS OF THE 21ST ANNUAL REUNION OF THE OREGON PIONEER ASSOCIATION FOR 1893 (1894), 53-219.

Includes letters from Marcus Whitman and a letter from Reverend H.H. Spaulding to Mrs. Whitman's father, giving an account of the Indian uprising in which the Whitmans were killed.

2904. ------. THE COMING OF THE WHITE WOMEN, 1836. AS TOLD IN THE LETTERS AND JOURNAL OF NARCISSA PRENTISS WHITMAN. Compiled by T.C. Elliott. Portland, Ore.: Oregon Historical Society, 1937. 113p. Reprinted from the OREGON HISTORICAL QUARTERLY 37:2 (June, 1936), 87-101; 37:3 (September, 1936), 171-191; and 37:4 (December, 1936), 276-290.

Extracts from Whitman's diary and letters.

2905. ------. MY JOURNAL, BY NARCISSA PRENTISS WHITMAN. Edited by Lawrence Dodd. Fairfield, Wash.: Ye Galleon Press, 1982. 73p.

2906. Whitman, Sarah Helen Power, 1803-1878. American poet and biographer of Edgar Allen Poe. POE'S HELEN REMEMBERS. Edited by John Carl Miller. Charlottesville, Va.: University of Virginia Press, 1979. 528p.

Correspondence 1873-1878 between Whitman, one-time fiancée of Poe and author of a defense of his works; and John Ingraham, author of a biography of Poe. Correspondence pertains chiefly to Ingraham's book.

2907. Whitman, Sarah Wyman. American art critic. LETTERS OF SARAH WYMAN WHITMAN. Cambridge, England: Printed at The Riverside Press, 1907. 254p.

Memorial edition published for Whitman's friends. Includes letters to Sarah Orne Jewett, Annie Adams Fields, Charlotte Greeley, and others to 1904; passages from a notebook, 1885; and undated fragments.

2908. Whitmore, Ellen Rebecca, later Goodale, 1828-1861. American teacher. THE JOURNAL OF ELLEN WHITMORE. Edited by Lola Garrett Bowers and Kathleen Garrett. Tahlequah, Okla.: Northeastern State College, 1953. 28p.

2909. Whitney, Clara A.N., later Kaji. American daughter of a Presbyterian missionary to Japan. CLARA'S DIARY: AN AMERICAN GIRL IN MEIJI JAPAN. Edited by M. William Steele and Tamiko Ichimata. Tokyo and New York: Kodansha International, 1979. 353p.

Diary 1875 to 1887 records daily life of an American girl growing up in Japan. She was a keen observer of Japanese society and describes with meticulous care the everyday customs and ceremonies of the country.

2910. Wilder, Laura Ingalls, 1867-1957. American frontier settler and author. ON THE WAY HOME: THE DIARY OF A TRIP FROM SOUTH DAKOTA TO MANSFIELD, MISSOURI, 1894. With setting by Rose Wilder Lane. New York: Harper & Row, 1962. 101p.

Describes the Ingalls family's move to Missouri from their drought-stricken farm in South Dakota.

2911. ------. WEST FROM HOME: LETTERS OF LAURA INGALLS WILDER TO ALMANZO WILDER, SAN FRANCISCO, 1915. Edited by Roger Lea Macbride. Historical setting by Margot Patterson Doss. New York: Harper & Row, 1974. 124p.

Letters written while visiting her daughter, Rose Wilder Lane, who was living in San Francisco, during the Panama-Pacific Exposition of 1915.

2912. Wildman, Mary, "Mollie" Kehler. American frontier settler. "Letters of Thomas G. Wildman, Mary B. Wildman and Augustus Wildman, 1860-1865." In REPORTS FROM COLORADO: THE WILDMAN LETTERS, 1859-1865. WITH OTHER RELATED LETTERS AND NEWSPAPER REPORTS, 1859. Edited with an introduction and notes by LeRoy R. Hafen and Ann W. Hafen. Glendale, Calif.: Arthur H. Clarke Co., 1961. p. 237-326.

2913. Wilkinson, Anne Biddle, d. 1807. American Quaker. "Letters of Mrs. Anne Wilkinson from Kentucky, 1788-1789." Edited with an introduction by Thomas Robson Hay. PENNSYLVANIA MAGAZINE OF HISTORY AND BIOGRAPHY 56:221 (January, 1932), 32-55.

Letters to her father, Philadelphia merchant John Biddle, from her new home in Lexington, Kentucky, where her husband, General James Wilkinson, worked for a law firm. Describes life on the Kentucky frontier.

2914. Wilkinson, Eliza Yonge. American colonist. LETTERS OF ELIZA WILKINSON DURING THE INVASION AND POSSESSION OF CHARLESTON, SOUTH CAROLINA BY THE BRITISH IN THE REVOLUTIONARY WAR. Arranged from the original manuscript by Caroline Gilman. New York: S. Colman, 1839. 108p. Reprinted, New York: New York Times Press, 1969. 108p.

2915. Wilkinson, Elizabeth, 1712-1771. English Quaker. "Extracts from the Journal of a Religious Visit to Friends in America, 1761-1763." FRIENDS HISTORICAL ASSOCIATION BULLETIN 18 (1929), 87-90.

Quaker diary, written while visiting the United States.

2916. Willard, Emma, 1787-1876. American educator, historian, and advocate of women's education. JOURNAL AND LETTERS FROM FRANCE AND GREAT BRITAIN. Troy, N.Y.: N. Tuttle, Printer, 1833. 391p.

Extracts from a diary and letters, December, 1830--May, 1831, written on a trip to Europe made for the purpose of visiting girl's schools.

2917. Williams, Eliza Azelia Griswold, 1826-1885. American whaler's wife. ONE WHALING FAMILY. Edited by Harold Williams. Boston: Houghton Mifflin Co.; and Cambridge: The Riverside Press, 1964. 401p.

Includes extracts from a journal written on the whaling vessel The Florida, September 7, 1858--October 26, 1861. Two children, William Fish Williams (b. 1859) and Mary Watkins Williams (b. 1861) were born on board.

2918. Williams, Helen Maria, 1762-1827. English novelist. LETTERS ON THE FRENCH REVOLUTION, WRITTEN IN FRANCE, IN THE SUMMER OF 1790, TO A FRIEND IN ENGLAND. CONTAINING VARIOUS ANECDOTES RELATIVE TO THAT INTERESTING EVENT, AND MEMOIRS OF MONSIEUR AND MADAME DU F--- [DU FOSSE]. Boston: J. Belknap and A. Young, 1791.

2919. ------. LETTERS, CONTAINING A SKETCH OF THE POLITICS OF FRANCE, FROM THE THIRTY-FIRST OF MAY 1793 TILL THE TWENTY-EIGHTH OF JULY 1794, AND OF THE SCENES WHICH HAVE PASSED IN THE PRISONS OF PARIS. London: G.G. and J. Robinson, 1795-1796.

Williams and her family were imprisoned in 1793 and spent several months in prison. According to Janet Todd, these letters leave an unsurpassed record of the immediacy and drama of the events and impressions of the times and give an accurate account of life in a French prison.

2920. ------. LETTERS FROM FRANCE. Facsimile Reproductions, with an introduction by Janet M. Todd. Delman, N.Y.: Scholar's Facsimiles & Reprints, 1975. 2 vols.

Photoprint of the 1796 edition.

2921. Williams, Isabella Burgess Riggs, 1840-1897. American missionary to China. BY THE GREAT WALL: LETTERS FROM CHINA. THE SELECTED CORRESPONDENCE OF ISABELLA RIGGS WILLIAMS, MISSIONARY OF THE AMERICAN BOARD TO CHINA, 1866-1897. Introduction by Arthur H. Smith. New York and Chicago: F.H. Revell Co., 1909. 400p.

Letters begin in 1854, when Williams (then Riggs) was living in Minnesota. She married Mark Williams in 1866, the same year they were appointed missionaries to China. Includes letters and extracts from the diary of her daughter, Henrietta Williams, written while at Oberlin College and in China, where she became head of a girls' school.

2922. Williams, Velina Stearns. American frontier settler. "Diary of a Trip Across the Plains, 1853." TRANSACTIONS OF THE 47TH ANNUAL REUNION OF THE OREGON PIONEER ASSOCIATION (1919), 178-226.

Overland diary April-September, 1853 written on the journey from Illinois to Oregon.

2923. Williams-Wynn, Charlotte Grenville, Lady, 1754-1832. CORRESPONDENCE OF CHARLOTTE GRENVILLE, LADY WILLIAMS WYNN, AND HER THREE SONS, SIR WATKIN WILLIAMS WYNN, BART., RT. HON. CHARLES WILLIAMS WYNN, AND SIR HENRY WILLIAMS WYNN, 1759-1832. Edited by Rachel Leighton. London: John Murray, 1920. 414p.

2924. Williamson, Ada Clendenin, 1880-1958. American artist. ADA CLENDENIN WILLIAMSON, 1880-1958: GLIMPSES OF THE ARTIST THROUGH HER DIARIES, LETTERS, AND SCRAPBOOKS. Mary E.G. Robinson and Carolyn D. McCreesh. West Chester, Penn.: Chester County Historical Society, 1982. 80p.

2925. Williamson, Nancy. American Lesbian teacher. She has conducted diary-writing seminiars. "From My Journal." THE LESBIAN TIDE 4:1 (August, 1974), 9.

2926. Willson, Ann, 1797/8-1843. American? Quaker. FAMILIAR LETTERS OF ANN WILLSON. Philadelphia: W.D. Parrish & Co., 1850. 270p.

2927. Willson, Elizabeth Lundy, d. 1838. American Quaker. A JOURNEY IN 1836 FROM NEW JERSEY TO OHIO, BEING THE DIARY OF ELIZABETH LUNDY WILLSON. Edited by William C. Armstrong. Morrison, Ill.: Shawver Publishing Co., 1929. 47p.

Travel diary, May-July, 1836.

2928. Wilmot, Catherine, ca. 1773-1824 and Martha Wilmot, later Bradford, 1775-1873. Irish sisters. AN IRISH PEER ON THE CONTINENT (1801-1803). BEING A NARRATIVE OF THE TOUR OF STEPHEN, 2ND EARL MOUNT CASHELL, THROUGH FRANCE, ITALY, ETC., AS RELATED BY CATHERINE WILMOT. Edited by Thomas V. Sadlier. London: Williams and Norgate, 1920. 227p.

Diary of a European tour, November 24, 1801--October 5, 1803, made with the Mount Cashell family.

2929. ------. THE RUSSIAN JOURNALS OF MARTHA AND CATHERINE WILMOT. BEING AN ACCOUNT BY TWO IRISH LADIES OF THEIR ADVENTURES IN RUSSIA AS GUESTS OF THE CELEBRATED PRINCESS DASCHKAW, CONTAINING VIVID DESCRIPTIONS OF CONTEMPORARY COURT LIFE AND SOCIETY AND LIVELY ANECDOTES OF MANY INTERESTING HISTORICAL CHARACTERS, 1803-1808. Edited by the Marchioness of Londonderry and H.M. Hyde. London: Macmillan & Co., 1934. 432p.

Catherine Wilmot's letters from Russia, 1805-1807; and the letters and journals of Martha Wilmot from 1806-1808. Vivid accounts of life at the Russian Court during the Napoleonic Wars, as the guests of the Princess Daschkaw.

2930. Wilson, Anne Campbell McLeod, Lady, d. 1921. Scottish wife of a British Civilian Officer in India. LETTERS FROM INDIA. BY LADY WILSON. Edinburgh and London: William Blackwood and Sons, 1911. 417p.

Letters 1889-1909, intended to give English readers an idea of the daily lives and interests of their countrymen in different parts of the Indian Empire. The letters are amplified by reminiscences.

2931. Wilson, Edith Bolling Galt, 1872-1961. American second wife of U.S. President Woodrow Wilson. A PRESIDENT IN LOVE: THE COURTSHIP LETTERS OF WOODROW WILSON AND EDITH BOLLING GALT. Edited by Edwin Tribble. Boston: Houghton Mifflin, 1981. 225p.

Love letters, April-December, 1951, chosen to form a narrative of their courtship.

2932. Wilson, Ellen Louise Axson, d. 1913. American first Wife of U.S. President Woodrow Wilson. THE PRICELESS GIFT: THE LOVE LETTERS OF WOODROW WILSON AND ELLEN AXSON WILSON. Edited by Eleanor Wilson McAdoo. With a foreword by Raymond B. Fosdick. New York: McGraw-Hill, 1962. 324p.

Love letters, dating from the beginning of their courtship in 1883 to her death in 1913.

2933. Wilson, Margaret. Scottish missionary to India. MEMOIR OF MRS. MARGARET WILSON OF THE SCOTTISH MISSION, BOMBAY. INCLUDING EXTRACTS FROM HER LETTERS AND JOURNAL. Edinburgh: Johnstone, 1838. 636p.

2934. Winnie, Caroline Frey. American Army surgeon's wife. "Letters from a Post Surgeon's Wife: The Fort Washakie Correspondence of Caroline Frey Winnie, May 1879--May 1880." ANNALS OF WYOMING 53 (Fall, 1981) 44-63.

2935. Winslow, Anna Green, 1759-1780. Canadian. DIARY OF ANNA GREEN WINSLOW, A BOSTON SCHOOL GIRL OF 1771. Edited by Alice M. Earle. Boston: Houghton Mifflin Co., 1894. Reprinted, Williamstown, Mass.: Corner House Publishers, 1974. 121p.

Diary 1771-1773, written as a running letter to her parents, describes her experience as a student at a Boston finishing school. Winslow died young of tuberculosis.

2936. Winthrop, Margaret Tyndall, 1591-1647. American third wife of John Winthrop, first Governor of

Massachusetts. SOME OLD PURITAN LOVE LETTERS: JOHN AND MARGARET WINTHROP, 1618-1638. Edited by Joseph H. Twichell. New York: Dodd, Mead Co., 1894. 187p.

Colonial love letters give a picture of domesticity and affection in an atmosphere of religion; household matters and business affairs have for the most part been deleted.

2937. Wister, Sally [Sarah], 1761-1804. American Quaker and daughter of a prosperous Philadelphia family. "Journal of Miss Sally Wister, 1777-1778." PENNSYLVANIA MAGAZINE OF HISTORY AND BIOGRAPHY 9:3 (1885) 318-333; 9:4 (1885) 463-478; and 10:1 (1886) 51-60.

In September, 1777, the British Army entered Germantown; the Wister family lived a few miles distant. Diary describes social conditions in the midst of some of the most important military operations of the Revolutionary War.

2938. ------. SALLY WISTER'S JOURNAL: A TRUE NARRATIVE BEING A QUAKER MAIDEN'S ACCOUNT OF HER EXPERIENCES WITH THE OFFICERS OF THE CONTINENTAL ARMY, 1777-1778. Edited by Albert Cook Myers. Philadelphia: Ferris & Leach, 1902. 224p.

American Revolutionary War diary September, 1777--June, 1778, begun when she was fifteen years old and addressed to her friend Deborah Norris in Philadelphia. Her family housed and sheltered Officers of the Continental Army at their estate near Germantown, Pennsylvania.

2939. ------. THE JOURNAL AND OCCASIONAL WRITINGS OF SARAH WISTER. Edited and with an introduction by Kathryn Zabelle Derounian. Rutherford: Farleigh Dickinson Press, and London: Associated University Press, 1987. 149p.

2940. Wister, Sarah Butler. American daughter of Actress Fanny Kemble and mother of author Owen Wister.

"Sarah Butler Wister's Civil War Diary." Fanny Kemble Wister. PENNSYLVANIA MAGAZINE OF HISTORY AND BIOGRAPHY 102:3 (1978) 271-327.

Civil War diary April 15--September 8, 1861, with annotations added in 1889. Her father, Pierce Butler, and her sister, Fanny Butler, were Confederate sympathizers; she and her mother, Fanny Kemble Butler, sided with the North.

2941. Wollstonecraft, Mary [Mary Wollstonecraft Godwin], 1759-1797. English feminist theorist and novelist. POSTHUMOUS WORKS OF THE AUTHOR OF A VINDICATION OF THE RIGHTS OF WOMAN. Edited by William Godwin. London: Joseph Johnson, 1798. 4 vols.

First publication of her letters. Volumes 3 and 4 contain her letters to Gilbert Imlay and to her publisher, Joseph Johnson.

2942. ------. MARY WOLLSTONECRAFT: LETTERS TO IMLAY. With a prefatory memoir by C. Kegan Paul. London: C. Kegan Paul & Co., 1879. 207p.

Wollstonecraft lived with the American sea Captain Gilbert Imaly, and wrote him a series of painful letters when they were apart. They separated in 1796, after she bore a child, Fanny.

2943. ------. THE LOVE LETTERS OF MARY WOLLSTONECRAFT TO GILBERT IMLAY. With a prefatory memoir by Roger Ingpen. Philadelphia: J.B. Lippincott Co., 1908. 177p.

2944. ------. FOUR NEW LETTERS OF MARY WOLLSTONECRAFT AND HELEN M. WILLIAMS. Edited by Benjamin P. Kurtz and Carrie C. Autrey. Berkeley, Calif.: University of California Press, 1937. 82p.

Letters written in Havre and Paris to Ruth Baldwin Barlow (1755-1818).

2945. ------. GODWIN AND MARY: LETTERS OF WILLIAM GODWIN AND MARY WOLLSTONECRAFT. Edited by Ralph M.

Wardle. Lawrence, Kans.: University of Kansas Press, 1966. 125p. Lincoln, Nebr.: University of Nebraska Press/Bison Books, 1977. 125p.

One hundred fifty-one letters, a remarkably complete correspondence, dating from the beginning of their courtship in 1796 to the day of Wollstonecraft's death.

2946. ------. COLLECTED LETTERS OF MARY WOLLSTONECRAFT. Edited by Ralph M. Wardle. Ithaca, N.Y. and London: Cornell University Press, 1979. 439p.

Definitive edition. Letters 1773-1797 to Jane Arden, George Blood, Henry Fuseli, William Godwin, Mary Hays, Gilbert Imlay, Joseph Johnson, Maria Gisbourne, and others.

2947. Wood, Anna Cogswell and Irene Leache. American "romantic friends." THE STORY OF A FRIENDSHIP: A MEMOIR. New York: The Knickerbocker Press, 1901.

Contains letters between Cogswell and Leach, and extracts from their notebooks.

2948. ------. IDYLLS AND IMPRESSIONS OF TRAVEL: FROM THE NOTE-BOOKS OF TWO FRIENDS. New York and Washington: The Neale Publishing Co., 1904. 264p.

Sequel to THE STORY OF A FRIENDSHIP. Chiefly an account of European travel, compiled from their notebooks and letters.

2949. Wood, Anna S. Prouty, 1844-1926. American frontier settler. "The Diary of Mrs. Anna S. Wood: Trip to the Opening of the Cherokee Outlet in 1893." H.D. Ragland. CHRONICLES OF OKLAHOMA 50:3 (1972), 307-325.

Diary of the trip to the Cherokee Outlet Wood made with her son in 1893. They secured homestead claims near present-day Alfalfa County, Oklahoma.

2950. Wood, Elizabeth. American frontier settler. "Journal of a Trip to Oregon, 1851." OREGON HISTORICAL

QUARTERLY 27 (March, 1926), 192-203.

Account of the overland journey from Fort Laramie, Wyoming, to Oregon, June-September, 1851.

Wood, Francis Anne Burney. See Burney, Francies Anne.

2951. Wood, Maria Lydia Blane. English wife of a Colonial Officer in India. FROM MINNIE WITH LOVE: THE LETTERS OF A VICTORIAN LADY, 1849-1861. Edited by Jane Vansittart. London: P. Davies, 1974. 188p.

Includes letters written while living in India, 1856-1860.

2952. Woodis, Ruth, 1889-1931. American frontier settler. DIARIES OF CLARK AND RUTH WOODIS.: THE STORY OF A COLORADO HOMESTEAD, 1913-1928. [S.I.] Woodis Enterprise, 1976. 150p.

2953. Woodman, Abby Johnson, b. 1828. American. PICTURESQUE ALASKA: A JOURNAL OF A TOUR AMONG THE MOUNTAINS, SEAS, AND ISLANDS OF THE NORTHWEST, FROM SAN FRANCISCO TO SITKA. Boston: Houghton Mifflin Co., 1899. 212p.

Tourist travel diary, April-May, 1888.

2954. Woods, Margaret Hoare, 1748-1821. Quaker. EXTRACTS FROM THE JOURNAL &ETC. OF THE LATE MARGARET WOODS FROM THE YEAR 1771 TO 1821. London: J.&A. Arch, 1829. 494p. Philadelphia: H. Longstreth and London: C. Gilpin, 1850. 378p.

2955. Woodward, Mary Dodge, 1826-1890. American frontier settler. THE CHECKERED YEARS. EXCERPTS FROM THE DIARY OF MARY DODGE WOODWARD, WRITTEN WHILE LIVING ON A BONANZA FARM IN DAKOTA TERRITORY DURING THE YEARS 1884-1889. Edited by Mary Boymton Cowdrey. Caldwell, Idaho: The Caxton Printers, 1937. 265p.

Account of life on a farm in the heart of the Bonanza farm district of the Red River Valley, Dakota Territory.

2956. Woolf, Virginia Stephen, 1882-1941. English novelist, essayist and feminist. A WRITER'S DIARY. BEING EXTRACTS FROM THE DIARY OF VIRGINIA WOOLF. Edited by Leonard Woolf. London: Hogarth Press. 372p. New York: Harcourt, Brace, 1953. 356p.

Extracts 1918-1941 focus on Woolf as a writer.

2957. ------. VIRGINIA WOOLF AND LYTTON STRACHEY: LETTERS. Edited by Leonard Woolf and James Strachey. New York: Harcourt Brace Co., 1956. 166p.

Literary correspondence 1906-1931 between two of the central members of the Bloomsbury Group.

2958. ------. THE LETTERS OF VIRGINIA WOOLF. Edited by Nigel Nicolson and Joanne Trautman. New York and London: Harcourt Brace Jovanovich, 1975-1980. 6 vols.

Volume 1: 1888-1912. Published in England under the title THE FLIGHT OF THE MIND. London: Hogarth Press, 1975. 531p. Volume 2: 1912-1922. Published under the title THE QUESTION OF THINGS HAPPENING. London: Hogarth Press, 1976. 627p. Volume 3: 1923-1928. Published as A CHANGE OF PERSPECTIVE. London: Hogarth Press, 1977. 600p. Volume 4: 1929-1931. Published as A REFLECTION OF THE OTHER PERSON. London: Hogarth Press, 1978. 442p. Volume 5: 1932-1935. Published as THE SICKLE SIDE OF THE MOON. London: Hogarth Press, 1979. 476p. Volume 6: 1936-1941. Published as LEAVE THE LETTERS TILL WE'RE DEAD. London: Hogarth Press, 1980. 556p.

2959. ------. THE DIARY OF VIRGINIA WOOLF. Edited by Anne Oliver Bell. New York: Harcourt Brace Jovanovich, 1977-1978. 6 vols.

2960. Woolley, Mary Emma, 1863-1947. American educator. THE LIFE AND LETTERS OF MARY EMMA WOOLLEY. Jeanette Marks. Washington, D.C.: Public Affairs Press, 1955. 300p.

Biography which incorporates letters into the

text. The largest extracts from her correspondence are found in Chapter 10, "Center of the World: Letters Home," which describes a trip to the Orient.

2961. Wordsworth, Dorothy, 1771-1855. English diarist and sister of William Wordsworth. RECOLLECTIONS OF A TOUR MADE IN SCOTLAND, A.D. 1803. Edited by J.C. Shairp. Edinburgh: David Douglas, 1894. 3rd ed. 316p.

Travel diary of a tour undertaken with Wordsworth and Samuel Coleridge, August 14--September 25, 1803.

2962. ------. THE JOURNAL OF DOROTHY WORDSWORTH. Edited by William Knight. London: The Macmillan Co., 1925. 554p.

2963. ------. THE EARLY LETTERS OF WILLIAM AND DOROTHY WORDSWORTH. Arranged and edited by Ernest de Selincourt. Oxford: The Clarendon Press, 1935. 578p.

Letters 1787-1805.

2964. ------. THE LETTERS OF WILLIAM AND DOROTHY WORDSWORTH: THE MIDDLE YEARS. Arranged and edited by Ernest de Selincourt. Oxford: Humphrey Milford, the Clarendon Press, 1937. 2 vols.

Letters 1806-1821.

2965. ------. THE LETTERS OF WILLIAM AND DOROTHY WORDSWORTH: THE LATER YEARS. Arranged and edited by Ernest de Selincourt. Oxford: The Clarendon Press, 1939. 3 vols.

Letters 1821-1850.

2966. ------. THE JOURNALS OF DOROTHY WORDSWORTH. Edited by Ernest de Selincourt. New York: The Macmillan Co., 1941. 2 vols.

2967. ------. SOME LETTERS OF THE WORDSWORTH FAMILY. WITH A FEW UNPUBLISHED LETTERS OF COLERIDGE AND SOUTHEY AND OTHERS. Edited by Leslie Nathan Broughton.

Ithaca, N.Y.: Cornell University Press, 1942. 131p.

Forty-four new letters of William and Dorothy Wordsworth to George Huntly Gordon.

2968. ------. JOURNALS OF DOROTHY WORDSWORTH, THE ALFOXDEN JOURNALS, 1798 AND THE GRASMERE JOURNALS, 1800-1803. Edited by Mary Moorman. Introduction by Helen Darbishire. New York, London, and Oxford: Oxford University Press, 1971. 231p. 2nd ed.

Revised, corrected and expanded version of the 1958 edition by Helen Darbishire.

2969. ------. "The Private Life: A Study of Dorothy Wordsworth's Journals." Rachel Mayer Brownstein. MODERN LANGUAGE QUARTERLY 34:1 (1973), 48-63.

2970. ------. "Dorothy Wordsworth's Journals, 1824-1835." Carl H. Ketcham. THE WORDSWORTH CIRCLE 9:1 (Winter, 1978), 3-16

2971. ------. "The Structure of the Picturesque: Dorothy Wordsworth's Journals." Robert Con Davis. THE WORDSWORTH CIRCLE 9:1 (Winter, 1978), 45-49.

2972. ------. THE LETTERS OF WILLIAM AND DOROTHY WORDSWORTH. Second Edition. Revised, arranged and edited by Chester L. Shaver, Mary Moorman and Alan G. Hill from the first edition edited by the late Ernest de Selincourt. Oxford: The Clarendon Press, 1967-1978. 5 vols.

Volume 1: The Early Years, 1787-1805, revised by Chester L. Shaver. Volume 2: The Middle Years, Pt. 1, 1806-1811, revised by Mary Moorman. Volume 3: The Middle Years Pt. 2, 1812-1820, revised by Mary Moorman and Alan G. Hill. Volume 4: The Later Years, Pt. 1, 1821-1828, revised, arranged, and edited by Alan G. Hill. Volume 5: The Later Years, Pt. 2, 1829-1834, revised, arranged, and edited by Alan G. Hill.

2973. ------. HOME AT GRASMERE: EXTRACTS FROM THE

JOURNAL OF DOROTHY WORDSWORTH, WRITTEN BETWEEN 1800 AND 1803, AND FROM THE POEMS OF WILLIAM WORDSWORTH. Edited by Colette Clark. Harmondsworth, Middlesex, England: Penguin Books, 1978. 301p.

2974. ------. LETTERS OF DOROTHY WORDSWORTH: A SELECTION. Edited by Alan G. Hill. Oxford: Oxford University Press, 1981. Oxford: Clarendon Press, 1985. 200p.

2975. Wordsworth, Dorothy, later Quillinan, 1804-1847. DORA WORDSWORTH: HER BOOK. With portraits and facsimiles. Edited by F.V. Morely. Boston and New York: Houghton Mifflin Co., 1925. 175p.

2976. ------. JOURNAL OF A FEW MONTH'S RESIDENCE IN PORTUGAL AND GLIMPSES OF THE SOUTH OF SPAIN. London: E. Moxon, 1847. 2 vols. New edition, with a Memoir by Edmund Lee. New York and London: Longmans, 1895. 288p.

2977. Wordsworth, Mary Hutchinson, 1770-1859. English wife of William Wordsworth. THE LETTERS OF MARY WORDSWORTH, 1800-1855. Selected and edited by Mary E. Burton. Oxford: The Clarendon Press, 1958. 363p. Reprinted, Westport, Conn.: Greenwood Press, 1979. 363p.

Letters to Thomas Monkhouse, Dorothy Wordsworth, William Wordsworth, Edward Quillinan, Isabella Fenwick, Mary Hutchinson, and others.

2978. ------. MY DEAREST LOVE: LETTERS OF WILLIAM AND MARY WORDSWORTH, 1810. Edited in facsimile by Beth Darlington. With a foreword by Jonathan Wordsworth. [Grasmere, Cumbria?]: Trustees of Dove Cottage, (Ilkey, Yorkshire: Scolar Press) 1981. 81p.

Edition of 300 copies.

2979. ------. THE LOVE LETTERS OF WILLIAM AND MARY WORDSWORTH. Edited by Beth Darlington. Ithaca, N.Y.: Cornell University Press, 1981. 265p.

Letters that came to light in 1977, including sixteen previously unpublished letters by Mary. Seven letters date from the summer of 1810, when William journeyed to Leicestershire with Dorothy Wordsworth to visit his patron Sir George Beaumont and to Wales to visit Mary's brother Thomas Hutchinson; Mary remained at Grasmere with their five children. Twenty-four letters date from the Spring and Summer of 1812, when William journeyed to London to patch up a misunderstanding with Coleridge, and Mary visited Hutchinson in Wales.

2980. Wormely, Katharine Prescott, 1830-1908. American Sanitary Commission administrator. THE CRUEL SIDE OF WAR: WITH THE ARMY OF THE POTOMAC. LETTERS FROM THE HEADQUARTERS OF THE UNITED STATES SANITARY COMMISSION DURING THE PENINSULAR CAMPAIGN IN VIRGINIA IN 1862. Boston: Roberts, 1898. 210p.

Official letters, April 27--July 25, 1862. Personal record of work with the United States Sanitary Commission during the Civil War. Wormely was chiefly involved in the Hospital Transport Service, which centralized relief work.

2981. Wright, Frances, later Madame D'Arusmont, 1795-1852. Scottish social reformer. VIEWS OF SOCIETY AND MANNERS IN AMERICA, IN A SERIES OF LETTERS FROM THAT COUNTRY TO A FRIEND IN ENGLAND, DURING THE YEARS 1818, 1819 AND 1820. By an Englishwoman. London: Printed for Longman, Hurst, Rees, Orme, and Brown; and New York: Printed for E. Bliss and E. White, 1821. 387p.

Travel letters, written to Wright's friend Mrs. Rabina Craig Millar, and revised for publication. Wright spent the winter of 1818 in New York, toured the northern states and Canada in the spring of 1819, and traveled as far south as Virginia in 1820.

2982. Wright, Myrtle Aldren, later Radely, b. 1903. English Quaker. NORWEGIAN DIARY, 1940-1945. London: Friends Peace and International Relations Committee, 1974. 255p.

2983. Wyndam, Joan, b. 1923. English author. LOVE

LESSONS: A WARTIME DIARY. Boston and Toronto: Little, Brown, & Co., 1985. 204p.

Diary August, 1939--May, 1942 by a young bohemian living in Chelsea; the diary closes as she volunteers for the W.A.A.F.

2984. Wynn, Frances Williams, 1733-1857. THE DIARIES OF A LADY OF QUALITY. By Miss Frances Williams Wynn, from 1797 to 1844. Edited by Abraham Hayward. London: Longman, Green, Longman, Roberts & Green, 1864. 359p.

Society diary, 1797-1844.

2985. Yates, Elizabeth, b. 1905. American author. MY DIARY--MY WORLD. Philadelphia: Westminster Press, c.1981. 187p.

2986. Yeoman, Mary, later Harding, b. 1780. English countrywoman. THE DIARY OF MARY YEOMAN OF WAINSTROW, COUNTY SOMERSET. Edited by R.D. Reid. No place, no publisher [printed at the Journal Office, Wells], no date. 24p.

Diary of one calendar year by a daughter of a prosperous country family with a pottery business in Wainstrow. Short entries originally written in a leather bound diary with ruled space for each day, describe social life; visits, parties, church events.

2987. Young, Caprice. American Senate Page. "Work/ Life: In the Corridors of Power: Diary of a 15-Year-Old Senate Page." MS. MAGAZINE 11 (March, 1983) 81-84.

Excerpt from a journal kept during an appointment as Page to Senator S.I. Hayakawa of California, September-December, 1981.

2988. Young, Janette (Lewis), 1858-1887. American. AN OREGON IDYLL: A TALE OF A TRANSCONTINENTAL JOURNEY, AND LIFE IN OREGON 1883-1884, BASED ON THE DIARIES OF JAN- ETTE LEWIS YOUNG. Edited by Nellie May Young. Glendale, Calif.: A.H. Clarke, 1961. 111p.

2989. Young, Josephine Churchill, later Birney, 1847-1915. JOURNALS OF JOSEPHINE YOUNG. New York: Privately printed at the De Vinne Press, 1915. 197p.

2990. Young, Mary Sophie, 1872-1919. American botanist. "Mary S. Young's Journal of Botanical Explorations in Trans-Pecos, Texas, August-September, 1914." B.C. Tharp and Chester V. Kielman. THE SOUTHWESTERN HISTORICAL QUARTERLY 3:1 (January, 1962) 366-375; and 3:2 (April, 1962) 512-538.

Relates Young's botanical explorations of the Davis Mountains and Ruidosa Hot Springs areas of Texas. The journal was chosen for publication because it graphically reveals the primitive conditions under which Young's pioneering collections were made, and because those who have read the original manuscript have been intrigued by both its charm and its historical significance.

INDEX OF AUTHORS BY PROFESSION OR SIGNIFICANT CHARACTERISTIC

INDEX OF NARRATIVES BY SUBJECT

INDEX OF NARRATIVES BY LOCATION

TITLE INDEX

FOR USE
IN
LIBRARY
ONLY